After three years of great loss and suffering on the Eastern Front, Imperial Russia was in crisis and on the verge of revolution. In November 1917, Lenin's Bolsheviks (later known as 'Soviets') seized power, signed a peace treaty with the Central Powers, and brutally murdered Tsar Nicholas (British King George's first cousin) and his children so there could be no return to the old order. As Russia fractured into loyalist 'White' and revolutionary 'Red' factions, the British government became increasingly drawn into the escalating Russian Civil War after hundreds of thousands of German troops transferred from the Eastern Front to France were used in the 1918 'Spring Offensive' which threatened Paris. What began with the landing of a small number of Royal Marines at Murmansk in March 1918 to protect Allied-donated war stores quickly escalated, with the British government actively pursuing an undeclared war against the Bolsheviks on a number of fronts in support of British trained and equipped 'White Russian' Allies.

At the height of British military intervention in mid-1919, British troops were fighting the Soviets far into the Russian interior in the Baltic, North Russia, Siberia, Caspian and Crimea simultaneously. The full range of weapons in the British arsenal were deployed including the most modern aircraft, tanks and even poison gas. British forces were also drawn into peripheral conflicts against 'White' Finnish troops in North Russia and the German 'Iron Division' in the Baltic. It remains a little known fact that the last British troops killed by the German Army in the First World War were killed in the Baltic in late 1919, nor that the last Canadian and Australian soldiers to die in the First World War suffered their fate in North Russia in 1919 many months after the Armistice.

Despite the award of five Victoria Crosses (including one posthumous) and the loss of hundreds of British and Commonwealth soldiers, sailors and airmen, most of whom remain buried in Russia, the campaign remains virtually unknown in Britain today. After the withdrawal of all British forces in mid-1920, the British government attempted to cover up its military involvement in Russia by classifying all official documents. By the time files relating to the campaign were quietly released decades later there was little public interest. Few people in Britain today know that their nation ever fought a war against the Soviet Union. The culmination of more than 15 years of painstaking and exhaustive research with access to many previously classified official documents, unpublished diaries, manuscripts and personal accounts, author Damien Wright has written the first comprehensive campaign history of British and Commonwealth military intervention in the Russian Civil War 1918–20.

Damien Wright traces his lifelong interest in military history back to his early childhood when he was shown a photograph of his Grandfather in Australian Light Horse uniform and allowed to take his medals to school for show and tell. His interest in the British campaigns in Russia were first piqued in his teens when reading a chronological list of Australian recipients of the Victoria Cross which showed two seemingly anomalous decorations for 'North Russia 1919' listed separately from the First World War awards. Some further digging revealed that both Australian VC recipients, one of whom was a fellow South Australian, had volunteered to serve in the same unit of the British Army. Further research proved difficult, so little had ever been published and the campaign seemingly largely unknown and ignored. The product of many years of exhaustive research, *Churchill's Secret War with Lenin* is his first book.

Churchill's Secret War with Lenin

*British and Commonwealth Military Intervention
in the Russian Civil War, 1918–20*

Damien Wright

Helion & Company

Helion & Company Limited
26 Willow Road
Solihull
West Midlands
B91 1UE
England
Tel. 0121 705 3393
Fax 0121 711 4075
Email: info@helion.co.uk
Website: www.helion.co.uk
Twitter: @helionbooks
Visit our blog at http://blog.helion.co.uk/

Published by Helion & Company 2017
Designed and typeset by Serena Jones
Cover designed by Paul Hewitt, Battlefield Design (www.battlefield-design.co.uk)
Printed by Short Run Press, Exeter, Devon

Text © Damien Wright 2017
Photographs © as individually credited
Maps drawn by George Anderson © Helion & Company 2017

Front cover: Captain Francis Lord, MC, MM, AIF attached Dunsterforce, on the lookout for Ottoman troops from an Armenian defensive position near Baku, September 1918 (Australian War Memorial G00803). Back cover: advertisement published in *The Times*, 10 April 1919, calling for volunteers for the North Russia Relief Force. The advertisement was published in newspapers throughout Britain (public domain).

ISBN 978-1-911512-10-3

British Library Cataloguing-in-Publication Data.
A catalogue record for this book is available from the British Library.

For details of other military history titles published by Helion & Company Limited, contact the above address, or visit our website: http://www.helion.co.uk

We always welcome receiving book proposals from prospective authors.

King George V of Great Britain and Tsar Nicholas II of Russia. (Public domain)

Dedicated to all those who served and suffered as a result of the Russian Civil War

Many skilful writers on Russia have eulogized her with descriptions of her vastness, her whiteness, her simplicity, her cruelty. With these more gifted people I cannot compete. But I can still say that Russia drew me with her mystery, calls to me even now after all these years with her mystery. The spell which she cast upon me will never die.

We may not have succeeded in what we had gone to do, but we tried our hardest and, successful or not, a tribute is due to all those personnel, officers and civilians, Russian as well as British, who gave of their best for a cause which we at any rate considered a just one.

Without their loyal help I alone could have done nothing.

Brigadier I I. N. H. Williamson, DSO, MC, RA.
British Military Mission, South Russia, 1919–20

Contents

List of Acronyms for Military Units and Formations

AEF Siberia	American Expeditionary Force Siberia
AIF	Australian Imperial Force
BEF	British Expeditionary Force
CEF	Canadian Expeditionary Force
CFA	Canadian Field Artillery
CSEF	Canadian Siberian Expeditionary Force
HLI	Highland Light Infantry
KRRC	King's Royal Rifle Corps
MGC	Machine Gun Corps
MMR	Mercantile Marine Reserve
NREF	North Russia Expeditionary Force
NRRF	North Russia Relief Force
RA	Royal Artillery
RAMC	Royal Army Medical Corps
RAN	Royal Australian Navy
RANB	Russian Allied Naval Brigade
RAOC	Royal Army Ordnance Corps
RE	Royal Engineers
RFA	Royal Field Artillery
RGA	Royal Garrison Artillery
RM	Royal Marines
RMA	Royal Marine Artillery
RMFFNR	Royal Marines Field Force North Russia
RMLI	Royal Marine Light Infantry
RN	Royal Navy
RND	Royal Naval Division
RNAS	Royal Naval Air Service
RNR	Royal Naval Reserve
RNVR	Royal Naval Volunteer Reserve
RNWMP	(Canadian) Royal North West Mounted Police
SBAC	Slavo-British Aviation Corps
TMB	Trench Mortar Battery
USN	United States Navy

Acknowledgements

Numerous people from around the world have generously provided information, research and assistance in the production of this book.

I would like to thank first and foremost the admirable Mrs Victoria Christen (Australia) daughter of Sergeant Samuel George Pearse, VC, MM, AIF and 45th Royal Fusiliers, a wonderful, warm lady with a remarkable life story who invited a stranger into her home and treated me to the greatest generosity and hospitality, and her son Mr Richard Christen, for their assistance with this project.

And sincere thanks to the following (in no particular order) without whom this book would not have been possible:

Jack Langley (Australia), spent many hours trawling through his extensive military reference library

Robin McColl (New Zealand), son of Private Hugh McColl, 46th Royal Fusiliers

Noel Miller (South Africa), son-in-law of Private Estcourt Cresswell-George, South African Brigade and 201st MGC

Keith Stephenson (UK), grandson of Sergeant Sidney Stephenson, MM and Bar, 201st MGC

Graham and Daphne Ransom (UK), son and daughter-in-law of Private Stephen Pettit, MM, No. 1. Special Company, Middlesex Regiment

Cathy McDermott (Australia), granddaughter of Private Wilfred Yeaman, AIF and 201st MGC

John Northover (UK), great-nephew of Major Albert Northover, MC, RE

David Mason (UK), grandson of Private James Mason, DCM, 45th Royal Fusiliers

Gary Cassidy (Australia) grandson of Sergeant Charles Tozer, RAMC

Jenny Martin (UK), granddaughter of Private John Lines, MM, RAMC, and for her assistance in researching the father of her neighbour, Lieutenant Ernest Harries, MBE, RM

Patrick Twomey (Ireland), grandson of Private Edward Gallagher, 45th Royal Fusiliers

Joan Chiles (UK), niece of Private Alec Beeson, 6th Battalion, RMLI

Christine Noe (UK), niece of Private Thomas Lechmere, MM, Tank Corps

Carrie Mowat (Canada), great-niece of Lieutenant Oliver Mowat, MC, CFA

Richard Flory (US), for his assistance researching services of officers

Barry Carr (Australia), for generosity and hospitality

Gordon Smith (UK), grandson of Yeoman of Signals George Smith, DSM, RN. Website: http://www.naval–history.net/

Sergei Gnezdov (Vyborg, Russia), who provided photographs of British soldiers' graffiti in his great-grandfather's cabin at Tulgas on the Dvina River

Angela Jones (UK), daughter-in-law of Private Jack Holloway, MM, 45th Royal Fusiliers

Richard Kearn (UK), grandson of Captain Alfred Kearn, OBE, RAOC

Mike Irwin (Australia), local Mildura historian and author of *Victoria's Cross*, a biography of Sergeant Samuel George Pearse, VC, MM

Alasdair Skeil (UK), grandson of Major Alexander Skeil, DSO, MC, Royal Scots Fusiliers

Alexei Suhanovsky (Arkhangelsk, Russia), local Archangel historian who has built a memorial cross at the location of Samuel Pearse's posthumous VC action

Al Richardson (UK), grandson of Captain Albert Richardson, MC, 45th Royal Fusiliers

Peter Broznitsky (Canada), CEF researcher specialising in Russians in the CEF. Website: http://www.russiansinthecef.ca/index.shtml

Richard Watts (New Zealand), grandson of Lieutenant Roy Stock, RAF who generously gave permission to reproduce his grandfather's photographs of RAF seaplanes on the Dvina River.
Colin Sayer (UK), son of Major Herbert Sayer, Tank Corps Training Mission South Russia
Michael Walshe (Australia), grandson of Joseph Michael Collins, MM, 45th Royal Fusiliers
Brenton Brooks (Australia), for generous assistance conducting research at the Australian War Memorial and National Archives, Canberra
Keith Chiazzari (South Africa), great-nephew of Air Marshall Sir Leonard Slatter, KBE, CB, DSC and Bar, DFC, formerly Flight Lieutenant, No. 47 Squadron, RAF, South Russia 1919–20
Ian Edwards (Scotland), grandson of Captain Jack Edwards, MC and Two Bars, 2/10th Battalion, Royal Scots
David and Mike Bremner (UK), nephew and son of Lieut. William Bremner, DSO, DSC, RN
Gareth Morgan (Australia), President, Australian Society of WW1 Aero Historians for assistance researching the service of Lieutenant Alfred Carey, RNAS and RAF
Tom Roberts (UK), great-nephew of Sergeant Benjamin Roberts, 45th Royal Fusiliers
Tom LeMoine (Canada), great-nephew of 2nd Lieutenant Claude LeMoine, RAF
Liz Pickman (UK), granddaughter of Sergeant Walter Jackson, RGA
R.C. Batten (UK), grandson-in-law of Lieutenant Samuel Kent, RN
David Treloar (Australia), son of Lieutenant George Treloar, DSO, MC, Coldstream Guards
John Stirling (UK), son of Captain John Stirling, MBE, Manchester Regiment
Anthony Huys (France), grandson of Major Edward O'Dell, MBE, North Staffordshire Regt.
Shaun Mitchell (Australia), son of Staff Sergeant James Mitchell, RASC
Geoff Earl (UK), grandson of Sergeant John Earl, RAF
Bill Gifford (Canada), son of Private John Gifford, Canadian Malamute Company
Margaret Tomlinson (UK), daughter of Private Robert Boggis, Royal Engineers
John Barton (UK), grandson of George Barton, Mercantile Marine Reserve
Irv Mortenson (USA), for assistance and guidance with the service of KRRC in North Russia
Ken Rouse (UK), grandson of Private Edwin Rouse, London Regiment
Val Ashbrook (UK), for assistance researching Petty Officer Charles Bailey, RN
Paul Barker (UK), grandson of Private Charles Barker, Royal Army Service Corps
Sue McAuley (Canada), granddaughter of Captain Gordon Galbraith, Worcestershire Regiment
John Metcalfe (UK), grandson of Private Edward Metcalfe, Yorkshire Regiment
Lorne Bohn (Canada), for assistance researching Private Lawrence Carr, 201st MGC
Mike Painter (UK), grandson of Mate Charles Painter, Mercantile Marine Reserve
Brian Tull (UK), grandson of Company Sergeant Major Henry George Tull, Tank Corps
Geoffrey Donaldson (UK), grandson of Regimental Sergeant Major Thomas Walsh, Tank Corps
David Sampson (UK) grandson of Private Thomas Kirkpatrick, Royal Sussex Regiment
Bill Woolmore (Australia), for assistance in research
David Clapp (UK), nephew of Private Percy Clapp, RAMC
Janet McCarthy (UK), granddaughter of Private Alfred McCarthy, British Military Mission
Rev. Seraphim Newman-Norton (UK), relative of Corporal Edward Norton, Tank Corps
David Butland (UK), grandson of Sergeant Edwin Lammas, Royal Marines Artillery
Matthew Broadbridge and William Harris (UK), for assistance researching Indian forces in Turkestan
Tom Roberts (UK) great-nephew of Sergeant Benjamin Roberts, 45th Royal Fusiliers
Duncan Rogers and Michael LoCicero, Helion & Company (UK), for enthusiasm and support for the project
Serena Jones (UK), for typesetting the manuscript and tabulating appendices, a laborious and difficult task done with exceptional attention to detail and skill
George Anderson (UK), for turning my rough sketches into maps suitable for publication

While still a young boy at primary school I became aware that my paternal grandfather, still alive at the time, had been wounded at Gallipoli and that my maternal grandfather had died in Russia and been awarded a posthumous medal for bravery. I often looked at and handled the medal because my mother kept it in our house.

The medal was a Victoria Cross. My maternal grandfather was Sergeant Samuel George Pearse, VC, MM. His parents had migrated to Australia from Wales and settled near Mildura, in north-western Victoria, before the First World War. In 1915, just before turning 18, Sam enlisted in the Australian Imperial Force and arrived at Gallipoli shortly before the ANZAC withdrawal. He was later awarded the Military Medal for bravery while serving on the Western Front in 1917.

In June 1919, Sam married Catherine Knox who he had met while on leave in England in 1918 but faced with a long wait for their joint passage to Australia, Sam enlisted for service with the British North Russian Relief Force, which paid more than twice the daily amount he had been receiving with the AIF. On 29 August 1919 Sam was mortally wounded during a successful assault on an enemy position, an unselfish act of supreme bravery while being exposed to heavy fire.

Sam's widow brought their four week old daughter with her to the presentation of the Victoria Cross by King George V at Buckingham Palace on 20 March 1920. My mother, Victoria Catherine Sarah Christen, now aged 96, had been named to have the initials 'VC'. Sam's intention was for his wife and child to live in Australia so my grandmother and mother duly arrived in Melbourne in May 1920.

One day during the mid 1950s I was amongst a group of high-school kids travelling to school by train when the conversation drifted into what our fathers did during the war. After patiently listening to other parental exploits I proudly mentioned that my father had served in the Navy throughout the Second World War and that both my grandfathers had been soldiers in the First World War; then added, somewhat smugly I suppose, that both my grandfathers were at Gallipoli, where one of them had been wounded, and that the other was wounded in France then later killed in Russia during fighting that resulted in the posthumous award of a Victoria Cross.

Naturally enough, plenty of scoffing ensued. 'A Victoria Cross?' … 'Killed in Russia?' … 'Who was fighting in Russia?' Sadly, I did not have sufficient knowledge at the time to adequately elaborate.

After school that day I explained the situation to my mother. She briefly mentioned details of her father's death then kindly allowed me to take the medal to school the following day. When not proudly displaying it on the train and at school the medal remained in my trouser pocket, firmly held there by hand until arriving back home.

In 1969 my parents stayed in Mildura during their journey from Sydney to Adelaide. In the foyer of the local Returned Services League Club they were pleasantly surprised to see a framed photo of Sam. Subsequent events there led to my mother meeting Sam's next youngest brother, Jack Pearse – her Uncle John.

Jack had been taken prisoner by the Japanese after the fall of Singapore in February 1942. During his time in captivity, which included the horrors of work on the Burma Railway, he retained possession of Sam's Military Medal, which Sam had sent to their parents in 1917. Jack stated that he always regarded the medal as his lucky charm.

Jack Pearse died in 1982. His son, Eddie, kindly gave Sam's Military Medal to my mother in 1985 when she visited Mildura to attend the opening of the 'Pearse VC MM Club'.

In June 2007 my mother suffered a severe stroke. Thanks to constant family encouragement, regular physiotherapy and her own fierce determination – a trait probably inherited from her father – my mother was eventually well enough to undertake assisted long-distance travel.

In November 2009 the Mildura RSL Club generously hosted us during their Armistice Day ceremony, during which my mother unveiled a statue of her father in Henderson Park. Many of the Pearse Clan were in attendance. It was a very happy occasion for my mother and we will always be extremely grateful to everyone who contributed towards honouring Sam in this way.

As the daughter of a Victoria Cross recipient, my mother was invited to attend the official reopening of the new Hall of Valour at the Australian War Memorial on 21 February 2011 (the day she turned 91). Before the actual ceremony we went to see Sam's framed photo. It had been positioned beside the one for Corporal Arthur Sullivan, VC, the other Australian volunteer to receive the Victoria Cross in the North Russia campaign, 1919. Arthur's medals were on display but not Sam's. This was when my mother decided that Sam's medals should rightfully be displayed alongside her father's photo.

From 1946 onwards there has normally been plenty of readily available information regarding the most significant world events before, during and after both World Wars. However the Allied attempt to suppress Communism in Russia after the 1917 Revolution was a dismal failure, seemingly best forgotten while concentrating on overall post-war recovery. No official war history was compiled. No campaign medals were awarded. Over the years very little was ever published on what actually happened in 1918 and 1919 during Russia's civil war.

The Allied intervention in Russia was well intended but the troops sent there were ill prepared, through no fault of their own, and too few for such an arduous task. Regardless of the eventual outcome, it was still wartime activity that should have been officially recorded with all due recognition given to those who served there. This book, a highly commendable effort from Damien Wright, is virtually an unofficial War History covering British and Commonwealth Military Operations in Russia 1918-1920. To the best of my knowledge it is the only such book in the English language and deserves to be first read and studied by all politicians seriously thinking about committing Armed Forces to a foreign war.

Richard Christen
Grandson of Sgt. S.G. Pearse, VC, MM, 45th Royal Fusiliers

Introduction

The primary objective of Allied intervention in the Russian Civil War was to reopen the Eastern Front against the Central Powers. The Kerensky Provisional Government took power in Russia after the Tsar abdicated in March 1918, but vowed to remain loyal to the Allies and continue fighting on the Eastern Front. In November 1917, a second revolution took place when the Bolsheviks, led by Vladimir Lenin, overthrew the Provisional Government and declared a cessation to all hostilities, considered by the Allies to be a gross betrayal.

Resuming hostilities on the Eastern Front would take pressure off hard-pressed Allied forces striving to fend off fresh German reinforcements which had been sent from east to west as a result of Russia ceasing hostilities. With German troops virtually in sight of Paris, the Allies were less concerned with who was ruling Russia as long as they would recommence hostilities on the Eastern Front. Some senior British generals were pressing the government of Lloyd George to remove the Bolsheviks and reinstate the Tsar, who would continue the war against the Central Powers. These officers received hearty support when Winston Churchill, a vehement anti-Bolshevik, became Secretary of State for War on 10 January 1919.

The German Spring Offensive of 1918 would not have been possible were it not for the entire German divisions that were freed up to fight on the Western Front. Major General Charles Maynard, who was to command 'SYREN' Force in North Russia, later wrote in his memoirs of the campaign the impetus for the Allies to intervene in the summer of 1918:

(a) Many more German divisions would have been withdrawn from Russia and employed against the Allies in France – possibly with decisive results.

(b) Germany, being free to draw on the immense resources of Russia and Siberia, would have been enabled to establish her national industries once again on a prosperous footing, and to supply the pressing needs of her civil population. The effect of our maritime blockade would thus be annulled.

(c) North Russian ports would have been converted into enemy naval bases, submarines operating from which would have circumvented our North Sea minefields and found our Atlantic commerce open to their attack. This, too, when the safe transport to Europe of America's armies was all-important.

(d) The chance would be lost of employing to any useful purpose either the army of Japan or the equivalent of several divisions of Czecho-Slovak troops of high fighting value, and full of enthusiasm for our cause.

(e) The anti-German movement at that time beginning to gain a hold in Russia would, if unsupported by the Allies, be quite unlikely to achieve any tangible result.[1]

British and Commonwealth military intervention in Russia, whether for the right or wrong reasons, was one of the most ill-conceived and poorly planned campaigns of the twentieth century. Overall it achieved little other than the loss of the life and maiming of many hundreds of soldiers, sailors and airmen who had already given so much during four years of war on the Western Front and in other theatres. The financial cost was also great, many millions of pounds were expended by a Great Britain which could ill afford to further squander its wealth during the period of post-war economic recovery.

---

1   Charles Maynard, *The Murmansk Venture* (Hodder and Stoughton, 1928), p.8.

The many different White Russian and anti-Bolshevik factions remained divided, failed to agree on strategy and were often no match for the increasingly organised, efficient and motivated Red Army under the leadership of Leon Trotsky. In many cases units of the White Army defected en masse to the Bolsheviks, sometimes murdering their officers before doing so. On more than one occasion, White Russian troops mutinied and murdered their British officers before going over to the enemy. Corruption and inefficiency from the lowest to highest levels of leadership plagued the White Russian forces.

Most of the Allied nations which sent troops did not border Russia nor have any obvious reason to get involved. Several countries sent forces or military missions to Russia. These ranged from YMCA canteens to the 70,000-strong expeditionary force sent by Japan to Siberia, by far the largest contribution of foreign troops. The US sent troops to both North Russia and Siberia as did the French, Italians and Serbs. Japanese interests in Russia were purely expansionist and limited to the maritime provinces of Siberia and China. They were also the last Allied interventionist forces to leave Russia. It was not until October 1922 that the Japanese reluctantly relinquished control of eastern Siberia to the Red Army.

By the outbreak of war in 1914, Russia was very much a nation stuck in a time warp. Despite the industrial revolution the country remained severely undeveloped. Domestic manufacture could not keep up with the demand of the rapidly mobilising Imperial Russian Army and there were significant shortfalls in arms, equipment and supplies. To assist their Russian ally to fight the Central Powers on the Eastern Front, Britain and France began planning to ship massive quantities of war stores to Russian ports. The objective of the 1915 Gallipoli campaign had been to knock Ottoman Turkey out of the war and open up the Black Sea to allied merchant ships but when the campaign stagnated and failed, the merchant ships were redirected via the Arctic route to Murmansk and Archangel in northern Russia.

Allied military missions had been sent to Russia as early as 1915 to aid in the distribution of donated war stores and training and equipping of the Imperial Army. In June 1916, at the request of the Allied governments and in order to coincide with the attack on the Somme, the Russians launched a massive offensive into western Ukraine which resulted in a number of German divisions being moved from west to the east to counter the offensive.

By mid 1917 over two million Russian soldiers were dead, five million wounded and two and a half million taken prisoner. Russia owed Britain over £600 million and France £160 million in war loans. During the war Russia had become completely dependent on loans and supplies from the Allies to continue its war against Germany. By the beginning of 1917 Russian factories could not operate due to a lack of manpower, there were widespread food shortages and the cost of living was exorbitant. These factors along with the massive casualties on the Eastern Front all contributed to a lack of support amongst the peasant and working classes for the Tsarist government. The climate of unrest led to many political factions gaining increasing support and becoming much more active and vocal.

On 11 March 1917, whilst the Tsar was visiting troops at the front, a revolution broke out in St. Petersburg and a Provisional Government installed. The Tsar abdicated from power and was placed under house arrest. The Provisional Government under Alexander Kerensky committed to maintaining hostilities with the Central Powers but by mid 1917 the Russian Army was in a demoralised state with troops abandoning the front en masse to return to their homes. A second group of Bolshevik revolutionaries saw their opportunity in the political and social upheaval and launched a second coup on 7 November, which removed Kerensky's government from power to be replaced by Vladimir Lenin who immediately proclaimed that Russia would cease all hostilities and withdraw from the war, repudiating all foreign debts, considered a gross betrayal by the Allies.

The Central Powers supported the rise to power of the Bolsheviks as their closure of the Eastern Front had made available the 80 German and Austro-Hungarian divisions that had occupied the front line with Russia, 35 of which were sent to France to form the crux of Ludendorff's spring 1918 offensive on the Western Front. Conversely for the Allies, the Russian government in power was incidental as long as hostilities were resumed on the Eastern Front. With the Allies so hard-pressed on the Western Front, it was critical to Allied interests that a government be installed in Russia which would not only resume hostilities but would also commit to repay the massive war debts incurred by the Tsarist regime.

On 22 December 1917, German and Bolshevik representatives met at Brest-Litovsk in the first stages of peace talks between the two nations, Lenin agreed to the terms on 3 March 1918. For the Bolsheviks the terms of the Brest-Litovsk treaty were extremely harsh. The Bolsheviks agreed to secede to Germany, Poland, Lithuania, Courland, Riga and part of Byelorussia, the former having a high population of Baltic Germans. In the Caucasus, Kars, Batum and Ardahan were relinquished to Germany's ally Ottoman Turkey. The Bolsheviks also had to endorse the independence of the German-protected government of the Ukraine. The land surrendered Brest-Litovsk accounted for 27 percent of the agricultural area of Russia, 26 percent of the population (46 million people), 26 percent of the railways and 75 percent of the country's iron and steel. As a final indignity the Bolsheviks were made to pay 3,000 million Roubles as compensation for waging war on Germany. With such harsh conditions it is at first difficult to comprehend why Lenin would accept such terms, but is understandable when viewed with the knowledge that he was solely concerned with the survival of Bolshevism in Russia and not the outcome of the war. Considering what the Bolsheviks were willing to sacrifice at Brest-Litovsk, it is unsurprising that the Allies considered the signing of the treaty a treacherous act.

Another factor which led to Allied intervention in Russia was a force of released Czechoslovakian prisoners of war known collectively as the 'Czech Legion'. Before the war thousands of Czechs and Slovaks emigrated to Russia from their native lands to the west. When war broke out in August 1914, many of these Czechs and Slovaks renounced their Austro-Hungarian citizenship and attempted to join the Russian Army but the Imperial Government was not enthusiastic about funding what could easily become a nationalist movement of disgruntled ex-soldiers. The Russian Empire was comprised of many different ethnic groups, some with nationalist aspirations, and it was not seen as wise to train and arm such a large group of Czechs and Slovaks. However the Russian Army suffered horrendous casualties during the first years of the war and as a compromise it was decided to form a limited number of Czechs into a brigade. After the March 1917 revolution, the Kerensky government expanded the brigade into a full corps which fought bravely during Russia's summer 1917 offensive, their last of the war as the Bolsheviks took power in November.

Thomas Masaryk, the leader of the Czechs (who would become the first President of Czechoslovakia), wanted to transfer the Corps to France to continue the war against the Central Powers. After massive losses the previous year at Verdun, and mutiny in the ranks, the French were eager to incorporate the Czechs into their forces and in December 1917 issued instructions to recognise the Corps as part of the French Army. The only problem was that the Corps remained in Russia.

In February 1918 it was decided that the Corps would leave Russia via Kiev in the Ukraine and travel along the 6,000 miles of the Trans-Siberian Railway to Vladivostok where Allied transports would be waiting to ship them to France. The Bolsheviks remained largely indifferent to the Czechs and were perhaps happy to see the departure of such a large force of armed 'foreigners'. White Russian General Alexeyev wanted to have the Czechs form an anti-Bolshevik Army but Masaryk had no intention of this. The Czech nationalist wanted his soldiers out of Russia at the earliest opportunity to fight in France where they could take part in the defeat of the Central Powers, and secure Czech nationhood from the defeated Austro-Hungarian Empire.

In March 1918, during the German advance into the Ukraine in response to the landing of Royal Marines at Murmansk, the Czechs fought side by side with the Bolshevik forces earning praise from their Soviet commander: 'The Revolutionary Armies of South Russia will never forget the brotherly aid which was granted by the Czech Corps in the struggle of the toiling people against the hordes of base imperialism.'[2] Soon after this glowing praise had been penned, the Bolsheviks revoked their support of the Czechs going to Vladivostok. Lenin's primary concern was that once the Czechs got to Siberia they would join the White Russian forces of Admiral Kolchak and that the Bolsheviks would next see the Czechs coming in the opposite direction. On 26 March 1918 Joseph Stalin, the People's Commissar for Nationalities, agreed to let the Czechs travel to Vladivostok but as citizens and not soldiers. Each trainload was allowed to carry 168 men armed with rifles and one machine gun. All other weapons were to be handed over to the Bolshevik authorities.

The British and French disagreed on where best to use the Czechs. The French wanted them for the Western Front whereas the British did not think it was productive to transfer 70,000 men from Vladivostok to France, a massive logistical undertaking, when they could be more effectively utilised in Russia itself. The desires of the Czechs themselves were entirely disregarded by the powers determining their fate. Britain and France eventually decided to split the Czech forces, half to go north to Archangel and be shipped to France through the Arctic Circle and the other half sent to Vladivostok to make their way to Europe via North America. The Czechs themselves had no wish to be further split, they were already separated across many thousands of miles of the Trans-Siberian Railway from the Volga River to Vladivostok and were not willing to be further separated.

On 5 April 1918, a large force of Japanese troops landed at Vladivostok on Russia's Pacific coast. The Bolsheviks took this to be a sure sign of invasion by the Allies and the Czech trains were stopped midway across Russia. Frustration grew amongst the Czechs to whom it appeared that the Bolsheviks neither wanted them to stay nor to leave. The Czechs decided to hand over no more weapons and also to recover those already surrendered.

In an incident at Chelyabinsk railway station in the eastern Ural Mountains on 14 May 1918, some railcars carrying Austro-Hungarian prisoners of war halted next to a train carrying Czech soldiers. There was a traditional animosity between the two nationalities, and as the two trains were about to leave an argument broke out and a Hungarian threw a piece of iron, striking a Czech. The Czechs were infuriated and all their frustrations over the previous months came to a head: they halted the prisoner of war train and lynched the assailant. The local *soviet* intervened and interned some of the Czechs as perpetrators. When Czech representatives came to the jail demanding the release of their comrades they too were imprisoned. Upon receiving word of what had happened, two Czech battalions marched into town, disarmed the Red Guards, freed their comrades and seized arms and stores, in the process taking control of the railway station.

To Lenin in Moscow this looked like unprovoked Czech nationalist aggression, confirming his suspicions of Czech intentions to join the Whites. Consequently a telegram was sent down the line to Chelyabinsk ordering that all Czechs be disarmed and pressganged into labour battalions of the Red Army. The Czechs were controlling the railway station and intercepted the telegram, and on 23 May decided that if necessary they would shoot their way through to Vladivostok and the Allied ships they believed would be waiting there to take them to France. Armed clashes broke out between Czechs and Bolsheviks all along the line. This spark set off a chain of offensives by White Russian factions and within two weeks vast areas of Russia and Siberia were wrestled from the Bolsheviks. The Czechs found themselves unwittingly supporting the Whites by default and becoming further and further entangled in a civil war in which they had no desire to take part.

On 25 June, some 15,000 Czechs whom had already arrived in Vladivostok decided to turn back towards western Siberia to reunite with their comrades. On 29 June, with the Allies' approval, Czech soldiers ejected the local *soviet* from Vladivostok and took over the city. On 6 July, the Czechs declared that they had taken all of Vladivostok and surrounding area under protection. They believed

2   John Silverlight, *The Victors' Dilemma: Allied Intervention in the Russian Civil War 1917–20* (London: Barrie & Jenkins, 1970), p.33.

that their conflict against the Bolsheviks had Allied support, whilst the Allies still believed that half the Legion was on its way to Archangel to be shipped to the Western Front. The Czechoslovak Legion's only ambition was to leave Russia with their compatriots and fight in France. It was to be two years before they were finally able to leave.

To the Allies, Russia appeared to be on the verge of disintegration. An amalgam of differing ethnic groups with unique languages, culture and customs, the Russian Empire was collapsing as states and territories declared independence. The Germans were free to occupy large parts of Poland and Ukraine, and were still menacing Petrograd and Moscow. There was the possibility of the Germans pushing east from Finland and capturing the year round ice-free port of Murmansk, and using it as a submarine base to menace Allied shipping in the Atlantic bringing the US Army to France. White Russian forces were slowly building strength to wage war against the Red Army. The Bolsheviks were not the strongest party in Russia, they were divided on strategy and how best to secure power. There were other parties who wanted to oust the Bolsheviks and impose their own leadership on the nation. The Allies desperately needed Russia to reenter the war and draw German reserves away from the Western Front, and were willing to support the reestablishment of the monarchy or a White Russian government to this end. There was hunger and unrest amongst the people and mutiny in the Russian forces. In the summer of 1918 the Allies decided to intervene.

Part I

North Russia: Murmansk ('SYREN' FORCE) 1918–19

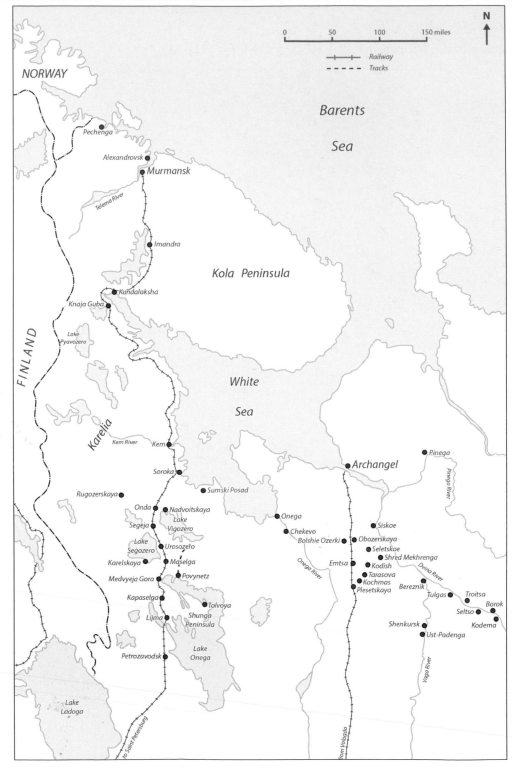

Map 1. North Russia, 1918–19

1

Murmansk: Operations in Karelia, March 1918–January 1919

The first landing of British troops on Russian soil was, quite ironically as it turned out, at the request of a local *soviet* council. In a confused series of events the Bolsheviks mistakenly believed that peace talks had broken down with Germany at Brest-Litovsk and that the German envoy was refusing to sign the treaty. This revelation, if proven to be true, would consequently mean that Germany could carry out its threat to advance eastwards from Finland (where thousands of German troops were based) towards Murmansk. The Murmansk *soviet*, fearing German attack on the town, requested that the Allies land troops to help in its defence.

Also at stake was the vital Murmansk–Petrograd Railway, the only link with the then Russian capital. From Moscow Commander of the Red Army Trotsky sent a telegram to the Murmansk *soviet* stating, 'The peace negotiations have apparently broken off. It is your duty to do everything to protect the Murmansk Railway … You must accept any and all assistance from the Allied missions.'[1]

The commander of the Murmansk *soviet*, Alexei Mikhailovich Yuryev, probably viewed this message with a certain amount of relief. A former ship's stoker and revolutionary, he was by no means a servient Bolshevik, and was independently minded and sometimes clashed on ideas with Moscow. Critical for the defence of Murmansk was that along with Allied help would come Allied troops and along with Allied troops would come desperately needed arms and supplies. In a reply to Bolshevik Foreign Commissar Chicherin, Yuryev wrote, 'Can you supply the region with food, which we are now lacking, and send us a force sufficient to carry out your instructions? If not, there is no need to lecture us. We ourselves know that Germans and Allies are imperialists, but of the two evils, we have chosen the lesser.'[2]

The Allies feared that if the Germans captured Murmansk they would have a ready made U-boat base from which the shipping lanes of the North Atlantic could be menaced unhindered, as the U-boats would not have to pass through the North Sea, heavily blockaded by Allied warships. It would have been politically disastrous if these troopships were sunk.

In February 1918 commander of the Royal Navy White Sea Squadron, Rear Admiral Thomas Kemp CB, CMG, CIE, Royal Navy (RN), requested an expeditionary force of 6,000 men to ensure the security of Murmansk. His request was denied as at the time every able-bodied man was needed on the Western Front. On 2 March the local *soviet* met with Kemp and a French Army captain to agree on the defence of Murmansk. It is questionable if Trotsky alone authorised Yuryev to ask for Allied help and allow a landing of foreign troops, but regardless, the telegram to the Murmansk *soviet* was later used as evidence in his trial under Stalinist rule.

Since the beginning of the First World War there had always been one of His Majesty's ships stationed in the Arctic to patrol shipping lanes and sweep for mines. The first British ship sent to North Russia was the battleship HMS *Jupiter*, followed by cruiser HMS *Vindictive* and battleship HMS *Glory*, which had been sent to Murmansk in the winter of 1917–18 to act as guard ship for the port.

1   Silverlight, *The Victors' Dilemma*, p.32.
2   *Ibid.*, p.42.

In January 1915 the Admiralty had received a request from the Imperial Russian government for assistance in the form of an ice breaking ship to keep the Arctic sea passage to Archangel via the White Sea open during the winter months. The Russian icebreaker had broken down and could not be repaired for some time.

HMS *Jupiter* (Captain Drury St. Aubyn Wake, RN) was a Tyne Guard ship, an old Majestic Class battleship that had been commissioned in 1895. Having left the UK for Archangel on 5 February 1915, *Jupiter* freed several ships in the White Sea that had been trapped in the ice. On several occasions *Jupiter* herself became icebound en route to Archangel. One of the merchant ships freed from the ice on 2 April was the SS *Thracia*, filled to the brim with vital war material for the Russian Army. The crew of *Jupiter* received a salvage bounty for the rescue, and remained stationed in the White Sea until May 1915 when the repaired Russian icebreaker resumed its post. The Tsar was extremely thankful for the efforts of *Jupiter*'s crew and awarded Imperial Russian orders to the ship's officers and the Medal of Zeal to her crew.[3]

Murmansk was little more than a frontier town in 1918. The port had been founded at the request of the British government in September 1915 to receive Allied arms and supplies to support Russia's war against the Central Powers on the Eastern Front. The town was constructed with British financial and technical assistance on the site of an existing fishing village and was initially named 'Romanov' in honour of the Tsar. The workers were mainly Chinese and Korean labourers but thousands of German and Austro-Hungarian prisoners of war were used as forced labour to construct a railway from Murmansk to Petrograd, many of the prisoners dying of starvation and disease in the process. It was said that a man died for every sleeper of the railway laid. Neither Murmansk township nor the railway were completed before the Tsar's abdication in 1917.

Due to the Gulf Stream Murmansk is ice-free year round whereas the only other port available to the Allies in European Russia, Archangel on the White Sea, is ice bound five months of the year. Even if Archangel was not encumbered by winter ice, it did not have the manpower, facilities or railways to effectively distribute the supplies it received. By the end of 1917 there were 12,000 tonnes of explosives and 200,000 tonnes of war supplies (which could have been put to good use by the desperately pressed Allies in France) lying exposed and rotting in and around Archangel's Solombola dock. At Murmansk, in 1916 alone over 600 ships landed more than one million tonnes of coal and over one and a half million tonnes of war supplies at Murmansk harbour but in the process lost 36 ships to U-boat attack. Nearly five million tonnes of war supplies were delivered to Russia by the Arctic convoys in the First World War, one million tonnes more than in 1939–45.

On 6 March 1918, a party of 130 Royal Marines and handful of sailors commanded by Major Henry Fawcett, Royal Marine Light Infantry (RMLI), disembarked at Murmansk harbour from HMS *Glory*. The battleship was the flagship of the British squadron in the Arctic commanded by Rear Admiral Kemp. The Marines marched into the town to an old log cabin that had been previously occupied by Russian sailors. They spent the next few weeks doing little more than repairing damage to their quarters and generally cleaning up the area as the sailors had left it in poor condition.

Reports received by Admiral Kemp of Germans advancing across the frontier towards Murmansk convinced the Admiralty that a threat to the town was imminent. Accordingly the cruiser HMS *Cochrane* (Captain James Farie, RN) was detached from the Grand Fleet to Murmansk whilst the French sent cruiser *Amiral Aube* and the United States cruiser USS *Olympia* to reinforce Kemp's Arctic Squadron.

Already in Murmansk harbour were Russian battleships *Chesma* and *Askold*, though through poor maintenance and upkeep both ships were unseaworthy, the *Chesma* partially aground. The *Askold* had an interesting history. It had narrowly escaped destruction in the Russo–Japanese war of 1905 and in

---

3   *The London Gazette*, 19 November 1915.

1. Distinctive five-funnelled Russian cruiser *Askold*. Having seen service during the Russo–Japanese war of 1905 and in the Pacific and Mediterranean 1914–17, *Askold* was seized by the British at Murmansk and rechristened HMS *Glory IV*. (Public domain)

1915 was sent to the Dardanelles to participate in the Gallipoli campaign. After the failure at Gallipoli, *Askold* was sent to Toulon and then Devonport for refitting. Whilst in Toulon, Russian exiles living in France influenced the crew and upon arrival at Murmansk *Askold's* crew mutinied, murdered the ship's captain and imprisoned its officers, right under the nose of the British ships in the harbour. This incident led to the other Russian ships in the harbour, including *Chesma*, following suit. Through the mutineers' neglect over the following weeks the commandeered ships became increasingly unseaworthy, however their guns remained serviceable, and that along with several hundred mutinous Russian sailors meant that the ships posed a real threat to the security of Kemp's squadron.

Across the border from Murmansk, Red and White Finns had been engaged in a three month struggle for power in which the Whites had emerged as victors. The Red Finns however were by no means beaten and bands of Red Finns continued to harry the Whites from within Finland. In April 1918, German-backed White Finnish troops pushed a band of Red Finns across the frontier into Russian Karelia. At request of Murmansk *soviet* leader Yuryev, Royal Marines from HMS *Cochrane* were despatched south along the Kola Inlet to the town of Kandalaksha. The presence of the improvised armoured train carrying the Marines was enough to dissuade the White Finns from pursuing any further and they fled back across the border. No shots were fired and there were no casualties.

Two weeks later Marines and sailors from HMS *Cochrane* fought the first British action during military intervention in the Russian Civil War. On 2 May the Murmansk *soviet* learned that a party of White Finns had captured Pechenga on the northern coast of the Murman Peninsula. It was feared that the White Finns would hand the town over the German forces advancing from Finland who would use the bay as a U-boat base. Admiral Kemp ordered *Cochrane* north to land 40 Marines under the command of Captain Vincent Brown, Royal Marine Artillery (RMA), a veteran of operations on the Western Front with the Royal Marines' siege guns, and an additional 100 British sailors and 40 Red Guards from Murmansk under Commander John Scott, RN, who would be awarded the DSO for his command of the defence of Pechenga.

The Red Guards were immediately despatched with two Maxim guns to occupy the three villages at the head of the Kola Inlet a few kilometres from Pechenga. Fifteen civilians with local knowledge were recruited as 'frontiersmen', expert trackers and skiers, to assist the Allied force and a running fight with the White Finns ensued. The Finns were excellent soldiers and were well camouflaged against the snow in white smocks. Equipped with skis, they were able to move much quicker than their opponents and initially forced the Marines and sailors from *Cochrane* to retreat.

On 6 May the Allied force at Pechenga was bolstered by the arrival of 35 Marines from HMS *Glory* with a Lewis gun section whilst 30 sailors returned to *Cochrane* taking with them a handful of White Finnish prisoners that had been captured. A naval 12 pdr was also landed with a naval crew from *Cochrane*. The White Finns used the only telephone line in the area for communications and the Marines were able to tap into it and with the help of local interpreters were able to discover their plans. The Marines went into action again on 8 May, Captain Brown and his men on sleighs and the frontiersmen on skis. Arriving at Lake Variema at 1500 and using information acquired on the telephone line and translated by the frontiersmen, the party set off for the Gubernatorski River, White Finnish scouts withdrawing as they approached.

In the early hours of the morning the small force reached the river and hut around which the enemy were camped. The Finns came rushing out of the house and the surrounding area. The Marines left their sleighs and advanced in open order, two lines of 15 men 10 paces apart with a Lewis gun on each flank. The Ross rifles that the Marines had been issued were frozen from the trip but the Lewis guns performed excellently. The Finnish force, numbering about 200, advanced under covering fire on the flanks on skis forcing the Marines to retire. The local reindeer sleigh drivers would have fled the oncoming Finns leaving the Marines stranded had it not been for the quick thinking of a Marine corporal who threatened to shoot the drivers if they moved. As the Marines reached the sleighs the Finns were only 100 yards distant, the Finns were apparently wary of the Lewis guns and did not continue their pursuit. As the Marines headed back to Pechenga they encountered the Royal Navy landing party and the remaining 40 Marines marching towards the location of the skirmish. Upon hearing the gunfire Commander Scott had headed out to reinforce Captain Brown's party only to encounter the Marines coming the other way. As the Finns were of superior strength and clearly had the advantage in operating on skis, Scott decided to return with the Marines to Pechenga.

On 10 May a small White Finnish force arrived in Pechenga village and boldly declared that they had annexed the town. The Marines surrounded the Finns, cutting off their line of retreat down the Kura road. The Royal Navy landing party was formed up below 'Observation Hill' when news was received that the small contingent of Red Guards at Pechenga had already ejected the Finns. In the meantime a large enemy force had appeared at 'Waterfall Hill' opening fire on the Marines who immediately mounted a counter-attack. The Marines became heavily engaged with the Finns and manoeuvred south to advance parallel to the Chelmozero road until they were halted by a Finnish machine gun. The Royal Navy landing party came up on the left and right and an intense battle ensued. Captain Brown unsuccessfully attempted to stalk the machine gun but was shot in the shoulder; he was so close that he could hear the machine guns' mechanism being cocked to correct stoppages and change ammunition belts.

A section of Finns manoeuvred to flank the pinned Marines but were driven off by the crew of the naval 12 pdr from HMS *Cochrane*. As the Royal Navy landing party led by *Cochrane*'s captain James Farie, RN appeared (Farie would be awarded the CMG for the defence of Pechenga) the Finns retreated. Pursuit was impossible, the snowfall being so heavy that a man could not move without the aid of skis or a sleigh. *Cochrane* fired off a salvo at the road, one 9.2 inch shell landing within 200 yards of the retreating Finns who proceeded to bolt, abandoning a substantial amount of their equipment.

This final skirmish concluded the Marines' fighting at Pechenga but operations there were to continue. The Finns, bloodied by rather more opposition than they expected, headed back over the border to their homeland. There were few British casualties in the fighting other than Captain Brown who was later awarded the DSC for his leadership during the fighting in and around Pechenga, the first decoration to be awarded for British military intervention in the Russian Civil War.

The swampy terrain at Murmansk froze solid during the winter and after the thaw became a muddy quagmire virtually impossible to cross. The roads during the summer months were little more than dusty tracks; in the spring they became swamps. The only reliable mode of transport in the region during the winter was the railway which ran directly south from Murmansk. The summers in Northern Russia were also notoriously harsh: a Royal Marine Artilleryman wrote in a letter home, 'Another sleepless night, a night passed in debating whether it were better to throw off the bed-clothes and expose ourselves to the onslaught of voracious mosquitoes, or to keep ourselves covered up in a bath of perspiration. At midnight the temperature stood at 80 [degrees] in the shade … How we hate the midnight sun!'[4]

On 13 May the RN/RM (Royal Marine) detachments set an ambush for a Finnish patrol that had been seen in the area but the Finns were alerted and escaped the net. The following day another 30 Marines from HMS *Glory* were landed to reinforce the small garrison at Pechenga. Information from informants was obtained on 18 May that the White Finns had lost 10 killed, four missing and several wounded in the fighting on 10 May and also a number of their strength had deserted and returned to Finland.

In the next few weeks the RN/RM force was occupied with fortifying their positions and further training. The Finns kept probing the Allied positions on Waterfall Hill so a 15-man Lewis gun section was established in an observation post on the hill. Within three days the Finns returned but were driven off by accurate fire from the Marines after which the Finns did not return. On 8 June the position was reinforced by another platoon of Marines who proceeded to build emplacements on all the commanding positions on the high ground. A small party of Finns tried to retake Chelmozero but were repulsed by the local frontiersmen using arms and ammunition supplied by the British. On 17 July HMS *Glory*'s Marines returned from Pechenga to Murmansk whilst the landing party from HMS *Cochrane* returned to their ship.

On 13 June a fire broke out at the rear of the Naval Transport Office at Murmansk which quickly spread and threatened to engulf the entire building. An armed party of six ratings and one Petty Officer under Sub Lieutenant G.N. Potts, RNR, was despatched from the armed yacht HMS *Salvator* (which had arrived at Murmansk on 21 May) to guard any salvaged material and keep on the lookout for further suspicious activity. Potts reported:

> When we were outside the house a shot was fired. Shortly afterwards a Russian civilian came running towards us stating that he was being fired at. He was pursued by several men, two or three of whom broke into our ranks, one producing an automatic pistol. The mob appeared to be closing in on three sides of us apparently with intention of attacking him, in consequence of which I gave the order to load. The mob then began to fall back … we had only gone a short distance when I heard a report of a rifle, and one of the guard fell to the ground wounded in the neck. The crowd was close at hand and thinking that the shot came from amongst them I gave the order to 'fix bayonets'.[5]

The wounded rating was carried away to have his neck bandaged whilst three men were arrested on the spot on suspicion of firing the shot. On arrival of more bluejacket reinforcements the crowd dispersed although there remained an air of disquiet. Writer 3rd Class Norman Preston was awarded the Meritorious Service Medal for this incident, for his coolness and presence of mind in salvaging money and confidential documents from a safe inside the Naval Transport Office whilst the building was ablaze.

---

4   Edward Fraser, *The Royal Marine Artillery: 1804–1923* (London: Royal United Service Institution, 1930), p.874.
5   The National Archives: ADM 137/3760: Report of Court of Enquiry into the burning of the Naval Transport House at Murmansk on 13 June 1918.

2. Murmansk harbour, winter 1918. Compared to its established sister city Archangel, Murmansk was little more than a collection of huts in 1918. (Public domain)

It was suspected that the fire and other incidents had been instigated by the crew of the Russian ship *Askold* in the harbour. To prevent any further disturbances the Russian crews were confined to their vessels with a warning that if they left their ships they would be fired on. This order led to a friendly fire incident between a section of Vickers guns from 253rd Company, Machine Gun Corps (MGC) on shore and a boat returning from the *Askold* containing a party from HMS *Glory* despite the fact that the latter was flying the Royal Navy White Ensign. A naval officer on board the launch recounted to the commander of the section on stepping ashore that he had 'a very exciting time', the launch receiving several bullet holes.

The Russian crews could not remain on their ships indefinitely so it was decided to disarm the *Askold*. Captain C.T. Brown, RMLI, with 50 of HMS *Glory*'s Marines, 50 French and 50 American Marines accompanied by some Army Staff Officers were assigned the delicate task. Most of the Russian crew had been tricked into coming ashore before the operation and the boarding party quickly took control of the ship, detaining the remaining crew on board and disabling the armament. After cleaning up the squalor left by the mutinous crew the ship was commissioned as HMS *Glory IV*.

The crew of *Askold* were paraded on Murmansk pier, covered by armed sailors and Marines. Major General Charles Maynard, CB, CMG, DSO, Devonshire Regiment, the recently arrived commander of the British Army's 'SYREN' training mission gave the mutinous Russian sailors the option to join the White Forces or be shipped south to join the Bolsheviks. The crew unanimously chose to join the Bolsheviks and were given two days' rations and sent south by train, from where they were probably sent to join the Baltic Fleet at Kronstadt.

In May 1918 the Admiralty remained concerned that during the oncoming summer in North Russia German forces from Finland might try to take the inlets on the northern Murman Peninsula for use as U-boat bases. The Army, hard-pressed as they were on the Western Front, could not provide further troops for protection of these inlets so a Royal Marines field force was created to be despatched immediately to act in defence of Murmansk and secure the railway running south towards Lake Onega.

Lieutenant Colonel Robert Paterson, RMLI, was appointed to command the hastily assembled 'Royal Marines Field Force North Russia' (RMFFNR) consisting of a field battery drawn from the RMA, a company of RMLI with platoons drawn from each of the four Royal Marine divisions and a machine gun section. Formed on 5 May 1918, the force left Eastney barracks two weeks later on SS *Porto* from Newcastle arriving at Murmansk on 29 May.

Commanding Officer:	Lieutenant Colonel R.C. Paterson, RMLI
RMA Battery (4 x 12 pdrs):	Lieutenant W.D. Craig, RMA
	2nd Lieutenant G. Jervis, RMA
	BSM C. Bryan, RMA
	85 Non-Commissioned Officers (NCOs) and Marines
RMLI Company:	Major L.A. Drake-Brockman, RMLI
	Lieutenant C.R. Lane, RMLI
(Portsmouth Platoon)	2nd Lieutenant L. Merchant, RMLI
(Chatham Platoon)	2nd Lieutenant R.C. Carvell, RMLI
(Plymouth Platoon)	2nd Lieutenant H.W. Stephens, RMLI
(Deal Platoon)	2nd Lieutenant E.A. Heaton, RMLI
	207 NCOs and Marines
Machine Gun Section:	2nd Lieutenant S. Matts, RMLI
	2nd Lieutenant H. McFarland, RMLI
	2nd Lieutenant E.B. Harries, RMLI
	60 NCOs and Marines

The Marines disembarked at Murmansk on 31 May and took over the barracks previously occupied by the Marine detachment from HMS *Glory* as well as three large buildings and storehouses, establishing 'Royal Marine Barracks Murmansk'. The Marines had to make do with what little they had and for some time the officers' mess was located in a railway car. The force was borne on the books of HMS *Glory* and was granted the title HMS *Glory III*.

The Marines did not sit idle and wasted no time getting busy. On arrival Lieutenant Colonel Paterson took overall command of the defence of Murmansk and sent 2nd Lieutenant Matts' machine gun section with some extra Marines south down the railway to Kandalaksha; 2nd Lieutenants Merchant and Harries with 60 NCOs and men went to Kolo on the north coast near the Finnish border, and 2nd Lieutenant McFarland was sent to Pechenga to train the local militia in the use of the Lewis gun. Major Drake-Brockman with 2nd Lieutenants Norris and Heaton with 150 NCOs and men were despatched to Kem on the White Sea to investigate reports of Finnish White Guards in the area.

On 8 June Lieutenant W.D. Craig, 2nd Lieutenants Matts and Carvell with Sergeants Butler RMA, Phillips and Jordan RMLI and Gunner Colgan RMA, Privates Young and Simonds, RMLI, along with three interpreters were sent to Knyajoya Gorka south of Kandalaksha to take over the training of the Finnish Red Guards there. They found the Finns emaciated, ill equipped and generally in bad spirits.

The three interpreters proved to be useless as they spoke only Russian and not Finnish, a considerable oversight. The obstacles were overcome as best as possible and by using demonstration and example the Marines began to drill the Finns who originally numbered only around 60 men. One of the Finns was a former officer in the Imperial Russian Army who understood some French and through translation from English to French to Russian the men were able to get a general understanding of instructions.

The Marines were granted temporary rank without pay for purposes of training the Finns: Lieutenant Craig acted in the role of a major whilst 2nd lieutenants acted as captains and sergeants became 2nd lieutenants, forming the command structure of what came to be known as the 'Finnish Legion'. After three weeks of hard training, 300 Finns were in good enough condition to be inspected by General Maynard who praised the Marines on their fine work. One Finnish company had mutinied but with firmness and the reduction in rank of the Finnish company commander to Private, the men were brought back into line.

Within six weeks there were 600 Finnish recruits uniformed in British khaki proudly wearing the red triangle badge and flying regimental colours that identified them as members of the British Finnish Legion. Of the creation of the Legion, Lieutenant Craig wrote, 'It would have been difficult to recognise in the Finnish Legion the scarecrows who, emerging from the woods alongside the railway, revealed themselves to our gaze a few short months previously.'[6]

The British command also raised a Slavo-British Legion company at Murmansk which was also initially put under training by the Marines, but it was never at full strength and within a few months had shrunk in size so dramatically through desertion that command was relinquished to White Russian control until further recruits came forward.

On 17 July, the Finnish Legion led by Lieutenant Craig engaged a party of White Finn Guards on the Finnish Border, 60 miles from the Finnish Legion base at Knyajoya. In the brief action four enemy were killed and several taken prisoner. To avoid any further incursions by the White Finns it was decided to occupy posts along the frontier to cover the route to Knyajoya.

On one patrol along the frontier Lieutenant Matts and his platoon were almost cut off but escaped after a skirmish in which some of his Finns were killed. Matts was suffering from an old leg wound and was invalided home shortly afterwards. Private Young, RMLI, took command of Matts' platoon and continued the men in Lewis gun and small unit tactics until relieved by army officers of the 'SYREN' Training Mission, a task well beyond his experience and rank. Lieutenant Craig maintained a Royal Marine presence on the frontier until September when all Marines except for two officers returned to Murmansk. Second Lieutenant Jordan remained behind in command of a company of the Finnish Legion whilst Lieutenant Carvell joined a Finnish company at Kem on the western coast of the White Sea.

Late in the night of 30 July HMS *Attentive* (which had arrived at Murmansk earlier in the month) with a number of other vessels including the seaplane carrier HMS *Nairana* (which had arrived on 7 July), HMS *Salvator*, Q-ship HMS *Tay and Tyne*,[7] USS *Olympia*, *Amiral Aube*, transports SS *Stephen* and SS *Asturian*, stores carriers *Westborough* and *Kassala*, and a number of Royal Naval Reserve (RNR) armed trawlers, left Murmansk with General Poole's 'ELOPE' Force training mission on board, as well as a section of machine gunners from 253rd Company, MGC, French 21st Colonial Battalion and a handful of Polish troops, to attack and capture the White Sea port of Archangel. The attack and occupation of Archangel was the first overtly offensive action by the Allies against the Bolsheviks and marked the commencement of offensive British military intervention in the Russian Civil War.

Lieutenant Harries and 2nd Lieutenant Merchant with 94 NCOs and men were detached from Murmansk to take part in the capture of Archangel and subsequent operations ashore on the banks of the Dvina River and were borne on the books of the monitor *M.25* until 1 June 1919 when they were administratively transferred to the books of HMS *Fox* (NREF).

---

6   Fraser, *The Royal Marine Artillery*, p.875.
7   Q-ships were heavily armed merchant ships with concealed weaponry to lure German submarines into making an attack.

Most of these Marines served with the Russian Allied Naval Brigade (RANB) at Archangel from September 1918 until the brigade's disbandment in late January 1919. The Marines thereafter served under Army command until recall to the UK with the remainder of the RMFFNR (which had remained at Murmansk) in July 1919.

At a War Office meeting on 16 May 1918 attended by representatives from the Dominions there was extensive discussion of the composition of the forces which might be deployed to North Russia, in response to which Australian, Canadian and New Zealand authorities put out a call amongst their forces for experienced volunteers of the rank of Sergeant and above for 'special service with the Imperial Army overseas'. Volunteers would not be informed of their destination nor of the duties required of them there until they were underway. Eventually sixteen Canadians, nine Australians and four New Zealanders as well as a number of British volunteers were selected for the mission, an order having been given that once selected it would not be possible to withdraw.

Command of the new force, designated 'North Russia Expeditionary Force' (NREF), was given to Major General Frederick Cuthbert Poole, CB, CMG, DSO, RGA and leadership of its two component training missions ('SYREN' and 'ELOPE') given to Major General Charles Maynard and Brigadier R.G. Finlayson respectively. Whereas 'ELOPE' was purely a training mission (which would later in the year incorporate RAF instructors) the expedition force troops were administratively placed under 'SYREN' Force command, namely 253rd Company, MGC, a company of 29th Battalion, London Regiment and 584th Field Company, RE.

Volunteers for 'ELOPE' Mission were isolated in the Tower of London where the authorities thought they would attract the least amount of attention whilst 'SYREN' were confined to barracks in a camp near Colchester. A third force codenamed 'DEVELOP' was envisaged to link up from Archangel with the Czech Legion in Siberia but did not progress beyond the initial planning stages.

Whilst awaiting orders to embark the rumour mill ran wild with potential destinations, everywhere from the Dardanelles to Siberia. The issuing of both summer and winter kit did little to dispel any of the rumours. There was no training, no briefings, the men spending their time playing cards and football. Some of the volunteers began to get 'cabin fever' and jumped the walls of the Tower in the middle of the night to stroll around the deserted streets. When the volunteers were instructed to have a stamped envelope ready to notify their next of kin of their address they expected that they would finally know their destination but instead they were told that their return address would be 'c/o ELOPE, GPO London'. It was not until embarkation on board SS *City of Marseilles* on the evening of 17 June that the rumour mill was put to rest and the volunteers were informed of their true destination, North Russia. There was no way that the men could have known that within two months they would be fighting an undeclared war with the Bolsheviks, particularly as the perceived enemy was still Germany and the Central Powers.

General Maynard was an old soldier who had seen service in Burma, South Africa and the Great War. In the manner of the time, he had been asked to head the 'SYREN' Force by an old friend over lunch at a club. Maynard accepted the job but having been invalided home from Salonika he could not pass the medical board. A friend who also happened to be a senior officer managed to convince the medical board that the 'job' overseas was of a type that would not require full fitness.

On 2 June at the Allied Supreme War Council meeting at Versailles, delegates from the Allied nations agreed on a joint effort to militarily intervene at Russia's northern ports. Chief of Imperial Staff General Sir Henry Wilson argued that no further German troops should be allowed to move from Russia to Germany and also that it was imperative to deny Russia's resources from the Germans. Wilson set out a number of British objectives of military intervention in Russia, namely:

1. To assist anti-German factions in Russia
2. To defend the north from possible use as U-boat bases
3. To protect Allied stores in the region

4. The use and protection of the Czech Legion

5. The restoration of Russia by economic means[8]

The US government agreed to participate in military intervention in Russia but not in the restoration of the Imperial Government nor, 'any interference with the political liberty of the Russian people.'[9] The US remained a reluctant participant in military intervention in Russia and was never comfortable about the use of its troops in active participation in the civil war.

The War Council decided that Allied forces in North Russia should consist of between six and eight battalions, most of which would be British, the force being placed under British military command. The Americans committed three battalions and three companies of engineers, the French and Italians would send one battalion each and the Serbs agreed to send a company of troops from Odessa to Murmansk.

Whilst organising logistics for the operation, Maynard approached the Treasury to get cash to buy lumber and pay for local labour for construction at Murmansk as there were not enough existing buildings to accommodate his troops. The General was refused and told that located at Vardo, Norway were thousands of barrels of salted herrings purchased by the British government that could be used as currency. Maynard was highly doubtful that salted fish would be any sort of substitute to a Russian workman for hard currency and had 'a strong objection to adding the running of a glorified fish shop to my other duties.'[10]

Disaster struck *City of Marseilles* en route to Murmansk: 22 of the Indian stokers were struck down with fever and died. The remaining stokers were too ill to perform their duties and volunteers were called for from amongst the soldiers on board who, not wanting to remain a sitting duck for German submarines any longer than was absolutely necessary, were eagerly forthcoming. The stokers had died from contraction of Spanish Influenza, which would ravage the globe killing millions of people over the following year. The *City of Marseilles* encountered rough seas during the journey, many of the passengers becoming stricken with seasickness. One Japanese officer on attachment with the Missions was noted to have not taken off either his riding boots or lifejacket for the entire trip. Even with the seasickness, nearly all the soldiers of 'ELOPE' and 'SYREN' training missions had seen extensive service on the Western Front and considered the expedition to be something of a holiday.

The machine gunners of 253rd Company, MGC, commanded by Major William Sheffield – who had been wounded on the Western Front with the Middlesex Regiment in 1914 before transferring to the newly created Machine Gun Corps in 1916 – were unable to assist in the engine room, as their Vickers machine guns were to be chambered from British .303 inch ammunition to the standard 7.62 mm Russian calibre, much of their time was spent busily stretching every pocket of the ammunition belts to take the new Russian round. They were also tasked with fitting four machine guns for protection in the event of submarine attack. General Maynard had previously been shelled by an enemy submarine in the Mediterranean and placed little value in the effectiveness of machine guns in the event of U-boat attack. The precautions were not without foundation as an enemy submarine was lurking in the area and was reported sunk on Tuesday 18 June by escorting Royal Navy destroyers.

Members of 'ELOPE' and 'SYREN' were given small Russian phrasebooks to learn by heart and attended lectures and song recitals led by a Russian officer. The men were generally optimistic about the operation and happy to be out of the trenches. Captain Peter Crawford, who would be awarded an MC with 253rd MGC in North Russia wrote, 'I personally looked upon the stunt as a good

8   Maynard, *The Murmansk Venture*, p.10.

9   General Tasker Bliss, US report at Allied Supreme War Council meeting, Versailles, 2 June 1918.

10   Maynard, *The Murmansk Venture*, p.17.

3. Royal Marines and Royal Navy sailors in North Russia. (Public domain)

chance compared with what we had at the time on the Western Front.'[11]

General Poole arrived at Murmansk ahead of Maynard's expeditionary force on board the US cruiser *Olympia*, which had seen previous distinctive service as Admiral Dewey's flagship during the Spanish–American War, in 1898. By 1918 Poole was a soldier of some experience with a number of campaigns under his belt. Having served on the North West Frontier of India and in the Boer Wars where he was awarded the DSO and thereafter Somaliland, Poole was serving in the rank of Major on the outbreak of war in August 1914 and had spent the first year of the war in various levels of command within artillery brigades of the BEF. Poole had seen previous service in Russia 1916–17 as Chief of the British Artillery Mission attached to the Imperial Russian Army and had some experience of Russian language, culture and customs.

The NREF arrived in Murmansk Harbour on 22 June in time to receive reports of armed men approaching the quay and several shots fired. British officers scuffled onto the deck with binoculars in an assortment of dress to observe what was happening, whilst Major Sheffield ordered his men to stand to their Vickers guns as a precaution against an armed mob which never appeared. It transpired that a group of Russian sailors had been trying to return to their ships which had been moved to make way for *City of Marseilles*.

General Maynard's impressions of Murmansk were hardly promising:

> Litter and rubbish were heaped on the foreshore and alongside the unkempt tracks that served as roads. Piles of fir logs, some partially shaped for building, but for the most part yet unfashioned, lay scattered about in seemingly hopeless confusion, suggesting that the land must be peopled by a giant race whose national game was spilikins. Outside many of the huts was such a conglomeration of unsavoury refuse that one shrank from the very thought of ever being compelled to enter them.[12]

Even a year later little had changed. Reginald Jowett was serving as a Petty Officer Telegraphist on HMS *Pegasus* when it docked at Murmansk in May 1919 and described a similarly bleak scene to that observed by Maynard a year earlier:

> The settlement itself consists of wooden houses built of roughly-hewn logs, with some attempts at architecture and artistic design. A great many of the houses are just wooden structures with a corrugated iron roof made like the top half of a barrel lying on its side. But some are really well-designed, and look

---

11   Christopher Dobson and John Miller, *The Day We Almost Bombed Moscow* (London: Hodder & Stoughton, 1986), p.50.
12   Maynard, *The Murmansk Venture*, p.23.

quite warm and substantial. There are two churches or Pagodas, tho' it is difficult to say what religion they represent, as none seems to know. Railway lines run everywhere and a great many of the allied soldiers live in railway coaches which are just shunted onto lines not in general use. There are very few roads worth the name and these are soft and sandy or muddy. Plank roads run nearly everywhere, but as they are only about two feet wide, it becomes necessary to get off them into the mud, whenever parties meet.[13]

Until other Allied Forces could arrive at Murmansk, Poole had to push on with what little he had. The British had brought with them to Murmansk an unwelcome stowaway in Spanish Influenza and a number of soldiers became ill shortly after their arrival in North Russia. There was not enough accommodation for the influx of sick at Murmansk, the town's limited number of huts and buildings were already occupied and could not cope with the number of incoming refugees let alone those requiring medical care. To overcome the shortfall tents and disused boxcars were set up as temporary hospitals for the sick. The need for buildings was so acute that General Maynard chose to use a railway carriage as his HQ.

On 27 June, Maynard headed south along the railway to inspect Kandalaksha. His train was held up at Imandra by the station master who refused to allow the train to proceed any further south. Maynard decisively resolved the situation by holding his revolver to the man's head: the stationmaster quickly reversed his decision. Once Maynard had reached Kandalaksha he found there a train full of 700 Red Guards on their way north, presumably to eject the Allies from Murmansk. Since the signing of the Treaty of Brest-Litovsk in March 1918, Germany had placed increasing pressure on the Bolsheviks to eject the Allies from Russia, threatening to send their own troops into Russia if the Allies were permitted to remain at Murmansk. Maynard was accompanied only by his aide-de-camp, Brigade Major, Chief British Intelligence Officer and a single platoon of infantry; however using bluff, guile and charm he managed to convince the Red commander to return south and even supplied the Red troops with some British rations.

Maynard had dodged an armed confrontation with the Bolsheviks, but only just. The Bolsheviks and Allies were not at war but tensions were increasing and unless the Allies withdrew from Murmansk the outcome of armed conflict between the British and Bolsheviks seemed inevitable.

A similar incident to that encountered by General Maynard at Imandra occurred at Kem not long after when word was received of the impending arrival of trains carrying 3,000 Red troops to escort the British back to Murmansk. Commanding British and local troops at Kem was Lieutenant Colonel Philip Woods, attached to 'ELOPE' Force from the Royal Irish Rifles as an infantry instructor. Having served with the 36th (Ulster) Division on the Somme where he was awarded the DSO, Woods had been placed in command of the local 'Karelian Regiment' headquartered at Kem.

The local detachment of 584th Field Company, RE under Captain William McKilligan and four sappers took to setting mines along the railway bridge whilst Lieutenants Norris and Heaton, RMLI, supervised the positioning of Royal Marine Lewis gun teams under Corporal Fryer along all the approaches and setting of range markers on the opposite bank of the river after the low lying scrub had been burned away. Headquarters at Murmansk had issued the somewhat contradictory orders that bloodshed was to be avoided if possible but also that Kem was to be held at all costs:

At length the enemy appeared, Commissar Spiridonoff and some 800 men in one train, which approached us slowly and stopped at the sight of the plank across the line and my clean glove extended somewhat in the manner of a traffic pointsman. Heads protruded from every window, and there was an amazed silence. The interpreter asked the occupants of the first compartment the whereabouts of Spiridonoff. Some way down the train a few carriage doors opened, and I told the interpreter to order them closed at once,

---

13   Victoria Haddon (ed.), *North Russia Expedition of Summer 1919: A Diary written by Mr R A Jowett* (CreateSpace, 2014).

that they were on top of a mine, and that if they disobeyed we would blow them out of existence. I then gave the pre-arranged signal to Fryer, who opened up with a few bursts of fire on both sides of the train, carefully not hitting it.

The Commissar, who was in the second carriage, was ordered out. He came up and wanted to talk, but I held out my hand for his revolvers and told him to instruct his men to throw their rifles out of the windows. This they did, with the moral persuasion of a few more bursts from Fryer's guns to hasten them. The interpreter then entered the train to see that all arms were properly jettisoned, finding a few. While Fryer took care of the train Spiridonoff walked with me to the station to be interviewed, but he was so astonished at his position that he forgot to smoke the cigarette I had given him. After the Commissar had been very comprehensively examined by Major Rowlandson, a Staff interpreter who had arrived for that purpose, he was escorted back to the train, which returned south with all its load of mischief, including their leader who was no doubt already turning over in his mind the possibilities of a future attempt in which he would not be so easily bluffed.[14]

The Karelian Regiment was a locally raised unit which recruited into its ranks the hardy frontiersmen who lived in the forests between the western shore of Lake Onega and the Finnish Frontier. From its formation the regiment was commanded by Woods with Royal Marine Lieutenant Heaton, Sergeant Walker and Corporal Fryer and two Serbian NCOs acting as company commanders and instructors. The regiment were uniformed and armed by the British but unlike enlistees into the Slavo-British Legion, did not swear an oath of allegiance to the British Crown. At the insistence of Woods, the regimental colour was a green shamrock on orange backing whilst the unit badge consisted of colour patches of green felt cut out into the shape of a shamrock; Woods referred to the regiment as his 'Irish Karelians'.

The regiment was also notable for the inclusion of an 'Auxiliary' unit of hardy Karelian women, experts in the use of small boats along the myriad of lakes and rivers criss-crossing the region. In an incident in August two young sisters, members of the Auxiliary unit, were in charge of a small supply boat when three White Finnish scouts who had been lying in wait in a concealed boat pounced on them as they passed. The order to halt being ignored, one of the Finns took aim and began firing near the girls with his rifle. The sisters stopped rowing and brought their boat about and began rowing slowly towards the Finns. As the boat came near, the Finns (who had stopped rowing) were taken by surprise when instead of slowing to a halt the sisters suddenly swerved and drove their boat with all their strength into the Finns' boat, crashing amidships with some force. One Finn was knocked overboard by the impact followed immediately after by his two comrades courtesy of a reign of blows by the two sisters, oars in hand. Two of the Finns drowned whilst the third made it to the river bank and was captured. Sisters Ackolina and Sasha Nicolina were both awarded the Military Medal by General Maynard for their bravery.

The raising of the Karelian Regiment had created suspicion amongst the provisional White Russian government. The Karelians were fiercely independent and sought assurances from the British that would assure their independence should the Imperial Government be reinstated. The Provisional Government did not support Karelian statehood nor the loss to Russia of any of the former empire and treated the Karelians contemptuously, even so far as to poison the Karelian Colonel Commandant at Kem. Woods believed that the murder had been carried out on the orders of White Russian Governor Yermoloff who was present at Kem at the time:

---

14 Nick Baron, *The King of Karelia: Colonel P.J. Woods and the British Intervention in North Russia 1918-1919: a brief history and memoir* (London: Francis Boutle, 2007), pp.159–160.

I am afraid that every British officer in Kem who knew the facts of this affair lost any degree of sympathy he might previously have entertained for the Russian cause. Indeed, in Mess I was obliged to assume a deafness from which I have never suffered in order to avoid having to comment upon suggestions of suitable reprisals in the interest of justice.[15]

By mid July, just over three weeks since the arrival of 'SYREN' Force, Maynard had occupied a significant area of land along the railway from Murmansk to Soroka. He was in a good position to repel a Bolshevik attack but it was the Germans that concerned him most. As late as September, Maynard wrote to Lieutenant Colonel Woods at Kem:

I cannot impress it too strongly on you and all Officers out here that neither the Finn nor the Bolshevik is our chief enemy. To me it is not a great matter whether you clear Karelia of White Finns or not. Your expedition is exceedingly useful, as it guards a certain extent of the western flank, gives your men experience, and enables you to get recruits. But I want such recruits to fight the Germans, who are the only people we need worry about very much.'[16]

By clearing the Bolshevik troops from the railway south of Murmansk, Maynard had freed his forces to take on his main enemy in the east. Had German forces in Finland made a concerted effort to take Murmansk it almost certainly would have been successful. German raiding parties had reached the railway south of Murmansk in June but had been withdrawn as Allied forces moved south. If the Germans or White Finns secured only a small portion of the railway, the British and White Russian garrisons south of Murmansk would have been completely cut off leaving a difficult traverse across the White Sea as their only hope of resupply or if necessary, withdrawal. The worst-case scenario that faced Maynard was a combined simultaneous White Finnish–German attack from the west and Bolshevik onslaught from the south in which event there would have been little that could be done, the result of which would have been disastrous for the British.

After the invasion of Archangel in early August, Poole gave command of the entire Murman area to Maynard and remained at Archangel with Brigadier Finlayson's 'ELOPE' Force. Maynard wanted to mobilise local forces in sufficient numbers for the purpose of manning a system of outpost garrisons east of Murmansk towards the Finnish border. This was achieved in a very short period of time, the Finnish Legion at Kandalaksha and the Karelian Regiment at Kem were rapidly expanded to patrol the likely lines of advance by the enemy.

There had been a series of strikes by labourers and railwaymen in Murmansk during the preceding weeks as local workers vowed to down tools until they received back pay they were due. The simple fact was that the Provisional Government did not have any cash and neither did the British. By November the currency situation had become so critical that Maynard left Murmansk to return to England to plea with the British Government for funds. He was promised £150,000 by the Treasury and the currency (Russian Provisional Government banknotes printed in England) transported to Murmansk via HMS *Dublin*. In an example of gross oversight the crisp, freshly printed notes had been printed with the coat of arms and monogram of the murdered Tsar. Every single note had to be individually and laboriously hand stamped to cover the Tsar's insignia. In the end the notes never went into circulation at Murmansk and were only ever used in Allied occupied areas at Archangel.

The Russian peasant remained suspicious of the new 'English rouble' and the introduction of the new currency was a complete failure. Of the currency problems, one keen observer wrote:

15 *Ibid.*, p.246.
16 *Ibid.*, pp. 305–306.

4. Major General Charles Maynard, CB, CMG, DSO, Devonshire Regiment, Commanding 'SYREN' Force, Murmansk 1918–19. (National Portrait Gallery 66386)

The country having been flooded with Kerensky and Bolshevik paper money, it was impossible to maintain any general European value, so a new rouble was issued called the 'English roubele', with a guaranteed minimum value based on deposits of securities with the Bank of England. But the peasants were not interested. They did not give up their old roubles for the new. So it became necessary to force matters. A schedule of depreciation of all old roubles was published. While the English roubles stood as guaranteed at forty to the pound all old or 'Russia' money, as the peasants called it, stepped down a ladder of fortnightly rungs from forty-eight to fifty-six, to sixty-five, to seventy-two, to eighty, to ninety, after which it was to have no value whatsoever. It was hoped, of course, that all people would avail themselves of the opportunity thus offered to dispose of their worthless money and the region would have a sound currency of some international value as a result.

Then, finding that it had a lot of old roubles on hand, the British paid their Russian soldiers and civilian labour in these old roubles that they had proposed to put out of circulation, at the same time making it impossible for the holder to spent this money in availing himself of any of the resources of the Military Intervention. Dozens of times I have seen Russian soldiers tear up this old money with which they had been paid and throw it on the floor in anger, because they could buy nothing with it.

Yet the old money stayed in circulation. When eighty was reached no attempt was made to press the process of depreciation any further. Old 'Nicolai' paper had gone out of circulation, and in the early days of August the peasants generally were preferring old roubles at eighty to new ones at forty. And there was a very general feeling among the Russian people that the Military Intervention had taken all the value out of their old roubles and in some mysterious way put it into its own pocket.[17]

In September, Maynard received his first reinforcements from Britain. The Canadians sent a 'Malamute Company' of experienced dogmen, the Italians an expeditionary force (67th Infantry Regiment) of 1,200 and the French a mobile ski-company. In the weeks leading up to the arrival of the reinforcements, reports were received of a large build up of White Finns assembling on the Finnish frontier. Maynard could not allow the Finns to threaten the railway and despatched a platoon of British infantry with 120 Serbs to advance down the railway line and probe the Bolsheviks' strength and positions south of Sumski Posad and prevent their interference with operations against the White Finns. The party was led by Captain Thomas Sheppard and performed exceedingly well against vastly superior forces. The British and Serbs were met and opposed by a Bolshevik force of battalion strength and at least 200 Cavalry. Sheppard's small band not only inflicted heavy casualties

17   Ralph Albertson, *Fighting Without a War* (New York: Harcourt, Brace & Howe, 1920), pp.100–101.

on the Bolsheviks but pushed them 30 miles down the line, a remarkable feat for such a small force against a numerically superior enemy. For his bravery and leadership in this action and on subsequent skirmishes on the same patrol Captain Sheppard was awarded the MC.

At the same time as Sheppard was wreaking havoc behind Bolshevik lines, Maynard sent two columns of troops westwards to take on the White Finns. One column was composed entirely of Karelian Regiment troops from Kem and the other of members of the Finnish Legion from Kandalaksha. The White Finns were not an easy foe to defeat and the two columns were met with stiff resistance, but on 11 September the Karelian column outflanked a Finnish guard unit and won a small but decisive victory at Ukhtinskaya on the northern bank of the River Kem. A considerable amount of arms and equipment was captured and found amongst the dead Finns were several uniformed German Army officers. The Finnish Legion Column under Canadian Major R.B.S. Burton, Manitoba Regiment, achieved similar successes and by October most of Karelia was cleared of White Finns up to the frontier.

In early October Commander-in-Chief, NREF, General Poole at Archangel requested that reinforcements destined for Murmansk should be diverted to Archangel. Maynard protested and the War Office compromised. Maynard had only to send one infantry battalion (17th Liverpools) which had only arrived at Murmansk on 17 October on board HMT *Keenum*); one artillery battery (421st Battery, Royal Field Artillery (RFA)); and a machine gun company (252nd Company, MGC) to Archangel whilst the remainder of the reinforcements would remain at Murmansk. Soon after, Murmansk and Archangel were made separate commands, both Maynard and the new commander at Archangel, Major General Ironside (who had replaced General Poole when he was recalled to London) would operate independently of each other although still under the umbrella of the NREF.

During the months leading up to the creation of independent commands Maynard had become increasingly agitated by the inequality that was being created between Murmansk and Archangel, both areas being administratively under GHQ NREF at Archangel. In a letter to the War Office Maynard lobbied for Murmansk to be granted limited autonomy:

> One of the points I wanted to discuss at home was the separation of this command from Archangel. I feel most tremendously strongly about it, and I'm certain no one who knows me will entertain the idea that I want the separation from personal motives. It is simply that, to my mind, the present system is objectless and harmful, and it would be almost as bad-though not quite-were Archangel to be under Murmansk. I say 'not quite' because cable communication between here and England is much more rapid than between Archangel and England, and written correspondence can reach here during the whole year [Murmansk is ice free year round whereas the White Sea and Archangel is frozen solid during the winter] This would enable the pith of important letters to be sent on by cable or W.T. if this place happened to be the G.H.Q. of the whole expedition. But I don't want this, as I consider one man cannot run both shows successfully.
>
> During the past ten days I've had many instances of orders received from Archangel with which it is quite impossible to comply, and which would never have been sent if any of the conditions here were known at Archangel.
>
> This has been the case especially as regards medical matters. For instance, I was ordered to send a stationary hospital of 200 beds to Archangel, when all I've got in the whole place is one General Hospital [No. 86 General Hosp., Royal Army Medical Corps (RAMC)]. Then I was ordered to send all the French medical officers who were in the French section of my General Hospital (which is chock full), leaving me with none here, and forcing me to withdraw French doctors from their proper French units down the line. When I pointed this out, I was told to comply, the words 'this is final' being added! Then too I get a wire saying they are evacuating to me at Murmansk 129 hospital cases. Most are 'sitting' cases, it is true, but my own hospital is absolutely full, and I've no place whatever to put them into. Setting aside the fact that they ought of course to have been evacuated from Archangel direct home, it simply shows complete ignorance of my position here.

Again, I was most anxious to get the Liverpool battalion down the line to Kem and Soroka. The railway was smashed at the time, and so I took the chance of sending them by sea, with three months' reserve of supplies. The ship had to go to Archangel en route to drop the howitzer battery for that side, but I let them know how keen I was to get the battalion to Kem as early as possible. Nevertheless they collared the battalion, and upset all my arrangements. I was already committed to Soroka, and am none too strong in the south. Now I have no prospect of reinforcing before three weeks, though there is a lot of sabotage, and the Bolsheviks are supposed to be organising an advance against me. Added to this, by holding up the supplies on board the ship at Archangel, my southern garrisons only just escaped having to go on half-rations.

A further instance. I lent 100 marines [of the Royal Marines Field Force] to Elope when they started for Archangel, and was promised them back in a fortnight. That was three months ago, and though I've asked for them continually I have not got them yet. I am told now that I cannot have them till I send winter clothing for them to travel in-and yet they send to me 120 hospital cases in an ordinary boat without their winter garments.

There are dozens of other cases I could quote, many of them quite small in themselves, but all leading to delay with no compensating advantages, and sometime to the feeling that due consideration is not being paid to this force-for we are all idiotically human. As a tiny example, out of the total number of 'immediate awards' allotted to North Russia, I have been sub-allotted only one-sixth, though my force is two thirds that of Archangel.

Don't imagine that I'm grumbling because I individually happen to be under Archangel. I agitate solely because I'm convinced that the formation of two independent commands is the only solution for North Russia.[18]

The day after the letter was received in London, a cable was sent to Maynard notifying him of the War Office's decision to grant Murmansk administrative independence from Archangel. With the departure of General Poole for England, the Commander-in-Chief position was abolished and the theatre broken up into the two separate commands.

On 11 November the Armistice was signed between the Allies and Germany effectively bringing the First World War to an end. British military intervention in Russia had been a direct result of the November 1917 Bolshevik revolution, the deposition of the Tsar and subsequent cessation of hostilities with Germany. The primary objective of Allied military intervention in Russia was the re-establishment of hostilities against the Central Powers on the Eastern Front. Thus, the Armistice should have resulted in the withdrawal of all Allied forces from Russia however the Allies did not leave and the British increasingly became entangled in the emerging Russian Civil War. Having aligned themselves with a number of anti-Bolshevik factions from South Russia to Siberia to the Baltic, after the Armistice the British objectives in Russia became solely the restoration of a White Russian government and removal of the Bolsheviks from power.

Even if orders had been immediately issued to withdraw all Allied forces from North Russia it would have been impossible to comply until at least spring 1919. With troops far into the Russian interior and beyond and with the Dvina River and White Sea beginning to freeze, within a matter of weeks or days Archangel would be completely frozen in and isolated from ice-free Murmansk. Archangel relied completely on Murmansk for communications with London and reinforcements so if Archangel had to be held over the long winter, so would Murmansk.

Disregarding the fact that the British were geographically entangled at Archangel until at least spring 1919, Maynard rather sentimentally stated, 'The Allies had contracted a debt of honour [to

18 Maynard, *The Murmansk Venture*, pp. 129–131.

Russia]; and the debt must be paid, however great the inconveniences and however loud the protests of those who might hold of small account their country's unwritten bond.'[19]

In the absence of despatch to Russia of large numbers of Allied troops, if there was to be any success in ejecting the Bolsheviks from power, the Allies would have to rely to a large degree on raising, training and equipping an effective White Russian Army. Recruiting had not been going as well as could be hoped, the total number of men volunteering at Murmansk had been just 400. The British raised and equipped Karelian Regiment was at almost full strength but they were disinclined to fight outside Karelia itself. Apart from Archangel and Murmansk, North Russia is sparsely populated and after three and a half years of war with Germany the number of men of eligible age for enlistment had decreased considerably. Those men of military age who were left were usually already employed in essential local services and disallowed by the Provisional Government from enlisting. In addition many men were disinclined to volunteer to join the White forces lest the Allies withdraw and the Bolsheviks defeat the Northern Provisional Governments.

General mobilisation was only one way to raise the numbers of recruits required to form the bulk of the White Russian forces in North Russia. Conscription was implemented gradually as there was a shortage of officers to lead the newly formed units. The mobilisation went well and revealed a large number of railway employees who had no real work to do due to the restricted rail service but had been preferring a comfortable local government job to voluntary enlistment.

Governor Yermoloff was confident that mobilisation in the Murmansk region would bring 5,000 recruits but in reality the total fell far short. The only other option to raise recruitment was to increase the area controlled by the Allies and this meant pushing southwards from Kem and Soroka to occupy more territory from which recruits could be conscripted.

To gather the forces necessary for the small offensive, Maynard was forced to withdraw a portion of the garrison from Pechenga garrison which was considered relatively secure in the wake of the capitulation of Germany. The small Allied force would need to be redistributed along the railway in preparation for winter, arctic equipment and sledges issued and the men formed into mobile columns and where possible trained in the use of skis.

Maynard's concerns were not limited to the Bolsheviks however: large numbers of White Finns remained in the Finnish frontier region and some had entered Karelia hell bent on taking revenge on soldiers of the Karelian Regiment by raiding their home villages. The White Finns would have to be monitored carefully.

Of equal priority to Maynard was the need to quell riots and disturbances instigated at the hands of Bolshevik agitators posing as released POWs returning to their homes in areas already held by the Allies. The current of unrest had at some times led to acts of outright hostility, the most serious of which were the destruction of railway bridges and attempted derailing of trains. Maynard would have to do his utmost to stamp these acts of sabotage out; during the winter months the repair of railway bridges would be a painfully slow process.

Ships were arriving at Murmansk every day bringing with them equipment, supplies and most importantly, men. Amongst the reinforcements arriving at Murmansk were 6th and 13th Battalions of the Yorkshire Regiment. The 6th Yorks had already had a terrible time before even setting foot on Russian soil. Their journey from England had been an epic of misfortune and bad luck.

They had travelled by train from Aldershot to Grimsby where on 15 October the battalion embarked on the *Traz-os-Montes*, a captured German transport ship whose best days were behind her, and her departure from port was delayed by mechanical problems. A delay of one to two days was expected whilst repairs were made and the men expected to be given shore leave for at least a few hours to stretch their legs rather than have to stay on board in port. Permission was refused but

---

19   *Ibid.*, p.136.

about 150 soldiers ignored the order and made for the docks and were summarily halted by Military Policemen and armed sentries. They disgruntled men were forced to return to the ship where they coaxed others that had remained on board to act together and rush the gates. Commanding Officer of 6th Yorkshires, Lieutenant Colonel George Lund, MC, drew his pistol and threatened to use it on any man that went down the gangplank. One of the rabble-rousers threatened that if he did, the men would fetch their rifles. The Colonel prudently holstered his revolver, which eased tensions and the men returned below decks. To prevent any more 'incidents' the ship was towed away from the dock where there was no avenue for the men to leave the ship other than jumping ship.

There were no further incidents and after repairs *Traz-os-Montes* sailed for Murmansk albeit with a slight list, but the Yorkshires were not long out of harbour when the engines broke down yet again. There was increasing concern as the ship started to drift towards an enemy minefield. One of the two escorting destroyers attempted to tow the ship away from danger but the cable snapped. Eventually a tug arrived and towed the stricken vessel to the Shetland Islands for repairs. On 4 November the ship put to sea once more only to break down for a third time. With a further two days of makeshift repairs complete, *Traz-os-Montes* headed out to the open sea once more and straight into a heavy storm. Most of the soldiers on board became violently seasick. The ship began to list in the water and her captain decided to anchor in a sheltered bay in the Orkney Islands and wait for the storm to pass.

On the morning of 8 November the ship started to drag its anchor and drift towards the shore. An SOS was promptly sent and distress rockets fired. The Yorkshires were taken ashore in relays by small boats, one soldier remarking when asked why he was removing the regimental badge from his headdress, 'I don't want Kitchener to know which mob I belong to.'[20] Lord Kitchener had drowned in the North Sea in 1916 when the cruiser HMS *Hampshire*, transporting him Russia for counsel with the Tsar, had been sunk by a mine.

There were only a handful of minor injuries during the disembarkation and the men celebrated the Armistice with the friendly inhabitants of the Orkneys until the arrival of SS *Huntsend* which took them the rest of the journey, it being decided not to tempt fate by making any further attempts to reach Murmansk on the *Traz-os-Montes*. It was not until 3 December that 6th Yorks entered Murmansk harbour, seven weeks after *Traz-os-Montes* had left Grimsby. After such a calamitous journey morale in the battalion was understandably low. It did not go straight into the front line but was instead initially used as a service battalion to assist Royal Engineers building a barracks and to do manual tasks around Murmansk, however the dissent within the ranks of the Yorkshires was not over.

In Murmansk, a series of suspicious incidents in and around the town had occurred, believed to have been perpetrated by Bolshevik spies and saboteurs. On 22 January a fire had broken out at Kandalaksha station (200 kilometres south of Murmansk) destroying five valuable engines and considerable rolling stock and material. On 1 February a fire broke out at one of the British barracks at Murmansk, razing it to the ground, killing Lance Corporals H. Asbury and John Holden, both of 248th Field Company, RE.

On Christmas Day, the body of 2nd Lieutenant Richard Plumpton, 6th Yorkshires, was found murdered in a ravine outside Murmansk. During a subsequent search of a White Russian barracks for contraband supplies, Lieutenant Plumpton's wristwatch was found in the possession of a White Russian soldier who was subsequently tried and executed for murder.

To compound the discomfort of the soldiers, there was a campaign by zealous teetotallers back in Britain not to send rum to the troops in North Russia. General Ironside at Archangel was furious: 'I wish I could have some of the placid prohibitionists on sentry-go for an hour in 72 degrees of frost and they would have changed their opinions as to whether it should be issued or not.'[21] As was the

20   Dobson and Miller, *The Day We Almost Bombed Moscow*, p.123.
21   *Ibid.*, p.185.

5. Three examples of 'Shackleton kit' in use in North Russia. The soldier on the left is Sergeant Bertram Perry, MM, AIF attached NREF, the soldier on the right is Sergeant Charles Tozer, RAMC. The soldier with rifle and webbing belt is unidentified. (Left image AWM AO5184, middle image public domain, right image author's collection)

custom on the Western Front, 'S.R.D.' rum ('Service Rum Dilute' or colloquially 'Seldom Reaches Destination') was issued to soldiers in North Russia and occasionally used as a form of payment for services rendered by local workers or as compensation for the hire of a *drosky* carriage (a local Russian horse-drawn buggy).

As poorly equipped as the NREF was in other areas, the 'Shackleton' cold weather kit designed by the famed Polar explorer Sir Ernest Shackleton (then serving as a Special List Major in the Army, officially appointed 'Staff Officer, Arctic equipment, North Russia Expeditionary Force'), and issued to the troops for the winter with its distinctive gloves and goggles, proved to be more than adequate apart from the much lamented 'Shackleton boot' which proved less practical. The canvas over-shoe was designed to be worn over standard issue army boots primarily for use with skis or snowshoes, had little grip on the soles, was very slippery on ice and was not completely waterproof. Use of studs made the 'Shackleton boot' slightly more suitable for garrison duty in winter blockhouses, however the shoes were rarely used in the manner for which they were originally intended.

The cold was so extreme that soldiers could not touch their rifles with bare hands for fear of skin sticking to the bare metal. No one ventured outside unless it was a short trip from one blockhouse to another. The fighting became largely static, similar to the Western Front but whereas in France and Flanders men could not advance due to massed machine guns and artillery, in North Russia movement was restricted due to the harshness of the winter.

In such extreme conditions, wooden blockhouses became crucial to holding the Allied line. Built in mutually defensible groups of three, each blockhouse was armed with a machine gun and seven riflemen, surrounded by barbed wire. A larger blockhouse equipped with two machine guns with arcs covering the three smaller blockhouses was built periodically along the line to provide defence in depth. Essential to each blockhouse was a large Russian wood stove kept constantly burning around which the occupants slept.

The RAF ground crew had an especially hard time. The engines of the aircraft froze solid, despite being constantly heated by fires and lamps, a technique used in Russia by the *Luftwaffe* during the Second World War. Another technique was to pour five gallons of boiling water through the engine

6. Sir Ernest Shackleton (second right) en route to Murmansk, October 1918. He wears the uniform and insignia of a British army staff officer Major including red and black brassard with white star insignia of the NREF. (Alfred Carey Collection, Naval Air Museum, Nowra, NSW)

in an attempt to defrost it, but after only a couple of gallons had passed through the engine would become frozen again. Valves, joints and throttles all froze to the point where lubricants could no longer be used. The wire bracing holding the wings taut frequently snapped under the intense cold. Mechanics had to work whilst wearing heavy winter clothing and cumbersome gloves. To remove the gloves was inviting the loss of fingers to frostbite. Bomb release levers were prone to freezing so the bombs were carried inside the observer's cockpit to be dropped by hand.

The cold also had a dramatic effect on the range of artillery shells. The British 18 pdr had to be ranged to 3,750 yards for the shells to have an effective range of only 2,000 yards in the sub-zero temperatures. Machine guns froze solid and artillery shell fuses did not detonate in the deep snow. An attempt was made to mix alcohol with the water cooling system of the Vickers machine gun to prevent freezing but when in the hands of Russian troops the spirits would often go missing.

Soldiers with experience of life in arctic conditions coped much better than the average British 'Tommy', especially the Italian and French alpine troops and the Canadian Malamute Company. A concerted effort was made to teach British troops to ski and in the use of snowshoes but the attempt largely failed, as it took too much time and required equipment that the Allies did not have to turn the average infantryman into a snow trooper. Men could not be spared from the front line to be trained in the arctic arts. On more than a few occasions soldiers had to be sent home with broken legs and other injuries sustained whilst undergoing ski training before the scheme was abandoned. General Ironside at Archangel had considered the necessity for ski troops so great that he wrote, 'Had we been opposed to bodies of good skiers of even one quarter our numbers we must have been turned out of the country. Mobility, when shown by either side, met with instant success.'[22]

By New Year 1919, Maynard was relatively content that he had enough men, supplies and equipment to defend Murmansk. His troops had completed fortifications and blockhouses for the

---

22 *Ibid.*, p.186.

winter and were well positioned to repel any Red Army advance on the town. The Germans and White Finns were out of the picture and Maynard no longer had to worry about the Finnish frontier to his east; any Bolshevik advance would inevitably come from the south following the railway.

No matter how well he had prepared, Maynard could not have expected the following 10 months of bitter fighting against a numerically superior enemy that was becoming increasingly skilled, organised and strong with every passing week. There would be difficult fighting during an Arctic winter and an unbearably hot and dry summer. What were initially small skirmishes would escalate into full scale offensives including naval flotilla actions and bombing and strafing by RAF aircraft operating from both sea and land.

2

Murmansk: General Maynard's Offensive, February–April 1919

On the Murmansk front, the beginning of 1919 brought with it the same problems that had plagued Maynard since his arrival: that of finance. When Yermoloff took over as Governor the British government was only able to provide the White Russian Provisional Government at Murmansk with one million roubles when the local Russian authority already owed 20 million roubles in wages alone. It was obvious to both men that it would be impossible to end the labour unrest and implement administrative changes if additional funding was not forthcoming immediately.

No repairs were being carried out along the railway and workmen refused to end striking until they were paid the considerable back pay owed. The significance of the cessation of repairs on the railway was brought to a head on 21 October 1918 when a train carrying two companies of 11th Battalion, Royal Sussex Regiment derailed between Murmansk and Kandalaksha causing 20 casualties, including several men killed. As the Royal Sussexes' service at Murmansk was almost entirely on garrison duties at Murmansk, Pechenga, Kola and Kandalaksha until their return to the UK in August 1919, they were virtually the only casualties sustained by the regiment in Russia. Discontent amongst the railway workers also began to manifest itself in an increasing number of attempts to destroy bridges and derail trains. After a number of cables back and forth between Maynard and London, the War Office and Treasury promised the immediate despatch of funds.

During February 1919, whilst General Ironside was fighting defensively at Archangel, Maynard initiated an offensive along the railway south of Murmansk. He planned to drive the Bolsheviks down the line from his base at Soroka to Segeja and Medvyeja-Gora on the banks of Lake Onega. If successful the offensive would secure for the Allies 3,000 square miles of new territory from which locals could be conscripted into the White Russian Northern Rifle Regiments. The British troops had only rudimentary experience and training in moving long distances in Arctic conditions so the experience of the Canadian Malamute Company was heavily drawn upon by Brigadier G.D. Price, Commanding 237th Infantry Brigade, NREF, in planning the operation.

On 30 July 1918 the War Office had requested 18 officers and 70 NCOs and men with experience operating dog sleds in Arctic conditions to be selected from the Canadian forces, for a special mobile unit being formed for service at Murmansk. Command of the detachment was given to Lieutenant Colonel John Leckie, Manitoba Regiment, a veteran of the Boer War who had been awarded the DSO with Lord Strathcona's Horse in 1901 and a CMG in 1917 for command of an infantry Brigade on the Western Front; whilst Major Lawrence Mackenzie, Nova Scotia Regiment, was made second in command. The special mobile unit was eventually dubbed 'Canadian Malamute Company' and sailed from Leith for Murmansk on board SS *Leicestershire* on 17 September, reaching Murmansk 10 days later.

Maynard had made significant preparations for transport and communications for the offensive. The Laplanders of the remote regions of Karelia, expert hunters and sleigh drivers, had been contracted to supply 600 reindeer sleighs alone. Four mobile columns, each of 200 men, were being formed and equipped with winter kit and were being trained in the use of skis, snowshoes and sleigh driving, all under the supervision and instruction of Antarctic adventurer Commander Victor Campbell, DSO and Bar, RN.

A serving naval officer, at the start of the war Campbell had been appointed by the Admiralty to command Drake Battalion, Royal Naval Division and was awarded the DSO for leadership of the battalion during the Gallipoli campaign and a Bar to the same award for services in the sinking of a German U-boat in 1917. On St. George's Day 1918, in command of Vice Admiral Roger Keyes' flagship, 'W' Class destroyer HMS *Warwick*, Campbell took part in the raid on Zeebrugge, an attempt by the Royal Navy to blockade the Belgian port from use by the German navy. By the time he was appointed for special service to the Admiralty as an Arctic adviser at Murmansk (much in the same manner as Shackleton, although Campbell was already a serving naval officer) he had had a very lively war. Both Shackleton and Campbell would add OBEs to their already impressive set of awards for services in North Russia.

Sir Ernest Shackleton, utilising his experience from expeditions in the Antarctic, was tasked with developing a system for packing the supply sledges of the offensive columns. Each sleigh would carry a specific amount of supplies and equipment for a specific number of men for a specific number of days.

Murmansk lies 200 miles within the Arctic Circle and during the months December–March is subject to one of the most severe winters on the planet. During these winter months it is excruciating enough to cope with day-to-day life let alone prosecute a war with the enemy. In such an environment it was exceedingly easy to lose a finger, toes or sometimes even limbs to frostbite, as Maynard was to experience for himself in March 1919:

> I was presenting decorations after an inspection parade at Soroka, and found it impossible to affix them to the tunics of recipients without removing my thick gloves. These I was careful to discard only for the few moments required for pinning on the insignia, replacing them during the narration of the circumstances in which the various awards had been earned.
>
> It happened, however that three men were to be decorated in connection with a gallant little affair in which they played a joint part, and one narrative giving the ground for award sufficed for all three. It fell to me, therefore, to affix three insignia in succession without my gloves. When decorating the third man, I found it exceedingly difficult to push the safety pin through – as I thought – the cloth of his tunic. I pressed harder still, but the tip of the pin would not appear; and it was only when I looked more closely to ascertain the cause that I saw blood oozing from my left hand. I had driven the pin deep into a half frozen finger, without being in any way aware of it.[1]

Due to the diligence and close supervision of officers and NCOs, cases of frostbite were, considering the locale, very few. One case that particularly saddened Maynard was that of an ex-Colonel of the Norwegian Army who had volunteered for the French ski company. He had been caught outside one night and unable to reach shelter before night fell. When Maynard visited him in hospital the gallant Norwegian had both his feet amputated and several fingers but was lucky to escape with his life.

In order to contemplate mobile operations during the winter, Maynard needed a force of competent ski troops. The Red Finns of the Finnish Legion were all excellent skiers but would not fight against the Bolsheviks. The only other troops available suitable for cross-country work on snow were the Canadian Malamute Company and small detachments from the Italian and French contingents and a few Serbs and local Karelians. It takes time to train the average foot soldier to become confident on skis and snowshoes and then to build condition to carry a rifle, pack, ammunition and supplies and to move quickly cross-country, and by the time adequate British troops could be trained it would already be spring with most of the snow long since melted.

Another important consideration for the offensive was the serviceability of railway communications. Maynard hoped to cover at least 60 miles to Segeja, so the repair of railway bridges destroyed by Bolshevik saboteurs was a primary concern. Maynard had informed Governor Yermoloff that he

---

1   Maynard, *The Murmansk Venture*, p.195.

thought it unwise to begin the offensive until at least mid February. Yermoloff agreed and it was decided that the next 4–5 weeks would be devoted solely to preparations for the attack.

Planning for Maynard's winter offensive was diverted in the New Year when orders were received from the War Office for the transfer of 6th and 13th Battalions, Yorkshire Regiment from Murmansk to 'ELOPE' Force at Archangel. Shackleton was assisted in planning the transfer by Lieutenant Joseph Stenhouse, DSC, RNR, formerly Master of Steam Yacht *Aurora* (expedition vessel of Ross Sea Party of Shackleton's 1914–16 expedition) during its 312 day drift stuck in sea ice.

After service in Antarctica, Stenhouse immediately returned to England and resumed naval duties. On 26 September 1917 whilst Gunnery Officer on Q-ship *Q61* captained by famed polar seaman Frank Worsley, Stenhouse participated in the sinking of a German U-boat in the Irish Sea for which he was awarded the DSC.[2] After the Armistice he was one of several polar explorers despatched by the Admiralty to North Russia where he assisted Shackleton in equipping Allied troops with Arctic kit and planning and logistics for the transfer of British troops from Murmansk to Archangel overland in sub-Arctic winter.

Planning for the transfer was meticulous. The 13th Battalion, Yorkshire Regiment (less 300 men transferred to Archangel via icebreaker) would travel in two columns overland from Soroka, situated on the western coast of the White Sea south of Murmansk. Each column of 200 men was divided into 13 sections of one NCO and 15 ORs with six horse-drawn sledges assigned to each section. Five of the sledges would carry three men each whilst the sixth sledge would carry the NCO and seven days rations with a total of 80 sledges per column.

A handful of experienced men trained in the cross-country skiing by Victor Campbell would travel in advance of the columns to establish rest and supply stops along the way. Each man would wear 'Shackleton kit' and where available fur caps, fur coats and moccasins with three pairs of socks. The move would be made under front-line conditions, each man would carry 120 rounds of rifle ammunition with battle kit and gas mask and all a full complement of 44 drums of ammunition for the Lewis guns. Each column would be accompanied by a RAMC (Royal Army Medical Crops) doctor and medical equipment loaned from 'SYREN' Force.

The advance party of one officer and 32 ORs left Soroka on skis on 4 February 1919 and established supply stops along the route and made arrangements for billeting overnight at Sumski Posad. The two main columns departed at intervals on 5 February and reached Nukta three days later. There being no billets after Sumski Posad the columns had to push on for a continuous 18 hour stretch before reaching Nukta where control of the columns was handed over from 'SYREN' Force (Murmansk) to 'ELOPE' Force (Archangel).

After a further four days overland in the snow the columns reached the Allied front line on the Archangel–Vologda railway front at Obozerskaya from where the Yorkshires were sent to garrison the ring of winter blockhouses. Of the conditions of the journey, 13th Yorkshires Commanding Officer Lieutenant Colonel Henry Lavie recorded:

> At about every 40 miles were depots with RASC rations for the Battalion; we started every day about 9 a.m. and marched from one town to another, the towns being about two hours march apart. On arrival all the men were put into billets so as to thaw their clothes and themselves, the cold being so intense that clothing, such as greatcoats, stood up by themselves, while all food and drinks were solid blocks of ice which had to be thawed before they could be consumed. Only one event of importance occurred on the way and that was when we ran into a blizzard, the temperature dropping to 57–70 degrees [Fahrenheit]

---

2   *The London Gazette*, 17 November 1917.

below zero; this lasted about ten hours and of course held up the march while it lasted, but no man suffered frost-bite during the whole march.[3]

The plan was repeated three weeks later by 6th Battalion Yorkshire Regiment which departed Soroka on 1 March arriving at Obozerskaya a week later. The total distance from Soroka to Obozerskaya was 350 kilometres travelled entirely on sledges and skis in severe sub-Arctic conditions without a single case of frostbite, thanks in no small part to the equipment, preparation and training provided by Shackleton and his team of polar explorers. Shackleton himself was proud of what he had achieved, 'The mobile columns there [North Russia] had exactly the same clothing, equipment, and sledging food as we had on the [Antarctic] Expedition. No expense was spared to obtain the best of everything for them, and as a result not a single case of avoidable frost-bite was reported.'[4]

Through networks of spies and informants the Bolsheviks likely knew the offensive was coming and sent a column of 300 men into southern Karelia. It was unlikely that this small force had any intention of occupying Karelia but were probably tasked with recruiting and spreading propaganda and establishing an advanced Headquarters.

It would be against Allied interests to allow the Bolshevik force to operate unhindered, as every recruit that joined the Bolshevik cause was one less that could be available to join the White Russian forces. The Bolsheviks were displaying more offensive spirit than Maynard had expected and had trained and equipped a force capable of rapid cross-country movement. It was unlikely that the Bolshevik force had any intentions on Soroka but Maynard could not take that chance. Something had to be done immediately.

Maynard needed as much information on the composition and intentions of the Bolshevik force as possible. A patrol under the command of French Lieutenant Angell, 'SYREN' Force interpreter Lieutenant Alfred Dicks, French Corporal De Hange and Sergeant E. Vickson, Canadian Malamute Company, made an initial reconnaissance on skis of the enemy positions to the south, covering 150 *versts* in 41 hours (a *verst* was a Russian unit of measurement equivalent to approximately one kilometre). As a result of Angell's report that the town of Rugozero (also known as Rugozerskaya) was lightly held by the enemy, Maynard issued orders that Captain Robert Adams, Canadian Engineers, assemble a small composite force of 14 men – Lieutenant Hordiliski, Polish Army, Canadian Sergeants Hayes, Gosney, Thornton, Thorsteinson and McLeod, Corporal Amadroff, Karelian Regiment and five Karelian 'frontiersmen' – to drive the enemy from the village.

Having left Soroka on 14 January, the operation was carried out two days later and was a complete success. The village was surrounded and rushed with the entire Bolshevik garrison either killed or taken prisoner. Lieutenant Hordiliski killed one old enemy soldier wearing an Imperial Russian Cross of St. George medal at only 10 yards range, counting 44 empty cartridge cases next to the body. The Bolsheviks were taken by such surprise that they did not have time to destroy any documents and their entire Headquarters papers fell into British hands. By the time the force returned to Soroka on 17 January they had covered on skis 256 *versts* in 70 hours. For his gallantry and leadership of the force, Adams was awarded the MC.

Having lost 280th MGC, 17th Liverpools, and 6th and 13th Yorkshires to Archangel, Maynard had to redeploy the British forces he had remaining which meant significantly reducing the already depleted garrison at Pechenga. Two hundred men of the mobile column of the 11th Royal Sussex Regiment made an overland march of 112 miles from Pechenga to Kola over rough and hilly territory in an Arctic winter in three and a half days, quite an achievement for garrison troops.

---

3   Robert Jackson, *At War with the Bolsheviks* (London: Tom Stacey Ltd, 1972), pp.3–4.
4   Sir Ernest Shackleton, *South* (London: Heinemann, 1919), p.327.

By late February preparations were complete for the offensive, although the use of reindeer sleighs as transport had to be abandoned when it was discovered that the reindeer would only eat a specific type of lichen moss which grew beneath the snow in Karelia but not along the western edge of Lake Onega, along the axis of advance down the Murmansk–Petrograd railway.

The Bolsheviks had learnt of the reduction of Maynard's force and were proclaiming they would drive the British at Murmansk into the sea. Maynard was keen to get the offensive underway to show the Red Army that even though he had lost significant forces to Archangel, he was still strong enough to take the initiative. The Bolsheviks main forward garrison was known to be at Segeja and it was decided that it was here that the offensive would begin. The Bolshevik strength at Segeja was estimated at 400 men, not including reinforcements available by train from Maselga north of Lake Onega.

With so few troops involved the word 'offensive' is perhaps too grandiose a term when used in comparison to offensives on the Western Front which involved hundreds of thousands of men and thousands of artillery pieces. Tiny in comparison with other First World War theatres, Maynard's entire offensive force numbered just 600 men, few of whom were British and most of the 'British' contingent were in fact Canadians from the Malamute Company which was operating without their sled dogs, as it was found they were unsuitable to operate in the terrain. The attack was divided into four columns which would operate independently of each other until all objectives had been taken.

The offensive force was divided into four columns:

No. 1 Column:	Major L. Mackenzie, Malamute Company
	15 Canadians, Malamute Company
	25 gunners 253rd Company, MGC
	50 Russians
	50 French ski troops
	3 x Lewis guns, 1 section, 237th Trench Mortar Battery (TMB)
No. 2 Column:	Captain A. Eastham, MC, Malamute Company
	15 Canadians, Malamute Company
	50 Serbians
	2 sections, 237th Trench Mortar Battery
No. 3 Column:	Colonel Marincovich, Serbian Company
	50 Serbians
No. 4 Column:	Major L. Drake-Brockman, RMLI
	75 men Karelian Regiment
	Captain R. Adams, MC, Canadian Engineers
	3 x Lewis guns

No. 1 Column was tasked to cut the railway and telegraph lines to the south of Segeja bridge before leaving a small detachment of Russian troops to cut off the enemy's retreat whilst the remainder of the column attacked Segeja from the south; No. 2 Column would concentrate at Parandova before attacking south along the road towards the village of Nadvoitskaya (also known as 'Nadvoitsa'). The Serbs of No. 3 Column were to move south from Parandova before detouring to the west to cut off the enemy post at Onda, whilst the Karelians of No. 4 Column would attack Segeja from the west.

The first bound of the offensive would not be easy. The Arctic mobility training that the men had been undergoing would be tested to its fullest as the temperature dropped. There were no marked tracks, and passages would have to be made over wild tundra and thick forests. Many of the bridges along the railway had been destroyed and not repaired and the frozen rivers and streams would create difficulties in crossing due to unstable and slippery riverbanks. Whilst there had been heavy fighting at Archangel since October, the February offensive would be the first significant action on

7. Some of the Canadian Malamute Company before sailing for Russia. The officer in the centre is Captain Alfred Eastham, MC, attached to the unit from the Canadian MGC. To his right is Sergeant Richard McNaughton, attached from the Central Ontario Regiment. Both Eastham and McNaughton were decorated with the DSO and DCM respectively for bravery during the attack on Nadvoitsa, 19 February 1919. (Author's collection)

the Murmansk front between the Allies and Bolsheviks and the first attack utilising the new British-trained and equipped White Russian forces.

The men rugged up in their cold weather gear and skis and snow shoes and set out south along the railway from Kem. The terrible weather delayed Major Drake-Brockman's No. 4 Column for so long that they arrived after Segeja had been captured by Major Mackenzie's No. 1 Column, which had made a march of 100 miles in 16 hours. The Canadian, British, French and Russian troops met stiff opposition but the accurate support of the trench mortars and machine guns gave the Allies the upper hand. Half the Red Army garrison was killed, wounded or taken prisoner.

Captain Eastham's No. 2 Column to their credit managed to keep their timetable and attacked on the morning of 19 February. The town of Nadvoitskaya was taken after a sharp battle before the force pushed on to capture the nearby railway siding 22, which necessitated an advance across the ice in full view of the enemy. Sergeant Ross McNaughton, Canadian Malamute Company, was awarded the DCM for good work with a Lewis gun and for driving a sleigh across 800 yards of open snow against an enemy position which was captured, surely the only occasion in history that the DCM was awarded for action with a sleigh. The Red garrison at Onda having heard the firing to their rear, began to withdraw down the line and walked straight into the Nadvoitskaya column. The Bolsheviks surrendered and no advantage was lost by the failure of the Serbs of No. 3 Column to reach their objective in time, delayed as they were by heavy snow.

Prior to the columns moving off to attack, a patrol had been sent down the line to make a break in the railway. Near the break, machine guns were set up in concealed positions. A White Russian officer posing as a Bolshevik established telephone communications with the Red garrison at Segeja and managed to elicit from the unsuspecting commissar on the other end of the line that reinforcements were being sent north. The train arrived at 1400, an engine pushing three carriages packed with Red troops. No lookouts had been posted and the engine driver at the rear of the train never saw

8. Captain Edwin Lance, DSO, Somerset Light Infantry, attached Karelian Regiment. Lance later fought in the Spanish Civil War for Franco, was captured by the Republicans and sentenced to death but released after an extended period of imprisonment. (IWM Q73476)

that the line had been cut. The wheels of the leading carriage left the tracks and brought the entire train to a shuddering halt as the engine crashed into the forward carriages, just as Captain Adams, Canadian Engineers, opened fire with his waiting Lewis guns at a range of less than 100 yards causing 'very heavy' casualties.

Some of the Red soldiers made it through the fusillade only to be cut down within a few paces by the waiting Russian and Karelian troops. Steam hissed from the damaged engine but the driver was able to get the locomotive moving and made a hasty retreat back down the line, robbing the Allies of the capture of the entire train and its surviving occupants.

At 0900 the following morning the Bolsheviks launched a determined counter-attack supported by an armoured train and 300 troops. The enemy occupied the high ground overlooking the approaches to Segeja and commenced to shell the village. Over the following seven hours the enemy fired over 300 high explosive and shrapnel shells along the Allied line. At 1430 the enemy located the sled-mounted Stokes mortar of 237th TMB which had been firing from a concealed position and dropped a shell directly on it with their first shot, killing Sergeant Frederick Johnson (attached 237th Trench Mortar Battery from 3rd Battalion, East Yorks) and wounding Captain R. Tyhurst and two men. Corporal R.J. Spencer (who had been attached to the battery from 13th Yorkshires in December and was consequently left behind when his battalion transferred to Archangel Command) was awarded the DCM for taking over the mortar and continuing to work it against the enemy armoured train, scoring several direct hits which were credited with forcing the enemy to retire, although the train had also likely exhausted its ammunition supply. After the failure of the counter-attack the Bolsheviks made no further efforts to retake their lost ground and quietly withdrew to Urosozero.

Under shell fire for the first time, the White Russian troops were showing signs of faltering until their gallant commander Captain Daidoff took to walking up and down the line with complete disregard to his own safety to bolster the men. By the time the armoured train had withdrawn, two Russian soldiers had been killed and another five withdrawn with shell shock.

Although the Canadian Malamute Company and 253rd Company, MGC formed the backbone of the forces attacking Segeja, the White Russian troops had performed exceedingly well, so much so that in his after action report Major Mackenzie praised Daidoff and his Russian troops as being 'a splendid fighting force, keen, alert, and self-reliant. When I asked Capt Daidoff for twenty five men to go out to cover our party detailed to destroy bridges at one A.M. on the 21st, the whole detachment volunteered and insisted on going on this arduous duty.'[5]

Major Mackenzie and Captain Eastham were both awarded the DSO, Mackenzie for his command of No. 1 Column in the capture of Segeja and Eastham for his command of No. 2 Column during the attack on Nadvoitskaya.

The initial offensive had liberated 3,000 square miles of recruiting area for the White Russian forces and most importantly the Segeja bridges had been captured intact. The Red Army had received a bloody nose and General Maynard had proven that operations by his troops in winter were possible. Whilst everything at the front was going relatively well, Maynard increasingly had to contend with trouble with his own troops behind the lines.

The Karelians did not consider themselves by any measure 'Russian' and felt that it had been a case of unfortunate luck that had led them to be incorporated in the Russian empire when in 1721 Karelia, which had been part of Finland, was annexed to Russia by Peter the Great.

For the period of the Allied military intervention at Murmansk the Karelians experienced virtual independence from any Russian authority, and they wanted to keep it that way. They had committed hundreds of troops and fought on the Allies' behalf against the White Finns before the White Russian Provisional Government had even mobilised their own troops. The Karelian leaders believed that if the great powers meeting in France to discuss terms of the defeat of the Central Powers were to become aware of Karelian sacrifices for the Allied cause then surely the Allies would concur with the creation of an independent Karelian state. The Karelian leadership submitted a petition to General Maynard. White Russian Governor Yermoloff would not even entertain any such request, and for political expediency Maynard had to act decisively to end the Karelian aspirations for statehood and reassure Yermoloff that the British had no intention to start carving up Allied occupied territory in North Russia. Karelia was an important part of the Russian frontier with Finland, forming a buffer zone between the two countries. As far as the Allies were concerned Karelia would remain a part of Russia.

Maynard sent his reply to the Karelians that he would take no steps to meet their request and that in the present state of affairs in Russia the Provisional Government could not consider Karelian autonomy. Maynard also very tactfully pointed out that a Karelian state could not survive as an independent nation; they had no natural wealth, no industry, railway or seaport of their own and no communications or transport apart from reindeer sleighs. For the time being the Karelians would have to support the Provisional Government and hope their deeds would be remembered after the Civil War. There could be no thought of an independent nation under the Bolsheviks.

There was no other course of action for the Karelians but to accept the status quo, but they did so reluctantly and advised they would dissuade any further Karelians from joining the White forces, and they would serve under British command but not White Russian. For this reason conscription of Karelians into White Russian units ceased and thenceforth only volunteers were accepted into the Karelian Regiment, a unit under British control.

There still remained the problem of Karelians serving under Russian officers in British trained and equipped White Russian units. It was an intention of Maynard's to have Russians involved in every possible facet of his command, so that when the time came for the British to finally leave the Whites would be able to function independently without British supervision and support. To this end Maynard wanted to gradually introduce Russian officers into the Karelian Regiment. To placate the Karelians, wary as they were of Russian leadership, Maynard gave an assurance that all battalion COs would be British and that the Karelian Regiment as a whole would remain under the command of Lieutenant Colonel Woods. The Karelian problem was thus temporarily solved but it

---

5   The National Archives: WO 97/5427: 237th Brigade War Diary, NOV18–MAY19.

left a prevailing feeling of unease between Karelian and Russian which never went away, and likely contributed to the ill feeling in the regiment which came to a head at Kem several weeks later.

Recruiting began at once for the Olonetz Battalion of the Karelian Regiment, which was made into a composite unit by drafting in elements of the small number of Slavo-British Legion volunteers on the Murmansk front, thus introducing Russians into the ranks as well as command structure. One of the new officers joining the battalion was a young Russian named Count Bennigsen. He had been a captain in the Russian Imperial Guards and spoke English fluently. Bennigsen had been on Yermoloff's staff and was later awarded the MC for gallantry in battle. The Count remained in Russia after the British withdrawal but fled to England as the Bolsheviks overran Archangel and Murmansk in early 1920.

The Karelians were not Maynard's only concern, political considerations surrounding the British-raised Finnish Legion was proving to be just as much a problem. Formed in June 1918 from 'Red' Finnish refugees who had fled across the frontier after the German-backed 'White' Finns took power in Helsinki, the Finnish Legion was one of the strangest units to serve under British command in North Russia. The men themselves were for the most part Bolshevik sympathisers who would under no circumstances engage in operations against the Red Army but would accept British support for operations along the frontier against White Finns crossing into western Karelia. To this end the 'Finnish Legion' was formed and command given to Canadian Major Robert Burton, Manitoba Regiment, attached from 'ELOPE' Force, who would be decorated with an OBE for his command of the Legion. The men who volunteered for service with it swore an oath of allegiance to His Majesty King George and were trained, equipped and uniformed by the British. By January 1919 the Legion numbered some 1,250 men and 30 women who served as stretcher bearers and auxiliaries. The Legion was organised into eight rifle companies, a ski company and mountain battery under the instruction of Lieutenant Joseph Littlehales, RFA, who would be awarded the MBE for his service in North Russia.

The signing of the Armistice in November 1918 and removal of the threat of a potential German-backed White Finnish attack from the frontier put General Maynard in a difficult position. The Finnish Legion were avowed Bolsheviks who would not fight against Russian Bolsheviks (indeed many thousands of Finns could be counted within the Red Army's ranks, some of their best troops) and with no further White Finnish enemy to contend with, Maynard was faced with having 1,000 enemy sympathisers under arms behind his own lines. Maynard considered disarming the Legion but did not have enough British troops at hand to perform the task.

Further complicating matters was the Finns' determination to return to their homeland at all costs. The British were understandably not keen to allow a force of 1,000 men, uniformed and armed by the British, to cross the frontier and begin an armed insurgency against the Finnish government. The Legion became increasingly recalcitrant, refusing to go on work parties and threatening to damage the railway if an attempt was made to force them. The Finns had much more to lose than gain by snubbing Maynard, the only person who could reasonably influence Governor Yermoloff on their behalf and in the end an uneasy understanding was reached. To keep a closer eye on the Finns, a detachment of 11th Royal Sussex were moved from Pechenga to Kandalaksha.

As well as indigenous troops, a unit of one of the foreign contingents also began to give trouble. A company of French ski troops had already seen action at Soroka when they received orders to rejoin their unit, but refused on the grounds that Prime Minister Clemenceau had not sent them to Russia to fight. Colonel Belgou of the French Military Mission led an investigation and recommended disciplinary action but in any case Maynard no longer had confidence in the company after the refusal and ordered it withdrawn from the line.

This was one of the first cases of refusal to fight amongst Allied troops but it certainly would not be the last. In his memoir of the campaign, *The Murmansk Venture*, Maynard refused to write negatively about his troops: 'I have … little desire to wash soiled linen before even a limited public, and still less to furnish it with a detailed laundry list; and I will therefore confine myself to the general statement that, before the undertaking reached its close, there were units of nearly every nationality upon which I could not rely with absolute confidence.'[6] In a dspatch to the War Office, Maynard sought to explain but not excuse the behaviour of the men under his command:

> Owing to the extreme shortage of civilian labour, I have been compelled to employ a great proportion of them [my troops] on permanent working and building parties, and on similar tasks of an uncongenial nature; their accommodation has not always been as suitable as I could have wished; the climate is severe, and trying even to the most healthy; leave to England is necessarily rare; local amusements are confined entirely to such as we are able to provide; any movement of troops by rail is attended by great discomfort, owing to the shortage of suitable rolling stock; and, during the winter, transport by sea and road entails unusual hardships. Moreover, my men have been surrounded for many months by an atmosphere of disorder, dissatisfaction, and lawlessness, which cannot but affect adversely even the best-disciplined troops.[7]

After a dark and freezing sub-Arctic winter, daylight hours at Murmansk began to increase in March (on 6 March the temperature rose above freezing for the first time since the previous year) although the thaw did not begin until early May. Within a week the environment changed from winter to summer, so dramatic was the change that it was hard to believe that two seasonal extremes could be only a week apart.

With the thaw came the curse of the North Russian summer, horde upon horde of huge, voracious mosquitoes. In all his years of campaigning Maynard had never seen such mosquitoes or in such quantity:

> Summer's advent ushered in at once a plague of mosquitoes more maddening than any from which I have been compelled to suffer, even by the jungle-covered banks of the Irawaddy or on the marshy flats of the Struma Valley.
>
> The explanation is doubtless simple; but to us it appeared either that our tormentors were unsurpassed as long-distance flyers, or that the hardiness and longevity of their larvae were beyond belief. At that we left it, thankful, as we flapped and cursed, that at least they were not of the genus *anopheles*; since, in such a case, malaria would have been likely to prove a far more devastating foe than either German or Bolshevik.[8]

On 17 March, Maynard received a telegram from the War Office informing that Trotsky, the Bolshevik Minister for War, was sending two fresh divisions against the Murmansk front. This information only reinforced the intelligence already at hand that a large Red Army attack from the south was being timed to coincide with an uprising in Murmansk itself. At once Maynard reinforced his front line with the few troops he could spare from Murmansk and outlying garrisons.

An Allied double agent who had gained the trust of the inner circle of the Bolshevik conspirators informed Maynard that the rising at Murmansk was to take place on 24 March to coincide with the anniversary of the deposal of the Tsar the previous year and if successful, risings would take place elsewhere down the railway line. The Bolshevik plan was to raid the White barracks for weapons to be joined by mutinying White troops. The several hundred prisoners on the battleship *Chesma* in Murmansk harbour would then be released and an attack made on the British General Headquarters at Murmansk. The insurgents believed they would also be supported by sympathisers within the Allied forces, including British soldiers who would openly side with the Bolsheviks once their

---

6   Maynard, *The Murmansk Venture*, p.190.
7   *Ibid.*, p.191.
8   *Ibid.*, p.197.

9. British uniformed recruits of the Finnish Legion. The Finns in the unit were 'Red' sympathisers and would fight their German-allied 'White' countrymen but would not take up arms against Russian Bolsheviks. (Public domain)

commanders had been arrested. Additionally, significant cash bounties had been placed on the heads of General Maynard and Governor Yermoloff.

On the night of 22 March, all guards and pickets were strengthened, and Governor Yermoloff's most trusted men sent out to capture the conspirators and all in their company as they slept. No Allied troops were to take part in rounding up the suspects but would parade in strength later in the day to show that there remained an organised force in Murmansk capable of supporting the Provisional Government.

The conspirators were taken completely by surprise, arrested and taken into custody. When those intending to participate in the uprising awoke they found their leadership incarcerated and the Allied forces clearly prepared for anything. The Bolsheviks took no action and the second anniversary of the March 1917 revolution passed almost without incident. After dawn, several noisy groups of workers gathered in the streets and some shots were fired but no damage done except the wounding of one Russian officer. Maynard's counter-coup had been entirely successful.

Word was later received that a group of conspirators had escaped capture the night before the planned coup and were promptly arrested. They were workers on board the repair ship *Xenia* docked in the harbour. The local Murmansk community couldn't care less for those Bolsheviks from areas outside the township who had been jailed, but the workmen on the *Xenia* had wives and families in Murmansk who began to lobby for their release. A petition was sent to Yermoloff requesting their release to support their families, additionally stating that the workmen had not been involved in the plot. Yermoloff was not sympathetic and refused the request. On this refusal a workers committee was formed threatening a general strike of railway and dockyard workers which would automatically come into effect if any member of the committee was arrested. With the Bolsheviks so active and the onset of spring, it may have been necessary to send troops down the railway to the front within a very short space of time, so a strike had to be avoided at all costs.

Yermoloff very shrewdly offered to release the *Xenia* workmen if the workers committee signed a document accepting parole for the crew and publicly rejecting the Bolsheviks. To Maynard's surprise the agreement was signed and copies posted across Murmansk. It was a good deal for Yermoloff whose public reputation increased whilst gaining a condemnation of the Bolsheviks and a guarantee of no street demonstrations. In the end the planned uprising resulted only in a boost for the Provisional Government rather than a coup and overthrow as the Bolsheviks had planned.

There were some disturbances at Alexandrovsk and Kandalaksha but they were mainly limited to small gatherings and some banner waving. Of more concern was the rumour that the commander of the Finnish Legion had been in contact with his opposite number in a Red Army Finnish unit recently sent to the Murmansk front to oppose the Allies.

The situation with the Finnish Legion continued to cause concern for Maynard but at no time more so than on 30 March when one of its trusted officers discovered that a plan was afoot for the entire Legion to mutiny, destroy two of the bridges that they were responsible for guarding and head southwards en masse to join the Bolsheviks. So serious was the threat that Maynard cabled the War Office requesting the immediate despatch of 400 naval reinforcements to take the place of the troops he intended to send to Kandalaksha to deal with the Finns in the event of a mutiny. The request was denied but Senior Naval Officer White Sea, Admiral Green agreed to release 120 of HMS *Glory*'s marines to Army command. All Maynard could spare were two platoons of 11th Royal Sussex to face off against the Finns, whose strength numbered several hundred, and an additional 500 in detachments along the frontier. All the Finns were experienced skiers and would have every advantage over the British should the first shot be fired.

Maynard had intended to visit Verner Lehtimaki, the leader of the Finnish Legion, in person, but was detained in Murmansk by reports of impending disruption by the populace. The Finns were unlikely to be willing to engage in talks with anyone other than the GOC so Maynard thought up a very simple ruse. The network of agents and informants was very thick in Murmansk, so much so that quite often the Bolsheviks knew of Maynard's movements and plans before any orders had actually been issued. This was utilised to its full advantage when Maynard boarded the train for Kandalaksha. He stepped onto the train in full uniform with entourage only to step out the other side a few minutes later alone, dressed in a soldier's uniform complete with balaclava, hat and spectacles. The only problem for Maynard was that it was dark and the spectacles designed for reading, and the General had quite a time negotiating himself back to headquarters.

Major Royes Turner, Manitoba Regiment (originally an infantry instructor with 'ELOPE' who would be awarded the DSO for service on the Archangel–Vologda Railway later in the year), Maynard's aide-de-camp, Colonel Ernest Lewin, DSO, RA (Royal Artillery), and 200 men of the 11th Royal Sussex arrived at Kandalaksha to find mutiny in the air. The Finnish representatives were informed that British Headquarters knew about the planned mutiny and had made all preparations. They were also told of the progress of negotiations to have the Finns returned to their homeland and that any man who stood against the British would forfeit their right to be repatriated. It was left up to the Finns to decide where their loyalties lay.

Lehtimaki and a core of hotheads at Knaja-Guba (who had not come to Kandalaksha to participate in the talks) remained of the view that the mutiny should still take place but they were left isolated when the majority of Finns at Kandalaksha were won over by the negotiations. Lehtimaki may have been the leader of the Finns at Murmansk, but the Legion was a British military unit and subject to the command of Major Burton who had given his guarantee that Lehtimaki would not be arrested if he attended the talks with the British: a guarantee that he had no right to give as his superior, Brigadier Martin Turner, CB, CMG, commanding 236th Brigade, NREF, wanted Lehtimaki arrested. This left Burton in an awkward position. In the end Turner conceded not to arrest Lehtimaki (no doubt to

10. British soldiers with reindeer sleigh transport, winter 1919. Reindeer were used
extensively by local Russian and Karelians during winter. (IWM Q17027)

protect Burton's integrity as CO of the Legion) and to allow him free passage to the Bolshevik lines. Lehtimaki and one other Finn took up the offer whilst the remainder of his former supporters at Knaja-Guba signed an oath to faithfully serve the Allies until their repatriation.

The following month Lewin, Burton and two Finnish representatives left for Helsinki to finalise a deal on the repatriation of members of the Legion to Finland. On 19 July a deal was reached to allow all but 100 men (who would have been arrested on sight) to return to Finland, Lieutenant Colonel William Warren, DSO, RFA, being appointed 'British Representative for Repatriation of Finnish Legion' for this purpose.

On 25 July, the Legion were issued orders to prepare for demobilisation and repatriation but some Legionnaires, worried about what might lie in store for them in Finland, openly expressed their desire to defect to the Bolsheviks. The assurances of the British agreement did little to appease the concerns of this faction of the Legion and they eventually deserted.

On 22 August the remaining Legionnaires agreed to surrender their weapons and embark on a train for the journey to Murmansk where they boarded the SS *Kursk* for Finland via Leith accompanied by a platoon of the 1st Battalion, East Surrey Regiment, recently arrived from England. On arrival at Helsinki *Kursk* was refused entry and forced to berth at the island of Villinki whilst further negotiations took place. Eventually most of the Finns were allowed entry whilst some of the 100 blacklisted men were granted permission to settle in Canada, thus bringing to an end the curious existence of the Finnish Legion.

In the weeks leading up to the unrest of late March, the Red Army had been considerably reinforcing its troops at the front and making preparations for an attack. On 7 April Red Finns attacked Siding 19, nine *versts* south of Segeja, but were driven off by the Russian–Canadian garrison under Major Peter Anderson (who had replaced Captain Alfred Eastham as commander of the Malamute Company in March), leaving behind four dead and one man prisoner. The prisoner revealed that the Bolshevik garrison at Urosozero 20 miles further down the railway had been significantly increased to 400 men and two field guns for the express purpose of attacking and recapturing Segeja. GHQ at Murmansk had issued orders that no further advance was to be made south of Segeja but in the knowledge that he would be unable to hold out against any attack in force, Anderson began preparations to launch a pre-emptive attack against Urosozero.

On the morning of 10 April, Polish Lieutenant Hordiliski and US Army Lieutenant Rogers of the 168th (Railway) Transport Company went forward by train, with a gang of Russian workers and 25 men of the Olonetz Battalion (technically a battalion of the Karelian Regiment but known interchangeably as Olonetz Battalion/Regiment) and a few Canadian NCOs acting as escort, to repair damage to the railway bridge leading to Urosozero. The tricky task of making repairs under enemy observation was made easier due to inclement weather and poorly trained enemy sentries, the work being completed before nightfall.

Anderson's plan was for the French armoured train with the bulk of the Allied troops on board (including Anderson, Captain Robert Hood and seven Canadian sergeants) to rush the town, taking the garrison (who would be unaware that the railway bridge had been repaired) by surprise, whilst a second train with 45 men of the Olonetz Battalion and a few Canadian NCOs under Captain John Nesbitt would follow 600 yards behind.

At 0200 on the morning of 11 April the two trains set out from Siding 19 towards Urosozero. The French armoured train got as far as 300 yards from the forward enemy positions before it was fired at. The French gunners on board the train immediately responded, knocking out the enemy machine gun post with a well-placed shot from a 3 pdr. At 800 yards from the village an enemy field gun entered the battle, firing two shots before it too was silenced by a direct hit by French artillery lieutenant Ardaillon, knocking out the gun crew.

Immediately on reaching the station, Captain Hood jumped from the train and rushed another enemy field gun, capturing it single-handed and killing the three enemy gunners with his revolver just as they were preparing to open fire on the train at point blank range, for which he was awarded the MC. The other troops on board the train quickly disembarked and swarmed through the village, sending the enemy fleeing 25 miles down the line to Maselskaya. The only fatal casualty during the operation had been Sergeant Cail Erickson (a Swede severing with the Malamute Company) becoming the first Canadian fatality on the Murmansk front, and Lieutenant Ardaillon, two Canadians and an Olonetz Regiment soldier wounded.

The Bolsheviks left behind around 50 dead and 40 prisoners along with two field guns with hundreds of rounds of ammunition, 22 freight cars (the last enemy troops had escaped with the engine), 200 pairs of skis and a variety of heavy equipment. In an ironic twist, on closer inspection it was discovered that most of the artillery shells and even enemy railway carriages had been manufactured in Canada and donated to Russia via the UK as war aid prior to the revolution. The Bolsheviks had been firing the Canadians' own shells back at them.

Anderson's surprise attack had completely routed a numerically superior enemy and captured an important railway station and village for which he was duly awarded the DSO for his planning and leadership of the attack. Anderson had emigrated to Canada from Denmark as a young man and had been serving with 1st Canadian Division in France where he was taken prisoner, subsequently becoming the first Canadian to make a successful 'home run' from captivity in Germany.

As successful as the attack and capture of Urosozero had been, it placed Maynard in an awkward position. He could now occupy the northern tip of Lake Onega but had been forbidden from offensive operations by the War Office, nor were the local White Russian forces sufficiently trained to be put into offensive action. If the northern shore of Lake Onega was occupied it would block any Bolshevik advance north along the railway whilst additionally considerably shortening the distance to the Finnish border towards which a wary eye must be maintained. If successful and all ground captured was held then the offensive might take some of the pressure off the Archangel front where the Red Army were showing a considerable increase in activity in the wake of the thaw of the Dvina River. Maynard believed that if he could capture and hold Medvyeja-Gora on the northernmost edge of Lake Onega he would greatly strengthen his tactical position. He asked the War Office for permission to continue the offensive south but his preparations were interrupted by further problems with the Karelians.

Finland saw the moves towards Karelian secession as an opportunity to regain lost territory. This left Maynard in a tricky situation. He could not appear to be overtly opposed to the Finnish aspirations for territorial expansion for fear of alienating the Karelian troops under his command. Karelia had been part of historical Finland until its secession to Russia in a treaty in 1721 and many Karelians supported a return to Finnish governance over Russian rule. Maynard had to be seen to support White Russian Governor Yermoloff's vehement opposition to losing a large part of the Finno–Russian frontier, a strategically important 'buffer zone'.

In early April, a large force of Finnish auxiliaries moved across the border into southern Karelia and on 26 April a force of some 5,000 Finns together with local Karelians moved on Olonetz and Petrozavodsk in an attempt to push the Bolsheviks from the area. Such a large force operating officially independent of the Finnish government within Allied controlled territory was of considerable concern. Maynard cabled the War Office requesting that an official guarantee be given by the Finnish government that any military action would be directed solely against the Bolsheviks and that any territory captured would be handed over to the White Russian Provisional Government.

A cabled reply was later received that the Finnish force in Karelia was composed entirely of volunteers and although equipped by the government of Finland was operating independent of their authority. In early May, Finnish Prime Minister Mannerheim made a statement that although his government was not pursuing a policy of Karelian annexation, they would not oppose Finns who assisted the Karelians in their struggle against the Bolsheviks. This statement confused Maynard somewhat: 'These were excellent sentiments but it struck me that if Karelian aspirations were confined to ousting the Bolsheviks, it was hard to understand why their efforts to pull with the Allies, whose aim this was, should show so sad a lack of enthusiasm.'[9]

With the possibility of Finnish-assisted secession, the number of men deserting from the Karelian Regiment reached such a crisis point that Maynard was forced to disband the unit and re-form it on completely different terms of service. The Karelians serving in the Olonetz Battalion (50 percent Russian, 50 percent Karelian) were good troops but had mainly been enlisted south of Kem and were of a different mould to those enlisted in the north who largely made up the ranks of the Karelian Regiment. The regiment as a whole had little offensive value and could not be counted on as a fighting force but there were a number of Karelian soldiers who were willing to continue fighting the Red Army. These volunteers were formed into a separate unit whilst the remaining Karelian troops were relegated to guard and labour duties.

On 20 May, the original Karelian Regiment was disbanded and the men offered enlistment under the following terms:

a) Volunteer Battalion, to fight the Bolsheviks anywhere on the northern front
b) Pioneer Company, for road and bridge construction near the front
c) Garrison Company, for guard duties in rear areas
d) Frontier Guard, for keeping watch on the Russo–Finnish border
e) Labour Battalion, unarmed and to take no part in fighting

Those who declined to voluntarily re-enlist would be eligible for conscription into the White Russian army. Unsurprisingly, the Labour Battalion and Frontier Guard Company were resoundingly popular. At its height the new Karelian 'Volunteer' Regiment comprised 4,000 men, most in non-

9   *Ibid.*, p.254.

combatant roles. The original regiment had numbered only some 600 on its disbandment, the difference having deserted due to 'subversive Finnish influences'.

The White Finn 'Volunteer Army' (not to be confused with the Karelian Regiment in its new incarnation as a 'volunteer regiment') in southern Karelia were soon driven out of Russia by the Bolsheviks. On their way back across the frontier the White Finns intimidated the local Karelians in an effort to sway any locals harbouring loyalty with the Northern Provisional Government. Maynard despatched a punitive expedition which arrested 15 of the instigators, resulting in a distinct improvement in behaviour on the behalf of the White Finns. Maynard had been rightly quite concerned about a large White Finnish force operating in his hinterland but as it transpired his worries had been unfounded. The Bolsheviks had solved the Allies' problem for them by promptly routing the Finnish force and sending it packing back across the frontier.

In April 1919, Maynard's small command was considerably bolstered by the arrival of two 'Special Companies' from the Middlesex Regiment and King's Royal Rifle Corps (KRRC), formed specifically for service in North Russia, as well as 65 American railway volunteers under Captain G.G. Jones, US Army Corps of Engineers. Even more importantly for Maynard was the arrival of additional artillery from 1203rd Battery, RFA and a battery of British-crewed French 65 mm mountain guns as well as stocks of ammunition for the continuance of the advance southwards.

RAF 'SYREN' aircraft from seaplane carriers HMS *Pegasus* and HMS *Nairana* would also contribute but on a small scale due to the scarcity of aircraft and bases from which they could operate. The first airstrip constructed on the Murmansk Front had been at Kem but it was a constant struggle to repair and maintain the landing strip, let alone the aircraft that were to be operating from it. Six RE8s with 14 officers and 57 other ranks had been sent out in November but the machines were well past their prime (only three aircraft were serviceable by April and these were very heavily patched up) and the aircrew were not able to utilise their machines to their full capabilities.

When Maynard had returned to the UK in December to meet with the War Office, he had pleaded for aircraft for Murmansk as a matter of priority. The Air Ministry informed that a report filed by one of their staff who had visited Murmansk stated that the area was totally unsuitable to operate aircraft. Maynard pointed out that the 'expert' had never left Murmansk township and therefore would have no idea of the conditions in the hinterland but regardless the Air Ministry refused to budge.

A new airstrip closer to Medvyeja-Gora would have to be built, the only suitable location being near the railway between Segeja and Urosozero alongside Siding 19. It would be no easy task to carve an airstrip out of the forest at Lumbushi adjacent to the siding, the work being supervised by Captain J. McLaren, RE, who was largely responsible for its completion. The airstrip remained far from ideal and by no means completely flat but the RAF made the best use of it they could. It did take a toll on the aircraft, however, and by the end of the advance one aircraft was all that could still fly, the remainder having either crashed on take-off or landing or been rendered unserviceable by the harsh climate or by being worn out.

In planning for the next stage of his offensive Maynard had a myriad of new conditions to consider. Due to the thaw, roads no longer existed and the few tracks that remained were virtually impassable. The railway was single track with many precipitous inclines that were less than ideal for the transport of guns or other heavy equipment, not to mention that nearly every bridge had been destroyed by the Bolsheviks to hamper any Allied advance.

The most arduous trek of the offensive would fall to the western column of the Olonetz Regiment. Their 100 mile long march would take them through some of the worst terrain in the region, much of it low-lying marsh and stream, making the transportation of supplies and equipment extremely arduous.

Of greatest consideration for Maynard was the difficulty of communications. The Allies had no portable wireless sets, no telegraph or telephone lines apart from the single direct line from Soroka to

Povynetz which was almost beyond use and there were no roads for despatch riders running east to west across the front. Issued maps were inaccurate, judging time and distance was extremely difficult and topographical information was unreliable. Maintaining command and control of the advance would not have been possible were it not for the gallant little band of Royal Engineers signallers of the 'SYREN' Force Signal Company.

Commanded by Captain Arthur Glover, RE, the company was the small, undermanned and overworked unit on whose shoulders the difficult task of establishing and maintaining communications for the offensive would rest. Glover's signallers performed sterling service under extremely difficult circumstances during the advance and indeed the entire campaign. Great strain was placed on the signallers during the offensive, they were almost constantly working to repair and maintain communications across the wide front which involved long treks back and forth along the line. For his outstanding services and leadership of the company, Captain Glover was awarded the MC whilst Sergeant C.T. Flinn was awarded the DCM. Glover may well have joked that he deserved a Polar Medal rather than the MC, his citation recalling that during the advance his duties included '...walking twenty miles in a night under severe Arctic conditions.'[10]

Given the logistical and strategic obstacles facing him, it is surprising that Maynard did not postpone the offensive until he was better prepared, but several considerations explained why he could not afford to delay. The Bolshevik flotilla on Lake Onega would soon be ice-free and there was a danger that these vessels would participate in combined operations along the northern shores of Lake Onega, threatening Murmansk. If Medvyeja-Gora was captured before Lake Onega had completely thawed the Allies would have the opportunity to launch and test their own flotilla – Mercantile Marine Reserve (MMR) volunteers were being specially enlisted to crew motor boats which would operate on Lake Onega under Royal Navy command – and begin the construction of seaplane bases for the aircraft expected to be delivered to Murmansk in May.

---

10   *The London Gazette*, 3 October 1919.

3

Murmansk: Railway Offensive, May–July 1919

The soldiers expected to carry much of the burden of the resumption of Maynard's offensive in May 1919 were men of two units hastily formed specifically for service in North Russia. Indeed without these reinforcements Maynard would not have been able to carry out his planned push down the railway from Medvyeja-Gora during the summer.

Designated King's Royal Rifle Corps and Middlesex Regiment 'Special Companies', the KRRC Company had been formed at Rifle Depot Winchester on 5 April from three platoons of KRRC and a fourth from the Rifle Brigade just four days before entraining for Russia; the Middlesex Company was drawn from men of the 2nd and 4th Battalions and formed at Mill Hill Depot on 3 April, just six days before entraining for Tilbury Docks where they boarded SS *Porto* with their sister unit, No. 1 Special Company KRRC. Both units disembarked at Murmansk 10 days later, 19th April 1919.

No. 1 Special Company, King's Royal Rifle Corps:

Commanding Officer:	Major F.V. Yeats-Brown
Second in Command:	Captain G.F. Hayhurst-France, MC
QM & Adjutant:	Captain C.P. Smith

No. 1 Platoon	Lieutenant D. Allhusen
No. 2 Platoon	Lieutenant, The Hon. J.C.C. Jervis
No. 3 Platoon	Lieutenant D.W.T. Gurney, Lieutenant S.C.F. de Salis
No. 4 Platoon	Lieutenant J.W.S. MacLure, Rifle Brigade

No. 1 Special Company, Middlesex Regiment:

Commanding Officer:	Major C. Drew, DSO
Second in Command:	Captain G.N.F. Cursons, MC
QM & Adjutant:	Captain E.J.B. Budden

No. 1 Platoon	Lieutenant F.T. Sobey
No. 2 Platoon	Lieutenant C.T. Whinney
No. 3 Platoon	Lieutenant S.F.M. Del Court, MC

On arrival at Murmansk both companies performed the usual garrison and guard duties before entraining for Siding 19 via Kem on 30 April. Upon arrival at the front line on 5 May, the companies were put to work constructing the rudimentary airstrip cut out of the forest at Lumbushi in preparation for the impending push south along the railway. With the arrival of the Middlesex and KRRC Companies, Murmansk Command's strength for the offensive had been bolstered to 3,000, of whom several hundred were British, a fraction of the total number of British forces at Archangel. On 29 April, Maynard received final word from the War Office granting permission for his proposed summer offensive.

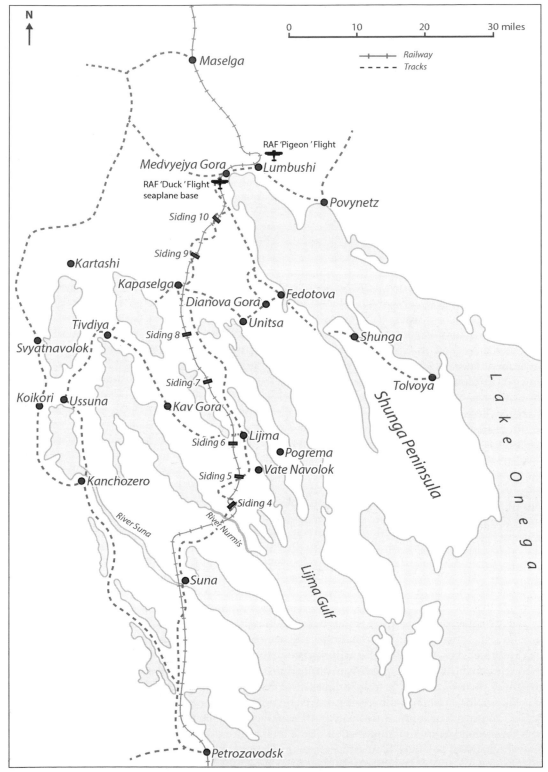

N

0   10   20   30 miles

+‒+ Railway
- - - Tracks

Maselga

RAF 'Pigeon' Flight

Medvyejya Gora
Lumbushi

RAF 'Duck' Flight
seaplane base

Povynetz

Siding 10

Siding 9

Kartashi

Kapaselga

Dianova Gora
Fedotova

Tivdiya

Siding 8

Unitsa

Shunga

Svyatnavolok

Siding 7

Koikori
Ussuna

Kav Gora

Tolvoya

Siding 6
Lijma

Shunga Peninsula

Siding 5
Pogrema
Vate Navolok

Kanchozero

Siding 4

River Suna

River Nurmis

Lijma Gulf

Suna

L a k e   O n e g a

Petrozavodsk

Map 2. Murmansk operations, May–September 1919

The advance was to be made by three separate columns operating independently of each other but with the same objectives to continue pushing southwards, eliminating pockets of Bolshevik resistance as they were encountered.

Centre Column:
>   Canadian Malamute Company
>   Royal Marines Field Force
>   French Company
>   French Armoured Train
>   6th Brigade, RFA

Left Column:
>   Daidoff's detachment, 9th Northern Rifle Regiment
>   Colonel Krugliakoff's partisans
>   Slavo-British Legion Company (Lieutenant Colonel Geoffrey Moore, KRRC)

Right Column:
>   1st (Volunteer) Battalion, Karelian Regiment (Lieutenant Colonel P. Woods, R. Ir. Rif.)
>   2nd (Olonetz) Battalion, Karelian Regiment (Major L. Drake-Brockman, RMLI)

Centre Column would drive the enemy down the railway simultaneous to an advance east of the railway by the Left Column whilst Right Column would push through the forest in a flanking movement once the Centre and Left Columns had broken the Bolshevik line.

On 1 May, the push south along the rail line began in earnest and after two days of fighting Maselga was captured by French and Canadian troops on 3 May. The 2nd (Olonetz) Battalion, Karelian Regiment arrived late in the afternoon and had been marching since 2115 the previous night, missing the battle entirely. Two days later the Karelian Regiment strolled into the small village of Podanie, abandoned by the Reds the night before on hearing of the fall of Maselga.

Canadian Captain John Nesbitt, Malamute Company (who had commanded an armoured train during the capture of Urosozero two weeks earlier) was conspicuous by his personal use of a Lewis gun in advance of the troops and for his work in setting one-man ambushes which caused a number of casualties for which he was awarded the MC.

Sergeant C.A. Fletcher, serving with 420th Battery, RFA, was awarded the DCM for bringing fire to bear on two enemy armoured trains which were holding up the advance, forcing them to retreat back to Maselga, then manhandling his gun forward some 2,000 yards before commencing fire on Maselga station, forcing the enemy armoured trains to retreat further down the line.

On 6 May, the same day No. 1 Special Company, KRRC, joined Centre Column, the Karelians were cooling their heels near the hamlet of Karelskaya waiting for damage to the line to be repaired by the accompanying US railway troops before resuming the advance. Word was being received from local villagers that the Reds who had fled Podanie on 4 May had since been reinforced by a party of 250 Bolsheviks which were threatening the Karelian positions at Karelskaya. By the night of 8–9 May, Lieutenant Colonel Woods was satisfied that Karelskaya could be held and implemented a rotating system of 24 hour patrols and pickets to detect any movement by the enemy.

One particular Russian officer had orders to take out a strong clearing patrol at 0400 along the roads leading to Karelskaya. A frequent and frustrating limitation to the use of White Russian officers was their complete lack of appreciation of the importance of carrying out orders at their specified time. Lieutenant Colonel Moore, attached to the Karelian Regiment, wrote of his frustration:

It is almost impossible to realise the elasticity of Russian ideas with regard to time. Any British officer or NCO, duly furnished with a watch, and ordered to despatch a patrol at a given hour, is more than likely to carry out the order. Not so the Russian. To him four o'clock and five o'clock mean much the same thing. 'After all,' he would say, 'both are early in the morning.'[1]

At midnight on the night of 8 May Major Lewis Drake-Brockman performed a final inspection of the Karelian pickets and outposts before turning in. Early in the morning he was woken to the sound of gunfire and bullets thudding into the wooden wall of the hut where he was been sleeping. The British officers ran outside to find the village under attack and a heavy barrage of machine gun fire making even crossing the street a dangerous endeavour. At least six enemy machine guns were in action and evidently a large enemy force in the woods preparing to attack. The location of the attack was the very direction the Russian officer had orders to take his clearing patrol at 0400 which he had failed to do at the designated time.

Drake-Brockman sheltered from the enemy fire behind the stone wall of the churchyard whilst taking stock of the situation, ordering one of his Olonetz companies to deploy to the enemy's flank whilst the remainder prepared to counter-attack under the cover of Lewis guns. As soon as the flanking party made an appearance led by the dashing Russian company commander, the holder of several Imperial Cross of St. George awards, the Red attack faltered and broke. Drake-Brockman led his men in the assault up a small hill and upon reaching the crest was giving orders to one of his Company Commanders, Captain Andousoff, when he was shot and killed by a sniper concealed nearby. The same sniper shot and killed a Russian officer and severely wounded a third before he was found in the shallow ditch from where he had been firing. The Red sniper only barely escaped a summary execution at the hands of the Olonetz soldiers by the timely intervention of a British officer. All six machine guns used by the Bolsheviks in the attack were captured as were a number of prisoners whilst the attackers left behind 50 dead.

Drake-Brockman was buried at Karelskaya churchyard, his grave since lost to time, but he continues to be commemorated on a plaque bearing his name in the Murmansk New British Cemetery. Total British and Russian casualties during the attack were three officers and five men killed and one officer and six men wounded.

On 6 May, the KRRC and Middlesex Companies were ordered south to join the offensive with Canadian Lieutenant Colonel Leckie's Centre Column with the Middlesexes held temporarily in reserve. The column advance the following day was held up when it was found that much of the line and most of the small wooden railway bridges had been destroyed by the retreating Reds. After a chilly night in the forest the advance was resumed early in the morning which resulted in a brief clash with the Bolshevik rearguard but the KRRC company still managed to take Siding 13 with relative ease. Here Leckie ordered a halt to the advance to allow the US Army railway engineers who were following the advance enough time to repair the line. In the meantime a number of patrols were sent down the line to probe the enemy further and on 9 May the KRRC managed to ambush a Bolshevik patrol, all but wiping it out with Lewis gun and rifle fire.

On 15 May, the Column was joined by the Middlesex Company at Maselga and resumed its push southwards towards Medvyeja-Gora. A couple of miles down the line the KRRC Company encountered the Bolshevik front line defences. The Reds were well dug in along a series of small ridges overlooking a cluster of huts and engaged Lieutenant Allhusen's platoon with rifle and machine gun fire. Allhusen's men returned fire whilst Lieutenant Jervis' Lewis guns moved to enfilade the Bolshevik trenches from the left and Lieutenant Gurney's platoon worked its way towards the right flank however the Bolsheviks were determined to fight it out and the Rifles attack

11. Lieutenant Colonel Phillip Woods, Royal Irish Rifles, Commanding Karelian Regiment. Woods had served as a young man with the South African Constabulary during the Boer War and with 9th (West Belfast) Battalion, Royal Irish Rifles, on the Western Front. Woods loved and respected the Karelian troops under his command dubbing them his 'Royal Irish Karelians'. (Public domain)

began to falter. Major Yeats-Brown seized command of the situation and charged through the Bolshevik fire to lead Allhusen's platoon in a bayonet charge towards the enemy. Unnerved by the charge, the Bolsheviks began to flee from their trenches, several being shot in the back as they fled.

As Lieutenant Gurney's platoon moved to the right flank it was met with a hail of fire and suffered casualties, Gurney and several rifleman being wounded. Major Yeats-Brown led Lieutenant Jervis' and Lieutenant de Salis' platoons in an attempt to turn the Bolshevik line and within a few minutes Corporal Fisher's Lewis gun was raking an enemy machine gun position forcing the Red gunners to scurry for cover. Without the machine gun the Bolshevik line began to crumble. As the remaining Reds fled their positions towards a wooded ridge 400 yards distant, Lieutenant Allhusen's and de Salis' platoons took up a position where they could engage the enemy, Rifleman Edward Boreham using his Lewis gun to great effect against an enemy Maxim for which he was awarded the MM.

On the right flank, Yeats-Brown was again at the forefront of the action leading Lieutenant Jervis' platoon and Lieutenant MacLure's Rifle Brigade Platoon uphill to suppress an enemy Colt machine gun position which was knocked out by accurate fire from Corporal Fisher's Lewis gun.

Lieutenant de Salis' platoon provided suppressive fire as Allhusen's men made a short advance simultaneously to a move by Lieutenants Jervis and MacLure on the enemy flank. During the advance Lieutenant Allhusen was wounded but the Bolshevik defence quickly crumbled under the weight of fire from the flanks and soon after abandoned their positions and fled.

The Middlesex Company was sent forward to harry the retreating enemy and after a brisk advance by Lieutenant Sobey's platoon against the enemy flank, an enemy machine gun was rushed and captured for which Sobey was awarded the MC.

As the KRRC Company rested, Lieutenant Sobey's and Whinney's platoons of the Middlesex Company, joined by a handful of Canadian scouts and Lewis gunners, pushed forward to Siding 12 with the intent to capture the siding and a field gun rumoured to be located there. A few enemy snipers were encountered but quickly sent packing. At 2100 the enemy's armoured train which had up to that point remained silent, made an appearance and opened fire on the advancing Middlesexes with machine gun and artillery fire. Responding with Lewis guns and rifle grenades, the Middlesexes pushed forward far enough that the commander of the enemy train withdrew from the engagement in fear of being overrun.

Lieutenant Whinney's platoon pursued the train down the track, bombing with rifle grenades before Whinney was held up by a large marsh on either side of the track. Whilst making their way across the mire the platoon came under fire from an enemy machine gun on a small hilltop on the opposite side of the railway which killed Private Leonard Thompson.

With night falling the Middlesexes abandoned the advance and dug in along the northern edge of the bog. The remaining two Middlesex platoons arrived the following morning and the advance was resumed, Siding 12 being captured with no opposition. The number of bloodstained dressings and abandoned uniforms and equipment strewn about gave some indication that the enemy had suffered a significant number of casualties. For his leadership during the day's fighting Lieutenant Whinney was awarded the MC. A tiny engagement by Western Front standards (indeed had it occurred on the Western Front it would have barely rated mention as a raid) the battle lasted 18 hours and cost the Bolsheviks more than 40 killed, at a cost to the British of one other rank of the Middlesex Company killed (Thompson) and two officers (Allhusen and Gurney) and eight men KRRC Company wounded.

On 18 May the British armoured train arrived at the Middlesex positions with the KRRC Company and reinforcements from the Royal Marines. Immediately on discharging its cargo the train steamed back up the line as the men took up positions on an exposed position dubbed 'Windyridge'. Not long had the British train departed than a Red armoured train arrived and proceeded to shell the British position for about an hour before steaming back down the line. Plans for a combined Marine/KRRC reconnaissance patrol had to be abandoned when the Royal Marine commander refused to allow his men to join the patrol on the grounds that they were exhausted, leaving the equally exhausted KRRC to undertake the patrol on their own. The following morning the KRRC Company, exhausted after 36 hours without sleep, formed up for the patrol without complaint, pushing through the forest adjacent to Siding 12 whilst the Marines remained behind at Windyridge.

Not far from Siding 11 a long burst of machine gun fire broke the silence through the forest and showered the men's heads with branches and twigs. The company's route down the forest path was blocked by the machine gun and an attempt was made to work around the position through the forest by use of compass. The route was found to be blocked by an area of marsh and it was whilst attempting to work around the mire that the Riflemen found themselves in the middle of a cluster of Bolshevik outposts. The KRRC had walked straight into an ambush. Immediately upon the Red gunners opening fire, Sergeant Charles Chapman from Jersey was badly wounded in the face and dragged back to cover. Shortly after, Lieutenant de Salis fell with a bad wound to the thigh. Platoon Sergeant Francis Hammond went forward to retrieve the stricken officer and courageously carried him under fire to the safety of the tree line. After applying a field dressing to the gaping wound and issuing orders to withdraw, Sergeants Hammond and Brace lifted de Salis onto a stretcher and carried him through the forest towards the railway line but became disoriented and lost amongst the maze of trees but after a long detour managed to find their way to the rear.

Lieutenant Jervis' platoon reformed and stood to inside the forest just in time to meet the Bolshevik attack which was defeated in no small part due to the bravery of Corporal William Pullinger who stood in full view of the enemy firing his Lewis gun from the hip, an action for which he would subsequently be awarded the MM. With the Bolshevik attack quashed and a lull in the battle, the KRRC Company withdrew through the forest to Windyridge arriving in a state of utter exhaustion but could not relax until they had loaded all their wounded onto a train for evacuation up the line. Later that day in the afternoon a loud explosion was heard as Bolshevik saboteurs who had infiltrated behind the British forward positions detonated a large explosive charge on the railway line cutting Windyridge off from reinforcements at Maselga. Expecting the explosion to be closely followed by an attack the British troops stood to in anticipation. About 30 minutes later the Bolshevik armoured train made another appearance, shelling and machine gunning the British from about a mile away. No casualties were inflicted, however, and eventually the train steamed away, probably having exhausted its limited supply of shells.

The KRRC felt that they had been let down by the refusal of the Royal Marines and left to carry out the half strength patrol alone. They were understandably relieved when word was received that the US Army railway engineers had repaired the broken line and their sister Middlesex Company was on its way south to Windyridge to replace the Marines who were being withdrawn. The Rifles were withdrawn to '60th village' (location of the 15th May action, nicknamed by the Riflemen after the KRRC historical regimental number) where they slept for most of the next 48 hours. For their bravery and leadership during the battles of 15 and 19 May Lieutenants Jervis and Gurney were awarded the MC and for gallantry in rescuing the wounded Lieutenant de Salis under fire and carrying him to safety, Sergeant Hammond received the DCM.

On 20 May the Middlesex Company, accompanied by Italian and French troops, resumed the offensive pushing south to Siding 11 and were surprised to find the Red forward positions which had caused so much trouble to the KRRC Company abandoned. In an anti-climax the Siding was captured with virtually no opposition. On the same night Lieutenant Del Court's Middlesex platoon pushed forward to attack the village

12. Captain Reginald Chichester, Somerset Light Infantry and Captain Reid (regiment unknown) attached Olonetz Battalion, Karelian Regiment.
Chichester was awarded an MC Bar with the Olonetz for operations at Medvyeja-Gora in May 1919, he later gave evidence at the 6th Battalion, Royal Marines Court of Enquiry. (IWM Q73456)

of Lumbushi which was captured with 10 prisoners taken after a half-hearted defence by the enemy.

On 21 May, Medvyeja-Gora at the northern edge of Lake Onega, the primary objective of the offensive, was captured by a combined force of the Right Column and Centre Column. The expected staunch defence by the Bolsheviks never transpired and the Middlesexes virtually strolled into the town, the Bolsheviks having abandoned their positions.

Captain Reginald Chichester was recommended for a DSO for his services during the advance as adjutant to the Olonetz Battalion although the award was downgraded to an MC Bar. Lieutenant George Fullman, a pre-war regular soldier who had served with the British Expeditionary Force (BEF) in 1914, was awarded the MC for his command of the 65 mm mountain gun section during the advance and particularly his work in dispersing the enemy assembled near Medvyeja-Gora station, to add to an MM awarded on the Western Front in 1916.

The KRRC and Middlesexes spent the remainder of the month taking turns with the Italian and Serbian troops on garrison duty. Rumours of an impending Red offensive and counter-attack never materialised and command at Murmansk took advantage of the relative quiet to reorganise and resupply. The troops also took the opportunity to rest up and thoroughly clean their weapons and equipment and enjoy the sunshine. During the lull, 20 men were selected from the KRRC and Middlesexes to form a 'Mounted Infantry' section for service with the Right Column, Major Yeats-Brown was evacuated to hospital and Lieutenants William Harrington, MC, MM, and Fisher, Northumberland Fusiliers, taken on strength to replace the wounded Allhusen and de Salis.

Acting in support of a three-pronged White Russian advance south of Medvyeja-Gora, a section of railway-mounted 4.5 inch howitzers of 420th Battery, RFA, under Major William Luck, MC, and the 65 mm mountain gun section under Lieutenant George Fullman, MC, MM, nearly met with disaster on 7 June when an advance by soldiers of 1st North Russian Rifles was held up by enemy rifle and machine gun fire. The Russian troops fell back on the guns whilst firing wildly in all directions allowing the Bolsheviks to push forward to the point where the railway was under threat of being overrun. Those officers and gunners that could be spared dismounted from the rail trucks on which the British guns were mounted to form a defensive line to allow the guns to be brought out of action, suffering three men wounded in the process. Luck was awarded an MC Bar for the action and BSM Tilbury the DCM for bringing up ammunition under fire.

On 10 June, a 500-strong force of White Russians was ordered to resume the advance south of Medvyeja-Gora and capture Siding 10 but the Russian troops refused to advance. The following day the Middlesexes and Lieutenant MacLure's Rifle Brigade Platoon with the remainder of the KRRC Company in reserve were ordered into the attack in their place. The Reds were dug into a strong position on a ridgeline with blockhouses with large fields of fire protected on the flanks by marshland. The British 4.5 inch howitzers were brought into action and laid down an accurate barrage on the ridge during which the enemy fire slackened and became increasingly inaccurate, Private Edward Felton, 253rd MGC, received the DCM for good work with his Lewis gun during the attack. By the time the Middlesexes and MacLure's men reached the crest of the ridge the Bolsheviks had long since fled.

On 19 June the Mounted Infantry section attacked the village of Kartashi, managing to infiltrate through the outer line of defences into the village itself where Private R. Sheead, attached from the Middlesex Company, encountered seven enemy soldiers getting a machine gun into action outside a house. Sheead charged the Bolsheviks, bayoneted one and shot another before the remaining five fired and wounded Sheead in two places. The Bolsheviks were soon after driven from the village, the capture of which was largely credited to Sheead's brave action for which he was awarded the DCM.

The days following were spent patrolling further down the line, and on 21 June the KRRC Company encountered a strong enemy position about four miles through the forest from the British line. The Rifles remained in contact only long enough to ascertain the extent of the enemy defences and withdrew without casualty.

On 23 June, the Middlesexes attacked the position with the KRRC in reserve. The battle was going in the favour of the British until a forest fire started by the Bolsheviks adjacent to the Middlesex advance was picked up by the wind and blown directly towards the attackers. At this point the Bolshevik armoured train reappeared and proceeded to spray the burning forest through which the Middlesexes were attacking with shell and machine gun fire. Having fought a six hour battle and in danger of being trapped by the forest fire, Major Drew ordered the company to withdraw having lost Private George Shadwell (CWGC records 'Showell') killed and several men wounded. The heat of summer and difficult trek through the forest had also caused a number of heat casualties. A summer shower put out the fire and gave some relief and the Middlesexes were perhaps fortunate to extricate themselves with so few casualties.

On 26 June, the Middlesexes and KRRC were recalled to Medvyeja-Gora to rest and replaced in the line by a company of Italian troops. Only a week later on 3 July, the Middlesexes and KRRC were rushed to the front line with all possible speed. The Italian company was on the verge of mutiny, its men seriously disaffected with their continued presence in North Russia so long after the Armistice.

The same evening that the KRRC returned to the front they took up positions just north of Kapaselga. The Bolsheviks had an estimated 250 to 500 men in the village and had weeks to prepare defences. They also had at their disposal two field guns and a railway-mounted 6 inch naval gun whilst an observation post in the belfry of the village church tower provided an excellent platform for Red artillery observers to direct the guns' fire.

13. Some of the KRRC and Rifle Brigade soldiers who served with 19 Company, KRRC in North Russia, 1919, pose with a captured Bolshevik Maxim machine gun. One soldier wears three horizontal stripes on his cuff indicating his wounding on three separate occasions. (Author's collection)

At 2200 on the night of 4 July (although at this time of year in the northern latitudes there was no night per se, rather one or two hours of twilight), Lieutenant Harrington with Sergeant Hammond and six men advanced to within 200 yards of the enemy front line in order to probe their forward positions. Hearing Russian voices ahead the party blazed away in the general direction of the enemy in an attempt to trick the Reds into firing back and revealing their positions. This the Bolsheviks duly did, revealing the location of their machine guns, indeed their firing continued for 30 minutes, long after Harrington's reconnaissance had withdrawn. Harrington received an MC Bar for the patrol to add to a previously awarded MM. Sergeant Ambrose Berridge and six men from Lieutenant Fisher's platoon carried out a similar probe on the right for which Berridge was awarded the MM.

For most of the following day the Red guns pounded the Allied positions until the British gunners on the armoured train blew the top off the church tower with a well-placed 18 pdr shell. The train kept up fire from its two 4.5 inch howitzers and single 18 pdr unopposed as without their observer in the church tower the Red artillery were firing blind. By the time the White Russian infantry reached the forward enemy trenches the Bolsheviks surrendered en masse and a number of machine guns were captured intact with thousands of rounds of ammunition. At midnight the KRRC Company moved forward into the village which had been set ablaze by the retreating Bolsheviks. The Riflemen did what they could to help the villagers rescue what few possessions they had but many villagers lost everything to the flames. The Riflemen spent the night in the churchyard and in the morning the Middlesexes arrived to relieve the Russians on outpost duty. The remainder of July was relatively quiet, the KRRC and Middlesex Companies spending their time rotating between manning defensive posts on the outskirts of the village, conducting patrols and garrisoning the village.

Offensive patrols were carried out nightly and with only two hours semi-darkness to provide cover the patrols had to be carefully planned. Some of the raids were particularly bold. During one such raid led by Captain Clement Smith (who would receive an MC for his service in North Russia)

14. KRRC and Middlesex Mounted Infantry at Svyatnavolok, summer 1919. (IWM Q16803)

an 18 pdr gun and ammunition limber was manhandled by gunners from 1203rd Battery, RFA, onto high ground within 1,000 yards of the enemy front line at Siding 8. A small party under Lieutenant MacLure and Sergeant Reeves crept forward to within 50 yards of the enemy and fired a flare for the gunners to aim on in the semi-darkness. MacLure's party hurriedly scurried away, chased on by a hail of enemy fire and signalled when they reached a safe distance. The 18 pdr and two Lewis guns opened fire and raked the outpost with 71 rounds of High Explosive and many drums of .303 inch Lewis gun ammunition. Their ammunition exhausted, the attackers snuck away as quietly as they had come. Somewhat head sore from the bombardment, the Bolsheviks made no attempt to follow the raiders but expecting a full scale attack to follow the bombardment, rushed reinforcements forward and opened fire in the direction from where the 18 pdr had fired from. For many minutes the Reds sprayed thousands of rounds of valuable ammunition at an enemy which had long since departed.

On another raid Lieutenant Harrington's platoon, accompanied by Major John Mason, MC, RE (who would be awarded the DSO for service in North Russia), and two Riflemen, crept all the way into Siding 8 to find the Bolshevik trenches unoccupied. Harrington decided to push forward another half mile down the line to investigate. Whilst investigating a small cutting next to the line a voice from behind the party shouted, 'Stoi!' ('Halt!') nearly directly into the British officer's ear. Harrington turned round to see the muzzle of a Bolshevik rifle pointed directly at his chest: the Red soldier was obviously intent on taking the party prisoner but Harrington had his revolver ready and had no such intention. In a rapid movement the young Lieutenant raised his revolver and shot the Bolshevik in the face, fleeing with Major Mason and the two Riflemen back up the line as fast as their legs could carry them. There was a great deal of shouting and firing going on behind them and one of the Riflemen cried that they were being chased by feared 'Mongolians!' Of all the 'types' of Bolshevik, the average British soldier in North Russia feared the nearly mythical 'Mongolian' the most:

The Mongolian was a legendary creature, Nobody had ever seen one, but they were rumoured to be similar to the Bolsheviks – in other words, habitually hairy and dirty and unable to speak English. The only difference was that Mongolians had long black moustaches. It was said that if the Mongolians captured you, the only way you got back to your comrades was in a paper bag.[2]

---

2   *Ibid.*, p.179.

The Bolsheviks did not continue their pursuit and the party reputedly 'broke all records in its sprint back to safety.'[3]

By early July the strength of the White Russians forces stood at 5,000 of which about 1,500 were untrained recruits. Although the Russian forces had increased in strength considerably, as Allied contingents began to be shipped home, the Allied force became weaker overall. At the end of 1 French troops were withdrawn from the front to be returned home in early June. On 7 June, orders were received for the Royal Marines detachment to be sent home and a few days later the Canadian government requested that all its forces be returned to the UK for repatriation including the valuable Malamute Company, which embarked for Canada via the UK the following month. In mid July, the two companies of American railway troops were also withdrawn. The manpower issues were compounded further when Maynard was informed that every British soldier who had arrived at Murmansk before 1 February 1919 must be sent home before the end of August. This instruction would affect a large number of the available British front line troops and a large part of the command and administration structure.

The departure of the RMFFNR was anything but convivial. In May they had been singled out by Maynard for praise for work they had done during the offensive but by June 1919, so long after the signing of the Armistice, and more than a year since they had landed at Murmansk, the mood of the Marines had changed dramatically. As early as February 1919, they were beginning to express their disgruntlement. That same month the small 55-strong detachment at Kandalaksha wrote a threatening letter to their CO complaining that an earlier letter outlining their grievances and wishes to be sent home had not been acted upon and that if no further action was taken they would 'down tools' for 48 hours in protest. Further than that, they threatened that if nothing further happened they would commandeer the first train going to Murmansk. Despite the threat of force in the letter, no further action was taken against those responsible.

If the Marines, many of whom were 'Hostilities Only' enlistees, were already disgruntled, their discontent boiled over on the night of 18–19 May when the Marines refused to proceed on a joint reconnaissance patrol with the recently arrived No. 1 Special Company, KRRC. There was a further disturbance in June when the Marines detachment commander stated to an Army brigade major that unless his men were relieved he could not be responsible for their holding the line. After volunteering to go on outpost duty for four days, the Marines had been left without relief at the front for 14 days in verminous clothing, and the men were ready to quit their posts. After more than a year in North Russia and having lost all faith that General Maynard would send the Royal Marines home before the final Allied withdrawal (Maynard had through necessity already broken an earlier promise that the Marines would no longer be used south of Maselga), the unnamed Royal Marines officer himself asked to be relieved of his command.

Although the dissent in the Royal Marines detachment appears to have gone unpunished, in June the War Office cabled the Admiralty: 'Regret to inform you that Royal Marine detachment has shown such exceedingly bad spirit that I am sending them from Medvyeja to Murmansk at once to await first opportunity for embarkation to England. I am very disappointed in behaviour of both officers and men.'[4] The Admiralty understandably resented receiving such a cable, particularly as the RMFFNR had served in North Russia the longest and had performed such sterling service, particularly the 100 Marines detached for the invasion of Archangel. An inquiry conducted by Senior Naval Officer White Sea, Admiral John Green with two Royal Navy captains and an RMA captain concluded that whilst there was no excuse for the Marines' refusals and insubordination there had been considerable mitigating factors.

---

3   *Ibid.*
4   Clifford Kinvig, *Churchill's Crusade: The British Invasion of Russia, 1918–1920* (London: Continuum, 2007), p.175.

15. Lieutenant George Fullman, MC, MM, 'A' Mobile Section, 6th Brigade, RFA. Fullman was a regular soldier who had served in France from August 1914 and had been awarded the MM in 1916. For his command of a 65 mm gun section during the advance to Medvyeja-Gora Fullman was awarded the MC. (Author's collection)

The inquiry found that the Marines 'had been on continuous active service in North Russia without leave for 14 months and longer than any other military unit'[5] and that the original field force had included only four regular officers, the remainder being temporary commissions whilst two thirds of the force were 'Hostilities Only' enlistees who should have been demobilised after November 1918. Furthermore the RMFFNR's commander, Lieutenant Colonel Robert Paterson, RMLI, had been transferred from command of the force to act as base commandant at Murmansk whilst another senior officer from the force, Major Lewis Drake-Brockman, had been transferred to serve with the Army. More so, the platoon which had caused the most trouble had been left to fight through a severe Arctic winter under the command of an officer temporarily commissioned from warrant rank with only a young and inexperienced subaltern to assist in command.

When the Admiralty had sent the Marines to Murmansk as a temporary measure in May 1918 they had expected that at most the Force would have remained for only three or four months before being relieved by the Army. When this did not occur, repeated requests were made by the Admiralty to the War Office for the RMFFNR to be returned to the UK but the War Office reply was always that the GOC Murmansk (Maynard) could not afford to lose the Marines. And so, 14 months later, the men of the RMFFNR remained in theatre, longer than any other unit which saw service in North Russia.

On 14 July, the Olonetz Battalion garrison at Tividiya under the command of Captain George Cursons, MC, Middlesex Regiment (Cursons came to North Russia with the Middlesex Special Company but was attached to the Karelian Regiment) was attacked by a force of 800 Red troops. The garrison managed to drive off the Bolsheviks with heavy casualties. For this action and earlier work in the capture of Kartashi, Cursons was awarded an MC Bar.

The Bolshevik counter-attack came on 24 July when a large force of Red Finns supported by naval artillery fire attacked Shunga on northern Lake Onega. British Field Artillery was sent overland to support Daidoff's Russians (9th North Russian Rifles) and a duel was fought between the shore-based British artillery and Red vessels on Lake Onega, one of which was sunk. The fighting on the Shunga Peninsula continued on and off for several more weeks, the White Russians slowly but steadily managing to push the enemy back from their advanced positions.

The series of counter-attacks illustrated the Bolsheviks' resolve to recover ground most recently lost to the Allies. A secret despatch had been was captured from a Bolshevik courier in which Lev Trotsky, the Bolshevik Commissar for War, stressed the importance of the recapture of Medvyeja-Gora. British

5   *Ibid.*

intelligence pointed to large concentration of Red troops south of Petrozavodsk where the Bolsheviks had gathered a significant force to tackle the White Finnish incursion, but now that the Finns had moved back towards the frontier the Bolsheviks were free to use the troops against the Allies.

With the capture of Medvyeja-Gora there was time for Maynard to consolidate and reorganise but he was determined to continue to strike further south whilst he still held the advantage. Orders were issued that the RAF would begin a programme of bombing the docks and railway junctions at Petrozavodsk and endeavour to destroy the railway bridge over the Suna River. This was one of the largest bridges between Petrograd and Murmansk and its destruction would create a bottleneck for the Bolsheviks that would take some days to clear.

The RAF raids were extremely effective and had a demoralising effect on the Red troops, who had nothing to put into the air to counter the British bombers. However, despite repeated attempts, the bombers could not destroy the Suna bridge, a very small target from the air which was heavily protected by machine guns on high angle anti-aircraft mountings.

Because of the difficult terrain and nature of warfare in North Russia, there was great scope for independent guerrilla and partisan operations. Maynard was fortunate that he had some officers of great resource under his command, and among them Captain Edward Small stands out. Officially serving as a General List interpreter, Small was an interesting and charismatic character, described by an army chaplain with whom he shared a tent for a short while as 'Bolo mad'. It is possible that Small's hatred for the Bolsheviks came from the fact that he was himself half Russian. Small commanded a group of about 40 Russian partisans with whom he would launch raids into Bolshevik-held territory. On one occasion with his small force he penetrated deep into Bolshevik territory and captured a complete enemy Brigade Headquarters including the brigade commander, regimental commander and 50 prisoners. He also rendered a 3 inch gun useless by removing its breech block.

When Small heard that the RAF had been unable to destroy the Suna bridge he volunteered to attempt to destroy it and set out with his partisans on 18 July. Creeping silently through the forest the guerrillas were forced to continually hide from Red Army patrols and it took the small band five days to reach their target. The Bolshevik guard was taken completely by surprise as the partisans set the bridge's wooden supports alight before fleeing back into the forest. The northern half of the bridge was destroyed before the Bolsheviks had time to react.

Thanks to the good work of Small and his band of partisans the bridge at Suna had been at least partially destroyed; it was now up to the RAF to make its repair as difficult and lengthy as possible by constant bombing and strafing of the bridge and its surroundings. For the raid on Suna bridge and the previous capture of the Red Army Brigade staff, Small was awarded the DSO.

Lieutenant Roy Smith-Hill of 6th Royal Marine Battalion was intrigued by Small and recorded in his diary:

> Someone told me also, when we were complaining about scarce rations amongst ourselves, that Small always has eggs and other luxuries for breakfast, and that he never inquired where they came from: they are left in the kitchen by someone or other for him. My narrator also asked if I had ever seen him with his Russians. He said it was like a huntsman and a pack of hounds. No one has ever seen him leave on his expeditions. He does not say anything about his departure, but merely disappears at night and reappears a few days afterwards. It struck me that that may be one of his secrets of success as no spies can arrange a trap for him. One evening I saw him with a girl at Svyatnavolok and was told that it was his wife, but he added 'I believe he has another at Kapaselga and another at Tividiya'. Another of his qualities seems to be his liking for whisky. He always takes a supply to his base and carefully locks it up. He told me that when Small's Russians have a Prousenik he turns a barrel of rum loose amongst them and lets them fight for it.[6]

---

6   Diary of Lieutenant Roy Smith-Hill, RMLI.

Smith-Hill was not entirely convinced by Small, however, and in a note in his diary made some years after his return from Russia wrote, 'Later, I was pretty sure that the enigmatic Small was also a Russian agent.'[7]

The White Russian regiments on the Murmansk front were being trained with utmost speed as Maynard found himself losing many of his best troops. The Canadians and Americans had gone home and the ever-reliable Serbs were expected to be recalled shortly. More importantly the White Russian forces needed time to gain experience before the British left, they would stand no chance against the Red Army without a core of experienced soldiers.

White Russian General Skobeltsin arrived at Murmansk from Archangel to take command of all White Russian forces. As a test of the Russian forces an attack utilising Russian troops only supported by British artillery was planned against Siding 10 south of Medvyeja-Gora. The attack failed miserably. The Olonetz Battalion performed well but the North Russian Rifles abandoned the advance as soon as the Bolsheviks opened fire. To bolster the North Russian Rifles Maynard detached experienced soldiers of the Serbian Company to serve within the Russians ranks. The Russo–Serb unit was given a relatively easy support role whilst an attack was carried out by British infantry and machine guns on 13 June. The supporting artillery completely demoralised the Bolsheviks who abandoned their positions after slight resistance. The Allies took Siding 10 without a single casualty. The Red Army counter-attacked heavily in the week following the capture of Siding 10 as the Allies pushed down the western shore of Lake Onega. The counter-attack was beaten back by White Russian machine guns ably commanded by Captain Peter Crawford of the Royal Scots, attached MGC, for which he was awarded the MC.

In July, Maynard received formal notification from London of the intent for all British troops to have left North Russia before the end of 1919. Even though it was well known the British would leave before the winter, Governor Yermoloff and General Skobeltsin still had to be personally informed. The news still came as a blow. The White Russian political and military leadership had held out hope that although combat forces were to be withdrawn a training mission and perhaps even British volunteers would remain behind. They were to be bitterly disappointed when informed that not a single British soldier in any capacity would remain behind in North Russia after the withdrawal.

On 5 July, a plot to mutiny and murder their officers was uncovered in a unit of the North Russian Rifles stationed near Lake Onega. A number of arrests were made and the ringleaders summarily court-martialled and executed by the very officers they had been plotting to murder.

By the end of July 1919, the KRRC Company had been recalled to Medvyeja-Gora and the Middlesex Company despatched to Kapaselga to garrison outposts on rotating shifts with the North Russian Rifles. On 6 August, the Bolsheviks launched a series of attacks on the Middlesexes' outposts and the KRRC were called forward in support but by the time they had arrived the British armoured train had already been in action laying down a heavy bombardment on the approaches through the forest and the enemy attack quickly petered out. Over the next two days strong patrols were sent forward but the Bolsheviks were found to have abandoned their positions.

Early in the morning of 13 August, the Bolsheviks attacked British forward positions at Kapaselga but were beaten off by heavy Lewis gun and artillery fire. So determined was the Middlesexes' counter-attack that one of their platoons charged directly into the enemy, killing a Red officer. Two further platoons were sent in pursuit but were not able to catch the retreating enemy. The following day Lieutenant Jervis and MacLure's platoons of the KRRC Company occupied the villages of Mogilniki and Maozero before handing over to White Russian troops.

To take advantage of enemy demoralisation, Brigadier General G.D. Price ordered his 237th Brigade to push the Bolsheviks down the line as far as possible in a general advance commencing

16. British-crewed French
65 mm mountain gun
of 'A' Mobile Section,
6th Brigade, RFA.
(IWM Q16786)

17 August. Carried down the line by the British armoured train, the Middlesexes, recently arrived 6th Battalion, Royal Marines and Olonetz Battalion disembarked north of Siding 8 and attacked down the railway with the British howitzers firing from the train carriages in support. The Middlesexes encountered four Bolshevik scouts in the siding who fled to their main positions on being fired upon. Heavy fire from the Bolsheviks pinned down the attackers for several minutes until the howitzers found their range. As the Middlesexes pushed forward they found the Bolshevik positions abandoned and large quantities of ammunition and several rifles were recovered. The advance continued but the Olonetz Battalion were showing signs of running out of steam and it took the efforts of their British officers to keep the local troops offensive.

The Middlesexes continued the advance, pushing on to Siding 7 four miles down the line. Encountering a strong enemy position just north of the siding, the entire attacking force leapt to its feet and charged the enemy which caused the Reds to turn and flee in panic, abandoning their positions and two machine guns. Nos. 3 and 4 Platoons of the Middlesex were deployed to face the Bolshevik counter-attack which did not eventuate. Having routed the enemy and advanced beyond where the British armoured train could support due to the destruction of several small railway bridges north of the siding, the Allied force withdrew to Kapaselga after destroying as best they could equipment and supplies left behind by the enemy.

On 21 August, the KRRC were relieved by recently arrived 6th Battalion, Royal Marines and 1st Battalion, East Surrey Regiment and received orders to return to Murmansk where the Riflemen spent most of the following month on garrison duties and work parties. After an additional four weeks in the line, the Middlesexes were withdrawn to Murmansk on 20 September. In the meantime the East Surreys had pushed the Bolsheviks as far as Siding 4, which would be the furthest extent of the British advance at Murmansk. Both KRRC and Middlesex Special Companies remained in Murmansk until the final evacuation of the North Russia Expeditionary Force, embarking on HMT *Ulua* on the night of 3-4 October, arriving at Glasgow eight days later.

4

Murmansk: Lake Onega Operations, June–September 1919

As the ice began to thaw on Lake Onega during spring 1919, General Maynard ordered the formation of the 'SYREN' Lake Onega flotilla to counter the threat of the Bolshevik flotilla known to operate on the lake. Originally comprising five boats transported over rail from Murmansk in various states of disrepair and several steam launches stuck fast in the ice and abandoned by the Bolsheviks when Povynetz was captured, command of the flotilla was given to Lieutenant Joseph Stenhouse, DSC, RNR, who had served as Master of *Aurora* during Sir Ernest Shackleton's ill-fated Imperial Trans-Antarctic Expedition 1914–16, and had brought the expedition vessel to safety after drifting 312 days in the Ross Sea ice.

On return to England, Stenhouse returned to naval service and was appointed as Gunnery Officer on Q-ship *PQ61* commanded by New Zealander Lieutenant Commander Frank Worsley, RNR, who had captained *Endurance* during the 1914–16 expedition and accompanied Shackleton on the epic open boat journey to South Georgia to seek help after *Endurance* was crushed by ice. On 26 September 1917, Worsley captained *PQ61* in the sinking of a German U-boat in the Irish Sea for which he was awarded the DSO and Stenhouse the DSC.

Stenhouse's chief administrative officer was another experienced Polar Medal recipient, Major James Mather, RE, who had served as a Petty Officer on Captain Robert Falcon Scott's equally ill-fated *Terra Nova* expedition, 1910–13, specially seconded Royal Naval Volunteer Reserve (RNVR) with the rank of Lieutenant Commander for the purpose.

The vessels discovered at Murmansk were hastily mounted on flatbed train carriages and sent south to Medvyeja-Gora post-haste and managed to get within two miles of Lake Onega before the destruction of a 60 foot railway bridge stopped the train in its tracks. Trees were felled, rudimentary rollers fashioned and the boats dragged overland to shore by hand. Two of the motor launches were put to sea and completed trials by the time the train which had carried them from Murmansk crossed the repaired bridge.

Three of the flotilla's vessels, *Wahine*, *Atlanta*, and *Georgia* were crewed by sailors from USS *Yankton* under Lieutenant Woodward, United States Navy (USN), whilst the remaining three boats were crewed with British artillerymen. The American-built submarine chaser christened *Jolly Roger* was made flagship of the flotilla and fitted out with a quick firing 3 pdr and no less than seven Vickers and two Lewis guns. Commanded by Captain Herbert Littledale, RGA, with 2nd Lieutenant William Wannell, RASC, as second in command, *Jolly Roger* was crewed by an assortment of gunners and drivers from 420th Battery, RFA, and one RE Corporal from 'SYREN' Force Signal Company, and after some tinkering with the engine by naval mechanics could reach a top speed of 30 knots.

Whilst awaiting the arrival of seaplanes from HMS *Pegasus*, Maynard ordered a further short advance to put his artillery in a position where it could support the flotilla operations from ashore. On 29 May, a short advance took place against Red positions on the railway eight miles south of Medvyeja-Gora. By the following day the Bolsheviks had been pushed from their positions and the Allied artillery brought into place.

The boats were long past their prime and were not ideal for the task required but were the best the Allies could assemble for the time being. Maynard had already received word from London that a detachment of MMR ratings was on its way to Murmansk with six 35 foot and four 40 foot Thornycroft motor boats to form the bulk of the flotilla, but their expected arrival would not be until

June at the earliest. Maynard had originally requested crews be sent from the Royal Engineers Inland Water Transport Section but they were heavily committed elsewhere, particularly on the Rhine and in Mesopotamia.

The MMR ratings and RNR officers who would command them (most of whom were discharged sailors and soldiers) had been specially enlisted for service in North Russia after responding to advertisements in newspapers calling for:

Naval Men for Service in North Russia: Bo'suns, A.B.s, motor mechanics (with experience of Bollinder engines), firemen (some with oil fuel experience), also complete crews (including officers) for six motor launches. The men will be required to sign an agreement for a maximum service of nine months. They will be under naval discipline and in uniform … Preference will be given to demobilised service ratings.[1]

One volunteer was James Gordon Gray from Melbourne who had previously served in the Royal Australian Navy (RAN) and Australian Imperial Force. Gray had been serving as an Able Seaman on HMAS *Pioneer* at the outbreak of war before jumping ship on 26 December 1914. *Pioneer* had been due to sail with the first convoy of Australian troops to Egypt on 1 November but her engines had broken down in Freemantle, being replaced in the convoy by HMAS *Sydney* which subsequently encountered and sunk the German raider SMS *Emden* on 9 November. On 24 December, the Admiralty requested that *Pioneer* be sent to the east coast of Africa to serve as part of the Royal Navy blockade of German East Africa. Probably smarting from the missed encounter with *Emden* and facing an uneventful war on blockade duties, Gray jumped ship and enlisted in the AIF in February 1915 under an alias, seeing three weeks service on Gallipoli in August with 8th Battery, Australian Field Artillery before being evacuated and invalided to Australia with enteric fever.

Whilst on Gallipoli, Gray had come clean about his desertion from the RAN and on his return to Australia and recovery from illness was permitted to re-attest under his real name in June 1916. Rejoining his unit on the Western Front, he was gassed in October 1917 and awarded the Military Medal for work repairing signal lines under fire during September 1918.

After being granted his discharge in the United Kingdom on expression of his intent to join the North Russia Relief Force (NRRF), Gray volunteered to enlist in the MMR detachment probably because he was a trained seaman. It is likely that at least several other Commonwealth volunteers also served with the MMR flotilla: Gray himself recalled that the motor boat on which he served on Lake Onega was crewed by four Australians, two South Africans and a New Zealander.[2]

The capture of Medvyeja-Gora on northern shore of Lake Onega on 21 May was followed by furious activity as work was done to consolidate the position. Boats zipped back and forth across the lake, camps were erected, roads repaired and defensive positions built. As there would be no further advance until the arrival of reinforcements in at least a month, emphasis was placed on making facilities more permanent.

The RAF worked quickly to build their sea base at Medvyeja-Gora and a rudimentary airstrip at Lumbushi. Four Fairey IIICs from the seaplane carrier HMS *Pegasus* designated 'Duck Flight' operated from the seaplane base whilst two RE8s designated 'Pigeon Flight' flew from the land base later bolstered by the arrival of other aircraft including a Sopwith Camel.

With the thaw of Lake Onega, it was imperative that the seaplanes arrived sooner rather than later, as without airborne cooperation the Allied flotilla stood to be badly mauled by their at least equal Bolshevik opposition. By the time the Medvyeja-Gora was captured on 21 May, the RAF had only a solitary RE8 flying, almost literally on a wing and a prayer. The seaplane carrier HMS *Nairana*

1   *Yorkshire Post* and Leeds Intelligencer, 29 March 1919.
2   *Evening Post*, 'Disorganised Russia, An Australian's Experiences', 12 April 1920.

17. Lieutenant Commander Frank Worsley, DSO and Bar, RNR and Lieutenant Joseph Stenhouse, DSO, DSC, RNR pictured in 1917. Both men had served with Shackleton's Imperial Trans-Antarctic Expedition, 1914–16 and would later serve in North Russia in 1919, Worsley at Archangel where he was awarded the DSO Bar and Stenhouse at Murmansk where he was awarded the DSO. (National Library of NZ 12-182001-F)

(whose planes had played a prominent part in the capture of Archangel the preceding year) arrived at Murmansk with replacement seaplanes at the end of May. Because the icebound White Sea denied access to Kem the decision was made to send the flight of Fairey IIICs and Short 184s to Medvyeja-Gora by rail. The aircraft arrived on 4 June and their assembly and servicing by the riggers and fitters of Duck Flight began at once. Two days later the first seaplane was operational on Lake Onega.

On 5 June, four heavily armed Bolshevik steamers were reported rounding the Shunga Peninsula heading towards Medvyeja-Gora. Under the command of Major Mather, the Allied flotilla went out to meet the enemy with the newly arrived seaplanes overhead. Mather encountered the Bolshevik vessels attacking several Russian launches which had been cornered in a bay near Shunski Bor and although significantly outranged and outgunned, boldly led the flotilla in to attack, driving the enemy southwards and allowing the Russian vessels to escape.

Wahine and the less glamorously named *Motor Boat No. 9* zigzagged to get within firing rage whilst the better armed enemy vessels opened fire, their first shots flying well overhead. Armed with only a single 37 mm gun, *Wahine* opened fire in reply but the range was too long and the shot fell well short. The enemy found their range and shells began falling around the two Allied vessels, one shell landed directly in front of *Wahine* before bouncing off the surface overhead, a lucky miss.

The Bolsheviks appeared to be completely taken by surprise by the presence of the seaplanes overhead, probably the first aircraft many of them had seen, and thought discretion the better part of valour, steaming southwards towards safety as fast as their boilers could take them. The Red flotilla was pursued but all four vessels managed to escape. Other larger actions would be fought on the lake but it was this first engagement that was the most critical for the Allies. If Maynard had lost control of the northern shore of Lake Onega he would have found it very difficult to maintain and hold Povynetz which would be vulnerable to seaborne attack. For his courage and devotion to duty during the action Mather was awarded the DSO, a rare award to an Army officer for services afloat.

On 9 June, a seaplane flown by Lieutenant Frederick Isaac with Observer Lieutenant Frederick Eades was investigating enemy positions off the Shunga Peninsula in heavy rain. Spotting the enemy below, Isaac flew the aircraft on a number of bombing runs from 300 feet whilst Eades threw bombs from the observer's cockpit and machine-gunned the Bolshevik troops below. Having expended all the bombs and ammunition, Isaac returned to the Duck Flight base at Medvyeja-Gora to rearm and refuel before taking off once more. Returning to the Shunga, an enemy gunboat was spotted which was attacked and driven ashore.

Two days later the pair were back in action in a Short 184 attempting to bomb the railway line to prevent the enemy from bringing up reinforcements. Flying from just 50 feet above the railway Eades managed to cut the line with bombs despite heavy fire from the enemy below. On hearing

18. Fairey IIIC seaplane landing at the RAF Duck Flight base at
Medvyeja-Gora on the banks of Lake Onega. (Author's collection)

that the enemy had repaired the damage overnight, Isaac and Eades took off again on the morning of 12 June and bombed the railway once more, this time from only 30 feet; the aircraft sustained damage from ground fire as well as shrapnel from their own bombs. Both Isaac and Eades were awarded DFCs for their gallantry and determination.

The flotilla was next in action on 10 June when *Jolly Roger* proceeded to shell the village of Fedotova on the western coast of the Shunga Peninsula. The enemy fled from the village leaving behind 30 dead. Throughout the remainder of June the flotilla spent most of its time bombarding enemy villages and transporting troops, guns and supplies across the lake to Shunga.

Encouraged by the proximity of Allied forces, the inhabitants of the northern shore of the Shunga Peninsula rose against the Bolsheviks in early June and sent an urgent request for arms and assistance. All Allied units had by this time been withdrawn to support and reserve roles for the White Russian units currently holding the front line, which meant the Russians could not be sent forward without leaving the front dangerously exposed. The only two units in any position to be despatched were Krugliakoff's partisans currently in transition to be incorporated into the army as a regular unit and 'Daidoff's Battalion' (9th Northern Rifle Regiment) at Povynetz. The decision was made to send Daidoff with a party of 400 men by boat across Lake Onega to the Shunga Peninsula with additional arms and ammunition for supply to the inhabitants.

It was a very risky operation. The boat convoy carrying the Russian troops would be extremely vulnerable to attack by the Bolshevik gunboats operating on the lake, even with an escort from the Allied flotilla. When Daidoff disembarked he might find that the Bolsheviks had quelled the uprising and his position would be untenable. Additionally, there would be the difficulty of resupply and communication with Daidoff's column via a waterborne route.

Maynard still did not know with any certainty when the promised fleet of motor boats and MMR men would arrive and until they were taken on strength it may have proven impossible to maintain a supply link with Daidoff should the Bolshevik flotilla show itself in any strength. The reward of hundreds if not thousands of potential recruits from the Shunga far outweighed the risk, and on 14 June Daidoff and his men were transported across the 20 mile long stretch of Lake Onega. Daidoff immediately pushed inland and in his first engagement with the enemy accounted for 70 Red troops. This success by exclusively White Russian troops brought much support from the local communities. General Maynard credited these early operations on the Shunga Peninsula with providing enough new recruits for the White Russian army to stand on its own feet with a 'reasonable prospect for success' in holding the territory captured by Allied troops during the push south to Medvyeja-Gora.

With the appearance of Daidoff's force on the Shunga it did not take a military genius to work out that not only had he and his men been transported over water but that they would have to be resupplied by the same route. Shortly after the Bolshevik flotilla was despatched to the head of the lake to cut off Daidoff from reinforcement and supply from Medvyeja-Gora.

The success of the White Russian operation caused its own problems. Maynard was faced with the decision either to evacuate Daidoff and leave the captured territory to the Bolsheviks and sacrifice the prospective recruits contained therein, or to consolidate his position by a further advance on land southwards along the railway from Medvyeja-Gora. He chose the latter option and on 11 June ordered an attack by Russian troops and the Olonetz Battalion on Siding 10 on the railway south-west of Medvyeja-Gora.

The Olonetz made steady progress but the simultaneous Russian attack along the railway faltered and failed. As soon as fire was opened up the attacking Russian troops fled, so rushed was their retreat that the Bolsheviks almost surrounded the supporting British gunners from 420th Battery, RFA, only the individual gallantry of the gunners and drivers saving the howitzers from being overrun. The Russians were ordered to make another attempt but refused, preferring instead to blaze away their ammunition in the general direction of the enemy. The Russian troops would advance no further and the attack lost what little momentum it had. The Bolsheviks could not be allowed to remain in possession of Siding 10 and in the absence of reliable White Russian troops Maynard issued orders two days later in direct contravention of his instructions from the War Office that no Allied troops were yet to be used for offensive action.

The flanking column of the Olonetz Battalion was bolstered by British artillery and Royal Engineers, a company of hardy Serbs and the newly raised Mounted Infantry section comprised of 20 volunteers from the KRRC and Middlesex Special Companies temporarily commanded by Maynard's ADC Lieutenant Colonel Ernest Lewin, CMG, DSO, RA, who had begged for the opportunity (Lewin reluctantly handed over command of the Mounted Infantry section to 2nd Lieutenant George Harwood, 3rd Dragoon Guards, the following month).

The Centre Column tasked with the actual capture of the siding was composed of KRRC and Middlesex Special Companies with a contingent of British machine gunners from 253rd Company, MGC. The Russians were given the easiest task, an attempt to force the left flank in an effort to link up with Daidoff on the Shunga. The attack was launched on 13 June and resulted in a complete rout of the defending Red troops. The Bolsheviks fled their heavily fortified positions without the British suffering a single casualty, the pre-attack bombardment greatly weakening the enemy's resolve to stay and fight. The flanking Right Column made good progress towards Kartashi meeting only slight opposition and the Left Column of Russians advanced almost as far as Fedotova without encountering the enemy.

Land communication with Daidoff had still not been established and a further advance was required. More so, the White Russian forces needed further victories to give them some much needed confidence. Their defeat at Siding 10 on 11 June, their first attempt at an attack without Allied assistance, had left many of the men dispirited. A further series of short and rapid advances with the Russian troops playing an increasing role may be just the antidote required for the Russians to recover from their apathy and lack of offensive spirit.

19. Improvised gunboat *Jolly Roger* with Army crew drawn from 420th
Battery, RFA, underway on Lake Onega. (IWM Q16772)

On 20 June, the Right Column captured Kartashi, inflicting heavy casualties on the Red troops garrisoning the town. The advancing Railway Column (now reinforced by British troops of the KRRC and Middlesex Special Companies) was delayed in thick forest which had been set alight by the Bolsheviks to delay the Allied advance. The British troops still managed to drive the Bolsheviks back and reached the outskirts of Kapaselga on 4 July. The Left Column of Russian troops linked up with Daidoff's force on 25 June and three days later attacked Dianova-Gora, the attack being such a success that their momentum led the attackers on to Unitsa which was also captured.

On 21 June, Lieutenant Guy Blampied with Observer Lieutenant Gerald Ross-Smith were returning from a raid on Dianova Gora when they spotted an RAF seaplane drifting several miles from the shore. Evidently the aircraft had suffered engine failure and was in danger of overturning. Landing next to the stricken seaplane, Blampied and Ross-Smith threw a cable and were able to gradually tow the aircraft northwards until met by one of the US Navy motor launches, which towed the seaplane the back to the Duck Flight base at Medvyeja-Gora.

The defining engagement of the advance occurred on the night of 5–6 July when a combined attack made by all three columns drove the Reds from Kapaselga taking many prisoners in the process. The Allies had now established an overland supply route and established communications with Daidoff's force. The capability of the newly trained White Russian troops in combat had at first not looked promising but with some reorganisation and a bolstering of Allied troops they had performed relatively well. It only remained to be seen if they could perform as well once the Allies had withdrawn from North Russia.

On 20 June, a curious incident had occurred when Bombardier William Wilson, 420th Battery, RFA, sunk the enemy vessel SS *Slutski* whilst firing his 4.5 inch howitzer from ashore near Unitsa, an unusual occasion of British land artillery sinking an enemy vessel whilst firing from ashore. For his services in North Russia, including the sinking of the enemy vessel, Wilson was awarded the DCM.

On 30 June, Lieutenant Guy Blampied and Observer Lieutenant Harvey were flying a reconnaissance mission near Kapaselga when their seaplane was struck by ground fire. Blampied recorded:

Went over Kapaselga with Harvey at 2,400 feet and machine was hit by a Bolshy machine gun. Hit in petrol tank and radiator, had to land in trees … one petrol tank was holed but I managed to switch to the other and keep the engine going. It heated up as one radiator had been holed … neither Lieutenant Harvey my observer nor I were hurt and we walked through the forest heading north (fortunately the sun was up to guide us) and after six hours we reached Lobska Gor. We found a farm … saw the farmer and drew a picture of a horse and cart, which he produced and drove us back to camp where we could reward him with plenty of rations.[3]

On 4 July, two seaplanes from Duck Flight at Medvyeja-Gora combined with *Jolly Roger* and other vessels of the flotilla joined in an attack on enemy positions on the western coast of the Shunga Peninsula. Four days later *Jolly Roger* was proceeding on a reconnaissance when suddenly a large explosion in the starboard petrol tank blew a hole in the stern of the boat, engulfing most of the aft section in flames. Despite the shock, Lieutenant Wannell assisted the mechanics from the smoke-filled engine room onto the deck, then took the helm and drove the boat at full speed towards the shore. Furious attempts had been made to throw ammunition overboard but a box of 3 pdr shells caught fire, causing a second explosion which wrecked the vessel. Still about a mile from shore, all those who had not been blown overboard during the initial explosion were forced to take to the water and attempt to swim ashore.

Captain Littledale's report of the incident credited that the men behaved 'magnificently', 'men who could swim volunteering to assist men who could not, and of these there were a large proportion.' Sadly five men were drowned in the incident, including two blown overboard in the initial explosion. Those killed were Corporal James Mitchell, 'SYREN' Force Signal Company, RE, Drivers Archibald Bremner and John Robinson and Gunners Arthur Hobbs and Henry Holliday, all of 420th Battery, RFA. Those who did not drown swam ashore, except for four men who were picked up by a seaplane which had been sent to investigate the heavy column of smoke caused by the explosion and subsequent fire.

Littledale's conduct was commended in a report made by Captain Norman Stewart-Dawson (who would be awarded the DSO for his command of Duck Flight to add to a DSC awarded with the Royal Naval Air Service in East Africa) of the RAF seaplanes involvement in the incident: 'Capt Littledale who had been in the water about 40 minutes had during the whole of this time been supporting one of his crew (an elderly man unable to swim and who was exhausted). His splendid action most assuredly saved this man's life.' The bodies of the five men drowned were never recovered and their names remain commemorated on the Archangel Memorial to the Missing.

Littledale was awarded the Royal Humane Society Bronze Medal for saving the life of one of his crew whilst Wannell was awarded the Military Cross for his efforts to bring *Jolly Roger* ashore. His citation credited his actions in the smoke and flame-filled engine room with saving the lives of the remaining crew.

On 10 July, a seaplane from Duck Flight scored a lucky hit with a 112 lb bomb on the enemy vessel *Carla Rosenberg* which ran aground off Unitsa. The stricken ship was crammed with troops who began to jump overboard but were machine-gunned from the air causing heavy casualties.

Six days after the sinking of *Jolly Roger*, Commander Robert Curteis, RNR, arrived at Murmansk with a party of 10 RNR officers and 50 MMR ratings (followed on 19 July by a further 25 ratings who had been left at Chatham due to a shortage of accommodation on the transport ships), bringing with them two 40 foot and four 35 foot motor boats to form the bulk of the 'Royal Navy SYREN Lake Flotilla'. Curteis divided the flotilla into three sub-units: 1st (British) Division, 2nd (Russian) Division and 3rd (Support) Division. Although a naval unit comprised of naval personnel, the flotilla, along with the Russian crewed motor boats, was administratively placed under the command of Brigadier G.D. Price's 237th Infantry Brigade.

3   Phil Tomaselli, *Air Force Lives: A Guide for Family Historians* (Barnsley: Pen and Sword, 2013), pp.39–40.

20. Officers and crew of 70 foot wooden gunboat *Jolly Roger*. Seated officers from left to right are Major James Mather, DSO, RE (seconded RNVR), Lieutenant Joseph Stenhouse, DSO, DSC, RNR, Captain Herbert Littledale, MC, RGA. (IWM Q16773)

In its new incarnation, at 0300 on 3 August the RN Flotilla saw its first action off the village of Tolvoya where 2nd (Russian) Division and RAF seaplanes attacked three enemy vessels whilst 1st (British) Division put ashore a landing party of MMR ratings under covering fire from *Chaser No. 15* (Lieutenant Shamardin, RNR), which fired 32 rounds of high explosive at the enemy trenches as the MMR ratings were landing. The sailors received sniper and machine gun fire from the vicinity of the church until the building was outflanked and the machine gun captured with its crew, for which Able Seaman Angus Mackenzie was awarded the MM, his citation recalling his coolness in manoeuvring his vessel under fire before disembarking and participating in the capture of the enemy machine gun. Daidoff's 9th Northern Rifle Regiment were then put ashore by the Russian motor boats and pursued the enemy inland. Lieutenant Arthur Lettington of Duck Flight was awarded the DFC for the action, for making repeated strafing runs against the enemy flotilla and assisting in driving three enemy vessels aground.

Opening fire at 2,500 yards range with seaplanes of Duck Flight overhead, 2nd (Russian) Division, drove two of the three enemy ships aground which their crews immediately abandoned. In command of 2nd Division, Russian Commander Kira-Dingan left chaser nos. 4 and 5 to cover the abandoned vessels and proceeded with *Chaser No. 1* southwards at full speed in pursuit of the escaping third enemy ship. The enemy paddle steamer was armed with a large 75 mm gun mounted aft and another on the bow, far more powerful than Kira-Dingan's single 6 pdr. A direct hit from the 75 mm would blow the Russian chaser out of the water. Both vessels exchanged fire during the chase until Kira-Dingan, his ammunition expended, ordered the chaser to break off the pursuit and return to Shunga.

In its first significant action with the enemy, the flotilla had captured the armed steamer *Silny* armed with two 3 inch guns and two machine guns, a submarine chaser armed with a 3 inch and two machine guns and the unarmed tug *Azod*. Combined with the 54 prisoners taken in and around the village by the MMR landing party, it had been a very successful operation.

The flotilla's next significant action was another combined flotilla–RAF attack which took place early in the morning of 29 August against the enemy-held village of Rimskaya on the western shore of

Lake Onega. At 0100 a landing party of 10 officers and 27 MMR ratings, 25 Russians and 25 Serbs with six Lewis guns were landed 500 yards north of Rimskaya, tasked to cut telephone lines and capture two groups of houses on the northern edge of the village. Upon capture of the houses the party was to signal the flotilla to put ashore the remainder of the landing party, who would then form up to attack the village itself. At 0500, RAF seaplanes would attack the village with bombs and machine guns, signalling the landing party with flares when their attack was completed, at which time the landing party would commence their attack. Once the sailors were in the village, 1st (British) Division would come alongside the local pier and land their crews who would proceed to the village to reinforce the attacking party. Commander Curteis commanded the landing party with Captain Herbert Littledale, RGA, one Chief Petty Officer and eight seamen with a Lewis gun forming landing party headquarters, whilst a further seven sections of one Chief Petty Officer and five ratings with a Lewis gun, grenades and rifles under a Lieutenant, RNR, would form the attacking parties: a total of 60 officers and ratings and eight Lewis guns, virtually the entire 1st (British) Division of the flotilla.

At 0530, *Silny* (one of the vessels captured from the enemy during the 3 August engagement at Tolvoya) opened a covering fire with her two 75 mm guns as the remainder of the flotilla formed a single line ahead and charged the shoreline at full speed, all guns blazing, until disembarking the main landing parties at 0615. Little resistance was encountered during the push from the shore and a thorough search of the houses north of Rimskaya and surrounding woods was conducted. Able Seaman William Logan and another rating discovered 18 armed enemy hiding in the forest who were immediately taken prisoner for which Logan was awarded the MM.

On completing the disembarkation and search of the area, the landing parties divided into three columns, Serbs on the left, Russians of 2nd Northern Rifle Regiment on the right and British in the centre, and commenced the advance on Rimskaya. The British encountered little opposition during the approach to the village, however the Serbs and Russians came under considerable machine gun fire on both flanks.

As Rimskaya was reached at 0900, Curteis ordered the British column to deploy by sections and prepare to rush the village under the covering fire of eight Lewis guns firing at 500 yards range. The extreme right section under Lieutenant Walter Woods, RNR, entered Rimskaya at 0945 and pushed to the south-east corner of the village taking 30 prisoners for which he was awarded the MC, whilst the other sections occupied the eastern and north-eastern approaches. Motor Mechanic 1st Class S. Erler distinguished himself during the attack by charging into a house from which a machine gun had been firing (with Motorman H. A. Barker following close behind), taking prisoner the 31 armed enemy inside as well as the machine gun for which Erler was awarded the DCM and Barker the MM.

During the attack Able Seaman John Buss advanced with his Lewis gun under heavy fire and was largely responsible for the capture of a further 50 enemy for which he was awarded a Bar to his DCM awarded as a Sergeant with 21st Battalion, London Regiment on the Western Front the previous year. One of the first to enter the village, Bosun Charles Mitchell personally took 12 prisoners and captured an enemy machine gun for which he was awarded the MM.

With Rimskaya occupied, Curteis handed over control of the village to 2nd North Russian Rifles and gave orders for the British column to rejoin the flotilla. The loss of the village with more than 100 prisoners had not been a critical blow to the enemy but in light of the impending evacuation did restrict the ability of the Bolsheviks to threaten Povynetz and the Shunga Peninsula.

The flotilla's final action took place on 14 September at the village of Vate Navolok south of Lijma and directly opposite Siding 5, in support of General Maynard's final offensive to drive the enemy southwards down the railway to secure the withdrawal of British troops to Murmansk. The plan was for 2nd North Russian Rifles and the lake flotilla to land at Vate Navolok and capture the village before pushing on to link up with the 1st East Surreys in a combined attack on Siding 5.

White Russian Colonel Hoffman, CO, 2nd North Russian Rifles, likely resentful of the departing British, refused to take part in the operation leaving Major Montague Burrows, 5th Dragoon

21. Test firing of Vickers machine guns on *Jolly Roger*. Standing middle
is Captain Herbert Littledale, MC, RFA (IWM Q16774)

Guards (commanding Russian partisans) and Commander Curteis to make the attack on their own. Hoffman did allow Burrows to call for volunteers from among his men and six officers and 87 other ranks came forward to join the four officers and 128 ratings (less than half of whom where British) from the lake flotilla.

The attackers crossed over 15 miles of Lake Onega in small boats and landed in a bay some 21 *versts* distant from Vate Navolok and had to march through the forest to the village where they arrived at 0630. After surrounding the village and cutting the telephone wire to reinforcements at Siding 5, the village was rushed and a Soviet Commissar and 17 other ranks captured. The Commissar was the commander of the Vate Navolok garrison and was persuaded through threats of torture and death to telephone the garrison at Pogrema and order the despatch of reinforcements to Vate Navolok by boat.

Leaving behind three officers and 55 men to defend the village and deal with the Pogrema garrison, Burrows left with eight officers and 60 men at 0930 to attack Siding 5 and link up with 1st East Surreys. Whilst trekking through the forest, Burrows encountered an enemy transport column which was rushed, capturing five men and 16 crates of ammunition. After an hour long trek through the forest the siding was reached without further incident. Burrows sent a demolition party down the line to blow the railway to the south to cut off the siding from enemy reinforcements. Siding 5 was attacked and cleared of the enemy who fled into the forest after putting up only slight resistance. In total 220 prisoners were taken by Burrows' party, more than three times the total strength of the attacking force. Burrows would be awarded the DSO for his gallant leadership of the operation to add to an MC awarded for the offensive against Medvyeja-Gora in May. Able Seaman R. Meadows was awarded the MM during the attack for advancing with his Lewis gun over open ground under heavy fire and making good use of it against the enemy.

When the party sent to blow the railway line returned stating that they had come under heavy rifle and machine gun fire and were unable to complete their task, Burrows ordered that as many train carriages as possible be derailed and all available transport collected to bring the captured machine guns and ammunition back to Vate Navolok. At 1140 an enemy train was seen approaching which was immediately rushed and two engines and a further 20 prisoners captured. On his return to Vate

Navolok, Burrows learned that during his absence the 26 men of the Pogrema garrison had come over in boats (as had been requested by the garrison commander under no small amount of duress) and been captured without firing a shot. During the night Commander Curteis and a small party left the village on a barge taking with them the 250 prisoners captured at Vate Navolok and Siding 5.

The night of 14–15 September was relatively quiet until a report of enemy boats approaching was received at 0100. The boats were allowed to come quite close before being met with a barrage of fire from the British and Russians ashore. The boats proved to have been carrying 46 armed enemy from the garrisons to the south, all of whom were at once taken prisoner.

At 0900 on 15 September, Lieutenant George Armstrong, RNR, led a patrol to Siding 5 to link up with the 1st East Surreys but on arrival found an enemy transport column in the middle of loading stores onto a train which had come up the line from the south. Armstrong ordered his men to open fire with Lewis guns and rifles, forcing the enemy to abandon the train and scatter into the forest from where they commenced returning fire. Without enough men to rush the siding, Armstrong decided to withdraw the patrol, contact being established with the East Surreys at 0800 the following day. Armstrong was awarded the MC for his leadership of the patrol and Bosun William Wise the MM for working his Lewis gun under fire until his ammunition had been expended.

A Bolshevik gunboat made an appearance during the night of 15–16 September, shelling the Allied positions ashore. Intelligence reports stated that the gunboat had orders to sink the tug *Azod* (captured by the flotilla during the 3 August engagement at Tolvoya) although the enemy vessel made no effort to push further north after expending its ammunition.

The flotilla was soon after withdrawn to Murmansk to prepare for the evacuation which took place during the first week of October. On their return to the UK the MMR volunteers who had enlisted under special conditions for the duration of their service in North Russia were discharged and returned to civilian life.

In 1920 Joseph Stenhouse was awarded the OBE for his services in command of *Aurora* in the Antarctic 1914–16. He returned to Antarctic waters as captain of *Discovery* during its 1927–29 oceanographic and research expeditions. During the Second World War he resumed active service and was reported missing, presumed killed in the Gulf of Aden on 12 September 1941 when his ship exploded and sank, likely having struck a sea mine in the Red Sea. His body was never recovered and he remains commemorated on the Portsmouth Naval Memorial.

The following awards were made to members of the Royal Navy 'SYREN' Lake Onega Flotilla:

Distinguished Service Order (DSO):	Commander R. W. S. Curteis, RNR
	Major (T./Lieut. Cdr., RNVR) J. H. Mather, RE
	Lieutenant J. R. Stenhouse, DSC, RNR
Military Cross (MC):	Captain H. F. Littledale, RGA
	Lieutenant G. W. Armstrong, RNR
	Lieutenant W. V. Wood, RNR
	2nd Lieutenant W. C. Wannell, RASC
Distinguished Conduct Medal Bar (DCM):	
	999397 Able Seaman J. Buss, MMR
Distinguished Conduct Medal:	639698 Motor Mechanic S. H. Erler, MMR
Military Medal (MM):	999383 Motorman H. A. Barker, MMR
	978725 Able Seaman W. Logan, MMR
	758966 Able Seaman A. MacKenzie, MMR
	978637 Able Seaman R. J. Meadows, MMR
	978592 Bosun C. H. Mitchell, MMR
	978901 Bosun W. O. H. Wise, MMR
Meritorious Service Medal (MSM):	978667 Bosun W. Chapple, MMR

5

Murmansk: Final Operations, August–October 1919

On 20 July 1919, in a calculated and planned uprising, White Russian troops at Onega mutinied and imprisoned a number of Russian and British officers before handing over control to the waiting Red Army. Onega was a strategically important seaport which connected Murmansk with Archangel via the overland route from Soroka, just 70 miles away. If the Bolsheviks pushed west from Onega and captured Soroka the Allied forces at Kem would be split from the front line at Medvyeja-Gora.

In June 1919, Maynard had lost his French, Canadian and American troops and the RMFFNR to be replaced by two 'Special Companies' of the KRRC and Middlesex Regiment, 1st Battalion, East Surrey Regiment and 6th Battalion, Royal Marines. The administration of the railways had been handed over from the Americans to Russian personnel and the drop in efficiency in operation had been immediately apparent. The same month as the new British reinforcements arrived the 1,200 Italian troops of 67th Infantry Regiment (incorporating mobile and machine gun units) which had made up a considerable portion of the original expeditionary force, left Murmansk on 10 August.

The urgent need for troops at Soroka necessitated the abandonment of the Pechenga garrison on the north Murman coast which had gradually been decreasing since November 1918. The garrison had been at Pechenga to protect the village in the event that White Finns made any moves across the frontier but by July 1919 the threat from the White Finns was much less than that of the Bolsheviks, and all indications were that the garrison would be needed at Soroka before they would ever be called into action at Pechenga.

An attempt was made to recapture Onega on 1 August by a force of White Russians stiffened by a core of British artillerymen and Royal Fusiliers of the recently arrived North Russia Relief Force (which despite its name operated only at Archangel) acting as Lewis gunners. Onega harbour was occupied for a time but the attack was a failure, the accompanying White Russian troops refusing to advance.

A further attempt was made on 30 August, preceded by a naval bombardment from the White Sea and a feint landing to draw attention away from the White Russian column advancing to attack the town overland. The Bolshevik garrison proved itself to be more resilient than expected and again the attack failed. The Bolsheviks knew that Onega split the overland communication route of the two Allied commands at Murmansk and Archangel and was of great strategic importance. The Allies would be compelled to continue attacking Onega until it was captured, all the Bolsheviks had to do was hold on to the town and inflict casualties each time an attack was made.

General Eugene Miller, the GOC White Russian forces North Russia at Archangel, became exceedingly anxious as the withdrawal date for the Allies drew ever nearer that Onega would be left under Bolshevik occupation. General Lord Rawlinson (recently arrived from England to oversee the evacuation as Commander-in-Chief, NREF) directed General Maynard to furnish a force to capture Onega as thus far all attacking forces had been detached from Archangel Command. Maynard at Murmansk would have struggled to release the 400–500 men necessary for the task and it was with relief that he learned that Lieutenant Colonel Woods' Karelians had forced the Bolsheviks from Onega on 8 September. Two days later troops from Archangel occupied the strategically important town.

As far back as November 1918, General Maynard had been emphasising the strategic importance of Murmansk and that if withdrawal from North Russia was decided upon that Archangel could be abandoned but Murmansk should be retained with all White Russian forces from Archangel concentrated at the ice-free port. On 11 August, Maynard and Governor Yermoloff travelled to Archangel for a meeting with Lord Rawlinson to plan the evacuation. It is interesting to note Rawlinson's recommendations:

> A careful study of the situation as described in the reports and appreciations of Generals Maynard, Ironside, and others, had convinced me that his [White Russian General Miller] best and safest course of action from the military point of view was to evacuate Archangel, while maintaining his position on the Murmansk front.
>
> I was anxious, however, before deciding definitely on the nature of the advice which I should tender to the North Russian Government, to make myself acquainted at first hand with General de Millar's political and military views as well as those of the commanders on the spot.
>
> I, accordingly, not only discussed the situation very fully and in all its aspects with Generals Ironside and Maynard (who had come over from Kem for the purpose) but also took the first opportunity of approaching General de Millar on the question of the defence of both fronts after our departure.
>
> These conversations only served to strengthen the conclusions I had already formed in my own mind, and I decided to recommend General de Millar to agree to the following proposals:
>
> (a) The abandonment of the defence of Archangel after our departure.
>
> (b) The evacuation to other parts of Russia of those amongst the civil population who might be victims of Bolshevik reprisals.
>
> (c) The transfer of the North Russian Government to Kem or Murmansk.
>
> (d) The concentration of all the best elements among the Russian troops for the defence of the Murmansk front.[1]

Located at Archangel, General Miller rejected the proposals as any victories he could hope to win along the Murmansk–Petrograd Railway would not compensate for the loss to the Red Army of Archangel.

At this same meeting approval was given to Maynard by General Rawlinson to extend his front line down the Shunga Peninsula towards Tolvoya. These last series of attacks to take place in September were aimed at delivering a decisive blow to the Bolsheviks on the Murmansk Front in much the same manner as the offensive operations that had taken place on the Dvina River in August. The attacks were planned to strike a decisive blow and leave the White Russians in the best possible position when the Allies finally withdrew.

Before commencing the push further south along the railway, the Shunga Peninsula would have to be secured to protect the Allied flank from attack. The task was detailed to primarily Russian troops (although some British liaison officers also took part) and proved to be highly successful. One advantage was that the White Russian troops were mostly fighting Red Finns and not their own countrymen. In conjunction with the Royal Navy Lake Onega Flotilla the Russians drove the Red Finns from the Peninsula in a final blow delivered on 21 August, the Finns suffering 140 killed and 90 prisoners with many machine guns and supplies falling into White Russian hands. Within two days the Peninsula was clear of all Bolshevik forces.

The evacuation of Archangel was planned to be completed on or as near to 25 September as possible, consequently evacuation of Murmansk could not commence until at least the first week of October. The river craft operating on the Dvina River would need to make their way across the White Sea to Murmansk to be refitted for the open sea journey to the UK, a process that would take at least a week. It was thus calculated that Murmansk could not be evacuated until at least 10 days after Archangel. To give himself enough time to make appropriate preparations and with these

---

1   Maynard, *The Murmansk Venture*, p.297.

22. Soldiers of 1st Battalion, East Surrey Regiment near
Siding 5, September 1919. (IWM Q16855)

considerations in hand, Maynard decided to begin his series of final attacks during mid September. Maynard described his plan:

> The object I had in view was twofold. First to strike the Bolsheviks such a blow that they would be unable to interfere with the final handing over of my front to the Russians, or with the withdrawal of my Allied troops immediately to follow. Secondly, to, inflict, if possible, such casualties as should spread demoralization in the enemy's ranks, and render them incapable of an early resumption of the offensive. Skobeltsin would thus, I hoped, be afforded time to consolidate his position on his new line or, should he consider it advisable, to resume his advance at the moment of his selection.[2]

The Allied evacuation would come as no surprise to the Bolsheviks. Rumour of the evacuation had been circulating as early as January 1919 and the British press had made no secret of the fact, some newspapers even guessing at the exact date when the troops might arrive home. The Bolsheviks knew that the withdrawal must be completed from Archangel by mid October or the White Sea and Dvina River freeze would preclude the Allies leaving until well into 1920.

It was also self-evident that the British would evacuate Archangel before Murmansk, thus when the withdrawal of British troops 250 miles from Archangel on the Dvina River began in mid September, Red Army commanders on the Murmansk Front knew they could expect a similar series of attacks as were experienced on the Dvina in August, in the very near future.

It would not have been effective for the British offensive to simply move the front line forward a few miles. The attacks would have to completely rout the Bolsheviks and crush their fighting morale to have been worth the effort. The objective would not be to make any strategic land gains but to inflict such losses on the Red Army that they would feel the effects for some time, allowing the British to withdrawal unhindered and giving the Provisional Government the maximum amount of time to reorganise.

General Maynard's plan was for a series of attacks along the railway south of Siding 10 and an overland attack along the Svyatnavolok–Koikori road:

2   *Ibid.*, p. 322.

Broadly speaking, the direct advance was to be made by two columns, one working down the railway, the other moving on the east, and being directed in the first instance on Yamka (6 miles S.E. of Siding 7).

Turning movements were planned to be executed by three columns:

(a) Wide on the west, from Svyatnavolok via Koikori and Ussuna on Konchozero.
(b) Also on the west, but on an interior line, from Tividiya via Kav Gora on Lijma.
(c) From Shunga Peninsula, with Siding 5 as its objective.

It was hoped that (a), if it succeeded in reaching Konchozero, would roll up the left flank of the enemy's forces, should they make a stand on the line of the Suna, and convert defeat into rout.

The object of both (b) and (c) was to get in rear of enemy positions on the railway known to be held by considerable garrisons. These, if all went well, would thus be caught between the flanking and central columns.

The scheme, in effect, amounted to an attempt to 'round up' the enemy at each of several successive stages of the advance. The central columns, too, were to make it their constant endeavour to work round the enemy's flanks and rear.[3]

Timings would be crucial to the success of the offensive. Of particular importance was how long it would take the road column to attack through the Svyatnavolok and Konchozero. The villages of Koikori and Ussuna, if not subdued quickly, would result in a bottleneck in the advance which would stall until both towns were captured. So crucial was their capture that orders were issued that both villages should be attacked and captured before the offensive began.

The newly arrived 6th Battalion, Royal Marines (which had sailed from the UK on SS *Czar* on 1 August, arriving at Murmansk a week later) were assigned the task to capture the villages with 20 men of the KRRC and Middlesex mounted infantry section and five field guns in support, with an additional 600 White Russian troops held in reserve. It was during this final offensive on the Murmansk front that the 6th Battalion, Royal Marines were thrust into battle only to fail miserably.

Immediately after the Armistice it was decided by the victorious Allies that a referendum should be held in the northern German province of Schleswig-Holstein to decide whether that province should remain part of Germany or be returned to Denmark, from where it had been annexed in 1864. A small force of British troops was to be sent to the province to supervise the plebiscite and prevent any public disorder, very much an early version of a modern day 'peacekeeping' mission. The Admiralty would contribute a specially raised Royal Marine battalion to the mission which was designated '6th Battalion, Royal Marines'.

Commanding Officer:	Lieutenant Colonel Arthur de W. Kitcat, RMLI
Second in Command:	Major A.W. Ridings, RMA
Adjutant:	Captain R. Burton, DSC, RMLI
'A' (RMA) Company:	Captain W.R. Boultbee, RMA
'B' (Chatham) Company:	Major A.C. Barnby, RMLI
'C' (Portsmouth) Company:	Major R.W. Laing, RMLI
'D' (Plymouth) Company:	Major J.P. Nind, RMLI

The battalion was concentrated at Bedenham near Gosport and commenced training on 8 July 1919. The training regimen was in drill and ceremonial parades as well as various administrative

---

3   *Ibid.*, p.304.

duties with virtually no land fighting training. Lieutenant Roy Smith-Hill, a platoon commander in 'B' (Chatham) Company, wrote how the men spent most of their time doing, 'an awful lot of polishing brasses and ceremonial drill' and added, 'We certainly did not expect to fight.'[4]

Major Arthur Barnby recorded that from the time he took command of 'B' (Chatham) Company at its formation to the time the battalion left the UK, his company had spent only 17 days training, most of which was spent on drill and ceremony for their expected duties in Schleswig-Holstein. Arm drill and dress were expected to be up to the standard of the 'King's Squad', the Royal Marines ceremonial troop.

Many of the Marines in the battalion spent the war at sea and had very little experience of land operations. The most experienced officer in land operations in the battalion was the Adjutant, Captain Richard Burton (who had been awarded the DSC with the RANB at Archangel in 1918 before brief repatriation to England) but he was the exception.[5] Virtually none of the other officers had any land fighting experience. Battalion CO Lieutenant Colonel Arthur Kitcat had spent his 29 years of service afloat, whilst Officer Commanding (OC) 'B' (Chatham) Company, Major Arthur Barnby, had spent his entire career in ships before transferring to the Royal Naval Air Service (RNAS) where he had trained as a pilot. OC 'C' (Portsmouth) Company, Major Robert Laing, had spent the war in ships of the Grand Fleet.

The company officers too were inexperienced, Captain Reginald Watts' 36 hours on Gallipoli before he was wounded being the cumulative total of service ashore by 'B' Company officers. Major Barnby estimated that within his company only 15 percent of the NCOs and men had any land fighting experience of any kind including the Company Sergeant Major (CSM) and Company Quarter Master Sergeant (CQMS) who had both spent the war on ships. Most incredibly, within the ranks could be found men who had been imprisoned for long lengths of time in German Prisoner of War camps, had been released since the Armistice and were now being sent to Russia after the war for which they had enlisted had ended.

Whilst 6th Battalion were in training for what was expected to be a relatively peaceful task, the Admiralty received from the War Office a request to send a Royal Marine battalion to North Russia to support the evacuation. In a matter of days 6th Battalion was on its way to North Russia, arriving at Murmansk on 8 August. Such was the need for reinforcements at the front that the Marines were entrained for Kem the same night of their arrival, arriving at the White Sea port township two days later. Within 24 hours of arrival in North Russia the battalion suffered its first fatality when Private W. Fazakerly of 'B' Company fell from the train during the journey south and was killed.

At Kandalaksha the battalion was billeted in 'Sussex Village' named after its first inhabitants from 11th Battalion, Royal Sussex Regiment. Whilst billeted in the village rumours began to spread amongst the Marines that newly arrived Commander-in-Chief, NREF, General Rawlinson had given orders for a general offensive to push the Bolsheviks all 250 miles south-west to Petrograd. Lieutenant Roy Smith-Hill wrote that his men were 'prepared to fight' and that they believed that, 'one good British battalion was worth more than ten Bolshevik battalions.'[6]

The 6th Battalion, Royal Marines saw their first action in North Russia on 17 August when 'C' (Portsmouth) Company supported by an armoured train, successfully attacked forward enemy positions and drove the Reds down the line. It was to be the battalion's only successful operation in North Russia.

On 27 August, an attempt by Russian troops and the KRRC/Middlesex Mounted Infantry section to capture Koikori nearly ended in disaster when the Bolsheviks strongly counter-attacked,

4   Diary of Lieutenant Roy Smith-Hill, RMLI.
5   Burton had been repatriated from Archangel, exhausted, then after a short recovery volunteered to return to North Russia with 6th Battalion.
6   Diary of Lieutenant Roy Smith-Hill, RMLI.

threatening to outflank the attacking force. Commanding the Mounted Infantry section, 2nd Lieutenant George Harwood, 3rd Dragoon Guards, was severely wounded by enemy machine gun fire and dragged behind the cover of some rocks by Corporal George Lidington (Middlesex Regiment). Rifleman Edwin Bridge (KRRC) kept the enemy at bay whilst Lidington went to fetch a stretcher, both men assisting to carry the wounded Harwood to safety under fire for which Bridge and Lidington were both awarded the DCM. Harwood was awarded the MC for his leadership during the attack.

On the morning of 28 August, the Royal Marines arrived at Medvyeja-Gora, 'C' Company being immediately despatched to the front line. During the night of 28–29 August, 6th Battalion's CO Lieutenant Colonel Arthur Kitcat led 'C' Company on an eight mile approach march to attack the enemy-held village of Koikori. During a break to take water, the assembled Marines were fired upon from the forest some 300 yards distant, killing a Serbian scout. The four gunmen responsible were seen scurrying back into the forest but with little chance of catching them, Kitcat ordered the march to continue to Koikori.

On reaching the outskirts of the village, 'C' Company was assembled under a ridgeline whilst Kitcat, OC 'C' (Portsmouth) Company, Major Robert Laing and Adjutant, Captain Richard Burton, went ahead to reconnoitre the ground. From a bend in the road leading into Koikori the party were able to observe the line of Bolshevik trenches and sangars in front of the village church about 500 yards distant, evidently the scouts who had fired on the party during the night had reported back to the village of the British advance.

Firing broke out along the enemy line as 'C' Company moved forward to attack, Lieutenant Colonel Kitcat found himself struck with indecision and unable to issue coherent orders:

> I tried to think what I ought to do and found I couldn't think at all. I felt it was foolish to remain in this road and yet couldn't bring myself to give the order to withdraw from it. There was some extraordinary reluctance to do so … There was a ridge some 200–300ft. behind which provided an excellent point of assembly. Then a subaltern who commanded the M.I. [Mounted Infantry] made suggestions. His advice was either to go into the wood or push down the ridge on our left where the ground was more or less open. I felt miserably undecided. If I had only had strength of mind to order Laing to form up his Company to the rear of the ridge this could have given me time for quiet thought. The Bolo was expecting us so there was no particular hurry. From this position I could have put in a strong attack either on its left or through the wood on the right. Further I might have given the men time for rest and food before moving. It makes me sick to think of what did happen.[7]

Kitcat overcame his malaise long enough to order a half-hearted attack on the left flank against the churchyard side of the village, the advance being initially unopposed until the enemy commander redeployed his forces and brought his machine guns into action causing a number of casualties amongst the advancing Marines. Kitcat himself was wounded at 1115, shot through the foot, having his wound bandaged by Captain Burton before being sent to the rear, Major Laing taking over command of the attack.

The attack soon petered out and failed, 'C' Company withdrawing back to Svyatnavolok. Five men had been killed and a number more wounded, the dead Marines recovered from the battlefield were buried in the small village churchyard. It was later discovered that Koikori had been occupied not by Bolshevik conscripts but by battle hardened Red Finns. With the Finns well entrenched with machine guns there would have been little chance the Marines could have taken the village even with

7   Major V.M. Bentinck, 'Mutiny in Murmansk': The Hidden Shame: The Royal Marines in North Russia 1918–1919 (Royal Marines Historical Society, 1999), p.67.

23. Lewis gun post of 1st Battalion, East Surrey Regiment on the
railway near Siding 5, September 1919. (IWM Q16850)

the benefit of surprise and more decisive leadership. The Marines were perhaps fortunate to have been able to withdraw with so few casualties.

After nearly 30 years service afloat, when the time came for Arthur Kitcat to lead his men into battle on land he had failed miserably, a failure he took particularly hard. In a letter to the Colonel Commandant of Royal Marines, written whilst on a hospital train back to Murmansk, a despondent Kitcat wrote: 'One thing stands out perfectly clear is that I am not fit to command troops either in the field or out of it. I feel I ought to be court-martialled and at least cashiered but if I am to be spared that humiliation I must at least retire from the service. I have served so badly.'[8]

The day after the failed attack on Koikori, having been relieved at Svyatnavolok by a company of 1st Battalion, East Surrey Regiment, the shattered remnants of 'C' Company were ordered by Major Martyn Strover, Royal Garrison Artillery (RGA), to occupy an outpost on the Svyatnavolok–Koikori road. The men refused and Major Laing as Company Commander had the unpleasant task of informing his Army superiors that the Royal Marines had refused duty. The reasons the men gave for the refusal were documented by Major Laing:

> A large number of the Company were under 19 years and therefore exempt from fighting. They had not been asked to volunteer for Russia. They wanted assurance of proper hospital arrangements before going on fighting. They, C Company, had done all the fighting up to date and it was time B or D Company did some fighting. That there were Germans fighting on the enemy side and we had made peace with Germany.'[9]

Perhaps as an indication of the drastic shortage of manpower and somewhat remarkably, no action was taken against the Marines other than to send back from the front three men who were under 19 years of age. It was to be an unfortunate precedent. The Marines had refused duty whilst on active service (one of the most serious crimes a soldier can commit) without consequence.

The morning after 'C' (Portsmouth) Companies failed attack on Koikori, 'B' (Chatham) Company entrained for Kapaselga and advanced positions on the Svyatnavolok road. The Marines spent the

8   Bentinck, *Mutiny in Murmansk*, p.69.
9   The National Archives: WO158/969: Court of Inquiry proceedings, 6th Royal Marine Battalion indiscipline.

next few days preparing for a second attempt to take Koikori including a session on forest fighting conducted by Major W. E. Williams, DSO, Middlesex Regiment.

Early in the morning of 3 September, 'C' Company set out for advanced positions on the northern approaches to Koikori, moving slowly and carefully with scouts deployed on either flank to ensure the forest on either side of the track was clear of any enemy. The following day RAF seaplanes from Duck Flight at Medvyeja-Gora strafed and bombed the village for 20 minutes although results of the bombing were inconclusive.

Some time later a Bolshevik deserter was seen coming down the road and taken prisoner. He had no boots, socks or rifle and said there were others in a similar state who wished to surrender. 'B' Company second in command, Captain Watts, took two sections forward to see if he could coax any more Red soldiers to come across but before getting anywhere near the village his party was fired on. On 7 September, the Marines were relieved in the advanced position by the Serbian Company who soon after lost a man to a random enemy shell.

At noon on 8 September, 'B' Company set out from Svyatnavolok to relieve 'C' Company in the front line posts whilst five miles to the west of Svyatnavolok, 'D' (Plymouth) Company was moving in to attack the enemy-held village of Ussuna. The attacking columns were divided as follows:

Koikori Column:	Major W. E. Williams, DSO,
ex Regiment	
'B' (Chatham) Company	6th Royal Marine Battalion
Half 'C' (Portsmouth) Company	6th Royal Marine Battalion
1 section	19th Battalion, MGC
Half section	55th Field Company, RE
2 x 4.5 inch howitzers	86th Battery, RFA
1 x 65 mm gun	135th Battery, RFA
Ussuna Column:	Major A. Ridings, RMA
HQ	6th Royal Marine Battalion
'D' (Plymouth) Company	6th Royal Marine Battalion
1 section	19th Battalion, MGC
Half section	55th Field Company, RE
2 x 65 mm guns	135th Battery, RFA
Reserve held at *Verst* Post 12:	
Half 'C' (Portsmouth) Company	6th Royal Marine Battalion

In order to reach their forming up line to attack Ussuna, 'D' Company had to cross Lake Pyalozero in boats in two lifts during the nights of 4–5 and 6–7 September. During the second lift the lamp set at *Verst* Post 9 to guide the Karelian boatmen had gone out and after futile attempts to locate the correct landing point the men had to spend an uncomfortable night in the boats until first light when the search was resumed and the pier located at 0600 on the morning of the 7 September, the remainder of the day being spent receiving ammunition and stores. A platoon under Lieutenant K. B. Previte which had landed the night before had a brief skirmish with enemy scouts but the landings were otherwise unopposed.

'D' Company's advance commenced at 0600 on the morning of 8 September, Lieutenant Previte's platoon leading as advance guard. The forward scouts were fired on during the approach march but quickly fled on return fire being opened up. The advance guard took a small hill overlooking Ussuna whilst the remainder of the company less HQ and one platoon pushed left to outflank the village whilst the half platoon under battalion adjutant Captain Burton attempted to completely outflank the village and attack from the rear: the plan being to attack the village from two sides simultaneously

24. Royal Engineers attend a church service on the deck of a transport ship in
Murmansk harbour, with HMS *Glory* in the background. (Author's collection)

with the company Lewis guns and a section of Vickers guns of 'B' Company, 19th Battalion, MGC,
and section of 65 mm guns of 135th Battery, RFA, providing supporting fire from a small hill.

As the Marines began forming up to attack, seaplanes from RAF Pigeon and Duck Flights
flew overhead, bombing and strafing the village until 1030. The forest through which 'D' Company
had to traverse became increasingly thick, reducing visibility and making it difficult to maintain
communication with the remainder of the company. A little too eager to engage the enemy, when
Burton's party finally located the remainder of 'D' Company, the forward scouts opened fire on their
own men. The firing only ceased due to the brave actions of two Marines of the main force who went
forward under fire to identify themselves.

By 1330, the main attacking force had reached the outskirts of the village but found their way
obstructed by haystacks and hedges which obscured direct observation of the enemy. There was no
time to reconnoitre another position as the machine guns and 65 mm howitzers opened fire, and the
attack had to commence. The enemy defensive fire was very accurate, much more so than had been
expected. Sergeant Jesse Mumford was sent forward with a section to scout the enemy positions and
was able to crawl within 80 yards of the enemy trenches which were discovered to be substantial and
well protected by barbed wire. For his gallantry Mumford was awarded the MM.

The Marines' attack was not going well and began to falter under the weight of enemy fire. In
an attempt to turn the enemy line, Captain Burton led a half platoon to the extreme left of the
main attack in the hope of flanking the Bolshevik positions but was shot and killed shortly after
(reportedly in a sniper duel with a Bolshevik adversary), and Regimental Sergeant Major (RSM)
Board wounded. Lieutenant William Hanson had also been wounded but refused to leave the line
and remained in command of his platoon for which he was awarded the MC. Burton was buried
in a small service conducted by a Russian Orthodox priest in Svyatnavolok churchyard. Smith-Hill
noted in his diary, 'He was very brave and cheerful. But of course sniping duels were not his job.'[10]

Having encountered a well entrenched and determined enemy, battalion second in command
Major Arthur Ridings, ordered the company to abandon the attack and to withdraw rather than

---

10   Diary of Lieutenant Roy Smith-Hill, RMLI.

risk further casualties. 'D' Company spent the remainder of the day and night digging in on the approaches to Ussuna and resupplying ammunition and water. Fire was exchanged with the enemy throughout the night but there were no further Marine casualties, in fact 'D' Company was lucky to escape without any fatal casualties during the day's fighting other than Captain Burton, although a number of men had been wounded.

During the night a report was made of enemy in the rear of the Marines position and a combined British–Russian patrol under Sergeant John Cannon, 19th Battalion, MGC, sent out to investigate. Lying in ambush, a strong patrol of 40 enemy were encountered and engaged at 20 yards range. For driving off the enemy and inflicting heavy casualties Cannon was awarded the DCM.

At dawn the enemy opened fire with two field guns which had been brought up during the night, forcing the Marines to withdraw from the right flank back into the forest. It being evident that the enemy defences could not be broken with the forces available, column commander Major Martyn Strover, RGA, ordered 'D' Company to withdraw from the line and make no further attempt to capture Ussuna.

With the distant sound of 'D' Company's attack on Ussuna and in the knowledge that 'B' Company would attack Koikori the following morning, word spread in 'B' Company that the men were keen that the officers should not do anything rash during the impending attack on the village of Koikori and, 'should not try and win any medals'.[11]

On the evening of 8 September, 15 Marines who had been ordered to take up outpost duty refused to do so. The following day Major Laing addressed 'B' and 'C' Companies and called for volunteers to man the outpost line. About 16 men from 'B' Company came forward but only three men from 'C' Company, the remainder refused. The number of volunteers being insufficient to man the outposts, Laing ordered Lieutenants Smith-Hill and Bramall to report the refusal to volunteer to local Headquarters. On his return to 'B' Company, Smith-Hill learned that 56 men had abandoned their posts and were marching to the rear. A cyclist was sent after the men to inform that if they approached Svyatnavolok they would be fired upon. Fortunately this did not occur and Smith-Hill found the men in their billets in the village.

He mustered the offenders and told them that they would be court-martialled and possibly shot for desertion on active service. The men did not believe they would be subject to any court proceedings let alone shot, recalling an incident when Marines of the RMFFNR had temporarily refused to fight and received no penalty. The following day at 0800, Smith-Hill found the men fallen in, at attention, dressed, clean and shaven and proceeded to take down their names and numbers for charges to be prepared against them.

At 0800 on the morning of 9 September, 'B' (Chatham) Company set out for *Verst* Post 15 where they encountered Lieutenant G.W. Beazley's platoon in skirmish action with enemy patrols although Beazley himself was absent having been evacuated to the rear sick. Enemy artillery was also in action, sporadic shells striking the trees above the Marines' heads, sending splinters of wood over the advancing troops.

At 1145 OC 'B' Company, Major Arthur Barnby, ordered Lieutenant Smith-Hill's platoon to increase the rate of advance as a 4.5 inch howitzer section of 420th Battery, RFA opened fire on the village in a preparatory bombardment. At 1200, Smith-Hill took the local Russian guide and Lieutenant Walter Morris, 19th MGC, forward to a small hill from which the enemy positions around the church could be observed. Hearing Russian voices nearby, Smith-Hill went back to fetch a section from his platoon whilst the MGC officer established his Vickers guns on the hill. By the time Smith-Hill had returned the Russian guide had fled.

---

11   *Ibid.*

Once the Vickers machine guns opened fire the rate of enemy fire slackened to only sporadic rifle shots as the Bolsheviks attempted to keep their heads under cover. One of the stray rounds mortally wounded Sergeant James McDonald, 19th MGC in the stomach. He was evacuated to Svyatnavolok where he died later in the day. Buried in the village churchyard, McDonald's grave has since been lost to time but he remains commemorated on a plaque in Murmansk New British Cemetery.

Major Barnby gave orders for Smith-Hill to take his platoon through the undergrowth around the base of the hill whilst Lieutenant Francis Bramall's platoon advanced on the right towards some hay carts near the church. Smith-Hill issued orders to send his three platoon scouts (Privates Arthur Jenkins, Thomas Pyle and another Marine) forward, the three men crawling to a gap in the hedgerow from where they could observe the enemy sangars. Having sighted the enemy positions, Smith-Hill called a Lewis gun forward to provide covering fire whilst Jenkins and Pyle crawled forward to clear the sangars with Mills bombs. Whilst bombing the enemy trenches Jenkins was shot and killed and Pyle badly wounded in the leg and left stranded under the enemy breastworks. A Marine crawled forward to rescue Pyle but was shot and killed in the attempt. Another man gallantly volunteered to make an attempt but he too was shot and killed. With no chance of being able to rescue Pyle under heavy enemy fire, Smith-Hill made the difficult decision to withdraw the platoon and leave the wounded Marine behind.

The badly wounded Private Pyle was taken prisoner after his comrades had withdrawn, his badly wounded left leg amputated by surgeons in a Bolshevik field hospital. Unlike most of the Marines in 6th Battalion who had not seen any land service, Pyle was an exception having previously served with 1st Royal Marine Battalion, Royal Naval Division, on the Western Front where he had been twice wounded. Held in Moscow until his release in a prisoner exchange the following year, Pyle was awarded the DCM for his gallantry in action bombing enemy sangars at Koikori and determination and loyalty displayed as a prisoner of war, the only such award made to a Royal Marine for service in Russia 1918–20.

At Koikori the Royal Marines' attack was on the verge of failure. The Red defenders were fighting back strongly, enfilading the Marines with a machine gun on the right flank and from snipers to the front and left. Even worse, the Marines in front began to receive fire from their own men on the hill behind. Under fire from three directions and with little chance of successfully forcing the Bolsheviks from their strong positions around the church, Lieutenant Smith-Hill gave the order to withdraw. As he stood to give the order, Smith-Hill again came under sniper fire from the hill behind his platoon position. When the firing failed to cease, the young subaltern realised that the enemy were in possession of the hill.

Smith-Hill rushed to 'B' Company HQ where he found Major Barnby wounded and Captain Reginald Watts in command. On receiving Smith-Hill's report, Watts issued immediate orders for the company to withdraw. Lieutenants Smith-Hill and Bramall blew furiously on their whistles to signal the withdrawal, counting their men as they came through. In Smith-Hill's platoon alone five men had been killed and four wounded, total casualties across the battalion during the failed attack amounting to eight killed and 23 wounded.

A local guide had led 'B' Company through the forest to the start off point for the attack on Koikori but even before the first shots had been fired he was conspicuously absent and could not be found. During a debriefing after his release from a Moscow prison, Private Thomas Pyle told how he had seen the guide in the Bolshevik camp after his capture chatting away to the Red soldiers. Evidently the plans of the attackers had been betrayed by the guide to the Bolsheviks before the attacks had even commenced.

With the Marines retreating in disorder, Lieutenant William Irvine-Fortescue of 55th Field Company, RE, took his section of sappers forward under covering fire of Lieutenant Walter Morris' section of Vickers machine guns, to hold the line and cover the Marines' withdrawal. Fortescue and

25. Red Army prisoners under guard by Royal Marines Artillerymen of
6th Battalion, Royal Marines, September 1919. (IWM Q16842)

Morris were both awarded MCs whilst Sergeant Frederick Major, 55th Field Company, RE, was awarded the DCM for holding the line with a handful of sappers until ordered to withdraw. Lieutenant Smith-Hill recorded the events that followed:

> On my return from speaking to Major Strover (Machine Gun Corps) I found the company collected in the road. On asking why they had left their positions they informed me that a Major in the MGC had told them to leave their Lewis guns and 'Get the hell out of it' as they were not needed and that he would find someone 'who was some use to the position.'
>
> I was told by the men that Major Strover had telephoned HQ informing them that he was sending the Marines out of it as he had no use for them and asking that they should be neither clothed nor fed.
>
> The word had been passed to the men that those who did not wish to fight could march back. The men fell in and obeyed orders.[12]

When 'B' Company OC, Major Arthur Barnby was wounded, command of the company had fallen to Captain Reginald Watts as second in command. On receiving Smith-Hill's report of Bolshevik troops occupying the hill to the rear of the attacking column, Watts immediately ordered the company to withdraw, an order which would subsequently result in his court-martial. Major W. E. Williams, DSO, Middlesex Regiment, provided the following testimony of Watts' behaviour at a subsequent Board of Inquiry held at Murmansk into the failure of the Royal Marines:

> On the Koikori road at 1535 hours on 8 September, Major Barnby rang me up and said that he was wounded and had handed over command to Captain Watts. About five minutes later Captain Watts rang me up and said that he was retiring his men (B Company) through C Company who would afterwards retire.
>
> I told him to put Lieutenant Morris MGC on the phone to speak to me. I told Lieutenant Morris to take command of front line and not to let anyone withdraw. I put Lieutenant Morris in charge because I knew he was the only officer I could trust.

---

12 *Ibid.*

Lieutenant Morris later rang me up and said that all was quiet and that he had reorganised the line, but that a party of thirty men of 'B' Company refused to stay up there and were creating a bad impression on the men of 'C' Company up there.

I sent up Lieutenant Fortescue RE with his half section and also ordered up one platoon (less two sections) of my reserve platoon of 'B' Company. About this time an officer rang up to say that Captain Watts had collapsed. I spoke to Lieutenant Morris on the phone and he said that Watts was very strange and had sent him down. Shortly after I saw a procession coming down the road half-carrying, half-pushing Captain Watts along.

Three men were holding him and about eight including the Company Sergt. Major carrying his equipment. I went up to Captain Watts and asked what as the matter. He seemed very dazed and incoherent and stated that all the bloody company was lost. I sent him back to the rear with his servant and fell in the rest and took them up the line.[13]

On 11 September, the remainder of 'B' Company was withdrawn to Svyatnavolok village and the mutineers rejoined the company for the time being. The battalion was finally withdrawn to Murmansk on 24 September where a Board of Inquiry was immediately convened into the failure of the Marines in action.

Maynard's final offensive, an attack in two columns along the entire Murmansk front, commenced on 14 September and would be the largest operation undertaken by Murmansk Command during the entire North Russian campaign. In common with the offensive operations on the Dvina River in August, the object of the offensive was to strike a serious blow to the enemy which would give the White Russian forces time to take up positions and prepare defences and allow for an orderly withdrawal of British forces from Murmansk in the first week of October.

Right Column:
    2nd North Russian Rifle Regiment (less one company)
Centre Column:
    Major A.G. Church, DSO, MC, 434th Battery, 6th Brigade RFA
    1st Battalion, Olonetz Regiment (detachment)
    Serbian Company (two platoons)
    65 mm gun, 135th Battery, RFA
    'B' Company, 1st Battalion, East Surrey Regiment (Captain R.C. Campbell)
Left Column:
    Lieutenant Colonel C.G. Ashton, OBE, 1st Battalion, East Surrey Regiment
(Railway):
    Major M.J. Minogue, DSO, MC, 1st Battalion, East Surrey Regiment
    Battalion HQ, 'A' Company, 'D' Company, two platoons 'C' Company, 1st Battalion, East Surrey Regiment
    19th Battalion, MGC (half section)
    British armoured train
    2 x 4.5 inch howitzers, 5 x field guns, 6th Brigade, RFA
(Road):
    Captain F.A. Browning, 1st Battalion, East Surrey Regiment
    2nd North Russian Rifle Regiment (one company)
    19th Battalion, MGC (half section)
    55th Field Company, RE (one section)

13   Bentinck, *Mutiny in Murmansk*, pp.33–34.

2 x 4.5 inch howitzers, 3 x field guns, 6th Brigade, RFA
two platoons 'C' Company, 1st Battalion, East Surrey Regiment
(Shunga Column):
Royal Navy 'SYREN' Lake Flotilla (acting as amphibious troops)

The Centre Column was tasked to move on Tividiya, 11 miles south-west of Kapaselga and the thence advance south-east to Lijma. The Left Column would advance parallel along the railway and road in close cooperation between Railway and Road sub-columns whilst the Shunga Column of Mercantile Marine Reserve sailors (mostly former sailors and soldiers specially enlisted for service in North Russia) would cross Lake Onega in coastal motor boats (CMBs) and small launches, landing near Lijma to cut the railway behind enemy lines.

At 0600 on the morning of 14 September, 'A' and 'C' Companies, 1st Battalion, East Surrey Regiment commenced the advance southwards with the British armoured train providing mobile artillery support for the 'Railway Column'. The East Surreys had disembarked from SS *Kildonan Castle* at Murmansk on 25 August and had been despatched from the UK specifically for Maynard's final offensive.

Commanding Officer:	Lieutenant Colonel C.C.G. Ashton, OBE
Second in Command:	Major M.J. Minogue, DSO, MC
Adjutant:	Lieutenant A.E. Cottam, MC
'A' Company:	Captain E.H.J. Nicolls, DSO, MC
'B' Company:	Captain R.C. Campbell
'C' Company:	Captain F.A. Bowring
'D' Company:	Major A.P.B. Irwin, DSO

The Surreys had not had a good introduction to fighting in the forests of North Russia. During their first engagement with the enemy the day before the offensive commenced, Lieutenant Robert Marshall had been shot through the chest in an ambush whilst leading a patrol 500 yards into the forest towards Siding 6. The ambushers did not press home their advantage and the patrol managed to extricate itself, Private George Street staying with the badly wounded Marshall and fighting off the enemy until he was able with assistance to carry the wounded officer out of the line of fire for which Street was awarded the DCM. Sadly, Marshall, twice wounded on the Western Front, succumbed to his wounds the following day and was buried along with Private Horace Terry, killed in the same ambush, in Kapaselga churchyard, the battalion's first combat casualties in North Russia.

At 0800, the two platoons of 'A' Company in the lead of the advance encountered a series of enemy outposts which opened up a heavy fire and prevented any further advance. The enemy eventually abandoned their positions on the appearance of 'C' Company pushing east from the railway. A number of enemy dead were found in and around the defensive positions whilst the East Surreys had suffered four men wounded, three of whom had been hit by friendly shrapnel fire from the British armoured train.

On the capture of the main position, a patrol of one officer and two sections 'C' Company set out to establish communications with 'Road Column' on the left flank. The patrol came under fire and in the brief skirmish which followed killed one enemy scout and took another six prisoner whilst the remaining enemy fled into the forest. 'A' and 'C' Company resumed the advance, reaching Lijma station at 1630 before pushing on to the railway bridge south of Lijma without any further encounters with the enemy.

During the night the enemy attacked the village of Mikheeva Selga, garrisoned by 50 men of the Karelian Regiment under Lieutenant William Little, Northumberland Fusiliers. The village was completely surrounded and repeatedly attacked over the following six hours during which Little was

26. British 4.5 inch howitzer mounted on train carriage. The officer standing
on the train at right is 2nd Lieutenant Gordon Miller, 1203rd Battery,
RFA who was killed in action 16 September 1919. (IWM Q16827)

wounded. Despite being heavily outnumbered the Karelians held out all night, driving the enemy off shortly before dawn for which Little was awarded the MC.

The following day, 15 September, 'D' Company arrived at 1st East Surreys' battalion HQ and replaced 'A' Company as advanced guard before resuming the advance at 0700. No enemy were encountered in the initial advance but there were clear signs of their hurried departure. On reaching Siding 6 the only living creature that could be found was a railway employee who was promptly taken prisoner and sent to the rear.

By 0920, 'D' Company had advanced to within two *versts* north of Siding 5 from where they could observe the enemy loading a train under steam. Major Irwin deployed his scouts and began to push forward, hoping to catch the train and cargo intact. As the scouts neared the siding the enemy opened fire with rifles and machine guns from the edge of the village and northern end of the railway siding, enfilading 'D' Company.

An attempt to storm the village failed under withering fire, the enemy's left flank being reinforced particularly strongly. Lieutenant George Cranham took a Lewis gun forward and engaged the enemy at close quarters for an hour and a half for which he was awarded the MC whilst Lieutenant John Brown was awarded an MC Bar for leading his platoon to enfilade the enemy. At 1620, Irwin decided to pull his men back to a position 400 yards north of the village and allow the British armoured train following the advance as mobile artillery support to bombard the siding. It was not surprising that the Surreys had encountered such heavy fire: a prisoner taken on the edge of the forest reported that the train had arrived with 400 Red Finnish reinforcements on board only shortly before the Surreys had attacked.

The artillery bombardment commenced at 1700 and lasted 30 minutes before another attempt was made to rush the enemy positions. The enemy put up little resistance, most of the garrison having fled during the bombardment, and both village and siding were captured along with a large quantity of rifles, ammunition and war material. 'D' Company continued on to the bank of the Chelbina River south of the village where forward outposts were established.

During the attack the Surreys lost Corporals Alfred Lett, Herbert Mardle and James Miller killed and six others wounded whilst 2nd Lieutenant Gordon Miller, attached to the armoured train from 1203rd Battery, RFA, was also killed by an enemy sniper whilst acting as forward observer with the infantry. The son of Lieutenant Colonel E.D. Miller, CBE, DSO, late 17th Lancers and Mrs Irene Miller, OBE, Gordon had been awarded the Boy Scout Gold Medal for Merit in 1912 for rescuing a drowning woman from a lake near Tarporley, Cheshire. Arriving in France in November 1918 he was too late to see any action and the following year volunteered for service in North Russia where he was killed aged just 19 years.

On the morning of 16 September, 'A' Company (temporarily under the command of Captain R.C. Campbell) was withdrawn to Siding 5, whilst 'B' Company (which had been up to this point with the Road Column) moved forward west of the railway and 'D' Company to the east. Both 'A' and 'D' Companies exchanged fire with enemy patrols but the advance continued unhindered until Siding 4 was reached where the enemy opened a heavy fire from a line of defences.

At 1630, a platoon was sent through the forest to work round the road and attack the Bolsheviks who were holding up the advance of the Road Column. At 1745 the platoon opened Lewis gun and rifle fire on the enemy-held village of Myanselga from the rear, allowing the Road Column to resume its push forward and link up with the platoon. CSM G.E. Nightingale and Sergeant Richard O'Brien, MM, were both awarded the DCM for working forward under fire with the company scouts to reconnoitre the enemy positions and for their work during the subsequent attack on the village. Twenty-five enemy prisoners were taken and a number of enemy dead counted in the village.

At 1900, both columns joined forces and pushed forward to Siding 4 where they encountered heavy fire from enemy positions on the high ground south of the siding. The Bolsheviks were eventually driven from the heights by 2200 and the position secured in depth. Twelve prisoners were taken bringing the total number of enemy captured by the East Surreys during the two days' operations to 120. The only casualties sustained by the Surreys during the fighting were 'D' Company, OC, Major Irwin and four other ranks wounded.

Commander-in-Chief, NREF, General Rawlinson (who had arrived at Archangel on 9 August to supervise the British withdrawal) was particularly pleased with the success of the offensive:

Maynard's attack has started well. The East Surreys have advanced several miles, and young Burrows of the 5th D.G.s, with his Russians has taken Siding 5 on the Murmansk railway with two locomotives and a good lot of rolling-stock. So far, 500 prisoners and two guns are reported captured, which is satisfactory.[14]

Some time later Rawlinson received an account of the capture of Siding 5 from Burrows:

The Russian troops, as well as the Serbs, refused to take part in the enterprise, because they said it was too dangerous. The Serbs did not trust the Russians, who were prompted by the commander of their lake flotilla. So Burrows got leave to call for volunteers. The whole of our own lake flotilla volunteered to a man, and 83 Russians as well, making a total of just under a hundred. With these Burrows crossed the Liguna inlet at night, surprised Siding 5, and took 300 prisoners.[15]

Rawlinson continued:

One sergeant-major, a South African, was asleep when they landed, and got left behind, and only woke up half an hour after they had started. Being an expert tracker, he thought he could easily find the column, but he missed his way, and eventually came out at Siding 4, instead of 5. There was a number of the enemy busily loading trucks. So, having settled himself comfortably in a good position, he proceeded to open fire at 700 yards range. Consternation ensued, and most of the Bolos bolted into the forest. Having given

14   Sir F. Maurice (ed.), *Soldier, Artist, Sportsman: The Life of Lord Rawlinson* (Boston: Houghton Mifflin Co., 1928), p.267.
15   *Ibid.*, p.267

27. British officers inspecting a Bolshevik train destroyed in the East
Surreys' attack on Siding 5, 15 September 1919. (IWM Q16822)

them 50 to 60 rounds, and getting short of ammunition, he set off again into the forest, where he met four Bolos who had also lost their way. These he took prisoners, but, as he could not get them away, he made them sit down under a tree, and taking out a Mills grenade, extracted the pin and secreted the bomb in the moss. He moved off quickly, when the bomb exploded, disabling the four Bolos, and so he got safely back. After the capture of Siding 5, an Australian wandered off to a cottage, into which he walked and ordered breakfast. While he was eating, five armed Bolos came in at the door. He promptly threw a Mills grenade on the floor, and jumped out of the window. Looking in again through the window, he found three Bolos dead, and the lady of the house complaining bitterly of the mess he had made. So he helped her to tidy up, and then rejoined his pals.[16]

By 15 September, the Allies held all the railway from Siding 4 through Siding 8 and on the following day reached the River Numis, the limit to which General Rawlinson had allowed British troops to advance and the final objective of Maynard's push south. Apart from the failure to take Koikori and Ussuna, the offensive had been an overwhelming success. A serious blow had been dealt to the Bolsheviks, the Red Army lost 1,000 men as prisoners alone. The RAF operating from Lumbushi airstrip and Lake Onega had also played an important role, their bombing machines sending home the largest ship on Lake Onega, a Bolshevik four-funnelled destroyer, on fire.

Any further advance would be at the discretion of General Skobeltsin, as British forces were already making preparations to return to Murmansk for a ship home. Had the Koikori and Ussuna attacks been successful and Konchozero taken, there would have been no reason to delay a further advance by White Russian troops but the lack of progress of the western column meant that the only prudent decision for Skobeltsin would be to consolidate the line and reorganise his forces before the British withdrawal.

With the White forces in a solid position, British troops began to withdraw almost immediately. By 22 September all Allied troops who had taken part in the offensive had either been concentrated at Medvyeja-Gora or were on their way to Murmansk. By 25 September the handover of vessels of the Royal Navy Lake Onega Flotilla and RAF aircraft had been completed and the entire front line occupied by White Russian troops. By the time HMS *Nairana* sailed from Murmansk on 6 October

16   *Ibid.*, pp.267–268

1919, her seaplanes had flown 616 hours of combat missions, dropped 1,014 bombs with a combined weight of 28 tonnes, 321 gas bombs, and 25,000 propaganda leaflets, fired 47,500 rounds of machine gun ammunition and photographed 250 square miles of enemy territory.[17]

The stress and strain of the long and arduous campaign had taken its toll on Maynard's already ailing health, and only days before the evacuation he broke down in exhaustion and was relieved of command by Brigadier H.C. Jackson of Lord Rawlinson's staff. On return to England, Maynard was knighted in recognition of his services as GOC Murmansk Command 1918–19.

Whilst other units were making preparations to withdraw from Murmansk in the first week of October, the officers and men of 6th Battalion, Royal Marines, would not return home without being held accountable for their failures. A Board of Inquiry was held at Murmansk from 24–27 September where several incidents involving the Marines were investigated:

1.   The refusal of the Portsmouth Platoon ('C' Company) to go on outposts on August 30th, 1919.

2.   The alleged withdrawal of a portion of the Chatham Company to camp at SVYATNAVOLOK in defiance of orders.

3.   The circumstances under which Captain Watts R.M., came back from the line. The general reasons for the failure of the attack on KOIKORI and USSUNA with the loss of under 20 casualties.

4.   The circumstances under which 15 men when called on to take up an outpost position on evening of 9th September on KOIKORI Road refused to do so and disappeared.

5.   Circumstances under which numbers 5 & 8 Lewis Gun Sections of number 2 Platoon 'B' Company under Lieutenant Eastman with exception of Corpl. Hartree refused to obey a direct order to go forward and reinforce Captain Noyes.

6.   The conduct of some 30 men who at the action at USSUNA on 8th September were detailed to carry out a flanking movement under Captain Burton and who retreated without due course at or previous to the time of Captain Burton's death.

7.   On September 9th at 12 Verst post certain men of 'B' and 'C' Company refused to go on outpost duty.[18]

RSM Douglas Board was one of the first to testify at the inquiry:

Since the arrival of the Battalion in Russia it has been split up, and those chiefly responsible for the discipline have not had much opportunity to use their influence in maintaining the discipline of the Battalion. I also think the Battalion was not long enough together as a Battalion to fit them for the work they were called upon to do there. A certain amount of unrest was caused in the Battalion through all the paper talk in England about troops being sent to Russia who were not volunteers … When a Marine joins the service he gets as good a foundation of infantry and physical training (ground work) as is possible to get. After which he goes to sea, perhaps for some years, where his work is entirely different from that of infantry. He consequently becomes a bit rusty in infantry work and somewhat soft for carrying out the arduous physical duties of an infantryman. Consequently on joining a Battalion for land duties a Marine requires brushing up in both physical and infantry training. I should like to say that anything I have said is not put forward as an excuse for any indiscipline in the Battalion.[19]

During 3–7 October, in the lead up to the British withdrawal, a field general court-martial was convened at Murmansk with Brigadier George W. St. G. Grogan, VC, CB, CMG, DSO and Bar (who had commanded 1st Brigade, North Russia Relief Force at Archangel) as President, and

17   Tomaselli, *Air Force Lives*, pp.39–40.
18   The National Archives: WO 158/969: 6th Royal Marine Battalion indiscipline.
19   *Ibid.*

Lieutenant Colonel R.O. Paterson, RMA, and Major Thompson, London Regiment, as Court Members. The court-martial was swift but thorough, most of the testimonies having been already taken during the Board of Inquiry. Two officers and 94 NCOs and other ranks (with one other rank awaiting trial in hospital) were tried on a number of charges, namely:

CHARGE 1: When on active service deserting H.M. Service in that they at 12 Verst post on 9th September, 1919, absented themselves from their company after having been warned that they would be required for outpost duty; until they were taken in charge at Svyatnavolok later in the same day.
CHARGE 2: When on active service disobeying in such a manner as to show wilful defiance of authority, a lawful command given personally by their superior officer in that on 8 Sept. 1919 they refused to reinforce the front line.
CHARGE 3: When on active service disobeying a lawful command given by a superior Officer in that they refused to take up an advanced position at the 7 Verst post on the Svyatnavolok-Koikori Road on 30 August, 1919, when ordered to do so.
CHARGE 4: (Private F. Pearson) When on active service negligently discharged his rifle on 8 Sept. thereby shooting himself in the foot.

Before sentencing, Commander-in-Chief, NREF, General Lord Rawlinson, ordered that Lieutenant Colonel Kitcat assemble all officers of the battalion exempting those from 'A' (RMA) and 'D' (Plymouth) Companies which had not been involved in the refusals. Rawlinson blasted the assembled Royal Marine officers:

Throughout the whole of my experience, and after four and a half years continuous fighting in France, I have never come across so bad a case of indiscipline, insubordination, and panic in the presence of the enemy … Had your foe been Germans, instead of Bolshevists, there are few either of you or of your men who would have survived. You have failed to maintain the high tradition of your Corps and, by your in-ability to infuse any motivation of fighting spirit in those under your command, you have seriously interfered with the general plan of operations…

I have found it necessary to try by court-martial a large number of N.C.O.s and men of this battalion. Their conduct in the presence of the enemy was such that I could not do otherwise, but the chief fault was not theirs, it rests with you, their officers, and particularly with you Colonel Kitcat, their Commanding Officer, for having permitted such a state of indiscipline to exist … Discipline can only be created and enforced by the officers, by their example, by their strict attention to duty, by their care in the welfare of their men and, above all, by the high standard of honour and military efficiency which they observe amongst themselves and exhibit in the training and the leading of the N.C.O.s and men. From enquiries I have made, I gather that you officers have done none of these things, and, consequently, your battalion has been found wanting … I had always understood that the discipline of the marines was of the highest, and I have been rudely deceived.[20]

Having berated the assembled officers, Rawlinson stepped down as the Marines who had been court-martialled were marched in and drawn up in a hollow square, leaving Colonel Kitcat to announce sentences. Lieutenant Smith-Hill noted that the men merely looked 'bashful' as their sentences to be served on return to England were read out.

Eighty-one of 87 other ranks charged with offences were found guilty whilst one other rank (Private Coombs) remained in hospital and would be tried on his return to England. Those charged with deserting their positions at *Verst* Post 12 near Svyatnavolok on 9 September were sentenced to

---

28. Murmansk New British Cemetery contains 83 burials and Special Memorials, and is maintained by the Commonwealth War Graves Commission. (Public domain)

two years imprisonment with hard labour whilst those convicted on the charge of disobeying a lawful command by refusing to take up advanced positions at *Verst* Post 7 on 30 August were sentenced to five years with hard labour. The 13 Marines convicted of the most serious charge of 'disobeying in such a manner as to show wilful disobedience of authority' when refusing to reinforce the line on 8 September (Charge 2) were sentenced to 'Death' although as a result of secret orders issued by King George that no further executions were to be carried out as a result of offences committed in Russia their sentences were commuted to five years with hard labour.

The lightest sentence passed was that awarded to Private Frederick Pearson, 42 days 'Field Punishment No. 1' for self-inflicting a gunshot wound to his foot. Apparently the only soldier from 'A' (RMA) Company to have been involved in the refusals, Sergeant A. Sturgess, was ordered to be discharged with ignominy from the service, commuted by General Rawlinson to reduction to the ranks. An entry was to be made on the service record of Corporal P.S. Geater, 'as to the lack shown by him of the qualities required in a Non-Commissioned Officer.' Several officers also received 'Administrative Punishments' including battalion CO, Lieutenant Colonel Kitcat, 'C' (Portsmouth) Company OC Major Laing and 'B' (Chatham) Company officers Captain Watts and Lieutenant Eastman. All surviving members of 'B' (Chatham) and 'C' (Portsmouth) Companies, with the exception of Captain Eric Noyes and Lieutenant Charles Godfrey, received an expression of the Lord of the Admiralty's 'grave displeasure.'

Kitcat had not been subject to any formal charge but he had found his leadership qualities in action wanting. As a result of his 'Administrative Punishment,' the Lords of the Admiralty ordered that he be immediately placed on the Half Pay list. In a letter to the Adjutant General Royal Marines Kitcat wrote, 'Our programme was to take Koikori and burn it. I ought to have succeeded in this without difficulty. I can now see that my best course would have been to have pushed through the wood. I should probably then have effected every object without a casualty. As it was we had 4 killed and 15 wounded.'[21] Kitcat's previously unblemished 29 year career in the Royal Marines was over.

OC 'C' (Portsmouth) Company, Major Robert Laing, was not subject to any charge but was still severely reprimand and placed on the Retired List. Laing had been present at the Messina

21   Bentinck, Mutiny in Murmansk, p.68.

earthquake in Italy in 1908 and had received a medal from the Italian government in recognition of his services in its aftermath. He had also received an expression of the high appreciation of the Commissioner of Weihaiwei for services during the Anti-Revolution rising in China in 1913 and had also seen action off the Falkland Islands in December 1914 in HMS *Kent*. Laing's record up to the time he joined 6th Battalion had been good apart from a drunken episode in New York two days after the Armistice on 13 November 1918. As punishment for his lack of leadership during the mutiny of his platoon, 'B' (Chatham) Company Lieutenant Harry Eastman was ordered to have his commission terminated.

Second in command of 'B' Company, Captain Reginald Watts, faced similar punishment. Watts was the only officer in 'B' Company to have seen previous service ashore during the war, a total of 36 hours on Gallipoli before he had been badly wounded, losing the use of an arm. Watts asked that his friend Lieutenant Roy Smith-Hill be his 'prisoners friend' and address the court on his behalf which Smith-Hill readily agreed to do. Watts had been charged with 'Cowardice' and 'using words calculated to create alarm and despondency'. Smith-Hill's closing address to the court is worth noting in its entirety:

The court has heard from Surgeon Codr. Wilkinson and others that accidents to the head are capable of producing the illness form which Captain Watts was suffering during the latter part of the 8th Sept. In Gallipoli he was shot in the right arm and sustained a 6 months illness followed by permanent disablement of the arm. During 1915 he fell about 30 feet down a coal-bunker in the *Cawdor Castle* and suffered a heavy shock. Earlier in the present year at Chatham he had a bicycle accident in which he became unconscious due to falling on the back of his head onto a slab of stone.

Surgeon Codr. Nicholls has told the court that the strain attached to the duties of Adjutant to the O.C. Troops at Kandalaksha had rendered him slightly abnormal. After the remainder of the Company left Kandalaksha, Captain Watts stayed behind and had a particularly difficult time turning over to his successor and this rendered him still more highly strung and less able to resist physical and mental strain.

It is obvious that Captain Watts' experiences had rendered him more susceptible to shock than the normal individual. On leaving Kandalaksha, Captain Watts travelled almost without a break to Svyatnavolok and thus had no time for a proper rest. The remainder of the Company rested at Med. Gora for 3 days. Two days before the attack on Koikori he was in charge of a minor action at 12 verst post. On the morning of 8 September he stood-to with the company at 3.30 a.m. and left at 4 a.m. in charge of a reconnaissance patrol which was engaged by the enemy near 16 verst post. Immediately on being relieved he came to the left flank and participated in the whole of the main attack. During the attack witness has been borne to the fact that none of his actions could be attributed to cowardice. He used up a stock of more than 6 field dressings when bandaging the wounded under fire.

When he arrived at the telephone position at about 3.30 p.m. he had been marching and fighting under the severest mental and physical strain for eleven and a half hours. It is most probable that he had no food that day since he had no opportunity. He himself is unable to remember any of the incidents that day.

During the retirement his mind was gradually succumbing to the strain. He was just able to telephone to Major Williams and it is important to notice that he did not report that the company had been wiped out. He collapsed before telephoning but Lt. Bisiker has stated that he recovered normal consciousness. After the second collapse he was abnormal and on medical evidence was not responsible for his actions or statements.

When he came under medical observation about a couple of hours must have elapsed since his remarks on the subject of the Company's casualties. Surgeon Lt. Codr. Nicholls has stated that during this time he may have been recovering and therefore he was not in his worst condition when he was examined at 12 verst post. I maintain that I have now shown the reason for Captain Watts' dazed condition. Namely shock produced by physical and mental strain on one rendered susceptible by experiences at Gallipoli and elsewhere.

The first charge against Captain Watts is 'Misbehaving in such a manner as to show cowardice in that he retired from the line supported by 2 or more men in a dazed condition'. No evidence has been brought forward to support such a grave charge as that of cowardice and no evidence to the effect that Captain Watts' condition was caused through cowardice. The last experience he may be expected to have in his mind when he succumbed was that of bandaging wounded men. He therefore talked disconnectedly of casualties; even though by this time he was not responsible for his statements. Thus with regard to the second Charge namely using words calculated to create alarm and despondency, Captain Watts, on medical evidence, was not responsible for anything he may have said.[22]

The mitigating circumstances were taken into account by the courts-martial and Watts was acquitted of the charge of 'Cowardice' but found 'Guilty' of the charge 'using words calculated to create alarm and despondency'. His sentence was to be dismissed from His Majesty's service. A suit of civilian clothes was found for the cashiered officer and he was sent on a collier home, his entry on the passenger manifest stating, 'R.H. Watts, Esq.' On return to England, Watts' sentence was reviewed and his conviction quashed but his dismissal from the service upheld. Watts later joined the Auxiliary Division of the Royal Irish Constabulary in Ireland during the post-war conflict in that country.

Eight of the Marines found guilty and sentenced who were under 19 at the time of the offence were given 'special consideration' in view of Army instructions that young soldiers were not, if possible to be employed in front line operations. Two of the young Marines had their sentences reduced to six months imprisonment whilst the other six were released. This decision brought the legitimacy of the entire courts-martial conducted at Murmansk under question.

Private Coombs, the Marine in hospital at Murmansk, was tried upon his return to England by district courts-martial at the Royal Engineers barracks in Chatham but was acquitted. All the other Marines charged with Coombs on Charges 1 and 2, 'Deserting H.M. Service' and 'Disobeying a lawful command', were found guilty. The ruling further contradicted the verdicts of the courts-martial held at Murmansk.

As for Lieutenant Roy Smith-Hill, he was informed he had incurred the 'severe displeasure' of the Lords of the Admiralty and had a note to this effect added to his officer's service record. He asked to be court-martialled but the request was refused: 'the Brigade Major later told me that it was not a bad thing for a young officer to receive their Lordships' severe displeasure because it would get his name known.'[23] This rather optimistic view of circumstances would not be far from the truth. When Smith-Hill finally retired from the Royal Marines it was in the rank of Brigadier and as holder of the CBE for his services.

Smith-Hill remained loyal to his Marines to the end and maintained the belief that during the battle itself his men had acquitted themselves well: 'During the attack on Koikori, the discipline and conduct of the men left nothing to be desired and no one left the scene of action before receiving the order to retire.' Although loyal to his men, Smith-Hill remained critical of the campaign and the senior officers who had sent them there:

> We had been ill-prepared for our attack on Koikori. Few officers and certainly none of the junior officers had any experience fighting in these circumstances. Our time had been at sea. We had thought that we were to act as a relieving force, while the evacuation of other battalions took place. In the subsequent court-martial it was obvious that the NCOs and men had lost faith in their officers … The other ranks suffered the most and deserved it least. Those sent to penal servitude and those wounded or killed were the victims of the

22   *Ibid.*, pp. 29–31.
23   Diary of Lieutenant Roy Smith-Hill, RMLI.

29. Seaplane carrier HMS *Pegasus* brought RAF Duck Flight's Fairey IIIC seaplanes to Murmansk and served on station in North Russia from April to October 1919. (Public domain)

ineptitude of senior officers. They were transported two thousand miles by sea and 450 miles by rail: they fought a minor action lasting two and a half hours – and returned home! They achieved nothing.[24]

Although (as far as the military hierarchy was concerned) the 6th Royal Marine Battalion had been a miserable failure, there had also been extraordinary examples of bravery exhibited by the Marines. When the two detachments of 'D' Company opened fire on each other early in the attack on Ussuna, two Marines went forward under fire to identify themselves at great risk to their own safety. As Private Thomas Pyle of 'B' Company lay wounded in an exposed position, a Marine ran forward without orders in an attempt to drag the wounded scout out of the line of fire, this man was shot and killed. Immediately another Marine, knowing full well the risk, crawled out into the exposed ground under fire in a gallant attempt to rescue Pyle. This second would be rescuer was also shot and killed.

The battalion embarked at Murmansk on SS *Elena* on the morning of 8 October bound for Glasgow where those sentenced to terms of imprisonment were separated and sent to prison in Edinburgh or south to Bodmin, Cornwall. On arrival at Chatham station Lieutenant Smith-Hill as acting company commander of 'B' Company received a message requesting that he keep the company at the station until the arrival of the divisional band to play them back to barracks:

> I felt that we would never be forgiven if we allowed ourselves to be played back in triumph, so I ordered the company to fall in quickly and reached barracks while the band was still getting ready to leave … I was sent for by the Colonel Commandant at Chatham Barracks and he asked me what had happened … As I explained what had happened he wept and his tears formed big pink blobs on his blotting paper.'[25]

24   *Ibid.*
25   *Ibid.*

The remnants of the battalion were quickly disbanded and the Marines either discharged or absorbed into other units. The whole affair was covered up, no news was released to the public, even the families of those imprisoned were not told for what crime their loved ones had been incarcerated.

Pressure from family members of the imprisoned Marines led to questions being asked in Parliament as to why Royal Marines were serving sentences in Bodmin Prison, 'for offences alleged to have been committed in Russia.' These questions were avoided and sidestepped until 22 December when First Lord of the Admiralty Mr Walter Long made the following statement:

> We have given these cases our most careful and anxious consideration, and have decided to deal with them in what we believe the House will regard as a spirit of clemency.
>
> About ninety men of the Royal Marines in North Russia were found guilty of insubordination and refusal to obey orders while engaged in active operations. They were serving with the Army in the field and were sentenced by military-courts-martial.
>
> Subject in all cases to good conduct in prison, we have decided on the following reductions in the sentences:
>
> Of the thirteen men sentenced to death commuted by the General Officer Commanding-in-Chief to five years penal servitude, to be released after six months.
>
> Fifty-one men sentenced to five years' penal servitude, to be released after six months.
>
> Special consideration has been given in the cases of men under nineteen years of age at the time of the commission of the offence in question, in view of the Army instruction, that young soldiers were not, if possible, to be employed in front-line operations. Two of those who continued in a refusal of duty when others obeyed, will, in view of their youth, be released after serving six months. The remainder – six out of eight – have been released. The extent to which it could be urged that bad leadership on the part of the officers contributed to these incidents has been fully considered, and, where merited, disciplinary action is being taken.[26]

No further questions were asked and no newspaper carried headlines of 'Russia Marines Death Sentences Revoked'. The whole affair was kept under such a veil of secrecy that neither Generals Rawlinson, Maynard nor Ironside mention the 6th Battalion, Royal Marines mutiny in their memoirs of the campaign.

By 10 October 1919, the refit of the Archangel river vessels had been completed and two days later the last Allied troopship left Murmansk escorted by battleship HMS *Glory*. The White Russian Provisional Government had requested that four CMBs be left behind to operate on Lake Onega but the Admiralty denied the request. There were reportedly at least a couple of British agents that stayed behind at Murmansk however no British serviceman would remain in North Russia. Australian 'ELOPE' Force volunteer Sergeant John Kelly spoke of the departure of the NREF:

> It achieved nothing, cost the British taxpayer 15 million, but most tragic of all was the number of splendid men who lost their lives in the venture, men who, after passing through the dangers of France, Gallipoli and other theatres of war, deserved a better fate.[27]

The Provisional Government did not hold out against the Red Army long. The Bolsheviks did not even wait for the sub-Arctic winter to end before capturing Murmansk on 13 March 1920 (Archangel had been captured on 21 February) only five months after the British withdrawal. The Bolsheviks showed restraint and although a number of its citizens who had cooperated with the

---

26   Hansard, 22 December 1919, Oral Answers House of Commons, First Lord of the Admiralty Mr. Long to Lieut.-Cdr. Kenworthy by Private Notice.

27   *Sydney Morning Herald*, 13 April 1979.

30. Special Memorial to Captain Richard Burton, DSC, RMLI in Murmansk New British Cemetery. Burton had been awarded the DSC (incorrectly shown on the memorial as 'DSO') at Archangel in 1918 with the Russian Allied Naval Brigade and volunteered to return to Russia with 6th Battalion, Royal Marines. He was killed in action 8 September 1919 during the attack on Ussuna. (Public domain)

Allies or opposed the Bolsheviks were imprisoned or put through mock trials and executed, the bloodbath expected by many did not occur.

Today, all that remains of the British presence at Murmansk 1918–19 is the small British military cemetery. Although administered by the Commonwealth War Graves Commission, the small cemetery is too remote and contains too few burials to warrant much attention from the CWGC and is shabby and un-maintained when compared to the immaculately kept military cemeteries in France and Belgium.

Part II

North Russia: Archangel ('ELOPE' FORCE) 1918–19

Archangel: Occupation and Operations August 1918–September 1919

For over 300 years the North Russian port of Archangel (or Arkhangelsk) had been used to ship to Europe North Russia's most valuable commodity, timber. The industrial revolution had resulted in increased demand for cheap building materials and with this demand came British merchant seamen and sawmill operators to Archangel.

Timber is so prevalent and accessible in North Russia that wood was a primary component of the construction of most local building. Houses were almost entirely made out of wood along with bridges, boats and even roads. The North Russian peasant was so skilled in the use of wood as a building material that using only a small, sharp axe, the most complex structures could be built without the use of a single nail. At Archangel there was electricity and trams ran through the centre of the city along the main street, Troitsky Prospekt, however there was neither sewage system nor running water.

Foreign activity in Archangel had increased dramatically since the beginning of the war in 1914. Until the year round ice-free port facilities at Murmansk were completed in 1917, Archangel remained Russia's only European port not blockaded by the Germans or Turks and became a key port for the delivery of Allied war supplies. Sprawled across the docks and warehouses lay millions of pounds worth of supplies and armaments purchased by the Tsarist government on war loans from France and Britain in particular.

By early 1918, Archangel remained largely as it had been in spite of the Bolshevik revolution of November 1917. Banks and private businesses continued to trade, priests continued to conduct mass and teach in the local schools. It was not until the arrival of the first 'Revising Mission' in May 1918 that the Bolsheviks actually took control of the city.

The role of the Mission was to maintain 'discipline' amongst the locals and conscript local men into the Red Army. The Mission was also tasked with the defence of Archangel from counter-revolutionary elements. The irony that the Bolsheviks themselves were counter-revolutionaries having taken power in a coup which overthrew the Provisional Government of Alexander Kerensky was likely lost on the average Red soldier.

On 30 July 1918 a combined Allied force set sail from Murmansk to capture and occupy Archangel. Army and naval landing parties would storm ashore under covering fire of HMS *Attentive*'s 4 inch guns supported by RAF seaplanes from HMS *Nairana* flying overhead. The operation would be the first time in history that the three services combined in a single amphibious operation. The landing force commanded by Brigadier R.G. Finlayson, CMG, DSO, RA numbered only 700 British troops of 'ELOPE' Force and a further 800 Allied troops of several nationalities.

Most of the British soldiers were members of the 'ELOPE' Force military mission that was to train and equip the Czech Legion when the Czechs reached the northern port. Although almost exclusively experienced veterans of the Western Front and other theatres, 'ELOPE' Force were certainly not assault infantry intended for use to storm ashore during an opposed landing.

Armed yacht HMS *Salvator*
    GOC NREF, Major General Poole
    Captain B.B. Bierer, USN, USS *Olympia*

Cruiser HMS *Attentive* (Captain Edward Altham, CB, RN)

Seaplane carrier HMS *Nairana* (Lieutenant Commander Eugene Smith, DSC, RN)
    SNO White Sea, Rear Admiral Thomas Kemp, CB, CMG, RN
    GOC 'ELOPE' Force, Brigadier R.G. Finlayson, CMG, DSO, RA
    OC Seaplanes, Major Francis Moller, MC, RAF

French cruiser *L'Amiral Aube*
    1 Officer, 4 ORs RAMC
    3 ORs RE Signals
    1 British liaison officer

3 x torpedo boats
    'A' French crew
    'B' British crew
    'C' American crew

Q-ship HMS *Tay and Tyne* (Captain Henry Albert Le Fowne Hurt, RN)
    10 x RNR trawlers
    Each carrying Lewis gun detachment, 1 NCO and 2 ORs, RA, 1 private, RAMC

Transport SS *Stephen* (Captain John Lewis Pearson, RN)
    OC Troops Major Bernard Musgrave, Loyal North Lancashire Regiment
    RAF Liaison, Lieutenant Maurice George Epstein, RAF
    'ELOPE' Force: 107 Officers, 344 ORs
    100 RMLI (attached from Royal Marine Field Force, Murmansk)
    50 USN (attached from USS *Olympia* at Murmansk)
    50 Polish Legion
    60 Slavo-British Legion
    1 Vickers section, 253rd Company, MGC (attached from 'SYREN' Force)
    1 Platoon, 29th Battalion, London Regiment (attached from 'SYREN' Force)
    9 officers 84 ORs, RAMC

Transport SS *Asturian*
    (Captain Joseph Pitts, MC, General List, attached as liaison)
    21st French Colonial Infantry Battalion

Transport SS *Kassala*
    50 USN (attached from USS *Olympia* at Murmansk)
    50 Polish Legion
    50 Slavo-British Legion
    1 Lewis gun detachment (8 other ranks)
    1 Officer, 1 OR, RAMC

Transport SS *Westborough*
    1 Lewis gun section
    1 Officer, 1 OR, RAMC

31. Adventure Class cruiser HMS *Attentive* which led the Allied fleet in the amphibious invasion of Archangel, 1 August 1918. (Public domain)

In advance of the invasion of Archangel, Lieutenant Colonel C.J.M. Thornhill, DSO, Indian Army, Poole's Chief Intelligence Officer, led a bold assault on the White Sea town of Onega, an important overland link between Murmansk and Archangel. Having assembled a small force of Russian volunteers and Serbs (Although described by British military authorities collectively as 'Serbs', only 20 percent of the company were ethnically Serbian, the remainder being a combination of Croats and Bosnians, mostly deserters from the Austro-Hungarian Army) with Captain J.J. Hitching, MC, 16th London Regiment, 2nd Lieutenant C.S. Richards, Special List (interpreter), 2nd Lieutenant Herbert Lee, West Yorkshire Regiment, Captain Denys Garstin, MC, 10th Hussars (formerly British Secret Service Petrograd), Canadian Sergeant Royce Dyer, MM and Bar, 8th Canadian Battalion, and Sergeant Allan Burke, 2nd Otago Regiment, an Australian serving in the New Zealand forces. Thornhill set out to capture the town and push south to capture the important railway siding at Obozerskaya. The story was subsequently relayed by a participant to a newspaper correspondent on assignment with the troops in North Russia and received extensive coverage in *The Times*:

> Colonel C.J.M. Thornhill, a fluent Russian speaker who had been Britain's chief of military intelligence in Tsarist Russia under the guise of Assistant Military Attaché, led a raid from Kem with the aim of cutting the Archangel–Vologda Railway at Obozerskaya…
>
> He gathered eighty nine officers and men, among them forty-seven of the ubiquitous Serbs, six Tsarist officers now serving as privates in the Slavo-British Legion, two peasants who joined as recruits and several British officers and NCOs…
>
> The party embarked on the *Michael Archangel* … In the bay the flag was taken down and the red one of revolution hoisted. On board the monks' boat there was suspicion of the Russian pilot. Colonel Thornhill, who speaks Russian like a native, never left the man's side; if there was to be treachery the pilot would be the first to pay the price.
>
> Onega was reached, and here the real drama began. The town was in the hands of the Bolshevists. The boat made fast to the pier; on shore, a Bolshevist guard of three or four men awaited her. The Colonel, disguised as a Russian soldier, ordered the whole of his party to stay below, and, leaning carelessly over the

rail, answered the questions of the guard. Was this the Monks' boat bringing food? It was. They laughed and jested, the Colonel stepped back into the alleyway, dropped his disguise, and, in the uniform of a British Staff Officer, leaped ashore. The attack was so sudden that the guard lost its head. One lunged at Thornhill with his bayonet, but the Colonel parried the blow with his arm and shot the man through the head.

Aroused by the firing, the party below deck disobeyed orders and came up. The Colonel was engaged, single-handed, with three Bolshevists. One of them raised his rifle and fired, but an ex-Russian Officer, Oluchakov leaped between Thornhill and the rifle; he took the bullet in the arm. Quickly, the gallant little party formed its plan of campaign; one or two of the guard had escaped to give the alarm, and by six a.m. street fighting was in progress and machine-guns were rattling. Four cardinal points were selected by Thornhill and by 11 a.m. resistance was over. There had been a force of 90 Bolshevists in the town under the leadership of Popoff, an ex-sailor. Our losses were one killed and one wounded; the Bolshevists lost one killed and two wounded. Thornhill's party took 60 prisoners, three machine-guns, 300 rifles and a large quantity of ammunition. Popoff escaped.

In the town there was much jubilation among the inhabitants. Seventeen Poles were released from prison where they were awaiting execution and they joined the expedition. At 2 p.m. the inhabitants gathered in the square and Colonel Thornhill explained the situation and reassured them.

… The party pressed on. Ten more Poles joined. They raised sixty horses and carts with peasant women as drivers. They shot a Bolshevik who had confessed to killing a Polish Lieutenant on his way to join Poole … They fought their way out of an ambush in a forest, then after marching all night clashed with a force of 350 Bolsheviks and fought them for six hours. They killed ten and lost five of their own number. Soon after this fight the scouts learnt that a force of some 2,000 Bolsheviks with field artillery had entrenched themselves across the raiding party's route. Thornhill decided that enough was enough. They now had no chance of cutting the railway line, but they had succeeded in diverting a major force of Bolshevik soldiers from the defence of Archangel. So they returned to Onega, burning bridges as they went, boarding the ship Kolo and arrived back at Kem safely.

Thornhill's expedition had lasted for twenty days and between August 1st and August 6th they had marched for some 140 miles.[1]

Thornhill was subsequently awarded a Bar to his DSO for the raid whilst Lee received an MC Bar, Dyer received the DCM and Private Vassily Prootkovsky, an ex-Imperial Officer enlisted as a private in the Slavo-British Legion, the MM. Dyer was promoted in the field to captain and given command of the 'one thousand criminals' of the newly raised 1st Battalion, Slavo-British Legion to whip into shape which he did very successfully. The Russian recruits revered their commander and when Dyer died of pneumonia on New Year's Eve 1918, a large photograph of the Canadian was carried at the head of the battalion, as was the tradition in Tsarist regiments. Command of the Battalion was subsequently transferred to Lieutenant Colonel Barrington Clement Wells, DSO, Essex Regiment although even after his death, as a sign of the esteem in which their leader had been held, 1st Battalion continued to be known as 'Dyer's'.

After the raid, Garstin joined the Dvina River force where he was awarded the DSO for his leadership in the capture of an enemy village and the single handed capture of an enemy armoured car. He was killed soon after and buried in Archangel Allied Cemetery (CWGC). Burke received an MM for actions in early 1919 and was subsequently promoted in the field and later received an MBE for his work in command of 2nd (Burke's) Battalion, Slavo-British Legion until handing over command to Lieutenant Colonel W. Morrison, DSO, MC, DCM, Gordon Highlanders, the following year.

1   The Times, 13 June 1919.

As Thornhill's force was storming ashore at Onega, Captain Edward Altham's flagship HMS *Attentive* was leading the convoy of attacking ships through the fog towards the mouth of the Dvina where the convoy arrived on the morning of 1 August. On 19 July, during a personal reconnaissance in the observer's cockpit of a seaplane from HMS *Nairana*, Altham had fired the first airborne shots of British military intervention in the Russian Civil War when the aircraft had come under fire from unidentified but presumably Bolshevik troops below. Altham let loose with a few bursts from the observer's Lewis gun which silenced the enemy fire.

As the flotilla steamed towards Archangel harbour they were spotted by an enemy battery of 6 inch and 4 inch guns on Modyugski Island. On board *Attentive*, Altham recorded:

> For the most part the batteries shooting was wild; but one 6-inch gun was evidently in expert hands. One shot shimmered over the forecastle, the next whistled over our heads on the bridge, and the next plunged into the base of the foremost of our four funnels and burst there, putting two boilers out of action and doing other damage.[2]

Ten minutes of counterfire by the Allied fleet and aerial bombing from a flight of Fairey Campania seaplanes from HMS *Nairana* under Major Francis Moller, MC, forced the Bolsheviks from their guns. The landing troops stormed ashore and cleared the island of opposition, the only casualties suffered by the Allies had been two French sailors wounded. Moller was subsequently awarded the DFC for his command of RAF 'ELOPE' Squadron at Bereznik whilst Leading Seaman Edward Eves of *Attentive* was awarded the Distinguished Service Medal (DSM) during the action for his work on a 6 inch gun under fire from Modyugski battery.

The fleet continued up the channel with one of the seaplanes spotting for the ships guns. With ample warning of the advancing Allied fleet, Bolshevik leadership in Archangel ordered two icebreakers scuttled in an attempt to block the passage up the channel, and evacuated the city. The Red Army in Archangel actually outnumbered the Allied force but the flypast of *Nairana*'s seaplanes was enough to convince them that the Allies were landing en masse and after mounting only token resistance the garrison fled the city. At 0400 on the morning of 2 August a coup which had been fermented by Russo–British agent Grigory Chaplin was launched to coincide with the Allied attack and was completely successful. The Bolsheviks had been removed from power in Archangel.

Sergeant John Kelly, an Australian veteran of the Western Front seconded for service with 'ELOPE' Force, disembarked at Archangel Quay in his distinctive slouch hat armed with a Lewis gun, accompanied by a party of Royal Marines from HMS *Attentive* and got quite a surprise when he stepped ashore:

> I had barely hit the wharf when a voice from the crowd called 'Hullo Aussie'. I stopped dead in my tracks. This was unbelievable. I sorted out the individual and questioned him as to how he came to recognise an Australian. The answer was simple. He was a Russian seaman who in his travels had picked up a little English. His ship had traded a lot in the Mediterranean and he had seen a number of diggers in Alexandria.[3]

One British sailor described Archangel:

> All along the front are huge buildings, mostly churches, with enormous domes and very imposing architecture. They are well spaced, and mostly white stone, sometimes with reddish coloured roofs. Some of the less important buildings are all red. Two of the churches are especially remarkable. One has a long

2   The National Archives: ADM 137-1711: White Sea SNO's Records 1918.
3   AWM: PR85/324, Recollection of John Kelly.

32. Some of the original members of 'ELOPE' Force, 1918. Seated back row left to right
(all sergeants): Bertram Perry, MM (Australia), Robert McCready (New Zealand), Wright
and Jones (British). Seated left to right: Arthur von Duve, MM (Australia), Torbett, MM
(British), Bain & Felwell, DCM, MM (Canada), John Kelly (Australia). Front row lying
left to right: Charles Hickey (Australia), Winning (British). (AWM P00454.002)

thin golden spire about 100ft long, and also some minor spires. The other has a great dome, and some
lesser ones in front. It would look very striking indeed, but for the rust and dirt that has accumulated on
it for some time past, which give it a very neglected appearance. Everywhere one can see the lovely green
stuff, trees, shrubs etc. that is so plentiful round here. The British ships … are anchored in the river which
is about a mile or a little over a mile wide, opposite Archangel. Also American and French ships are here.
The town looks to be a large one, say 40,000 Russian population but with the Allied soldiers etc., it must
be considerably greater … There is very little on the south side of the river, and what there is, has mostly
been built by the Allies. Solom Balskie [Solombola], appears to be a sort of Dockyard and manufacturing
place.[4]

British agent Grigory Chaplin had seen extensive service with the Imperial Russian Navy during
the war with Germany, several months of which was on secondment with British submarines in the
Baltic. When the Bolsheviks launched their coup in November 1917, Chaplin had been in Petrograd
and immediately went into hiding and began recruiting former Imperial Army officers for service
with Denikin's Volunteer Army in the South. The British realised that Chaplin could be of great
value if utilised correctly and messages began to be passed between Chaplin and General Poole.
In June, Chaplin arrived in Archangel and immediately started to organise the coup which was to
pave the way for the landings. For this task Chaplin went by the name 'Commander Thompson' of

4   Haddon, *North Russia Expedition of Summer 1919*.

the British Naval Mission in Petrograd and was supplied with a British passport and Royal Navy uniform. Organising the coup in some cases was surprisingly easy as despite the arrival of the small Bolshevik mission in May, many White Russians still held positions of power in Archangel.

Whilst in Archangel, Chaplin met with Nikolai Vassilevich Tchaikovsky who was to lead the new White Russian Provisional Government that would be installed upon the successful conclusion of the coup. A relative of the great composer, Tchaikovsky was in mid 1918 almost 70 years of age. He had been imprisoned in St. Petersburg under the Tsar and had spent half his life in exile. For 26 years he had lived in England, and another six in America. Tchaikovsky had been planning to join the Czech Legion in southern Russia when he was persuaded to head to Archangel and join the White Russian cause there. On 1 August 1918, as the small Allied fleet entered the White Sea, Chaplin gave the signal to initiate the coup as the fleet sailed into Archangel Harbour.

General Poole's official despatch to the War Office gave a report of the success of the landings:

> During the night the Bolshevik Government decided to evacuate the town, after having ordered two icebreakers to be sunk in the fairway to block our passage up the channel. On August 2nd the revolution planned by our supporters broke out at 4 a.m. and was completely successful. The Bolshevik Government was overthrown. The new government cordially invoked our aid, and declared itself pro-Ally, anti-German, and determined not to recognise the Brest Litovsk treaty. After some delay caused by exploring a passage between the sunken icebreakers, we were fortunate enough to find that there was just sufficient room to allow a passage for the ships. We then made a triumphal procession up the channel to Archangel, being everywhere greeted with enormous enthusiasm.[5]

Three rather curious decorations were awarded for the capture of Archangel. Captain Sir Ivor Heron Maxwell, General List, Captain Walter MacGrath, RE, and Lieutenant Commander Malcolm MacLaren, RNVR, all received awards of the MC for work leading up to the landing and specifically for maintaining communications with Murmansk, fermenting the coup itself and coordinating the anti-provisional government factions.

It was immediately evident to Poole upon disembarking at Archangel that one of the main aims of the landings, to recover the war stores warehoused there, had been pre-empted by the Bolsheviks with a considerable amount of the supplies having already been shipped away to Petrograd and Moscow.

The Allied contingent in Archangel was small and ill equipped and the threat of a Bolshevik instigated counter-uprising so real that Poole imposed martial law over the city. Poole's attitude towards Russian civilians was such that when Maynard's civilian railway workers went on strike for lack of wages, Poole recommended that he use force to get them back to work. Not without reason, Poole did not endear himself to the population of Archangel. Immediately upon arrival he requisitioned the largest and finest residence in the centre of the town as NREF Headquarters. He ejected the sawmill owner and his wife from the large stone building and it was not until the lady of the house told him that he was 'worse than the Bolsheviks' that Poole allowed her and her husband to occupy four rooms in the back of the large house. Even when the town had been under Bolshevik control the owners had been allowed to occupy a portion of the house. As the sawmill owner was a wealthy businessman this was quite conciliatory action for them to take. The same was the case for many other of Archangels substantial buildings which were occupied by various branches of the NREF. The British Consul at Archangel reported to the Foreign Office, 'Whole school buildings

5   *The London Gazette*, 6 April 1920.

33. Troitsky Prospekt, Archangel's main street with electric tramline in foreground.
Cathedral of the Archangel Michael after which the city was named is visible
in the background at the mouth of the Dvina River. (Public Domain)

were requisitioned, and in large rooms capable of holding four or five people might be seen one
officer and one table.'[6]

The Consul, Douglas Young, was critical of the invasion of Archangel and telegrammed the
Foreign Office advising against military operations without the consent of the Bolsheviks which
even if locally successful would ultimately backfire on the Allies and entangle them further into
Russia's internal affairs. Young's American equivalent had made much the same point to the US
Secretary of State. He hypothesised the consequences of Allied intervention with what would later
prove to be unerring accuracy:

> Intervention will begin on a small scale, but with each step forward will grow in scope and its demands
> for ships, men, money and materials. Intervention in the north of Russia will mean that we must feed
> the entire north of Russia containing some 500,000 to 1,500,000 population. Intervention cannot reckon
> on active support from Russians. All the fight is out of Russia. Intervention will alienate thousands of
> anti-German Bolsheviks. Every foreign invasion that has gone deep into Russia has been swallowed up.
> If we intervene, going father into Russia as we succeed, we shall be swallowed up. I cannot see that the
> fundamental situation in Russia is changed even if it were proven that Lenin, Trotsky, Sverdlov, etc., drew
> monthly pay checks from the Berlin Treasury.[7]

British agent in Petrograd, Robert Bruce Lockhart, was aghast when he learnt that the British
had landed so few soldiers, barely enough to hold Archangel let alone usurp the Bolsheviks and
remove German influence in Russia. Lockhart did not hold back:

---

6   Dobson and Miller, *The Day We Almost Bombed Moscow*, p.130.
7   Silverlight, *The Victors' Dilemma*, p.59.

34. View of Archangel looking East. (IWM Q 16254)

We had committed the unbelievable folly of landing at Archangel with fewer than 1,200 men. It was a blunder comparable with the worst mistakes of the Crimean War. Indirectly, it was responsible for the Terror. Its direct effect was to provide the Bolsheviks with a cheap victory, to give them a new confidence and to galvanise them into a strong and ruthless organism.[8]

The landing at Archangel actually almost led to an alliance between Germany and the Bolsheviks. On 28 July, German Ambassador Karl Helfferich arrived in Moscow to replace Count Wilhelm Mirbach, assassinated earlier in the month in an apparent Franco–British plot. Helfferich wasted no time in applying pressure on the Bolsheviks to eject the Allies from Russia.

The Archangel landings caused such a stir amongst the Bolshevik leadership that it was rumoured that they would open a corridor through Russia to allow German troops to advance to Murmansk and Archangel to eject the Allies. There remained a real fear that a combined German–White Finnish force with the acquiescence of Moscow would advance on Murmansk and Archangel from Finland. It was not until the great Allied offensives on the Western Front of late 1918 ended any hope of Germany winning the war that fears of German troops ejecting the Allies from North Russia also ceased.

In the months following the Archangel landings, a rumour reached General Maynard at Murmansk, 'to the effect that there was jealousy, and even friction between Archangel and Murmansk, with the resultant evil of unharmonious working. For this whispered calumny there was no foundation whatsoever'. Despite the fact that Poole on more than one occasion 'poached' troops from Murmansk Command, Maynard considered him, 'a Chief under whom I served most gladly, and between whom and myself there was always a close understanding.'[9] Not everyone got on so well with Poole.

Poole's command was six times the size of England with less than 1,500 men to defend it. Poole acted quickly by sending sailors and marines from USS *Olympia* down the railway on the heels of the fleeing Bolsheviks, the French 21st Colonial Battalion in support of the Americans and a day after

8   R.H. Bruce Lockhart, *Memoirs of a British Agent; being an account of the author's early life in many lands and of his official mission to Moscow in 1918* (London: Putnam, 1932), p.211.
9   Maynard, *The Murmansk Venture*, p.56.

their arrival at Archangel on 25 August on board SS *City of Cairo*, 'A', 'B' and 'C' Companies, 2/10th Battalion, Royal Scots ('D' Company for the time being remained at Archangel) under battalion second in command Major W.C. Whittaker, up the Dvina River in barges escorted by river steamers rudimentarily converted to gunboats.

This left Poole with only a few hundred men with which to guard Archangel and monitor a population of uncertain loyalty, he had little faith in the leadership of Governor Tchaikovsky to do the same. Archangel and the surrounding district was placed under martial law with French Colonel Donop appointed as Military Governor. If something needed to be done, Poole would order Allied troops to carry out the task and would subsequently send a note to Tchaikovsky informing of the action taken, if he bothered at all. In a letter to Tchaikovsky, Poole wrote, 'I have the honour to inform you that the city of Archangel as well as the whole province are at present under martial law. I have given orders to the military not to permit any display of red flags in Archangel.'[10] A British Foreign Office diplomat wrote in retrospect, 'General Poole treated Archangel and the surrounding territories as a conquered territory.'[11]

A number of Allied diplomats who had fled Petrograd to Murmansk in July 1918 arrived at Archangel a week after the landing by the Allies. As civilians, they did not approve of the heavy-handed manner in which Poole was running the district. In a letter to Poole the British *Chargé d'Affairs*, diplomat Francis Lindley, wrote of the importance that an effective local Russian government should be seen to be in control of Archangel:

> Unless our adventure here is to begin and end with the occupation of a small district, it is absolutely necessary that a Russian authority should exist which the population can regard as their own government, and capable of being expanded or absorbed into the government of the whole country. In order to assure this, the existing government must appear to have real authority.[12]

On 17 August, a seaplane flown by Lieutenant Thomson with Lieutenant William Umpleby as observer took off from HMS *Nairana* on a reconnaissance over enemy territory. The aircraft was forced down over Olimpi into the River Vuig due to a severed fuel line. The seaplane could not be salvaged owing to its location behind enemy lines and had to be abandoned by the two airmen, who having escaped the wreck swam ashore and made their way back to Archangel on foot, arriving the following day. Two days later a flight of *Nairana*'s seaplanes destroyed the wrecked aircraft by incendiary machine gun fire from the air, preventing its salvage by the enemy.

Relations between the White Russians and Poole had deteriorated considerably by September 1918. The Allies remained in charge at Archangel and apart from issuing self-praising proclamations there was little for Tchaikovsky's government to do. In one incident, Tchaikovsky ordered that a local anti-socialist newspaper be put out of production. Poole demanded that production should be immediately resumed. Public gatherings were banned. Supplies began to run short when promised food ships from England did not arrive. To the average citizen of Archangel it appeared that it was the Allies who were firmly in charge and not Tchaikovsky's government, and that little had changed in the transition of rule from the Bolsheviks to the Allies.

The handful of units under Poole's command were by late August a considerable distance from Archangel and fighting in the difficult conditions of the Dvina River in summer. The manpower shortage was eased with the arrival of US 339th Infantry Regiment along with US Army engineers and a field hospital on 4 September. Influenza had broken out on the troopships en route to Archangel and several hundred men were stricken with the illness. Medical facilities at Archangel

---

10   Silverlight, *The Victors' Dilemma*, p.74.
11   *Ibid.*
12   *Ibid.*

were rudimentary and much of the intended medical supplies had accidentally been left in the UK before the ships sailed. As there were no facilities ashore that could handle such a large influx of patients, the sick men had to stay on board the troopships. Almost as soon as the US troops stepped ashore they were embarked for the front, one battalion going up the Dvina to the River Front and another by train to the Railway Front.

Tchaikovsky's leadership had proven to be a hindrance to Poole and it was no surprise that when rumour of a plot to remove the elderly Russian and his government from power started to circulate. The British General publicly disapproved of such an action however no guard was placed on Tchaikovsky's residence nor were patrols in the city increased. On the night of 4–5 September, in a plot which seems implausible to have not been ordered by Poole, Russian–British agent Grigory Chaplin with a group of former Imperial Army officers kidnapped Tchaikovsky and exiled him and his cabinet to Solovetski Island in the White Sea. In a proclamation addressed 'To the citizens of Archangel! To the citizens of the Northern Region!' Grigory Chaplin declared that Tchaikovsky's administration had 'proved to be incapable of handling the task it had assumed' and that 'we must build the welfare of our country with our own Russian hands … let us put aside party strife … Long live a free, great and undivided Russia.'[13]

Russian workers resented that the Allies had allowed Tchaikovsky, a Russian leader sympathetic to the plight of the worker, to be illegally removed from office, and promptly went on a general strike. Armed peasants began to arrive in Archangel from regional areas to demand that Tchaikovsky be reinstated. A British warship was sent to retrieve Tchaikovsky and his ministers from their exile in the White Sea and Poole, although unrepentant, went into damage control. It was US President Wilson who finally forced the issue. On 9 September, through Secretary of State Lansing, President Wilson informed the British government that if Tchaikovsky was not reinstated all US forces would be withdrawn from Archangel. Poole had little choice but to comply with Wilson's ultimatum.

To calm the waters Tchaikovsky offered to remove some of the more socialist-leaning ministers in his cabinet and to introduce more moderate policies; the new cabinet was renamed, 'Northern Provisional Government'. In response, Poole agreed to relieve the French Military Governor, Colonel Donop, of his position and to allow a Russian Governor General to be appointed. Poole was recalled for 'consultations' with the War Office on 14 October and never returned to North Russia but was sent instead to South Russia to act as head of the British Military Mission to General Denikin's Volunteer Army.

Poole was replaced as commander of 'ELOPE' Force by his Chief of Staff, Major General William Edmund Ironside who had only arrived at Archangel a week earlier. Ironside had served as an artillery officer in the Boer War and with the BEF in France in 1914. By September 1918 he had served in the 4th Canadian Division (where he met his faithful Russian-born servant 'Piskoff' whom he took with him to North Russia) and commanded a British infantry brigade. There are many myths surrounding Ironside's service as a young officer in South Africa. Among the more interesting are that as a result of his natural flair for languages he had accompanied a German punitive expedition against a native tribe in German South-West Africa for which the German Government reputedly awarded Ironside a campaign medal.

Nicknamed 'Tin-ribs' and 'Tiny' due to his enormous stature, Ironside was physically a strong man who can be seen in contemporary photographs towering over his fellow officers. One White Russian officer described the General:

He is six feet four inches tall without shoes, weighs 270 pounds, and is only thirty-seven years old. He is descended from the last Saxon king of England, was dismissed from St. Andrew's School when

---

13   *Ibid.*, p.76.

35. General William Edmund Ironside, towering over his naval contemporaries at Archangel. Nicknamed 'Tiny' due to his six foot four inch frame, Ironside was a noted master of languages and veteran of the Boer War and the Western Front when he was appointed to command 'ELOPE' Force. (Public domain)

he was 10 ½ years old because he whipped the teacher. He was the first British officer to land in France; in fact he landed on the night of August 2, before England had entered the war on August 6 [sic]. He was in command of a division on the French front, when he was ordered to Russia. He relinquished his command and cleared in an aeroplane for England. After a flight of three and one-half hours he landed somewhere in England, spent three days acquainting himself with Russian conditions and left for Archangel; he does everything that way.[14]

In the final weeks of September conditions in Archangel became exceedingly bad. There was a drastic shortage of food, which inversely supported an explosion of prices on the thriving black market. The YMCA (both Canadian and US YMCA operated at Archangel) stopped selling chocolate when they discovered that it was being resold at a considerable premium to locals.

Despite Tchaikovsky's promises of 'one hundred thousand' volunteers, recruitment into the fledgling Northern White Russian Army had been so poor that conscription had to be introduced. When recruitment had been opened at Archangel on 5 August, quite apart from the rush of volunteers which had been expected, only a single man came forward:

The staff were very busy unpacking uniforms etc., for the expected arrival of the advanced guard, it is supposed, of the hundred thousand loyalists promised by Tchaikovsky, panting to avenge their country's wrongs … the net result of the day's work was a solitary recruit … he was a young English-speaking Russian sailor who enlisted, so he said, as he had nothing else to do.[15]

In late 1918 the War Office was unable or unwilling to send to Ironside the reinforcements that he so desperately needed and just weeks after the arrival of the US contingent at Archangel, President Wilson had announced that no further US troops would be sent to North Russia. When it became apparent that an effective White Russian Army could not be raised in North Russia the US Government declared that 'all military effort in northern Russia be given up except the guarding of the ports themselves and as much of the country round them as may develop threatening conditions.'[16]

14   Leonid Ivan Strakhovsky, *Intervention at Archangel; the story of allied intervention and Russian counter-revolution in North Russia, 1918–1920* (Princeton: Princeton University Press, 1944), p.91.
15   Imperial War Museum (IWM), 9906/P76: Private Papers of A.G. Burn.
16   Dobson and Miller, *The Day We Almost Bombed Moscow*, p.136.

On 11 November 1918 the Armistice was signed, ending hostilities between the Allies and Central Powers and thus the need to reopen the Eastern Front, the primary objective of Allied military intervention in Russia. Whilst many of the Allied sailors, soldiers and airmen in North Russia would have reasonably believed they would soon be recalled and sent home for demobilisation, the White Sea had already frozen over, cutting off Archangel from Murmansk. It would not be possible to evacuate Archangel until the White Sea sufficiently thawed to allow the passage of shipping in May 1919.

The White Russian forces raised by the British in North Russia 1918–19 will be less remembered for any actual fighting prowess but rather for the endemic mutiny and desertion which plagued the Northern Rifle Regiments from their inception until the final British evacuation. On 29 August 1918, only four weeks into recruitment, some recent enlistees of the Slavo-British Legion fired on their British officers and deserted. Two months later on 29 October, Russian conscripts at the Alexander Nevski Barracks refused to go on parade. The reasons they gave were 1. Their Russian officers were still wearing Tsarist badges of rank; 2. They would not fight for the English King; 3. They would not salute; 4. They wanted larger rations.

The situation escalated on 11 December when 1st Archangel Regiment refused to turn out for parade. Upon hearing the news, General Ironside immediately made his way from GHQ to the Archangel prison which had been converted into a barracks, taking with him a company of 2/7th Battalion, Durham Light Infantry, force troops held in reserve at Archangel. On arrival at the barracks, Ironside found a Russian general crouching behind a building. He later recalled:

Numbers of red flags were being waved from every window, and we could see the heads of the men craning out to see what happened. A few shots were being fired from the roof, apparently haphazard into the air. The general was quite calm and collected. He ordered up a Lewis gun, manned by Russian N.C.O.s doing a course at the machine gun school. By loud-speaker he ordered the company to come out and fall in. The only result was renewed shouting and more waving of flags. Two Stokes mortars were then brought up, manned by Russian officers who were doing a course. They came into action, steadily and well, and the first round went over the barracks, bursting in the stone quadrangle behind with a tremendous noise. The second burst right on the roof of the building, and before a third could be fired the main door was burst open and the men came out with their hands in the air. As if by magic, all the flags came fluttering down from the windows and all shouting ceased. The men fell in on the parade ground, most of them half-dressed and looking very frightened. It was difficult not to smile at the whole affair, though I felt very much relieved. The ringleaders were tried by court martial, found guilty of mutiny and sentenced to death. I was able to commute their sentences to terms of imprisonment.[17]

The event many have been cause for Ironside to 'smile' but he omits to state his own role in the eventual fate of the mutineers. Ironside recounted that the mutineers were sentenced to death commuted to life imprisonment, but CSM Fred Neesam, DCM, of 2/7th Durham Light Infantry, an eyewitness to the events which followed, recalled a different story:

The man on the mortar was an Irishman. The General [Ironside] said to him: 'Paddy, put one over the barracks into the parade square on the other side.' So Paddy dropped a bomb into the square, and as soon as it went off the Russians in the barracks started to cheer and wave; they thought he couldn't hit them. Then the General said: 'Paddy, put one into the middle of 'em.' So he did, and the next thing that happened was that a score of rifles appeared at the windows, with white flags tied to them.

The mutineers were ordered to throw out their rifles. Then they were paraded outside the barracks, and Ironside asked them who the ringleaders were. They wouldn't talk, so he ordered every tenth man to

36. Cathedral of the Archangel Michael with its huge external frescos visible. The cathedral was destroyed by the Soviets after Archangel was captured in 1920; in 2008 construction of a replica building was commenced on the site of the old Cathedral, due to be completed in 2017. (Author's collection)

step forward and told them they would be shot if they didn't hand over the guilty ones. They talked, and thirteen men were rounded up. They were court-martialled and sentenced to death. Their own men shot them; they made them dig their own graves and then shot them in the back of the neck.[18]

Ironside should have known better than to state in his book *Archangel 1918–19* that the sentences were commuted to life imprisonment, as it was he who had signed the death warrants. There had also been no Russian general on the scene, Ironside had been writing about himself in the third person. Another witness recorded: 'The firing party of so-called volunteers was furnished by the company implicated, and behind the party, machine-guns were placed as a hint that the firing was to be effective … The whole of the proceedings were summary, there being no court-martial as is customary in our service.'[19]

The following day, White Russian General Maroushevsky issued a proclamation:

Yesterday, December 11, there occurred in the Archangel Regiment some trifling misunderstandings which were terminated immediately. In informing the people of the city of Archangel about this occurrence, I appeal to everyone to remain calm. I hereby issue a warning that also in the future I shall not tolerate any incidents which might disturb the population.[20]

Whilst Ironside was dealing with disruptions at Archangel, the Red Army had launched its winter 1918–1919 offensive, culminating in the capture of the strategically important Canadian–British held town of Shenkursk on the Vaga River on 25 January 1919. The Red Army had demonstrated

---

18   Jackson, *At War With the Bolsheviks*, pp.93–94.
19   IWM: 9906/P76, Private Papers of A.G. Burn.
20   Strakhovsky, *Intervention at Archangel*, p.122.

no lack of offensive spirit, launching an offensive in severe sub-Arctic conditions. Whilst the Allies remained static in their defensive winter blockhouses waiting for the spring and return of the river gunboats (which had been withdrawn to Archangel once the Dvina and Vaga Rivers began to freeze in mid October 1918) before resuming the advance, the Bolsheviks made no such considerations and the offensive was a tremendous success.

The Bolshevik victory at Shenkursk demonstrated the weakness of the Provisional Government and Allied forces in North Russia to hold ground, even with a defensive advantage. With the Bolsheviks in possession of Shenkursk, the Allies positions on the Railway and River Fronts were in danger of being outflanked. Ironside desperately needed reinforcements to have any hope of holding the line once the thaw came. He urgently requested reinforcements from the War Office but hard-pressed as the British Army was on the Western Front, no troops were available. Instead two infantry battalions (6th and 13th Battalions, Yorkshire Regiment) and 252nd Company, MGC, which had arrived at Murmansk on 26 November, were transferred from Murmansk to Archangel, much to Maynard's displeasure: he still had not been returned the forces lent for the invasion and occupation of Archangel in August 1918. Of the 5,000 British soldiers originally despatched to Murmansk, only a small number remained. Maynard knew that there was nothing to be gained by dwelling on the issue and so in his quiet professional manner, set about changing plans for his upcoming spring 1919 offensive to take into account the reduced strength.

Transferring the troops from Murmansk to Archangel would be an epic in itself. During winter the White Sea is completely frozen and roads buried by snow. All food for pack animals had to be carried with each small convoy as there would be none to be found en route. An icebreaker would carry 300 men and half 252nd MGC directly from Murmansk to Archangel whilst the remainder of the contingent, some 2,000 men, would travel by horse-drawn sledge and on foot from Soroka to Onega.

Upon arrival at Archangel, 6th Yorkshires were sent straight to the defensive front line at Seletskoe but once there, a serious refusal occurred within their ranks. Private Riley Rudd, RAMC, witnessed the chain of events:

Great doings at Seletskoe. 1000 troops there now, battalion Yorks, 2 Platoons Liverpools and 2 sections M.G.C. All these have gone on strike. Held meetings in I.M. last night and passed resolutions that they must be withdrawn from Russia immediately. Others to the effect that Censorship be removed from letters in order that the people in England may get to know the true state of affairs out here and that a cable be sent to L. George demanding immediate withdrawal of all troops in Russia. They all positively decline to go up the line or to obey any orders but are conducting themselves in an orderly manner. The general has been sent for.[21]

Ironside was furious and recalled:

I had never in my life experienced a mutiny amongst British troops, and I hated to think that the first signs of indiscipline should have come from them, of all the Allied contingents...He [the CO] had only been with the battalion for a few days, and was astounded when the adjutant reported that the men had refused to fall in. He went straight down to the men's billets, and ordered the battalion to fall in without arms. When this was done two Sergeants immediately stepped forward and told him that the battalion would not do any fighting. Without a moments hesitation, Lavie walked to the right of the line and ordered a lance-corporal to take a file of men and fetch their rifles...He then ordered the two sergeants

---

21   IWM: 4615/81/21/1, Diary of R. Rudd.

into close arrest and told the lance-corporal to take them to the guard room. The only other British personnel he had were half a dozen men of the R.A.S.C.

I interviewed the two sergeants in the guard room, where I found them very nervous and crestfallen. I told them of the gravity of the crime they had committed and that they would be brought before a court martial as soon as one could be assembled. They were two men who had done no fighting, having served all the war in the Royal Army Pay Corps in England. After the March 1918 retreat, when men were needed for infantry units, they were transferred to the Yorkshire Regiment and were eventually sent to Murmansk … They were duly tried by court martial, formed of officers sent up from the base, found guilty of mutiny and sentenced to be shot. In accordance with my secret orders from His Majesty that no death sentences were to be carried out after the Armistice I commuted their sentences to life imprisonment.[22]

Attempts by British headquarters to suppress rumblings of rebellion were not aided by some of the articles on Russia being published in newspapers back in England. One article published in *The Daily Express* on 3 January 1919 summed up the average Briton's feeling on military intervention in Russia:

We are sorry for the Russians, but they must fight it out among themselves. Great Britain is already the policeman of half the world. It will not and cannot be the policeman of all Europe. We want to return to industry and to restore the ravages of war. We want to see our sons home again. In fact, we want peace. The frozen plains of Eastern Europe are not worth the bones of a single British grenadier.[23]

The low fighting morale was not limited to British troops. US soldiers had been suffering from similar disaffections. On 4 March 1919, the same day the British Cabinet made the decision to withdraw from North Russia before the winter, Sergeant Silver Parrish of the US 339th Infantry Regiment wrote a letter to his superiors requesting an explanation, 'why we are fighting the Bolos and why we haven't any big guns and why the English run us and why we haven't enough to eat and why our men can't get proper medical attention and some mail.'[24] Parrish was brought up before his CO and informed that what he had done was punishable by death. None the less, two weeks later Parrish was awarded the British Military Medal for bravery by General Ironside.

Parrish, like many Allied soldiers in North Russia, was sympathetic to the hardships of the local peasantry:

The way these kids and women dress would make you laugh if you saw it on the stage. But to see it here only prompts sympathy (in the heart of a real man) and loathing for a clique of blood-sucking, power-loving, capitalistic, lying, thieving, murdering, tsarist army officials who keep their people in this ignorance and poverty … after being up here fighting these people I will be ashamed to look a union man in the face … The majority of the people here are in sympathy with the Bolo and I don't blame them, in fact I am 9/10 Bolo myself and they all call me the Bolo Leader and my platoon the Bolo platoon.[25]

A particular bugbear of the US troops was the status of British 'temporary' officer ranks. In the British Army, an officer could be temporarily promoted to a higher rank in order to perform the duties of that rank whilst remaining substantively a junior officer. In most cases this meant a lieutenant could serve as a captain and a captain as a major as needs required. If there was a change in manpower requirements the temporary rank would be relinquished and the officer would revert

22   Ironside, *Archangel 1918–19*, pp.112–113.
23   Dobson and Miller, *The Day We Almost Bombed Moscow*, p.181.
24   Bentley Historical Library, The University of Michigan, Silver Parrish diary.
25   *Ibid.*

37. Typical street scene on Troitsky Prospekt, Archangel. The British flag flies over the Headquarters building of the North Russia Expeditionary Force. (Public domain)

to the duties of their substantive rank. There was no such system in place in the US Army and some American troops saw the temporary rank system as a calculated means to ensure that British officers would at all times be senior to their American counterparts.

In early March 1919, the French 21st Colonial Battalion, on leave in Archangel, refused to return to the Archangel–Vologda Railway Front stating that they would take no further part in any further offensive action other than the defence of Archangel. Two hundred French ski troops at Murmansk also refused, although it is unlikely that the two incidents were coordinated. Being of no further use, both units were soon after sent home. On 29 March, 'I' Company, US 339th Infantry Regiment briefly refused to return to the line over a number of grievances but eventually fell in.

In a letter dated 13 April 1919, Lieutenant Colonel Sharman, CO, 16th Brigade, Canadian Field Artillery (CFA), reported that an unnamed section of Canadian artillerymen had refused to obey orders for a period of 24 hours in protest over non-payment of 'Arctic Pay' whilst British troops were entitled. On 6 February, Ottawa had declined to pay its troops in North Russia the Arctic Pay allowance of one shilling per day for NCOs and six pence for privates. Ironside advocated that Canadian troops be allowed the special pay and on 27 May made a submission to the Canadian government which was accepted and payment of the allowance approved by the Canadian government shortly before the Canadian gunners' departure.

In early March 1919, Lieutenant Cecil Dickson, Cheshire Regiment, CSM Fred Neesam, DCM and Sergeant J. Colman, both of 2/7th Battalion, Durham Light Infantry, were detached from their battalion for service with a special 'Allied Military Mission' being formed to travel overland from Archangel and connect with Admiral Kolchak's forces in Siberia.

Departing Archangel on 8 March, the Mission consisted of small detachments from a number of the Allied contingents in Archangel as well as a party from the Provisional Government and a number of Russian soldiers. Travelling overland through forest, swamp and mountain, the Mission arrived in Omsk on 21 May and having delivered despatches and performed their diplomatic duties, made the arduous trek back to Archangel where they arrived on 22 June, covering more than 3,000 miles in the return journey. For his command of the British contingent of the Mission during the remarkable journey, Dickson was awarded the MC and Imperial Russian Order of St. Vladimir and Neesam and Colman the MM and Imperial Russian Medal of St. George.

In June, all four companies of 17th Liverpools returned to Archangel ('A' Company had remained at Solombola as Force Troops whilst 'B' and 'D' Companies had served on the Railway Front and 'C' Company on the Dvina) to prepare to embark for home after a difficult period of service fighting through the Arctic winter. The battalion spent the remainder of their days in Russia working on fatigue parties around the city with daily bathing parades held to provide some respite from the heat. During one such parade on 28 June, Private Bernard Murray drowned, the last battalion fatality in North Russia.

The same month, 2/10th Royal Scots, the stalwarts of the North Russian theatre, embarked for home. The Scots had been the first British unit to arrive at Archangel in August 1918 and had taken part in the fierce early battles of October and November 1918, most notably in the defence of Tulgas on 11 November 1918. The Scots suffered more casualties than any other British or Commonwealth unit which served in Russia 1918–20, most suffered during a four week period October–November 1918.

On 17 June 1919, a fire broke out on a Russian motor launch transporting ammunition in Archangel Harbour. A Russian tug and picket boat from USS *Olympia* set out to render assistance but were driven back by an explosion on board the motor launch. As the tug came alongside, Samuel Haines, a Junior Officer in the Mercantile Marine Reserve, went on board the burning vessel. Realising that he would be unable to extinguish the fire, Haines waved the other vessels away, went below and began bringing out boxes of ammunition as well as rifles and fuel. Calling the picket boat from *Olympia* alongside, Haines passed the rifles, ammunition and fuel to the US sailors. The fire was eventually got under control as more boats came alongside but the motor launch was gutted. For his gallantry in going aboard the burning vessel despite the danger of an explosion, Haines was awarded the Albert Medal. He later volunteered for the Auxiliary Division of the Royal Irish Constabulary and served with them in Ireland during 1920–21. In 1929 he rescued two boys aged 18 and 14 from a burning cinema at Welling, Kent, sadly both boys died from their injuries. His own son Sergeant Hugh Haines was killed in action in Burma in 1945 aged 31.

On 26 August, 2nd Battalion, Highland Light Infantry (HLI) arrived at Archangel where 'A', 'B' and 'C' Companies marched into barracks at Smolny whilst 'B' Company took up garrison duties at Bakharitsa. The battalion had been sent to act as General Rawlinson's Force Troops to keep order and take part in the defence of the city in the event of an uprising or collapse of the White Russian Provisional Government.

The battalion's first duty the day after their arrival was to provide a funeral party under the command of Captain F.K. Simmons, MVO, MC, for the burial of Lord Settrington, Irish Guards attached 45th Royal Fusiliers, the badly wounded officer plucked from a swamp under fire by Corporal Arthur Sullivan on 10 August for which Sullivan would subsequently be awarded the VC.

On 2nd September a huge fire broke out at the timber yard at Solombola (also known as 'Maimaxi') which quickly spread owing to a strong wind. The fire swept further inland and caused a great amount of damage, burning everything along a mile long stretch of the docks and timber yard leaving little standing in its wake. Such was the intensity of the fire that the flames jumped 1,000 yards to the opposite bank of the Dvina, the British-owned timber and sawmills on both sides of the river for three miles were engulfed and razed to the ground.

By the time the fire burnt out two days later the total damage was estimated at £600,000. There was no evidence that the fire was deliberately lit although it seems likely based on probability that sabotage was the cause. Luckily no lives were lost in the conflagration.

On 10 September, Private James Quigley was shot in the leg whilst guarding stores at Bakharitsa. It was believed that the shot had been fired form within the compound and suspicions were that a White Russian soldier was responsible. Two days later 'D' Company was transported across the

38. General Sir Henry Rawlinson, Commander-in-Chief, NREF, August–October 1919. (NPG 44090)

White Sea to Kandalaksha on the Murman Peninsula to take part in an operation to clear a force of Red Finns from their hideout within British controlled territory. The Finns were deserters from the British-sponsored Finnish Legion who had refused to sign an agreement to faithfully serve the Allies until their repatriation to Finland could be arranged, opting instead to desert and go into hiding.

On 22 September, a mixed platoon from 'D' Company under Major L. Gartside, DSO, and 2nd Lieutenant C.D.C. Leslie with three intelligence officers attached, set out in four local fishing boats on a river that led to the enemy hideout. The Finns knew the British were coming and the following day the Scotsmen were ambushed whilst still in their boats with the loss of 12 men killed and four wounded. One of those wounded, Private Abraham Gotts aged 19 from Ormesby, Yorkshire, died of his wounds four days later and was buried in Murmansk New British Cemetery, making him the last British servicemen to die as a result of enemy action in North Russia. The HLI spent the remainder of their time in Archangel performing garrison duties until finally being evacuated to Murmansk 27 September and thence to England with the remainder of the NREF in the first week of October.

In October, after news that all British forces had withdrawn from North Russia and having heard nothing from her son, the mother of 18-year-old Private Percy Brentnall wrote to HLI regimental headquarters seeking information on his whereabouts. Brentnall had served under the alias 'Jack Ferguson' and had not listed any next of kin on his enlistment. It would have come as a sad shock to his mother in Nottingham when a letter arrived in response to her enquiry stating that her son was reported 'Missing Believed Killed 23.9.19'.

The following month, Lieutenant Leslie composed a condolence letter to Percy's mother:

> I fear that there is very little to tell but I will tell you as much as I can because I knew and liked your boy well and I am deeply grieved at his loss and can sympathise with you. We left on a raiding party and were surprised by the enemy before we got to our destination; after the show the boat your boy was in was missing, but we found it afterwards four inches deep in blood and water and riddled with bullets, but what happened to its occupants is impossible to say.[26]

A single decoration was awarded for bravery during the ambush, a Military Medal to Corporal Thomas Mitchell from Dumfries. It was also the only decoration for gallantry in the field awarded to 2nd HLI in North Russia. Mitchell was a regular soldier who had been taken prisoner in 1914 and released in 1918 in time to rejoin the colours and embark with the battalion for Archangel.

---

26   IWM: 997/88/7/1, Private Papers of P. Brentnall.

On 9 August 1919, Sir Henry Rawlinson arrived at Archangel to take up the role of Commander-in-Chief, NREF. Rawlinson described the command as 'a nasty job' but decided to accept the appointment out of a sense of duty. It was probably not necessary for Rawlinson to come out to Russia to oversee the evacuation as both Ironside and Maynard had the situation well in hand, and both probably would have preferred an extra battalion of troops for their final offensives rather than a new Commander-in-Chief.

As the date of the final evacuation quickly approached, the feeling among the local population and White Russian forces became increasingly anti-British. With some justification they felt betrayed and abandoned. Ironside described one 'unhappy incident' which occurred shortly before the evacuation:

A distinguished Russian colonel who had fought well under the Allies and who was well known to me personally asked permission to see me. He had been awarded a British D.S.O., of which he was very proud. He entered my office and saluted me. He then threw his D.S.O. on the table between us. For two minutes he told me what he thought of the Allies and their behaviour. He then saluted again and marched out of the room. I sat in silence looking at the discarded Order which he had so gallantly won.[27]

One proclamation issued by a local official of the Provisional Government pleaded with the British to stay:

Do for your faithful Ally Russia, who has shed so much blood in your cause, what you have done for your enemy Hungary, who caused you to pour out your blood. In the name of a tortured Russia we ask help from the Allies, not as a beggar asking alms at the Church door, but as a duty the Allies owe her…Have we not in fact in the war saved Paris, saved Italy, saved all the Allies? We have lost hundreds of thousands of our best sons to save you … It is not only necessary that you do not turn Russia into an enemy, but also that you keep her as a friend.[28]

Ironside's own sympathy for the White Russian leadership was by the time of the evacuation virtually exhausted: 'I found it difficult to have any sympathy with men who had done so little to help themselves. They had realized too late what was about to happen to them.'[29]

On 9 September, Rawlinson's GHQ, NREF, was closed down and on 23 September, all British troops withdrawn to Archangel city. On 17 September, the water level of the Dvina fell to a level which made it impossible for some of the vessels to get past the sandbanks downriver to Archangel which necessitated the urgent scuttling of two of the flotilla monitors which had seen sterling service. Both *M.25* and *M.27* met this fate as Captain Altham, RN, later recalled, 'It was sad to see these poor stout little craft, which had done such good work, being blown to atoms by skilfully-placed gun-cotton charges. At least it saved them from the ignominy of the shipbreakers' hammer.'[30]

On 19 September, White Russian General Miller desperately cabled London requesting that any British officers and men who wished to volunteer to stay on in North Russia after the evacuation might be allowed to do so:

The North Russian Government proposes to engage a certain number of Britishers who have been demobilised from the British Army to serve in North Russia with the Russian Armies. It is proposed to form a brigade (with machine gunners) and artillery. No contract can be entered into with officers or

27   Ironside, *Archangel 1918–19*, pp.176–177.
28   *Ibid.*
29   *Ibid.*
30   *Ibid.*

other ranks now serving in the British Army, but any who are prepared to engage themselves with the North Russian Government can give their names and obtain all particulars here in Archangel.

The conditions of service were equal to that which they would have received under service of the Crown:

> Rations, clothing, equipment, arms – same as in the English army – provided by us. Pensions for invalidity and to families – same as in the Russian Army – Salaries – same as received by the English in the North Russian Expeditionary Corps ... To married soldiers, an additional 200 roubles a month. Travel to and fro provided by us.[31]

There may have been at least a few British soldiers who would have stayed behind to the end given the opportunity to do so but after so many mutinies and betrayals by the local Russian troops and their general lack of any aptitude for fighting, likely few British soldiers would have volunteered. In any case they would have to return to the UK to be discharged before being able to return to North Russia to take up the offer. Small contingents of volunteer Danes, Swedes and Finns who took up the Provisional Government's offer did make it to Archangel but they were too few too late to have any real influence on events.

On 21 February 1920, units of the Soviet 154th Regiment entered Archangel and were met by the population with traditional Slavic greeting of bread and salt. As the Red Army troops were entering the town, General Miller and the last of his White Russian officers were escaping on an icebreaker through the ice bound White Sea. They stepped ashore in Norway and from there were scattered to the winds, many, including Miller, fled to France and the large White Russian exile community there.

An epitaph to Allied military intervention in the Russian Civil War might best be left to an American YMCA worker who wrote:

> No mention was made of this expedition in the Armistice of November. Hence it had in some subtle way ceased to be part of our war against Germany. It had become a new war, a war against Bolshevik Russia, an unlegalized war, and this it continued to be as long as the expedition lasted. Yet no declaration was forthcoming, either of war or peace. Particularly wanting was a declaration of purpose. Weary months of stubborn fighting for our men were unrelieved by any single word of definition of the fight from their government. There consequently was antagonism to the campaign on the part of the soldiers. I do not say loss of morale, because the term would be misunderstood. Our men fought. But they hated the fight, they resented fighting without a cause.[32]

---

31   Strakhovsky, *Intervention at Archangel*, p.233.
32   Albertson, *Fighting Without a War*, p.6.

7

Archangel: Dvina River Front September–December 1918

For all his difficulties at Archangel in August 1918, Poole's major problem was that he simply did not have enough troops to advance up the Dvina. No sooner had 2/10th Battalion, Royal Scots disembarked at Archangel on 26th August and marched down the dock accompanied by the US Marine band from USS *Olympia*, 'A', 'B' and 'C' Companies were embarked onto shallow-draught barges and shipped up the Dvina. 'D' Company remained at Archangel for the time being but on 4 September despatched a platoon for service with the RANB on the Onega Front. The Scots had been serving in Ireland before mobilisation for North Russia and had accepted drafts of a number of men on attachment from other battalions stationed in Ireland to bring the battalion up to strength for active service.

Commanding Officer:	Lieutenant Colonel H. Sutherland, DSO, Royal Highlanders
	Major A. Skeil, MC, Royal Scots Fusiliers (after Oct. 1918)
Second in Command:	Major G. Gilmore, DSO, MC, Royal Sussex Regiment
'A' Company:	Captain L. Shute, Royal Scots Fusiliers
'B' Company:	Captain J. Edwards, MC and Bar
'C' Company:	Captain J. Penman
'D' Company:	Captain A. Bright

A company of French 21st Colonial Battalion was also promptly loaded onto trains and sent south-west to the Archangel–Vologda Railway Front. The local Red Army commander on the Archangel front, bolstered by the arrival of a unit of Red Guards, factory hands from Petrograd, set up a series of blocking parties in the villages and sidings along the river and railway as the British and French troops advanced. The barges carrying the Royal Scots were in constant danger of beaching on the numerous sand bars or worse, to hit one of the mines floated up the river by the Bolsheviks. The barges were occasionally sniped at from the riverbank whilst the railway boxcars were fired on from the forest.

The Scots took the town of Bereznik near the junction of the Dvina and Vaga rivers on 3 September which Poole planned to use as his base for the winter. On the Railway Front, the Allied troops got as far as Obozerskaya before halting to construct a winter line of defensive blockhouses. Only one week after the arrival of the Royal Scots, the Allies were positioned 125 miles from Archangel up the Dvina River and 75 miles down the Archangel–Vologda Railway, not bad for one week's work.

On 4 September 1918, the American contingent arrived at Archangel, almost 4,500 men of US 339th Infantry Regiment, 310th Engineers, 337th Field Hospital and the 337th Ambulance Company. Given command of the American North Russian Expeditionary Force (ANREF) in North Russia, was New South Wales-born Colonel George E. Stewart, a Medal of Honour recipient for the campaign in the Philippines at the turn of the century during the Spanish–American War. No sooner had the US troops arrived at Archangel, than half the regiment was sent down the line to Obozerskaya on the Railway Front to reinforce the French troops there whilst the other half sailed down the Dvina to Bereznik to reinforce the Royal Scots and Poles holding the line.

By sending US troops to the front, General Poole had contravened US President Wilson's instruction to the British government that US troops were to be used only for guarding stores and to

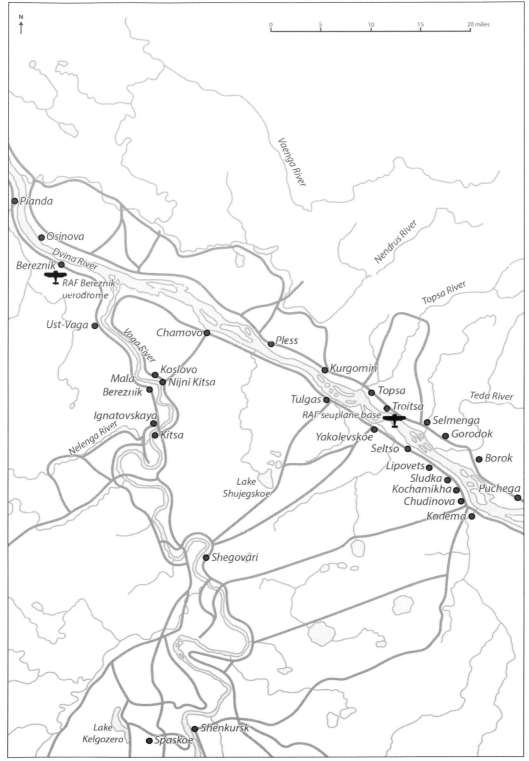

Map 3. Dvina-Vaga operations, August 1918–September 1919

give, 'such aid as may be acceptable to the Russians in the organization of their self-defence.' Wilson had left no doubt that the US soldiers were not to, 'take part in organised intervention … from either Vladivostok or Murmansk and Archangel.'[1]

The reason why Poole had disobeyed the instructions of the President of one of Britain's closest Allies was simple. Including the Marines and sailors of USS *Olympia*, Poole had 4,800 US troops under his command, twice as many as he did British soldiers. Of the 2,420 British troops at Archangel, a significant number were base and support troops and members of the 'ELOPE' Training Mission. Also, many of the British troops were of a physical category so low that they were officially classified as unfit for active service; conversely the US soldiers were fit, healthy, and keen, albeit inexperienced. Poole could not afford to keep 4,500 trained men in Archangel guarding stores whilst he had only 1,000 men facing the Red Army on each of the two fronts.

Amongst the small Allied contingents in North Russia were the 900 men of French 21st Colonial Battalion recruited almost exclusively from French colonies in North Africa and unsuited for service in the sub-zero temperatures of North Russian winter. A small force of 350 Serbs were hardy fighters but most had served in the Austro-Hungarian Army, spent years in Russian prisoner of war camps and were well overdue for relief. Completing Poole's 'foreign' contingents were a handful of Poles (designated 'Polish Legion'), consistently excellent fighters, and an even smaller number of raw recruits from the newly formed British trained and equipped Slavo-British Legion, untried and untested.

There being not enough soldiers to occupy territory already captured from the Bolsheviks, Poole requested that Admiral Kemp under Admiralty authority, order the creation of a 'Russian Allied Naval Brigade' (RANB) to consist of local Russian recruits trained and led by petty officers, sailors and Royal Marines from the Allied warships at Archangel. Formed in August, the RANB comprised seven ratings and a petty officer from HMS *Attentive*, eight French sailors from *Amiral Aube*, one officer and eight sailors from USS *Olympia* and one officer and 16 other ranks, Royal Marines. Soon after its formation, the 94 officers and Marines detached from RMFFNR at Murmansk for the capture of Archangel were also attached to the RANB. The bulk of the brigade would be comprised of locally recruited Russian sailors, trained at Smolny Barracks in land warfare and drill by the Allied naval contingents, for all intents and purposes a naval equivalent of the Army's locally raised 'Slavo-British Legion'. Local Russians enlisted into the brigade observed naval traditions and wore cut down Leading Seaman's insignia on their headdress.

Command of the Brigade was given to Captain George Burt, RN, with Lieutenant Commander Patrick Edwards, RNVR, second in command and Captain Richard Burton, RMLI, as Adjutant. The first 100 recruits were formed into 'A' Company under Captain Burton and after four weeks training at Archangel, were sent to the town of Onega on the White Sea to conduct a weeks further training in the field before despatch to the front line at Chekevo south of Onega. Within a week, Edwards had received orders from General Poole to proceed to Onega to take command of all Allied troops in the region after Captain Burton was ordered home sick on 5 September, for which Edwards was seconded to Army command and given the temporary rank of Lieutenant Colonel.

Edwards certainly had credentials for command of the Brigade. He had served with Howe Battalion, Royal Naval Division, on Gallipoli where he was one of a handful of Howe men to reach the Turkish trenches during the Third Battle of Krithia on 4 June 1915, where he was wounded. Edwards was again in action with the RND on the Somme at the Battle of Ancre on 13th November 1916 where despite severe wounds (which would result in the loss of an eye) he continued to direct an attack on a German redoubt. After recovering from his wounds, he next saw action in command of one of HMS *Vindictive*'s storming parties during the St. George's Day 1918 raid on Zeebrugge in which he was again severely wounded and evacuated to England.

---

1   President Wilson's Press Statement, 5 August, 1918.

39. Some of the original members of 'ELOPE' Force. The soldier in slouch
hat at right is Sergeant Arthur von Duve, MM, AIF. (AWM A00250)

The Russian Allied Naval Brigade remained in action on the Onega Front during September–November when Captain Burton was repatriated to Archangel sick and exhausted. Two army officers were appointed to the Brigade to fill the gaps left by Edwards' promotion to CO and Burton's hospitalisation. Captain John Card, East Surrey Regiment was given command of 'A' Company and Lieutenant Stephen Mann, 2nd Battalion, London Regiment, the newly formed 'B' Company. Mann had previously served as a Sergeant with 'ELOPE' Force and had been commissioned in the field for gallantry near Onega during the months following the capture of Archangel. Both men were to die within two days of each other in March the following year, Card being posthumously awarded an MC for gallantry with the RANB during New Year 1919 whilst Mann was posthumously awarded the MM for gallant work as a Lewis gunner in an attack near Onega shortly before being commissioned; his award, gazetted in 1920, being one of very few MMs gazetted with citation.

During an engagement with the enemy near the village of Gorka on 1 October 1918, Sergeant Walter Marriott, RMLI, left his trench to stalk a sniper, managing to crawl within 15 yards of the enemy before killing him. Marriott further distinguished himself when Captain Burton was pinned down by enemy machine gun fire, opening up on the enemy with a Lewis gun to keep their heads down to allow Burton to escape to safety. Burton credited Marriot with 'undoubtedly saving my life', strongly recommending the gallant Marine for award of the DSM which was duly gazetted the following year.

After recovering in hospital at Archangel, Captain Burton was repatriated to the UK in time for the gazetting of a DSC for his work as Adjutant of the Brigade from August–November 1918. Determined to return to Russia, in mid 1919 he volunteered for service with 6th Battalion, Royal Marines which had been formed for service overseeing a referendum in northern Germany but was instead diverted for active service at Murmansk. He was killed in action during an attack on the villages of Ussuna and Koikori on 8 September 1919 and buried in a local churchyard, his grave since lost to time.

In early January 1919, the RANB was disbanded as a naval unit and its members absorbed into Army command. At the time of absorption the Brigade numbered some 400 men, mostly Royal Marines and Russians but with smaller numbers of Polish and Lettish volunteers, and comprised two infantry companies, a machine gun section (four Vickers and four Lewis guns), an artillery section (two French 75 mm and four Stokes mortars) and a mounted scouts section.

Critical to the success of the Allied advance upriver was the hurriedly assembled flotilla of Royal Navy monitors and an assortment of locally outfitted gun barges, steamers and tug boats, known as the 'River Expeditionary Force' under the command of Captain Edward Altham, RN, who would command the River Force until the final evacuation of North Russia the following year. Immediately after the capture of Archangel, preparations were made to utilise a number of local vessels abandoned by the Bolsheviks for service on the Dvina in support of the advance. The armourers and shipwrights of HMS *Attentive* worked furiously during the following two weeks after the capture of Archangel, outfitting and equipping the vessels with an assortment of armament of all manufacture and calibres, including French, Russian and British guns, including two naval 12 pdrs put ashore from *Attentive*. The first two vessels ready for service upriver were the Russian vessels *Advokat* (Lieutenant Edward Henry Richardson, AM, RN) and *Gorodok* (Gunner William Henry Kewish, RN), with crews from *Attentive*. Both vessels left Archangel on 8 September and steamed upriver towards the furthest extent of the Allied advance at Bereznik.

The Bolsheviks had their own river flotilla of much faster and better armed vessels which severely shelled *Advokat* and *Gorodok* as they approached Bereznik, wounding a number of crew including captain of *Gorodok*, Gunner Kewish, RN. Commander Charles Cowan, RN had been observing the uneven exchange of fire from a motor launch and immediately took command of *Gorodok* after Kewish was wounded, ordering a withdrawal under fire for which he was Mentioned in Despatches.

At Archangel, frantic efforts had been made to fit out the Russian screw steamer *Opyt* (with Russian crew under Commander Kaskoff, Russian Navy) as a small gunboat, arming the vessel with five 76.5 mm guns and a 3 inch howitzer. Two paddle steamers, *Razlyff* (Lieutenant Malet, RAF) and *Tolstoy* (Russian crew) were also armed and fitted out whilst two smaller motor launches *ML.1* (Sub Lieutenant Royer Dick, RN) and *ML.2* (Lieutenant Henry Cavendish, RN) were fitted with 3 pdrs and machine guns. By 10 August, the 'Naval Gunboat Squadron' was placed under the command of Lieutenant Cavendish and set out for the front line. Arriving at Bereznik two days later, Cavendish found the advance party dug in ashore with four Bolshevik gunboats holding up any further advance. Command of the gunboat *Gorodok*, without a captain after Gunner William Kewish was wounded, was given to Lieutenant Daniel Fedotoff White, an English-speaking former Imperial Russian Army officer who had been locally enlisted into the RNVR as an intelligence officer at Archangel.

The two Royal Navy monitors *M.23* and *M.25* were not able to join the remainder of the flotilla upriver from Puchega until 25 August due to their draught of six to eight feet which had necessitated a cautious traverse between the sand banks further downriver. On 28 August, *M.25* made a 'very dashing' attack on the enemy flotilla during which Surgeon Lieutenant John Dobson, RN, had a miraculous escape. An enemy shell exploded less than a foot from where he was standing in the passage between the Ward Room (fitted as a dressing station) and the Captain's cabin. Shielded by a cross iron, he was blown to the floor but survived with the loss of an eye and numerous shrapnel wounds across the right side of his body. Despite his wounds, Dobson immediately formed a stretcher party to attend to the wounded 6 inch gun crew on the quarter deck and worked continuously, dressing and treating the wounded for three hours, when having no further casualties to treat, he administered himself a dose of morphine and collapsed on his bunk. Dobson was subsequently awarded the DSO whilst Private James Metcalf, RMLI, received the DSM for remaining on duty on the quarterdeck despite his wounds.

40. Captain Edward Altham, CB, RN, Senior Naval Officer commanding the Royal Navy Dvina River Flotilla, 1918–19. (Public domain)

Under continued relentless and determined attacks from the Bolshevik gunboat flotilla, the River Expeditionary Force withdrew back to Bereznik on 29 August, *M.25* and gunboats taking up positions from where they could cover the Dvina–Vaga junction. Further reinforcements of Royal Scots arrived on 31 August accompanied by Captain Altham on *ML.2* who immediately transferred his Senior Naval Officer (SNO) pendant to the yacht *Kathleen*.

On 7 September, after a week of relative quiet, Lieutenant Richardson, RN took *Advokat* forward to reconnoitre the position of the enemy gunboats before landing a party of sailors to clear a house in the village of Shedrovo known to hold a telephone being used by the Bolsheviks. Enemy observers wearing 'long grey coats and soft round hats with stars on the front' had been seen posting sentries along the river and Richardson was keen to clear them out. He steamed *Advokat* forward to shell the enemy observation posts and was greeted by inaccurate machine gun and rifle fire from ashore.

With *Opyt* in support, the two gunboats advanced on Shedrovo, shelling the river bank as they went, forcing the enemy machine gunners into the forest. Leaving *Opyt* to provide covering fire, Richardson took *Advokat* abreast of 'Telephone House' and put ashore a landing party of six bluejackets and four Russian sailors under Stoker Petty Officer Sydney Wragg, RN.

The landing party stormed the house which had been abandoned by the Bolsheviks on the arrival of the two gunboats, and secured the telephone as well as a number of documents which were delivered to *M.25*. For leadership of the landing party and a later action ashore in which he took command of a Lewis gun and used it against the enemy to great effect, Wragg was subsequently awarded the DSM. Richardson was also awarded the DSC for his command of *Advokat* to add to an Albert Medal awarded for service at Archangel in 1916 in assisting to evacuate the injured from a burning cargo ship packed with explosives.

The following morning a platoon of Royal Scots arrived on the tug *Elma* to clear Shedrovo completely of the enemy. The tug carrying the Scots was escorted upriver by *Advokat* and *Opyt* and got as far as the village itself before the Bolsheviks opened fire with machine guns and pom-pom (small calibre automatic artillery, usually used for anti-aircraft defence although equally deadly when used against ground targets) from the reoccupied 'Telephone House' and another house closer to the small village church. The pom-pom fire was well directed, a hit being scored on *Elma*'s main steam pipe, wounding three Scots. At a painfully slow pace the tug's captain was able to make his way downriver out of sight of the enemy whilst *Advokat* and *Opyt* shelled the village to provide cover, setting fire to the enemy headquarters in 'Telephone House'.

In early September reports had been received of a force of 500 Red troops advancing on the Dvina–Vaga junction south of Bereznik. 'A' Company, 2/10th Royal Scots, a detachment of Poles and two field guns were sent out to intercept the Bolshevik force. On the night of 11–12 September the Bolsheviks attacked but were repulsed, 'A' Company bearing much of the brunt of the attack. Over the following two days the Company pushed forward with the support of the guns of HMS *M.23* (Lieutenant Commander Andrew Oliver St. John, RN) and HMS *M.25* (Lieutenant Commander S.W.B. Green, RN) and drove the Bolsheviks from the villages of Prilutski and Korbalski.

Early in the morning of 14 September, 'B' Company, Royal Scots under Captain John Edwards, MC and Bar, was ordered to advance from Ust-Vaga on the Vaga River to Chamovo on the Dvina's eastern bank. After a 10 mile march through dense forest and marshland, Mala Bereznik was reached where a platoon under Lieutenant Harry Braham (who had been commissioned from the ranks of the Liverpool Regiment) was detached to hold the village whilst the remainder of the column advanced on Chamovo. The going was so bad in some places that the column had to halt and wait whilst local Russian soldiers constructed rudimentary log walkways over the worst parts of marshland. It was some eight hours before the exhausted column finally reached their objective which was found occupied by the enemy.

HMS *M.25*, *Advokat* and *Razlyff* (Sub Lieutenant Royer Dick, RN, who would be awarded the DSC for his command of the ship and would end his career after the Second World War as a Vice Admiral) pushed up the Dvina to support the infantry ashore at Chamovo where another landing of Royal Scots was to take place. One of the enemy's most powerful and fastest gunboats, the *Magoochy* (reportedly capable of 14–15 knots) was surprised whilst moored alongside the riverbank at Chamovo. The gunboat opened fire on *M.25* but was quickly silenced by the monitor's 7.5 inch guns, a shell tearing through the paddle, stopping both engines, and bursting the boiler. Most of the Bolshevik crew took to the water where they were rescued and taken prisoner by *M.25* which came alongside the wrecked vessel and took a further 20 prisoners, 10 of whom were wounded, and cleared the ship of all charts and documents. The Russian pilot on board *Magoochy* was immediately pressganged into service for the British, subsequently proving himself to be, 'most faithful and useful' which was a boon for the River Flotilla as the two pilots picked up at Bereznik on the way upriver were described in rather unflattering terms: 'useless, completely paralysed with fright, and nearly had us aground twice on the way up.'[2]

On arrival at Chamovo to cover the second landing at 0800 on 14 September, there could be found no sign of any Allied troops although a field gun firing from next to a wood stack near the village church was targeted and quickly silenced. The enemy flotilla also made an appearance but were quickly driven off after a few salvos from *M.25*. Without any infantry ashore the flotilla remained vulnerable to short range fire from the village or surrounding forest; however rather than withdrawing and allowing the enemy to reoccupy Chamovo Lieutenant Commander Green, RN, in *M.25,* took matters into his own hands and led ashore a landing party of 33 petty officers and ratings, three Russians and four naval Lewis gunners from the motor launches to hold the village and its approaches until the infantry arrived.

The small force was divided into three sections: a 'Right Flanking Party' under Bosun Gutless, MMR, with two Lewis guns and a Maxim, 'Left Flanking Party' under Russian interpreter Lieutenant W.G. Waganoff, RN (who would lose his life a year later in the HMS *Glowworm* explosion) including the Russian seamen and a Lewis gun section from *Advokat* under Petty Officer Wragg, and a 'Centre Party' under Petty Officer Osborn with two sections of seamen.

As the landing party cautiously made its way into the village it came under heavy rifle and machine gun fire from enemy concealed in the forest. Three ratings – Able Seamen Charles Boyles, Ernest Buckingham, and Stanley Wright – were shot and killed in the fusillade and another sailor wounded. Green ordered his men to withdraw to the river bank where there was good cover to allow *M.25* and *Advokat* to shell the approaches to the village. Fire from the British vessels was rapid and accurate, completely silencing the enemy machine guns within minutes. With little chance of a

---

2   The National Archives: ADM 137/1695: White Sea River Expedition.

41. Captain John Edwards, MC and two Bars, 2/10th Battalion, Royal Scots poses with two officers of 339th US Infantry Regiment in a Vickers machine gun pit, September 1918. (Ian Edwards)

landing party ever being able to hold the village, Green ordered his men to remain in cover by the riverbank until fire from another concealed enemy field gun ashore forced the party to reembark.

With the landing party back on board, *M.25* and *Advokat* pushed upriver out of range of the enemy guns where they engaged the enemy gunboats but again came under fire from a concealed battery ashore. With the infantry attack yet to materialise, Captain Altham gave the order to withdraw downriver, both vessels having to run the gauntlet of fire from both banks of the Dvina, firing continuously with all guns as they went, one shell from *M.25* knocking out a field gun on the right bank. Late in the evening the Royal Scots finally arrived and took Chamovo without resistance, reporting as many as 40 enemy bodies in the village, killed by shell fire from *M.25* and *Advokat*.

With no time to rest, a platoon commanded by 2nd Lieutenant Graeme Orr, MM, accompanied by a Russian detachment pushed forward and after a brisk fight captured half of the village and with it a 3 inch gun, which the Reds tried to recapture at dusk but were beaten off by accurate rifle and Lewis gun fire. During the night the Scots and Russians surrounded Chamovo and finally cleared it completely, capturing a number of prisoners, pack horses and supplies.

Further down the Dvina from Bereznik on the western bank, the Bolsheviks had fortified the outskirts of the village of Pless where they were supported by artillery and gunboats. 'A' Company was ordered to make a long trek through the forest to outflank the defences. After a long and weary march through rain and mud the column encountered a marsh through which passage was impossible. The men were so exhausted that column commander Major Alexander Skeil, MC recounted, 'occasional plops would be heard of tired men slipping from trees against which they had been leaning into the icy water.'[3]

After a night of severe discomfort, early in the morning of 16 September the column resumed its advance. The exhausted troops struggled on all day, some collapsing along the way, until they found a small mill in which they sheltered for the night. After a slightly more comfortable night in the forest the column set out at dawn for Kurgomen, eight miles south-east of Pless, to find the village abandoned by the enemy, the locals telling how the Red garrison had fled in terror in the mistaken belief that brigades of British troops were about to attack rather than an under-strength company of exhausted, hungry Scotsmen. 'A' Company's exhausting trek through the forest had lasted three days without adequate food and water.

On 15 September, Captain Altham ordered *M.25* forward to Chamovo to provide cover the Royal Scots already ashore and another landing taking place on the opposite bank. Steaming up to Chamovo, the monitor caught the Bolshevik armed steamer *Dedoushka* moored alongside the partially submerged *Magoochy*, apparently in an attempt to salvage ammunition from the stricken gunboat. A 7.5 inch shell from *M.25* struck the wooden steamer, setting *Dedoushka* alight and causing

3   Major John Ewing, MC, *The Royal Scots, 1914–19* (Edinburgh, London: Oliver and Boyd, 1925), p.746.

a number of casualties. Accompanied by much cheering from ashore, the enemy vessel sank opposite Chamovo, most of its superstructure remaining visible above the waterline in the shallow water.

On the same day the Royal Scots marched into Pless, US troops fought their first engagement in North Russia when a Bolshevik gunboat appeared off Chamovo and opened fire on the breakfasting soldiers before disembarking a landing party of riflemen. Sergeant Silver Parrish of the US 339th Infantry Regiment recorded in his diary:

> Almost every man was rattled until I went down over an open field hollering for our men to follow and I formed a skirmish line and with the assistance of a few Russian regulars and one platoon of Scots we drove them back on their boat and then our gunboat [M.25] hove in sight and sunk the enemy boat.'[4]

With the guns of *M.23* and *M.25* clearing the way for the Royal Scots following in barges a day behind, the River Expedition pushed upriver to Tulgas where on 18 September, an attempt was made to capture an enemy battery just beyond the village. A small party of sailors and marines under Lieutenant Fedotoff White, RNVR, was put ashore to carry out the task which was successfully achieved without casualty.

Steaming forward from Tulgas, the village of Puchega was reached on 19 September, the main force of Royal Scots arriving the following day. The Bolsheviks had set a trap, however, and as the River Expedition passed the bend of the river they were engaged by an enemy land battery and the Bolshevik gunboat flotilla. With the flotilla under heavy fire, *Gorodok*, in the lead of the Russo–British flotilla, gave cover fire to allow the advanced parties ashore to withdraw to Puchega before pulling back beyond the bend in the river. For leadership in the capture of the enemy battery at Tulgas and gallantry in action covering the withdrawal of the Royal Scots under fire, Lieutenant Daniel Fedotoff White was awarded the DSC.

Frequent gun battles with the enemy followed until 23 September. On the 24th a flanking movement by enemy troops on the left bank of the river was discovered when the enemy opened fire with a land battery brought up during the night on the right bank. In command of the ground force component of the expedition, Lieutenant Colonel John Josselyn, DSO, OBE, Suffolk Regiment, issued orders to that the Royal Scots ashore withdraw further downriver under cover of the gunboats.

On 19 September, the first enemy sea mines were encountered, sighted in the river between Kurgomen and Pless, an event which dramatically changed the nature of naval operations on the river and would remain the single greatest threat to the lives of the crews of the River Flotilla during the following year of operations on the Dvina. Keen to investigate the mines himself, Captain Altham, RN, went aboard a Russian launch for a closer inspection and to sweep the mine to shallow water where it could be inspected and destroyed. Whilst approaching the mine the engine on the launch was cut out with the intention of drifting closer, however the Dvina's strong currents pushed the launch directly over the mine causing it to detonate, blowing the stern off the vessel and killing three of the Russian crew. Altham himself amazingly escaped with only bruises and a torn uniform. Knowing full well the danger from the mines, on the following day Private Albert Turton, MM, of the Royal Scots volunteered to row a boat five miles through the minefield under direct observation of the enemy to deliver a message from his OC to Battalion headquarters at Tulgas. In spite of falling shells from the Bolshevik flotilla, Turton not only delivered his message but recorded the location of the mines for which he was awarded the DCM.

The only craft available for minesweeping operations were shallow draught paddle steamer tugs *Viune* and *Petrograd*, which began sweeping the same afternoon that the first mine was sighted. There

---

4   Bentley Historical Library, The University of Michigan, Silver Parrish diary.

being no proper sweeping gear available, lengths of thick wire were utilised to 'scoop' the mines, a total of 24 sea mines being cleared and destroyed by both vessels up to advanced positions at Puchega.

In early September 1918, General Ironside had been recalled urgently from the Western Front to the War Office where he met with the Chief of the General Staff, Sir Henry Wilson, who matter-of-factly informed him, 'Your business in North Russia is to hold the fort until the local Russians can take the field. You are to prepare for a winter campaign. No joke that!'[5] Ironside embarked for North Russia only days later on board SS *Stephen* which was also transporting the Canadian Malamute Company bound for Murmansk and 16th Brigade, CFA under Lieutenant Colonel Charles Sharman, an experienced artillery officer and former mounted policeman, to Archangel. The Canadian gunners had been sent to Russia after a request by the War Office to the Canadian government for a field artillery brigade to support the US contingent in North Russia, which had no artillery of its own. Sharman had served during the Boer War with 5th Canadian Mounted Rifles but arrived in South Africa too late to see any active service. Whilst serving pre-war with the Royal North West Mounted Police (RNWMP), Sharman had been commissioned into the Canadian militia artillery. With the outbreak of war in August 1914 and Canada's pledge to form an expeditionary force, Sharman was given command of 1st Brigade, CFA, being wounded with them on the Western Front in 1916. The following year Sharman commanded the Canadian Artillery School in England before appointment to command 16th Brigade, CFA, shortly before its departure for North Russia, taking his pick of officers and men from the gunnery school with him.

After disembarking at Archangel on 3 October, the Canadian artillerymen embarked on barges on 8 October for the journey up the Dvina. At the Dvina–Vaga junction the two subunits of the brigade separated: Major Walter Hyde's 68th Battery was despatched down the Vaga for service on that front whilst Major Frank Arnoldi's 67th Battery continued up the Dvina. Both officers were recipients of the DSO and veterans of artillery operations on the Western Front in support of the Canadian Corps. A small detachment of 17 gunners under Lieutenant Sydney Evans, DCM, did not embark on barges but were instead sent overland down the Archangel–Vologda Railway to Obozerskaya where they were assigned to crew an 18 pdr gun on the British armoured train there. The train was commanded by Lieutenant Commander Edward Hilton Young, DSC, MP, RNVR, an elected Member of Parliament. Young had been decorated with the DSC for service with the Royal Navy siege guns in Flanders and had been Mentioned in Despatches for his command of one of the landing parties in the raid on Zeebrugge, where he was wounded and lost an arm.

Unlike his predecessor General Poole, Ironside chose not to remain exclusively at GHQ Archangel, preferring to make long trips to the front many hundreds of miles up the Dvina River. He travelled to and fro on a horse-drawn sleigh and would appear unannounced at some of the units under his command in remote locations causing more than a few startled faces.

Command of a multinational force would be difficult under any circumstances, however Ironside was particularly hampered by the low morale of some of the contingents from other Allied nations involved in the expedition and himself harboured some harsh views. Ironside accused the French of 'general ill-discipline and slovenliness' as well as a proclivity to refuse to fight. His words were much more positive, albeit perhaps a little exaggerated, towards the American troops whom he described as inexperienced but 'troops of good heart'. Ironside recorded one of his first encounters with the US troops:

> The inexperience of the U.S.A. troops at once became evident in the first company we visited. The whole company was lined out, peering into the forest with their arms at the ready. No clearings had been made for even a modest field of fire. I explained to the company commander what he should do, so that

---

5   Ironside, *Archangel 1918–19*, p.13.

42. Monitor *M.25* frozen into the White Sea at Archangel, winter 1918–19. The Royal Navy Dvina River Flotilla was withdrawn to Archangel in October 1918 to avoid being cut off as the river froze. (Author's collection)

a few sentries should watch while the remainder of his men rested or took their meals. He stared at me in obvious amazement and then burst out with, 'What! Rest in this hellish bombardment!' At the moment a few shells were falling wide in the forest … They had a lot to learn, but like all troops of good heart they shook down to their difficult task.[6]

A notable feature of some US accounts of service in North Russia is the resentment felt by many US troops against their treatment by what they perceived to be arrogant and condescending British officers. Ralph Albertson, an American YMCA worker who served in canteens up and down the Dvina recorded the frustration felt by many of his countrymen:

> British colonels did not give their orders to American colonels to be passed down the line. In fact, they had very little use for American colonels. They went to the captains, the lieutenants, and even the sergeants and corporals and the men themselves. They ignored American officers most noticeably. They set their own petty officers upon the Americans in a manner that was most irritating to American national self-esteem and bitterly resented.[7]

This resentment may have contributed to an event which followed at Obozerskaya on 31 January 1919 when Private Frank O'Callaghan, US 339th Infantry Regiment, shot 2nd Lieutenant John Allan Watson, RGA, in the chest at close range without any apparent motivation. O'Callaghan was apprehended and disarmed, diagnosed as insane and repatriated to the US. The US Army held an internal investigation but made no ruling as to O'Callaghan's motivation. Watson, a native of Crieff, Scotland, who had served with the Glasgow Yeomanry and Scottish Rifles before commissioning into the RGA, was buried in the small cemetery at Obozerskaya, his grave since lost to time.

During late September 1918, reinforced by 'C' Company and US 339th Infantry Regiment newly arrived from Archangel, 2/10th Royal Scots continued the advance upriver as far as Nizhne-Toimski where they were halted by a numerically superior force dug in and heavily fortified. On 27 September, the Scots pulled back to Borok where they set to work constructing a winter defence line of wooden

6   *Ibid.*, p.31.
7   Albertson, *Fighting Without a War*, pp.38–39.

blockhouses. The following day, 'A' Company was transferred to the eastern bank of the river to provide the inexperienced US troops with assistance in constructing defences. On 29 September, all Allied forces operating south of Archangel on the Dvina were redesignated 'Dvina Force'. On 2 October, a mixed US–Russian force pushed southwards far up the Vaga River to Shenkursk where a winter defence line was established.

Two days later on 5th October, *M.25*, which had given such sterling service in support of operations since the capture of Archangel, was recalled downriver to avoid being frozen in with the onset of winter. Archangel and the White Sea froze over in early October whilst the Dvina–Vaga junction did not freeze until 10 days later. This gave the Reds the advantage of being able to operate their gunboats south of the junction with nothing to oppose them during those critical 10 days.

On the same day, as *M.25* was being recalled downriver, a number of engagements were fought between the Royal Scots and Bolsheviks. After a heavy bombardment by the Red gunboats, the Bolsheviks attacked Borok on the left bank but were beaten back by heavy fire from the entrenched Royal Scots. The following day, 'B' Company proceeded forward to clear the forest of any remaining enemy but ran into an ambush. The Bolshevik fire was not very accurate, however, and the Scots were able to withdraw with the loss of one man killed, 21-year-old South Londoner Private John Clubb.

By 7 October, a Russian 5.1 inch howitzer with British crew arrived at Borok to counter the Red gunboats with a company of US troops to reinforce the line. On the same day, after a short bombardment by the howitzer, the Royal Scots and US troops attacked the Bolshevik advanced positions to the east of Borok. The Reds were quickly routed leaving behind a pom-pom, two machine guns and a number of killed and wounded. The only Scots fatality was Lance Corporal David Michie, aged 26, from Kirkcaldy, Fife.

On 9 October, the Bolsheviks retaliated with a series of counter-attacks over the following 24 hours. The British line gave way slightly but the attacking force was eventually driven off. The Bolsheviks still maintained the advantage with their river flotilla, some 30 vessels strong including a number of gunboats, and were quick to exploit this advantage. On 13 October, after several days of intermittent but heavy shelling, the Scots withdrew from Borok to a new defence line at Kurgomen under threat of being overrun. Over 100 stretcher cases were evacuated under constant fire from the Bolshevik gunboats and attacks by Red troops. The Scots suffered five men killed including CSM Harold Simpson, DCM, and one officer and five men wounded.

During the attacks 7–9 October, Sergeant F.G. Hofman along with two other Scots found themselves completely isolated from the remainder of their company but continued to work their Lewis gun, repulsing three attempts by the enemy to storm their post for which Hofman was awarded the DCM. Captain John Penman, Lieutenant William Bassett, and 2nd Lieutenant Graeme Orr, MM, were also all awarded MCs for the defence of Borok. Penman was credited with organising the defence of the village and leading a number of counter-attacks in which he personally killed several of the enemy, whilst Bassett's award was for repelling enemy attacks and capturing a machine gun, and Orr's for defending the outpost line from determined enemy attacks. Orr was wounded during a subsequent enemy attack four days later whilst Bassett was killed in action during the disastrous ambush near Kulika later in the month.

The medical services too were recognised for their gallantry during the defence on Borok, Captain William Gourlay, RAMC, received the MC and Nurse Selma Amy Valentine, Voluntary Aid Detachment (VAD), the MM, the only such award made to a nurse for Russia 1918–20. Both awards were for command of the hospital at Borok during the attacks and for work in the care and evacuation of wounded to a hospital barge.

On the same day that the enemy attacks on Borok were finally repulsed, Lieutenant Robert McNair, RNR, arrived in command of a barge fitted with a 130 mm gun which was brought into immediate action against the enemy flotilla. Fire from the barge struck one of the enemy gunboats sending plumes of smoke and steam into the air, for which McNair and his 13 crew members became entitled to prize money for the sinking. Nearly a year later in September 1919, the Head of Legal Branch of the Admiralty cabled Dvina River Flotilla commander Captain Altham to advise that as no declaration of war had been made between the British and Bolshevik governments, crews were not entitled to naval prize money for sinking enemy vessels, although the Admiralty graciously agreed to grant equivalent to a bounty to McNair and his crew.

The presence of McNair's 130 mm gun and the sinking of one of the enemy vessels came as a nasty surprise to the Bolsheviks who withdrew out of range of Borok but continued indirect fire on the British gun barge, joined by a 9 inch gun near Kodema on the western bank. McNair counted 150 rounds falling around him but the fire was inaccurate, none of the enemy shells landing any closer than 50 yards from the barge.

The following day, the Bolsheviks extended their attacks to Seltso on the opposite bank but were forced back into the forest with many casualties, which allowed the remainder of the withdrawal to the Kurgomen-Tulgas defensive line to be carried out unhindered on 14 October. All field artillery on the western bank was successfully withdrawn but on the eastern bank all guns were lost, a French 4.7 inch mounted on a barge which had run aground, two naval 12 pdrs and two Slavo-British Legion 18 pdrs stuck in the mud, all guns being destroyed to prevent their capture and use by the enemy.

From 15–20 October 1918, McNair's 130 mm gun barge was constantly in action keeping the enemy flotilla at bay, and also against enemy troops ashore although accuracy was impeded by persistent fog. On 18 October, the fog cleared enough that McNair scored a direct hit on an enemy landing party with a 130 mm shell. The following day the young naval officer engaged four enemy gunboats, driving them upriver without too much difficulty until another enemy gun opened very accurate fire from ashore from a concealed position which neither McNair nor his Canadian artillery observer could spot. The Russian crew of the tug attending the British gun barge fled overboard by the time the second enemy round was fired, leaving McNair and his crew stranded in full view of the enemy gunners. With no visible target to return fire against, McNair ordered his gun crew to take cover on the barge as best as they could until an enemy shell scored a direct hit, blowing a large hole through the bulkhead which rapidly filled with water and sending the barge to the bottom of the Dvina, although due to the shallowness of the river (at that time of year less than 10 feet) the deck of the barge remained above the waterline. The resulting list rendered any further firing of the 130 mm gun impossible and for the first time since the attack of 14 October, the enemy were able to bombard the Allied forward line without reply. During the period 11–20 October, the British gun barge was in constant action, single handedly keeping the Bolshevik river flotilla at bay for which McNair was awarded the first of two DSCs he would receive for service in North Russia.

The British line was further strengthened with the arrival of 67th Battery, CFA, on 17 October and all efforts directed to preparations for the impending Red attack. Enemy reconnaissance patrols were frequently sighted and it was expected that an attack in strength could come at any time. At this critical point, command of Dvina Force was given to Major Alexander Skeil, 2/10th Royal Scots, who ordered that the number of blockhouses built on both banks of the river should be increased to 12 on the west bank and 14 on the east, all well wired-in with cleared fields of fire. Attempts had been made to dig trenches and other fortifications but it had been found impossible to dig due to the depth of the water table.

On 23 October, the Bolsheviks launched a large attack on the west bank of the Dvina and were met by the Scots and US troops who had spent their time clearing fields of fire well and the attack was driven off without loss to the defenders. The Scots would not fare as well during an attack against the Bolshevik line at Kulika near Topsa four days later. Two platoons of 'B' Company and three of 'C' Company with a detachment of Poles and Lithuanians with eight Canadian and Royal Marine gunners in tow under the command of Lieutenant John Penman set out through the forest during a snowstorm, expecting that the Bolsheviks would be taken by surprise in the bad weather. The Scots

43. NCOs of 85th General Hospital, RAMC, Archangel, winter 1918–19. (Author's collection)

walked directly into an ambush and were cut down in swathes by Red machine gun and rifle fire leaving many dead and wounded in the snow as they withdrew. Ironside recounted:

> The Lithuanians immediately bolted. The platoon officers of the Royal Scots became casualties and the enemy then delivered a counter attack. The Royal Scots turned and fled, throwing away their arms and equipment in a state of absolute panic and demoralisation. The Poles on the left flank were the only troops who behaved well and did not succumb to panic. They covered the retirement and brought back all their wounded. Four Canadian artillerymen and four marine artillerymen who accompanied the Royal Scots in the attack behaved very gallantly and were the last to be withdrawn after making their presence very severely felt on the enemy.[8]

When a roll was taken after the retreat, the party had lost 26 men killed and dozens wounded. Royal Scots Medical Officer Lieutenant John Morrison was awarded an MC for treating the wounded under fire whilst Bombardier Charles Colwell, 67th Battery, CFA, was awarded the DCM for fighting his way out of the ambush and leading the Canadian gunners and Royal Marine Artillerymen to safety. The only officer killed in the ambush, Lieutenant William Bassett (attached from 10th Black Watch) would be awarded a posthumous MC for his actions in defence of Borok earlier in the month.

On 11 November 1918, the day the Armistice was signed ending hostilities between the British Commonwealth and the Central Powers, the Red Army launched its largest attack yet, landing soldiers on both banks of the Dvina under the cover of the morning mist and a heavy barrage from the Red gunboat flotilla. The attack on the east bank was driven back but on the western bank near Tulgas, 300 Red troops formed up under the cover of a steep embankment before attacking and managed to push through gaps between the blockhouses. Defending Tulgas were 'B' Company, US 339th Infantry Regiment, 'A' Company, 2/10th Royal Scots and two 18 pdrs of 67th Battery, CFA. Such was the rate of the Red troops advance that they captured a field hospital and very quickly threatened the guns of 67th Battery some distance behind the defensive line of blockhouses.

---

8   Ironside, *Archangel 1918–19*, p.45.

Sergeant Francis Frape of the Canadian Army Veterinary Corps and Corporal Fred Wheeler, both of 67th Battery, grabbed their rifles and took charge of a number of drivers and gunners and began to fight off the attackers from the stables behind the gun positions. Both men were awarded the DCM for their gallantry and leadership, their citations recounting that they personally accounted for several of the enemy each. Gunner Walter Conville was shot and killed and for several minutes it appeared that the Canadian guns would surely be overrun, until drastic action was taken by two platoons of Royal Scots led by Lieutenant Robert Hastings, who charged the enemy and drove the Bolsheviks back from the gun pits for which Hastings was awarded the MC. In the ensuing hand-to-hand fighting, Sergeant Christopher Salmons charged directly into the enemy, firing his Lewis gun from the hip until he was brought down by bullets and bayonet. He was posthumously awarded the DCM for rescuing a wounded officer under fire on 10 October and leadership during the disastrous raid on Kulika.

A flanking attack by 200 Reds was observed advancing out of the forest, the opposite direction to which the 18 pdrs were facing. The Canadian gunners had to manhandle the guns out of their pits to face the enemy. Sergeant William Armstrong, MM, a pre-war militia artilleryman, rolled his gun out, faced it to the rear and fired over open sights for six hours driving off the attackers for which he was awarded the DCM. Corporal Stanley Wareham, MM, was shot and killed standing by his gun.

Enfilading fire from the blockhouses inflicted further casualties and prevented reinforcements from reaching the attackers. As the sun began to set the Bolsheviks filtered back to the cover of the riverbank as best they could, leaving behind dozens of dead and wounded. Had the attacks from the riverbank and forest been coordinated the guns may well have been overrun and the blockhouses attacked from the flanks, but the mud, mist and spirited defence by the Canadian gunners and drivers all conspired to defeat the attackers. Major Frank Arnoldi, OC, 67th Battery, CFA, was awarded a Bar to his DSO earned on the Western Front for command of the defence of Tulgas whilst Captain John Watson, RAMC, was awarded a Bar to his MC for gallantry in evacuating wounded under fire, and Captain George Edwards, RE, an MC for steadying the defending troops when the enemy had almost reached the gun positions.

It was estimated that over 1,000 Red troops had taken part in the attack and that their casualties had been very heavy, possibly as many as two thirds of the attacking force either killed, wounded or taken prisoner. A number of Red soldiers found themselves separated and lost in the forest, many of whom walked around in circles in the sub-Arctic conditions before eventually dying of exhaustion and exposure. One group of stragglers stumbled into British positions on the Vaga River days later having wandered many miles through the snow. Total Allied casualties for 11 November 1918 were three US soldiers, 17 Royal Scots and two Canadian gunners killed and a number more wounded. In skirmishes over the following three days an additional five US troops and one Royal Scot were killed.

The Bolsheviks brought up reinforcements in the days following, 2,500 troops eventually being committed. On 12–13 November the Bolshevik gunboats pounded the British and American positions, scoring a direct hit on a blockhouse manned by the Royal Scots killing Private Clarence Yacamini.

After two days of intermittent bombardment the Bolsheviks resumed their attack on 14 November but were held up by deep snowfalls on the western bank. On the eastern bank the Bolsheviks managed to rush a forward position of the Royal Scots, killing 2nd Lieutenant John Dalziel. By midday the bombardment ceased and the gunboats returned to Kotlas, leaving the Bolshevik troops to hold the line as best they could without artillery support. Despite four days of bombardment and attacks, when fighting patrols were ordered out that afternoon the exhausted Scots and US troops formed up in the snow without complaint. Over the next few days patrols along the enemy line of retreat discovered the bodies of Bolshevik soldiers frozen stiff in the snow. Some had been wounded and left behind and others appeared to have died of exhaustion and cold.

Over the four days of fighting, 11–14 November, US 339th Infantry Regiment suffered seven killed and 74 wounded, the Canadians lost four killed (including Bombardier David Fraser and Gunner Frank Russell, killed when their mounted patrol was ambushed in the forest) whilst 2/10th

Royal Scots suffered 20 men killed with dozens more wounded. The Red Army suffered heavily with an estimated 350 men killed. Ironside particularly praised the good work of Major Alexander Skeil and 2/10th Royal Scots and Captain Robert Boyd of US 339th Infantry Regiment. Both Skeil and Boyd were awarded the DSO for gallantry and leadership during the river fighting, Skeil for the Royal Scots epic trek through the forest in September and Boyd for the defence of Tulgas. Indeed the Royal Scots would suffer more casualties in Russia than any other unit which served there.

For the untried troops of US 339th Infantry Regiment, the battles of 11–14 November had been the largest yet experienced and they had learnt much from the experienced Canadian gunners. One American officer wrote:

> During this fight, or rather after it, the Canadians taught our boys their first lesson in looting the persons of the dead. Our men had been rather respectful and gentle with the Bolo dead who were quite numerous … but the Canadians, veterans of four years fighting, immediately went through the pockets of the dead for roubles or knives and even took the boots off the dead as they were pretty fair boots.'[9]

Most of the troops involved in the defence of Tulgas did not learn of the Armistice until days later. When news reached Archangel, Ironside described the city as:

> Like a hive of bees. Everywhere there was an underlying hope that, even at this late hour, something might happen to save us from our winter campaign … And then on the very afternoon of Armistice Day, there arrived the news of heavy fighting on the Dvina. All the vain hopes of a peaceful evacuation or a quiet winter campaign, which so many people had cherished, disappeared in a flash.[10]

By mid November the brutal sub-Arctic winter brought offensive operations by both sides to a standstill. As the temperature plummeted far below zero, it became so cold that the range of the 18 pdr artillery shells was significantly reduced and care had to be taken to avoid the buffer oil freezing over. There were attempts to mount patrols but in such extreme temperatures offensive operations were impractical. One small relief was that the clouds of mosquitoes disappeared with the onset of winter.

In late November the Dvina south of Tulgas froze completely over leaving the Bolsheviks without the firepower advantage from their gunboats. The British line was further bolstered by the arrival of 'D' Company, 2/10th Royal Scots under Captain Arthur Bright which had been fighting on the Railway Front since October. In their only major engagement on the Railway, 'D' Company had been attacked in strength on 19 October by a large force of Red troops preceded by a heavy barrage from a Bolshevik armoured train. Safe in their blockhouses, the Scots drove off the attackers without too much difficulty, sustaining one fatal casualty only, 21-year-old 2nd Lieutenant Kenneth Croal.

By December heavy snowfall further restricted operations although patrols were still sent out with sledges, skis and snowshoes. The Canadian gunners of 67th Battery countered the short range of their artillery in sub-zero temperatures by building a heavy sledge on which could be loaded a single 18 pdr. Using this method, on the night of 5 December the Canadians boldly advanced 1,500 yards in front of the British line of blockhouses and began a rapid fire bombardment of the Bolshevik line. Inexplicably, the Bolsheviks did not respond with their own artillery or send out any patrols and the 'sleigh gunners' were able to make their way back to their blockhouses without difficulty. So successful was this tactic that it was repeated several times thereafter.

Few of the British soldiers had any experience in winter pursuits and much of the month was spent training in new modes of transport. Those with particular aptitude were selected to form snowshoe

---

9   Roy MacLaren, *Canadians in Russia 1918–19* (Lewiston, N.Y.: Maclean-Hunter Press, 1976), p.65.
10   Ironside, *Archangel 1918–19*, pp.50–51.

44. General Ironside and Staff, Archangel 1918–19. (Public domain)

and ski platoons which roamed the frozen forests looking for the enemy but encounters were very uncommon and the men spent much of the winter in blockhouses and billets doing their best to keep warm. As a consequence fires were common and it was largely due to the experience of local Russians in dealing with such conflagrations that significant damage or loss of life was not incurred.

In late December, Ironside set out to visit his command taking particular interest in seeing conditions on the frontline. During one of his sleigh trips he had his own close encounter with the enemy:

> I suddenly heard a shout, followed by a rifle shot from the right front. My driver stopped at once and threw himself out in the snow to the left, still holding on to his reins. Several more shots went off and I heard bullets swishing into the bushes behind us. Then there was a regular fusillade from Piskoff and Kostia, letting off their automatics. I tumbled out into the snow by my driver, and grabbing the rifle at the bottom of my sleigh, I ran up to join Piskoff. I could see the flashes of the enemy rifles about twenty yards off, and managed to get off a couple of rounds in their direction. I heard a pony scream and a man shout, and then all was silence. The three of us then stalked the place from where the shots had come … Here we found an overturned sleigh with a dead pony. Close beside them was a wounded man. There was a lot of blood about the sleigh and the snow round it. We propped the wounded man up and gave him a good tot of rum, which roused him a bit, but he was badly hurt … Piskoff managed to get something of a story from him … before the man collapsed and died.[11]

The White Russian forces in North Russia will generally be remembered as mutinous, traitorous and of only occasional value on the battlefield, but some extraordinary men could also be counted amongst their ranks. One such standout was the fighter ace Alexander Kazakov. He had entered the Imperial Army's Air Service at the outbreak of war and completed his flying training in February 1915, forcing down his first enemy aircraft (a two-seater Albatross spotting for German artillery) the following month by ramming with his undercarriage. The Albatross went down over the Russian lines whilst Kazakov made a hasty crash-landing. The intensity of air-to-air combat on the Eastern

---

11   *Ibid.*, pp.96–97.

Front was minimal compared to the dogfights over France and Flanders but none the less Kazakov's score continued to climb and by November 1917 he had downed 17 German and Austro-Hungarian aircraft, making him the highest-scoring Russian ace of the war.

When the Bolsheviks took power in late 1917, many pilots of the former Imperial Air Service were pressganged into Bolshevik service. Kazakov, along with a handful of pilots, observers and ground crew, was able to escape the Bolsheviks with the assistance of British spy George Hill, nominally a Lieutenant in the RAF and thrice decorated for his work with the British Secret Service in Russia with the DSO, MBE and MC. In a report of his work recruiting former Imperial Air Service pilots, Hill wrote, 'I guaranteed 10,000 roubles to the pilot of each aeroplane landed with all accessories in the Czecho–Slovak lines: 2,500 roubles to each observer on condition that they went over in flights or squadrons.'[12] Kazakov eventually reached Archangel soon after the Allied invasion, bringing with him 37 pilots and ground crew of the old Imperial Air Service who were accepted into service by the British and designated 'Slavo-British Aviation Corps' (SBAC). Without any aircraft the SBAC existed in name only and with only enough aircraft in theatre to supply the RAF contingent, the Russians were instead provided with some Sopwith Strutter and Nieuport scout aircraft discovered unassembled in their shipping crates at Bakharitsa docks.

The fledgling Red Air Force had few aircraft in the northern theatre, estimated at a few Nieuport scouts and a handful of seaplanes. Air to-air encounters were extremely rare and the RAF and SBAC sat out most of the winter but did fly the occasional mission to strafe and bomb enemy-held villages and perform reconnaissance duties.

When the Bolsheviks launched a series of counter-attacks in October, Kazakov's forward airfield at Siskoe was cut off. The ground crew dismantled the aircraft and loaded them in parts onto sleighs and set out for the Allied lines. Taking refuge in a convent, the airmen fought off the Bolsheviks with Lewis guns taken from the aircraft, keeping the enemy at bay for a week before being relieved. Once clear of the Bolsheviks, the aircraft were reassembled and made operational once again. For his bravery and leadership, Kazakov was made a Major in the British Army and awarded the DSO.

In early September, an RAF 'ELOPE' Squadron was formed specifically for service at Archangel. South African Lieutenant Colonel Kenneth van der Spuy was given command of the new unit, likely because of his previous experience in command of air expeditions in remote areas such as the campaign in East Africa. Van der Spuy was given a freehand in selecting personnel from across the Commonwealth for the squadron:

> Among the officers selected by me were three South Africans, three Australians, two Canadians and a few men who had experience in the colonies and dominions. I included these because in my experience I had found that such men were well fitted to adapt themselves to strange and severe conditions. I was fortunate, on arrival in Archangel, to find a few more Colonials who, with the experience they had gained there, proved a great asset. I was fortunate, too, in obtaining the services of two officers who had been with Scott on his ill-fated expedition to the South Pole.[13]

Until spring 1919, the squadron was almost exclusively equipped with obsolete RE8 reconnaissance-bomber aircraft, although both Flight Commanders flew Sopwith Camels and later Sopwith Snipes for strafing.

One of the Canadians in the squadron, Lieutenant Frank Shrive, had been born in Northamptonshire but emigrated with his parents to Ontario in 1906. He had enlisted into the 129th Battalion, CEF, in January 1916 and was wounded by shrapnel on Vimy Ridge in June 1917. Whilst hospitalised

12 George Hill, *Go Spy the Land: Being the Adventures of IK8 of the British Secret Service* (London: Cassell & Co. 1932), p.104.
13 Major General K. van der Spuy, *Chasing the Wind* (Cape Town: Books of Africa, 1966), p.112.

in England recovering from his wounds he became intrigued by aircraft on training flights that would frequently buzz overhead. After recovering from his wounds Shrive volunteered for the Royal Flying Corps (RFC) and was duly accepted for training as an artillery observer, likely because of his experience as a gunner in France. On 5 September, Shrive made an entry in his diary:

> Well we got the news this morning, and it looks like being official. Six of us observers, all Canadian, are on a special assignment most likely to Russia. They also say Canadians have been chosen because we are going to a cold climate. Must be North Russia, but no one states this specifically.[14]

The squadron embarked on SS *Stephen* at Dundee on 21 September and steamed into the North Atlantic the same day. Although all officers had been sworn to secrecy with regards to their destination, the cab driver that took Shrive to the harbour seemed to know all about the North Russia expedition as he had spent all morning ferrying latecomers to the docks. It wasn't until he boarded the ship that Shrive finally met the rest of the squadron:

45. Russia's highest-scoring First World War ace Major Alexander Kazakov in uniform of the SBAC. (Alfred Carey Collection, Naval Air Museum, Nowra, NSW)

> We have had several meetings and have met our O.C., Colonel Van du Spey [sic], and also two captains who will be our flight commanders. There are thirty two R.A.F. Officers, who, we understand, will be divided into Headquarters, A Flight, and B Flight. Some of the observers, (about half) are from Blandford, while the remainder are Army and not known to us. None have flown on active service. The pilots, however, are a mixture of British, Canadian and South Africans; about half of them have seen active service.[15]

SS *Stephen* arrived at Archangel on 1 October, however the RAF men were confined to the ship and did not disembark until the following day. It was to be the last day that all members of 'ELOPE' Squadron would be in the same place at the same time:

> There are as far as we are concerned three fronts, the railway already mentioned, and due south of here; another on the River Dvina, a hundred or possibly more or less miles south of here; and a third at Pinega, which is to the east and somewhere behind those forests which I have mentioned. Eight of our officers are leaving for this Pinega front tomorrow.[16]

After a couple of weeks fitting out in Archangel, Shrive and 'B' Flight left for Bereznik on the Dvina River Front on 26 October. HQ at Archangel were so ill equipped at the time that the aircrew were not even issued the most basic items required of a squadron on active service, 'There are just no

---

14   Frank J. Shrive, *The Diary of a P.B.O. (Poor Bloody Observer)* (Erin, Ontario: Boston Mills Press, 1981), p.40.
15   *Ibid.*, p.42.
16   *Ibid.*, p.59.

46. Russian aircrew of No 1 (SBAC) Squadron, Bereznik aerodrome, summer 1919. Russian ace Alexander Kazakov is seated fourth from left and New Zealander Lieutenant Colonel Roderick Carr, RAF, seated to his left. (Alfred Carey Collection, Naval Air Museum, Nowra, NSW)

good maps, the only thing available being some pen and ink sketches which H.Q. has issued to us, but as for scale or any attempt at accuracy they are badly missing.'[17]

Eventually four RAF 'Squadrons' were formed locally in North Russia although their squadron numbers bore no connection to RAF Squadrons outside of Russia. The SBAC was formed as 'No. 1 Squadron' at Bereznik, as was RAF 'No. 3 Squadron' whilst the RAF Flight at Obozerskaya was designated 'No. 4 Squadron' and that at Pinega as 'No. 2 Squadron'.

Shrive's 'B' Flight (latterly No. 3 Squadron) RE8s were to precede the squadron personnel and would be waiting at Bereznik aerodrome when the barge carrying the observers and ground crew arrived. Whereas the trip from Archangel to Bereznik by air would take two hours, the barge would take four days in extremely cramped conditions, so tight that the officers had to 'hot bunk', sleeping in shifts. As it transpired, out only five of the six RE8s were able to complete the flight from Archangel to Bereznik. The aircraft flown by Lieutenant Grant, a Canadian formerly of Princess Patricia's Canadian Light Infantry (PPCLI), was forced down in a marsh by engine failure:

A cylinder blew right off the engine and as the engine jammed, the propeller broke up. Grant put the aircraft into a glide and landed in the first place he was able to, which was a marsh, but as it was fairly well frozen over he had no trouble. He stayed in the cockpit all night, but was picked up the next morning.[18]

Grant landed the RE8 in an inaccessible area and it was found impractical to recover the aircraft due to the thick snow and heavy forest. Instead, a team of fitters went out and recovered as much of the aircraft and engine as they could before leaving the airframe to the elements.

'B' Flight's barge arrived at Bereznik on 3 November and work immediately commenced to unload stores and equipment. Three days later, Shrive with pilot Lieutenant Tyley (a South African veteran of the campaign in East Africa) flew their first mission over Red Army lines:

17   *Ibid.*, p.62.
18   *Ibid.*

Tyley and I took off with eight Cooper (20lb) bombs and five machine gun drums. Our target was a town called Kotlas, some thirty miles across the line. When within ten miles of it we ran into thick cloud, so had to turn back. We dropped the bombs on some barges in the river, figuring that that might do a bit of harm. Neither Tyley nor I like the idea of bombing innocent civilians. We may of course change our thinking but for the moment we'd rather have military targets.[19]

Constructing 'B' Flight's airstrip near Bereznik on the banks of the River Dvina was not going to be a significant difficulty, the country was fairly open already, however at the home of 'A' Flight (latterly No. 4 Squadron) at Obozerskaya on the Railway Front, dense forests spread for many miles on either side of the railway. It took two weeks to cut a swath through the forest large enough for a short runway, so short in fact that the RE8s barely had enough room to take off with a full bomb load. Each side of the airstrip was fenced in by 100 foot tall pine trees on all sides making take-off and landings particularly tricky. Almost as soon as the axes and saws were downed, 'A' Flight became operational.

Life at the airfields was made easier by the presence of camp followers who helped out with duties around camp. Young boys, dubbed *malchiks* helped out around the train carriages being used as a barracks for the aircrew whilst older girls known as *barishynas* helped with laundry and in the kitchen. In return the men usually paid for their services with local roubles or cigarettes and gifts of food. In particular demand was tobacco, tea, sugar and flour, all commodities highly prized by the locals. Some of the Allied soldiers developed strong paternal bonds with the *malchiks* and *barishynas* and more than a few were formally adopted by soldiers who took the children with them back to England.

The limited hours of daylight in the northern latitudes during winter meant that the operational effectiveness of the RAF squadrons was severely limited. During November there was an average of eight hours daylight in 24 but by mid to late December it had fallen to four hours and the temperature well below zero. The RAF had their hands more than full just operating in the environment, let alone conducting offensive missions against the enemy.

The Armistice, signed on 11 November 1918, brought an end to four years of war between the Allied nations and Central Powers. Whilst their brothers in France and Belgium were celebrating the end of the war, some of the largest battles of the Allied military intervention were being fought around Tulgas on the Dvina. At the aerodrome at Bereznik, Armistice Day turned out to be rather memorable for Shrive and Tyley although for an entirely different reason.

Both men were taking off in an RE8 on a bombing mission armed with eight small 20 lb 'Cooper bombs' and one 200 lb bomb mounted between the undercarriage. In addition to the pilot, observer, machine gun and four drums of ammunition, the aircraft was at its maximum take-off weight. On take-off Shrive noticed that it was taking longer to become airborne than was usual. When the RE8 finally got off the ground it had exceeded the length of the relatively short airstrip and when only a few feet in the air the aircraft struck a large tree stump, knocking the left wheel clean off. Tyley regained control of the aircraft and shouted to Shrive, 'drop those bloody bombs!' Shrive pulled the left bomb lever only to discover that nothing happened, the four bombs under the left wing were stuck in place. He then tried the right lever and the other four Cooper bombs went whistling down to the earth below. 'Three exploded in the bush, but the first one landed in Headquarters yard, making a nice-sized hole and causing one hell of a panic there. They mistook us for Bolshie aircraft and started peppering us with machine gun fire.'[20] With the centre section wires damaged the wings became unstable and liable to snap. It was too risky for Tyley to bank the aircraft so he began a flat turn to the left which brought them out over the Dvina. Shrive took the opportunity to release the 200 lb bomb, 'When it hit the water, only a couple of hundred feet below us, we were lifted a good fifty feet by the explosion.'[21]

---

19   *Ibid.*, p.63.
20   *Ibid.*
21   *Ibid.*

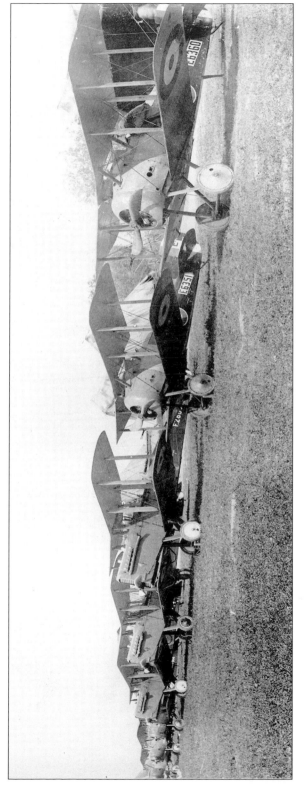

47. Sopwith Snipes and Airco DH9As on the flight line at Bereznik aerodrome, summer 1919. (Alfred Carey Collection, Naval Air Museum, Nowra, NSW)

Tyley flew the aircraft downriver for a couple of miles before turning into the wind to begin a descent towards the airfield. It was during the landing that Tyley demonstrated his skill as a pilot by touching down on the right wheel only: 'When no more than 10 feet from the ground, Tyley banked the machine sharply to the right. The right wing and wheel hit the ground at the same time and there was a sharp jolt, the prop shattered, and the engine nosed into the ground.'[22] The aircraft stopped so abruptly that Shrive's Lewis gun broke free of its mounting, striking him in the back. The four Cooper bombs still on board did not explode, the safety devices were fortunately intact and because of Tyley's skilful landing, the bombs never made contact with the ground. The right wing, right undercarriage and propeller were damaged beyond repair and the RE8 was cannibalised for spare parts for the other aircraft. Tyley and Shrive were immediately grounded but both men had their stories straight and said that the bombs had fallen off because of the initial collision with the stump and not because Shrive had pulled the release leaver whilst directly above the HQ building. As a result of the accident, 'Standing Orders' were issued that Cooper bombs were not to be carried in conjunction with larger bombs and vice versa as the landing strip was too short for error. 'The only real damage done, apart from the aircraft was the out-house at H.Q., which will require considerable remodelling.'[23]

On 10 November, No. 3 (Bereznik) Squadron was joined by Kazakov's flight of White Russian airmen and ground crew of the SBAC. Although the former members of the Imperial Russian Air Service would fly missions with RAF pilots and observers in RAF aircraft, the SBAC would not be officially members of the RAF and would retain their unique identity.

News of the Armistice reached the front on 12 November but it remained unclear to the soldiers, sailors and airmen exactly how the cessation of hostilities on the Western Front would affect them in Russia. Most servicemen in Russia were 'Hostilities Only', those that had either volunteered or been conscripted for the duration of the war. Now that the war with the Central Powers was over and no war had been declared by the British Government on Bolshevik Russia, many expected they would soon be recalled home. Shrive had no such illusions:

Captain Albu, our Flight Commander, has just called us together. He said I have some good news for you and also some which is not so good. First, an Armistice has been signed and the war is over. This took place at eleven a.m. yesterday. Now, he said, as far as he knew this would not affect the North Russian expedition and until further word was received we were to carry on according to orders. This second announcement did not surprise us much as we had discussed this probability quite often previously and were not too surprised.[24]

Missions continued to be flown and on 13 November bad news reached Bereznik:

Moffoot and Gordon did not return from a flight this morning. They were on a reconnaissance toward Kotlas. The weather had cleared over night. The C.F.A. at Kurgomen, which is a village at the front line, saw the R.E.8 pass over but did not see it return. Of course it is long past the time of its endurance and must be down in the forest somewhere; we hope it is this side of the line, but hardly think so as the troops which are on both sides of the river would have seen it.[25]

As the peoples of western Europe celebrated the Armistice, many in the NREF could not help but feel that they had been forgotten by the world, On 14 November, Shrive made the entry in his diary:

22   Ibid.
23   Ibid., p.64.
24   Ibid.
25   Ibid.

They are sure having a great time in London and all the big cities. There is never a mention of our little force up here; we sure seem to have been forgotten. When the excitement has settled down someone may remember us.[26]

Two days later Shrive found himself in the rear cockpit of an RE8 flown by Lieutenant Green, the usual observer having been stricken with the flu. The mission should have been an easy one: fly to a small village about 15 miles inside Bolshevik lines and bomb the house with a blue roof. A snow fall had covered the village overnight so Shrive decided to drop their bombs on some barges tied up at a nearby dock. Shrive also had orders to drop over enemy lines handfuls of propaganda leaflets nicknamed 'bumph'. Never having been on such a mission before, the Canadian believed that throwing handfuls of printed 'bumph' out of the observer's cockpit would have been quite simple. In practice it was much more dangerous than he first thought:

A lot of this paper junk caught in the slipstream, flew back and caught in the rudder control wires and Green groaned that his rudder would operate only one way. In other words we found ourselves doing wide circles, as the rudder was well jammed to starboard. The only solution was for me to crawl down the inside of the fuselage towards the tail of the aeroplane and, when I got as far as possible, punch a hole in the fabric and pull out the offending paper. This I did, but getting back to the cockpit was another matter, as my feet threatened to go through the bottom canvas, and to be honest I sure was scared. After what seemed an hour, only five minutes or less really, I managed to get back and touching Green on the shoulder, I said let's get the hell out of here, I've had enough. We made the aerodrome safely, but no more bumph dropping until a better method is devised.[27]

Subsequently 'bumph' was distributed from the air in cigarette packets complete with a single cigarette inside which was evidently a much safer method of delivery.

On 17 November, good news was received after Lieutenants George Moffoot and Robert Gordon walked into British lines at Kurgomen. Both men had badly frostbitten feet and lost a lot of weight during their four days behind enemy lines but were alive. Their aircraft had been hit by machine gun fire and forced down in a forest. Unable to set the aircraft fully alight before hearing Red troops approaching, the two men struggled through the snow until dark when they decided to stop and wait for sunrise in case they lost their direction in the dark and wasted the night walking around in circles in the dense forest. An old peasant was encountered the following morning who agreed to guide the two men to British lines and after a further 30 hours of hard trekking through the snow, both pilot and observer crossed over the line at Tulgas where a company of 2/10th Royal Scots were manning several blockhouses. Moffoot and Gordon were both subsequently awarded the DFC as much for their services in the air as their difficult escape on the ground.

By New Year's Eve the front lines had remained largely static since mid November and it seemed unlikely in the extreme climatic conditions that the Bolsheviks would attempt any offensive actions until at least the start of spring 1919. The Allied lines of blockhouses were well constructed, protected by trenches and barbed wire and relatively comfortable. It would take a well planned and executed offensive by a highly motivated enemy to eject the Allied troops from their positions. The Allied leadership in North Russia did not believe the Red Army capable of launching such an offensive in the midst of a brutal sub-Arctic winter. Not for the first time, they badly underestimated their opponent.

---

26   *Ibid.*, p.65
27   *Ibid.*, p.67.

8

Archangel: Railway Front September 1918–September 1919

No sooner had Archangel been captured, than the commissioning of an armoured train to support the advance southwards from Archangel along the Archangel–Vologda Railway commenced. The train was fitted out with a 3 inch howitzer and 2.5 inch gun in a forward carriage protecting the engine and two 3 inch howitzers and a naval 3 inch in an artillery carriage behind the engine. More than a dozen Lewis guns were also distributed across the carriages for use as protection against enemy infantry. The crew would be truly Allied in nature, 80 French 21st Colonial Battalion, 20 Slavo-British legionnaires, a small detachment of Polish gunners, one corporal and seven privates, Royal Marines, and one sergeant each from RFA and RGA.

Command of *Miles* as the train was christened (after an RFC pilot who had been killed on the Western Front) was given to Lieutenant Commander Edward Hilton Young, DSC, RNVR, a serving Member of Parliament who had seen more of the war than many of his naval contemporaries. Enlisting into the RNVR in August 1914, Young had served on HMS *Iron Duke* with the Grand Fleet during the first year of the war before being appointed as Rear Admiral Troubridge's mission to the Danube in 1915, the same year he was elected in absentia as Member of Parliament for Norwich. Young served most of the war with the Royal Navy Siege Guns in France and Flanders before participating in the Zeebrugge Raid on HMS *Vindictive*, where he was severely wounded in the arm, necessitating its amputation.

The armoured train left Archangel on the night of 17 August and fought its first engagement the following day near *Verst* Post 493 (VP493) when *Miles* came face to face with a Bolshevik contemporary whilst round a bend in the line. Young recalled:

> Our howitzer cracked five seconds before the enemy's gun, and our shell burst visibly amongst the trees just beyond him; his shrieked over us again. We were advancing slowly in order to make it more difficult for him, and he was stationary. The little howitzer was proving very handy, and we were firing faster than he; the splitting cracks at my ear were gaining on the rose coloured flashes that kept on leaping from the little black box at the end of the straight. 'It wont last long at this short range' I thought. His next shell burst on the line a couple of hundred yards ahead of us, and ours burst on the line by his side. Two more of ours went there close beside him, and then he decided that it would not do.[1]

This was perhaps the first time in history that British forces fought an engagement between armoured trains. There was no time for self congratulation however as an enemy field gun opened fire but withdrew after only six rounds. Believing that there were enemy infantry lurking in the tree line, Young ordered the Slavo-British Lewis gunners to open fire:

> At the sound of my whistle the twelve Lewis guns burst into a deafening uproar. Firing them had the charm of novelty for the young Russians, and they made the best of it. The din rose in wave on wave of uproar, and at once there came an answering crackle of brisk rifle fire from the forest ahead and on either side of us. Most of the bullets passed whistling overhead, but now and then one hit the cars or the engine

---

1   E. Hilton Young, *By Sea and Land: Some Naval Doings* (London: T.C. & E.C. Jack, 1920), pp.320–321.

48. Royal Engineers assembling 'M' gas bombs on the airstrip at Obozerskaya. The tree line beyond the airstrip gives some indication of the dense forest which covered much of North Russia. (Public domain)

with a whack. 'Heaven protect the steam pipes,' I thought. Suddenly there came a terrific flash and smack from No. 2 car, behind the engine. 'Hit!' I thought; 'No. 2 is knocked out. Is the line fouled?' But it was not a hit on No. 2; it was my garrison gunner sergeant, Halwell, who was captain of No. 2 car, joining in the fray with the little Vickers gun, firing it through the trees at the sound of the Bolshevik rifles.[2]

Having pushed as far forward as was sensible without infantry support, Young gave orders to steam back up the line to safety. For his gallantry during this engagement, Young recommended Sergeant Edward Halwell, RFA, for the Military Medal.

In early October the Polish detachment were recalled to Archangel and replaced by 20 gunners from the newly arrived 16th Brigade (68th Battery served on the railway and 67th Battery on the Dvina), CFA under Lieutenant Sydney Evans, DCM, who brought with them a rail mounted 18 pdr.

With the Canadian gunners on board, the advance was resumed down the line and a further engagement fought on 14 October with entrenched enemy supported by artillery. Young recalled the engagement:

Evans' 18-pounder leaped and cracked like a machine gun; the range was so short that the crash of the lyddite shell as it burst followed close on the crack of the gun. The howitzers behind were playing on the trench on the right, the Lewis gunners were sweeping the edges of the wood. There was a row of telegraph poles by the side of the line, and at one report of the 18-pounder I saw three or four of them snap and topple over like nine-pins…I caught sight of a barricade on the line ahead, level with the enemy's trench. Evans was bursting his shells right and left of it, where the Bolshevik machine guns were, making with his one gun a perfect storm of lyddite … We had rolled to within a hundred yards of his trench, still crashing and hammering, when we heard at last a feeble spurt of rifle-fire, and immediately afterwards we saw dimly, at the far ends of the trench, a few scattered parties running away at full speed into the woods. We reached the barricade still hammering, stopped, and went astern … When my whistle could make itself heard above the clamour of the Lewis guns the train ceased fire and we waited, all eyes on the trench, in a silence that was tangible after the deafening noise … there was no movement from the enemy's trench.[3]

Simultaneous to the push down the line by the armoured train, a combined force of French and US troops had been making their way through the forest to attack the Bolshevik positions at VP455 from the flank. Second Lieutenant Guy Chantrill (a General List interpreter with 'ELOPE' Force) had previously made a reconnaissance of the enemy positions far behind enemy lines and volunteered to lead the US troops ('I' and 'M' Companies, US 339th Infantry Regiment) through the forest to their objective. The attack failed but Chantrill was awarded the MC for his work.

By 17 October, the train had pushed as far forward as VP444 north of Emtsa where the line was badly broken. With neither Bolshevik nor Allied armoured train able to advance any further, the two trains spent the following three days fighting an artillery duel back and forth. Corrections for guns on board the Allied train were provided by 2nd Lieutenant Herbert Collison, RFA, who had climbed a telegraph pole with a field telephone. Thanks to his corrections, direct hits were scored, driving the enemy train further down the line.

In addition to the duel between the two trains, a series of confused battles were fought up and down the line between the French infantry and Bolshevik troops, each side advancing and retreating over the same ground several times. On one occasion Collison had the nerve-wracking experience of sitting atop a telegraph pole whilst Bolshevik scouts ran by below without spotting the British officer perched above their heads. For his work during the day's fighting Collison was awarded the MC and on the recommendation of Major M.J. Donoghue, US 339th Infantry Regiment, the US Distinguished Service Cross.

In conjunction with two companies of US troops which had arrived from fighting further up the line, the Allied armoured train resumed the advance to cover the work of US rail troops as they worked to repair the line. By the end of the day the line was repaired and Young ordered the train forward:

Coming round the corner in the twilight, we had a glimpse of the dark square of the enemy's train, visible for a second between wreaths of smoke that were rising from buildings burning in the station. Evans at the 18-pounder got his shot in first, and pluckily keeping his crew in action at their exposed gun in spite of a sharp rifle-fire, he drove back the train, and so plastered the defences of the clearing with lyddite that the heart went out of the enemy's resistance.[4]

In recognition of their gallant services on the armoured train during the period 14–17 October, Young recommended both Evans and fellow Canadian Gunner William Birkett for the MC and DCM respectively. Birkett would go on to be awarded a DCM Bar for gallantry in March the following year when he ran into no man's land under fire to retrieve a message from a fallen runner.

A week later orders were received to halt the advance, consolidate and make preparations to construct a winter defence line with a forward chain of blockhouses at VP444 and an advanced base at VP454 and headquarters at Obozerskaya. With no further role for the Allied armoured train during the winter, Young was returned home in December to be awarded a DSO for his command of the train to add to a DSC earned with the Royal Navy siege guns in France. Young went on to a successful career in politics and business, being knighted in 1927 before his death in 1960 aged 81.

The Seletskoe detachment of two 18 pdrs from 68th Battery, CFA, arrived in the village of the same name on 10 October and proceeded south for 21 *versts* to the village of Mejnovskaya where they were met by Lieutenant John McRae of the same battery who had gone ahead to arrange billets,

---

3   *Ibid.*, pp.355–356.
4   *Ibid.*, p.359.

49. A North Russia blockhouse, this example manned by Australian machine gunners of 201st MGC on the Railway Front, summer 1919. Note the Australian flags draped over the front of the blockhouse and flying on a flagpole behind. (Author's collection)

arriving there three days later. The Allies were attempting to push south-west to the Emtsa River towards the railway and south down the Mekhrenga River to Tarasova.

On 5 December 1918, 'D' Company, 17th Battalion, Liverpool Regiment (Captain E. A. Dickson) at Tarasova received word from a Red deserter that the Bolsheviks were preparing to attack early the following morning. Dickson decided that rather than wait for the attack, he would take his company forward and surprise the enemy in their assembly positions.

With 30 Russian partisans acting as scouts, two officers and 76 other ranks of 'D' Company left Tarasova at 2215 that same night and after a 16 *verst* trek through the forest took up positions behind the chain of enemy blockhouses which were attacked and captured in turn without loss to the Liverpools, the enemy suffering seven men killed and four taken prisoner.

The party went on to set an ambush along the Tarasova–Kochmas road and lay in wait until 0800 when an enemy convoy of 18 limbers and three field kitchens were observed travelling in the direction of Kochmas. The trap was sprung and the entire convoy taken intact, several of the drivers being killed in the initial burst of fire and an additional three prisoners taken. On inspection the limbers were found to contain supplies as well as two Maxim machine guns and thousands of rounds of ammunition.

Enemy snipers forced the ambushers back into the safety of the forest where they pushed forward to the enemy supply dump at Kochmas which was attacked and captured after a stiff fight in which the determined enemy defenders suffered a number of casualties. Despite being only a single *verst* from the main enemy positions and increasing enemy resistance, Dickson was determined to push forward as rapidly as possible but by 1030 the company was held up by heavy machine gun and rifle fire within 120 yards of the enemy line, estimated to be held by 600 enemy.

'D' Company's firepower was significantly reduced with all Lewis guns out of action as a result of snow freezing working parts, which broke under the stress of extended firing. By 1145 ammunition was running low and Dickson gave the order to withdraw into the forest, taking with them five horses, two machine guns and seven prisoners, but not before shooting the 38 horses captured from the convoy and at the supply dump at Kochmas. The enemy hotly pursued the Liverpools into the forest and it was found impossible to get the pack horses away so the two captured Maxim guns were quickly stripped and the parts thrown into the undergrowth.

The battle had not been all one sided and on return to Tarasova the Liverpools counted their casualties. Sergeant Percy Greany, MM, had been carried in critically wounded and died shortly after whilst Privates Charles Ainsworth, Robert Brown, James Houghton, Alfred Owens and Henry Turner had all been killed and 2nd Lieutenant A. Cousins, MM, and four other ranks wounded. Another man had been separated from the column during the retreat and was missing but subsequently stumbled out of the forest, exhausted but alive.

On 30 December, 'D' Company was again in action attacking an enemy trench system on the Tarasova–Kochmas road. One section of Liverpools reached a point just 80 yards from the enemy trench but had to withdraw due to the refusal of the Archangel Regiment troops to advance. Private Ben Sugden was killed during the attack, his body carried back to Tarasova by his platoon mates.

Little fighting took place on the Railway Front during the first weeks of January, both sides preferring to remain relatively comfortable in their blockhouses rather than carrying out any offensive operations. It is likely during this period that the Bolshevik strength on the Railway Front was significantly reduced to provide further troops for the successful Bolshevik offensive against Shenkursk on the Vaga later in the same month.

The only significant actions to take place in the New Year were a series of attacks on Tarasova during the period 24–29 January 1919. After repeatedly and determinedly attacking the village through the snow, on 29 January the Bolsheviks broke through the outer line of blockhouses and opened fire with rifles and machine guns from only 200 yards range. In one of the blockhouses, Private Edward Crook, 252nd MGC, kept his Vickers machine gun in action continuously over the four days of attacks, repulsing three attempts by the enemy to capture the position. Crook remained at his post until almost overrun before getting his section away safely for which he was awarded the DCM.

Battery Sergeant Major (BSM) Charles Grayson, 'C' Mountain Battery, RGA, was awarded the DCM for actions on the same day for withdrawing a howitzer in difficult circumstances from a position where it was threatened by the enemy whilst Lieutenant Edward Toms, 252nd MGC, was awarded the MC for taking command of a Vickers gun on which the No. 1., Private William Lyne, had been killed and another wounded on 25 January.

On 7 February 1919, 'B' Company, 17th Liverpools with a detachment of Royal Marines from the Russian Allied Naval Brigade, 252nd MGC, a detachment of trench mortars and a company of French and Russian troops, attacked the enemy-held village of Kodish under covering fire from 421st Battery, RFA. The plan was for the French force to advance through the forest and attack Kodish from the rear, capture the enemy field guns and push through the village from the south whilst the Liverpools and Marines would proceed through the forest to rendezvous with the White Russians near the Kodish road junction. The Russian troops would then make a diversionary attack whilst the Marines moved into position to coordinate their attack with the French to the south.

Enemy scouts detected the Liverpools and Marines moving through the forest and Bolshevik artillery began to shell the approaches to the village, one shell landing on the RAMC aid post, killing Sergeant William Tombler and wounding for a second time a Marine who was having his wounds dressed and the Liverpools' CSM.

A veteran of the Western Front from the Battle of Loos in September 1915, Private Riley Rudd was serving with the RAMC detachment in the attack and recorded in his diary:

Got nearly into Kodish and heard tremendous firing ahead. Bullets were coming our way very plentifully. Lt. Hopkinson, K.L.R., came running down the road, told us the men were being attacked on their left by a strong force and were withdrawing to the river … At 12th verst pole they [Royal Marines] met with two block-houses which held them off and wounded many. The men were too exhausted to continue

50. Brigadier Arthur Turner, CMG, DSO, RA, Commanding Allied Forces, Railway Front 1918–19. (IWM Q73485)

or to capture the block-houses. Then they were attacked on their left flank and had to retire to avoid being cut off from the river.[5]

A section of seven French troops detailed to capture the two enemy field guns firing from the far side of the village got to within 20 yards of the battery position before being spotted, the enemy gunners fired two rounds at point blank range, both of which flew overhead. The Frenchmen stormed the positions, put the guns out of action and captured two horses, three of the seven men being wounded in the process by fire from the guns of 421st Battery, RFA. The village was captured and in Allied hands by 0820, however both captured guns had to be spiked and abandoned due to a strong counter-attack by Red troops from the neighbouring village of Auda.

In the meantime the Royal Marines attack on the right flank had been held up at *Verst* Post 12 by two blockhouses which could not be bypassed, causing a number of casualties. The enemy counter-attacked from the left, forcing the Marines to withdraw under covering fire of the British artillery to avoid being cut off from the river. The Marines became stranded in the forest and there were fears that they had been cut off and captured en masse until they began arriving in British lines several hours later.

During the attack, 2nd Lieutenant Eric Stevenson (attached to the Liverpools from the Yorkshire Regiment) was last seen to have been severely wounded but could not be evacuated due to the volume of enemy fire. He was reported missing but subsequently confirmed killed although his body was never recovered, nor was that of 19-year-old Private William Graham, killed in the same attack. An additional four men were also wounded and Private 'Jock' Baxter of the Royal Marines reported missing although he walked back into Allied lines two days later.

Major Oliver Body of 421st Battery, RFA was awarded the DSO for his command of the howitzers during the battle and for making a personal reconnaissance under fire to locate the enemy, whilst Lieutenant John Peter, a doctor attached to 17th Liverpools from RAMC, was awarded the MC for attending wounded under heavy fire and organising the evacuation of stretcher cases on sleighs. Privates Frederick Bolton, Harry Gingell and David Welsh of the Royal Marines were also awarded MMs for the attack.

Sergeant James Howarth of 'B' Company, 17th Liverpools was recommended by Major M.J. Donoghue of US 339th Infantry Regiment for an award for defending two advanced posts with 30 men for seven hours under heavy rifle and machine gun fire. Remarkably, Howarth led his men out of the relative safety of their position to counter-attack the enemy head-on with Mills grenades. It was only when he discovered that the enemy outnumbered his own small force by five to one that he ordered his men to withdraw and was the last man to cross the Emtsa River to the British front line.

5   IWM: 4615/81/21/1, Diary of Private R. Rudd.

Equally remarkably, Howarth had previously been recommended by Donoghue for recognition for his gallantry in an action near Kodish exactly four months prior on 7 October 1918, when Howarth led a series of attacks on a fortified line of blockhouses, exposing himself to the enemy to better direct the fire of a Lewis gun crew covering the withdrawal of the wounded. For his gallantry in action in North Russia, Howarth was awarded both the DCM and MM, one of very few British servicemen to be twice decorated for service in North Russia, and also awarded the US Distinguished Service Cross, the highest award the US could confer on a foreign soldier.

Another recommendation was made by Major Donoghue for the failed attack on Kodish, that to Captain Richard Smyrden, 17th Liverpools who rallied a group of retreating Russian troops and with his own company counter-attacked and reestablished the original firing line. Smyrden then led an attack against the enemy driving them back into the line of blockhouses. For his gallantry and leadership, Smyrden was also awarded the US DSC.

A company of 1st (Dyer's) Battalion, Slavo-British Legion under its new commander, Lieutenant Colonel Barrington Clement Wells, DSO, Essex Regiment, performed with distinction during the attack on Kodish attached to 17th Liverpools. The Russian legionnaires were awarded one DCM and four MMs for bravery in the attack. Initial signs had not been good when the legionnaires had first been attached to the Liverpools in December, four deserted to the enemy and another 25 were arrested on suspicion of being sympathetic to the Bolsheviks. The legionnaires redeemed themselves during the Red Army offensive of January 1919 when one sergeant and nine men held out to the death in a blockhouse until they were overrun.

Two days after the failed attack on Kodish, at 0430 on the morning of 9 February, the enemy opened up a heavy bombardment on the 'B' Company blockhouses on the extreme right and left of the British positions at Seletskoe, before attacking in force. The attack on the western most blockhouse was driven off with heavy losses but at the eastern most position the enemy managed to storm the blockhouse, killing six men.

The Bolshevik attack on 'B' Company at Seletskoe had been timed to coincide with a concurrent attack on 'D' Company further south at Shred Mekhrenga. Patrols from 'D' Company had encountered a strong enemy force the previous day and had been forced to withdraw to the safety of their blockhouse defences post haste. 'D' Company drove off the enemy attack inflicting heavy casualties without loss to themselves.

On 9 February, Red Artillery bombarded Shred Mekhrenga all day until late afternoon when enemy infantry were seen advancing along the frozen river in preparation to attack. Of the eight blockhouses protecting approaches to the village, the enemy captured three (despite accurate supporting fire from the guns of 68th Battery, CFA) but were driven from them by the Liverpools' counter-attack. Miraculously, despite the large volume of fire during the attack and counter-attack, there had been no 'D' Company fatalities.

On 21 February a Sopwith Strutter of No. 1 (SBAC) Squadron flying out of Bereznik aerodrome piloted by Lieutenant P. Kravetz (SBAC) with Irish-born Canadian Observer Lieutenant Noel Nunan, RAF, was forced down (either due to enemy fire or engine failure) on a reconnaissance mission over Onega. Both aircrew survived the forced landing but were subsequently shot by Red troops, Kravetz was killed outright and Nunan died of wounds three days later.

On 31 March 1919, Lieutenant Francis Tattam, RAF, accompanied by wireless operators J.E. Johnson and McCardle were ambushed on the road from Obozerskaya to forward positions at Bolshie Ozerki where they were to have acted as wireless operators for an artillery shoot. Tattam was wounded, Johnson killed outright and McCardle mortally wounded. Left for dead, a British patrol found McCardle some time later and rushed him to the field hospital at Obozerskaya where he succumbed to his wounds the following day aged just 19. Johnson and McCardle were buried next to each other in the small churchyard at Obozerskaya, their graves since lost to time. Both men are commemorated in the Archangel Allied Cemetery. The wounded Tattam was taken prisoner and

51. South African North Russia Relief Force volunteer Private Estcourt Cresswell-George wearing MGC collar badges and the distinctive white star on navy blue background shoulder insignia of the NRRF. (Author's collection)

endured months of incarceration in Moscow before release in a prisoner exchange the following year.

During the period 15–17 March, 13th Yorkshires (which had been transferred from the Dvina River to the Railway Front less 'D' Company) were in action supported by 4.5 inch howitzers of 'Right Section' 421st Battery, RFA (Major O. G. Body, RFA, Lieutenant H. P. Hart, RFA and 58 other ranks) defending Shred Mekhrenga from a series of Bolshevik attacks. For actions during one particularly heavy attack on 17 March, Captain Maurice McCall and Lieutenant Charles Jameson were awarded the MC and Sergeant E. McLaughlin the DCM.

On 19 March, a party of 50 NCOs and men dubbed 'Special Company', 13th Yorkshires under Lieutenant Walter Butteriss (including 2nd Lieutenant Arthur Morrall attached from Leicestershire Regiment) and Lieutenant John Holroyd-Sergeant) were attached for service with their sister battalion, 6th Yorkshires near Bolshie Ozerki. The town had been earlier captured by the Red Army from a unit of French troops as an attempt by the Bolsheviks to cut the overland supply route from Murmansk to Archangel.

On 23 March, 'A', 'B' and 'C' Companies, 6th Yorkshires with 'Special Company', 13th Yorkshires and 'H' Company, US 339th Infantry Regiment attacked Bolshie Ozerki. The US troops were to attack first and extend to the south side of the road whilst 'C' Company, 6th Yorkshires would extend to the northern side and form up with the attacking Americans. The village was bombarded by three French 75 mm guns firing from the direction of Obozerskaya from 0700 to 0900 when the infantry attack commenced. The US troops immediately came under fire from a blockhouse as they extended to the northern side of the road instead of the southern side as planned. This left Captain Frank Parker with no option but to take his 'C' Company to the southern side which was more exposed that the Americans' position.

Parker led the company from 50 yards in front as the sniper and machine gun fire intensified. Up to his waist in snow he turned around and rallied his men, 'Come on boys; their bullets are going over our heads … come on Yorkshires.' As the company advanced Parker called for Lewis guns to come forward, Corporal Fred Hearfield and Lance Corporal Isaac Rhodes responded and went forward with their guns.

The enemy could be seen moving amongst the blockhouses and trees: Hearfield attempted to provide suppressing fire but found his Lewis gun to be frozen and unworkable so sent it back and took up a rifle. Rhodes was slightly more successful and used his Lewis gun to some effect by standing in the deep snow and firing the weapon from the shoulder.

The Bolsheviks lowered their fire and began causing casualties amongst the attackers, Captain Parker was fatally shot in the head and chest and Lance Corporal Rhodes mortally wounded. Second Lieutenant Frederick March, MM, took command of the company but could advance no further due

52. Second Lieutenant Frederick March, MC, MM, 6th Battalion, Yorkshire Regiment, awarded the MC for leadership during the 23rd March 1919 attack on Bolshie Ozerki after his company commander had been killed. (Author's collection)

to the volume of enemy fire, and unable to bring any effective return fire due to the rifles being clogged with snow and the Lewis guns jammed and at risk of being enveloped by the enemy he had no choice but to issue orders to gather the wounded and withdraw.

Corporal Hearfield and Private Lloyd attempted to recover Captain Parker's body but as soon as Hearfield reached the body the volume of fire from two nearby machine guns intensified and made recovery of the body impossible. Unable to drag the gallant captain out of the line of fire through the deep snow, Hearfield was only able to recover his commander's belt, revolver, haversack, fur hat and wrist watch. Hearfield shouted to Lloyd, 'Don't come on, we cannot do it – make a run for it.'[6] Both men managed to rejoin the company although Lloyd was twice wounded in the headlong rush. The wounded were evacuated on stretchers over the snow, the battalion chaplin Reverend Wilfred Brown acting as a stretcher bearer dragging wounded through the snow and dressing their wounds, bravery for which he was awarded the MC.

In addition to the loss of Captain Parker, Lieutenant Howard Hart and Lance Corporal Isaac Rhodes were killed and a further 16 men wounded and two missing. Second Lieutenant March was awarded the Military Cross for taking command of the company and the skillful withdrawal, the same award being granted to Lieutenant Walter Butteriss to add to an MM awarded with the Leicestershire Regiment on the Western Front.

Orders were issued for the attack to be resumed the following morning but protests were made amongst the Yorkshires that they had not had a hot meal since they left Onega and had only had some hot tea brought up by the YMCA. Their rations were frozen and inedible and the men were exhausted. The company was withdrawn to Chinova which they reached at midnight, having marched 245 miles in 10 days and fought the action at Bolshie Ozerki. The following day 68 men of the company reported sick through exhaustion.

'D' Company of the 6th Yorkshires had been detached away from the battalion for service on the Dvina and at Pinega and had taken part in an assault on the hamlet of Zemstovo on 25 March. Heavy machine gun fire and deep snow conspired against the attackers who were forced to withdraw with their casualties under fire. For gallantry and determination during the attack and in evacuating casualties, Lieutenant George Richardson was awarded the MC and CSM William Rutter and Sergeant Ernest Harrison the DCM. The Yorkshires lost Sergeant Arthur Newton and

---

6   *The Yorkshire Post*, Wednesday, 15 October 1919.

Private Reginald Best killed and three men wounded. A number of men suffered frostbite during the withdrawal and had to be evacuated to hospital at Archangel. By the end of the month the thaw had set in and the snow-covered and frozen ground became increasingly marshy and difficult to traverse, and a further attack on Zemstovo planned for 27 March was abandoned.

On 2nd April another attempt was made to capture Bolshie Ozerki by 'A' and 'C' Companies with 'B' Company in reserve, but was again repulsed with the loss of Captain Tom Bailey (who would be posthumously awarded the MC for the attack on 23 March) and Private Herbert Clayton killed and Lieutenant C.W. Goodlass, 2nd Lieutenant Oscar Barkes, 2nd Lieutenant Frederick March, MM (who lost both feet), CSM Jarrett and nine other ranks wounded and an additional two men missing. Lieutenants Charles Marshall and Ashton Mills both distinguished themselves during the action, Marshall for going back 300 yards under fire to retrieve two Lewis guns and Mills for defending his position for five hours against repeated enemy attacks, preventing his company from being cut off, for which both men were awarded the MC.

Second Lieutenant Robert Dodds, RE Signals, was also awarded an MC for his work maintaining signals communication under fire during the period 23 March–2 April, to add to a DCM and MM received for service on the Western Front. Dodds would be serving as OC Signals at Onega at the time of the White Russian mutiny in July and would spend the remainder of his time in Russia in Moscow as a prisoner of war until his release in a prisoner exchange in March 1920.

On 3 April a large Bolshevik force attacked 'D' Company, 6th Yorkshires' positions at Shred Mekhrenga isolating a forward post held by 2nd Lieutenant Morrall and 15 men on the Alexandrova road. With just two Lewis guns and rifles, Morrall and his men kept an estimated 500 Red troops at bay for three hours before being forced to flee towards a blockhouse. In the meantime, reinforcements under Lieutenant Holroyd-Sergeant were making their way forward and encountered Morrall's party fleeing in the opposite direction. The Bolsheviks were close on the heels of the retreating Britons and opened fire on the relieving force from both flanks, but the fire was inaccurate and Morrall and Holroyd-Sergeant were able to withdraw with the loss of Corporal Alfred Beak and Privates John Bates and Arthur Morrell, both officers being subsequently awarded the MC; Private P. Hughes received the DCM for good work with a Lewis gun preventing the party from being cut off.

On 5 April, the Bolsheviks resumed their attack on the village but were held off for 13 hours by blockhouses manned by 'A' and 'B' Companies. It was touch and go for much of the engagement until the arrival of two platoons from 'D' Company from Seletskoe turned the battle in favour of the British. Over 100 enemy dead were recovered from in front of the British blockhouses and 80 prisoners captured including the Red battalion commander. Fortuitously, the Yorkshires suffered no fatal casualties.

Sergeant G.A. Hay, RAMC, was awarded the DCM for his work organising a party of stretcher bearers and leading them under heavy fire to collect wounded, being credited with the saving of several lives. Corporal Harry Byart of 421st Battery directed fire from the village church tower during the attack, being credited with single handed playing a significant role in breaking up the attack, for which he was awarded the MM.

Simultaneous to the attack on Shred Mekhrenga, the Bolsheviks made a much larger attack on the 13th Yorkshires' garrison at Seletskoe but walked directly into a trap. Private Riley Rudd, RAMC, recorded in his diary:

At 4.30 am. This morning, Bolo made his long threatened attack in force, after a heavy artillery bombardment. However we must have had information of a reliable nature from the prisoners taken yesterday and were prepared. The result was that the Bolo came a disastrous cropper. Our fellows let him get through our wire and up to the blockhouses, which they, by pre-arranged plan temporarily left and then opened fire with machine guns and rifles from their rear and both sides and in front. Being fired at from all sides completely nonplussed Bolo, who could see he was in a trap from which there was no

53. Australian NRRF volunteers guard captured Red Army troops after
the attack on Emtsa, 29 August 1919. (Author's collection)

escape. The net result was annihilation for the Bolos, the machine guns doing terrible executions. It was calculated that 200 were killed and wounded … 125 prisoners taken. Bolos total losses being about 350. This in one hour's action![7]

Including casualties and prisoners taken in the failed attack on Shred Mekhrenga, the Bolsheviks had lost 500 men in a single day.

On 17 April, word was received that the Bolsheviks had abandoned Bolshie Ozerki, 6th Yorkshires moving to occupy the village the following day. By the end of spring 1919, the frequency of Bolshevik attacks on Bolshie Ozerki petered out and virtually ceased although both sides remained active patrolling along the Alexandrova road. Occasionally, British and Red Army patrols encountered each other resulting in brief but fierce skirmishes. During the night of 8–9 June, 2nd Lieutenant James Ellis of the 'Special Company', 13th Yorkshires led a combined British–Russian patrol to attack Bolshevik positions near Alexandrova. Despite a gallant effort by Ellis to capture an enemy position with only eight men, the attack failed due to the withdrawal of the White Russian flanking party.

On 15 June, Ellis was in command of a patrol of 12 other ranks which encountered a company strength enemy patrol in the forest estimated to be 100 men strong. The Bolsheviks attacked and for three hours Ellis led his small patrol in a running fight until reaching the safety of the British lines at Bolshie Ozerki, for which Ellis was awarded the MC.

The 13th Yorkshires spent most of the remainder of June on garrison duties at Shred Mekhrenga and saw no further action and in July received orders to return to Archangel to embark for a troopship home the following month. Their sister battalion 6th Yorkshires departed North Russia a month later in early September.

The execution of Slavo-British Legion mutiny ringleaders at Troitsa on the Dvina in early July did nothing to avert a far more serious mutiny of White Russian troops at Onega two weeks later on 20th July 1919. Two days prior to the insurrection, No. 2 Company of 5th North Russian Rifles had been

---

7   IWM: 4615/81/21/1, Diary of Private R. Rudd.

sent forward to defend a length of railway track after two lines of White Russian trenches had been captured by the Bolsheviks. The company commander left the position to visit British Headquarters and whilst absent Bolshevik agitators used the opportunity to execute a planned mutiny that night, arresting the White Russian officers in their beds. The battalion was distributed throughout several small villages and it was not until the afternoon that the mutineers captured local HQ and with it several British officers, one of whom, Captain George Roupell, VC, East Surrey Regiment, serving as Staff Captain to Brigadier Turner (Roupell was reputedly the only officer in the British Army allowed to wear a beard by special permission of King George), was unlucky enough to have been visiting Onega at the time of the mutiny. Roupell recalled:

> I noticed considerable activity in one or two parts of the village down below me; soldiers fully armed running about in a rather excited way, a shot was fired and it dawned on me that this was perhaps the beginning of trouble and perhaps a mutiny of the local White Russian troops ... My suspicions were confirmed when I saw one or two Russian officers being led off under arrest ... I was surrounded by a party of what looked like comic-opera brigands: they wore their army uniform and had armed themselves with every sort of weapon which they could find; the chief brigand had a rifle slung over his shoulder, a revolver in his hand, bandoliers of ammunition and, slung on his belt a number of hand grenades; if the situation had not been so serious it would have been comic, but the humour of it did not really appeal to me at that moment.[8]

In his diary, Sergeant John Kelly, one of nine Australian Imperial Force officers and NCOs despatched to North Russia in 1918 as part of 'ELOPE' Force, wrote of the mutiny at Chekevo village south of Onega:

> The first to go down was one of our well liked Aussie officers, Captain Brown. Before they got him though he accounted for six of the Bolshies. It would seem therefore that Captain Brown was doomed to die in Russia as it was highly unlikely that he would have stood by and watched this slaughter without a fight and there is no doubt in my mind the Reds would not have spared him.[9]

Captain Allan Brown was the only serving member of the AIF to be killed in Russia during the Allied military intervention period. Brown had enlisted in the AIF in August 1914 and served at Gallipoli where he was wounded before arriving in France in 1916 where he was again wounded at Messines in 1917. Brown was posthumously twice Mentioned in Despatches and awarded the Imperial Russian Orders of St. Anne and St. Stanislaus by the Provisional Government. He was the last serving AIF soldier to be killed in action.

After the capture of the British and Russian officers, the remaining White Russian units in the region including a machine gun detachment, machine gun training school, cavalry detachment, supply and medical units, all joined the mutineers and occupied Onega for the Bolsheviks. In apparently coordinated attempts it was discovered that 6th North Russian Rifles on the Railway Front and 7th North Russian Rifles at Seletskoe were also planning to revolt but the plot was discovered and both units withdrawn from the line. The events of July 1919 proved beyond doubt that Bolshevik infiltration of the North Russian forces was endemic.

The loss of Onega was a significant strategic setback for Ironside. The town was a vital overland link between NREF commands at Murmansk and Archangel and if the Red Army pushed eastwards from Onega they would threaten to flank Archangel itself. If the Bolsheviks pushed westward they

8   IWM: 12008 PP/MCR/56, Private Papers of G.R.P. Roupell.
9   AWM: PR/85/324, 419/31/50, Memoirs of John Kelly.

would threaten Maynard's lines of communication at Soroka. It was critical that Onega be recaptured immediately.

On 23 July 1919, monitor *M.26* (Lieutenant Commander Arthur Fawssett, RN) commenced bombarding Onega just as the Bolsheviks were marching the remaining British prisoners out of the town. Some of the shells landed very close to the prisoners causing the Bolshevik guards to scatter, giving the captives just enough time to escape and flee towards the docks in the confusion. On board *M.26* the escaped prisoners could be seen waving frantically from ashore and a boat was sent to rescue them. One of those rescued was Lieutenant Colonel Cecil Uniacke, RA, who would be awarded the OBE for his services in North Russia, including his leadership during the escape.

A combined force comprising RFA gunners, Royal Fusiliers of the newly arrived 2nd (Sadleir-Jackson's) Brigade, North Russia Relief Force, a naval landing party and Russian troops was assembled to attempt an amphibious assault and recapture of Onega. The composition of the force was as follows:

Monitor HMS *M.24*	Lieutenant Edward Grayston, RNR
Monitor HMS *M.26*	Lieutenant Commander Arthur Fawssett, RN
Tug *Alku* (naval landing party)	Lieutenant Robert McNair, DSC, RNR
HMS *Walton Belle* (Russian troops)	Lieutenant Ernest King, DSC, RNR
Barge *Keret* (Royal Fusiliers, 443rd Battery, RFA)	Major Douglas Campion, RGA
Details 45th & 46th Battalion, Royal Fusiliers	2nd Lieutenant Robert Nason, Argyll & Sutherland Highlanders

In the early afternoon of 1 August, Fawssett led the force into the mouth of the Onega River under covering fire of the guns of *M.26* and *M.24*. At 1312 the tug *Alku*, under the command of Lieutenant Robert McNair, RNR (who had been awarded the DSC for command of a gun barge on the Dvina River the previous year) reached the quay followed two minutes later by paddle steamer HMS *Walton Belle* commanded by Lieutenant Ernest King, DSC, RNR. Both vessels were made fast on the quay, *Belle* putting ashore a party under Captain Moir to clear approaches to the quay, but the Russians on board refused to disembark and no amount of coaxing could get them ashore. Eventually a handful were convinced to move by means of the use of belaying pins and other 'persuasive weapons' but remained determined to avoid taking part in the fighting.

The enemy had been taken completely by surprise by the attack but quickly reorganised and began a heavy fire on the quay. Lieutenant Ian Findlay, MC, 443rd Battery, RFA, took two gunners and six Fusiliers and rushed to the crossroads 200 yards distant, cleared the nearest house with grenades and placed two Lewis guns under Bombardier Arthur Gurr in opposite second floor windows from where they could enfilade the approaches to the quay.

Whilst Findlay was setting up his Lewis guns, a handful of Russians were reluctantly coming ashore from *Walton Belle* and ordered out to the left and right flanks. With the quayside cleared and occupied, *Keret* came alongside with Major Douglas Campion, RGA, and two 3.7 inch mountain howitzers on board. On advice from Captain Moir that it would not be possible to establish an observation post ashore, Campion had lashed the wheel and trails of the howitzers to the barge, intending to fire from the deck, using *Keret*'s bridge as an observation post. BSM Frank Seymour, RGA attached 443rd Battery, took command of directing fire from the bridge for which he was awarded the DCM.

At 1338 fire was opened on the enemy from the 3.7 inch howitzers at ranges of 600 to 1,200 yards. Although the Bolsheviks had recovered from the initial surprise, they did not push their counter-attack forward and seemed content with advancing only as far as encountering British fire. Shells from the howitzers set some wooden houses 1,000 yards from the quay ablaze, the strong wind fanning the flames and causing the fire to quickly spread until the sky was filled with thick black smoke, further obscuring the gunners' visibility.

At 1430 a runner from Lieutenant Findlay's advanced post at the crossroads reported that the enemy were dug in in a series of trenches 100 yards west of the village church and that a machine gun was firing from the church belfry. As only one of the 3.7 inch howitzers could be brought to bear on the church, Major Campion ordered Lieutenant Herbert Steele, MC, to take a gun ashore which opened fire on the church, silencing the enemy machine gun. Corporal Arthur Rowan, 443rd Battery, an American volunteer serving in the British Army, was awarded the DCM for his bravery in keeping the howitzer in action under heavy fire.

Corporal Thomas Lee, MM, 443rd Battery, distinguished himself during the fight by the skilful use of his Lewis gun and for rescuing wounded Russian soldiers who had been left by their comrades under very heavy machine gun fire. Lee was wounded during the battle but continued to fire his Lewis gun until he was ordered to return to the quay. He was awarded a well deserved DCM to add to an MM earned on the Western Front.

By 1700 the situation remained in stalemate, the British unable to push out from the quay and the Bolsheviks unable to force their way to the docks. Having expended half of his ammunition, Campion ordered a reduction in the rate of fire just as an enemy field gun came into action dropping shells between *Keret* and *M.26*. Leading Seaman Leslie Cox of *M.26* distinguished himself by his actions as coxswain of *Alku* in making numerous trips back and forth ferrying the wounded under fire. In order to steer the tug, Cox had to stand in an exposed position and could not take cover from the incoming enemy fire for which he was awarded the DSM, as were Able Seaman Robert Etherington and Frederick Foster, also of *M.26*.

At 1900 an enemy pom-pom opened fire scoring several hits on *Keret* and *Walton Belle* although no casualties were sustained. Fire from *M.26* silenced the pom-pom gunners and no more was heard from them. The failure of Colonel Danilov's Russians to push forward had left the attack in a stalemate which ultimately led to its failure. At 2300 orders were issued for all forces to withdraw to the quay to reembark.

Shortly before midnight *Keret* and *Walton Belle* pulled away from the quay, all available Lewis guns, rifles and both howitzers firing on the approaches to the quay as they withdrew. About 30 Russians had not embarked and were nearly left behind but were brought on board under fire with some difficulty. Last man aboard was also the first ashore, Bombardier Arthur Gurr, 443rd Battery, who was awarded the MM for his command of a Lewis gun section which he used to great effect during the battle. Two British soldiers had been killed during the action, Gunner John Bulmer, 443rd Battery and Private Alfred Doyle, 46th Royal Fusiliers, their bodies retrieved under fire by their comrades. More than a dozen soldiers and sailors had also been wounded.

The drama on board *Walton Belle* did not end with the refusal of the Russian troops on board to disembark. Whilst returning to Archangel, five Bolshevik prisoners captured during the operation managed to disarm their guard and take over the entire ship, farcically subduing some 200 armed White Russian soldiers who put up no resistance to the takeover. The Bolshevik prisoners had all but taken the wheelhouse when one of the Mercantile Marine ratings took the situation in hand and stepped onto the deck with a shotgun, blowing the heads off two of the hijackers.

The *Belle*'s arrival at Archangel harbour was met with considerable excitement. An officer ashore, upon seeing an SOS flare fired from the steamer, took the signal to mean that the ship was still in the hands of the mutineers and ordered his men to open fire with Lewis guns until the order was countermanded a few moments later. A boarding party from HMS *Fox* came alongside to put an end to the affair and did not discriminate in the meting out of punishment to the Russians on board.

Lieutenant Commander Fawssett was awarded the DSO for his command of the failed operation whilst Lieutenants King and McNair both received DSC Bars for their command of *Walton Belle* and *Alku* respectively giving McNair the unique distinction to be the only naval officer to be twice awarded the DSC in Russia.

Lieutenant Grayston of *M.24* was awarded the DSC for that monitors part in covering the attack (he had previously been recommended for the award by Captain Altham for service on HMS *Cicala* on the Dvina) as was Surgeon Lieutenant Walter Castle, RN, who was decorated for treating wounded under fire. Lieutenant Findlay received an MC Bar for his command of the assaulting force and for rescuing one of his wounded gunners under fire. The Onega threat remained very real until, fearing a stronger Allied attack, the mutineers scorched the town and fled south on 8 September, leaving the scorched remains to the British.

On 17 July 1919 a composite force of three platoons, 45th Royal Fusiliers (Captain William Newbold, MC), one platoon, 46th Royal Fusiliers (Lieutenant Maxwell Perry), a section of 385th Field Company, RE, and the 'Australian Section' of 'C' Company, 201st Battalion, MGC (Major Harry Harcourt, DSO, MC), arrived at Obozerskaya from Archangel by train, where they set up rows of bell tents at VP455 and made preparations to go up to the front line of blockhouses at VP448. Although

54. Privates Estcourt Cresswell-George (South Africa) and Michael Greatorex (Australia), Australian Detachment, 'C' Company, 201st Battalion, MGC. Both men wear Australian slouch hats and the white star on navy blue backing shoulder insignia of the North Russia Relief Force. (Author's collection)

the three platoons of 45th Royal Fusiliers were made up exclusively of Australian volunteers, the 'Australian Section' of 201st MGC was much more 'Commonwealth' in composition. Commanded by Lieutenant Curtis Snodgrass, attached MGC from Bedfordshire Yeomanry, the section included one New Zealander, two Canadians, three South Africans and 21 Australians. For the sake of uniformity the entire section including officers were issued with distinctive Australian slouch hats regardless of nationality, a unique occurrence of soldiers from Commonwealth countries other than Australia being granted permission to wear Australian slouch hats whilst serving in the British Army.

Arriving at the front line blockhouses at VP448 a day later, the Australians did not have to wait long before seeing their first action in North Russia. At 0530 on the morning of 22 July the men were awoken to the sound of rifle fire and rushed outside to be greeted by bullets whizzing through the camp. Private Wilfred Yeaman, an Australian volunteer serving with 201st MGC recorded in his diary:

At first think it's the Russkies on the revolt but find that the direction of fire is coming from the wood on other side of railway … By this time the Russkies have their M.G. going in full swing & the French '75s' do some fine shooting, the shrap bursting just below the tops of the trees at 2 & 300 yards range. After about 25 minutes the Bolshies give it best. At 6.30 No 1 & our team go by armoured train on patrol towards the front line but only get to 449 (6 versts) and train stops owing to the B[olshevik] blowing up the line in 2 places. A party goes ahead to see how things are going at 448 & we follow about half a mile with gun as covering party. Hear Bolshie has had a go at 448 but doesn't do much damage … Object of attack seems to be that the Bolshies & the front line Russkies had made it up to join & cleaned up all the English in reach of them. Some of the ring leaders being shot for being disloyal the day previous & front

55. Soldiers of the Australian Detachment, 201st MGC at rest in their forest camp.
Note British, Scottish and Australian headdress. (Author's collection)

line relieved by fresh troops last night otherwise things wouldn't have gone too well for us. Our casualties only amount to one Rusky. N.Z. flag in front of our tent gets 3 bullet holes through it & the Aussie flag manages to get one.[10]

The incident mentioned by Yeaman, a plot between the Bolsheviks and White Russian troops to stage a mutiny, had occurred two days prior and is interesting in that General Ironside's account of events and that of an eyewitness differ significantly. In Ironside's brief account, on 20 July 1919, plans for a mutiny amongst White Russian troops manning the chain of blockhouses south of Obozerskaya were uncovered when an engine driver was found with a letter plotting the mutiny which detailed that the White Russian troops would mutiny within two hours, murdering their officers before surrendering the blockhouses to the Bolsheviks.

As the detachment of Poles serving on the Railway Front were disarming the White Russian troops, two suspected mutineers fled towards the forest and were promptly shot. Further questioning revealed that both men had been ringleaders.

The recollection of Private William Baverstock, a clerk from Melbourne serving with 201st MGC, and a witness to the events was quite at odds to that of Ironside. The Russian company was ordered from the line on the pretence that there had been an outbreak of cholera amongst soldiers who had spent time in the blockhouses. On reaching the armoured train they were told to deposit their arms in one of the carriages, presumably being told that they would be returning to Obozerskaya, away from the front where new uniforms would be issued. Only after the arms were safely locked away were the mutineers assembled and told that their plot had been uncovered whereupon a detachment of Polish troops emerged from the forest with rifles at the ready. The Russian colonel in charge of White Russian troops on the Railway Front ordered that the ringleaders be handed over within one minute or every tenth man would be summarily executed. None of the assembled mutineers moved. The officer walked through the ranks counting off every tenth man who were immediately

10   AWM: PR91/126, Diary of W.C. Yeaman.

taken into the forest by the Poles. Baverstock recalled in an article published nearly 50 years later: 'We waited for a few minutes in uneasy silence, then through the timber came the sound of shouted orders followed by staccato volleys of rifle fire.'[11] Some of the Australians took photographs of the executions but were later ordered to destroy them.

When the mutiny planned for 20 July was foiled, the Bolsheviks launched their attack the following night and managed to capture nine of the 12 blockhouses held by White Russian troops who were not implicated in the plot to mutiny. Three blockhouses held out until reinforcements arrived from the Australian Company, 45th Royal Fusiliers and 201st MGC. After a brisk fight the Australians ejected the surviving Red troops from the captured blockhouses, forcing the enemy to flee headlong into the forest.

On 24 July a White Russian officer reported a large force of Bolshevik troops in a clearing in the forest. Major Harry May, DSO, MC, RFA, Officer Commanding Royal Artillery on the Railway Front, assembled a party of 70 Australian 45th Royal Fusiliers, nine 201st MGC machine gunners and a trench mortar crew from 238th TMB to go into the forest to locate the enemy. May followed the track into the forest until he neared the clearing where his scouts reported three enemy outposts. The Red troops spotted the advancing Australians and opened fire with machine guns which were suppressed by accurate fire from the Fusiliers Lewis guns. With a signal of three blasts of his whistle, May led the force less the trench mortar section (which had been unable to keep up with the rapid rate of advance) towards the clearing. The Australians advanced at the double for 1,500 yards through the forest without encountering much opposition until the enemy camp was reached. Finding themselves counter-attacked the Fusiliers formed up and charged the clearing, routing the enemy, shooting or bayoneting the Bolshevik machine gunners at their guns.

Australian Fusilier Lance Corporal Allan Lutherborrow, a veteran of the Western Front, was badly wounded in the head and both thighs but remain at his Lewis gun and continued to direct fire at the enemy until passing out from pain and loss of blood for which he was subsequently awarded the DCM.

Private Estcourt Cresswell-George, a South African serving with the Australian Section of 201st MGC, volunteered to go on the patrol and excitedly recalled in a letter to his parents sent a few days later:

On Thursday last, I got in my first night scrap in Russia. I volunteered with 8 others from the 'Aussie' Coy of the battalion for a patrol which was to last all night. We're on the Vologda Front and have not joined our battalion, but are a mobile unit together with details of the 45th and 46th Fusiliers. Well this night about 80 of us – 45th Aust Company, Fusiliers, and nine of my section 201 Battalion MGC set out from our camp at 6 p.m. We went right into the forest for about 10 versts and struck a camp of Bolos. They had 5 maxim guns waiting for us in a clearing and opened fire. We charged and took their guns, taking 2 prisoners and killing and wounding a fair number. The rest went for their lives. We then formed a square in readiness for a counter attack, as with the exception of narrow surveyors clearing running East and West, all was thick forest. The major in command then called for volunteers – 1 Sgt and 5 men to patrol about half a mile in the direction the Bolos had run. So I volunteered with 4 Aussies and an Aussie Sergeant. We struck a batch of 20 Bolos about 300 yards from our square and killed several, putting the rest to flight. We gathered lots rather important information and found large stores of gun cotton and detonators. After we returned we made enough stretchers to carry back the wounded – two Aussies and a Bolo. It was raining all night and the ground was all swampy so it was awful carrying the stretchers over this ground and through the thick forest country. I had four goes at carrying them. Some shady things were done that night to Bolos!!! We left over 35 dead Bolos. I've got a cap off one of them …

---

11   William Baverstock, 'Death for Every Tenth', *Australasian Post*, 26 December 1956.

56. South African Lieutenant Colonel Jack Sherwood-Kelly, VC, CMG, DSO, Norfolk Regiment attached as Commanding Officer, 2nd Battalion, Hampshire Regiment. A fiercely brave and independent thinker with strong moral principles, Kelly's criticism of the conduct of the campaign in North Russia would come at great personal cost. (IWM Q68324)

The Sergeant who went on that special volunteer patrol with five of us, got the M.M. for it.[12]

The Sergeant mentioned as receiving the MM was John Francis Roche from Sydney who had previously served in an AIF trench mortar battery on the Western Front. One other Australian was also decorated: Private William (alias Walter) Jones received an MM Bar for the defence of VP448 on 22–23 July and the raid two days later, his first MM having been awarded for gallantry with the AIF in France the previous year when he had been severely wounded. Major May was also awarded an MC Bar for his command of the patrol and for his leadership during the failed enemy attack on VP448.

On 22 July 1919, 'HQ', 'Y' (Dorsetshire) and 'Z' (Wiltshire) Companies of 2nd Battalion, Hampshire Regiment (originally titled '1st Composite Battalion' due to its multi-regimental composition) which had disembarked from SS *Stephen* at Archangel on 27 May, embarked on barges for Bakharitsa before transfer by train to Obozerskaya on the Railway Front, to bring Brigadier Arthur Turner's column up to strength after the departure of US 339th Infantry Regiment in early June at the request of President Wilson. On 25 July, 'Y' Company was deployed to relieve Russian forces manning the forward defensive positions at VP446 and 448 whilst 'Z' Company moved to VP455 the following day. The Bolsheviks were quick to note the Hampshires' arrival and began a heavy artillery barrage which destroyed a blockhouse killing Private Henry Begley of Dublin, one of 39 men attached to the Hampshires from the Connaught Rangers. The Hampshires spent the following three weeks strengthening the advanced defences against shell fire.

In the lead up to a raid on Bolshevik blockhouses near the village of Alexandrova planned to take place on 17 August, the Hampshires were trained by Royal Engineer specialists in the use of poison gas projectors intended to be used in the attack. Believing the raid to be largely pointless and that the use of gas in the forest presented too great a risk to his own men, Hampshires CO Lieutenant Colonel John Sherwood-Kelly, VC, CMG, DSO, Norfolk Regiment wrote a letter to Brigadier Turner requesting that the raid be abandoned, 'if the proposed operation is left to my discretion I shall not carry it out. I am continuing to make all preparations in case you order me to carry out the raid.'[13]

Neither Turner nor Ironside were pleased with Sherwood-Kelly's recalcitrant response which along with the Hampshires' failed attack on Troitsa in June and reports of Kelly's disparaging

12   Private letters of E. Cresswell-George.
13   Philip Bujack, *Undefeated, the Extraordinary Life and Death of Lt. Col. Jack Sherwood Kelly, VC, CMG, DSO* (Great Britain: Forster Consulting, 2008), p.193.

57. Australian sentries from 201st MGC guard the rear entrance to a blockhouse on the Railway Front. The message reads 'Bolos Welcome' above an outline map of Australia. (Author's collection)

comments regarding senior officers in North Russia and the conduct of the campaign, appeared to be forming part of a pattern of insubordinate behaviour.

On the same day that the letter was received at Archangel, Ironside decided to relieve Sherwood-Kelly of his command and replaced him with another highly decorated South African, Lieutenant Colonel D.M. McLeod, DSO, MC, DCM, 4th South African Infantry (South African Scottish). Before making a final decision what to do with Sherwood-Kelly, Ironside asked Brigadier Turner for a report on the South African. Turner pulled no punches: 'He is a hot-headed and quarrelsome man who has rows with practically everyone with whom he comes in contact.'[14]

The raid on Alexandrova went ahead on 19 August as originally planned without Sherwood-Kelly, 'Y' (Dorsetshire) and 'Z' (Wiltshire) Companies performing well despite heavy fire from the enemy blockhouses. Corporal Robert Burns, one of 22 men attached to the Hampshires from the Royal Irish Fusiliers, crawled forward with wire cutters and proceeded to cut a gap in the wire through which Corporal Thomas Porter, Dorset Regiment, led his platoon commander, 2nd Lieutenant Herbert Wheeler, DCM, and three other soldiers, in a charge to capture an enemy trench mortar. Burns and Porter would both receive the DCM and Wheeler the MC for the raid whilst Lieutenant Claud Sheppard, Manchester Regiment, would also receive the MC for his work as an artillery observer.

In the meantime 'W' (Somerset Light Infantry) and 'X' (Hampshire) Companies had remained on the relatively quiet Pinega River Front. In terms of troop numbers the front was the smallest in comparison to other areas of operations in North Russia. Most of the units deployed to the front were Russian, trained and equipped by a handful of British military advisers. The only British forces on the front were at varying times a company or two of infantry which had usually been rotated from the Dvina or Vaga Fronts and No. 2 (Pinega) Squadron, RAF, which was in reality only Flight strength. Periodically a Russian or British party bumped into the Bolsheviks on patrol followed by a

14   Dobson and Miller, *The Day We Almost Bombed Moscow*, p.205.

brief inconclusive skirmish but these encounters were few and far between and the troops themselves considered Pinega to be pretty tame.

There was little action for the Hampshires on the Pinega but both Companies took part in a number of reconnaissance patrols during one of which CSM Samuel Norris and Corporal Frederick Tilley of 'X' Company were awarded the MM for a particularly successful encounter in which several Bolsheviks were killed and prisoners taken.

On 24 August 1919, Lieutenant Moscrip (pilot) and Observer Lieutenant P.R. Bowen, MC, DFC, were flying an RE8 of No. 3 (Bereznik) Squadron on a mission to bomb enemy gunboats and barges on the Pinega River. When just north of the Bolshevik airfield at Toima, Bowen noticed two Red Air Force Nieuports being wheeled out of hangers. Moscrip did not have time to attack the enemy aircraft on the ground and rather gamely decided to wait for the Nieuports to come up and 'have a scrap'. The first Nieuport pilot was extremely cautious and kept a wary distance from the RE8. Bowen held his fire until the enemy pilot came closer but the much faster Nieuport got in a lucky burst from 400 yards distance, hitting Bowen in the right arm and Moscrip in the left arm and shoulder, shattering his elbow. Although wounded, Bowen fired a drum from his Lewis gun as the Red pilot turned away although it did not appear that any of his shots found their mark.

Minutes later the badly wounded Moscrip fainted at the controls leaving Bowen to fly the plane himself by leaning forward from the rear cockpit and using his left hand on the control column, his right arm being virtually useless. Although he had never piloted a plane before Bowen flew the entire 100 miles back to Bereznik this way. As Bowen prepared to make a crash-landing Moscrip regained consciousness for just long enough to touch down perfectly and even taxied to the canvas hanger where he again passed out. Welsh fighter ace Captain Ira Jones, DSO, MC, DFC and Bar, MM, was at the airfield and recorded:

> Moscrip's cockpit was one horrible mass of congealed blood, and with a face like parchment he was carted off to hospital, but Bowen, in spite of his wound, the strain and the weakness caused by loss of blood, walked about and refused to go to bed until 9.30 p.m. Up the Welsh! It was really a wonderful show.[15]

Bowen was subsequently awarded a DFC Bar for his bravery. Moscrip was perhaps unlucky not to receive any recognition himself, he did after all, despite serious wounds that had caused him to remain unconscious for some time, manage to land the aircraft safely. Bowen could neither use the rudder pedals nor throttle from his position in the observer's cockpit, not to mention his wounded right arm. It would have been very unlikely that Bowen would have been able to crash-land the aircraft without causing both pilot and observer further serious injuries, if not death. With his arm shattered, Bowen was sent home but once recovered volunteered for service with the Lithuanian Air Force with whom he served until July 1920. On return to the UK, Bowen was recruited to work as a British agent in Ireland. His body was found lying face down on Herron Street, Dublin on 27 October 1920, assassinated by the IRA.

Another air to air encounter with the enemy occurred a few days later when Lieutenant 'Roddy' Waugh was attacked in a Sopwith Snipe by a Bolshevik Nieuport over Pinega. The Bolshevik pilot fired about 200 rounds at the Snipe and then turned for home, none of his shots registering a hit and the encounter ended inconclusively.

The final straw for 2nd Hampshires' CO, Lieutenant Colonel Sherwood-Kelly, came when he wrote a letter to a friend in England which was intercepted by the censor at Archangel. In the letter Kelly criticised the entire North Russia operation, calling it a

15   Ira Jones, *An Air Fighter's Scrapbook* (London: Nicholson & Watson, Ltd., 1938), p.148.

Useless, aimless and ill managed campaign ... I have seen enough to convince me that we were wasting good men and money by remaining in North Russia, and, further, that our work, such as it was, was unskilfully and badly done ... I simply could not bear any longer to see splendid soldiers, who had given years of devoted sacrifice in France, uselessly killed in a useless, aimless, and ill managed enterprise.

He was brought before Commander-in-Chief, NREF, General Sir Henry Rawlinson who informed that the letter was 'most improper and constituted an offence which would normally be tried by court-martial.' In view of Kelly's distinguished military record however, Rawlinson decided against court-martial and instead gave orders for the South African to be relieved of his command and returned to England.

Sherwood-Kelly believed he had made a deal with Ironside that in return for the General not forwarding Turner's adverse report on Kelly to Rawlinson (which, in conjunction with being discovered writing a letter highly critical of his commanders to a member of the public, would almost certainly have ended his military career) Kelly would also refrain from writing a letter to

58. Lieutenant Colonel Jack Sherwood-Kelly, VC, CMG, DSO on the way to his court-martial at Middlesex Guildhall, 28 October 1919. (Public domain)

Rawlinson detailing his criticisms of the campaign and its commanders. It wasn't until his return to England that Kelly learnt that Rawlinson had overruled Ironside and that Turner's report would not be withdrawn, and with nothing left to lose wrote three scathing open letters to the press.

The Daily Express headline for Saturday, 6 September, 1919, read; 'Archangel Scandal Exposed; Duplicity of Churchill Policy in Russia; The Public Humbugged; Famous VC appeals to the Nation'. In his open letter published in the press Sherwood-Kelly publicly lambasted the campaign:

Sir, I have just returned from North Russia under circumstances which compel me to seek the earliest possible opportunity of making known in England certain facts in connection with North Russia which otherwise might never come to light.

I wish to state that in so doing I am actuated by no personal motives, but solely by considerations of public policy. I know that my action will render me liable to professional penalties, and will prejudice my future in the Army, but I am prepared to take all risks in carrying out what I know to be my duty to my country and to my men.

I volunteered for service with the North Russian Relief Force in the sincere belief that relief was urgently needed in order to make possible the withdrawal of low category troops in the last stages of exhaustion, due to fierce fighting amid the rigours of an Arctic winter.

The wider advertisement of this relief expedition led myself and many others to believe that affairs in North Russia were about to be wound up in an efficient and decisive manner. And we were proud to be accorded the privilege of sharing in such an undertaking. I was placed in command of the 2nd Battalion the Hampshire Regiment, in the brigade commanded by Brigadier-General Grogan, V.C., C.B., C.M.G., D.S.O.

Immediately on arrival at Archangel, however, towards the end of May, I at once received the impression that the policy of the authorities was not what it was stated to be. This impression hardened as time went on, and during the months of June and July I was reluctantly but inevitably drawn to the following conclusion: That the troops of the Relief Force which we were told had been sent out for purely defensive purposes, were being used for offensive purposes on a large scale and far into the interior, in furtherance of some ambitious plan of campaign the nature of which we were not allowed to know. My personal experience of those operations was that they were not even well conducted and they were not calculated to benefit in a military or any other sense a sound and practical British policy in Russia. They only entailed useless loss and suffering in troops that had already made great sacrifices in the Great War.

I discovered, what is now a matter of common knowledge even in England, that the much vaunted "loyal Russian Army,' composed largely of Bolshevik prisoners dressed in khaki, was utterly unreliable, always disposed to mutiny, and that it always constituted a greater danger to our troops than the Bolshevik armies opposed to them. This was tragically demonstrated early in July when the Russians mutinied and murdered their British officers.

I formed the opinion that the puppet Government set up by us in Archangel rested on no basis of public confidence and support, and would fall to pieces the moment the protection of British bayonets was withdrawn.

At the same time I saw British money poured out like water and invaluable British lives sacrificed in backing up this worthless army and in keeping in power this worthless Government, and I became convinced that my duty to my country lay not in helping to forward a mistaken policy, but in exposing it to the British public.

I ask you, sir, to publish this letter, so that people in England may know the truth about the situation in Archangel and may be able to take steps to right it.

J. SHERWOOD-KELLY, Lieut.-Col., Late Commanding 2nd Battalion the Hampshire Regiment.

The War Office went into damage control and issued a statement in response that Sherwood-Kelly's letter was 'biased and entirely unfounded.' The official response continued:

It should be realised at once by everyone that Colonel Kelly has never been in a position nor been long enough in North Russia to know either the political position at Archangel or the mental attitude of the North Russian people. He was an individual battalion commander whose duty took him to the front, and would not know the factor influencing the situation. Nor does he, indeed, profess to be giving more than his personal impressions of the matters on which he ventures to write. One may safely assume that a record of personal bravery is not of itself sufficient to enable a man to form any reliable opinion on the military and political situation in North Russia.[16]

The official explained that what Sherwood-Kelly had described as 'far into the interior' was in fact an advance of just 10 miles to consolidate the front line already in existence. The War Office official line was, 'There is not, nor ever has been the slightest intention of deviating a hair's-breadth from the settled policy of evacuation.'[17] This despite correspondence between Ironside and the War Office as recently as June in which the capture of Kotlas (150 miles from the forward most British positions) was being discussed in earnest.

---

16   *Aberdeen Journal*, 9 September 1919.
17   Dobson and Miller, *The Day We Almost Bombed Moscow*, p.207.

59. Commonwealth volunteers of 45th Royal Fusiliers and 201st MGC shortly before going into the attack on the Bolshevik battery position at Emtsa, 29 August 1919. They wear strips of calico material on their arms for ease of recognition of friend and foe during the confusion of battle, as the Australians had done at the Battle of Lone Pine on Gallipoli. (AWM AO3723)

The content of the Sherwood-Kelly letter met with the approval of many British soldiers who remained behind in North Russia. Petty Officer Telegraphist Reginald Jowett of HMS *Pegasus* wrote:

Lt Colonel Sherwood Kelly's scathing indictment of the Government's policy, and general conditions in this area, published in papers about Sept 8th which have just reached us, is causing a good deal of comment here, as we all know how true it is. The 'High Official' in the War Office, who terms his statements as 'Biased and unfounded' is that peculiar animal known as an 'armchair critic', who probably has never been within a thousand miles of Archangel. To those who have been here, his statement against Kelly simply makes him look foolish, but I expect his is just trying to shield the Govt. as usual … All the men who have been up-river, are unanimous in declaring that the conditions spoken of by Lt.-Colonel Kelly in his articles in the press, are absolutely so. I wonder how the High Official at the War Office would answer all these witnesses.[18]

Any hope that Sherwood-Kelly could avoid a court-martial were dashed upon the printing of his letters in the press. The Army was reluctant to pursue a court-martial and create further publicity, but Secretary of State for War, Winston Churchill, was adamant that a court-martial be convened without any reference to conduct in North Russia in order to avoid giving Sherwood-Kelly a platform to further voice his criticisms of the campaign. The whole affair had become too public and the Army and War Office needed to save face and make an example. On 13 October 1919, Sherwood-Kelly was arrested and at Middlesex Guildhall on 28 October, plead guilty to writing three open letters to the press contrary to King's Regulations. In his defence Kelly stated:

---

18   Haddon, *North Russia Expedition of Summer* 1919.

60. Sergeant Samuel George Pearse, VC, MM, 45th Battalion, Royal Fusiliers, late AIF, awarded a posthumous Victoria Cross for bravery at Emtsa, 29 August 1919. (AWM H06653)

61. Pearse's grave in the small churchyard at Obozerskaya, since lost to time and the elements. (AWM 3120)

I plead with you to believe that the action I took was to protect my men's lives against needless sacrifice and to save the country from squandering wealth she could ill afford. I leave this matter in your hands, hoping you will remember my past services to my King and country.[19]

The court members were sympathetic and Sherwood-Kelly's only sentence was that of a severe reprimand, but his military career was over and he relinquished his commission two weeks later retaining the rank of Lieutenant Colonel. It was a sad end to a distinguished career. In later years Sherwood-Kelly attempted on several occasions to rejoin the Army but his applications were on all occasions rejected. He later unsuccessfully stood for a Conservative seat in Parliament and pursued a number of business projects in South America and Africa. Lieutenant Colonel John 'Jack' Sherwood-Kelly, VC, CMG, DSO, died of malaria contracted during his time in Africa in a London nursing home in 1931, aged just 51. As a holder of the Victoria Cross he was buried with full military honours at Brookwood Military Cemetery.

The final offensive operation on the Archangel–Vologda Railway Front, an attack on the Bolshevik battery position near Emtsa in which the entire force of Australian volunteers which had arrived in July would take part, was planned to take place on 29 August. The force set out the night before to trek through the forest to an assembly point and were in place to commence the attack at 0530.

In the days preceding the attack, DH9A aircraft of No. 4 (Obozerskaya) Squadron, RAF, flying from the airstrip cut out of the forest next to the railway siding at Obozerskaya, dropped improvised 'M' gas bombs (manufactured by Tasmanian NREF Gas Officer Major Thomas Davies, DSO, MC, RE at the Royal Engineers workshop in Archangel) onto enemy-held villages. The use of aerial gas bombs eliminated the need for the favourable wind conditions required for the successful use of ground based gas cylinders and was revolutionary at the time. More than 200 small 'M' bombs were dropped on Emtsa during the two days leading up to the attack, the gas proving extremely effective in incapacitating the enemy but was not considered fatal. General Rawlinson noted in his diary after the 29 August attack, 'Went round hospitals and saw Bolo prisoners who had been gassed. Good gas.'[20]

The attacking force was divided into two columns. Captain William Newbold's three platoons of Australian 45th Royal Fusiliers and two companies of North Russian Rifles comprised, 'May's Force' under the command of Major Harry May, RFA, whilst Lieutenant Maxwell Perry's platoon of 46th Royal Fusiliers and Lieutenant Curtis Snodgrass' Australian Section, 201st MGC formed 'Harcourt's Force' under Major Harry Harcourt, MGC.

Early on the morning of 'Zero Day', 29 August, local guides led the attackers on the final trek to the start line but either did not know the terrain well or misunderstood their instructions (or were Bolshevik sympathisers) as they were unable to lead the British troops to their correct assembly points.

'Harcourt's Force' was tasked with attacking the strong enemy positions from the right front with 'May's Force' attacking simultaneously from the south. With 20 minutes until 'Zero Hour', Harcourt found himself near the railway siding with 'May's Force' somewhere further south. There being no time to reach the original objective, Harcourt decided to attack the siding and push north to take the battery position hoping that the sound of firing would attract May's party.

After a brisk fight, 'Harcourt's Force' took the siding capturing five machine guns, a 6 inch gun and 80 prisoners before immediately pushing north towards the fortified enemy battery position. On the outbreak of firing the Bolsheviks sent an armoured train down the line to drive off Harcourt's attack which ran straight into a platoon of Australian Fusiliers which had found itself distanced from the fighting. Private William Quarrell, an Australian volunteer from the small country town of Mayanup, Western Australia, who had been twice gassed in France, charged the train, hurling two

19   *The Times*, 29 October 1919.
20   Kinvig, *Churchill's Crusade*, p.246.

62. Exhausted Australian 45th Royal Fusiliers sleeping after the
battle at Emtsa, 29 August 1919. (AWM A4886)

Mills grenades into a carriage which contained a naval gun, killing all the gunners and knocking the
gun out of action before being wounded for which he was awarded the DCM.

Sergeant George Murphy, 201st MGC, brought his gun to within 10 yards of the engine of the
armoured train and poured a deadly fire into one of the forward carriages, killing or wounding a
number of enemy before turning the gun on the engine, compelling the driver to retreat towards
Emtsa, for which Murphy was awarded the DCM.

As anticipated, Major May had quickly brought his force towards the sound of firing and by the
time Harcourt had pushed north to attack the enemy battery, 'May's Force' was coming up on the right
flank to join the attack. The battery position was protected by a series of blockhouses ringed by barbed
wire which had to be cut before the Fusiliers could knock out the guns themselves. During the early
stages of the attack Major May was shot through both thighs and received a bullet through his slouch
hat and was evacuated to Obozerskaya, leaving command of the column to Captain Newbold. Major
Harcourt too was wounded, handing over command of his column to Lieutenant Snodgrass.

Australian machine gunner Private William Baverstock recalled the attack on the right flank:

Captain Newbold leaped from behind a tree and with a yell, led his men forward to attack the Bolshevik
position. Some Fusiliers were killed and wounded as they rushed from tree to tree approaching the enemy.
In the short but fierce exchange of fire, one-by-one the blockhouses were silenced. The sole remaining
blockhouse proved to be extremely difficult to approach and a number of men were lost in the process.[21]

Corporal Horace Gipps distinguished himself during the capture of one of the blockhouses by
dashing forward immediately as the wire was cut, bombing the blockhouse and killing the occupants,

21   Mike Irwin, *Victoria's Cross: the story of Sgt. Samuel George Pearse, V.C. M.M.: from ANZAC to Archangel* (Victoria: Northland
Centre, 2003), p.62.

63. The distinctive profile of an Australian NRRF volunteer watches the rounding up of Bolshevik prisoners after the capture of the enemy battery position at Emtsa, 29 August 1919. (Author's collection)

putting a machine gun out of action, for which he was awarded the DCM. Gipps, from St. Kilda, Victoria, had enlisted in the AIF in August 1914 and served as an artilleryman at Gallipoli and on the Western Front before being commissioned. Gipps voluntarily relinquished his rank of lieutenant in order to enlist in the NRRF as a private.

During the attack several men were shot trying to cut through the rows of barbed wire protecting the approaches to the remaining blockhouses. Australian Fusilier Sergeant Samuel George Pearse, MM, a Welsh-born 23-year-old trapper from Mildura, Victoria, and Private Charles 'Chilla' Hill, a 19-year-old clerk from Sydney, inched forward under heavy fire cutting their way through the wire. Hill stood up, attempting to hurl a Mills grenade through the firing slit of the blockhouse but was immediately shot down with a huge wound to the upper thigh. Hill was dragged to safety by his comrades who applied a field dressing to staunch the bleeding.

Having seen his friend shot down and despite knowing the danger, Pearse continued to cut his way through the wire entanglements. Baverstock continued:

> Pearse called for a pair of wire-cutters and a bag of Mills bombs. Laying on his back he hacked at the strands of barbed wire until he had cleared an aperture. Through this he entered the open area in front of the blockhouse. He was seen to rush to one side of the blockhouse and to drop bombs into the interior. Explosions followed and he was seen to move across when an unexpected burst of fire came from within.[22]

Private Ben Williams, a 20-year-old coachsmith from Arncliffe, New South Wales, immediately rushed forward and emptied his Lewis gun into the blockhouse, killing all the occupants. Pearse's biographer wrote poignantly of the gallant Australian's last moments:

> The men gathered round him knew instinctively it was a death wound. He was going pale as his life blood soaked the ground beneath him. They made him as comfortable as possible with one man cradling his

---

22 *Ibid.*

head in his lap. Sam was fading fast and uttered some words that were incoherent as he lapsed in and out of consciousness … He then closed his eyes and passed away.[23]

Pearse's body was transported back to Obozerskaya where his mates erected a Celtic cross in the small village cemetery alongside several other British burials, their graves since lost to time.

Samuel George Pearse had been born at Penarth, Glamorganshire in 1897 and emigrated to Australia with his family as a young boy. Settling in Mildura, Victoria, Pearse enlisted into 7th Battalion, AIF in Melbourne in July 1915 aged 18. Seeing only a week's service on Gallipoli before the evacuation, Pearse was wounded in action at Pozieres before transferring to 2nd Australian Machine Gun Company with whom he was awarded the MM during the battle of Passchendaele for bombing an enemy listening post in no man's land and bringing in wounded under fire. Promoted Corporal shortly before being wounded for a second time in May 1918, he was evacuated to a military hospital in England. After a court-martial for being three weeks AWOL, Pearse spent the remainder of the war at a machine gun depot in England.

For his gallantry in cutting a path through the wire under fire and storming the blockhouse, Captain Newbold recommended Pearse for award of a posthumous Victoria Cross. Newbold himself received an MC Bar for 29 August to add to the MC awarded for actions 24–25 July, making him one of few soldiers to be twice decorated during service in North Russia.

As noted, Sergeant Samuel Pearse slipped past the AIF policy allowing only unmarried men to join the NRRF. Private Edward Rawlins did the same, marrying a 'Lancashire Lass' he had met in England in 1916 whilst recovering from wounds. Pearse had been married for only a short time before leaving for North Russia but long enough for his wife Kitty to become pregnant with a daughter born the year after his death. In honour of her husband and the decoration he was posthumously awarded, Kitty named the child 'Victoria Catherine' or 'V.C. Pearse'. Kitty was presented with her husband's VC by the King at a private investiture at Buckingham Palace on 25 March 1920; Queen Mary took delight in nursing one month old Victoria, remarking how sad it was that the child would grow up without her father.

In May 1920, as the widow of an Australian soldier, Kitty emigrated with her daughter to Australia and married another former soldier, taking her new husband's surname which she also gave to Victoria. Growing up as a child in Australia during hard times, 'Vicky' knew that her father had been awarded the VC and to her that meant her mother's husband. It was not until she came across the Victoria Cross in a trunk of old belongings that she discovered that the name on the medal was not that of the man she believed to be her father. Having learnt the truth, for many years after Vicky resented the medal awarded to the father she never knew. Instead of a father she had a medal and she believed that had her father survived, her childhood would have been much easier and happier.[24] On 11 November 2009, a life-size statute of Samuel Pearse was unveiled in his honour in his home town of Mildura, his daughter Victoria, aged 89, proudly in attendance.

Interestingly, Private Estcourt Cresswell-George, a South African serving with 201st MGC, noted in a letter to his parents that two recommendations had been made for the VC for the attack including 'one posthumous'.[25] It is possible that of the two DCMs awarded to Gipps and Quarrell, one was originally a recommendation for the Victoria Cross, the remaining recommendation being the posthumous award to Pearse. Cresswell-George himself stated that he was recommended for the DCM for going behind the enemy armoured train and blowing up the line. Although no British award was ever gazetted to Cresswell-George, he did receive the Russian Cross of St. George awarded by the Provisional Government, presumably for the same incident, which he wore in North

---

23   *Ibid.*, p.63.
24   Interview with author, 29 August 2004.
25   Private letters of E. Cresswell-George.

Russia although he was never granted official permission to wear the award after his return to the UK.

The reason for this anomaly was that Russian commanders were authorised to award on the spot the Medal and Cross of St. George for bravery with or without the sanction of the War Office and a number of British soldiers received Russian decorations awarded in the field at a unit parade by Russian commanders, details of which were subsequently published in Ironside's GHQ Archangel Routine Orders. Only later did the War Office retrospectively limit the number of Russian awards 'granted permission' for acceptance and wear (as opposed to actually awarded) using a quota system. Many soldiers awarded Russian decorations who wore the medal or ribbon in North Russia, were later not granted permission in a 1921 War Office 'Confidential List' to wear their awards on return to the UK. No awards made to British and Commonwealth servicemen during the Russian Civil War period were ever published in the *London Gazette* as they had been prior to the Revolution. In many cases, those British soldiers who had distinguished themselves in the campaign and had been awarded a Russian

64. Australian NRRF volunteers Privates Wilfred Robinson and Ernest Gaffey, 45th Royal Fusiliers at Netley Hospital in October 1919. (Public domain)

medal, but had not received a British decoration, were put forward and subsequently granted official permission to accept and wear their Russian decoration. It is telling that neither of the two VC recipients for North Russia received a Russian decoration.

Charles 'Chilla' Hill, who had suffered a severe leg wound shortly before Pearse was killed, was evacuated to Obozerskaya and then to Archangel where his leg was amputated. A number of other Australian Fusiliers had also been wounded during the attack, one of whom, Private Wilfred John Robinson, a 20-year-old shipping clerk from Ivanhoe, Victoria, miraculously survived a rifle bullet to the heart. Robinson had been enfilading the enemy trenches with his Lewis gun resting on the barbed wire fence near where Pearse had cut through when he was shot in the chest, the force of the bullet being largely absorbed by a pocket New Testament, Comforts Fund diary, and wallet in his breast pocket. After evacuation to Netley Military Hospital where he witnessed the presentation of Australian Fusilier Private Joseph Purdue's DCM for carrying a wounded officer through forest and swamp during the withdrawal from the 10 August attack on the Dvina, Robinson was reenlisted into the AIF in London on 16 March 1920 for the return journey to Australia, giving him the distinction to be the last man to enlist in the AIF. Many years later Robinson donated the bullet damaged wallet, diary and bible to the Australian War Memorial where they remain in permanent collection.

Major Harcourt was awarded a DSO Bar for his command of the composite company to add to a previously awarded MC whilst MCs were awarded to Lieutenants Charles Rhys (Grenadier Guards), Arthur Saunders (Royal Berkshire Regiment) and John Winsor (Devon Regiment) attached 45th Royal Fusiliers and Lieutenant Maxwell Perry (Devon Regiment) attached 46th Royal Fusiliers. Lieutenant William Wilken, RE, was awarded the same decoration for devotion to duty in defusing 15 mines which had been left in the captured enemy positions and for supervising repair of the

65. Australian and South African machine gunners of 201st MGC moving off from a captured Bolshevik blockhouse. This is believed to be the blockhouse near Emtsa which Sergeant Samuel Pearse attacked during the action, for which he was awarded a posthumous Victoria Cross. (AWM 3725)

railway, working continuously for 60 hours after the battle. Sapper Jack Chinnery of 385th Field Company, RE., was awarded the MM for 'great dash and resource' in joining the Australian troops attacking the enemy battery position as an infantryman.

Harcourt continued to serve in the British Army post-war and after a short stint in the Indian Army, emigrated to Australia in 1930. During the Second World War he was appointed to command 2/6th Independent Company, 2nd AIF, and served on the Kokoda Trail in New Guinea 1942–43 and was awarded the US Silver Star. Post-war Harcourt was awarded a Civil OBE in 1957 for services to 'Legacy', a charitable organisation devoted to the care and welfare of families of deceased servicemen. Settling in Tasmania on retirement, Harcourt died in 1970.

In a report to his superiors Soviet General Samoilo recounted the attack on Emtsa from the Bolshevik perspective:

> Attacked on our right flank and came at us out of the forest. They reached our artillery positions and took them after six hours of fighting. They went on to try to capture Armoured Train No. 20 but although the crew was killed, it was started and went to the aid of the 1st Light-Artillery battery and took it to safety. The Interventionists set Emtsa on fire and destroyed the water tower. By midnight they had overrun all our frontline positions but 500 of our men plus ten machine-guns and four minethrowers managed to break out. The 155th regiment managed to hold on to the railway station for nearly two days. But no reinforcements could get through. The British attacked again and again and set the station on fire. Our men were exhausted and surrendered.[26]

The Emtsa operation had been a success. The enemy battery position was captured along with the railway siding for the loss to the enemy of eight field guns, the same number of machine guns and 30 enemy killed or wounded and another 180 taken prisoner. On the British side, in addition to the

---

26 Dobson and Miller, *The Day We Almost Bombed Moscow*, p.217.

loss of Sergeant Pearse of 45th Royal Fusiliers, Private John Stoddart from Glasgow was killed and Private John Cairns of Belfast died of wounds, both of 46th Royal Fusiliers, and a number more were wounded including Majors May and Harcourt and Australian Fusiliers Privates Wilfred Robinson (shot in chest), Charles Hill (leg amputated), Ernest Gaffey, John Kevan (shot in head), Jack Peiti and William Quarrell. Kevan was dangerously wounded with a bullet wound to the head which smashed his left eye. Eight years after returning from North Russia, shrapnel was discovered in his brain and surgically removed:

> To carry in his brain for eight years a piece of shrapnel without being aware of it has been the amazing experience of John McClure Kevan, an official in the Bank of New South Wales. The piece of shrapnel was a quarter of an inch square. Kevan lost an eye when wounded, and has suffered from fits and loss of memory until an operation last Thursday eased the pressure and he is now recovering.[27]

Two platoons were left to garrison the captured blockhouses and battery position whilst the remainder of the force stood to in preparation to attack Emtsa village six versts distant upon the arrival of the North Russian Rifles. The Russians took longer to clear their objectives than planned and when they finally rendezvoused with the Fusiliers the Russian commander was adamant that his men would make the attack themselves without British support. The time lost in waiting for the arrival of the Russians gave the Bolsheviks ample opportunity to reinforce and prepare defences and the attack failed.

The new front line at the battery position was held until 9 September when the British force began to withdraw back to Archangel, the evacuation being completed 10 days later. During this period life in the captured villages was quite comfortable. For the first time in North Russia the men had the luxury of sleeping indoors: 'To be able to get a change of clothing and to have a real blanket to sleep in was akin to being billeted in Brussels direct from Ypres.'[28] On 1 September, 300 Bolshevik troops supported by a light field gun launched an attack on a forward position four versts from Bolshie Ozerki. The post was at the time garrisoned by a single platoon of soldiers from 'Z' (Wiltshire) Company attached 2nd Hampshires under 2nd Lieutenant Victor Auton, MC, DCM. Despite being attacked from three sides simultaneously, Auton led the defence of the position for two hours before the enemy finally withdrew after a patrol of Hampshires led by 2nd Lieutenant Harold Finch, RASC, circled round the enemy and attacked from the rear, cutting off their line of retreat. Private J.B. Jasper of the Wiltshires personally killed an entire Bolshevik machine gun team before he was himself wounded, but remained on duty, killing a further three of the enemy and wounding a number more during the enemy counter-attack, for which he was awarded the DCM. Finch himself personally killed four of the enemy and wounded a number more during the engagement for which he was awarded the MC, whilst Auton received an MC Bar for his defence of the position against an enemy many times his own number. Lieutenant John Churchley, RFA, was also awarded an MC for his gallantry in directing fire from his section of 18 pdr guns against the attackers from an exposed observation post which became the target of the enemy field gun. One soldier was killed in the defence, Private James McKenzie, 8th MGC, who had served on the Western Front with the Gordon Highlanders. Extraordinarily, the father of Private McKenzie was also serving in North Russia at the time as a private in the RAOC stationed at Bakharitsa dock and was granted leave to travel to Obozerskaya to attend his son's funeral.

For the two weeks following the defeat of the enemy attack on Bolshie Ozerki, the front remained relatively quiet, most of the Hampshires' time was spent conducting patrols through the forest and

---

27   *Northern Times*, 18 June 1927.
28   G.R. Singleton-Gates, *Bolos and Barishynas: Being an account of the doings of the Sadleir-Jackson Brigade, and Altham Flotilla, on the North Dvina during the summer 1919* (Aldershot: Gale & Polden, 1920), p.149.

along approach routes to Bolshie Ozerki. On 15 September, on the last patrol before withdrawing to Archangel, a mixed platoon of 23 men from the Hampshires and 'D' Company, 8th Battalion, MGC, under 2nd Lieutenant Harold Finch, RASC, and Lieutenant George Dallas, MGC, was sent on a routine patrol along the Bolshie-Ozerki–Chamavo road, leaving the forward British positions at noon.

As they made their way into the forest the party stumbled upon a force of 750 enemy preparing to attack Bolshie Ozerki. The patrol was attacked from all sides, Dallas gave the order to take cover moments before he was shot and killed. The patrol put up a plucky fight, one Lewis gunner expending eight drums of ammunition and another corporal accounting for nine of the enemy who, perhaps taken aback by the heavy resistance and unsure of the size of the British force, did not press home their advantage and simply walk over the British patrol.

On being attacked the patrol had split into two groups, one of which had a compass and made the British lines at Bolshie Ozerki after a rapid withdrawal. The other group had no compass and after escaping the enemy wandered through the forest for 20 hours before finally returning to British lines. Given the circumstances, the patrol was lucky to not have been wiped out entirely. In addition to the loss of Lieutenant Dallas, Private Frederick Read, 'Z' (Wiltshire) Company, 2nd Hampshires was killed and 2nd Lieutenant Finch and two 8th Battalion, MGC other ranks and a Hampshires soldier wounded.

On 27 September, having withdrawn from the front line earlier in the month, the last soldiers of the North Russia Expeditionary Force and North Russia Relief Force departed Archangel on troopships bound for Murmansk and then home.

9

Archangel: Vaga River Front January–September 1919

After shelling Shenkursk intermittently for two weeks, on 19 January the Bolsheviks launched their winter offensive to capture the strategically important city. Ironside described Shenkursk as 'the most important city in North Russia' after Archangel and was determined to hold the line. Garrisoning the city and advanced positions were 'C' Company, 17th Battalion, Liverpool Regiment, US 339th Infantry Regiment and most critically, two 18 pdr field guns of 68th Battery, CFA, which had arrived in late December under Captain Oliver Mowat.

During a visit to Shenkursk by General Ironside and Lieutenant Colonel Sharman (Commanding 16th Brigade, CFA) on the day of the offensive, firing was heard from nearby Ust-Padenga and a detachment of eight gunners under Lieutenant John Winslow with Corporal Thomas Greaves, promptly despatched to bolster the gunners of the 1st Russian Light Battery there.

On 20 January, the garrison at Ust-Padenga (primarily US troops) was subjected to the heaviest bombardment yet experienced, a preliminary to a strong infantry attack on three sides the following morning by Bolshevik troops camouflaged against the snow in white smocks. Overwhelmed by the attacking force, the American soldiers withdrew from their forward positions back into Shenkursk, the platoon in the westernmost position suffering severely in making their escape.

Fire from the Canadian artillery and American machine guns was very effective and heavy casualties were inflicted on the enemy. The Bolsheviks did not have an opportunity to consolidate the captured forward line before a counter-attack led by US Captain Otto Odgaard drove the Red troops back into the tree line from where they had attacked. Odgaard's force of 450 US and White Russian troops had driven off an attack three to four times their number but had suffered some 50 casualties during the fight.

The Bolsheviks continued to shell the advanced position at Ust-Padenga throughout the following two days but Allied patrols found no indication of preparations being made for another attack. On 22 January, a Bolshevik attack by 200 men was made at the village of Sergievskaaya on the eastern flank and behind Ust-Padenga. The following day the enemy attacked Ust-Padenga, bombarding the White Russian 18 pdr guns of 1st Russian Light Battery so heavily that the inexperienced crews abandoned one of their guns which had to be recovered under fire by Lieutenant Winslow and the Canadian gunners. Running the gun up to a small crest, Winslow directed its fire over open sights against the enemy infantry below whilst Gunner John McLean and Driver Murdoch Kennedy (both awarded the MM for the defence of Ust-Padenga) took a Lewis gun forward to protect the exposed left flank.

With little hope of holding the line, orders were received from Shenkursk to abandon Ust-Padenga, Lieutenant Winslow taking command of the evacuation of the Russian artillery. With considerable difficulty he rallied the Russian gunners and coordinated the withdrawal of the two 18 pdr guns until the inexperienced Russians, unused to driving horses under fire, showed signs of wanting to abandon the guns. It was immediately apparent to Winslow that if the guns were to be saved, the Canadians would have to do it themselves and he gave orders for his men to pull their Lewis guns back from the column rearguard and take charge of one of the Russian guns which was evacuated to the next line of defence at Shalosha. The remaining 18 pdr was abandoned to the enemy after being rendered inoperable. The only Canadian casualty in the defence of Ust-Padenga had been Gunner G.B. Thompson, who

66. Some of the Allied officers who took part in the defence of Shenkursk. From left to right Lieutenant Harry Mead and Captain Otto Odgaard, 339th US Infantry, Lieutenant John Winslow, 68th Battery, CFA. Both Winslow and Odgaard were awarded the Military Cross for the defence in which Odgaard was wounded. (Public domain)

was wounded in the back during the defence of the village but only conceded to evacuation after ordered by Winslow to leave.

In the meantime, a gun section under Captain Mowat had been sent from Shenkursk to Spaskoe to cover the retirement of the Ust-Padenga column. The Bolsheviks remained hot on the heels of the retreating Allied troops and at 1000 on the morning of 24 January launched a three-pronged attack on Spaskoe. Despite the fire from Mowat's two 18 pdrs and an additional two naval 12 pdrs, the enemy continued to gain ground with the inevitable conclusion that Spaskoe could not be held.

The following day, Bolshevik attacks on both flanks forced Column Commander Brigadier C.C. Graham, DSO, to withdraw his forces to the outskirts of Shenkursk itself. Captain Odgaard established a skirmish line on the edge of a bluff as the Canadians dug in their 18 pdr across the road from the church. The Bolsheviks brought up artillery mounted on sledges and began to mercilessly pound the city.

Bellowing at the top of his lungs, Capt. Mowat acts as forward observer, directing fire from the belfry. Oddly, the Soviet commander does not order an infantry assault; either he considers it unnecessary, or perhaps his soldiers would rather not charge the Canadians, who have a vicious reputation for mowing down infantry with shrapnel. The Americans dig in among the graves in the churchyard as Soviet shells strike closer and closer to their aiming point, the church tower, until an airburst right beside the belfry sends a hunk of shrapnel clanging off one of the bells. In the momentary silence that follows, Capt Mowat sings out, like the barker at a country fair, 'One cigar!', and the soldiers on the skirmish line collapse in giggles.

A few hours later, Capt Mowat is strolling across the road from the churchyard to the gun position when he is cut down by a Soviet shell. The gunners pack him into a sledges for the four-mile trip to Shenkursk, and the American soldiers hear his voice again: 'Tell the captain I couldn't wait.'[1]

By mid afternoon the signal line to Bereznik directly in the Allies line of retreat was cut by either a small guerrilla force operating behind Allied lines or saboteurs. The news received from Spaskoe was also not good. Captain Oliver Mowat had been severely wounded in the thigh by an exploding artillery shell. The same shell killed Corporal Cecil Worthington and wounded Bombardier Benjamin Lawrence and Captain Odgaard. In one blow both commanders had been knocked out of the battle.

Surrounded by dead and wounded, Corporal Walter Hughes (who had been acting as No. 1 of the 18 pdr before the shell had struck) found himself in charge of the force until the arrival

1   Charmion Chaplin-Thomas, 'The Fourth Dimension', *The Maple Leaf*, Vol. 8, No. 2, January 2005.

of Sergeant John Beddow. By this point of the battle the 18 pdr had been hit several times and put permanently out of action. It was impossible to bring the gun out of the line due to damage to the wheels and limber so Beddow removed the breech block and sights, rendering the gun useless to the enemy. For their gallantry during the action Beddow was awarded an MM Bar and Hughes the MM.

The 'A' Company, US 339th Infantry Regiment garrison at Shenkursk under Lieutenant Harry Mead had suffered numerous casualties during the enemy attacks and shelling and with no hope of holding the line any longer without risking the overrun of the entire garrison, Mead gave the order to pull back taking the wounded with them. Faced with the prospect that he could be completely encircled at any moment, Brigadier Graham ordered the evacuation of Shenkursk to take place that night, 25 January. Frantic preparations were made to evacuate the wounded on sleighs whilst stores and equipment that could not be carried out were destroyed.

Orders were issued that the town be evacuated by all military personnel by 0300 and anyone seen on the street after that time would be shot on sight. All ranks were to carry three days rations and the march was to be carried out in strict silence. If the enemy were encountered during the withdrawal, bayonets only were to be used to avoid giving away the column position.

67. Captain Oliver Mowat, 68th Battery, CFA, died 27 January 1919 of wounds sustained in the defence of Shenkursk. Mowat had been awarded the MC for bravery and leadership in action at Kodema, 15 December 1918 but did not live long enough to receive the award. On the withdrawal of Canadian forces from North Russia in June 1919 his comrades smuggled his body out of Russia back to Canada. (Carrie Mowat)

Due to the critical lack of transport ponies and sleighs, the hospital convoy at the head of the column did not leave Shenkursk until 0130, an hour over schedule. The going was tough due to sub-zero temperatures and total darkness but the column slowly wound its way past areas known to be held by the enemy and somehow, miraculously, Shegovari was reached without incident. The Bolsheviks pursued the retreating column right up to the banks of the Dvina but after a few days of patrolling gave up on any chance that there were stragglers separated from the main column.

The Canadian gunners of 68th Battery (rightly regarded by Ironside as some of the best soldiers in the NREF) had performed exceptionally but not without the loss of their detachment commander. Captain Oliver Mowat was evacuated with the wounded to the hospital barge at Bereznik where he succumbed to his wounds three days later. Lieutenant Colonel Sharman was able to visit Mowat shortly before he died and pin on his chest the ribbon of the Military Cross which he had just been awarded for gallantry in charge of his guns at Kodema in December. Sharman recorded in his diary:

They amputated his leg during the evening and the poor boy never regained consciousness. I was with him when he died and pinned on his shirt the Military Cross which he had just been awarded, also cut off a lock of his hair and sent it with a letter to his people.[2]

Prior to the return of 16th Brigade, CFA, to England in June 1919, Mowat's body was secretly exhumed and smuggled back to Canada in a sealed coffin as part of the battery baggage. His body was collected by his family and buried with full military honours in his hometown of Campbelltown, New Brunswick, making Mowat the only Commonwealth soldier to die in North Russia whose body was subsequently returned home. All other Commonwealth casualties remain buried in North Russia, either in the Commonwealth War Graves Commission cemeteries at Murmansk and Archangel or in plots long since overgrown and lost in outlying areas.

The RAF had played their own small but important role in the evacuation of Shenkursk. On 23 January, Lieutenant Frank Shrive, a Canadian serving in the RAF as an observer, with pilot Russian ace and commander of the SBAC Major Alexander Kazakov was called to Lieutenant Colonel Sharman's headquarters where the Canadian gunner commander outlined to the two airmen the seriousness of the situation and the task required of them. The Allied garrison was too small to hold out much longer and Kazakov and Shrive were instructed to fly a reconnaissance mission along the roads from Shenkursk to discover if there were any safe routes for the garrison to withdraw to Bereznik. Once the reconnaissance had been completed Kazakov was to land and report his findings to Major Hyde, commanding 68th Battery, CFA.

Kazakov and Shrive left at first light on 24 January in a SBAC Sopwith Strutter armed with eight 20 lb Cooper bombs and five drums of Lewis machine gun ammunition. The temperature registered well below zero as the two airmen struggled into their cumbersome flying suits before taking off in the bitter cold.

Shenkursk was easy to find from the flashes on the horizon of Red Army gun positions shelling the city. Having ascertained a safe route to evacuate Shenkursk, Kazakov should have landed and reported to Major Hyde but the Russian was unable to resist the temptation of bombing a Bolshevik battery position.

Kazakov indicated with hand signals for Shrive to ready the bombs, as they made their first pass over the position Shrive released two of the Cooper bombs, straddling the position without effect. Kazakov brought the aircraft round, turned to make another pass but this time the Red gunners were ready and waiting. Shrive recalled:

As I let the bomb go I noticed two men in front of one of the huts. They had brought out a machine gun, raised it on one of their shoulders and in no time I felt the thud of bullets on the machine. I hurriedly let go the fourth bomb, and then turned my machine gun on to the men on the ground. Only one bullet fired, the one in the barrel. The Lewis had frozen.[3]

Kazakov looked over his shoulder at Shrive and pointed a finger at the ground, something was very wrong. Shenkursk was only a mile or so ahead and within minutes they were gliding down for a hurried landing on the frozen river:

As the machine stopped (the captain had turned off the ignition before we touched down), I moved to speak to him, and then I saw that all was not well. His head was on his chest and he was groaning badly. Quickly I jumped out on the wing to see further and then saw that blood was all over his flying

2   Public Archives of Canada, EE-112, Private Diary of Lieutenant Colonel C.H.L. Sharman.
3   Shrive, *The Diary of a P.B.O.*, p.74.

suit. I could see at once he was badly wounded. I jumped from the wing and did a strange thing. On our approach I had noticed some soldiers in an observation tower, and I thought they looked like C.F.A. chaps. Facing them I sent the word 'help' in semaphore, and within a minute a sleigh, driver and two gunners were on their way to the machine. Between us we lifted Kazakov from the cockpit, and he was hurried away to the monastery, which was now being used as a hospital.[4]

A Canadian sleigh took Shrive to the local HQ where the observer informed the staff that the river road was occupied by the enemy and there was only one road open through which the town could be evacuated. Shrive headed over to the monastery to check on his pilot where he found Kazakov fully conscious and coherent. A bullet had entered his chest, gone through his lung and come out his shoulder. The gallant Russian was expected to make a full recovery and would be evacuated with the rest of the wounded.

In the meantime, a Russian mechanic had looked over the aircraft which seemed to be serviceable enough to be flown back to Bereznik. The only problem was that there was no pilot, Kazakov was unfit to fly and was being evacuated. It looked likely that Shrive would have to destroy the aircraft to prevent its capture until a very curious event occurred. A man in typical Russian peasant clothing had been looking over the aircraft before strolling up to Shrive and asking in broken English if he intended to return to Bereznik. Shrive replied in the affirmative and the Russian offered to fly the plane back himself with Shrive in the observer's cockpit.

After a discussion through the liaison officer and translator from 17th Liverpools, it was decided that the man was legitimately a qualified pilot and allowed to take the Sopwith on a circuit to prove his ability. The Russian had no difficulty and made a perfect landing. With a pocket full of despatches from Colonel Sharman, Shrive and his new pilot (whose name Shrive never knew) took off for Bereznik. The sun was setting as the Sopwith came in to land at Bereznik aerodrome. On landing the mechanics were amazed to see that the pilot was not Kazakov but a stranger. It is likely that the Russian had served as a pilot with the Russian Imperial Air Service during the war (possibly even flying the Sopwith Strutter) and had returned to his home town of Shenkursk after the revolution.

Immediately on landing Shrive dashed to Dvina Force HQ with Colonel Sharman's despatches which included his orders to evacuate Shenkursk that night:

We have now the satisfaction that all the field guns but one, all machine guns, all troops, including wounded and some five hundred civilians, got out safely … although at one point were within a mile of the enemy they were not attacked.[5]

After his adventures over Shenkursk, as a former Canadian gunner on the Western Front, Shrive spoke to Major Francis Moller, MC, DFC (Commanding RAF Bereznik) about the Bolshevik battery near Kitsa and suggested that No. 3 (Bereznik) Squadron try a directed artillery shoot in conjunction with Canadian signallers and gunners from 68th Battery Although common practice in France, up to late January 1919 no artillery observation missions had been carried out by the RAF in North Russia.

Shrive flew two artillery observation missions on 29 January, mostly targeting the road behind Kitsa that the Red Army used as a supply route. On 11 February, he went on a shoot with SBAC pilot Lieutenant Biadok in a Sopwith Strutter. As Shrive gave corrections via code to the gunners on the ground, the CFA shells fell around the Red positions:

4   Ibid.
5   Ibid., p.75.

The first shell burst well beyond the Bolo gun, so using the clock code and after some six firings we had the gun well bracketed. We then switched to target two and did the same. The third target was treated in the same way. One might ask why bracket the guns when the range was reasonably accurately known. In this case it was because the C.F.A. are daily expecting a sixty-pounder to arrive, and when it does it will be an easy task to use the information and apply it to the heavier gun. In other words a dead hit from a sixty will do far more destructive work than could be done with the eighteen-pounders we were working with yesterday. This method was used at Vimy Ridge with very devastating results.[6]

Shrive was hospitalised in March with exhaustion. He was not the only airman to be medically barred from further flying. The constant strain put on aircrews due to the shortage of personnel was taking its toll. Shrive makes several brief references earlier in his diary that he was already not too popular with higher command and it is not until his hospitalisation in March that he explains why:

I have never been backward in making certain suggestions to H.Q. As this body of people is located in Archangel and know very little of the difficulties we have had up here, I have several times made it a point to bring things to their notice. This I have found is no way to win a popularity contest. However, I have found all my fellow officers here at Bereznik are with me one hundred percent. As we up here see it, when the Armistice in November was signed, a good number of the Archangel gang figured that was it. We up here, though, had no Armistice, and with continuing depletion of personnel, those of us left now doing double and probably treble.[7]

After a transfer to No. 4 (Obozerskaya) Squadron (periodic transfer of aircrews between 'squadrons' in North Russia to meet needs was common) and another accident when his pilot flew into a snowdrift on take-off, Shrive proceeded to Archangel on leave. The mood he found in the city was not one of enthusiasm for the expedition. Shrive met aircrew in the city who had spent little time on missions through either sickness, casualty or conniving and others who flatly refused to serve at the front. Barely withholding his disdain Shrive recorded:

In three days I go back, and yet here in Archangel there are at least a dozen chaps who have done nothing, and from all accounts do not intend to … To be honest, since being in Archangel I have found that there is very little enthusiasm. A Royal Scot officer I met last night said he was in France just after Mons, served at Ypres, then on the Somme, and as he put it, we only signed up for one war and he was quite bitter in getting caught in another which to us now seems a lot too political.[8]

The malaise amongst soldiers in North Russia after the Armistice was understandable. The vast majority of the NREF were 'Hostilities Only' enlistees who had either volunteered or been conscripted into service for the duration of the war. By the time Shrive arrived in Archangel on leave the war had already been over for four months and no one was in a hurry to catch 'the last bullet' in a campaign which had only vague and dubious objectives, particularly if they had already survived years of war.

By his own admission Shrive himself became increasingly cynical of the campaign during his time in North Russia and his leave in Archangel did nothing to quell the anger growing inside him:

A good number of us have been away from home three years or more and also have served some time in other branches of the service and seen Active Service. We are all receiving letters saying how the lads are

6   *Ibid.*, p.76.
7   *Ibid.*, p.77.
8   *Ibid.*, p.80.

getting home and are now in civvies. We know now pretty well for sure that we will be on our way back to England within three months. The rub is, though, that for about two more months we are going back to engage in a war which our hearts are not in … As I see it this is not our war.[9]

On 28 February the garrison commanded by Captain Archie Henderson, Norfolk Regiment, in the village of Vistafka just south of Mala Bereznik on the opposite bank of the Vaga River, was heavily shelled all day as a prelude to a determined enemy attack at 1700 by 500–600 Red troops camouflaged in white smocks supported by an estimated 10 field guns including two heavy howitzers. The garrison of 17th Liverpools and 4.5 inch howitzers of 'Right Section', 421st Battery, RFA (Captain L.G. Duff, MC, RFA, Lieutenant Bernhard Martin, DSO, RFA, and 50 other ranks) defended the village equally determinedly, the gunners firing the howitzers over open sights directed by Lieutenant Algey Palmer, Northumberland Fusiliers from his observation post on the roof of a house for which Palmer was subsequently awarded the MC. Signalman Chapman distinguished himself during the defence by taking a Lewis gun forward in to the open to better engage the advancing enemy. Despite the numerical advantage, the attack faltered and failed, the enemy sustaining heavy casualties.

The Bolsheviks made a second attempt on 2 March after another heavy bombardment which set a number of houses on fire but both waves of attacks were also repulsed. The following day at 0600 the enemy made a third attempt to capture the village from the Allied side, cutting Kitsa and Vistafka off from the road to Tulgas. The attackers were repulsed for a third time after getting so close to the British gun positions that one of the howitzers came under sniper fire, slightly wounding Gunner Earle. Reverend Wilfred Brown, a chaplain attached to 6th Yorkshires, was awarded the MC during the attack for going forward and attending the wounded under fire and organising their evacuation, as was Lieutenant Bernhard Martin, 421st Battery, for skilful handling of his guns and Lieutenant Walter Newton, 68th Battery, CFA, for his work in an observation post for five days without rest.

Captain Henderson was awarded the DSO for his command of the defence of Vistafka during the attacks 28 February–4 March 1919; Sergeant Claude Winegard of 68th Battery was awarded the DCM for his gallantry during the attacks 1–3 March, for extinguishing a fire which had broken out in the stables and ammunition dump and for work on 3 March when he led a patrol to within 50 yards of an enemy machine gun outpost before attacking with Lewis guns, forcing the enemy to withdraw the machine gun from the attack.

Determined to push the British from their positions on the Vaga and having failed to dislodge the defenders at Vistafka, on 8 March the Bolsheviks attached Kitsa, their heaviest attack yet. The Reds reportedly used gas shells during the prelude bombardment but their use appears to have been ineffective, either due to wind or inaccuracy, as no British gas casualties were reported there.

The enemy managed to bring a machine gun forward to within 300 yards of one of the 4.5 inch howitzers and opened fire, killing Gunner Robert Middlemas outright. The Bolsheviks made three attempts during the day to push into the village but were repulsed at every attempt before withdrawing into the forest. Sergeant Hannibal Bond of 421st Battery was awarded the MM for his gallantry and leadership during this final attack.

Much of the village had been destroyed and set alight during the enemy bombardments and with the enemy outnumbering the defenders and with little prospect of repulsing any further attacks, the order was given to withdraw and abandon Kitsa to the enemy.

In late April, a Bolshevik deserter arrived at British lines bringing with him valuable information on the enemy defences on the Vaga River Front, and in particular the location of the Red Army Headquarters, down to a description of the building. Brigadier Finlayson (GOC Dvina Force) did

---

9   *Ibid.*, p.81.

not want to miss an opportunity to strike directly at Red Army command and requested the RAF bomb and strafe the enemy headquarters. South African Lieutenant Colonel Kenneth Van der Spuy volunteered for the mission and arranged to borrow Kazakov's personal Sopwith Camel for the operation. Anticipating that the mission would be a short one Van der Spuy did not take the opportunity to eat breakfast before setting off, a decision he was to greatly regret.

After take-off Van der Spuy flew up the Vaga River towards the enemy-held village and was immediately able to identify the headquarters building from the description given by the Bolshevik deserter and proceeded to bomb the Red Army HQ, although his bombs missed the target. He turned his aircraft for home and flew for about 40 minutes back up the Vaga before the engine suddenly cut out mid-air. As the Sopwith rapidly lost altitude the South African made a desperate attempt to restart the engine but was unsuccessful and was compelled to make a forced landing.

Dense forest far out to the horizon precluded an attempt to land on either side of the river and Van der Spuy had only seconds to make a decision. The only area clear of obstacles was on the small sandy bank of the Vaga itself:

Having selected a dangerously small clearing to land on, between the river and the fringe of the forest, I side slipped in, as I was able to, over the tall trees, flattened out at about ten feet above the ground and waited for the drop. What I had calculated was that the machine when pancaking on to the ground from that height would collapse its undercarriage, turn over on to its back, and that I would then be able to loosen my safety belt and drop out, set fire to the machine and make my getaway. What I did not reckon on was that the fall might be so heavy as to cause not only the undercart to collapse but the upper plane as well! This is exactly what did happen: a drop, a hard, tearing crash as the undercart went, a half summersault, another jarring crash as the centre-section struts collapsed and, instead of finding myself hanging nicely upside down in my seat ready to loose the safety belt and drop down on to mother earth, I found myself hard on the ground with my head sticking out of the padded, curved side of the cockpit, trapped!

By rights my neck should have been broken. To make matters worse, petrol was pouring over me. For a minute or two I panicked, because the fear of fire, in which case I would, of course not have a hope. I could, also, hear people shouting; fortunately they were on the opposite bank of the river. Somehow, I managed to free one hand and commenced furiously to scrape a hole in the earth until it was large enough to squeeze one shoulder through and, by slow degrees, my body. How long this took I don't know-it seemed an age, and all the time the shouting was coming nearer. Once out, there was no time to collect anything, much as I would have liked to have my revolver and the compass, and I bolted for the shelter of the trees. Hardly had I reached these when machine-gun fire broke out and, looking back, I could see splinters fly from parts of the aircraft.

For a while I remained hidden, perched in the lower branches of a tree. Soldiers passed within yards of me, obviously searching. Later, when the coast seemed clear, I made my way deeper into the forest and trudged all day through deep snow in the direction of our lines. I found the going difficult and tiring, floundering into holes and constantly striking hidden snags, logs and other obstacles hidden under the snow which, at that season, had softened. Once I went right through the upper crust and found myself in a deep donga, about ten feet below the surface. The sky was overcast so I had no sun to help guide me, but later in the day I heard gunfire and subsequently – after my release – learned that General Finlayson had given orders for the guns to fire, hoping that this would assist me to find my way in the event of my having escaped injury or capture. I was very glad of this because I was afraid of going in the wrong direction; to make a course in dense forest, without the sun to guide one, is difficult, and should I have walked in the wrong direction it would, through starvation and exhaustion, have been the end of me. I also discovered, subsequently, that the crash had been seen and photographed late that same afternoon by our flyers and that I had figured in the casualty lists as 'missing, believed killed.' No news of my safety reached my next of kin until many months later.[10]

For two days Van der Spuy evaded Red patrols, trudging through the snow in flying boots which stuck with every step. Late in the third day the South African was crossing a field towards the security of the forest when a mounted patrol appeared on a nearby road. He dropped to the ground and remained completely still, waiting to see if he had been spotted. Once the horsemen had passed, he made a sprint for the tree line only to run headlong into another mounted patrol. Within seconds the downed flyer was surrounded with a dozen rifles pointed at his chest. After three days on the run in enemy territory with no food, Van der Spuy became one of the highest-ranking British officers to be taken prisoner by the Bolsheviks during the Russian Civil War.

After an inspection of the inadequate defences surrounding Kitsa on 18 April, orders were issued for the evacuation of Ignatovskaya on the western bank of the Vaga to be carried out the same day to prepared positions at Mala-Bereznik, the evacuating troops leaving a number of booby-traps for the Bolsheviks before departing. Perhaps having got wind of the British withdrawal, the enemy shelled Ignatovskaya with shrapnel just as the Canadian 18 pdr section from 68th Battery was leaving, wounding Lieutenant John McRae who had been awarded the MC for the defence of Kodish, 5–6 January 1919.

The long-awaited arrival of the four 60 pdr guns at Archangel in early April significantly increased British firepower on the Dvina and Vaga Fronts. Lieutenant John Roberts, 68th Battery, CFA, who had been awarded the MC for leading an infantry attack in October noted in his diary:

> The long promised 60 pounder gun actually arrived at Mala Bereznik and it was astonishing the sense of extra security that the possession of one such gun gave to the Column even though most of us had been in France where the presence or absence of one or more guns was not of sufficient importance to mention. But this was a distinct event in our life in Russia as it meant that at least we had range supremacy and could 'talk back' however weakly, a thing we had not as yet been able to do.[11]

With the withdrawal to Mala Bereznik, all the artillery of the Vaga Column was concentrated in the one place, the newly arrived 60 pdr, 4.5 inch howitzers of 421st Battery, RFA. 'Right Section' and 18 pdrs of 68th Battery, CFA. The 421st Battery had an unfortunate start to their service in North Russia, suffering their first casualty soon after arrival at Archangel in October the previous year when Lieutenant Bernard Aldwinkle was accidentally shot in the head during revolver practice and died the following day.

On 1 May, the Bolsheviks made a concerted attack on Mala Bereznik, defended by 'C' Company, 17th Liverpools and a section of 280th MGC. A number of enemy shells started fires within the village, smoke adding to the general confusion of the battle. At 1000 the enemy attacked on the right flank with such determination that almost a whole company of Red troops breached the forward barbed wire defences before they were pinned down in the dead ground between the 'Pimple' and 'Summer House' positions by Stokes mortars and 4.5 inch howitzers of 421st Battery. The enemy continued to shell the village and probe the defences all day until their withdrawal on the commencement of a heavy thunderstorm at 2100. The British and Canadian defenders had killed 66 of the enemy and taken prisoner a further 30, for the loss of a single casualty from 17th Liverpools wounded.

2nd Lieutenants Samuel Dudley and Leslie Worgan, 17th Liverpools, were both awarded MCs for their command of forward blockhouses during the attack. Dudley's post comprised himself,

10   van der Spuy, *Chasing the Wind*, pp.131–133.
11   MacLaren, *Canadians in Russia 1918–19*, p. 84.

68. A gunner of 421st Battery, RFA sighting a 4.5 inch howitzer on the Kodish Front, summer 1919. (Author's collection)

one NCO and eight men which he took out of the blockhouse to boldly attack the enemy from the rear. Worgan determinedly held his post with 20 men against an attack by an estimated 200 enemy, driving them off with the loss of 40 killed and 21 taken prisoner.

Four days later the Bolsheviks bombarded Mala Bereznik for 15 hours before repeating the attack but were again driven off with heavy losses. Lieutenant Edward Bradfield, 280th MGC, was credited with opening a machine gun barrage with his Vickers section on the edge of the wood, preventing the enemy from advancing any further, for which he was awarded a Bar to his MC, the earlier award for gallantry on the Western Front when his entire machine gun section was wiped out. The attack of 5 May was repulsed but not without loss to the Liverpools: Private Joseph Murphy was killed and a further four other ranks wounded.

Sergeant Arthur Parsons, attached to Royal Engineers Signals from 2/10th Royal Scots, was also decorated for gallantry during the two attacks for going out under fire to repair damaged signal wires. Working for 23 hours without rest he kept up communications between the forward outposts, allowing the artillery observers to communicate with the battery of guns at Mala Bereznik for which Parsons was awarded the DCM.

During the night the Bolsheviks made a further attack on the town, this time from the river. In an extraordinarily bold and innovative move, two large barges loaded with eight field guns were silently towed up the Vaga to a position opposite Mala Bereznik where they opened fire at 2200, just as the sun was setting. The range was too short to have been effective and after a barrage lasting 20 minutes the barges withdrew under counter-battery fire from the Canadian and British guns in the village. To protect against any further bold moves by the enemy, Captain Altham despatched the large China gunboats HMS *Cricket* and HMS *Cicala* from the Royal Navy Dvina River Flotilla to take up station further down the Vaga from the Dvina junction.

On 9 May the Bolsheviks resumed their attempts to capture Vistafka, opening a 10 gun bombardment followed by strong infantry attacks which threatened to overrun the village. Corporal Walter Hughes of 68th Battery took his rifle up a tree and sniped a number of enemy in the vicinity of his gun pit without being detected. Apparently unaware of the precarious position of the small Allied garrison, the Bolsheviks did not attempt to storm the village, allowing the garrison to escape with Lieutenant Winslow's 18 pdr section to Kitsa and thence northwards to Ignatovskaya where they joined a further two guns of 68th Battery. The only Canadian casualties during the defence of Vistafka were Gunner William Webster wounded in the back by shrapnel and Bombardier William Birkett (who had been awarded the DCM for service on an armoured train in October and DCM Bar for rescuing a wounded messenger under fire in March) shot in the arm by a stray bullet.

By April 1919, preparations for the despatch of 1st (Grogan's) Brigade of the North Russia Relief Force (officially titled 238th 'Special' Brigade, so named in the Russian style after its commander, Brigadier George W. St. G. Grogan, VC, CB, CMG, DSO and Bar) were well underway. Born in St.

Andrews, Fife, Grogan had begun the war as a Captain in the Worcestershire Regiment but by 1918 had risen to the rank of Brigadier General commanding 23rd British Infantry Brigade on the Western Front. In command of the brigade during the German 'Spring Offensive' of 1918, Grogan walked up and down the line to rally his troops after his horse was shot from under him. He continued to rally his men under heavy fire, an act for which the gallant Brigadier was awarded the Victoria Cross.

69. Brigadier George W. St. G. Grogan, VC, CB, CMG, DSO and Bar, Worcestershire Regiment, GOC 1st (Grogan's) Brigade, North Russia Relief Force, 1919. (Public domain)

One of the battalions selected for service with the Brigade was 1st Battalion, Oxfordshire and Buckinghamshire Light Infantry (originally titled '2nd Composite Battalion' due to its multi-regimental composition), formed as a cadre, whose regular officers and men (some of whom had been prisoners of war released after the Armistice) were recalled in April 1919 to Aldershot in preparation to embark for active service by the end of the month. With the rapid reduction of the post-war army and commitments elsewhere, there were not enough soldiers from the Oxs and Bucks alone available for service in North Russia so the War Office decided to bring the battalion up to strength by drafting in soldiers from other regiments.

'HQ' and 'A' Company would be comprised of soldiers from the Oxs. and Bucks, 'B' Company, Royal Warwickshire Regiment, 'C' Company, Devon Regiment, and 'D' Company, Royal Berkshire Regiment. Additional platoons would also be drafted in from other regiments and distributed across the battalion to bring the unit up to full strength. By the time the battalion sailed for Russia no less than 20 regiments were represented, there were so many Scotsmen that the battalion was known as 'Oxs and Jocks'. All soldiers serving with the battalion would be allowed to retain their regimental uniform, headdress, hat badge and traditions.

The eventual composition of the battalion when it sailed for North Russia was as follows:

Commanding Officer:	Brevet Colonel W. Marriott-Dodington, CMG, Oxs and Bucks LI
Second in Command:	Major L.J. Carter, DSO, Oxs and Bucks LI
'A' Company:	Oxs and Bucks LI (Captain Cuthbert Baines, DSO and Bar)
'B' Company:	Royal Warwickshire Regiment (Captain A.J. Peck)
'C' Company:	Devonshire Regiment (Major A.F. Northcote)
'D' Company:	Royal Berkshire Regiment (Major A.G. MacDonald, DSO)

On 3 April, *The Times* ran a headline: 'Grave peril of our troops in North Russia: Reinforcements urgently needed' in which the author recounted the official line that only volunteers were being sent to Russia for which recruiting offices would open shortly. Similar assurances were made in Parliament despite the fact that both battalions of 1st (Grogan's) Brigade, NRRF (1st Oxs and Bucks and 2nd Hampshires) were composed entirely of regular troops who had not volunteered to serve in North Russia.

It was repeatedly stated that the British soldiers who fought on the North Russian Front [in the NRRF] were all volunteers. Despite the fact that these statements were made by people who should have a full sense of their responsibility, there is no question whatever that they were not true.

What happened in the case of the Devonshire Regiment certainly happened elsewhere, and may be taken as typical of the procedure. I am writing now, not from hearsay, but from facts which came under my own personal observation. This was how the thing was done. In the first place, a request was made for a stipulated number of volunteers … the number of volunteers asked for was quickly forthcoming, and then there was another order that the Devonshire Regiment had to provide one company for a Composite Battalion which was being formed.

These men were provided in the way in which drafts were provided for the Army in France throughout the war. They were 'warned'. That is to say they were ordered to go. They were not consulted as to their wishes in any way. Nor were the authorities concerned with the period of service which the men had yet to complete. Men who were daily expecting demobilisation, returned prisoners of war, men who were married with long families, men who had served four years in France and elsewhere. All these men were bundled off to fight again. Probably three-quarters of the Devon Company were obtained in this way. These were the 'volunteers' of which the officials at the War Office talked so loudly.[12]

In addition to the usual drills and training, instruction was given on Russia and Bolshevism which unfortunately gave a perhaps one-sided impression of the enemy:

> The Battalion was given to understand by these lectures that the expedition was to be a picnic; that the Bolsheviks were cowards and the forest fighting against them was not difficult. The officers were told that North Russia abounded in game, and were advised to take fishing-rods and guns, the better to enjoy a summer holiday; and that mosquitoes were likely to prove more formidable foes than the Bolsheviks.[13]

On 11 May, the brigade embarked at Southampton on board SS *Stephen* bound for Archangel where they arrived on 27 May, having waited five days at Murmansk for the last of the White Sea ice floes to thaw. Despite the weariness of four years of war, the brigade's departure was cheered by crowds of public with, 'foghorns, sirens and whistles from every conceivable craft.'[14] On disembarking at Archangel, Brigadier Grogan was greeted by leaders of the White Russian Provisional Government with the traditional Slavic welcome of bread and salt. Speeches were given and translated before a march past down the main street, Troitsky Prospekt, towards billets at Olga Barracks on the north-east side of the town.

1st Oxs and Bucks spent their first days in Russia performing ceremonial and guard duties, the officers being invited to various lavish dinner parties held by local Russian Generals and dignitaries. On 30 May, all Allied troops in Archangel took part in a parade led by the US contingent to commemorate those who had died in the American Civil War. On the King's Birthday, 1 June, the Oxs and Bucks attended a ceremony to present the Slavo-British Legion with 'King's' colours.

The following day, brigade mates 2nd Battalion, Hampshire Regiment (formed as '1st Composite Battalion') commanded by South African, Lieutenant Colonel John Sherwood-Kelly, VC, CMG, DSO, embarked on barges for the trip down the Dvina. The barges arrived at Bereznik on 5 June and shortly thereafter along with 238th TMB and half a company of 8th Battalion, MGC, were sent further downriver to relieve the lines at Kurgomen and Tulgas. Two weeks earlier Tulgas had been the scene of bitter fighting before its recapture by troops from US 339th Infantry on 18 May. The

12   *The Western Times*, 15 October 1919.
13   Captain J.E.H. Neville, M.C., *History of the 43rd and 52nd (Oxfordshire and Buckinghamshire) Light Infantry in the Great War, 1914–1919* (Aldershot: Gale & Polden, 1938), p.310.
14   *Ibid.*, p.311.

70. Soldiers of 1st (Dyer's) Battalion, Slavo-British Legion parade at Archangel for presentation of King's Colours on the occasion of the King's Birthday, 1st June 1919. (Public domain)

village had been abandoned to the Red Army by 3rd North Russian Rifles on 25 April when soldiers from that unit mutinied and went over to the Bolsheviks.

The arrival of both brigades of the NRRF in May and June increased the total number of Allied troops at Archangel significantly, however all US and Canadian troops as well as the stalwart 2/10th Royal Scots departed Russia in June, leaving Ironside increasingly dependent on the British-trained and British-equipped White Russian 'North Russian Rifle Regiments' which were unreliable to say the least. 3rd North Russian Rifles had mutinied at Tulgas on 25th April and less than a month later on 14 May, a company of 8th North Russian Rifles refused to embark for the front and killed two of their officers. Ironside had 15 of the ringleaders shot and disarmed the remainder, forming them into a labour company.

1st Oxs and Bucks had landed in North Russia less than a week before suffering their first fatality. Lieutenant Quartermaster George Dancy, MC, DCM, a veteran of the Mesopotamian campaign and former RSM of the battalion, had been described as 'ill' before leaving England and had worked himself very hard in the lead up to the move down the Dvina. On the afternoon of 2 June, Dancy was found with a self-inflicted gunshot wound to the head and died shortly after.

Lieutenant J.E.H. Neville, MC (who would write the regimental history of the Oxs and Bucks during the Great War), was serving with the Oxs and Bucks and described the terrain and conditions in which the battles of the spring and summer 1919 were fought:

The country can be described by two words; forest and swamp. The forest, consisting of pines and silver birches, was extremely think and gave a visibility of about fifteen to twenty yards in broad daylight. Added to which, impenetrable bramble undergrowth, ten feet high and more, was often encountered on any deviation from the tracks. Once in the forest it was very difficult to keep direction without a vestige of a landmark to march on and with forest tracks radiating in all directions. A compass was soon found to be essential. The forest tracks were only passable by men in single file. No matter how brilliant the sunshine, the forest was always dank, sombre and sinister; and teemed with all manner of insect life. To stray from a forest track often entailed floundering up to the knees in swamps, cunningly disguised by nature with soft, spongy moss.[15]

The Oxs and Bucks took up advanced positions at Nijni Kitsa and Mala Bereznik on the Vaga River where the battalion suffered its first combat casualty on 9 June when a Bolshevik machine gun team crept forward to the edge of the forest and opened fire on a British post nicknamed 'The Pimple', wounding a man from 'A' Company in the groin.

On 11 June, the battalion lost Lance Corporal Alfred Phillipson, a Cheshire Regiment soldier serving in 'C' (Devonshire) Company, in a drowning accident in the river. Phillipson and his platoon sergeant had disobeyed orders and gone swimming in the Vaga at midnight. Phillipson had become tangled in some reeds and by the time the sergeant was able to return to the river with help, Phillipson was still submerged. Lieutenant John Moulding dived in and brought the body to the surface but it was too late. Phillipson was pronounced dead by a US Army doctor and buried in Ust-Vaga churchyard, his grave since lost to time.

Sadly, Phillipson was one of a number of British servicemen to die from drowning in North Russia. The rivers and swamps claimed a number of lives during the campaign and virtually every infantry battalion that served in North Russia lost at least one man to drowning. To counter the risk of accidental drowning, GHQ Archangel issued orders that bathing was to take place only in organised 'bathing parties' but drownings still occurred. The fast-flowing currents of the Dvina were particularly treacherous, any man falling into the river who was not plucked out immediately, even if a strong swimmer, was at a very strong risk of drowning. Some contemporary accounts state that men who fell into the Dvina were unlikely to ever surface again.

The Oxs and Bucks did not waste time in making their presence on the Vaga felt as CO, Colonel Dodington immediately began planning an offensive raid against the Bolshevik forward positions at Ignatovskaya, a small village south along the Vaga. Dodington's plan was to advance through the forest down the left bank of the Vaga and capture the Bolshevik front line near Mala Bereznik, then proceed down the Moscow road past Ignatovskaya and spike the Bolshevik guns mounted on artillery barges at Maksimovskaya before a rapid withdrawal to British lines.

'A' (Oxs and Bucks) and 'C' (Devons) Companies would make the advance to Ignatovskaya on the left bank whilst 'B' (Warwicks) and gunners from 55th Battery, RFA would advance on Kitsa on the right. A handful of sappers from 384th Field Company and Royal Engineers signallers as well as RAMC field ambulance detachments would also accompany the force. Machine guns and trench mortars from Bereznik would fire in support of the attack, bombarding the enemy line seconds before the British attack went in.

The 1st Oxs and Bucks battalion history unashamedly records a rather unsavoury exchange between OC 'A' Company, Captain Cuthbert Baines and Sergeant Bristow of No. 2 Platoon on the fate of any 'Chinese' prisoners that might be taken:

Sergeant Bristow, with a broad grin on his jovial face, wanted to know whether 'Chinks' were to be taken prisoners or otherwise disposed of … it was unanimously agreed by all present that no trouble should be taken to preserve any Chinese prisoners from harm. On the other hand, the poor benighted Bolshevik was to be treated kindly, for he might be enlisted into the Slavo-British Legion as an ally.[16]

---

15   *Ibid.*, pp.320–324.
16   *Ibid.*, p.337.

It might seem unusual for a regimental history to include details of an agreement before a battle to kill prisoners however in North Russia the murder of prisoners by Allied troops was not uncommon practice. One observer recorded:

A friend of mine was walking unarmed on a lonely road near the front one day when a Bolshevik soldier came out of the woods and made a friendly approach. He asked my friend if it was safe to go in and give himself up as a prisoner and was assured that it was. They went in together, the guard at the barricade took charge of the prisoner, taking him to headquarters. Ten days later my friend learned that this prisoner had been shot, and the only reason given was that he had refused to give certain desired information as to the enemy. I have heard an officer tell his men repeatedly to take no prisoners, to kill them even if they came in unarmed, and I have been told by the men themselves of many cases when this was done … when we caught the Commissar of Borok, a sergeant tells me we left his body in the street, stripped, with sixteen bayonet wounds. We surprised Borok, and the Commissar, a civilian, did not have time to arm himself. The sergeant was quite exhalant over it. He killed Bolsheviki because they were barbarians and cruel. This was the only thing his government had ever told him as to why they would be killed.

I saw a disarmed Bolshevik prisoner, who was making no attempt to escape and no trouble of any kind, and who was alone in charge of three armed soldiers, shot down in cold blood. The official whitewash on this case was that he was trying to escape. I have heard of many other cases of the shooting of Bolshevik prisoners. At one time this had become so common that the Officer Commanding troops issued and had posted up an order forbidding it and calling attention to the fact that there were many Bolshevik soldiers who wanted to come over and give themselves up but feared to do so because they had heard about our shooting prisoners, and warning our men that the Bolsheviki might retaliate by shooting our men whom they held as prisoners.[17]

After a late meal, anti-mosquito ointment concocted by the regimental doctor from tar and lard was distributed to the troops in an attempt to provide some relief from the swarms of mosquitoes which inhabited the forest. A common feature of virtually all accounts of service during spring and summer 1919 in North Russia is description of the 'tropical' climate and swarms of ravenous mosquitoes. During the heat of the day the insects sought refuge in the shade of the forest only to emerge en masse at sunset. Lieutenant Neville, Oxs and Bucks, wrote of the limitations of using mosquito head-nets in North Russia:

Swarms found their way through the meshes where the net itself touched the skin round the collar. Through the seams of trousers and breeches, through lacing holes, they found room for the insertion of the proboscis. They settled like hairs upon the troops' hand, and crawled up their sleeves and inside their shirts. Added to this torture, there was the maddening wheezing hum of the little devils and the sudden intensified scream as one or more settled in your ears and buzzed out again. The air was charged with them … No description of them would be an exaggeration: they had to be seen and felt to be believed.[18]

Shortly after 2200 on 27 June, the guns of 55th Battery, RFA opened fire, 'Suddenly there was a terrific crash behind the enemy's lines; then another – and another – until the Bolshevik position was blotted out completely in clouds of smoke and dust.'[19] The Oxs and Bucks moved off at 2215 sharp through the clearing in front of the British positions and into the dense forest. At 2300, just as 'A' and 'C' Companies were moving into position, the bombarded recommenced:

---

17   Albertson, *Fighting Without a War*, pp.86–88.
18   Neville, *History of the 43rd and 52nd*, p.328
19   *Ibid.*, p.337.

71. Gunners and Drivers of 421st Battery, RFA and 1152 Company, RASC which served in North Russia. The soldier with the swagger stick is Sergeant Walter Martin, 421st Battery, RFA. A veteran of the Boer War, Martin was awarded the DCM for work as a forward observer near Alexandrova on the night of 13–14 July 1919. (Author's collection)

The noise was simply terrific when the guns and machine guns opened fire. The echo and reverberations of bursting shells and flying bullets were deafening, and, though there were only nine guns firing, it seemed as if there might have been nine hundred as the noise of each shot resounded through the forest.[20]

Tragically, three shells in quick succession landed on 'A' Company's position, Lieutenant Hugh Sturges was severely wounded in both legs and his platoon scattered. During a momentary pause in the bombardment the Bolsheviks opened fire with machine guns but were quickly forced into cover when the British shelling resumed. As the creeping barrage moved beyond the Bolsheviks' forward trenches, the Oxs and Bucks emerged from the forest and scaled the high barbed wire fence in front of the position. The Red troops had long since fled and the British faced virtually no resistance. The frontline appeared to be deserted but two Maxim guns and 17 prisoners were taken at the cost of just one man from 'A' Company slightly wounded.

Time was critical to the success of the operation and leaving some men behind to destroy the Bolshevik positions and equipment, the remainder of the party continued on to the wire in front of Ignatovskaya where they were met by heavy but inaccurate rifle and machine gun fire. Sergeant John White of 'A' Company, a Mesopotamia veteran and recipient of the Military Medal, left his platoon to try and find the enemy flank but was shot in the head and killed.

In the meantime, 'C' Company had been held up by an enemy blockhouse across their route to Ignatovskaya. OC 'C' Company, Major Northcote had been assured that the blockhouse would be knocked out during the preliminary artillery bombardment but after one hour of shelling it was yet to receive a direct hit. There was no choice but to try and capture the blockhouse intact. The leading platoon under Lieutenant Norman Hughes almost reached the blockhouse before they were spotted and fired on, Hughes was hit and badly wounded in the stomach in the initial burst of fire.

The heavy fire pinned down 'C' Company in a depression just 50 yards from the blockhouse, bullets struck the trees above the men's heads sending shards of wood and bark below. Pinned down in front of the blockhouse, Lieutenant Marcus Wilcox spotted a party of Red troops attempting

---

20 *Ibid.*, p.339.

72. A 4.5 inch howitzer position of 421st Battery, RFA on the Kodish Front,
summer 1919. The huts had been built by Canadian gunners the previous year to
house their 18 pdr guns during the harsh winter. (Author's collection)

to outflank the Devons by advancing down a trench leading towards the river. Wilcox directed his Lewis gunners to suppress the trench, killing several of the enemy.

Pinned down and unable to advance, a runner reached Major Northcote with a message from Colonel Dodington ordering 'C' Company to withdraw. The company had been split in half when taking cover from fire from the enemy blockhouse and it was left to a volunteer to make the risky dash across the exposed road running between the company halves, to pass the message to withdraw. Lieutenant Harry Gibbons volunteered and dashed across the road under heavy fire immediately in front of the blockhouse but by a miracle was not hit. For his leadership and personal bravery during the raid, Gibbons was awarded the MC.

'C' Company had suffered numerous casualties and a number of gallant attempts were made to retrieve the wounded but the would be rescuers were all shot down in turn and several wounded men, including the badly wounded Lieutenant Hughes, had to be left behind to the enemy.

'A' Company were not having an easier time than their comrades in 'C' Company. Pinned down in front of rows of barbed wire and unable to advance, a stray bullet struck 'A' Company OC Captain Cuthbert Baines in the groin causing a severe injury.

Unable to capture Ignatovskaya without more troops, his communications with Mala Bereznik broken and the prearranged time for a box barrage on the approaches to Ignatovskaya fast approaching, Colonel Dodington had no other option than to order a complete withdrawal. A final, desperate attempt was made by men from 'C' Company to extricate the wounded Lieutenant Hughes from the line of fire before the bombardment but intense enemy fire made any further attempt nearly suicidal.

The bombardment by 55th Battery resumed but was too weak to cut the enemy wire and resulted only in a greater fusillade of fire from the enemy once the shelling stopped. At 0250, Colonel Dodington (whose HQ position was also under fire) gave the order to withdraw. As the British were pulling back, Bolshevik artillery made an appearance, shelling the road down which the British had to withdraw. The barrage crept forward, following the British column as it rapidly retreated however the firing was sporadic and inaccurate and no further casualties were incurred.

All who participated in the raid were shocked at the determined resistance put up by the well-dug in Bolsheviks and were forced to reconsider the low impression of the Red troops given on their way to Russia:

It was obviously necessary to readjust the estimate of the enemy's power of resistance as advertised in England before the Regiment had sailed. Their guns and machine guns had been surprisingly well served; and the enemy had repulsed a determined attack against all expectations … either the Relief Force troops had not the valour of the old, as alleged by *The Times*, or the Bolsheviks were better soldiers than had been reported.[21]

There was little elation as the troops made their way through the forest back to Mala Bereznik. The journey was worst for the wounded who had to be carried on the back of springless local *drosky* carts which constantly jolted over the slightest bump. At 0500 the column passed through the forward British positions at Mala Bereznik where the wounded and 17 Red Army prisoners were loaded on to barges for transport to the British hospital at Bereznik. The wounded Captain Baines suffered particularly badly, he was immediately evacuated to Bereznik where his leg was amputated.

Despite the loss of Lieutenant Hughes and seven other ranks killed and Captain Baines and Lieutenant Sturges severely wounded, the raid on Ignatovskaya achieved little of military value. Other casualties wounded during the raid included Lieutenant E. S. Browne, 55th Battery, RFA, a sapper from 384th Field Company, three machine gunners from 8th Battalion, MGC, and 27 NCOs and men from 'A' and 'C' Companies, 1st Oxs and Bucks, four of whom were reported 'Missing Presumed Killed' but later confirmed as prisoners of war. Compared to France and Flanders the casualties were light but certainly heavier than Dodington had expected. To lose soldiers who had survived years of war on the Western Front and Mesopotamia only to die in a forest in a little known campaign was particularly hard to bear.

The attack failed mainly due to the legacy of Western Front tactics and thinking which were not applicable to the forests of North Russia. The bombardment from so few guns did not cut the enemy wire in front of Ignatovskaya and served only to warn the Bolsheviks of the impending attack. Insufficient time was given to the flanking platoons to reach their starting positions before the attack. The attacking force did not have enough experience of the time it took to navigate through the dense forest and individual platoons found themselves dispersed and overlapped. In its first action in North Russia the Oxs and Bucks proved that movement and not artillery were the key factors to a successful attack. Dodington immediately set about planning another operation in which he would put these hard learned principles into practice.

Just after midnight on the night of 2–3 July, Colonel Dodington led his battalion into the forest in a second raid on the Bolsheviks' positions outside Ignatovskaya, this time without any prearranged artillery bombardment to alert the enemy. Dodington was determined for the raid to succeed where the first attempt had failed. What he did not know was that his positions at Mala Bereznik were being constantly watched and just 200 yards into the forest Bolshevik scouts opened fire on the column before melting back into the shadows.

Progress through the forest was tediously slow with very few landmarks to aid navigation. As the trees thinned towards the clearing at Ignatovskaya, Lieutenant James Neville, MC, of 'A' Company took Sergeant Charles Botley and three men as scouts ahead to locate the enemy position. Neville would later pen the regimental history in which he modestly makes no reference to himself by name, only as 'an officer':

When I was plumb in the middle of the clearing I realized instinctively that my men were not following. I had a cold and lonely feeling. I looked round and saw them lying down on their bellies. Then it was that Sergeant Botley whispered 'Bolos' and pointed to his right rear … I had hardly uttered – when there was

---

21   *Ibid.*, p.344.

a cracking of whip lashes all around me. In a split fraction of a second I must have turned about for I just caught a glimpse of the machine gun which had fired at my back.[22]

Neville fortuitously escaped with only a bullet through his water bottle and an arm wound but remained on duty.

As the Bolsheviks fired wildly into the forest it became immediately apparent that the enemy positions had not been outflanked as anticipated. The order was given to fix bayonets and assault the enemy line. Immediately as the platoons cleared the tree line the men realised they had not advanced far enough to flank the seven foot barbed wire fence the Bolsheviks had erected in front of their positions.

'A' Company led the attack with Lance Corporal Charles Martin bravely rushing forward with a Lewis gun. Resting the barrel on a rung of the fence, Martin raked the enemy trenches at close range, an act for which he was subsequently awarded the MM. Captain George Naylor and Sergeant Taylor led the remainder of the force forward in the mad scramble over the fence and charged a Bolshevik machine gun which was still firing. Sergeant Cleary bayoneted one of the gun crew whilst Captain Naylor finished off the rest with his revolver.

The British troops swarmed over the position only to discover that most of the enemy had fled into the forest and the blockhouses and trenches had been deserted; only one machine gun and eight enemy dead were left behind. The raiders searched the position for documents and set demolition charges in two of the blockhouses before withdrawing through the forest back to Mala Bereznik.

Casualties for the second raid on Ignatovskaya were far lighter than the first, only Lieutenant Neville and two other ranks lightly wounded. The raid once again illustrated the difficulty of navigating a column through the forest to an objective within a set timeframe. For his gallantry and leadership during both raids on Ignatovskaya, Captain Naylor was awarded a Bar to his MC previously awarded for service during the siege at Kut-Al-Amara, Mesopotamia, where 1st Oxs and Bucks were besieged for four months. Captured by the Turks, more than half of their number died of privation and disease during nearly three years of captivity.

On 14 July, a strange incident occurred when Lance Corporal John Ferries, one of the Royal Scots attached to 'C' (Devons) Company who had been reported 'Missing, Presumed Killed' after the first raid on Ignatovskaya, wandered back into British lines from the forest. He was questioned by the battalion intelligence officer Lieutenant Guy Tamplin, MC, RGA, who was told that after his capture, Ferries had been put to labour but had escaped when the chance presented itself and had walked 30 *versts* along the river to reach the British lines at Mala Bereznik. Further questioning revealed that Ferries was lying and had in fact been offered freedom by the Bolsheviks in exchange for his agreement to spread propaganda and dissent amongst his comrades and undermine the authority of the officers. Ferries was put under arrest and sent downriver where he was not heard from again. Extraordinarily, he is still recorded by the Commonwealth War Graves Commission as being killed in action on 27 June 1919, and to this day a plaque bearing his name remains in the CWGC cemetery in Archangel.

The remainder of the month was relatively quiet but the calm did not extend to 1 August when 400 Red soldiers of 156th Regiment launched an attack on the Oxs and Bucks positions west of Mala Bereznik, accompanied by a barrage from Bolshevik artillery at Ignatovskaya. The British responded with their own artillery and trench mortars and drove the Bolsheviks back just as they reached the British wire.

Thirty minutes later the Bolsheviks could be heard digging in just inside the tree line and Lieutenant John Clews, DCM, and Lieutenant William Dibben, MC, of 'B' (Warwicks) Company were sent out with patrols to locate the enemy who were found 'digging in like rabbits'. Dibben

---

22   *Ibid.*, p.349.

charged the enemy, driving them back into the forest where he encountered 200 more enemy troops preparing to attack. Sprinting back to the trench mortars of 239th TMB (Captain J. L. Carr, Oxs and Bucks), Dibben gave the location of the enemy and 15 rounds of rapid fire did the rest, dispersing the Bolshevik attack and forcing the enemy further into the forest. For his gallantry Lieutenant Dibben was awarded a Bar to his MC awarded on the Western Front.

On 19 August, a curious event occurred at Ust-Vaga when a Bolshevik seaplane flew low over the town and landed on the nearby Vaga River. Both pilot and observer promptly disembarked and surrendered. Later in the same day, presumably part of a prearranged plot, a Bolshevik Nieuport fighter landed near Troitsa on the Dvina River, the pilot surrendering his aircraft intact to the British garrison.

On 1 September a Bolshevik force infiltrated through the forest behind British lines to attack Ust-Vaga from the flank. The town was garrisoned by a meagre force of HQ staff, a handful of men from 'B' (Warwicks) Company and 'C' (Devons) Company, two sections of 8th Battalion, MGC, details from the RASC and RAMC and one company of dubious quality from 4th North Russian Rifles. At 0030, civilian guides led Bolshevik troops into the town after cutting the telephone line to reinforcements at Seltso on the Dvina. The Red troops quietly crept upon two of the MGC blockhouses, killing Private William Fisher and capturing the remaining crews.

The enemy moved silently towards the log cabin in which the British officers were billeted, easily discernible by the bunch of berries placed by a either a civilian or one of the North Russian Riflemen to identify its location for the attacking force. The British officers had earlier noticed the berries but had thought it a local custom or superstition and thought nothing of it. The British sentry was well alert and noticing movement dashed inside the cabin, bolted the door shut and woke the sleeping officers. A grenade was thrown and the Bolsheviks opened fire on the cabin with rifles and a light machine gun. The British officers and their batmen inside the cabin responded by snap shooting at the Red troops as they came forward.

Their element of surprise lost, the Bolsheviks withdrew out of sight of the cabin and must have been shocked to see Major A. F. Northcote, OC 'C' Company with Lieutenants Henry Gibbons and Maurice Beck advancing in wellington boots with greatcoats covering their pyjamas, possibly the only occasion in British military history that a counter-attack has been led by officers clad in pyjamas and wellington boots.

Unable to advance closer to the officers' billet, the Bolsheviks turned their attention to the next most conspicuous building which was in fact the Vaga Column hospital. The North Russian Rifles had long since fled or joined the attackers and it was left to Major Northcote and his platoon of Devons to clear the remaining Red troops from around the hospital. In the meantime the RAMC Medical Officer, Captain Frederick Chandler, had been gallantly defending the besieged hospital with his hunting shotgun in lieu of a more useful weapon. Lieutenant Beck had a face-to-face encounter with the Bolshevik commander in the middle of the street, both men emptied their revolvers at each other with neither scoring a hit. Some of the fleeing enemy had taken the opportunity to occupy the two captured MGC blockhouses and were able to enfilade the Warwicks and Devons in their attempt to clear the village. Northcote turned his attention to the blockhouses and mounted a deliberate attack, none of the Bolsheviks inside either blockhouse showed any desire to surrender and all were killed.

By 0630, after four hours of fighting, the plucky Devons had cleared Ust-Vaga of the enemy. Fourteen Bolsheviks had been killed and eight taken prisoner, seven of whom were also wounded. A local later reported that another 15 enemy bodies had been removed from the battlefield by Bolshevik cavalry. The two Vickers machine guns of 8th MGC taken from the blockhouses by the retreating enemy were later found abandoned in the forest. British casualties had been six killed and 12 wounded. Those killed were Private William Fisher 8th MGC, Sergeant Charles Wilkes and Private Denis Ponting, 'B' (Warwicks) Company, Private John Nelson, King's Own Scottish Borderers attached Oxs and Bucks, Private Nathan Pimm, 239th TMB and Corporal George Almond, 1102nd Horse Transport Company, RASC.

For their gallantry and leadership during the attack, Major Northcote was awarded the DSO, Lieutenant Gibbons the MC, CSM Samuel Lee, 'C' (Devons) Company, the DCM and eight other ranks the MM. One of the MMs was awarded in rather unusual circumstances to Private Arthur Warren, 'D' (Berks) Company attached 239th TMB. Warren was a patient in the Ust-Vaga hospital at the time of the attack but defended the hospital with a rifle despite considerable pain from his injuries. He was credited with killing two Red soldiers and wounding one.

On 8 September, the warning order for evacuation was finally received from GHQ Archangel. The Oxs and Bucks spent most of the next two days booby-trapping roads, bridges and houses with Mills bombs and gun cotton and loading stores and equipment onto barges. On 13 September, machine gun and trench mortar fire broke out at Mala Bereznik as enemy patrols probed the British forward posts. Evidently the Bolsheviks had no intention of letting the British leave quietly. The forward

73. Private William Sparks, 'C' (Devons) Company, 1st Battalion, Oxfordshire and Buckinghamshire Light Infantry, awarded the MM for bravery during the Bolshevik raid on Ust-Vaga during the night of 1 September 1919. (Author's collection)

posts had reported the sound of Mills bomb booby-traps exploding sporadically through the night and all indications were that the enemy were moving to make an attack on Koslovo on the opposite bank of the river. At 0630, Bolshevik artillery opened fire on Mala Bereznik and kept up an intermittent bombardment all day until 1600, caving in one of the forward positions and wounding one man, however the expected attack did not materialise.

On the evening of 15 September 1919 the long awaited order to move out finally came. After throwing surplus supplies and ammunition into the Vaga River and down village wells, a party of Royal Engineers under Lieutenant John Wakeford set gun cotton charges to blow the wooden bridges across the Vaga. As the Oxs and Bucks marched northwards towards Bereznik they passed old women who came out of their houses to watch the column pass, 'howling and beating their chests in paroxysms of grief'.[23] Soon after midday the Oxs and Bucks took over positions of 46th Royal Fusiliers who had also withdrawn to Bereznik from advanced positions further down the Dvina. Although both units had been in North Russia for some months it was the first time soldiers of the two regiments had met.

The following day, soon after the Oxs and Bucks had left Bereznik, firing was heard in the distance and word received that the Bolsheviks had captured Ust-Vaga from the local Russian forces. All reports seemed to indicate that a rearguard action would have to be fought but the Bolsheviks seemed content to harry the column from a safe distance rather than attack outright. An unfortunate event occurred as the last of the Dvina Force barges made their way towards Archangel, when a Bolshevik machine gun crew firing from the river bank at the confluence of the Dvina and Vaga inflicted a number of casualties amongst men of 45th Royal Fusiliers. Among those killed were Captain Alistair Pearse, MC, Middlesex Regiment attached 45th Royal Fusiliers (officers in 2nd (Sadleir-Jackson's) Brigade, NRRF, served on attachment from their parent units) and Sergeant

---

23   *Ibid.*, p.375.

Percy Petter, both of whom would be posthumously decorated for an action at Kodema just a week earlier, Pearce receiving an MC Bar and Petter the DCM.

A platoon of Royal Marines commanded by Lieutenant Clive Sergeant, RMLI, was landed and made short work of the enemy ambushers but not before four Royal Fusiliers had been killed and a further seven wounded. The Oxs and Bucks had been responsible for securing the confluence of the rivers and were not to embark themselves until six hours after the last barge had passed Bereznik but the order had been altered and the timings changed, and on arrival at Bereznik Colonel Marriott-Dodington was not informed that the last of the Dvina Force barges had not yet passed.

The Oxs and Bucks arrived at Archangel on 21 September and four days later received orders to board hospital ship *Braemar Castle* and transport *Czar* bound for Liverpool via Murmansk. In contrast to the fanfare of their departure, the Oxs and Bucks' return attracted little interest amongst the public. The battalion disembarked in the midst of the Railway Strike of 1919 and the 'civic welcome' they were told to expect was rather subdued. After an address by the Lord Mayor of Liverpool, the battalion marched off to their billets; the battalion history records, 'of public interest there was none … the Regiment marched up to Knotty Ash Camp, receiving many hoots and jeers from the assembled strikers, and was lucky under the circumstances to escape bottles and other welcoming missiles.'[24]

The end for 1st Oxs and Bucks 'composite' battalion was an unglamorous one. Over the following week the various drafts of attached men began to slowly disperse to their parent regiments. On 13 October, HQ and 'A' Company moved to camp at North Ripon where the men were sent on leave to await demobilisation. The 1st Battalion, Oxfordshire and Buckinghamshire Light Infantry was for the time being at least reduced to a cadre only.

24   *Ibid.*, p.383.

10

Archangel: Dvina River Front January–June 1919

By the end of January 1919, with the Bolsheviks in possession of Shenkursk and threatening to push further north, General Ironside issued immediate orders to further strengthen the road, river and rail heads through which the enemy must advance. The nature of warfare in North Russia was very different to that on the Western Front, there were no front lines per se but rather a series of junctions, usually a village or railhead, separated by many miles of dense forest. To control territory captured during the advance from Archangel in August, Ironside had ordered the construction of a series of blockhouses and other defences to protect these junctions.

Australian 'ELOPE' Force Sergeant John Kelly described the nature of defensive warfare in North Russia:

> The area under our control was roughly 50,000 square miles in extent, but fully 90% of it required no defence at all owing to the peculiar natural features of the country which consisted of pine and fir tree forests so densely timbered that it was utterly impossible for anyone to establish communication of any kind through them; there was also the additional barrier in the winter months of many feet of snow and in the summer months the melting of this snow transformed the ground surface into a squelching bog. Through these forests ran several rivers and streams, the railway and a few isolated tracks leading to a lonely village here and there. To defend the area it was therefore only necessary to plug up these road, river and rail heads. Our defences somewhat resembled a huge fan, with Archangel as the hub, and a force operating at the end of each of the ribs. These posts might be anything up to 250 miles from the Base according to the district in which they were situated. Being completely isolated from other posts, each Command acted independently, fighting its own battles and acting entirely on its own initiative. The result was that instead of a continuous front line such as we knew in Gallipoli and France, there were several Fronts known as the 'Railway Front', 'Dvina River Front', 'Kotlas Front' and so on. Fighting was conducted principally from blockhouses under Indian or guerrilla warfare conditions.[1]

On 27 January, word was received at Archangel that the Bolsheviks had fired three poison gas shells at British positions on the Railway Front. Ironside immediately cabled the War Office: 'Report that three gas shells fired by enemy. My one gas officer has gone up to investigate.'[2] Discussion by members of the British government on the use of poison gas against the Bolsheviks had always been controversial. The War Office was reluctant to use such a weapon against the Bolsheviks when the Red Army had not used gas shells themselves.

Churchill was ablaze at the suggestion that the British would not use all available weapons against the Bolsheviks. In a letter to the Chief of Imperial Staff dated 25 January 1919, Churchill wrote:

> What is the reason for the injunction given at 'A' [Archangel]? Because an enemy who has perpetrated every conceivable barbarity is at present unable, through his ignorance, to manufacture poisoned gas, is that any reason why our troops should be prevented from taking full advantage of their weapons? The use

---

1   AWM: PR85/324, Recollection of John Kelly.
2   Kinvig, *Churchill's Crusade*, p.128.

74. Tasmanian Major Thomas Davies, DSO, MC, RE, displaying the construction of 'M' aerial gas bombs dropped by the RAF in North Russia. (IWM Q16335)

of these gas shell having become universal during the great war, I consider that we are fully entitled to use them against anyone pending the general review of the laws of war which no doubt will follow the peace conference.[3]

Word that the Bolsheviks had used gas shells at Archangel was a boon to Churchill who wasted no time in announcing to the press that the Reds had used poison gas first and a ship would soon sail from the UK carrying gas shells for North Russia. On 7 February, formal instructions were cabled to Ironside at Archangel and Maynard at Murmansk authorising that, 'fullest use is now to be made of gas shells with your forces or supplied by us to Russian forces, as Bolsheviks have been using gas shells against Allied troops at Archangel.'[4]

The Bolsheviks reportedly used poison gas shells against the British in North Russia on at least two occasions, both on the Railway Front, but on both occasions their use was limited and ineffectual. By the withdrawal of British troops from North Russia in October, the British had fired from artillery and dropped from aircraft more than 1,000 gas shells and improvised gas bombs. The gas used was non-fatal tear gas which incapacitated those affected, consequently there were very few fatalities attributed by the British to its use. Ironside wrote of the unsuccessful attempts to use gas:

It was found impossible to empty the gas by ordinary hand discharge owing to the lack of wind in the thick forest. For a month we waited for a north wind and this method of discharge had to be abandoned.[5]

The gas projectors subsequently sent by the War Office were found to be in an unusable condition leaving no effective means to deliver poison gas to the enemy. Seeing a solution to the dilemma, Major Thomas Davies, DSO, MC, RE, an Australian mining engineer and chemist, devised aerial poison gas bombs which could be dropped by aircraft. Dubbed the 'M-bomb', the device was essentially a poison gas canister with metal fins welded on to provide some aerodynamic properties. The bombs were manufactured by the RAOC on board the repair ship HMS *Cyclops* under the supervision of Major Davies. Close to 1,000 were eventually made and several hundred dropped on the enemy, primarily by DH9s of No. 4 (Obozerskaya) Squadron flying from Obozerskaya during attacks on Emtsa and Plesetskaya, 27–29 August.

The gas caused coughing, vomiting and sore eyes but very few deaths, in fact, after an interrogation of enemy prisoners who had been gassed it was officially reported to Ironside that the gas was 'non-lethal'. One British officer deliberately exposed himself to the gas to ascertain the effects for himself and was violently ill for two days but recovered very quickly thereafter. Although non-lethal,

3   This letter is today held in the Churchill Archives.
4   Kinvig, *Churchill's Crusade*, p.128.
5   Dobson and Miller, *The Day We Almost Bombed Moscow*, p.204.

the invention of the 'M-bomb' met with considerable success and Ironside reported, 'Gas bombing proved highly successful and materially helped the Russian situation.'[6]

On 26 January, a Red force attacked Tulgas (garrisoned at the time by soldiers of US 339th Infantry Regiment and 2/10th Royal Scots) and captured the town but were driven out by a determined counter-attack by the Royal Scots and 'Doughboys' the following morning. Bolstered by their success at Shenkursk, the Bolsheviks continued to attack over the following three days until Ironside, unsure if he could hold the line, ordered the town evacuated four days later after Tulgas had been set alight and nearly burnt to the ground. The Bolsheviks failed to take advantage of the withdrawal and the Allied troops reoccupied the town soon after.

By early 1919 the Bolsheviks were enjoying significant advantage over the Allies on the Dvina both in manpower and particularly artillery. The Bolsheviks had brought up large calibre guns which far outranged the Canadian 18 pdrs and could shell the British held villages without concern for counter-battery fire. Intelligence reports were continually received that after their success at Shenkursk, the Reds were building strength to continue their advance further up the Vaga. Without enough troops to hold the advanced Dvina positions and the Vaga junction, it was unlikely that Ironside would be able to hold his hard-earned gains without reinforcements. Ironside cabled the War Office to this effect which resulted in his 'poaching' of 6th and 13th Yorkshires from Murmansk Command, much to General Maynard's chagrin, stretched thin as his own forces were.

In February, the column on the Northern Vaga was bolstered with the arrival of 'A' Company, 2/10th Royal Scots and in early March, 6th Battalion, Yorkshire Regiment, recently transferred from Murmansk. Their sister battalion 13th Yorkshires (less 10 officers and 175 other ranks who remained behind in Murmansk) with 280th Company, MGC had been transferred from Murmansk a month earlier. Both battalions had arrived at Murmansk in the final week of November providing a significant boost to Maynard's troop strength only for both units to be called away to Archangel in February.

After the difficult trip from Kem to Seletskoe via Obozerskaya the Yorkshires were deployed along the Dvina–Vaga junction in preparation for an expected push north from Shenkursk as part of a continuation of the Bolshevik winter offensive.

Perhaps as a means to quell some of the ill feeling and reassure the troops that they were not forgotten, on 4 April the War Office authorised General Ironside to make an announcement to the soldiers of the NREF who had fought through the winter campaign:

> Although you are cut off from your country by the ice, you are not forgotten. Your safety and well-being, on the contrary, is one of the main anxieties of the War Office, and we are determined to do everything in our power to help you and bring you safely home. You were sent to North Russia to help draw off the Germans from attacking our armies in France, and undoubtedly you helped last year to keep large numbers of German troops away from the battlefield and so enable a decisive victory to be won.
>
> Whatever may be the plan of action towards Russia decided on by the League of Nations, we intend to relieve you at the earliest possible moment, and either bring the whole force away or replace you by fresh men. These reliefs are being prepared now, and will come through the ice to your aid at the earliest moment when the ships can break through. Meanwhile, your lives and your chance of again seeing your home and friends and your fellow-country-men, who are looking forward to giving you a hearty welcome, depend absolutely upon your discipline and dogged British fighting qualities. All eyes are upon you now, and you represent the British Army which has fought and won and which is watching you confidently and earnestly. You will be back home in time to see this year's harvest gathered in, if you continue to display the undaunted British spirit which has so often got us through in spite of heavy odds and great

---

6   *Ibid.*, p.204.

75. Bolshevik Nieuport 21 captured on the Dvina River Front near Troitsa, summer 1919. The pilot had landed in British lines and defected. Souvenir hunters have already been at work stripping fabric from the fuselage. (Author's collection)

hardships. Only a few more months of resolute and faithful service against this ferocious enemy and your task will have been discharged. Carry on like Britains fighting for dear life and dearer honour, and set an example in these difficult circumstances to the troops of every other country. Reinforcement and relief are on the way. We send you this personal message with the most heartful wishes for your speedy, safe and honourable return.[7]

On 5 April, a Sopwith Strutter flown by pilot Lieutenant Kropinov with Observer 2nd Lieutenant Smernov, both of the SBAC, took off from Bereznik aerodrome on a reconnaissance mission when the engine failed soon after take-off. Kropinov attempted to bank the aircraft but stalled and crashed, killing Kropinov outright on impact and badly injuring Smernov who was dragged from the wreckage unconscious but died before reaching Bereznik Hospital. Lieutenant Colonel Robin Grey, commanding RAF HQ Archangel, wrote of the tragedy, 'Lt. Kropinov was one of the best Russian pilots and both officers are a great loss to the SBAC.'[8]

On the Dvina Front the British were very much on the back foot after the Red Army's successful winter offensive and loss of Shenkursk. The Bolsheviks knew that they held an advantage until the thaw allowed British river gunboats and monitors to steam upriver, an advantage the Reds had every intention of taking. At 0800 on the morning of 25 April, 300 men of 3rd North Russian Rifles mutinied near Tulgas, murdering some of their White Russian officers before going over to the Bolsheviks. The mutineers and Red troops then joined forces and proceeded to attack the town which was garrisoned only by remnants of the battalion which had remained loyal and a newly formed battery of Russian field artillery. A Russian artillery officer and three gunners managed to half drag, half row a small boat across the thawing river under fire to bring news of the mutiny to the gunners of 67th Battery, CFA on the opposite bank at Kurgomen, who had heard the firing but believed Tulgas to be under attack.

Attached to the Russian artillery battery at Tulgas, Captain Godfrey Whistler, RFA found himself in the midst of the mutiny. Whistler shot one of the mutineers who was threatening two White Russian officers and took charge of the situation, ordering the Russian gunners to limber the guns, carry out a retirement and bring the guns out of Tulgas to safety for which Whistler was awarded the MC.

On learning that a mutiny was underway, the Canadian gunners at Kurgomen turned their guns and opened fire in close support of Whistler's loyal Russians who signalled at 0930, 'Cannot hold out any longer; support withdrawal of guns.' Under cover of a box barrage fired by the Canadians from across the river, the Russian gunners limbered their guns and escaped just as the mutineers were encircling their position.

The loss of Tulgas was a great blow to Ironside and created a significant strategic problem as the Bolsheviks now held the left bank of the river some 10 miles behind the Allied line. The river bank at Tulgas was also much higher than the opposite bank at Kurgomen giving the Bolsheviks an elevated position from which they could shell the Canadian gunners below. Over the following four days the Bolsheviks made repeated unsuccessful frontal attacks on the right bank against Kurgomen, supported by firing from Tulgas, but the Kurgomen garrison held firm.

By 30 April, the ice had thawed enough for the Bolshevik river fleet of some 29 vessels armed with guns as large as 6 inch calibre to make their first appearance since the Dvina froze over in October the previous year. On 1 May, the Bolsheviks changed tack and launched a massive coordinated attack on both banks of the Dvina supported by eight field guns and two heavy howitzers on the Tulgas side and 12 field guns (which outranged the Canadian 18 pdrs) against Kurgomen on the right bank. To defend Kurgomen the British had 550 all ranks including 75 loyal Russian troops, 160 British infantry from 6th Yorks, 140 Canadian gunners of 67th Battery, CFA, and a handful of locally auxiliaries and odd men from other units.

The Bolshevik artillery at Tulgas was very effective in pinning down the Canadians who were unable to bring their guns into action against the attack. When the two British 60 pdrs with their superior range opened fire on the enemy gunboats and barges, the Bolsheviks made the critical mistake of moving the fire of the guns at Tulgas from the Canadian battery onto the 60 pdrs some distance away. No sooner had the Bolsheviks shifted fire, the Canadian gunners jumped from their pits and within three minutes the Bolshevik guns at Tulgas had been silenced with shrapnel. Shells from the 60 pdrs drove the enemy flotilla back whilst the Canadian 18 pdrs finished off the Red infantry. The Bolshevik attack quickly crumbled and over the following four days British and Canadian artillery drove off further attacks, inflicting heavy casualties.

The arrival of the badly needed 60 pdrs at the front in April had been an epic in itself. Special sledges had to be constructed at Archangel to transport the huge guns and the ammunition required to keep them in action. Separate sledges were constructed for the gun barrel, gun carriage and wheels, each pulled by 10 of the small but strong Russian ponies. The gun buffer required a six horse sledge alone, the ammunition followed in 50 single-horse *drosky* carriages.

By 6 May, the ice had thawed enough for dynamiting to take place to permit the gunboats and monitors of the Royal Navy Dvina River Flotilla to steam upriver. The Flotilla fired in support of the recapture of Tulgas on 18 May by a combined force of White Russian troops and 'D' Company, 6th Yorks, an action for which Lieutenant John Whetton was awarded the MC. By the beginning of June all four companies of 6th Yorks had returned to Archangel and spent their final days in Russia in barracks awaiting the transport ship which would take them home, no doubt looked on jealously by their sister battalion, 13th Yorkshires, who remained behind.

By 28 May, the Canadian gunners had fired their last shots in action in North Russia and will justifiably be remembered as amongst the best troops to serve in the campaign. Of his men Major Frank Arnoldi (awarded a DSO Bar for command of 67th Battery on the Dvina) wrote:

Many times in France, I had talked with other chaps and discussed what a corker of an outfit one could make if one had the choice of men from the whole Corps. Well, I had them. Men from every unit, at least every brigade, including new men from Canada. Picked from a reserve of some 8,500, including the cream of the School of Gunnery. The men were even beyond my expectation and never during our eight months existence on the front were there any signs of discontent among them. Always game for a fight or a laugh and it was generally both.[9]

At Archangel on 10 June, after strict instructions from the Canadian Government that all Canadian troops be withdrawn from North Russia, Lieutenant Colonel Charles Sharman paraded the brigade for inspection by leader of the White Russian Provisional Government at Archangel, General Eugene Miller, who presented the Order of St. Vladimir to Sharman and a number of other decorations to officers and men of the brigade including Medals of St. George awarded in the Russian custom by ballot amongst the men to elect their 10 bravest. In the afternoon the brigade paraded for a final inspection by General Ironside who proclaimed his endless admiration and thanked the gunners for their gallant service during the difficult days of late 1918 and early 1919. On the afternoon of 11 June 1919, the 22 officers and 455 men of 16th Brigade, CFA embarked on SS *Czaritsa* for Leith and a troopship to Canada.

In May and June 1919 the exhausted units of the original NREF which had arrived at Archangel in August and September 1918 finally received orders for home. They had lived and fought through sub-Arctic winter conditions that had not been experienced by British or Commonwealth troops in any other theatre of the Great War. Before embarking for home, Ironside read to the assembled troops a message from the King:

I had many anxieties about your isolated forces at the commencement of the long Arctic winter, but as time wore on these anxieties were allayed by the splendid way in which you have mastered all difficulties. On the arrival of the special relief contingent, I desire to congratulate you and your troops, together with their Allied and Russian comrades, on their achievements in the face of so many hardships, difficulties and perils.

GEORGE, R.I.[10]

In order to prevent the Red Army from interfering with the evacuation and to give the North Russian Provisional Government the time it needed to prepare to go it alone, the War Office gave instructions for the raising of a force specifically for service in North Russia. The force would deliver a series of aggressive attacks along all fronts rendering the enemy unable to interfere with the evacuation of Archangel. A concerted effort would also be made to link up with Admiral Kolchak's Siberian Army at Kotlas, an important river and rail junction on the Dvina.

Implementation of the plan would require large-scale reinforcements of which the British Army had none to spare. The Army, Royal Navy and Royal Air Force had been rapidly demobilising since the Armistice and those that remained in uniform were committed to the Armies of occupation in Germany and the Balkans and in a number of smaller conflicts.

Without the possibility of diverting enough serving soldiers from other theatres, a call was put out for trained volunteers to form the 'North Russia Relief Force'. On 9 April 1919, the first recruiting posters went up around London with newspaper advertisements published the following morning. The posters assured that, 'A discharged or demobilised soldier, if accepted, will rejoin in the rank,

---

9   MacLaren, *Canadians in Russia 1918–19*, p.112.
10 Ironside, *Archangel 1918–19*, p.6.

76. Advertisement published in *The Times*, 10 April 1919, calling for volunteers for the North Russia Relief Force. The advertisement was published in newspapers throughout Britain. (Public domain)

RELIEF FORCE FOR RUSSIA

THE RELIEF FORCE which is being formed for Service in North Russia will include the following: R.F.A., R.E. (Field, Signals, Postal), Infantry, M.G.C., R.A.S.C., R.A.M.C., R.A.O.C., R.A.V.C., A.P.C.

WHO MAY JOIN

The Force will be mainly composed of VOLUNTEERS drawn from the sources mentioned below :—
(a) Demobilised and discharged trained soldiers.
(b) Trained duration of the war soldiers serving at home.
(c) Soldiers at home serving on normal engagements or for 2, 3, or 4 years.

All men re-enlisting must be :—
(a) Fully trained in the Arm which they desire to join.
(b) Fit for General Service.
(c) 19 years of age and over.

A discharged or demobilised soldier, if accepted, will rejoin in the rank, substantive or acting, he held at the time he left the Colours.

PAY AND ALLOWANCES

PAY, ALLOWANCES and BONUS as now given to Men in the Armies of Occupation.

On completion of the period of service all men will be given two months' furlough or any longer period to which they may be entitled on full pay and allowances.

PERIOD OF SERVICE

The period of enlistment for recruits will be one year, or such shorter period as may be required, but no man who re-enlists for this duty will be kept longer than required for this special service.

WHERE TO ENLIST

Qualified men should apply at once to the nearest Recruiting Officer; to Officers Commanding local Regimental Depots; or to the Chief Recruiting Staff Officer, Great Scotland Yard, London.

substantive or acting, he held at the time he left the colours.' This may have been the original intent but it did not occur in practice, many ex-officers joined as NCOs and NCOs as privates.

Rates of pay and leave were also attractive. Soldiers on return from Russia would be granted two months paid furlough before discharge. A North Russia Relief Force volunteer in the rank of private would receive 14 shillings per day including allowances which in total was more than double the normal daily rate of pay, an extremely attractive remuneration for discharged soldiers for whom jobs in the depressed employment market flooded with thousands of returned soldiers was uncertain. After 1 September 1919 a further 'Russia' allowance of four shillings for officers and two shillings six pence per day for other ranks was paid to British soldiers serving in Russia (a 'Russia' allowance of one shilling for NCOs and six pence per day for other ranks had been payable since 1 February) making the North Russia Relief Force volunteers the highest paid soldiers in the British Army at the time. In order to enlist, volunteers completed 'Army Form B250A Short Service':

You will engage to serve His Majesty as a Soldier in the Regular Forces for one year provided your services are no longer required for the Special Service for which you have been enlisted, you will be discharged with all convenient speed.

There would be no time to conduct any training, volunteers were required to be fully trained in the branch in which they were volunteering. British officer volunteers remained members of their parent British regiments and served on attachment to units within the Relief Force.

Public opinion regarding the formation of the force was mixed, with some newspaper editors more supportive than others. *The Daily Herald* criticised 'the gambler of Gallipoli, Winston Churchill', suggesting that the operation was doomed to meet the same fate as the disastrous Dardanelles campaign. Despite public war-weariness and a wary public, the call for recruits was met with an overwhelming response. *The Daily Mail* wrote, 'The fighting spirit of the old army is aflame. Yesterday hundreds of veterans of the Great War were crowding Great Scotland Yard, Whitehall, to join the North Russia Relief Force.'[11]

The Relief Force was notable for the large number of British officers (approximately 40[12]) who voluntarily relinquished commissions to serve as 'Other Ranks'. Men who were rejected because they were no longer fit, many bearing the scars of previous wounding, wept as they left the recruiting offices. One officer of the new force described the scene:

> They are a motley crew. Here a late Major, with the Distinguished Service Order; he commanded a battery of field guns at Ypres in 1917. There an ex-Captain of Lovat's Scouts, with the Military Cross and Mons Star; a late R.F.C. pilot; many subalterns; ex-sergeant-majors, with Distinguished Conduct Medals; quartermaster-sergeants; corporals-but private soldiers all.[13]

Appointed OC, 'A' Company of the 45th Royal Fusiliers, Major Edward Allfrey, MC and Bar, KRRC, who had started the war as a private in the Ceylon Planters Rifle Corps, wrote of the men assembling at Park Royal Depot on 5 May:

> Recruits are still pouring in dressed in civilian clothes with medal ribbons on their waistcoats and red handkerchiefs round their necks. They have all seen previous service and look the most ideal material from which to form a battalion. The officers too are excellent, several having thrown up their appointments to command companies.[14]

Private Estcourt Cresswell-George, a veteran of service with the South African Brigade on the Western Front, was awaiting repatriation to Durban when he spotted posters calling for volunteers for North Russia:

> This intrigued me tremendously and I made enquiries and found out that I could join … When I went round to join the queue at Scotland Yard to join up, the queue went right around two blocks … I went the following day very, very early, and I was standing in queue, which even then was fairly long, when a Sergeant-Major in an Australian uniform came round saying, 'Any machine gunners here?' I thought 'Ah!' So I said 'Yes, I'm a machine gunner.' He said, 'Come with me, we want you!'[15]

Private Norman Brooke, an Australian veteran of the Western Front who would be awarded the DCM in North Russia, knew nothing of the campaign there until encountering a group of soldiers in discussion in one of the AIF holding camps one day in May 1919:

> I was crossing the space between huts one day and I saw a group of men and a couple of officers and sergeants talking away and I walked over towards them and another man came from the group towards me so I stopped him and asked him what they were talking about and he said they were looking for recruits for the North Russian Relief Force. So I went over and asked about it. I had heard of Russia from school geography and thought it was a country I would like to see sometime so I thought there might be a chance to go and see it. I was unsettled after France and didn't feel like going home immediately.[16]

---

11   Dobson and Miller, *The Day We Almost Bombed Moscow*, p.197.
12   Hansard, 14 May 1919, Oral Answers House of Commons, Captain Guest to Commander Bellairs.
13   Singleton-Gates, *Bolos and Barishynas*, p.3.
14   IWM: 3450 86/86/1 Private Papers of E.M. Allfrey.
15   Private letters of E. Cresswell-George.
16   AWM: S00180, Interview (1984) with Private N.M. Brooke, DCM.

The Relief Force was notable for its large contingent of Australian volunteers. When the call for volunteers went out there were large numbers of Australian soldiers stagnating in camps in England awaiting a slow troopship home to the other side of the world. In the months following the end of the war shipping was at a premium and the return of Commonwealth troops to their countries of origin a low priority. Although soldiers from other parts of the Commonwealth including South Africa, Canada, and New Zealand volunteered individually or in small groups to join the NRRF, only the Australian contingent were enlisted in any significant number thanks in no small part to the efforts of one of the officers attached to the new force: Major Harry Harcourt, DSO, MC, Royal Dublin Fusiliers attached 201st Battalion, MGC, a Gallipoli veteran who had a number of interactions with Australian troops during the war, and Australian Sergeant Major Charles Oliver (the 'Sergeant Major in Australian uniform' mentioned in Cresswell-George's account), ex-AIF, who had served as an instructor at Royal Military College Duntroon before the war and would also serve with 201st MGC.

One of the Australian volunteers, Private Ernest Heathcote, recalled the manner in which he volunteered:

> Our camp at Longbridge … On Salisbury plains was invaded one morning by an Imperial Army officer belonging to one of the Guards regiments. He had insignias on his tunic in the shape of a white five pointed star on a blue background. We were naturally curious and we soon got the wind that he was giving a picture on the North Russian situation in the canteen at twelve thirty. As you may expect the whole camp turned up to the lecture and he explained to us that he had been sent down to the Australian camps by the War Office to recruit volunteers to join the North Russia Relief Force. He was 'howled down' by the diggers and told to 'go home'. It was painful scene – especially for the officer – but it was only a humorous interlude in a monotonous routine for the diggers.
>
> A good deal of discussion was carried on by the diggers and at that time there was a lot of unrest on account of the time the Australian authorities were taking to get us back home and we were all fed up with being in camp doing nothing. We all wondered if there would be any volunteers who would go to North Russia as members of the Imperial Army. There were some two hundred volunteers and by the end of the following month an Australian Machine Gun Section was formed.[17]

Born in 1902, Heathcote had been so desperate not the miss the war that he had enlisted in the AIF in July 1918 under the assumed name 'Frederick Manning Whatson', declaring his age to be '19 years, 6 months' although he was just 16 at the time. Listing an 'uncle' in Illinois, USA as his next of kin, he arrived in England three days after the war ended where he spent the next six months amongst the thousands of AIF men cooling their heels awaiting a troopship home. He wasn't rumbled until July 1919 after his mother sent a letter to AIF authorities, by which time Heathcote had discharged from the AIF and was serving with the British Army in North Russia under his assumed identity, aged just 17.

In order to enlist in the North Russia Relief Force, Commonwealth soldiers first had to discharge from the service of their respective nation, in the case of the Australian volunteers, the Australian Imperial Force, and enlist as a private in the British Army for a term of 1 year with the promise of two months leave on return from Russia. The British authorities also took responsibility for repatriating ex-AIF volunteers to Australia after their return from Russia.

A large number of Australians expressed interest in joining the Relief Force but perhaps put off by the requirement to revert in rank to private and the prospect of no longer being under Australian command, only approximately 110 completed the enlistment process. One of the AIF volunteers,

17   AWM: PR89/140, Recollection of Ernest Heathcote.

77. Captain Arthur MacIlwaine, Major David Earp, Colonel Lancelot
Tomkinson and Captain Harrison inspecting a seaplane supply barge, Dvina
River, summer 1919. Tomkinson was Senior RAF officer Dvina River and was
awarded the DSO and AFC for his service in North Russia. (Richard Watts)

Horace Gipps, had served as an artillery officer on the Western Front and voluntarily relinquished his AIF rank of lieutenant in order to volunteer as a corporal in the Relief Force.

The AIF authorities allowed only unmarried men to discharge in the UK to join the Relief Force and a number had their discharges cancelled or not processed due to dependents although it is likely that some slipped through. One who did was Sergeant Samuel George Pearse, a Welsh-born Victorian who had served with 7th Battalion, AIF, on Gallipoli and 2nd Australian MG Company in France with whom he had been awarded the MM at Ypres. Pearse had discharged from the AIF, enlisted in the British Army, was posted to 45th Royal Fusiliers and only then married his English sweetheart Catherine 'Kitty' Knox (who had been serving in Queen Mary's Army Auxiliary Corps) before sailing for North Russia.

Approximately 80 of the Australian volunteers were posted to the 45th Battalion, Royal Fusiliers and another 30 to 201st (Special) Battalion, MGC. Most of the Australian 45th Royal Fusiliers were form into an 'Australian Company' which served on the Archangel–Vologda Railway Front whilst a further 'Australian Platoon' served with 'D' Company, 45th Royal Fusiliers on the Dvina River Front. Likewise, most of the Australian 201st MGC volunteers were formed into an 'Australian Section' (which also included a small number South African, Canadian, New Zealander and British volunteers) which fought alongside the 'Australian Company' on the Archangel–Vologda Railway Front whilst another 'Australian Detachment' served with the 201st MGC on the Dvina River Front. 201st MGC was noted for its contingent of South African volunteers described in the unit war diary as having 'great experiences of bush fighting in East Africa'.[18] Four ex-AIF volunteers who had been

18   The National Archives: WO 95/5430, 201st Battalion, MGC, War Diary.

born in Russia were appointed as interpreters and given the rank of Acting Sergeant, nominally as members of the Middlesex Regiment although that regiment did not serve at Archangel.

A number of unprecedented conditions of service were granted to Australian volunteers as an enticement to enlist. They would be permitted to continue to wear their AIF uniforms, badges, unit colour patches and slouch hats despite no longer serving with the Australian forces, and although commanded by British officers, the NCOs would all be ex-AIF men. Indeed there were so many ex-AIF volunteers in 'C' Company, 201st MGC on the Archangel–Vologda Railway Front that all soldiers serving in the 'Australian Section', regardless of nationality, were issued with the distinctive Australian slouch hat.

Presumably not by coincidence, the man given command of 45th Royal Fusiliers was also Australian, Lieutenant Colonel Charles Davies, attached to command the battalion from the Leicestershire Regiment. Having run away from home in Australia as a boy, Davies worked his way to England where he enlisted into the Leicestershire Regiment and saw service in South Africa during the Boer War. Later commissioned into the same regiment, Davies continued to serve as a regular officer before returning to Australia where he was appointed to command 8th Australian Infantry Brigade in late 1915, having just enough time to marry his Australian sweetheart that same year. Davies was awarded a DSO for command of 32nd Battalion, AIF at Polygon Wood in September 1917 before rejoining the British Army on termination of his commission with the AIF in 1919 when he was given command of 45th Royal Fusiliers. The distinct 'colonial' influence on the unit did not meet with the approval of some members of the battalion. OC 'A' Company, Major Edward Allfrey, MC and Bar, attached from KRRC, recorded in his diary that he thought the Australian influence was cause for some of the indiscipline amongst the men: 'I think the chief trouble is that this battalion is run largely on Australian lines.'[19]

Another colonial, a South African, was placed in command of 46th Royal Fusiliers, the second volunteer battalion being raised for the Relief Force. Lieutenant Colonel Herbert Jenkins had served during the Bechuanaland Rebellion and Boer War and with the 2nd Kimberley Regiment in German South-West Africa in 1915. As an officer with 1st South African Infantry on the Western Front he had twice been wounded and awarded the DSO before appointment to command 46th Royal Fusiliers.

Volunteers for the NRRF generally came in two categories: those who had seen very little active service or arrived too late for the war altogether and those who had seen extensive service in multiple campaigns, and either through lack of availability of jobs, boredom or for the familiar security of service life wanted to continue serving. Many soldiers returned home after the war to find the 'land fit for heroes' was anything but what they had been promised, and with unemployment and uncertainty in the air they chose the familiarity of the colours over the uncertainty of the unemployment office. Many young men had spent their entire adult life and formative years in uniform and knew little else.

AIF volunteer Keith Attiwell, who had arrived in England too late to see service on the Western Front, wrote of his surprise to be serving in the ranks with soldiers who had only weeks earlier been commissioned officers:

> Among the Relief Force were many ex-officers who had joined as privates, simply for adventure. Our signalling officer was Lord Settrington, heir to the Earl of March … Our battalion quartermaster sergeant was a lieutenant colonel in France, and in my platoon was a certain corporal who it was well known was a baronet. The presence of so many ex-officers was due to two causes – firstly, the difficulty of obtaining satisfactory employment in England; secondly the chance of returning to the reckless life to which they had grown so used in France and other theatres of the war.[20]

19   IWM: 3450 86/86/1 Private Papers of E.M. Allfrey.
20   *Observer* (Adelaide, South Australia), 17 April 1920.

Although few volunteers could have given any real explanation of the larger political situation in North Russia, the papers of the day carried stories of a beleaguered British garrison of exhausted men on the verge of being forced into the sea by an increasingly powerful Red Army. Vividly imaginative tales of Bolshevik atrocities were also not in any short supply, one recounting how Red soldiers broke into a house where a mother and her four children were dining, 'cut off the mother's head and threw it in the soup tureen; then the children's, one of which they put on each plate.' The same type of propaganda pieces playing on the public's patriotism and fear had been published about the German Army in Belgium in 1914. 'No one – least of all a nation which so recently engaged herself for a broken word – would abandon a helpless people to such a fate.'[21]

Both sides used tales of the others brutality in their propaganda but not everyone was so easily fooled. One American observed:

> The men of this expedition were told many stories of Bolshevik atrocities. No care or effort was spared in printing these stories in both English and Russian and getting them into the hands of the soldiers. It was important to inspire fear and hatred of the Bolsheviki in the hearts of our men, more important than the verification of the stories. After the evacuation of Shenkursk we were told, with complete details, of the murder of the nuns and the Abbess, and of the members of several families who were well known to us ... We were told of rape and of tortures, all in convincing circumstantial setting ... In July, however we learned the truth. Three Russians whom I had known all winter and in whom I have the utmost confidence, went to Shenkursk, stayed there incognito a week, and came back. They told me that they had seen the nuns, and talked with the people who were supposed to have been murdered.[22]

Eventually a force of 5,000 men in two brigades was raised, manned both by volunteer and regular soldiers. The 1st Brigade (officially titled 238th 'Special' Brigade) would be commanded by Brigadier George W. St. G. Grogan, VC, CB, CMG, DSO, Worcestershire Regiment, and was composed of serving regular soldiers ordered to North Russia (despite assurances to the public by the British Government that only volunteers were being sent) whilst the 2nd Brigade (officially titled 239th 'Special' Brigade) commanded by Brigadier Lionel W. de Vere Sadleir-Jackson, CB, CMG, DSO and Bar, 9th Lancers, would be composed entirely of volunteers. The integration of an additional Lewis gun company and Stokes Mortar platoon into the composition of the Royal Fusilier battalions in the Relief Force was for the time revolutionary and would be credited by Sadleir-Jackson as being a key factor in the Brigade's success in North Russia.

Sadleir-Jackson had served as a subaltern with 9th Queen's Royal Lancers during the Boer War with whom he was wounded and awarded the DSO. Transferring to the Royal Engineers Signal Service before the outbreak of war, Jackson served in France from 1914 and was awarded the CMG for services during the retreat from Mons. He was then posted to command 1/10th London Regiment followed by 54th British Infantry Brigade whom he led during the 1918 German offensive on the Somme. Badly wounded in the knee during the offensive, Jackson was awarded a Bar to his DSO whilst recovering from wounds in hospital. Between the Armistice and his appointment to command 2nd Brigade, NRRF, Jackson was further gazetted for the award of Companion of the Order of the Bath.

As newly raised units specifically for service in North Russia, the 45th and 46th Battalions of the Royal Fusiliers were presented with their colours by Commander-in-Chief, NREF, General Lord Henry Rawlinson at Sandling Camp, Kent on 22 May. Five days later 1st (Grogan's) Brigade arrived at Archangel on SS *Stephen* having left the UK on 13 May in company with SS *Czar* and sister ship

---

21   Singleton-Gates, *Bolos and Barishynas*, p.5.
22   Albertson, *Fighting Without a War*, pp.84–85.

Czaritsa amidst much fanfare. Grogan's Brigade would have arrived several days earlier but the convoy had to wait five days for the last of the ice in the White Sea to clear before sailing into Archangel. The convoy had been escorted by the cruiser USS *De Moines* with Admiral Newton McCully, USN on board. McCully was returning to Russia having first been sent there as an observer during the Russo–Japanese war of 1904–5. After service in North Russia he was sent by the US Navy to the Crimea where he remained until the final withdrawal after White Russian General Baron Pyotr Nikolayevich Wrangel's forces finally collapsed in November 1920. McCully's links to Russia did not end there. He took with him back to the US six Russian children whom he adopted. In 1927 he married a Russian refugee with whom he raised the adopted children as their own.

The greater part of 2nd (Sadleir-Jackson's) Brigade (less approximately 200 men) sailed for Archangel on 28 May, 45th Royal Fusiliers on board the SS *Porto* and 46th Royal Fusiliers on board the *Praetorian*. Their departure had not been without drama. There was trouble when the men were denied permission to go ashore to

78. Brigadier Lionel W. de Vere Sadleir-Jackson, CB, CMG, DSO and Bar, 9th Lancers, General Officer Commanding 2nd Brigade, North Russia Relief Force. (NPG 85370)

buy cigarettes and personal comforts and about 40 of the 45th Royal Fusiliers rushed the gangway demanding to be allowed ashore. Allfrey described events:

> Things looked rather threatening and I thought something must happen at once … I got up on one of the boats and started talking to the men. I told them that we were all volunteers, and the sooner they started to soldier the better it would be for the Battalion. I told them that if they could not undergo a small inconvenience such as this I did not think they would be any damn good to the Russian Relief Force … I used every argument I could, and finally quite a lot returned to the ship … The nett result was that only a few got ashore; some jumped over the side and some rushed the gangway. How the War Office have the audacity to put 1,400 men alongside an amusing town and order them not to go ashore I'm blowed if I know.[23]

Allfrey's account of the public send-off gives some indication that although the public were weary of sending their husbands and sons off to war, and the campaign in North Russia was generally unpopular, some of the patriotism and zest of the early years of the war was yet to wear off:

> Thousands of people turned out to cheer us as we went off, and the whole thing was most impressive. Hundreds of ships sounded on their hooters, and all the water side was packed with waving and cheering people. I have never seen anybody get a better send off.[24]

---

23   IWM: 3450 86/86/1 Private Papers of E.M. Allfrey.
24   *Ibid.*

Allfrey also wrote of the arrival of some of the more recalcitrant members of the battalion:

> Quite a lot of last night's deserters came running along the quay after the boat had started. Several were very drunk, and the whole scene, although showing damn rotten discipline, really was most amusing. They came off on small launches, etc., and climbed up the side of the ship on a rope ladder. How some of the most drunk got on board I really don't know. Only one fell into the sea, and a young seafaring civilian went in after him and gave him a life belt … The C.O. [Davies] created a sensation by personally escorting three very drunk men of D Company to the Guard Room. Every now and then he gave them a great clout on the head.[25]

The trip to Russia was also far from uneventful, the Regimental Sergeant Major making an attempt to kill the Lewis gun Sergeant Major whilst he slept: 'Luckily the attempt was not successful although he put a bullet into the pillow of the man he tried to do in.'[26]

SS *Porto* and *Praetorian* arrived at Murmansk on 3 June and Archangel three days later, where on 10 June the Relief Force was formally welcomed to the city in an elaborate parade and march-past. After accepting the traditional Russian greeting of bread and salt, Brigadier Sadleir-Jackson spoke a few words translated to the assembled crowd. One of the newly arrived Fusilier officers noted, 'our first impressions of Russian troops were appreciative of their bearing and their qualities. Alas! We were the more deceived.'[27]

Fifty men of the first contingent, having disembarked only five hours earlier, were immediately despatched upriver to Pinega to defend against an expected Bolshevik attack. The attack did not materialise, and four days later the party were sent to Osinova on the eastern bank of the Dvina River to establish the rows of bell tents and stores depots that would become the advanced base for 2nd (Sadleir-Jackson's) Brigade.

The second contingent of approximately 200 men of 2nd (Sadleir-Jackson's) Brigade included the 'Australian Company' of 45th Royal Fusiliers, a platoon of 46th Royal Fusiliers, the 'Australian Section' of 'C' Company, 201st Battalion, MGC and a section of 385th Field Company, RE, which would serve on the Archangel–Vologda Railway independent from the remainder of the brigade. The contingent sailed from Leith on board SS *Steigerwald* on 3 July taking with it a number of aircrew and mechanics as RAF reinforcements. Captain Ira Jones, DSO, MC, DFC and Bar, MM, RAF, an air ace who had shot down 40 enemy aircraft over the Western Front, becoming one of the most highly decorated British and Commonwealth fighter aces in the process, was one of the RAF contingent and witnessed one late arrival make his way aboard:

> One of the men, an Australian, is a real tough nut and deserves to join the party. Apparently he volunteered for this trip but for some reason was not accepted, so he came to see his pals off. Just as the ship was leaving the quayside this man took a swift run and made a mighty leap on board, his comrades waiting for him with open arms. The effort was cheered to the echo for several minutes and when the man was brought before Guard he decided that he was of the right type to battle with the Bolshies, so he was added to the roll.[28]

The departure was an anti-climax: as soon as *Steigerwald* left the quay her engines came to a stop and she spent the next two days undergoing repairs in the harbour. After the two day delay, she set out once more, the men on board spending most of their time preparing equipment, learning a few

25 *Ibid.*
26 Dobson and Miller, *The Day We Almost Bombed Moscow*, p.199.
27 Singleton-Gates, *Bolos and Barishynas*, p.11.
28 Jones, *An Air Fighter's Scrapbook*, p.111.

79. 'A' Flight, RAF Dvina River Seaplanes onboard *Seaplane
Supply Barge 1*, summer 1919. (Richard Watts)

words of Russian and on Lewis gun practice from the stern of the ship using empty packing crates thrown overboard as targets. The composite force arrived at Archangel on 12 July and disembarked on what Private Wilfred Yeaman, an Australian serving with 201st MGC, recorded in his diary as the 'hottest day since leaving Egypt. (112 degrees in shade)'.[29] The composite force made final preparations in Archangel before entraining for Obozerskaya on the Railway Front on 16 July.

Military authorities had imposed strict restrictions on the use of private cameras on the Western Front lest sensitive photographic negatives fall in to enemy hands, however there was no such restriction in effect in North Russia. Many soldiers brought with them an Eastman-Kodak 'Brownie', the first compact, mass-produced camera. As a result of the prevalence of cameras brought by British troops to Murmansk and Archangel, the photographic record of the British soldier in North Russia far exceeds that of the Western Front where only official war photographers were permitted to take photographs which were heavily censored before publication. A number of soldiers determinedly set out to document their service in North Russia photographically and on return to the UK produced extensive albums of their time there.

Some Relief Force officers had been thrilled by tales of fishing and hunting in lakes which 'boiled with fish' and skies 'black with duck', bringing with them to Russia fishing poles and shotguns, 'valises of enormous proportions contained more sporting accoutrements than those needed for the prosecution of war.'[30] The tales of a fisher and hunter's paradise were not apocryphal, and the poles and shotguns were put to good use supplementing tinned rations such as 'Maconochie's Beef and Vegetables' which quickly became monotonous.

---

29   AWM: PR91/126, Diary of Wilfred Yeaman.
30   Singleton-Gates, *Bolos and Barishynas*, p.12.

Interactions with the locals were mostly limited to bartering for goods and food. In particular demand were sable and fox furs which fetched enormous prices in England. One entrepreneurial soldier of the North Russia Relief Force brought back to England a silver fox pelt which he had purchased for less than £5 and sold on to a London dealer for 300 guineas.[31] Many of the soldiers spoke some French as a result of years on the Western Front but Russian was a different challenge entirely, although it did not take the average soldier long to learn the most useful words: *skolka* – how much? *Dobra* – good, *niet dobra* – not good, *kharasho* – alright. The scarcity of consumables in North Russia put the British Tommy at a significant bargaining advantage:

> Many men exchanged a packet of cigarettes for a large loaf of bread or a pound of fresh butter. In this country money has very little purchasing value, but one can get anything for a few cigarettes or some tobacco or chocolate. In fact cigarettes are carried by the men instead of roubles.[32]

After a week in Archangel, the bulk of the Sadleir-Jackson Brigade embarked on barges for the day-long journey upriver where they had their first encounter with the northern Russian mosquito. Nearly every diary and recollection by British soldiers of service in North Russia makes at least one reference to the voracious sub Arctic species:

> For over 200 miles of the Dvina the whole Brigade fed the Russian mosquito as that insect had never before been fed … the pestilent brutes attended the barges in their tens of thousands. Patent remedies and deterrents merely acted as choice cocktails.[33]

Petty Officer Telegraphist Reginald Jowett on board HMS *Pegasus* described the painful bite of the Dvina River mosquito: 'Their bites are very poisonous, sometimes raising a swelling as much as 3 or 4 inches long, on the fleshy parts of the body. Some people seem to suffer a great deal.'[34]

After five days cooped up on the barges, the brigade disembarked at Osinova on the western bank of the Dvina where a base camp was established. The long summer days were spent preparing equipment and training but there was also time for a little enjoyment. On 21 June the brigade held its first and only sports day which incorporated rather unconventional activities such as wrestling on horseback which resulted in a broken leg for one sapper who fell from his mount.

On 2 June, 2nd Battalion, Hampshire Regiment, part of 1st (Grogan's) Brigade, commanded by South African Lieutenant Colonel John Sherwood-Kelly, VC, CMG, DSO, embarked on barges for the trip down the Dvina to the frontline. Sherwood-Kelly was a highly regarded fighting soldier who had seen much distinguished service throughout several campaigns. As a 16-year-old he had first seen action in Matabeleland in 1896, served with the Cape Mounted Police in the Relief of Mafeking, the Somaliland Burgher Corps during operations against the 'Mad Mullah', and took part in suppressing the Natal Rebellion of 1906. Emigrating to Norfolk, he joined the Territorial Force with whom he served until enlisting in the regular army as a private in 1914, shortly before being commissioned with his brother into King Edward's Horse. Kelly commanded a battalion of Kings Own Scottish Borderers (KOSB) on Gallipoli and was later CO, 1st Battalion, Royal Inniskilling Fusiliers when he was awarded the VC at Cambrai in 1917. *The Daily Express* wrote of him:

> He fought in Matabeleland and Somalia and was so anxious to go to the front in the recent war that he enlisted as a private under an assumed name. He was promoted on the field during the second battle

31   *Dundee Evening Telegraph*, 27 November 1919.
32   IWM: 3450 86/86/1 Private Papers of E.M. Allfrey.
33   Singleton-Gates, *Bolos and Barishynas*, p.12.
34   Haddon, *North Russia Expedition of Summer 1919*.

of Ypres, went to Gallipoli in 1915 and returned in the battle of the Somme. He won the VC after the Cambrai battle in 1917 by his skill and gallantry in covering the passage of a canal by his battalion of Inniskilling Fusiliers. He led the first company of the battalion over the canal then, under heavy fire, reconnoitred the enemy's position, and when his left flank was held up, brought a Lewis gun into position to cover the advance through the wire. He wears five wound stripes and was seven times mentioned in despatches.[35]

Like their brigade mates in 1st Battalion, Oxfordshire and Buckinghamshire Light Infantry, 2nd Hampshires were also a regular army composite unit. Originally titled 'No. 1 Composite Battalion', the cadre of Hampshire soldiers had been brought up to battalion strength by drafts of soldiers from other regiments. Within 'W', 'Y' and 'Z' Companies there were also smaller drafts of men from no less than 25 different regiments. The eventual composition of the battalion when it sailed for North Russia was as follows:

Commanding Officer: Lieutenant Colonel J. Sherwood-Kelly, VC, CMG, DSO, Norfolk Regt.
Second in Command: Major N.E. Baxter
'W' Company: Somerset Light Infantry (Captain C.C. Smythe, MC, Hampshire Regiment)
'X' Company: Hampshire Regiment (Captain F.G.J. Berkeley, MC)
'Y' Company: Dorsetshire Regiment (Captain G.N. Woodhouse, MC)
'Z' Company: Wiltshire Regiment (Captain J.M. Ponsford, MC)

The Hampshire barges arrived at Bereznik on 5 June and shortly after, along with 238th Trench Mortar Battery and half a company of 8th Battalion, MGC, were sent further down the river to relieve 2/10th Royal Scots and units of US 339th Infantry Regiment in the lines at Kurgomen and Tulgas. 'HQ', 'W' and 'Y' Companies relieved the Royal Scots on the eastern bank whilst 'X' and 'Z' Companies relieved the US troops on the western bank. The small town of Tulgas had recently been the scene of bitter fighting and had only been recaptured by US troops two weeks earlier. Red gunboats shelled the British positions daily, and it was of little consolation to the newly arrived Hampshires when the veteran Scots and US troops informed that the shells were actually intended for the British gunboats on the river but due to bad shooting on the part of the Reds, were continually falling short.

The Hampshires occupied trenches and blockhouses vacated by the Scots and US troops, thankful that winter had since passed. The thaw of the Dvina meant that the RN gunboats and river monitors could once again proceed upriver to provide cover to the army ashore. The better climate and extended hours of daylight also meant that the RAF Seaplane Flight could provide almost constant cover.

On 13 June, patrols were sent out on both banks with orders to reconnoitre towards Troitsa. Sherwood-Kelly personally led a patrol from No. 3 Platoon, 'W' Company on the eastern bank into a small hamlet which had been reported as 'neutral'. As he turned the corner of a cabin, a Bolshevik soldier stuck a rifle around and fired. Sherwood-Kelly grabbed the barrel of the enemy weapon and shot the Bolshevik at point blank range in the chest, another Bolshevik scout was killed and one wounded without the Hampshires suffering a casualty. The patrol on the opposite bank also encountered the enemy and in a brief skirmish killed a Russian scout without loss to themselves.

On 16 June, Sherwood-Kelly again took out a platoon on an all day patrol during which he covered 35 miles in 17 hours but no enemy were sighted. Sherwood-Kelly's aggressive leadership was

35   Dobson and Miller, *The Day We Almost Bombed Moscow*, p.199.

clearly the kind of soldiering that Brigadier Grogan, himself a VC recipient, and General Ironside applauded. In a communiqué from Brigade HQ, Kelly was congratulated by Grogan:

> The GOC wishes to personally thank you on the very gallant way you led the patrol on June 13th, 1919 which resulted in you killing three of the enemy at great personal risk to yourself. The information obtained by you was very valuable and the result of your encounter cannot but increase the morale of our men.[36]

On 14 June the remaining US troops at Archangel boarded SS *Menominee* and sailed for Boston via Brest. The American North Russia Expeditionary Force (who had nicknamed themselves 'Polar Bears') had fought well but returned home to very little fanfare, only in the Polar Bears' home town of Detroit was there any form of official welcome and a memorial erected.

Also in June, the hardy 2/10th Royal Scots and gallant 16th Brigade, CFA, who along with US 339th Infantry Regiment bore the brunt of the fighting in North Russia during the winter, embarked at Archangel for home. The Royal Scots in particular had seen the most fighting and suffered the most casualties of any British unit which saw service in Russia 1918–20. With the departure of the US and Canadian contingents, Ironside had become almost solely dependant on British forces, the 'Northern Rifle Regiments' (more commonly known as 'North Russian Rifles') showing increasing sings of insurrection. On 14 May, a company of 8th North Russian Rifles refused to embark for upriver and killed two of their White Russian officers. Ironside had the ringleaders shot and disarmed the remainder, forming them into a labour company. It was an omen for much worse to come.

The War Office plans for a link-up of the Northern and Siberian fronts at Kotlas was finally shattered when news reached London on 17 June that General Radolo Gajda of the Czech Legion, commanding Kolchak's Western Army tasked to take Kotlas, had been repulsed by the Red Army. The news added further weight to the arguments of those in Whitehall opposed to military intervention that British troops should push no further into the Russian vastness, lest they become further entangled and require even more troops to be despatched to retrieve them. Major Allfrey wrote in his diary on 2 July:

> Ironside told the C.O. that he had received a telegram from England to suspend all hostilities out here at once. This telegram merely makes Ironside smile, as he has no more intention of ceasing hostilities than the man in the moon, nor is it possible to do so, for the British force out here is involved pretty deeply in the operation and there is nothing between the Bolsheviks and thousands of Russians but us and they would all be murdered at once if we withdrew. It is not known why the telegram was sent, but it is pretty certain it is, as usual, just a weak government pandering to the Labour people. The rumour is that the coal miners have threatened that unless the British force in Russia is home within forty days they will all come out on strike on the grounds that we are interfering with the rights and freedoms of the Russian people. In other words they too are Bolsheviks and wish to support the Bolshevik movement.[37]

Ironside telegraphed the War Office on 19 June stating that he would not allow 'British forces to get into such a position that they would require relief or that they could not withdraw.'[38] He also added that Kotlas could not be captured if the enemy 'puts up a stubborn resistance.' Regardless of his misgivings, the following day Ironside initiated the first stage of his final offensive. With the arrival of the NRRF, Ironside's ground forces had been considerably strengthened as had the

36   Bujack, *Undefeated*, p.189.
37   IWM: 3450 86/86/1 Private Papers of E.M. Allfrey.
38   War Office, *Army: The Evacuation of North Russia, 1919* (London: HMSO, 1920) p.38.

Royal Navy with the arrival of additional river monitors, gunboats and six CMBs. RAF 'ELOPE' had also been reinforced with new aircrews, mechanics and riggers, bringing the RAF at Archangel to its peak strength during the campaign.

Unfortunately for Ironside the Red Army too had been bolstered with reinforcements and equipment. The Soviet 6th Army under former Tsarist-turned-Bolshevik General Alexander Samoilo had by June 1919 become a formidable fighting force. His rifle regiments were supported by a full complement of field guns, machine guns and trench mortars as well as observation balloons and Nieuport fighter aircraft. Samoilo also had at his disposal a small but effective river flotilla which were a constant thorn in the side of the RN vessels operating on the northern Dvina. The depth of the Dvina was unusually low in the spring and summer of 1919 which aided Samoilo to send supplies downriver from Kotlas whereas access to the British front was restricted due to huge sandbars and low water levels.

The Nieuport fighter planes had been shipped in crates to Russia by the French government prior to 1917 for use by the Tsar's Imperial Air Service. Following the revolution

80. Lieutenant Russell, RAF Dvina River Seaplanes, on mine watch duty on *Seaplane Supply Barge 2*. (Richard Watts)

and mobilisation of the Red Army, a large amount of Imperial Army arms and equipment fell into the hands of the Bolsheviks. The pilots and aircrew that did not flee to areas controlled by the Whites remained to form the fledgling Red Air Force.

The RAF had almost unopposed control of the air in North Russia, the few serviceable aircraft that the Red Air Force could field rarely ventured into the skies above the Dvina and the few that did in most cases fled on the slightest sign of British aircraft. Operating independently of No. 3 Squadron at Bereznik, the 'Dvina Force Seaplane Flight' provided close cooperation air support to both the River Flotilla and troops on the ground, flying from their seaplane base on a large sand bar near Troitsa, and two mobile 'Seaplane Supply Barges', 'SSBs'.

For all the danger of combat flying over the Western Front, for Captain Ira Jones the prospect of peace meant an end to flying. One day in early 1919 whilst visiting the Air Ministry, Jones noticed several posters calling for volunteers for a 'Relief Force' being sent to Archangel, North Russia. Jones was excited by the prospect of more combat flying and hurried to the RAF club where he hoped to meet like-minded pilots nearly out of a job.

At the club he met fellow ace Major Geoffrey 'Beery' Bowman, DSO, MC and Bar, DFC, a distinguished fighter ace who had commanded No. 56 Squadron on the Western Front where he claimed 32 aerial victories. Jones greeted Bowman and enquired if he had seen the advertisements calling for volunteers. Both men subsequently volunteered at the Air Ministry as aircrew reinforcements and served in North Russia during summer 1919.

On 9 June, Jones and the RAF reinforcements bound for North Russia left Edinburgh harbour on SS *Steigerwald* with Army members of the North Russia Relief Force, bound for Archangel via

81. Captain Oliver Bryson, MC, DFC, AM, RAF. Bryson had been awarded the AM for the rescue in March 1917 of his observer after his aircraft crashed and caught fire. Awarded the MC the following year, Bryson was awarded the DFC for service in North Russia and a DFC Bar for further flying on the North West Frontier in 1931. (Public domain)

Murmansk. The week long journey gave Jones plenty of time to contemplate the enormity of the task before them:

I am mystified by the seemingly complete unpreparedness of the Allies for a gamble with so much at stake. To attack a vast country like Russia with a handful of men and arms seems on the face of it to be the apotheosis of madness. There is every indication at the moment that the gamble is a wild one, and that the future historian will only be able to record that this adventure resulted in the loss of much British gold, of a few British lives, and merely enhanced the high morale of the British soldier under vastly differing climatic conditions. It seems that this wild gamble is made on the single naïve assumption that a handful of trained officers and men who have been through the War in France are sufficient to inspire the white counter-revolutionary forces in North Russia with the will to action against the Soviets' as yet untrained levies.[39]

Another volunteer member of the RAF contingent was Captain Oliver Bryson, an ace with 12 victories in the skies over the Western Front. Bryson had been awarded the Albert Medal in 1917 for gallantry in rescuing his wounded observer from the wreckage of their burning aircraft after a crash-landing to add to an MC awarded in France. Already a highly decorated airman by the time he sailed for Russia, for service flying a Sopwith Snipe over the Dvina and Pinega during the summer of 1919, Bryson was awarded the DFC and for service on the North West Frontier during 1930–31, a DFC Bar.

Some of the new pilots were so keen to take on the Bolsheviks that they wasted little time getting into action. On 17 June, soon after arriving at Bereznik aerodrome from Archangel, New Zealander Major Charles Carr took off in a Sopwith Snipe on a lone mission to attack the enemy aerodrome at Puchega. Carr strafed the airfield and hangars from very low altitudes for 30 minutes, setting fire to a Bolshevik Nieuport and a hanger which contained a further three aircraft which were also destroyed, for which he was awarded the DFC. Carr was later selected for Sir Ernest Shackleton's final expedition to Antarctica as the pilot of the aircraft carried on the expedition ship *Quest*. Shackleton died of heart failure at Grytviken, South Georgia in January 1922 with expedition medical officer Alexander Macklin, (who had been awarded the OBE for service in North Russia) by his side, and the expedition was abandoned. Serving during the Second World War in a number of senior RAF appointments, Carr was knighted before retiring with the rank of Air Marshall.

On one of his first missions over Bolshevik lines on 21 June, one of the replacement RAF pilots, Lieutenant Clarence Knight, who had been credited with the destruction of two Gotha bombers

39   Jones, *An Air Fighter's Scrapbook*, p.118.

whilst flying Sopwith Camels over the Western Front, was killed. No. 3 (Bereznik) Squadron's bombing machines had been operating in conjunction with the infantry in the latter stages of June and a number of gains had been made into Bolshevik territory. The aircraft piloted by Knight with Observer Lieutenant Neill was seen to be forced down by ground fire over enemy territory. Both men were initially reported as 'Missing Presumed Killed' until late in the evening of the same day a bedraggled figure staggered into Bereznik aerodrome. Neill, his head and arm in bandages, in an exhausted state relayed the story of Knight's fate. A burst of ground fire had hit the aircraft wounding Knight in the stomach and Neill in the head and arm. The badly wounded pilot was just able to land the stricken aircraft before collapsing in pain and weakness from loss of blood. Neill jumped out of his cockpit and began to unbuckle the wounded pilot but he had only one good arm. The wound to Knight's stomach had torn a hole from the left to right side of his abdomen just above the waist. The pain was so intense that when Neill attempted to move his dying comrade, Knight asked that he be left

82. New Zealander Major Charles Carr, DFC, AFC, No. 3 (Bereznik) Squadron, RAF. (Fielding Public Library, NZ)

alone in the cockpit and for Neill to make a run for the cover of the trees before Red troops arrived. Neill knew that there was nothing he could do for his gallant pilot and made haste. Knight was probably dead before Neill had covered the distance to the tree line.

As he lay low in the woods, Neill could hear Bolshevik soldiers searching the forest but despite his wounds managed to evade the enemy and make his way to White Russian lines. The Russian troops thought the strange apparition coming out of the forest to be a Bolshevik and opened fire; fortunately their aim was wild. As best as he could with a smashed arm, Neill called out in English and stumbled into the White Russian positions. The Russians were extremely apologetic for having shot at the wounded airman and bound his arm and head wounds as best as they could.

Knight's body was recovered the following day by a patrol from 2nd Hampshires, by whom he was buried with full military honours in Topsa churchyard. Ira Jones records that Neill was recommended for the DFC and 'he well deserves it' however no decoration was ever awarded for his courage and bravery. Knight's grave has since been lost to time and he remains commemorated on a Special Memorial in Archangel Allied Cemetery.

11

Archangel: Dvina River Front June–July 1919

On 20 June 1919, Ironside renewed his attempts to push forward down the Dvina towards Kotlas. In a coordinated attack, 3rd North Russian Rifles would attack Topsa at the northern end of the chain of Bolshevik blockhouses whilst Sherwood-Kelly would take 'W' (Somerset Light Infantry) and 'Y' (Dorsetshire) Companies of the Hampshires, a section from 238th TMB and Vickers guns from 'C' Company, 8th Battalion, MGC, through the forests on a long trek behind enemy lines to attack Troitsa at the opposite end of the chain. Simultaneous to the 'W' and 'Y' Company attack on the right bank, 'X' (Hampshire) and 'Z' (Wiltshire) Companies with a section from 8th Battalion, MGC and two sections 238th TMB, would attack the enemy south-east of Tulgas on the left bank.

The Bolshevik defences at Topsa and Troitsa consisted of a series of blockhouses forming a large semi-circle which encompassed both villages with the open end of the semi-circle facing the cliffs on the bank on the Dvina. The approach march was long and would require a wide detour through the forest before attacking the enemy from the flank and rear 24 hours later.

HM Ships *Humber*, *Cockchafer*, and *Glowworm*, and monitors *M.27 and M.33* were detailed to provide naval gunfire support for the attacks, *Humber*, *M.27* and *Cockchafer* to bombard the enemy ashore whilst *Glowworm* and *M.33* would stand ready to engage the enemy gunboats. At 0700 on the morning of 19 June, the monitors and gunboats moved into position. Commanding the RN River Flotilla, Captain Altham's intention was to keep the appearance of the flotilla (visible to enemy observers in Troitsa church) as normal until the time came to commence the bombardment. He could then steam the additional monitors and gunboats forward from behind a bend in the river. In any case his plans for stealth were foiled when at 0930 the enemy gunboats attacked. The usual inconclusive exchange of fire followed until the enemy were driven off but not before *Glowworm* had been struck by a shell which luckily caused little damage and no casualties. There was rumour that the Bolsheviks knew of the British plans in advance.

At 1600 on 19 June, the two columns with 60 pack mules in tow set out on the 30 km approach march through the forest to attack the Bolshevik line. The march went well until the forest path petered out and the British encountered a large marsh around which there was no alternative route. The pack mules quickly became bogged making it necessary for the supplies to be unloaded and hauled by hand. The men suffered in the oppressive heat of the midday sun and the stinging mosquitoes and horseflies did little to ease their hardship. The Hampshires suffered their first fatality before a shot had even been fired: Private F.V. Chapman, one of five officers and 70 other ranks attached to the battalion from the Somerset Light Infantry, accidentally drowned when he fell into the marsh. Heavily laden with equipment, Chapman sank below the surface and died a terrible death before his comrades could extricate him.

The detachment of 155th Field Ambulance, RAMC, detailed to follow the attacking column and establish a forward aid post, also had a most difficult trek. The party, commanded by Army doctors Lieutenant Colonel T.E. Harty and Captain Knight, had travelled only half a mile into the forest when they realised they were heading in the wrong direction and would need to change course and follow a forest track. As the party trudged along a shot rang out from the direction from which they had just left but as there was no further fire, Harty put it down to an accidental discharge and ordered the march to continue. Immediately on resuming the march the RAMC men came under machine gun and rifle fire from the direction of Kurgomen. The White Russian troops manning advanced

83. RAF Dvina River Seaplane Flight on the sandbar at Troitsa, summer 1919. (Richard Watts)

positions of the front line had not expected that the RAMC party would have changed direction so dramatically and opened fire on what they believed to be an enemy column marching down the forest road.

Harty and Knight ordered the medics to lie down to take cover from the fire but not before Private Stocker was badly hit in the left shoulder and lung. Every attempt by the two medical officers to signal to the White Russian gunners only attracted a greater volume of fire. Eventually Knight was able to improvise a makeshift white flag and led a stretcher party carrying the critically wounded Private Stocker towards the Russian positions. On reaching the Allied line the Russian soldiers were extremely jumpy and made as if they wanted to shoot Knight on the spot, despite his British uniform, but a few stern words in English which the Russian soldiers clearly did not understand but could well comprehend the meaning, saved the medical officer from summary execution.

After some very arduous going the Hampshires column reached its starting off point two miles from Troitsa at 2300, some 19 hours after they had set off from Kurgomen. The men were given permission to rest and collapsed in exhaustion, taking the opportunity to get what little sleep they could before the impending battle. Whilst his men rested, Sherwood-Kelly went forward with a small party to reconnoitre the enemy positions. He had hardly returned before giving the order to move out to the starting line for the attack to commence at 0500 on the morning of 20 June.

The silence was broken at 0400 by the preliminary bombardment from the Russian-crewed 60 pdrs and RN gunboats and monitors. *M.27*'s concentrated fire from triple-mounted 4 inch guns burst around the enemy observation post in Topsa church, however strict orders had been issued not to hit the building itself in case it could latterly be used by the British for the same purpose. At 0430 fire on Topsa ceased to allow 3rd North Russian Rifles to commence their attack on the village, which was captured despite a determined defence, with the loss to the Bolsheviks of two field guns, ten machine guns and 400 prisoners.

The monitors and gunboats detailed to provide artillery cover immediately steamed upriver to repeat the process against Troitsa, firing a salvo every 30 seconds, their range corrected by the Naval Observation Post at Tulgas on the opposite bank manned by Lieutenant Clive M. Sergeant, RMLI, Lieutenant Francis Blessing, RNVR, and three signals ratings. A seaplane flown by Lieutenant Henry Bockett-Pugh with Observer 2nd Lieutenant George Lansdowne from the RAF Dvina River Seaplane Flight was also airborne, providing corrections to the naval gunners from overhead. A second Short 184 seaplane flown by Lieutenant V.W. Lamb with Observer 2nd Lieutenant A.J.

Redman was also detailed to have flown reconnaissance but it crashed on take-off, both officers plucked from the river unhurt. Once ranged, the ships commenced rapid fire for 15 minutes before ceasing to allow the Hampshires to commence their attack on the village.

At 0445 the column was in position and Sherwood-Kelly gave the order to attack. With the trench mortars and Vickers guns providing suppressive fire, 'Y' Company of the Hampshires emerged from the edge of the forest and proceeded to open fire with rifles and Lewis guns on the enemy trenches. 'W' Company moved through 'Y' Company as the trench mortars and Vickers continued their barrage. The village was much better defended than anticipated and the Bolsheviks were proving to be much more determined than intelligence reports had suggested. As the Hampshires were becoming increasingly pinned down, groups of Red soldiers could be seen advancing on the column's flanks. An enemy field gun was firing at point blank range and at 1000 OC 'C' Company, 8th Battalion, MGC reported that he had only 2,500 rounds left, only enough for a further 30 minutes firing. The machine gunners could not get back to the mule train to bring more ammunition forward due to the increasing enemy fire from the flanks. Only the slight depression the Hampshires clung to for cover prevented more men from being hit.

The Hampshires had not yet received any word of the success of the White Russian attack on Topsa, the failure of which would leave the British column cut off, and Sherwood-Kelly, conscious that if the fire became too heavy and the enemy turned his flanks he would have to leave casualties behind, had a difficult decision to make: 'There was no doubt to my mind that I must either withdraw or be cut off ... At 1030 hours I reluctantly ordered the withdrawal.'[1] When instructed by Brigadier Grogan to resume the attack, Sherwood-Kelly refused and ordered his men to continue the withdrawal, which was apparently reluctantly approved by Grogan from Brigade HQ as the discretionary decision of the commander on the ground.

During the withdrawal back to Topsa, Sherwood-Kelly was livid. Lieutenant G.E. Hill, attached to the brigade as an intelligence officer, testified at Kelly's subsequent trial that during the withdrawal he had been openly critical of senior officers of the NREF and the reliability of the White Russian forces, saying

'You cannot expect the show we are going on to succeed when we are commanded by a lot of people with no service like all these people out here. We will have to go through with this show, but it is no damn good. It is all very well for those damn people who sit on their ruddy backsides behind and run the show to tell us the Russians are going to fight, but I know they are not and we shall have to do the whole thing.'[2]

By the time the column reached Topsa, which had in the meantime been captured by 3rd North Russian Rifles, the men were completely spent. The failure of the attack and loss of Sergeant John Batten killed, an experienced NCO with 17 years service, had been a blow to the morale of the Hampshires.

Sherwood-Kelly's criticism of the campaign had been particularly targeted at the command and leadership of General Ironside, whom he described as 'weak and not fit for the job'. The two certainly had no love lost for each other. In his book, *Archangel 1918–19*, published in 1953, Ironside included a rather mendacious account of the failed Hampshires attack on Troitsa and accused Sherwood-Kelly (who is not mentioned by name) of significant errors in judgment and command and losing his head during the attack, which almost entirely contradicts Kelly's own report of operations written only two days after the events which it described.

1   The National Archives: WO 95/5422, 2nd Battalion, Hampshire Regiment War Diary, North Russia 1919.
2   Bujack, *Undefeated*, p.194.

The Russian attack (on Troitskye) was a complete success. Over 500 prisoners taken and 100 dead were counted on the position. Unfortunately the Hampshires failed to take any part in the fight. Had they obeyed orders the result would have been an overwhelming success. The story was this. They duly arrived at their appointed position some minutes before the zero hour, after a march of nine miles through the forest. They laid a cable behind them as they went and were all the time in communication with brigade headquarters. Just before the attack commenced some twenty or thirty of the enemy were seen coming up from their rear towards their front, apparently quite unaware of enemy troops being behind their line. The C.O. [Sherwood-Kelly] considered that he was being outflanked and withdrew his men some distance along the path by which he had come. He neither engaged the enemy party which he though was outflanking him nor informed the brigade of what he was doing. Later he withdrew to his starting point without making any attempt to join in the fight which had then started.

When I interviewed the C.O. the next day he could not explain why he had acted as he had. He had obviously lost his head, thinking he had overshot his position and gone too far forward. It was a clear case of disobedience of orders, aggravated by the fact that he could have communicated with his superior at any moment. The effect of the non-co-operation of the British troops had a grave effect upon the Russians just at the very moment when they needed an overwhelming success to raise their morale. Had the CO been a regular officer I should certainly have had him court martialled. He had fought brilliantly throughout the war and now appeared to me to be worn out with the responsibility of having had to act in an isolated position. To put an end to the unfortunate incident I withdrew the battalion from the line, sending the CO down to base with orders that he should be sent home for demobilisation.[3]

Kelly's biographer responds to Ironside's accusation:

That Ironside included this event at all in his account was a deliberate attempt to put his side of the story and blacken the name of Kelly after his subsequent but not consequent court martial … to say that Jack was worn out with responsibility of leading in an exposed position ignores the fact that he had been in this pointless position before at Cambrai [where he was awarded the VC] and elsewhere, where after terrible sacrifice by his men, they waited for relief and support for two days before being asked to withdraw. He had no wish to repeat that experience with the lives of his men in North Russia, of all places, where there was absolutely no chance of support. He was not worn out with responsibility at all, he was simply unwilling to order brave men to die as a morale building exercise for unreliable Russian units and no doubt then be told to withdraw again … Ironside's account was not only at odds with Kelly's version but also totally contradictory with the Regimental History.[4]

The Hampshires' War Diary gives further context to Sherwood-Kelly's actions during the attack on Troitsa:

Attacked 04.45. At 10.30 as no news was heard or seen of 3rd N.R. Rifles on our right who were attacking Topsa and the enemy who were fighting very well had nearly surrounded us, the C.O. decided to withdraw from the position we had reached round Troitskoye village. After having withdrawn about two miles news was heard that the 3rd NRR had taken their objectives and Topsa so we marched into Topsa via the woods to the South.[5]

Sherwood-Kelly's report on the action:

3   *Ibid.*, p.196.
4   *Ibid.*, p.195.
5   The National Archives: WO 95/5422, 2nd Battalion, Hampshire Regiment War Diary, North Russia 1919.

84. British Stokes mortar position on the Dvina, summer 1919. The
men wear mosquito nets over their caps. (Public domain)

Difficulty in getting through the marsh ... supposed to have been rendered passable by the R.E. but in a
great many places little work had been done ... no telephone cable linking the positions ... running out
of ammunition ... the chief reason for me having to withdraw was the fact that I had no information of
the success or otherwise of the attack on Topsa.[6]

Further evidence that Kelly had not 'lost his head' and ordered the Hampshires to withdraw
'without making any attempt to join in the fight' can be gleaned from a letter from a young subaltern
with the Hampshires who wrote of the attack:

They gave us a very warm time but our own better shooting told heavily. However we were nearly
surrounded and cut off so, fagged out as we were – we had to retreat at 930 am in the blazing heat, no rest,
little food. My platoon was the last to leave, the enemy had worked up to within seventy yards, covering
us with very heavy fire the whole time. We just got out and had to trek right back over our old trail, and
we got back to TOPSA at 12 midnight.[7]

Kelly's actions in ordering the withdrawal were also supported by Major Edward Allfrey, MC and
Bar, KRRC, OC 'A' Company, attached 45th Royal Fusiliers who wrote in his diary:

In my opinion, and also Colonel Davies [CO 45th Royal Fusiliers] the show is tactically wrong ... After
five years of war good troops ought never to be placed in such a rotten predicament by some damn fool

6   *Ibid.*
7   Bujack, *Undefeated*, p.196.

of a muddle headed broken-down old regular soldier.[8] [a reference to Brigadier C.C. Graham who had planned the attack on Topsa and Troitsa.]

Kelly's biographer further states that Ironside had deliberately attempted to besmirch Kelly's character:

> To dress this matter up in a way that flagged up Kelly as the main reason for failure and not either Churchill's vacillation and duplicity, his own indecision and performance as a Commander, the hopelessness of the strategic situation or the massive problems of trying to work with loyal but disrupted White Russian units. Thus Ironside painted a picture of a man totally inept and who panicked.[9]

An obstinate and at times difficult man, Sherwood-Kelly was determined not to let Churchill, Rawlinson, and Ironside get away with what he believed was the gross manipulation of the British public regarding the true situation in Russia and the cause for which British soldiers were dying. He began writing letters openly critical of the campaign, its commanders and the White Russian forces, something which would later embroil him in a public scandal and end his military career.

Few decorations were awarded for the failed attack on Troitsa, however Lieutenant George Hill, a Special List interpreter, was awarded the MC for volunteering to lead to safety under heavy machine gun fire three platoons which were in danger of being cut off, whilst 2nd Lieutenant Arthur Warwick, RE, received the same decoration for volunteering to bring up ammunition from the pack ponies to the firing line under machine gun fire and for getting the horse transport away during the withdrawal after the transport officer had been wounded.

Flying low overhead in support of the attack, Observer Lieutenant Bernard Heeney was severely wounded by ground fire but managed to fly back to Bereznik. On landing, Heeney was immediately transferred to a hospital barge for Archangel where he spent 35 days in hospital before evacuation to England. An original member of 'ELOPE' Squadron who had served through the winter, Heeney was awarded the DFC for his services in North Russia.

Simultaneous to the attacks on Topsa and Troitsa, Major N.E. Baxter, commanding 'X' and 'Y' Companies on the left bank, despatched a force of men under Captain Berkeley, MC, with detachments of 384th Field Company, RE, 8th Battalion, MGC and 238th TMB, to flank the enemy line and attack from the rear over the Moscow road. The enemy were found to be well entrenched on an embankment, 20 feet high with a commanding view of the road, a large open bog between the forest and the enemy positions providing a further physical barrier.

With an impossible task before him, Captain Berkeley gave the order to withdraw but not before Lieutenant D.T. Gorman, MC (who had served with the AIF on Gallipoli) had been badly wounded in the stomach, Privates William Seviour and George Taylor killed, and Private Percival Hunt wounded and missing. Seviour, one of eight officers and 184 other ranks attached to the battalion from the Wiltshire Regiment, had been severely wounded with a gunshot wound to the neck and back and fell into a bog from which he could not be rescued, those who attempted to pull him to safety nearly becoming trapped themselves.

At 2100, that same night, upon hearing word from Russian villagers that the enemy had abandoned their position on the embankment, Baxter immediately despatched a strong force to occupy it. A party under Captain J.M. Ponsford, MC, Wiltshire Regiment, who had taken part in the attack, was sent out to search the ground and bring in the bodies of Privates Taylor and Hunt but only Taylor's body could be found, his tunic and boots had already been stripped by the enemy. The search party

---

8   IWM: 3450 86/86/1 Private Papers of E.M. Allfrey.
9   Bujack, *Undefeated*, p.196.

also located a bloodstained tunic with a bullet hole above the hip. This was determined to have been the tunic belonging to Private Hunt, the bullet having traversed from the left hip to right thigh, but there was no sign of the missing soldier.

Questioning of local inhabitants resulted in conflicting statements, some saying that the Bolsheviks took two British soldiers prisoner but most stated that only one soldier was taken prisoner. It appeared based on the abandoned tunic and statements by the villagers that the badly wounded Private Hunt had been taken with the Red troops when they abandoned the position.

Lieutenant Gorman died of his wounds two days later and was buried in Troitsa churchyard. Chaplain of 2nd Hampshires, Reverend Harold Master, wrote to Gorman's mother:

> He died on the 22nd at Kurgoman where he had been taken to the Field Hospital. His body was brought here on the same day, and was buried with full military honours yesterday morning. I myself conducted the funeral service, which was attended by all the Hampshire Officers on this side of the river and by a large body of the men of this Battalion. A cross of blue cornflowers (the only flowers available) was placed upon the body by his men. A Sergeant who fell in action on the same day is buried beside him...[10]

Private Percival Hunt was never heard of again. On 28 December 1920, his name was raised in parliament when the Secretary of State for War, Winston Churchill, was asked what information could be given as to Hunt's whereabouts, 'last seen at Tulgas wounded in the thigh, surrounded by Bolsheviks on 20 June 1919, reported prisoner.' Sir Archibald Williamson, MP, replied:

> The military authorities in Russia were enabled to report that he had died on the field. No corroboration whatever has been received of the unofficial statement that Private Hunt became a prisoner of war, and I regret that there is no ground for doubting the accuracy of the official report of his death.[11]

Having defeated the British attempt to take Troitsa, the Bolsheviks counter-attacked on the morning of 21 June but were repulsed by accurate fire from HMS *Cockchafer* which had steamed up Kurgomen channel at great risk of running aground. Assistance in piloting the gunboat through the channel was given by Lieutenant Robert McNair, DSC, RNR, who had commanded the 130 mm gun barge during operations on the Dvina the previous year, by June 1919 one of the most experienced officers on the river.

On 24 June, Tunnel Class minesweeper HMS *Sword Dance* (Lieutenant Alan Halliley, RN) struck a mine, killing Leading Seaman Archibald Hansford. Although wounded, Halliley continued to captain the minesweeper during the ensuing confusion for which he was awarded the DSO.

Just over a week later on 3 July, *Sword Dance*'s sister ship HMS *Fandango* (Chief Boatswain Thomas Vosper, RN) also struck a mine which killed Gunner James Livesey, RN and seven ratings. Both vessels had swept over 40 mines since the thaw but the loss of both ships served as a reminder if any was needed of the danger posed by Bolshevik mines floated downriver and the inherent danger of minesweeping on the Dvina.

A naval officer recalled the important work of the two plucky ships before their demise:

> Whenever H.M.Ms Sword-Dance and Fandango, preceded by the two little 'searching' steamboats, showed themselves beyond the bend of the river, it was only a matter of seconds before a lofty column of spray and a distant boom told that the Bolo was busy. But nothing could discourage those sweepers. Time after time the sweep would part, and they would manoeuvre, slowly and deliberately, in the narrow mine-

---

10   National Archives of Australia: AIF Service Record, Gorman, T.
11   *Hansard*, 28 October 1920, Written answers House of Commons, Mr Mitchell to Sir. A. Williamson.

85. Large China gunboat HMS *Cicala* on the Dvina, summer 1919. (Public domain)

infested channel, without the slightest regard for the shells falling all round them, join up a new sweep, and carry on. One square hit from a 5.9 would have meant practical annihilation, and they frequently escaped only by a matter of a very few yards.[12]

HMS *Fandango* was completely sunk and *Sword Dance* partially so, with bridge and stern still visible above water. Both ships remained submerged until they were destroyed on 17 September just prior to the final evacuation from the Dvina, to prevent their recovery by the Bolsheviks.

On 26 June, 'W' and 'Y' Companies, 2nd Hampshires moved to take over advanced posts south of Topsa to relieve 2/4th North Russian Rifles. Two days later, 'X' and 'Z' Companies rejoined the battalion from the western bank of the river and on the following day the Hampshires took up new positions at the village of Zinovievskay, four kilometres south-east of Troitsa.

On 30 June, White Russian troops attacked Selmenga with supporting fire provided by 238th TMB. The attack failed after two of the Russian company commanders were killed and the men broke and ran. The trench mortars then came under heavy artillery fire but were able to extricate themselves without casualty. During the attack a seaplane flown by 2nd Lieutenant William Boyd with Observer 2nd Lieutenant J.B. Prowse scored a direct hit on an enemy gunboat with a 20 lb Cooper bomb, although due to the small size of the bomb there was no significant damage done.

On 27 June large China gunboats HMS *Cricket* and HMS *Cicala*, which had spent the winter frozen in at Archangel, were ordered to steam upriver to push the Bolshevik flotilla further back towards Kotlas to allow 2nd (Sadleir-Jackson's) Brigade to land at Troitsa, which was at the time under observation from Bolshevik spotters in the church tower at Yakovlevskoe across the river. The gunboats opened fire at 1000 as HMS *Step Dance* and HMS *Morris Dance* swept the channel for mines. The gun duel between the British gunboats and Bolshevik flotilla and shore battery went on for more than an hour, neither side apparently scoring any hits although there were several very near misses. An officer on board *Cricket* recalled:

---

12   Singleton-Gates, *Bolos and Barishynas*, p.59.

86. Captain Norman Fraser, MBE, AFC, commanding 'B' Flight, RAF Seaplanes Dvina River, summer 1919. (Richard Watts)

Hour after hour it went on, steadily and with deliberation. As the Bolo found our range, we shifted slowly from place to place, keeping carefully in the swept channel, and giving a wide berth to the left bank, where the ugly spiked heads of a number of large sea mines were just visible on the surface.[13]

A heavy shell landed a few yards from *Cricket* sending a large pillar of spray and splinters into the side of the gunboat. The next shell landed immediately in front of the bow, followed by two more a few seconds later. The officer continued:

By all the rules of the game, the next should have landed fair and square on the quarter-deck, but he didn't get it off in time – he probably had a misfire – and the extra seconds allowed us to get clear, as the next one, faultless for direction, burst well astern. Swerving to port, we ran into the little bay, where we were either invisible to the enemy or else well camouflaged against the background. He still continued to put them down in the same place, and searched the lower side of the bay, evidently using the ruined belfry of Topsa Church as his aiming mark. But they all passed harmlessly over us.[14]

At this point of the battle the monitor *M.33* arrived to resupply *Cricket* with ammunition, after which both ships steamed into action, pushing the Bolsheviks a further three miles upriver, guaranteeing the safety of Troitsa Bay which would remain the Dvina Force advanced base until the final evacuation in September.

Commanding *Cricket* was Lieutenant Commander Frank Worsley, DSO, RD, RNR, who was by 1919 something of a maritime legend. Worsley, a New Zealander from Akaroa, had been Captain of *Endurance* during Shackleton's ill-fated Imperial Trans-Antarctic Expedition 1914–16 and it was largely due to his skill as a sailor that all 28 men of the expedition were eventually rescued. In an epic feat of seamanship, Worsley captained a 22 foot whaleboat *James Caird*, named after one of the expedition donors, with Shackleton and four other men on board on a 16 day, 800 mile journey across the treacherous South Atlantic to the island of South Georgia. On arrival on the island, Shackleton, Worsley and Tom Crean trekked for 36 hours over the mountains to salvation at the whaling station at Grytviken. The welfare of his men ever-present in his mind, Shackleton made all efforts to return to Elephant Island to rescue the remainder of his trapped crew, but due to the Antarctic winter was unable to return to the island until three months later, nearly two years after *Endurance* had been crushed and sunk by pack ice.

Worsley's service in North Russia remains a bit of a mystery although it is known that he spent time in command of local troops ashore behind enemy lines in early August 1919, for which he was awarded a Bar to his DSO previously awarded for services in action with enemy submarines in 1917.

13   *Ibid.*, p.62.
14   *Ibid.*, pp.62–63.

On 4 July, an incident occurred on HMS *Cicala* when orders were received to relieve *Cricket* in the gun line: the seamen on board *Cicala* refused to weigh anchor in protest of the lack of fresh meat and poor rations. Captain Altham was brought on board to hear the men's grievances and said he would make arrangements to improve the quality of rations but also that there would be an investigation and those responsible would be punished. The following day, all seamen were interviewed separately and the three leading seamen ringleaders identified, disrated and sent to other ships in the flotilla. Given the harshness of naval punishment the perpetrators got off relatively lightly for such a serious crime committed on active service.

On 3 July, the Hampshires were relieved at Troitsa by 1st (Dyer's) Battalion, Slavo-British Legion and returned to Bereznik. On 6 July, rumour was received of an impending Bolshevik uprising behind the British lines. At 1500 the Hampshires embarked at Bereznik in full kit ready to take on any Red insurgents should they make an appearance. However no uprising occurred and the battalion was diverted north to the Railway Front, two companies continued upriver to the strategically important garrison at Ust-Pinega on the junction of the Dvina and Pinega Rivers which had recently seen increased enemy activity. The rumours of a Bolshevik uprising were not unfounded and the following day 1st Battalion, Slavo-British Legion mutinied in the most treacherous event to take place during British military intervention in Russia 1918–20.

The British eagerly and actively recruited local Russians and other ethnic minorities into the Slavo-British Legion and North Russian Rifle Regiments, however in their haste to bolster the White Russian forces before the withdrawal, many of the recruits were entirely unsuitable. Enlistment into the Slavo-British Legion had been so low that recruits had been sought from former Bolshevik POWs and petty criminals imprisoned in Archangel's jails. The Provisional Government was extremely sceptical of the whole Slavo-British Legion scheme, considering many of its men fit only for a prison cell. Ironside brushed aside critics of the scheme in the belief that the quality of British officers commanding the legion would instil discipline and prestige and whip the troops into top fighting shape.

Ironside also formed a 'Junior Battalion' administratively attached to the Legion from the urchins and orphans who had washed up at Archangel. The boys were issued the smallest size British uniforms that could be found (which were still much too big), given haircuts and trained as batmen to British officers. Command of the Junior Battalion was given to Major Harry Cautley, Suffolk Regiment, subsequently awarded an OBE for his services at Archangel. Many units adopted *malchiks* (usually orphans) as unit mascots, some of whom were evacuated with their guardians back to the UK and Canada.

On 1 June, General Ironside presented the Legion with 'King's Colours' at a ceremony at Archangel with the whole town in attendance:

> The colours had been woven by the women of Archangel and after they had been blessed by a bishop of the Greek Church they were handed over to a Russian ensign, escorted by two bearded Russian soldiers. On the march past even General Miller, who took the salute, was moved to salute the companies as they passed him with such words as, 'Excellent company.' 'Good company.' I had great hopes that we had created something good in the making of this fine battalion.[15]

Born to Russian–German parents in Latvia in 1867, General Evgeni 'Eugene' Miller graduated from an elite cavalry school at the age of 19 and spent the pre-war years as Imperial military attaché in Belgium and Italy. During the war he served variously in command of a dragoon regiment and as a staff officer and commander at Corps and Army level. In 1917, just prior to the revolution, he was

---

15   Ironside, *Archangel 1918–19*, p.143.

87. Corporal Davies, Lieutenant Norbert Russell, and Sergeant John Calderwood on the sand bar at Troitsa which served as a base for RAF seaplanes. Russell received an MiD for North Russia whilst Calderwood was awarded the MSM. (Richard Watts)

appointed chief of the Russian military mission to Italy. After the Bolsheviks took power he was one of a multitude of Imperial officers opposed to the new regime who washed up at Archangel where he would face the most challenging period of his military career.

On 14 January 1919, Provisional Government President Nikolai Tchaikovsky appointed Miller in the dual role of Governor General and Commander-in-Chief of the provisional government, White Russian General Maroushevsky was given command of all Russian troops in the region under General Miller's authority.

Despite Miller's best efforts to weed out Bolshevik agitators and sympathisers from local recruits, they remained rife within the ranks of the White Russian forces. Those men recruited that were not already Bolshevik sympathisers were susceptible to being turned once in a British-supplied uniform. One British officer described the White Russian forces with overt condescension: 'Officers, with very few exceptions … were afraid of their own men, physical cowards, drunkards and thieves. They appeared to lack all moral sense, or sense of shame … corrupt in the extreme.' He went on to describe the other ranks with only slightly more admiration as 'easy converts to Bolshevik propaganda … capable of great powers of endurance … impervious to weather and have iron constitutions. They got drunk on anything … Aviation petrol included.'[16] Regardless of the quality of the White Russian troops themselves, actually getting them into action was almost a battle in itself. Of a total nominal strength of 4,000 men in the 'Northern Rifle Regiments' at Archangel, rarely could more than half that number be actually assembled and sent into battle.

On the night of 6–7 July, 1st Battalion, Slavo-British Legion were billeted on the western bank of the Dvina River near Topsa, 'B' and 'C' Companies were billeted in the village of Tuisamnika close to Topsa, whilst the rest of the battalion were billeted further inland.

---

16   The National Archives: WO 95/5430, Sadleir-Jackson Brigade War Diary.

At 0230, during the period of semi-darkness that is a summer night in the sub-Arctic latitudes, a party of eight men led by Corporal Nuchev and Private Leuchenko crept towards the hut where the British and Russian company and platoon commanders were sleeping. Corporal Nuchev shot Captain Aubrey Finch (Seaforth Highlanders) through a window as he was sleeping, killing him outright, whilst the seven others in the group stormed the hut shooting and killing four British and four Russian officers and three batmen.

Captain David Barr (East Lancashire Regiment) was badly wounded with bullet and bayonet wounds but managed to evade his attackers and flee out of the hut into the twilight, swimming across the Dvina to one of HMS *Humber*'s picket boats. For his gallantry in fighting his way out of the billet under fire and courage and endurance despite his wounds, Barr was awarded the MC but sadly succumbed to his wounds six days later and was buried in the Archangel Allied Cemetery.

The other British officers killed were Lieutenant Gerald Gosling, MC, Gloucestershire Regiment, Lieutenant Cecil Bland, MC, Royal Berkshire Regiment, and Lieutenant Thomas Griffith, Loyal North Lancashire Regiment.

The killing of the 'B' and 'C' Company officers was the signal for the mutiny to begin. About 150 men of the two companies fled towards the Bolshevik lines in small groups. Almost simultaneous to the Slavo-British Legion mutiny there was an uprising amongst 200 men of 4th North Russian Rifles billeted in nearby Troitsa. In a carefully organised and coordinated plot, two of the attached British officers were arrested by the mutineers and locked in the village bath house whilst the remainder took over the battalion position by force. Subsequent investigation revealed that the mutinies had been planned long in advance by Bolshevik agents within the White Russian ranks.

Brigade Intelligence Officer Major Straker and Staff Captain G.H. Pickering were awoken by the gunfire and peered outside a window in their billet to find a few Russian troops milling about apparently unconcerned, and 'there being no accounting for what a Russian soldier may or may not do', the pair retired back to their bunks.

Another minute passed and rather than abating, the gunfire increased. The two officers decided that the prudent course of action would be to investigate. Making their way outside, the two men were mobbed by a horde of shrieking mutineers seemingly intent on killing the British officers outright. After a couple of terrifying moments menaced with rifles and bayonets, their lives were spared, both men were locked in the bath house under armed guard.

Fearing their likely fate at the hands of the mutineers, Straker and Pickering hastily formulated a plan to stage a breakout using Straker's pocket knife to attack the guard but before the desperate plan could be carried out the door burst open and a further two captives were bundled in, Colonel Lowrie of the Royal Marines and a newspaper correspondent. As the men huddled together to discuss their options, a shell flew overhead and burst near enough to the bath house that splinters tore into the log wall of the hut. Another shell landed nearby and then a third which completely took the roof off the building, showering the men below with debris.

The mutineer guard had fled on arrival of the first shell, leaving the small party to flee back to the temporary safety of their billet. The officers who had remained behind had not had a happy time, the mutineers blasted the windows with rifle and Lewis gun fire, one Royal Engineers officer noted as being 'of monumental proportions', caused some apprehension by his inability to conceal himself completely below a window. The arrival of Straker and Pickering, both of whom had been believed captured and executed, was met with great relief. After a few more shells had burst around the billet the firing stopped.

On the outbreak of the mutiny, General Grogan had made a personal reconnaissance to investigate and found Troitsa village in the hands of the mutineers. He raced back to a Russian artillery battery on the outskirts of the village and after a frustrating delay in communicating to its non-English speaking commander where to fire his shells, the battery opened fire on the village, sending the mutineers fleeing into the forest.

88. Lieutenant Colonel Charles Davies, CMG, DSO (seated centre) and officers of 45th Battalion, Royal Fusiliers serving on the Dvina River Front, summer 1919. (IWM 16436)

Grogan then coordinated the assembly of a mixed force of signallers and RASC men to pursue the mutineers and round up any stragglers. At 0300 orders were given for the assembly of a naval landing party of as many men as could be raised. After a hurried issue of rifles and bandoliers, the naval detachment under Chief Staff Officer Commander Frank Bramble, RN and a Royal Marine detachment unde to do some one in r Lieutenant Clive Sergeant, RMLI, were landed and assisted to hold the village until the arrival of reinforcements of Royal Fusiliers from Osinova.

The rifle and Lewis gun fire had alerted the British garrisons on both sides of the Dvina that something terrible was afoot and furious cables were sent up the line to the Fusiliers camp at Osinova for reinforcements. At first it was thought that Bolshevik saboteurs had attacked the White Russian positions but it was soon all too obvious that the cause of the shooting was a mutiny of White Russian troops. CO, 46th Royal Fusiliers, Lieutenant Colonel Herbert Jenkins, took 'C' Company, 46th Royal Fusiliers (Captain John Blackburn, MC) on board the river steamer *Retvisan* as reinforcements with a sad and worried-looking General Ironside accompanying them on the run to Troitsa. As a precaution, a signal was also sent ordering the immediate disarmament of 2nd (Burke's) Battalion, Slavo-British Legion at Archangel.

During the mutiny, Slavo-British Legion company commanders Captain William Beavan, Welch Regiment and Alfred Barrett, Royal Berkshire Regiment, formed their men on parade despite the mayhem going on around them, and by their determination held the men steady with the assistance of 2nd Lieutenant Sydney Brooker, General List, who was commanding one of the platoons in Beavan's company. All three men were awarded the MC for their courage and determination.

Control of the situation was regained by fire from the river flotilla and the arrival of 'C' Company, 46th Royal Fusiliers. The Fusiliers fanned out into the woods in an attempt to cut off the armed mutineers from their line of retreat. In the brief skirmish that followed two mutineers were killed and several wounded. Two hundred mutineers managed to escape through the forest to the Bolsheviks who took advantage of the upset to attack and capture the village of Selmenga. 'C' Company, 46th Royal Fusiliers was rushed to the village whilst 'A' and 'D' Companies, 45th Royal Fusiliers were hurried to reinforce the line from Osinova on board requisitioned Russian paddle steamer HMS *Borodino*.

The day after the mutiny, during the early morning of 8 July, Bolshevik gunboats pressed forward to support a push by their troops on the western bank of the river, apparently timed to take advantage of the mutiny. The enemy gunboats were reported only 1,200 yards from the Royal Navy Dvina Flotilla anchorage and RAF seaplane base at Troitsa and the situation looked dire.

HMS *Humber* was rushed forward to join *Cicala*, *M.27* and *M.33* in the gun line as the smaller craft pulled back. *M.33* was hit by a heavy shell which destroyed the wardroom but caused no casualties to either the ship's crew or the wine store and the monitor was able to remain in action. *M.27*'s triple 4 inch guns were brought into action against the enemy flotilla with great effect. *Cicala* developed mechanical problems due to continual fire at high elevation and had to be relieved in the line by *Cricket*.

By midday the firing died down with reports that the enemy had retreated to Selmenga. The sailors on board *M.33* took the opportunity to catch a little sleep which was interrupted when the monitor came under 'a perfect storm' of machine gun fire from the riverbank just 50 yards distant. The crew quickly jumped into action and responded with their own deck-mounted machine guns as sister ship *M.27* blasted the forest, silencing the enemy and allowing *M.33* to make its way to the other side of the river. *M.33* had been riddled with bullets in the exchange but miraculously none of the monitor's crew had been killed and only two ratings wounded. When a landing party was put ashore to investigate the location of the enemy machine gun, a number of enemy bodies were counted, mostly victims of *M.27*'s guns.

Throughout the afternoon of 8 July, Red troops continued to snipe the monitors of the British flotilla from the riverbank, anyone seen above decks for a second or two received a bullet fired in their direction. The fire was not accurate but dangerous none the less:

> There was one persistent gent – evidently an officer of Dyer's Battalion, as he was wearing khaki and a Sam Browne belt – who seemed determined to do someone in. He could be seen constantly dodging from cover to cover. Our gunner had a long argument with him with a Lewis gun, but the duel ended without a score.[17]

At 1600, the Bolshevik flotilla resumed firing from the bend in the river and *M.27* and *M.33* boldly steamed forward to Seltso, the extent of the cleared minefield, to take the enemy on. The monitors came under a maelstrom of fire from three directions, from artillery at Selmenga on the eastern bank and Seltso on the western bank in addition to the Bolshevik gunboats to the front. At 1640, *M.33* was struck by a 5.9 inch shell amidships on the starboard side below the waterline, causing the monitor to list badly and begin to sink. An attempt to steam out of range failed when the added draught from the list caused the monitor to ground on a submerged sand bar directly under the steep riverbank from which the enemy machine gunners had peppered the ship earlier in the day. Stuck fast, broadside to the enemy, the crew of *M.33* could do little more than watch as enemy shells began falling closer and closer as the Bolshevik gunners corrected their range. One crew member recorded that the following 10 minutes were, 'excessively unpleasant.'

> It was with enormous relief that we saw the bow gradually paying off and the ship moving again. Once afloat, we legged it down river, firing our after gun, and the enemy shots following – ahead, astern and on

---

17   Singleton-Gates, *Bolos and Barishynas*, pp.66-67.

89. Six recipients of the VC on board SS *Stephen* en route to Archangel, May 1919. From left to right standing: Colonel Henry Douglas, VC, CB, CMG, DSO, RAMC, Lieutenant Colonel George Grogan, VC, CB, CMG, DSO and Bar, Worcestershire Regiment, Lieutenant Colonel John Sherwood-Kelly, VC, CMG, DSO, Norfolk Regiment, Lieutenant Colonel Charles Hudson, VC, MC, Notts and Derby Regiment. Seated left to right Captain Montague Moore, VC, Hampshire Regiment, Captain Oswald Reid, VC, Liverpool Regiment. (Public domain)

both sides – the water creeping up and up, in spite of the pumps, till the engines were heaving round in three feet of water. In ten minutes or so we reached Troitsa Bay, a few hundred yards beyond the enemy's extreme range, a few minutes before the fires were put out and everything stopped.[18]

The gap made by the withdrawal of the damaged *M.33* from the gun line was quickly filled by HMS *Humber*, and the monitor's 6 inch guns combined with numerous attacks by RAF seaplanes eventually drove the Bolshevik flotilla further upriver. HMS *Cricket* had also fallen victim to the enemy guns during the defence of Troitsa. The gunboat was so badly damaged that it took four weeks of repairs undertaken in the shallow waters near Tulgas before she was again ready for action, by which time she had become stuck aground on a sand bar and had to sit out the attack of 10 August. It took the tremendous efforts of Commander Hugh Beaumont Robinson, RN, to refloat the ship before it was immediately despatched upriver to counter the enemy flotilla. Robinson would later be awarded a DSO for services on board HMS *Humber* during the period 7–10 July.

The RAF were also heavily in action on 8 July, engaging the enemy almost immediately upon taking off from the seaplane base at Troitsa anchorage. During one mission to bomb the enemy flotilla, the Fairey IIIC Seaplane flown by Lieutenant M. Hilton with Observer Lieutenant G.J. Ross was hit by ground fire whilst immediately above the enemy flotilla. The petrol tank was found to have been pierced by an enemy bullet and leaking. Ross put his foot over the hole and by furiously pumping the hand pressure pump was able to keep the aircraft airborne until it reached base.

At Troitsa, 'A' Company, 45th Royal Fusiliers under Major Allfrey had remained behind to guard the disarmed remnants of the Slavo-British Legion and to isolate any Bolshevik agitators and ringleaders. Forty mutineers were summarily sentenced to death and put under a Fusilier guard with orders to shoot if there was any trouble. Major Allfrey went to see Legion CO, Lieutenant Colonel Wells: 'He is very overdone, poor fellow, and is also a good deal gone in the nerves.'[19]

---

18   *Ibid.*, p.68.
19   IWM: 3450 86/86/1 Private Papers of E.M. Allfrey.

The Times war correspondent at Archangel recalled in his memoir of service in North Russia a meeting with his old pals Finch and Barr shortly before the mutiny:

It didn't take me long to sense a certain disappointment. These two fellows had been so proud of their special work at Bakharitsa, training the erstwhile Bolsheviks. They had done so well with practically nothing of the language at their command. They had served in France and were out there in order to prolong the adventures of war. Laughing, chaffing Scots – when they were in Archangel. Just the fellows to kick dullness out of an evening; and so staunch in their friendship for each other that they were known as the Scots Twins.

The boys sat on my camp-bed in the bell tent. I said:

'Come on, Davy, tell us all you know. You look as happy as a pack of playing cards in a cathedral. They tell me you're going in to a scrap this week.'

'Ay'

Where was the old enthusiasm? The cheery fellow who used to sing with gusto? Finch was equally quiet and reserved.

'How did the old 'Bolos' behave coming up? I asked. 'Do you think they'll put up a good fight?'

'They may, Andrew'

'And they may not?'

'And they may not,' said Barr.

'You've had trouble with them on the way up?'

'A bit,' said Barr.

'What happened?'

'Oh, we nipped the trouble in the bud, as ye might say. Had to get rid of ten of them – the ringleaders; they were making mischief among the others.'

Yes, the old spirit was gone; they were visualizing something about which they didn't care to talk.

I said good-bye to the boys and they went up-river with their contingent.

It was the last time I saw them alive.[20]

The Slavo-British Legionnaires who had not participated in the mutiny were marched into the Fusiliers camp where Allfrey took dramatic precautions to prevent a repeat of the mutiny:

I have established machine-gun posts all round the camp they are to occupy when they arrive, and if there is the slightest trouble I shall pump lead into them harder than they have ever seen bullets fly before. The machine-gun nests are quite neatly arranged, and are concealed, each one being in a bell tent, which is quite a common sight round these parts and will not be suspected.[21]

On the following day the Bolsheviks sent out a large patrol with the aim of guiding those mutineers still dispersed within the forest towards the Bolshevik lines. They walked straight into the Australian Platoon, 'D' Company, 45th Royal Fusiliers:

The next day they were amazed to see a mass of Bolos advancing, waving and shouting, many clearly unarmed … Some of Dyer's Battalion had refused to mutiny, so the Australians persuaded these fellows to stand on the parapets and wave to the advancing Bolos. Great was the joy of the enemy when they saw their 'comrades'. The Australians allowed the mob (no other term applies) to get within two hundred

---

20   Andrew Soutar, *With Ironside in North Russia* (London: Hutchinson & Co., 1940), pp.137–138.
21   IWM: 3450 86/86/1 Private Papers of E.M. Allfrey.

90. Brigadier Sadleir-Jackson (with cane under arm), General Ironside (partly obscured by Sadleir-Jackson) and White Russian General Miller (with moustache, standing closest to camera) await disembarkation of 2nd (Sadleir-Jackson's) Brigade at Archangel. (Public domain)

yards of our lines. Then they opened fire, and mowed down the foe as corn before a reaper. There were few escapes.[22]

Among the Legionnaires, Allfrey found a female private who had been a company commander in a women's battalion of the Imperial Army which had defended the Tsar's winter palace. One man was an English-speaker who had been condemned to death for taking part in the mutiny. He explained that he had lived in Scotland and that his wife was still there working in a coalmine. Allfrey decided that this man was unlikely to be a murderer and lobbied for and secured his release.

Twenty-six Russian soldiers were eventually charged with offences relating to the mutiny, their court-martial carried out in the field over two days, 12–13 July. Eight men were acquitted whilst the remaining 18 charged were sentenced to death, six of these having their capital sentences commuted to 10 years penal servitude leaving 12 mutineers sentenced to execution. Ironside had originally wanted to shoot 'about 20' mutineers as an example but the War Office were quick to quash any such action:

> The execution of so large a number of men as 20 cannot be approved unless the circumstances are such that you are unable to maintain your authority without having recourse to such drastic measures. It is thought that it should suffice to shoot but a small number of examples, and unless the evidence against the remainder is such as to render them liable to conviction for murder, the number executed should not exceed the numbers who lost their lives as a direct result of the mutiny.[23]

22   Jones, *An Air Fighter's Scrapbook*, p.134.
23   Peter Quinlivian, *Forgotten Valour, The story of Arthur Sullivan VC, shy war hero* (Frenchs Forest, NSW, Australia: New Holland, 2006), p140.

On 14 July, one of the condemned prisoners was shot whilst attempting to escape. Another convicted mutineer, Private Starkoff, sentenced to 10 years imprisonment, was also shot whilst attempting to escape on 18 August. Ironside ensured that 500 new White Russian recruits were present to witness the executions as a none too subtle warning.

On 17 July at 0800, the condemned men were brought out to meet their fate. Ace pilot Captain Ira Jones, RAF, was witness to the executions:

> I have to-night seen something which I never want to witness again. An execution. I've kept my eye on a living Being, like myself, and I've watched that Being suddenly transformed into an unsightly lump of flesh.
>
> The mutineers of Dyer's battalion were shot in one lot at a selected place across the river. I watched the whole performance.
>
> There were three acts. Act I. The prisoners – thirteen [sic] in all – were in tents and a priest went to bless them and take any messages to relatives. Each one was sprinkled with Holy water, and the priest kissed each one.
>
> Act 2. The prisoners were marched under escort to the place of execution, where Russian and English troops formed three sides of a square, the other side being taken by spectators. The doomed men were placed in a row with their backs to the place of execution and their sentences read out. Two were reprieved and sentenced to imprisonment.
>
> Act 3. Those to be shot were blindfolded and the stripes of a fine looking sergeant were torn off his coat sleeves. Each man was then taken by the arm by British soldiers and led to posts where they were tied arms and feet.
>
> A disc was placed on their breasts opposite their hearts, as a target. Some of the cowardly ones cried hysterically, but the sergeant was a real stoic, and I felt (my feelings were shared by others) that it was tragic to have to kill such a brave man, but you cannot cheat Nemesis.
>
> The men were being shot by their own comrades who had not mutinied, each of the condemned men having a machine-gun all to himself [although each loaded only with a belt of 5 rounds] at ten yards range. It was an eerie sight because the executioners were themselves covered from behind by machine-gunners from the Royal Fusiliers, in case they suddenly changed their minds and turned their weapons on the British present!
>
> A Russian officer was in charge of the execution, although a British A.P.M. [Assistant Provost Marshall] was present. The signal to fire was when the officer dropped his raised sword, then a strange thing happened which lengthened the lives and agony of those Bolos for about one minute. A little dog appeared from somewhere and trotted up to one of the prisoners and sniffed at his legs. The dog had to be got away before the officer dropped his sword. I shall never forget the rattle of those machine guns and the wriggling bodies as their life was shot out of them.
>
> The executioner of the sergeant either deliberately missed him or became very nervous, because when the smoke of the guns had cleared away the N.C.O. had pulled off his handkerchief and was shouting 'Long live Bolshevism.'
>
> The officer, pulling out his revolver strolled up to him – I was secretly hoping he would not shoot – and as he did so pointed the revolver at the disc on his heart. The sergeant spat at him. Bang! Bang! Bang! And two more for his head.
>
> Afterwards, all the bodies were buried in one big grave which the victims had themselves dug in the morning.[24]

Of the mutiny one officer wrote:

---

24   Jones, *An Air Fighter's Scrapbook*, pp.138–40.

In their innermost hearts the loyal Russians were not sorry. They regretted the butchery of British officers, but the mutiny itself they regarded as the natural and inevitable outcome of the whole effort. They merely shrugged their shoulders as if to say, 'We told you so.'[25]

On 14 July a sad event occurred at Ust-Pinega on the Pinega River Front. Driver Nathaniel Croucher of 238th Signal Company (1st (Grogan's) Brigade, NRRF) drowned in the river. Sick Berth Attendant Ernest Daish, RN, recorded in his diary:

> The funeral took place today of a RE soldier who was killed several days ago. The men have a habit when taking their horses for a wash in the river of hanging on to their tails. This is all right if the horse is swimming but a dangerous game if standing in the water. It was so in this case. The man was bathing and hanging on to the horse's tail when it kicked out striking him in the forehead stunning him. He sank and was carried out by the strong current. His body came ashore three days later. It was intended to bury him in the churchyard and a grave was dug but at the last moment the priest objected. So he was taken to a little cemetery outside the village and buried there with full military honours.[26]

In the weeks following the mutiny there was relative calm on the front, however the RAF Seaplane Flight at Troitsa remained active. On 14 July, whilst on a bombing/reconnaissance mission over enemy lines, a Fairey IIIC seaplane flown by Lieutenant Marshall with Observer Lieutenant George Lansdowne was forced down by ground fire near the river bank adjacent to the enemy gunboat flotilla. Both men attempted to set the aircraft on fire but were unsuccessful so decided rather ambitiously to try and swim downriver to British lines, but were captured not long after entering the water. Watching the drama unfold from above, other RAF seaplanes circling overhead made attempts to set the stricken seaplane alight with tracer fire but were also unsuccessful and by the time an afternoon rain shower had passed the aircraft had been loaded onto a barge and taken away by the Bolsheviks.

Lansdowne was gazetted for the award of the DFC for his work with the RAF Seaplane Flight whilst still a prisoner in Moscow, where he remained imprisoned until released in a March 1920 in a prisoner exchange.

The following day, a seaplane flown by 2nd Lieutenant W.G. Boyd with Observer 2nd Lieutenant J.B. Prowse sustained damage during a mission to machine gun Seltso. Ground fire wounded Prowse in the knee but Boyd remained unhurt and quickly turned for home where Prowse was treated for his wounds before evacuation on the hospital barge to Archangel.

On 18 July, several seaplanes flew missions to bomb the enemy flotilla, one gunboat was set alight by a direct hit whilst the observer in another seaplane managed to destroy an enemy sea mine from the air. Tragedy followed two days later when a Fairey IIIC flown by Lieutenant A.J. Rankin crashed into an ammunition lighter on take-off, and Observer 2nd Lieutenant Jean Gondre was knocked unconscious and drowned. Rankin remained unharmed but was badly shaken.

On 1 August, Russian ace Alexander Kazakov died when his Sopwith Camel crashed soon after take-off from Bereznik airfield. To those that witnessed the crash there was little doubt that the gallant Kazakov had taken his own life. Captain Ira Jones witnessed the whole sad event:

> Ever since the rumour started that we were going to evacuate, Kosikoff has been a different man, silent and morbid. To-day, he has been noticeably sullen and appeared to have lost all interest in life, and refused to give an answer to an invitation to dinner which we were giving to the Russian pilots as a farewell 'do' …
> August 3rd: Kosikoff is dead. He died in my arms. About five-thirty Kosikoff walked into a hangar and

---

25   Ibid., p.25.
26   Private diary of Ernest Ethelbert Daish.

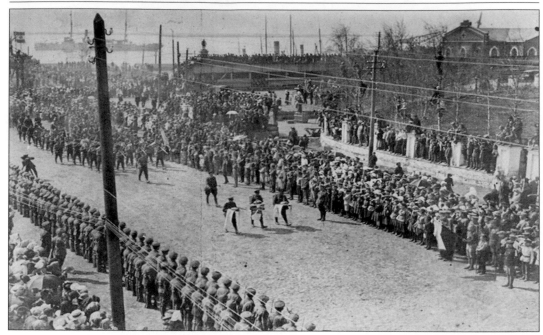

91. Arrival of bulk of 2nd (Sadleir-Jackson's) Brigade, North Russia Relief Force at Archangel, 10 June 1919. The Russian soldiers at the head of the procession carry the traditional Slavic greeting of bread and salt. (Author's collection)

instructed some Russian mechanics to bring out a Camel machine and start up the engine. I noticed him approach the craft with bowed head, and, accompanied by Lieutenant Carter, I walked up to try to induce him to speak, and, possibly, find out whether he was going to attend the dinner to-night. Kosikoff's behaviour was peculiar. Instead of 'revving' up the engine gradually, he opened the throttle sharply, and the engine stopped. I was about to venture a facetious remark, but Kosikoff's glare showed that he was ablaze with anger. The 'prop' was sung, the engine roared, and the Russian ordered the chocks to be moved. The machine took off, and Kosikoff made no attempt to gain height, but kept the craft at twenty feet for a good distance in order to gain speed. Then, suddenly, he pulled her up in a sharp climb as if to loop. The little craft reached the top of the loop, stalled badly, and then dived vertically into the centre of the aerodrome. I dashed up to the wreckage and pulled the gallant major out of the cockpit. His head was resting on my arms while the ambulance was rushing to the scene, but before it arrived I saw the film of death creep over his eyes. He spoke not a word, and a great soldier passed into Valhalla ... I am convinced that Kosikoff brought about his own death and staged it in the most dramatic manner.[27]

27 Jones, *An Air Fighter's Scrapbook*, pp.141–42.

Archangel: Dvina River Front August 1919 offensive

The final two months of operations on the Dvina River, August and September 1919, would see some of the fiercest fighting between British and Red Army troops of the civil war. The brunt of the fighting during this period was borne by units of the North Russia Relief Force, in particular 2nd (Sadleir-Jackson's) Brigade, comprised of volunteers who had seen extensive service in campaigns on the Western Front, Gallipoli, Palestine, Italy, the Balkans, East Africa and Mesopotamia and had specifically volunteered for further service in North Russia.

The objectives of Sadleir-Jackson's plan for a major offensive on both banks of the Dvina in early August were threefold: 1. To strike a strong blow at the enemy so as to lower his morale; 2. To compel him to withdraw his river fleet to obtain room for mining operations and unhindered evacuation; 3. To raise the morale of the White Russian troops.[1]

The forces opposing the British were considerable. During August the strength of the Soviet 6th Army had risen to 6,000 men deployed along a front six miles long and 10 miles deep. Sadleir-Jackson's under strength brigade numbered only 2,200, a further 300 men having been deployed to the Railway Front.

To reach their objectives well behind enemy lines the attacking columns would have to trek for up to three days undetected through treacherous forest and swamp just to reach the starting line. It was hoped that the Bolsheviks would not expect an attack so far behind their front line, giving the attackers the advantage of surprise.

Sadleir-Jackson's plan was for columns on either bank of the Dvina to make a silent march several miles behind enemy lines and after a prearranged bombardment by field artillery and RN gunboats, to simultaneously attack a chain of six enemy-held villages, three on each bank of the river. 'Z' Day would be 10 August 1919. Objectives for 45th Royal Fusiliers on the western bank were the villages of Seltso, Sludka-Lipovets and Chudinova and for 46th Royal Fusiliers on the eastern bank, the villages of Selmenga, Gorodok and Borok. The day after the attack the western bank column would split, leaving a garrison to protect the captured villages whilst another force commanded by 45th Royal Fusiliers CO, Lieutenant Colonel Charles Davies, would push directly east towards the Bolshevik-held township of Shegovari on the Vaga River, attacking the enemy's gun line, cutting off their retreat. On 'Z' Day plus two, after a concentrated poison gas bombardment, Vaga Force and the Dvina column would link up and vigorously attack north along both banks of the Vaga towards Ust-Vaga killing or capturing all those Red troops who had been unable to escape the Dvina–Vaga pocket. Any guns captured were to be turned on the enemy.

Each of the two attacking columns, 45th Royal Fusiliers on the western bank and 46th Royal Fusiliers on the eastern bank would be further divided into three columns, each named for the villages which were their respective objectives.

On the western bank, 45th Royal Fusiliers attacking columns:
Lieutenant Colonel C. Davies, DSO
Seltso: 'C' Company (Major G.C. De Mattos)

---

1   The National Archives: WO 95/5430, Sadleir-Jackson Brigade, War Diary.

Sludka-Lipovets:	Major Harry Heaton, MC and Bar
	'A' Company (Major E.M. Allfrey, MC and Bar)
	'D' Company (Major S. Le F. Shepherd, MC and Bar)
	Detachment, 55th Battery, RFA
	Detachment, 201st MGC
	Detachment, 240th LTMB
	Detachment, 250th Signal Company, RE
	Detachment, 385th Field Company, RE
	Detachment, 155th Field Ambulance, RAMC
Chudinova:	'Carroll's Cavalry', detachment 3rd/4th Northern Rifles
	Regiments (Lieutenant Colonel J.W.V. Carroll, CMG)

On the eastern bank, 46th Royal Fusiliers attacking columns:
Lieutenant Colonel H. Jenkins, DSO

Selmenga:	Half 'Lewis Gun' Company (Captain A.E. Wass, MC)
Gorodok:	Major A. Percival, DSO
	'D' and half 'C' Companies (Captain Guy de Miremont, DSO, MC)
	2 platoons, 'Lewis Gun' Company
	Detachment, 241st LTMB
	Detachment, 55th Battery, RFA
	Detachment, 155th Field Ambulance, RAMC
Borok:	'A' Company (Major G.W. Nightingale, MC)
	Detachment, 241st LTMB

CO, 46th Royal Fusiliers, Lieutenant Colonel Herbert Jenkins, DSO, would accompany the Borok column in overall command of the eastern bank whilst CO, 45th Royal Fusiliers Lieutenant Colonel Charles Davies, DSO, would accompany the Sludka-Lipovets column on the western bank and would take command of the Dvina column in its push westwards towards the Vaga on 'Z' Day plus 1.

Each column would depart the start line at Yakovlevskoe together, and at staggered intervals individual columns would break away and march through the forest to their forming up positions to await Zero Hour. All six columns were anticipated to be in position on both banks of the river before the naval barrage commenced. The columns consisted primarily of soldiers of the 45th and 46th Royal Fusiliers and 3rd and 4th Northern Russian Rifles together with detachments of 240th (left bank attached 45th Royal Fusiliers) and 241st (right bank attached 46th Royal Fusiliers) Trench Mortar Batteries, 201st Battalion, MGC, 55th Battery, RFA, 250th Signal Company, RE, 156th Field Ambulance, RAMC, and 385th Field Company, RE. The Chudinova column on the western bank was comprised exclusively of White Russian troops including 'Carroll's Cavalry', a small unit of White Russian mounted infantry led by column commander Lieutenant Colonel John Carroll, CMG, DSO, Norfolk Regiment. The cavalry force was critical to the southernmost operation. After the capture of Chudinova, Carroll's Russian troops were to push on to Puchega and seize the village and its boats, before crossing the river to the eastern bank to cut off the enemy line of retreat from Borok.

Before the offensive could commence, a chain of three enemy blockhouses obstructing the axis of advance on the eastern bank near the Selmenga River had to be eliminated, the task falling to two platoons of 'C' Company, 46th Royal Fusiliers and two sections 241st TMB under the command of Lieutenant Thomas Williamson (Notts and Derby Regiment). The force left British lines at 2300 on the night of 31 July and shortly before midnight were in position awaiting the machine gun and mortar barrage which would precede the assault. After five minutes of firing the Lewis gun and mortar fire ceased and 'with a rousing cheer' the assault parties went in. The northern assault party killed four of the enemy in a trench and a further three with grenades as they attempted to flee. They then pushed forward capturing two blockhouses which were promptly set on fire before withdrawing under cover of the Lewis guns back into the forest. The western assault party ran into deep marsh and could advance no further, abandoning the attempt to capture the third blockhouse. A few minutes after the Fusiliers had withdrawn into the forest, the Bolsheviks recovered and apparently expecting a full-scale British attack, opened heavy fire in the general direction of the British lines with machine guns and artillery for more than an hour expending large amounts of ammunition.

Total British casualties suffered during the raid were one officer killed and four Fusiliers wounded. The officer was Lieutenant Gwynne Jacob, DCM, MM and Bar, 46th Royal Fusiliers. Jacob had seen more war than most before his service in North Russia. Arriving in France just prior to Christmas 1914 with KRRC, he

92. South African Lieutenant Colonel Herbert Jenkins, CMG, DSO, commanding 46th Battalion, Royal Fusiliers. (Public domain)

had earned the MM in 1916 and an MM Bar and DCM the following year. Commissioned into the RFC he trained as a pilot, transferring to the RAF on its creation on 1 April 1918. Having relinquished his RAF commission in order to resume army duty as a 2nd Lieutenant in the East Yorkshire Regiment in April 1919 (possibly specifically to enlist in the North Russia Relief Force), he immediately volunteered for service in North Russia. Jacob was buried the following day in the small cemetery in the Troitsa churchyard. His grave lost to time, he remains commemorated in Archangel Allied Cemetery.

Of particular concern to Sadleir-Jackson in the lead up to the attack was the lack of accurate maps. The existing Russian maps which British commanders had been issued did not show significant seasonal obstacles such as swamps and were useful as a general guide to the terrain only. Brigade Intelligence officer Major Straker, who had survived the Slavo-British Legion mutiny the previous month, set about creating new maps of absolute detail and accuracy.

Transport was also an important consideration. Without a forward railway or suitable roads; reliance was placed almost entirely on the recruitment of local drivers and their *drosky* horse carts. To meet the demands of the offensive every available *drosky* and owner on both banks of the river was conscripted into service, payment being in the form of an amount of flour, sugar and tea for each day of service. Over 1,000 horses were eventually requisitioned and nearly as many *droskies* and peasant drivers. One soldier noted that 'the entire Dvina Force had gone "drosky mad" … Never before in the history of North Russia had there ever been such a collection of droskies, drivers and ponies'.[2]

During a reconnaissance on the eastern bank in the days leading up to the attack, a patrol under Sergeant John Whammond, 46th Royal Fusiliers, was spotted by the enemy and fired on. When Whammond did not return to British lines it was thought that he had been killed or captured or become lost in the forest. Those that knew the plucky Scot were the least surprised when he arrived days later, 'a little grubby and unshaven, but with a happy smile and a notebook full of most wonderful information.'[3] By the time he left North Russia, Whammond had added a DCM, an MM and an MiD to his MC awarded on the Western Front as a lieutenant in Lovat Scouts.

Whammond had been born in Arbroath in 1883, where he worked as a stable boy before travelling to South Africa to enlist in the Cape Mounted Police. In 1915 he fought with South African forces during the campaign in German South-West Africa finishing as a Regimental Sergeant Major before commissioning into Lovat Scouts. After service in North Russia he returned to South Africa and the Cape Mounted Police with whom he was awarded the Meritorious Service Medal in 1934 as a Sergeant Instructor. In 1940 he again volunteered for service and was appointed Lieutenant Colonel in charge of a unit of South African Military Police. Lieutenant Colonel John Whammond, MC, DCM, MM, MSM, died in Pretoria on 14 May 1941 aged 58.

On the afternoon of 7 August Bolshevik 4.2 inch artillery opened fire on monitor HMS *M.33,* lying mid river at anchor in an advanced position. Unable to escape the salvo, *M.33* was twice hit as the monitor was making

93. Lieutenant Colonel John Whammond, MC, DCM, MM, MSM, in the uniform of South African forces during the Second World War. Whammond relinquished his commission in Lovat Scouts to volunteer for service as a private with the NRRF. He was promoted sergeant and awarded the DCM and MM within weeks of each other to add to an MC awarded on the Western Front. (Public domain)

steam, the second shell crashing through the starboard side petty officers' mess and into the engine room, where it lay unexploded. Serving in the engine room of *M.33*, Chief Engine Room Artificer Sydney Rutland, RN, wrote in his diary of the incident:

I shall never forget the feeling of the minutes following the shell's entrance and I saw she had not exploded. I think everyone's heart was in one's mouth … Fortunately for everyone in the engine room it did not explode but it caused a few tense moments.[4]

A third shell grazed the monitor, tearing the canvas awning, and another exploded between the ship's propellers before the Bolsheviks turned their attention to targets on shore. The battered *M.33* was withdrawn downriver where a more thorough assessment of the damage could be carried out. She was replaced in the line by *M.27*, which also came under fire until an attack by RAF seaplanes from Troitsa silenced the enemy gunners.

On the night of 9 August, two bombing missions were flown by No. 3 (Bereznik) Squadron against Gorodok on the eastern bank. Six DH9s, five DH9As and two Sopwith Snipes from the

3   *Ibid.,* p.88.
4   IWM: 209/91/11/1, Diary of S.J. Rutland.

94. Royal Fusiliers assembled at Osinova before moving off to the front. Comprised almost entirely of veterans of the 1914–18 war, 45th and 46th Royal Fusiliers were the most battle hardened units in the British Army in 1919, a number of officers relinquishing their commissions to serve in the ranks. (IWM Q16080)

airfield at Bereznik dropped a total of three tonnes of bombs in the two raids, the results of the bombing being noted as 'most successful'.

Early on the morning of 10 August, seven DH9s and two DH9As armed with phosphorous and high explosive bombs flew further missions against Bolshevik-held villages on both banks but due to thick fog only two of the nine aircraft actually located their target and on return to Bereznik found the aerodrome covered by a thick mist. Fires were lit to illuminate the airstrip and flares fired but by 0530 only five of the nine aircraft had landed. One of the missing aircraft flew north all the way to Pinega where a phosphorous bomb detonated on landing, badly burning the pilot. During a separate mission in one of the RAF Seaplane Flight aircraft, Lieutenant Bentley with Observer 2nd Lieutenant Abbey also became lost in the fog. Bentley made a number of attempts to locate the seaplane base but the fog was so thick that he had to resort to making an emergency landing on the Dvina. Fortunately for the two airmen they had landed on the British side of the line and in fact where only a short distance from the anchorage at Troitsa from where they had taken off.

With an easier traverse than their sister battalion across the river, 46th Royal Fusiliers left British lines on 'Y' Day, 9 August, and advanced silently through the forest to their start lines. As the columns made their way through the forest, British and Russian artillery fired several hundred poison gas shells into the Bolshevik-held villages which were the objectives of the attack. Muddy forest trails and marshland made the journey hard going but by 1100 on 'Z' Day, 10 August, the Fusiliers were in position to await the final preliminary bombardment which would signal commencement of the attack.

Late in the morning of 10 August, at the prearranged time of 1100, HM Ships *Humber*, *M.27*, *M.31* and *M.33* and no less than 60 Vickers machine guns of 201st MGC, situated on a large sand bar in the middle of the Dvina, opened fire on enemy positions on both banks of the river. HMS *Cicala* joined the barrage when enemy gunboats made an appearance at 1200, one enemy gunboat was hit and reported as retiring with heavy list. Due to the inclement weather the RAF had been unable to fly artillery cooperation missions, so the gunners had to fire by map and observation only.

It was miraculous that *Cicala* was even in action on 'Z' Day. During the night of 5 August, whilst measuring the depth of the river, the leadman dropped his lead directly onto a mine causing it to explode and blow a 12 foot hole in the ship's side. Fortunately there were no casualties and amazingly the ship was back in action five days later after only rudimentary repairs.

The preliminary bombardment was the largest fired by British forces in North Russia. In addition to the naval bombardment, a total of eighteen 18 pdrs, eight 4.5 inch howitzers, two 155 mm heavy guns and two 60 pdrs crewed by naval gunners commanded by Lieutenant Ralph Martin, RN, fired in support of the attack. Some of the 18 pdrs had arrived only the day before the bombardment and due to a shortage of artillerymen were crewed by RASC men under the instruction of three RFA gunners. Despite taking over the 60 pdrs just three days prior to the attack and having had no prior experience of operating land guns, the naval gunners performed exceptionally well. One of the 60 pdrs had been recovered from the bottom of the Dvina after an unfortunate unloading accident. Navy divers and cranes recovered the gun and after repairs and testing it was put straight back into service.

95. Lieutenant Walter Curtis, MC, Somerset Light Infantry attached 46th Royal Fusiliers, wounded in action and awarded the MC for gallantry during the attack on Borok, 10 August 1919. During the Second World War, Curtis served as second in command of No. 8 (Guards) Commando before appointment to command 4th Battalion, SLI whom he led in Normandy in June 1944. (Author's collection)

Sub Lieutenant Basil Brewster, RN, serving as second in command of the naval gun battery, recounted just how inexperienced in land operations the detachment was:

> Not knowing any better we had selected a nice little hillock overlooking the enemy, giving us a clear view of his defences, so that we could see what to aim at. This promptly brought an Army Major to the scene who yelled at us, 'Get your bloody guns off the skyline!!!'-and having assisted us with this, and listened to our explanations, sent a gunner subaltern to explain to us the mysteries of 'indirect fire' employed by land artillery.[5]

The two platoons of 46th Royal Fusiliers under Captain Arthur Wass, MC, tasked to attack Selmenga, reached their objective early in the morning and were able to rest until forming up shortly before the bombardment. Selmenga was captured by the Fusiliers with little opposition and no casualties. The North Russian Rifles, having got lost in the forest during the approach, were conspicuous by their absence but still managed to take a number of Bolshevik stragglers prisoner.

---

5   IWM: 10815 PP/MCR/237, Private Papers of B. Brewer.

Wass was subsequently awarded the DSO for his service in North Russia and his command of the Selmenga column. Early on the morning of 11 August, the column pushed on to Gorodok, captured during the previous day's fighting, which was reached at 1100.

Under the command of Major G.W. Nightingale, MC, Borok column consisting of 'A' Company, 46th Royal Fusiliers, two sections of 241st TMB, six Russian guides and an interpreter, a total of eight officers and 191 other ranks, moved through the British lines at 2100 on 9 August. Whilst awaiting Zero Hour, a peasant family were seen approaching the ravine where the Fusiliers were resting and were arrested and temporarily detained until the column got underway.

When the attack on Borok commenced, the Bolsheviks put up a stiff defence in which two Fusilier platoon commanders became casualties: Lieutenant William Tayler (attached from Royal West Kent Regiment) was killed and 2nd Lieutenant Walter Curtis (attached from Somerset Light Infantry) suffered a wound to the eye leading his platoon up a hill to outflank and capture a strong enemy position, for which Curtis was awarded the MC. Lieutenant Alexander Matson (attached from Royal Welsh Fusiliers) took control of the two leaderless platoons whilst maintaining command of his own for which he was awarded the MC for gallantry and leadership. As Matson was preparing to move on to the next objective he nearly walked directly into the British bombardment and was fortunate to escape injury. The enemy were holed up in the cemetery and on a strong hilltop position with a number of well-dug trenches providing an excellent field of fire.

Just before 1400, Lieutenant Colonel Jenkins called for an artillery barrage on Borok village which was duly provided by HMS *Humber,* driving the remaining Bolsheviks into the forest. After three hours of hard fighting, by 1425 all objectives had been captured along with two Japanese field guns and a number of machine guns and rifles. Bolshevik losses amounted to about 60 killed, mostly in the cemetery and in the positions on the hill, and 102 prisoners, many of whom were wounded. The Fusiliers' casualties included Captain Harry Driver, DSO, MC (attached from Bedfordshire Regiment) and Sergeant Harry Jackson killed and one NCO and seven men wounded.

The column tasked to attack Gorodok comprised 'D' Company, 46th Royal Fusiliers, two companies of 1/3rd North Russian Rifles, section 55th Battery, RFA, section 241st TMB, and was the largest of the three attacking columns. Command of the column was given to Major Arthur Percival, DSO, MC, who would be awarded a DSO Bar for the attack. Percival would later gain infamy during the Second World War whilst holding the position of GOC Malaya when he surrendered to the invading Japanese at the fall of Singapore in February 1942.

The column set out at 2115 and faced the same hard going as the Borok column which had left 15 minutes earlier, particularly in crossing the Selmenga River. Thereafter the terrain improved and after a trek of several hours the column was in position to await the preliminary bombardment leading up to Zero Hour.

The attack would be made by two flanking columns. The right column under the command of 'D' Company OC, Captain Guy de Miremont, DSO, MC, would attack towards the village church whilst the left column led by Russian Captain Postniekov, MC, would attack from the eastern side with the two companies of 1/3rd North Russian Rifles. Additionally, howitzers, trench mortars and Lewis guns would provide suppressive fire from the tree line before the attack went in.

At 1200, the heavy barrage lifted as the pack howitzers and trench mortars opened fire from close range in a furious barrage as the Fusiliers and Russian riflemen crept forward, one of the mortars getting off 40 rounds in the first minute. Captain de Miremont had trouble getting his company into position due to a marsh blocking their path but by Zero Hour was ready to advance on the village. On the barrage ceasing five minutes later, the attackers raced forward and were met with only half-hearted resistance despite the Red troops holding a commanding ridge feature protected by rings of barbed wire with a number of entrenched machine guns.

So quick was the right flanking party's advance, they nearly walked into their own howitzer and mortar bombardment. The Fusiliers could advance no further until the close supporting fire ceased, and a runner was sent back to halt the barrage ahead of schedule. After recovering from the initial barrage the Bolsheviks on the western side of the village put up a determined defence, stubbornly barricading themselves in some of the log houses. Lieutenant William Culbert, attached to the Fusiliers from the Connaught Rangers, brought his section of trench mortars into action on the enemy occupied houses and with several well-aimed shots routed the dug-in Bolsheviks for which he was awarded the MC.

Private Hugh McColl, a Fusilier signaller attached to 'D' Company witnessed the final attack on Gorodok:

96. Private Hugh McColl, 46th Royal Fusiliers, a witness to 'D' Company's bayonet charge against Gorodok. (Robin McColl)

I witnessed a pretty bayonet charge, such as I never wish to see again. The next wave was advancing slightly on our right, and we were sending over covering fire. When they got a hundred yards away from the Bolo line I saw them leave the trenches to meet our chaps, then our officer [Captain De Miremont], with stick in one hand and revolver in the other, gave the word, and our chaps rushed forward with bayonets drawn. It was splendid, but horrible to see. Our fellows simply carried everything before them, although the odds against them were great. They were letting out blood-curdling yells all the time, and the scene-well it can be imagined, better than explained, but when Bolo retired he left a nice little pile of corpses behind him, all with bayonet wounds.[6]

By 1300, the remaining enemy had fled and the village was in Allied hands with 300 prisoners taken, 85 of which were captured by the section commanded by Sergeant H.F. Gascoigne-Roy, an Australian from North Sydney who had served in the British Army, for which Roy was awarded the DCM. A number of enemy troops fled across the plain towards the village and the river but were shot down by rifle and Lewis gun fire. 'D' Company pushed forward to Gorodok ridge where the enemy counter-attacked, McColl continues:

We had got as far as 100 yards distance from the Ridge when all of a sudden a severe musketry and machine gun fire rattled out ... We got over the Ridge, and a pretty sight met our eyes. The Bolo, who had been driven out of Gorodok, was making his counter attack on our new positions, and he was, literally speaking, coming over in thousands. All that we could see was one black mass of humanity moving over a vast stretch of plain-two regiments it was, as we afterwards noted with much satisfaction ... With many thumpings of the heart, I watched the black mass move over the ground, and the hands which held my rifle trembled more than once. I realised how inadequate our numbers were, compared to the enemy ... The Colonel, let it be said, was very cool and collected withal, and gave the order in the most matter of

---

6   Private Diary of Hugh McColl.

97. Royal Navy-crewed 60 pounder on the Dvina, summer 1919. (IWM 35014)

fact tone imaginable. When the Bolo had come within firing range, he merely smiled and said, 'Go on, let 'em have it boys', and the boys did, believe me.[7]

Lieutenant Charles Moorhead (attached from Manchester Regiment) was wounded during the counter-attack but remained in command of his platoon for which he was awarded the MC, whilst Lieutenant Albert Jones (attached from North Staffordshire Regiment) and Sergeant T.G. Goodchild were awarded the MC and DCM Bar respectively for capturing four field guns, two trench mortars and 21 prisoners during the attack on Gorodok. Goodchild's first DCM had been awarded for service on the Western Front in 1917 with the Lincolnshire Regiment Corporal A.W. Card, who was also awarded the DCM for bringing his Lewis gun section forward to meet the counter-attack and supervising their fire.

The attackers were cut down in droves and the charge faltered, scores of Red soldiers dropped their rifles and came forward to surrender. After mopping up resistance in the houses on the western edge of the village, Captain de Miremont despatched a platoon under Lieutenant Albert Jones to take out an enemy 3 inch gun battery on the edge of the forest which was shelling the village. The Bolsheviks defended the guns stubbornly and three attempts by the Fusiliers were repulsed by heavy fire. In an after-action report held in the Sadleir-Jackson Brigade War Diary there is an unsubstantiated report that when the guns were finally captured later in the day they had been crewed by 'German' gunners.

Apart from the Eastern Baltic where German troops directly engaged British forces in combat as late as October 1919, and the early operations against White Finns at Murmansk in May 1918, there are several anecdotal descriptions of German troops fighting against the British in other theatres of Russia (including German pilots flying for the Bolsheviks in South Russia) but very little actual evidence to support such claims. During the mid 18th Century, germanophile Catherine the Great invited large numbers of ethnic Germans to settle in southern Russia, mostly on the Volga River frontier. Many German speaking 'Volga Deutsch' were conscripted into the Red Army after 1917, some of whom undoubtedly fought against the British and may have been captured. It is possible that this is the origin of the rumour.

For his gallantry and leadership of 'D' Company during the attack and capture of Gorodok and subsequent counter-attack, Captain De Miremont was awarded an MC Bar whilst Captain Clive

---

7   *Ibid.*

Featherstone, a South African who had seen action at Delville Wood, serving with 241st TMB and Lieutenant Francis Lewis, 55th Battery, RFA, were awarded MCs.

With the capture of Gorodok the British forces on the eastern bank of the Dvina had cut off a large Bolshevik force at Selmenga which would attempt to break out of the encirclement. When the Red troops mounted their counter-attack at 1545 on the afternoon of 10 August, the Fusiliers were waiting: they opened fire with rifles, Stokes mortars and Lewis guns and drove the attackers towards the northern side of the village where they again came under fire, an outlying Lewis gun able to completely enfilade the enemy. A number of Bolsheviks threw down their weapons and surrendered, others fled headlong into the forest. The Fusiliers were kept busy throughout the night as small groups of demoralised stragglers gave up their efforts to break through and surrendered.

When a final count was taken, the column had inflicted a heavy toll on the Bolsheviks at Gorodok with 40 men killed and 750 prisoners (including a regimental commander and two battalion commanders), nine field guns, 16 machine guns, five mortars, 900 rifles and 70,000 rounds of ammunition. A number of important documents were also abandoned by the enemy, supplying the British with information on Red Army orders of battle and dispositions. The 46th Royal Fusiliers had lost two officers and five soldiers killed and a number more wounded in the attack.

Despite the difficult traverse through the forest to their objectives, 46th Royal Fusiliers had successfully captured all three villages, depriving the Bolsheviks of nearly 1,000 men in a single blow for which the attackers suffered only light casualties. Their sister battalion on the Dvina's western bank would not be as fortunate.

In order to attack the Bolshevik-held villages south of Seltso on the western bank, 45th Royal Fusiliers would have to traverse a large area of marshland through which there were few suitable routes. In place of entrenching shovels the men were issued machetes to cut through the thick undergrowth. Due to the distance required to be traversed on foot, the attacking columns set out on 'W' Day, 7 August, three days in advance of the attack. The route through the dense forest was disorienting and confusing and made navigation extremely difficult, the only reliable method being to plan legs set to a bearing using pacing to judge distance. Orders had been given that no fires were to be lit and rifles carried unloaded to prevent any accidental discharge which would give away the position to the enemy. As the column proceeded through the forest to a clearing and flour mill where it would halt for the night, a steady rain began which barely stopped for the three days leading up to Zero Hour, deteriorating the forest tracks and turning the terrain through which the attackers would have to advance into marshland.

In the weeks leading up to the attack, Royal Engineers sappers from 385th Field Company had been frantically busy, amongst many other tasks, constructing a landing pontoon on the eastern bank which they named 'Luby's Landing' after the unit OC, Major M. Luby, DSO, MC. Pioneers had also been sent to work on road building far from the front line to create an impression that the British attack was planned for elsewhere. Signallers from 250th Signal Company, RE, were kept busy laying cable on elevated poles as far forward as possible to facilitate the rapid laying of line to keep up with the attack. Wireless stations were established on both banks of the river as were a number of visual signalling stations further forward. It had been intended that the signallers would advance with the attacking columns, laying cable from pack ponies as they went, but the ground on the western bank of the river was so bad after the rain that the ponies were sent back and the signallers continued laying the cable by hand, a very difficult task. Further complicating matters during the early stages of the advance, sappers from 385th Field Company tasked with clearing tracks through the forest had cut down trees on which cable had been laid causing communications to be cut until the signallers located the break and repaired it.

On the following 'X' Day, 8 August, after a hard night of marching, the Seltso column broke off to await Zero Hour at their designated start line whilst the remaining columns continued on, spending an uncomfortable night resting in the forest.

98. A 3.7 inch howitzer of 443rd (Campion's) Battery, RFA in
the forest, Dvina River, 1919. (IWM Q16191)

A Red deserter was brought in early on the morning of 8 August, and revealed under questioning that the Bolsheviks were not expecting a British attack. Subsequent events showed that this was likely not the case. That evening the Seltso column deployed west to take up positions in the forest and await the attack, however not long after leaving the main column they found their way blocked by an impenetrable marsh through which the pack animals, carrying everything from Vickers machine guns of 201st MGC, to trench mortars, pack artillery, ammunition and supplies, could not pass.

Two days silent marching through forest and swamp with little rest took its toll on the Fusiliers. The men were so exhausted that when communication was lost with the Seltso column no runner was sent out as it was not thought he would have been able to reach the column before Zero Hour the following morning. During the night 'Carroll's Cavalry' and 2/4th North Russian Rifles joined the column, bolstering the strength of the force, but the Russians were so exhausted after their 25 mile ride through marshland and forest that they had to be left behind when the column resumed its advance, to catch up later.

The final approach march on 'Y' Day, 9 August, was the worst yet, exhausted after three days of hard marching the men struggled through the worst terrain yet encountered, their feet blistered, webbing belts chafing, rifles and packs feeling like they weighed a ton, the men trudged on. To make matters worse it rained all day compounding the men's misery and turning the forest floor into mire.

On 'Y' Day, the column split yet again into Sludka-Lipovets and Chudinova columns. The gunners of 55th Battery, RFA, had made valiant efforts to drag their pack mules through the swamp but it was evident that they would not make the start line in time for the attack which would have to go in without local artillery support. After having come so far the mule train was ordered to turn around and return to Yakovlevskoe, taking the vitally needed howitzers, ammunition and stores with them. The battery war diary notes, 'It was a bitter disappointment to all ranks that in spite of all exertions they were unable to assist in the operations.'[8] Although the attack would still have significant artillery support from larger calibre field artillery and the RN gunboats (including the two naval 60 pdrs and Russian 18 pdrs firing poison gas shells), the loss of the more accurate pack howitzers and additional stores was a serious blow.

'Carroll's Cavalry' also became stuck in the mud but continued to push on as best they could, but it was not expected that they would reach their objective of Chudinova by zero hour, leaving the two companies of 2/4th North Russian Rifles to make the attack on their own.

Sadleir-Jackson's plan called for No. 3 (Bereznik) Squadron, RAF, to fly reconnaissance missions from Bereznik in the days leading up to the offensive and to carry out a number of bombing missions against the Bolshevik-held villages and gunboats in the hours leading up to the attack. Several aircraft would also bomb Bolshevik positions on the nearby Vaga River at Kitsa, Ignatovskaya and Shegovari to soften up those villages for the planned attack on 'Z' Day plus 1 and also to confuse the enemy as to the intended direction of the British assault. All of the RAF's available Sopwith Snipe fighters would also be airborne to drive off any concentrations of enemy troops that might form. Despite detailed planning, due to the inclement weather the day before the attack, the aircraft could not operate and remained grounded.

At Seltso village, as the naval barrage lifted at precisely 1200, 240th TMB's mortars went into action, hammering the enemy positions. The mortars had only fired for a matter of minutes when a white flag was hoisted from one of the enemy blockhouses. A party went forward to call the Bolsheviks out to accept their surrender but was fired upon and had to scurry back to the safety of the tree line. At 1210, the infantry attack went in but the Fusiliers quickly found themselves enfiladed and pinned down, and a number of men were hit. Sergeant Reginald Mouat, a veteran of the Western Front who had been awarded the MM with the Hampshire Regiment in 1917, was taken aback by the ferocity of fire, 'hellish and worse than anything I met in France.'[9]

Sergeant C. Hunter showed extraordinary determination bringing his Lewis gun into action against the enemy, during which he was wounded. Despite his wounds and the heavy fire directed at him, Hunter continued to engage the enemy until the Lewis gun was hit and put out of action. He then took command of an abandoned enemy machine gun and turned it on the enemy, continuing to fire until ordered to withdraw for which the plucky Fusilier was awarded the DCM.

Lieutenant Arthur Colledge (attached from Worcestershire Regiment) was killed and Lieutenant G.J. Kirkaldy wounded from 45th Royal Fusiliers whilst Lieutenant Patrick Sylvester, Somerset Light Infantry attached 3rd North Russian Rifles was also wounded. At the head of his men, Seltso column commander Major Gerald de Mattos did not escape the initial volley of fire and was mortally wounded. South African Captain H.L. Sumner, MC, MM of 240th TMB immediately took command but the attack was already faltering. Given the Bolsheviks' determined response to the attack it appeared likely they had been forewarned that the British were coming.

By 1230, having failed to break the Bolshevik line, orders were given for the column to withdraw under fire. Shortly after, at 1245, the reserve platoon of 45th Royal Fusiliers was sent forward on the left flank. Charging the enemy's positions the reserve platoon managed to break through their forward defences but could advance no further due to concentrated fire from enemy positions in depth. The Bolsheviks were able to bring forward their machine guns from positions not under attack and rained a terrible hail of fire onto the Fusiliers. By 1300, the situation became dire for the attackers when the Bolsheviks began their counter-attack. The first two attempts were checked but on the third charge the Red troops broke through and rapidly moved to outflank the Fusiliers. To

8   The National Archives: WO 95/5430, Sadleir-Jackson Brigade, War Diary.
9   IWM: 2650/94/11/1, Private papers of R.S. Mouat.

99. Major Stanley Shepherd, MC and Bar, Northamptonshire Regiment attached 45th Royal Fusiliers, killed in action 10 August 1919. (Public domain)

prevent the column's line of retreat being cut off, Sumner issued orders to withdraw with all wounded under covering fire of the Lewis guns.

The strongest of the three columns attacking on the western bank was tasked to attack the villages of Sludka-Lipovets, commanded by 45th Royal Fusiliers second in command, Major Harry Heaton, with 'A' and 'D' Companies under Major Edward Allfrey and Major Stanley Shepherd, MC and Bar (attached from Northamptonshire Regiment) respectively. Attached to the column was 45th Royal Fusiliers' hardy Australian commander, Lieutenant Colonel Charles Davies. Although Davies remained in overall command of the attack on the western bank, he would not take personal command of the columns until 11 August when, after handing over the captured villages to White Russian troops, all three columns would combine to drive west to cut off any enemy caught behind the British advance.

Progress for the Sludka-Lipovets column had been particularly slow, the alternating terrain of forest and marsh proving so difficult to traverse that by 'Z' Day the pack mules could advance no further and all the column stores had to be unloaded and carried by the troops themselves to the start line some four *versts* distant. Captain Henderson and Lieutenant John Penson, MC, 385th Field Company, RE, made a reconnaissance of the terrain south-west of Sludka and found the forest tracks impassable for animals. It seemed impossible that the column would have any hope of reaching its objective by Zero Hour so Lieutenant Colonel Davies gave the order to attack the villages of Kochamika, Jitna and Zaniskaya (slightly south of Sludka) instead and push northwards along the banks of the river towards Lipovets.

Penson was awarded a Bar to his MC for good work guiding the column through the forest during the three day march to a position 400 yards west of Kochamika without being observed. Private Norman Brooke, an Australian volunteer from Melbourne, went forward to reconnoitre the enemy positions and returned with information which enabled Lieutenant Edward Sutro (attached from 4th Battalion, Royal Fusiliers), commander of the 'Australian Platoon', 'D' Company to advance without casualties for which Brooke was awarded the DCM.

By 1105, the column was in position just in time for the prearranged naval bombardment. No sooner had the bombardment ceased, than Sutro led the 'Australian Platoon' in a charge through the village. *The Sydney Morning Herald* later jingoistically recounted, 'they [the Bolsheviks] were charged with bayonets fixed by the British battle scarred heroes of France and Belgium who slowly advanced in shorts and shirt sleeves regardless of the machine gun fire'.[10]

Private Norman Brooke recalled the attack:

10 *Sydney Morning Herald*, 11 September 1919.

We were given the order to go and we went and not a shot was fired until we got to the edge of the river bank. Looking over there we could see the gunboats on the river ... They were in close range, up to eight or nine hundred yards away, we opened up with machine guns and rifles ... the gunboats simply turned around and went up stream and pasted us from out of our range. Unfortunately one of the first shells fired killed about seven or eight including our commanding officer ... We got off fairly lightly.[11]

When news of the 10 August 1919 attack filtered back to Australia the following month, virtually all of the major Australian newspapers carried a short article titled variously 'Australian Heroes: Exploit in Russia' and 'Diggers in Russia: Good Work with the Bayonet':

The Australians participated in an attack which was characteristically daring ... when the barrage ceased 20 cheering Diggers led the company through village after village on the bank of the Dvina taking 50 prisoners ... The senior British officer attributed the bayonet successes to the 'devilish keen spirits of the Aussies'.[12]

The three villages of Kochamika, Jitna and Zaniskaya were captured with little resistance and the river bank quickly reached. Four Vickers machine guns from 201st MGC were brought forward and opened fire on the assembled Bolshevik barges and paddle steamers at close range. Accompanying the machine gunners were a number of sappers from 385th Field Company who having fulfilled their role as pioneers during the advance had joined the attack as infantry.

In response to the British fire from the river bank, one of the Red gunboats opened up with its 6 inch gun. One of the shells landed close to Private Ernest Heathcote's Vickers gun, putting the crew out of action, 'his first shot blew the gun on which I was No. 1 into the air killing No. 2 and 3 men and left me out of action with a broken leg, a wound in ankle and elbow smashed.'[13]

Another shell from the Bolshevik gunboat landed directly onto column HQ, killing Major Shepherd and wounding Captain Alexander Ficklin (attached from Norfolk Regiment) and eight others, command of the attack was assumed by Major Robert Mayne, 201st MGC. With Kochamika secured and under fire from the Bolshevik gunboats, the force pushed north towards its original objective of Sludka.

At 1415, a party of 100 Red sailors landed at Kochamika in an attempt to encircle the column. Lieutenants Stewart Harrison, MC (attached from Irish Guards and Guards Machine Gun Regiment) and Charles Armstrong (attached from East Surrey Regiment) commanding two platoons of Vickers guns of 201st MGC, rallied some stragglers into an improvised line of defence and brought their Vickers gun sections under Sergeant Sidney Stephenson, MM, into action against the landing party. Heathcote recalled, 'they never got 20 yards as they made a lovely target.'[14] After decimating the landing party and holding the Bolsheviks off for 20 minutes, Harrison and Armstrong withdrew their guns and rejoined the column.

Thus far in the attack, 'D' Company had done all the fighting and it was now the turn of Major Allfrey's 'A' Company to lead the column in the attack on Lipovets.

Sergeant Watson sprang out of the wood and opened fire on some Bolos only 20 yards away. This at once gave away our position, and a proper inferno of bullets started at once from both sides. Our shooting was far better than theirs, and eventually I saw some of the enemy on our right starting to retire. I took this opportunity to order a charge, and immediately we got up and they saw our bayonets, the whole lot simply dashed off as hard as they could, and we ran down close behind them into the village, shouting and

11   AWM: S00180, Interview (1984) with Private N.M. Brooke, DCM.
12   *Sydney Morning Herald*, 11 September 1919.
13   AWM: PR89/140, Recollection of Ernest Heathcote.
14   *Ibid.*

firing at them. I emptied Jos's Salonika revolver into them, and got one or two of the best. The Bolos were simply terrified, and went helter-skelter into any house they could. The cracking of single rifle shots went on for about a quarter of an hour while my men were digging the Bolos out of all sorts of extraordinary places such as up chimneys and underneath mattresses.[15]

During the attack and capture of Lipovets, 'A' Company lost Private John Bell killed and another nine men wounded including platoon commander Lieutenant Charles Fuller (attached from Middlesex Regiment) shot through the stomach. Fuller had to endure an excruciatingly painful 48 hour journey through the forest on a stretcher to Yakovlevskoe. He was subsequently awarded the MC for his gallantry and leadership during the attack on Lipovets and was invalided out of the service with a disability pension on return to England.

Evacuation of the wounded was coordinated by 45th Royal Fusiliers Medical Officer Captain James Vallance, RAMC, who would be awarded the MC for dressing and evacuating wounded to safety under fire during the attacks. Stretcher bearer Private Herbert Sharpe, a pre-war Lincolnshire Regiment regular soldier who had been one of the first British troops to set foot in France with the BEF in August 1914, was awarded the DCM for bravery in dressing and evacuating wounded Fusiliers under heavy rifle and machine gun fire.

The local Bolshevik commander and his orderly were taken prisoner and swiftly executed, and the village captured and occupied by 1645. Having routed the enemy at Kochamika, Sludka and Lipovets, the column had accumulated nearly 600 prisoners, far outnumbering the strength of the column itself. Some of the prisoners became 'restless' and were shot 'as a precaution' to keep the others in line. British accounts of military intervention in Russia, including official accounts, are surprisingly candid when it comes to the issue of shooting prisoners. Although German prisoners were undoubtedly summarily shot on the Western Front, the details would not be expected to be written up in the unit war diary or published after the war in a unit history as was the case with operations in North Russia. One of the operational orders issued by Sadleir-Jackson Brigade HQ in the lead up to the attack was, 'Metallic poisoning of wells can be rapidly tested by giving it to prisoners or inhabitants.'[16]

Sadleir-Jackson's original battle plan had been for the Sludka column to link up with the force which had attacked Seltso after both villages had been captured. Little was Major Mayne to know that the attack on Seltso had failed and the column at Sludka was thus cut off from British forward HQ at Yakovlevskoe. In the late afternoon orders were issued from Brigade HQ for the Seltso and Sludka-Lipovets columns to join forces in an attack on Seltso at 1820, preceded by a barrage from every available gun on the front. The attack was initially held up by Bolshevik machine gun fire but by 1850 the remaining enemy were fleeing the village and large numbers of prisoners were taken. Some stragglers fled to the banks of the Dvina where they came under concentrated machine gun fire from the Vickers guns of 201st MGC on the sand bar mid river. A Royal Navy CMB was also in action, zipping up and down the river adjacent to the villages, firing on groups of enemy stragglers as they reached the river bank. Shortly before 2100, a landing party of 39 marines under Lieutenant Clive Melbourne Sergeant, RMLI, and a naval party of 35 ratings under Lieutenant Meredith Spalding, RN, were put ashore to mop up stragglers for which both officers were subsequently awarded the DSC.

Having struck a serious blow to the enemy (although not without loss to themselves) and with little food, water and ammunition and the attacking troops exhausted, there was little hope of holding the captured villages in the face of a Red counter-attack. Major Mayne gave the order to withdraw northwards back to Yakovlevskoe at 1900 on 10 August. The withdrawing British columns

---

15   IWM: 3450 86/86/1 Private Papers of E.M. Allfrey.
16   The National Archives: WO 95/5430, Sadleir-Jackson Brigade, War Diary.

100. Sergeant Sidney Stephenson, 201st Battalion, MGC, standing left, awarded an MM Bar for bringing a section of Vickers guns into action against the enemy gunboats at Kochamika on 10 August 1919 and during the crossing of the Sheika River the following day: the action for which Corporal Arthur Sullivan, 45th Royal Fusiliers was awarded the VC. Sidney's younger brother, seated, served with the Royal Navy flotilla on the Dvina River. (Keith Stephenson)

took with them dozens of Bolshevik prisoners pressganged into carrying stretchers for the wounded under the supervision of Fusiliers Medical Officer Captain James Vallance, RAMC. Several civilians were also pressed into service to guide the column through the forest on the long trek to British lines.

Further south, 'Carroll's Cavalry' had arrived at Chudinova to find the village already in the hands of 2/4th North Russian Rifles. A detachment of cavalry under Captain Frederick Cavendish (Leinster Regiment attached 45th Royal Fusiliers) withdrew to report the capture to Lieutenant Colonel Davies but in their absence the Russians abandoned the village to the enemy. In his subsequent report on operations Lieutenant Colonel Carroll stated that the Russian officers, 'were not competent and did not display any qualities of leadership.' Davies went further when he wrote scathingly, 'The Russian troops on both banks of the river were of very little use. This applies to all columns. The 2/4th NRR were not worth ten British soldiers.'[17]

With so many prisoners and wounded, the column returning to Yakovlevskoe made slow progress. By 0230 on the morning of 11 August, the column had covered only nine miles when the civilian guides found their progress blocked by the Sheika River and a large marsh on either side. The marsh extended about 250 yards either side of the river and could only be crossed by means of a single wooden plank bridge. Evacuating heavily laden and exhausted soldiers and their equipment and wounded on stretchers over the slippery walkway would be a tediously slow task.

About half the withdrawing troops had crossed the marsh when word was received from the column rearguard that Red soldiers were rapidly approaching. Minutes later shots rang out as the rearguard engaged the pursuing enemy in an effort to give the column as much time as possible to cross the marsh but with only a wooden plank walkway to cross, going was slow. The rearguard were quickly overwhelmed and fled through the forest towards the plank bridge. The Red troops were quick on their heels and opened fire on the retreating British column as they were crossing the walkway. Some of the Bolshevik prisoners forced to carry stretchers dumped their wounded cargo into the morass in an attempt to escape to the opposite side of the marsh. A number of Fusiliers were hit and fell into the swamp. One of the stretcher cases hurled into the marsh was Captain Alexander Ficklin (Norfolk Regiment), wounded by the same shell which had killed Major Shepherd. Ficklin

---

17   *Ibid.*

101. Portrait of Lord Settrington serving as Lieutenant Charles Henry Gordon-Lennox, Irish Guards attached 45th Royal Fusiliers. Lord Settrington was badly wounded 11 August 1919 as the withdrawing column was crossing the Sheika River and was plucked from the swamp under fire by Corporal Arthur Sullivan, who was subsequently awarded the Victoria Cross. Evacuated to Archangel, Lord Settrington succumbed to his wounds on 24 August and is buried in Archangel Allied Cemetery. (IWM HU 126338)

was fortunate enough to be able to drag himself out of the marsh and was rescued, others were not so lucky. Wounded Australian machine gunner Private Ernest Heathcote described the scene: 'Many fell only slightly wounded but once in that soaking, sucking morass there was no hope of escape.'[18]

Despite the danger, as bullets flew around him, Corporal Arthur Sullivan of the Australian Platoon, 'D' Company, 45th Royal Fusiliers, immediately jumped into the swamp and one by one brought in an officer and three wounded men under heavy fire from the Red troops only 100 yards distant. Sullivan, a bank clerk from Crystal Brook, South Australia, had enlisted in Adelaide in April 1918 and arrived in England in late September, too late to see action in France before the Armistice. Having missed serving at the front, he was waiting for a troopship home when the call for volunteers for North Russia went out. The wounded officer Sullivan plucked from the mire was 20-year-old Lieutenant Charles Henry Gordon-Lennox, Irish Guards attached 45th Royal Fusiliers, who as son of the Earl of March, served under the title 'Lord Settrington'.

In 1903, aged four years, the young Lord had attended the Prince of Wales' birthday and in 1911 had been a page boy at the coronation of King George V. Like many of the public school educated youth of his generation who came of age during the war, there was no time for Oxford or Cambridge, the young Lord Settrington went straight from Eton to officer training at Sandhurst before commissioning as a 2nd Lieutenant in the Irish Guards aged just 17. He was taken prisoner in April 1918 during Ludendorff's Spring Offensive and spent the remainder of the war in prison camps before volunteering for service with the North Russia Relief Force in 1919. After his rescue by Sullivan from the marsh, Settrington was evacuated to Yakovlevskoe and thence to Archangel but succumbed to his wounds two weeks later on 24 August. General Lord Rawlinson, who had corresponded with the Earl of March on receiving news of the critical wounding of the young Lord, noted the sad event in his diary.

For his gallantry in rescuing the wounded from the swamp under fire, Sludka-Lipovets column commander Major Harry Heaton recommended Sullivan for award of the Victoria Cross. Heaton himself received a DSO for his command of the column during the 10 August attack to add to a Military Cross and Bar awarded for service on the Western Front with the Durham Light Infantry.

---

18   AWM: PR89/140, Recollection of Ernest Heathcote.

Keen to return to Australia after his discharge from the British Army, Sullivan elected to return home without having his VC presented by the King. When he was eventually presented with the decoration by the Prince of Wales at a ceremony held at Government House, Adelaide, on 12 July 1920, the Prince remarked, 'Aren't you the man who ran away from my father?'

Within weeks of the presentation of his award, Sullivan fell sick and was hospitalised with malaria. At first the Department of Repatriations refused to cover his treatment. His case was not assisted by the local Medical Officer who stated that as North Russia did not have malarial mosquitoes he could not have contracted the illness there. It was clear that Sullivan did not have the illness before leaving Australia with the AIF and the illness could only have been contracted during his service overseas but the Department continued to refuse to pay any benefits until a malarial expert (who incidentally was also a Russian refugee) intervened to support the claim that the disease could only have been contracted during service. The Department reluctantly took responsibility.

Sullivan returned to work as a bank clerk, eventually rising to become a branch manager. As a recipient of the Victoria Cross, in 1937 he was given the opportunity to return to England as a member of the Australian Army Coronation Contingent for the coronation of King George VI and was enlisted as a Gunner in the Royal Australian Artillery. He took with him to England the ashes of his friend Sergeant A. Evans, VC, DCM, of the Lincolnshire Regiment who had died in Australia. Shortly after returning the ashes to the family, on 9 April, Sullivan was returning to his room at Wellington Barracks, strolling along Birdcage Walk resplendent in his uniform, slouch hat and ostrich feather plume, when he was besieged by a crowd of enthused Royal watchers keen for the opportunity to obtain an autograph from a VC holder and member of the Australian Coronation Contingent. Dubbed the 'Shy VC', Sullivan quickly crossed the street in an attempt to avoid the crowd but was struck by a bicycle and fell, striking his head on the gutter. The 'Shy VC' did not regain consciousness and died soon after.

Sullivan's coffin lay in state at Wellington Barracks, 18 years earlier the same chapel used for the memorial service for Lord Settrington, the wounded officer Sullivan pulled from the swamp under fire. Granted a full military funeral, the Australian Army Coronation Contingent lined the road leading to Golders Green crematorium where with a number of dignitaries including General William Birdwood (who had commanded the ANZACs on Gallipoli and the Australian Corps in France) and nine Victoria Cross recipients in attendance, his ashes were handed over for return to his widow Dorothy and daughters in Australia. When the Australian Coronation Contingent took part in the coronation procession four weeks later, a blank file was left in the ranks to mark Arthur Sullivan's place.

The King conveyed a message of sympathy to Australian Prime Minister Stanley Bruce:

> The Queen and I were distressed to hear the sad news of Gunner Sullivan's death. Please convey our sincere sympathy to his relatives and to the members of the Australian contingent in London for the loss of a distinguished comrade.[19]

In 1938 a plaque bearing the insignia of the Australian Commonwealth Military Forces and the Victoria Cross was installed by his comrades of the Coronation Contingent on the railings of Wellington Barracks. In 1956, Dorothy Sullivan was invited to attend the Victoria Cross centenary celebrations on behalf of her deceased husband.

Under fire from the rear and in danger of being overrun, Captain Sidney Walker (attached from 24th London Regiment) turned his platoon about to face the enemy and with the assistance of the Vickers guns under Lieutenants Harrison and Armstrong, 201st MGC, drove the attackers back beyond the

---

19   *The Age*, 12 April 1937.

102. Corporal Arthur Percy Sullivan, VC, 45th Royal Fusiliers, late AIF, from Crystal Brook, South Australia, awarded the Victoria Cross for gallantry on 11 August 1919. (AWM 2497)

103. HRH the Prince of Wales presents the Victoria Cross to Corporal Arthur Sullivan at Government House, Adelaide, 12 July 1920. Sullivan wears the white star on navy blue background insignia of the NRRF. (State Library of South Australia B456748)

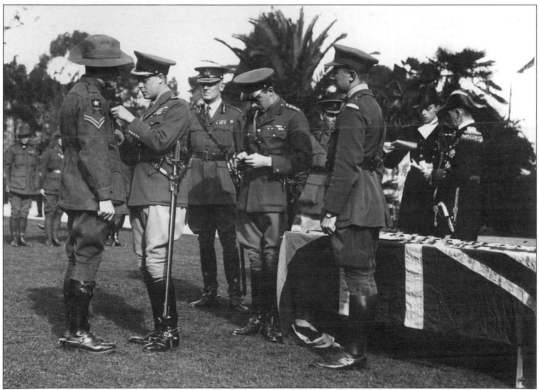

104. Funeral procession for Gunner Arthur Sullivan, VC, Australian Coronation Contingent, 12 April 1937. (AWM P07480)

105. Plaque erected near Wellington Barracks at the spot where Sullivan was killed. It reads: "To The Glory of God And In Ever Living Memory Of Gnr. ARTHUR. P. SULLIVAN. V.C. who was accidentally killed on April 9th 1937 whilst serving as a representative of his country at the Coronation of H.M. King George VI. THIS TABLET WAS ERECTED BY HIS COMRADES OF THE AUSTRALIAN CORONATION CONTINGENT 1938. (Public Domain)

tree line. Determined not to let their quarry escape, the Reds made a further three attempts to push the British into the swamp but each time were driven back by machine gun fire until the attackers thought better and withdrew deeper into the forest. For their gallantry in repulsing the attack Walker and Harrison received MC Bars and Armstrong the MC whilst Sergeant S.T. Stephenson received a Bar to his MM earned with the MGC on the Western Front the previous year.

Armstrong remained in the Army and saw further service in Iraq, 1920 and the North West Frontier of India. He commanded a battalion during the withdrawal to Dunkirk for which he was awarded the DSO and later in the war served with Special Operations Executive (SOE) in Yugoslavia, 1943–44 before jumping with the Polish Independent Parachute Brigade into Arnhem with 1st British Airborne Division.

The column had suffered heavily in the attack. Heathcote recounted, 'I saw some sad sights along the remainder of that swamp – legs and arms sticking out of the mud and others on their last gasp.'[20] The Bolsheviks also lost heavily to Harrison and Armstrong's Vickers machine guns. The 201st MGC War Diary records that 50 dead Bolsheviks were counted, 'all killed by M.G. fire'.

During the confusion of the attack the column had split into several smaller parties which, without guides to lead them, had to make their own way back to Yakovlevskoe as best as they could. In Heathcote's party there were 39 men 'fit to fight' and Heathcote and two officers as stretcher cases. The party had with them around 80 prisoners, some of whom volunteered to guide the party north to Yakovlevskoe but instead led them directly into a Bolshevik camp.

The camp was occupied by only 20 Red troops who were quickly rushed and killed or captured. Justice for the prisoner who led the party to the camp was swift, 'the guide was immediately shot'. Without guides and utterly lost, the party continued aimlessly through the forest and by the following day had exhausted their rations and nearly run out of water, for which there was little chance of finding a resupply other than in one of the Bolshevik-held villages. Small parties of Fusiliers scattered throughout the swamp and forest faced a similar predicament.

The torment for the wounded can only be imagined. Lieutenant Charles Fuller had been shot through the stomach and hip leading 'A' Company into Lipovets and had to suffer through two days carried through the forest on a stretcher. Private Ernest Heathcote had suffered a broken femur, dislocated elbow and shrapnel wound to the ankle. The pain of being carried for days through the difficult terrain on a stretcher must have been unbearable.

Heathcote described how his party wandered about the forest all day without food or water, afraid to rest on account of the numerous Bolshevik patrols. One of the Red Army patrols located and attacked the party on the night of 12 August, but the British pickets were alert and 18 of the attackers were killed and 20 wounded with the loss to the British of only one Fusilier wounded. The unarmed Bolshevik prisoners with the party had suffered particularly badly in the attack, several of their number being killed and wounded. Some of the other prisoners, seeing an opportunity to escape in the confusion, fled into the forest. One Fusilier in the party suggested shooting those that remained but the officer in command scolded any such ideas, as without the prisoners it would be impossible to evacuate all the stretcher cases.

The party continued to wander about the forest for the next two days, unable to find their way out. They had had no food since before the attack and no water for two days. On the morning of 14 August, four days after the attack, one of the Fusiliers strayed from the party and found a fresh water source from which the men gulped furiously before filling their water bottles.

The RAF were active in attempts to guide the attackers back to British lines, sending up an observation balloon from No. 51 Kite Balloon Section, RAF (which had operated on the Dvina since 13 July) lit up by searchlights at night as a landmark and during the day sending aircraft to fly low

20   AWM: PR89/140, Recollection of Ernest Heathcote.

over the forest firing flares, while buglers from the Fusiliers band played at regular intervals at the edge of the forest in an attempt to lead the stragglers out.

During the night a number of enemy patrols were heard in the forest and by 0500 on Friday, Heathcote's party was surrounded. The Fusiliers held the attackers at bay for an hour and a half but after a brief lull in the battle the Reds resumed the attack. Heathcote recalled that there were only 20 exhausted Fusiliers left who could shoot back. To avoid being overrun even the wounded were forced to do their part, 'I was lying on my left side on the stretcher and noticed the chap next to me roll over on his back and I saw he was shot through the forehead so I made an effort and got his rifle and did my best with it.'[21]

By 0800 the party had nearly exhausted its ammunition and were on the verge of being overrun. The Bolsheviks pushed forward for a third and final time, about 20 of their number entered the British position where a hand-to-hand fight ensued. The situation looked hopeless when a cheer was heard and a half-company of 45th Royal Fusiliers came charging through the forest with bayonets fixed, driving the attacking Bolsheviks back in panic. One of the rescuers forced some rum between Heathcote's lips and he remembered little else until awaking six hours later to find himself being carried through the forest. A stretcher bearer asked if the young Australian would like anything to eat and offered Heathcote a tin of bully beef, his first food in six days: 'I don't think I ever enjoyed anything better in all my life than that and a drink of water.'[22]

Heathcote's party was rescued on 15 August, some eight days after it had set out from Yakovlevskoe. The party had been wandering in the forest without food and very little water for five days. They had participated in an arduous three day advance behind enemy lines through treacherous forest and swamp, fought a costly series of engagements and withdrawn back through the same forest and swamp carrying their wounded, encumbered by prisoners, the entire time under threat of attack.

When Heathcote's boot was cut off at the aid station at Yakovlevskoe his wound was found to be septic, 'my leg was broken above the knee and my right arm was dislocated at the elbow but with all this I was satisfied as it meant one thing to me – Blighty.'[23] Heathcote was given tea, rum and plenty to eat which despite his exhausted state he took to heartily.

The seriously wounded were evacuated downriver on a hospital barge to Archangel, where they remained until transportation became available for repatriation to the UK. Heathcote arrived at Archangel on 22 August and left North Russia three days later. On 29 November 1919, he embarked with a number of other Australian Relief Force veterans on the SS *Sofels* bound for Australia. On return to civilian life Heathcote dropped his alias 'Whatson' and resumed his real identity on joining the NSW police, with whom he rose to the rank of Sergeant. Ernest Heathcote died in 1984 having rarely spoken to his four daughters about his service in North Russia.

Memories of the march through the forest and swamp back to Yakovlevskoe would remain an enduring memory for those who lived through it. OC 'A' Company, Major Allfrey recorded:

We had a terrible march which I shall never forget; and how we overcame the difficulties such as carrying the stretchers over the marshes and getting them through the felled trees, I cannot think. The only thing I do know is that everybody was dead beat, and our feet, owing to the fact that we had not taken off our boots for ages, were in most awfully bad condition.[24]

Lieutenant Colonel Davies himself had a similar and only slightly less harrowing experience in returning to British lines. Davies' small HQ party, which had been cut off from the remainder of

21 *Ibid.*
22 *Ibid.*
23 *Ibid.*
24 IWM: 3450 86/86/1 Private Papers of E.M. Allfrey.

106. Australian 45th Royal Fusilier Private Joseph Purdue being presented with his DCM on the steps of Netley Hospital, whilst recovering from a bullet wound to the leg. (AWM 5011)

the column on the arrival of the Bolshevik landing party, included himself, Captain Charles Booth (attached from Border Regiment), Lieutenant John Penson, RE, Chaplain Norman Knock and two runners. Fleeing into the forest, the party lost a member when Lieutenant Penson went forward to investigate some shouting in Russian and did not return.

Down to five men, the party pushed north towards British lines until their path was blocked by Red troops and were again fired on. They stumbled onwards through the forest in the drenching rain, periodically encountering the enemy who invariably let loose in their general direction but not so accurately that the party could not escape further into the forest.

Three White Russian riflemen and a Bolshevik prisoner were encountered hiding in the forest and ordered to join the party, one of them offering to not only guide Davies to advanced HQ at Yakovlevskoe but to also light a fire to dry the Colonel's socks. Throughout the night the three officers took turns on watch, little faith being placed in the Russian soldiers to keep an adequate guard.

Awoken by rifle fire at 0500, the party quickly moved on until encountering a recently used track with field telephone wire visible although it was not possible to tell if it was British or Bolshevik troops who had passed. Further north the party was separated when the White Russian troops spooked themselves and fled into the forest. Anticipating an imminent ambush, the officers followed suit and in the confusion Chaplain Knock was separated from the party. The Reverend was fortunately rescued by a patrol of Fusiliers in the forest and eventually reached Yakovlevskoe on the night of 11 August, but there remained no sign of the CO.

Davies and Booth spent the night soaked through, dining on what little sweetened water and army biscuit they had, but were forced to abandon their campsite during the night when rifle shots were heard nearby. The three Russians did their best to show their indebtedness by attempting to keep the officers as comfortable as possible, lighting fires, drying socks, the Bolshevik prisoner even offering to carry the officers across creeks and streams so as to keep their feet dry.

By dawn the two men were exhausted and feeling the ill effects of lack of food and rest. No doubt an extraordinary sense of relief was felt when on the morning of 12 August, an RAF observation balloon was spotted over British lines. Their ordeal did not end on arrival at Yakovlevskoe however.

As the two exhausted men trudged wearily down the forest track leading towards the village, a Royal Navy sentry fired two shots at the officers with his rifle.

The arrival of the CO at Yakovlevskoe was greeted with much excitement and great relief. It was feared that Davies had at best been captured or at worst killed. The brigade intelligence section had already cabled GHQ at Archangel informing they had plenty of Bolshevik battalion commanders in the prisoner cage ready for immediate exchange. As an expression of thanks to the Bolshevik prisoner who had tried so hard to assist during the trek, Booth drove him to the prisoner cage rather than subject him to marching under armed guard. It was the Red soldier's first time in a motor car and he no doubt turned heads arriving in style, chauffeured by a British officer no less.

There were many individual acts of bravery during the disastrous withdrawal through the swamp and forest. Sergeant W.D. Fox, 45th Royal Fusiliers, found himself detached from the main body and in charge of 250 enemy prisoners with only a small party of Fusiliers. For two and a half days without food or water, Fox led the party through the forest, all the while harassed by the enemy. For his 'great pluck' and devotion to duty Fox was awarded the DCM, as was Private Joseph Purdue, an Australian volunteer serving in 'D' Company, decorated for carrying a wounded officer for four hours through the marsh and forest and aiding in repelling the enemy attack near the Sheika River during which he was wounded in the leg.

A number of other decorations were also awarded for the attack on the left bank of the Dvina. Lieutenant Robert Ramsay (attached to 45th Royal Fusiliers from Royal Highlanders) received a Bar to his MC for temporarily taking command of the column immediately after the death of Major Shepherd. Lieutenant Llewellyn Jones (attached from Royal Welsh Fusiliers) received an MC for scouting work and bringing out all his casualties despite the danger of encirclement whilst Lieutenant Edward Sutro received the same award for leading his 'Australian Platoon' in the bayonet charge on Sludka, capturing of 350 prisoners.

MCs were also awarded to Royal Engineers Lieutenant Harold Platts, 385th Field Company and Captain John Tinker, 250th Signal Company for repairing the track over which the Sludka-Lipovets column had to cross over difficult ground, and for maintaining communications through the forest during the three day approach and attack.

CSM Edward Almey, 45th Royal Fusiliers, was awarded the DCM for leading a small party against an enemy machine gun which was firing on the right flank, capturing both the gun and 50 prisoners. Corporal George Baker, MC, also of 45th Royal Fusiliers, was awarded the MM for commanding his section in the capture of 30 prisoners at Sludka and his work evacuating wounded. Baker had previously been awarded the MC on the Western Front as a 2nd Lieutenant in the Leicestershire Regiment and had voluntarily resigned his commission in order to enlist in the North Russia Relief Force. At the outbreak of the Second World War, Baker was serving with the Hong Kong Police and was interned on the island until its liberation.

Private Jack Holloway, 45th Royal Fusiliers, was also awarded the MM for gallantry during the capture of Sludka. He personally reconnoitred approaches to the village under heavy machine gun fire before leading his section into the village, capturing an enemy machine gun in the process. Holloway would go on to serve with the Royal Irish Constabulary in Ireland during the war of independence in that country.

Recommendations for awards of the Military Medal during the First World War and post-war campaigns were destroyed during the Blitz, and consequently there are many tales of bravery for which MMs were awarded in North Russia 1918–19, particularly during the 10 August 1919 attacks on both banks of the Dvina, which cannot be recounted in this chapter; unless the original award certificates and citations signed by General Ironside still exist, the deeds for which the decorations were awarded are sadly lost forever.

One soldier who was not decorated in North Russia was Corporal Adam Thompson Stewart, 45th Royal Fusiliers. A resident of Glasgow, Stewart had been a pre-war Territorial soldier and

107. Lieutenant Alexander Adams,
DFC, RAF Seaplanes Dvina River,
summer 1919. (Richard Watts)

had first gone to France with the 5th Battalion, Scottish Rifles in 1914. Commissioned and transferred to the Machine Gun Corps (Motors), he was awarded the MC as a Battery Sergeant Major and an MC Bar as 2nd Lieutenant, MGC. Returning to England on leave, Stewart was accused of passing bad cheques, court-martialled, cashiered out of the service, had award of his MC and Bar cancelled and was sentenced to three years imprisonment with hard labour on 11 November 1918, the day the Armistice was signed.

Whilst imprisoned at Maidstone Gaol, Stewart lodged several petitions to be given the chance to redeem himself, particularly as he had a wife and child to support. Eventually the Army Council relented and allowed Stewart to enlist into the North Russia Relief Force. Remarkably, for his gallantry and devotion to duty in North Russia, the King gave approval for Stewart's name to be published in the *London Gazette* as having his MC and Bar restored in recognition of distinguished services.

Despite the restoration of awards, the Army Council refused to grant Stewart an officer's gratuity for war service and after his return from Russia, when reenlisting in the Territorials, he was told he could never be considered for a commission. It is almost certain that Stewart would have received a further decoration for service in North Russia had his previous awards not been cancelled.

Given the stiff resistance put up by the Bolsheviks at Seltso, and their determination to counter-attack at Kochamika and pursue the Fusiliers into the forest, it was lucky for Sadleir-Jackson that the 10 August attack on the western bank of the Dvina did not end in complete disaster. Despite a prevailing attitude amongst the Relief Force troops that the Bolsheviks weren't 'worth a damn' as fighters, the Fusiliers had learnt a hard lesson that the Red troops were much more determined, tough fighters than they had been given credit for.

Although inclement weather severely restricted the operation of aircraft on the day of the attack, before noon the weather cleared slightly and a flight of five DH9s from No. 3 (Bereznik) Squadron, RAF, were despatched to bomb and strafe the Bolshevik-held villages, reportedly causing much damage. One of the aircraft flew low over Kochamika whilst 45th Royal Fusiliers were awaiting to attack and was fired on by a Bolshevik anti-aircraft gun. Only three of the five aircraft returned safely, one crashed at Kurgomen and was destroyed by the accidental detonation of a bomb and another force-landed at Rostovskoe and remained unsalvageable, although the aircrew in both cases survived. Two Sopwith Snipes of the same squadron also attempted to fly missions on 10 August but on both occasions were forced to land at Kurgomen in bad weather. At 1430 an attempt was made by a further two DH9s to reach targets at the front but both aircraft could not continue due to bad weather, one landed at Kurgomen and the other near Troitsa. Throughout operations on the Dvina during August–September 1919, the 120 mile round trip from the airfield at Bereznik to the forward area of operations proved problematic.

A flight of three aircraft from RAF 'ELOPE' was also in action, bombing and strafing enemy gunboats. Of the three aircraft which took off for the raid, one flown by Captain John D'Arcy-Levy with Observer Lieutenant Bugg became lost in the low-lying mist. D'Arcy-Levy had been a pilot in the RNAS early in the war and had been taken prisoner in 1914. Released shortly after the Armistice he immediately volunteered for service in North Russia. The mission was his first over enemy lines since he was captured in 1914.

With no way to determine in which direction to return to Bereznik and with every bend of the river and pine forest looking identical in the bad weather, Levy decided to land at the nearest friendly troops and ask for directions back to Troitsa. Below, the airmen could see a White Russian position and accepting the embarrassment he would face on arrival back at Troitsa, Levy decided to land and ask for directions. Levy landed easily but decided not to taxi the aircraft to take-off position until he knew for certain in which direction to fly. As he left the cockpit and walked towards the position, he hoped that there would be a White Russian officer that spoke some English, or perhaps even a little French, as many of the educated Russian officers did. He spoke to the first soldier he encountered and tried to explain using a pointing motion and repeating the word 'Bereznik?' The stunned expression on the soldiers face when he heard the word 'Bereznik' immediately told D'Arcy-Levy that these men were not White Russians at all and he had in fact landed in Bolshevik controlled territory.

The Red Army soldier raised his rifle but Levy knocked it out of his hands, turned on his heels and ran as fast as his legs could carry him. In the meantime Bugg, who had remained behind in the observer's cockpit watching events unfold, turned his Lewis gun onto the Bolshevik soldiers. Levy jumped into the cockpit, his heart thumping through his chest, and started the engine, probably in his panic too quickly, and the engine choked and stalled. He jumped out to swing the propeller but was clubbed to the ground. Seeing some of their number felled by fire from Bugg's Lewis gun, the Red troops took their anger out on the Levy as he lay on the ground, bayoneting him to death as Bugg looked on. Within seconds, Bugg too was wrestled from his observer's cockpit and thrown on the ground. Fortunately he was wearing mechanic's overalls, and that is what the Bolsheviks took him to be: Bugg's life was spared and he was taken prisoner. He was eventually transported to Moscow and imprisoned there with other British troops taken prisoner in Russia, where he remained until a prisoner exchange in March 1920.

In the final analysis, the 10 August 1919 offensive was considered a success. Contrary to the shambles of 45th Royal Fusiliers' attack on the western bank, the attack of their sister battalion 46th Royal Fusiliers on the eastern bank went off without a hitch, all of the objectives were captured with very few casualties. The Red Army had lost significant numbers of men killed, wounded and missing, many of whom had been taken prisoner. A number of the Bolshevik casualties had been incurred in the initial bombardment which included the firing of some 600 poison gas shells. Sadleir-Jackson's estimate of enemy casualties were 500 men killed, 800 wounded, 300 gassed and 200 died from exposure in the forest and a further 2,164 prisoners of whom 98 were wounded. Calculating casualty figures is not an exact science, however, and it is difficult to determine how Jackson came to the figures he did other than statements made by prisoners, but if he was correct the 6th Red Army opposing the British on the Dvina Front had lost 4,000 men in a single action, more than half the 6th Army's total strength.

Sadleir-Jackson credited the success of the operation to the gallantry of the Fusiliers:

> The pluck and endurance of the British Infantry was beyond all praise, the troops were without food for 24 hours before the attack but despite this and though dead tired, and soaking wet, the dash and spirit with which they attacked was beyond all praise.[25]

---

25   The National Archives: WO 95/5430, Sadleir-Jackson Brigade, War Diary.

108. Monitor HMS *M.25* which saw sterling service on the Dvina River from August 1918 to 17 September 1919, when she met the inglorious fate of being scuttled with sister ship *M.27* after the water level of the Dvina fell to a level where it was no longer possible to return to Archangel. (Public domain)

He also noted that in a campaign where the machete was a more valuable tool than the shovel, it took time for the company officers to overcome the influence of trench warfare doctrine and gain a sense of mobile rather than static operations and an eye for terrain and tactical movement.

Recommendation was also made that in the present type of warfare RAMC personnel should be armed with revolvers. There was an incident during the attack where White Russian troops assigned to protect stretcher bearers of 156th Field Ambulance, RAMC, deserted into the forest: unable to defend themselves, eight RAMC personnel were taken prisoner.

British casualties had been heavy; the heaviest suffered on a single day by the British Army in North Russia 1918–20, with 145 men killed, wounded and a number more missing. The 45th Royal Fusiliers on the western bank (Sludka–Lipovets–Chudinova) lost four officers, four NCOs and 20 men killed whilst 46th Royal Fusiliers on the eastern bank (Selmenga–Gorodok–Borok) lost one officer, one NCO and five men. Dozens of men were wounded and a number who did not make it out of the forest posted as 'missing'.

Compared to warfare on the Western Front, casualties were light but the number of men involved was also relatively small and warfare in the forest and swamps of North Russia was very different to that in the trenches and massed artillery and machine guns of France and Belgium.

Although Seltso had been captured, the village remained isolated from resupply by the Soviet minefield on the Dvina. Before naval transports could resupply the advanced positions at Sludka and Chudinova, the minefield at Seltso would have to be cleared. The task was assigned to the RN Flotilla's Chief Mining Officer, Lieutenant Commander Arthur Murray, OBE, RN, who determinedly set about collecting and defusing mines from the day after the attack. One of his officers, Lieutenant Cyril McLaughlin, RN, knew full well the danger he faced as his predecessor, Lieutenant Roger Fitzherbert-Brockholes, RN, had been killed whilst attempting to defuse a mine on 2 July. Sadly the same fate awaited McLaughlin who was killed during an attempt to render a mine safe on 11 August.

Murray himself was severely wounded when a mine pistol fuse detonated prematurely, but not before relaying a number of mines to catch out any Bolshevik gunboat which might attempt to steam downriver to interfere with the evacuation the following month. After the deaths of McLaughlin and Fitzherbert-Brockholes in nearly identical circumstances, plans to clear the minefield were abandoned, the risk of losing more men so close to the evacuation outweighed the advantage of the monitors and naval transport being able to reach advanced positions at Chudinova.

Although attempts to clear the minefield ceased, the Royal Navy continued its own mine-laying activities, laying some 30 mechanical and 30 horned mines in the Dvina during the period 28 August–2 September, whilst an additional 10 mechanical and 20 horned mines were laid in the northern Vaga.

Despite the massive blow to the enemy on the Dvina, the RAF had little rest in the weeks following the attack, flying missions against the Bolshevik flotilla and enemy-held villages every remaining day of the month. Some 20 minutes into a Short 184 seaplane engine test flight flown by 2nd Lieutenant Claude LeMoine with Sergeant Walter Quantrell in the observer's cockpit on 20 August, the aircraft was seen to descend into a dive which developed into a vertical spin ending in the aircraft crashing directly into the Dvina. LeMoine was killed instantly, however, quite miraculously, Quantrell survived with serious injuries.

In a letter to Claude's parents, Lieutenant Colonel Lancelot Tomlinson, OC, RAF Seaplanes, HMS *Pegasus* wrote,

> It is with the deepest regrets and sorrow that I venture to write to you to explain the details of your gallant son's death through a seaplane accident that occurred on August 20th and also to offer you, and not only me but all my officers, deep sympathy on the occasion of your loss. Claude LeMoine had taken up his seaplane for an engine test and had been flying well for some 20 minutes: unfortunately he became a little over-confident and put the seaplane into a very steep Bank – whilst spiralling down. From this position the seaplane 'took charge' and got into a vertical spin and hit the water at a great speed, vertically, and with tremendous force. Your son was killed instantly and the Flight Sergeant, whom he had up as a passenger, was seriously injured. His loss is a very great one to me: he was always so naive, cheery and contented and as a pilot held all our admiration. His gallantry during the recent offensive when we completely defeated the Bolshevik, was splendid. He was buried with all the military honours we could give him and all his brother officers who could be spared attended to give him honour. I enclose a photograph of his grave and also of Troitsa Church, Dvina River, where his body now lies. Once again accept my deepest sympathy.[26]

Quantrell was subsequently recommended for award of the Air Force Medal for his work as senior NCO of the fitters and engine mechanics of the RAF Seaplane Flight from HMS *Pegasus*, although the recommendation was downgraded to that for the Meritorious Service Medal which was seen as more fitting by RAF command.

The night of 24/25 August 1919 was like any other on the Dvina in the late summer of 1919. The large China gunboat HMS *Glowworm*, one of six such vessels operating on the Dvina, in company with HMS *Cockchafer* (Commander Quintin Preston-Thomas, RN) was steaming down the river to relieve HMS *Cricket* and HMS *Cicala* at the gun line, both of the latter ships having been ordered to return to Archangel for the evacuation. *Glowworm* had a complement of 54 officers and men and was at the time under the command of Commander Sebald W.B. Green, RN, who had been awarded the DSO for services in command of *M.25* in the capture of Archangel and initial operations on the Dvina almost exactly a year earlier.

The crew of *Glowworm* would have been less concerned with the threat from the Bolshevik gunboats operating on the river than the sea mines which the enemy floated downriver, carried by the currents towards Bereznik. These mines had already taken a toll on the Royal Navy Flotilla: tunnel minesweeper HMS *Sword Dance* had struck a mine on 24 June killing one rating whilst sister ship HMS *Fandango* had been struck on 3 July 1919, killing seven sailors with many more wounded.

---

26   Letter to LeMoine family.

The day before *Fandango* was struck, a mine was sighted floating downriver towards a stationary hospital barge. The Flotilla's Chief Mining Officer, Lieutenant Roger Fitzherbert-Brockholes, RN, set out in a small skiff with his usual crew (Leading Seaman John Sexton, RN, Ordinary Seaman T.M. Cheesebrough, RN and AM1 Henry W. Scudder, RAF) and paddled over to the mine which could be seen protruding above the water line. Moments later the mine exploded, killing all four men instantly.

For his work in charge of minesweeping operations, SNO Dvina River, Captain Altham recommended Brockholes for the Victoria Cross although the Admiralty deemed that such an award was not appropriate and did not forward a petition to the King for its award. There being no scope under the existing warrants to award the DSO or DSC posthumously, Brockholes was instead Mentioned in Despatches. Conversely, Lieutenant Cyril McLaughlin, RN, killed defusing a mine more than a month later on 11 August, was recommended for the DSO before his death and consequently received that award.

As HMS *Glowworm* and HMS *Cockchafer* neared Bereznik, the watch on *Glowworm* spotted a barge on fire mid river. The Mercantile Marine and Russian crew of Army barge NT326 *Edinburgh* had raked out the galley fire as usual before heading to their hammocks for the night. Closer to midnight, two of the crew awoke to find the aft cabin ablaze. An attempt was made to put out the fire, but unable to stem the flames, some of the crew fled the barge in a small boat. They had good reason to flee the inferno, as they knew what Commander Green on *Glowworm* almost certainly did not: that the barge was being used to transport ammunition and was loaded with 70 tonnes of high explosive.

As Green brought *Glowworm* alongside, the crew of the gunboat rushed with hoses to fire-stations on the foredeck in preparation to put out the conflagration. It so happened that on that fateful night Commander Green had been hosting three guests on *Glowworm* who rushed to the bridge to watch the commotion. They were Lieutenant John Zigomala, MBE, Irish Guards attached RE, Lieutenant W.G. Waganoff, RN (Russian interpreter) and Captain Dugald MacDougall, DFC, a Canadian from Manitoba serving with the RAF awarded the DFC for work flying seaplanes over the Dvina during the advance from Archangel. All three officers joined Commander Green and on the bridge, peering over the deck at the blazing barge below. Likewise, many of *Glowworm*'s crew not involved in fighting the fire crowded the foredeck to watch the burning spectacle before them.

As the crew of *Glowworm* attempted to bring the flames under control, *Cockchafer*, some distance away, was brought to approach the barge from the opposite direction. A crowd gathered ashore to watch the activity, few of whom could have known the horror which was to follow. As the crowd watched, a huge explosion sent a wall of flame high into the night sky. A moment later a second and then third enormous flash blanketed the countryside followed by a deafening roar and shockwave as the explosion ripped through the night, sending debris as far as a mile away.

As the crowd ashore recovered from their shock, hastily cobbled-together rescue teams began to row out to *Glowworm* in whatever vessel they could find. As the ad hoc rescue teams boarded her, they were met with a scene of utter destruction. Virtually the entire superstructure had been scorched and bent; debris and bodies of the crew lay everywhere. Being closest to the explosion, the foredeck had suffered the most damage. *Glowworm*'s firefighting crews had been wiped out at their hoses. Captain Ira Jones, RAF, was in one of the first boats to reach the still smouldering ship:

> The ghastly sight that faced us of dead and mutilated British sailors, whose bodies were strewn all over the deck, is one that we should like to, but never will, forget. Death came to them at their posts. Many were killed by flying projectiles, while others succumbed to the effects of the terrific detonation of four hundred tons of explosives in the barge. Bowman and I knew that a great friend, Captain MacDougal, was aboard, so we dashed up the bridge to search for him. On the way we had to pass through a room, where I noticed two sailors sitting on chairs. I asked them if they were all right. One was obviously stunned, and did not

reply, but the other, somewhat incoherently, exclaimed, 'Write to my mother!' I asked him where he came from, and the reply was, 'Hull.'

Producing a pencil and paper, I asked him to write his mother's address, and, meanwhile, Bowman and I continued our way to the bridge. There, again, we were faced with death.

Commander Green, the captain of the vessel, Captain MacDougal, and five sailors all lay prostrate and beyond human aid. We decided to return to the two sailors. Imagine our astonishment in finding them both dead, sitting in upright positions and with their eyes open.[27]

As rescuers came across wounded sailors they were carried to the relatively undamaged afterdeck and laid in rows for the medical staff to attend to. The first doctor on the scene was Major Kenneth Black, RAMC. The doctor made his way to the foredeck but realised there was little he could do there as virtually all who had been standing there at the time of the explosion were dead. Black hurriedly made his way up the two flights of stairs towards the bridge. At the top of the first flight of stairs he found the lifeless body of Surgeon Lieutenant R.M.R. Thursfield, RN. The ship's doctor had obviously been killed by the second large explosion whilst making his way to the bridge to assist those wounded in the first blast. Seeing there was nothing that could be done for Thursfield, Major Black hurried up the second ladder to the bridge to find the bodies of Commander Green, his three guests and other sailors.

Black was able to determine that they had been killed looking down over the bridge at the burning barge below when the explosion occurred. Commander Green was found lying mortally wounded at the rear of the bridge, barely holding on to life (it is impossible to tell if this was before or after Ira Jones and his group had made their way to the bridge). Green was only able to communicate for a short time by squeezing Black's hand before drifting into unconsciousness. He was evacuated from the smoking hulk of *Glowworm* to the hospital barge at Bereznik but did not regain consciousness and died an hour later.

In the meantime Commander Preston-Thomas had brought *Cockchafer* to her stricken sister ship's aid. *Cockchafer* lit *Glowworm*'s deck with searchlights to aid the rescue efforts whilst coming alongside. From the bridge Thomas directed the rescue crews through a megaphone. Jones recalled:

> The sailors worked with a coolness and precision as if they were carrying out practice drill in their barracks, although their hearts must have been heavy with the loss of comrades who had stuck gallantly to their work of attempting to save the ammunition barge, knowing the tremendous risks involved.[28]

Sick Berth Attendant Ernest Daish, RN witnessed the tragedy and recorded in his diary:

> Today was devoid of incident till 11pm when the most disastrous event of the Northern campaign occurred. I was lying in my bunk reading when there came a terrible explosion apparently right over the barge. I thought the Bolos were firing 6–inch shells and had got the exact range. Getting dressed I had just reached the top deck when a louder explosion occurred and a rain of shrapnel fell on the roof. Then followed a terrific burst, the whole sky was lit up. Shrapnel fell like a mighty hailstorm and I saw an ammunition barge blown up and sink. All the windows on our port side were blown out and several on the starboard side. The full force of the disaster fell upon the monitor Glow-worm whose commander had taken his ship alongside the burning barge in an attempt to extinguish the blaze. He surely could not have known the nature of the cargo and yet he ought to have known. Close to the burning barge was a big iron lighter loaded with about 500 tonnes of cordite, lyddite, 6–inch shells and small arm ammunition. If

---

27   Jones, *An Air Fighter's Scrapbook*, p.150.
28   *Ibid.*

109. Large China gunboat HMS *Cockchafer*, one of six Insect Class gunboats to serve on the Dvina, including HM Ships *Cicala, Cricket, Glowworm, Moth* and *Mantis*. (IWM FL22629)

this had blown up there would not have been left a ship in harbour, we should all have been wiped out. It was an anxious time. One 6–inch shell fell right into a case of cordite passed through singeing the cordite and yet did not explode it. Not till next day was it known how narrow had been our escape. As to the Glow–worm (which had only come up the day before to cover our retreat) she was simply riddled with shell and shrapnel. About 40 holes in the port side of her hull, the funnel was just like a huge sieve, her bridge and masts were shot away and her guns damaged. But the worst part of the business was the loss of life – 23 of her brave fellows were killed outright. The commander was wounded along with many others. As the Glow–worm drew off and came alongside her sister ship HMS Cockchafer she rammed her on the starboard side tearing a big rent below the water line and another larger one just above. The next morning a terrible sight met our gaze. Several of the men were simply torn to pieces and all were badly smashed. The doctor was killed and a flying corps captain. It was a sad sight to see them all lying side by side. A few hours before all were jolly and well and now out of a crew of 75 [sic] only 25 were left unhurt. The commander died at 2 o'clock without regaining consciousness, his wounds were terrible. Two others died towards night. I went on board the Glow–worm. I'm not likely to forget the spectacle very soon.[29]

The following day the full scale of the tragedy became apparent. Of the 54 crew on board *Glowworm* at the time of the explosion, 24 had been killed outright (including the two guests of Commander Green) and 15 wounded. Additionally two MMR men and two Russian seamen on board a nearby ammunition barge had been killed by flying debris, and three other MMR men wounded.

There were many individual acts of bravery that night, some of which were later recognised by the Admiralty in the form of decorations to those singled out for praise. It fell to Lieutenant Anthony Thorold, RN, the senior surviving officer of HMS *Glowworm*, to write a report of the events that led to the loss of so much life. In the report, Thorold makes mention of the gallant deeds of some of *Glowworm*'s crew that fateful night:

---

29   Private Diary of Ernest Ethelbert Daish.

I have the honour to submit the names of the following officers and men who showed great presence of mind and devotion to duty on the occasion of the explosion of the ammunition barge at Bereznik on August 25, 1919.

Mr Wildbore, Gunner, though wounded in the first explosion took charge aft, and on my being blown overboard by the second explosion, took command, anchored the ship, and carried on until he fainted through loss of blood.

Petty Officer Withington, though wounded in both arms, greatly assisted Mr Wildbore in anchoring the ship and rallying the survivors, after which he had to be carried to the steam boat for conveyance to the hospital barge.

Chief Engine Room Artificer Samuel Wilton, when boiler tubes were cut through by splinters from the second explosion, there was a large escape of steam, the cause of which could not be located. Unsuccessful attempts were made by Stoker Petty Officer Kirby to shut off steam to the capstan, which was finally done by the Chief Engine Room Artificer after Kirby had been scalded.

Able Seamen Patterson and Horsford showed great coolness and presence of mind in throwing overboard a cordite case which had been hit by a splinter of hot metal.

Sickberth Assistant Gregory showed much ability and resource in dealing with the wounded under the circumstances, using rifles as splints etc.

From evidence which I have since collected, it is submitted that in my opinion the discipline under the circumstances was exceptionally good throughout, as shown by the fact that although so many were killed and wounded, the ship remained under the control of the only surviving officer on board.[30]

Thorold's report was submitted to Captain Altham, commanding the Dvina River flotilla, who forwarded with his own recommendations to Rear Admiral John Green, CB, RN, SNO, White Sea:

Sir, I have the honour to forward the attached report from Lieutenant Anthony H.G. Thorold, senior surviving officer of HMS Glowworm, on the occasion of injuries to that ship from the explosion of an Army ammunition barge. The presence of mind displayed by Mr Wildbore, Gunner and PO Withington in anchoring the ship undoubtedly saved her from grounding or damage by collision, which in the strong current might have been serious. The conditions after the action were exceedingly trying and I beg that suitable notice may be taken of the high conduct of the officers and men by Lieutenant Thorold, who himself displayed much coolness and presence of mind on the occasion.[31]

Gunner Albert Wildbore, RN, subsequently received the MBE and Petty Officer William Withington the MSM, whilst Lieutenant Anthony Thorold was MiD for his services. Chief Engine Room Artificer Samuel Wilton also received the DSM for his services in North Russia, although not specifically for the *Glowworm* disaster.

The damage to *Glowworm* was significant. She was towed back to Archangel for refitting and repair, but although able to return to England under her own steam the gunboat was too worn out to continue service, and was paid off almost immediately on arrival at Chatham on 18 November and eventually scrapped in 1921.

In 1935, a 'G' Class destroyer was christened with the same name and went on to become famous as the destroyer that rammed the German cruiser *Admiral von Hipper* off Norway on 8 April 1940. Of the ship's complement of 149 officers and ratings, only 31 survived. All the survivors spent the remainder of the war in POW camps and it was not until their release in 1945 that reports were submitted to the Admiralty of the events leading up to the sinking of *Glowworm*. As a result of these

---

30   The National Archives: ADM 137/1695, White Sea River Expedition.
31   *Ibid.*

reports, ship's captain, Lieutenant Commander Gerard Roope, RN, was awarded a posthumous VC, whilst the only surviving officer, Lieutenant Robert Ramsey, RN, received the DSO and three of *Glowworm*'s crew the Conspicuous Gallantry Medal (CGM).

On 29 August 1919, a curious incident occurred when *M.33* spotted a man signalling for help from the river bank. A launch was sent out to investigate and returned with a soldier from the Royal Scots, attached Hampshire Regiment, who had been taken prisoner on the Railway Front on 21 July, but had escaped and spent three weeks walking through the forest before finally reaching the Dvina and sighting a British ship.

It was lucky that he arrived when he did, as the water level of the Dvina had begun to fall during August and by the end of the month the vessels of the Royal Navy River Flotilla were being progressively withdrawn downriver, with the exception of *M.25*, *M.27* and the yacht *Kathleen* which had been caught out by the rapid fall in water level and were stranded. Dredging and depth charging the obstructing sand bank was attempted but with only limited success. *M.25* got over two sandbars and *M.27* one, but even with the removal of armour plating, guns, mountings, fuel, ammunition, stores and both main engines, the monitors became trapped once again; they met an inglorious fate when on 17 September they were packed with gun cotton and blown up, where they lay along with stricken HMS *Sword Dance* and HMS *Fandango*.

HMS *Sword Dance* had nearly been salvaged thanks largely to the efforts of Lieutenant Commander Philip G. Rouse, RNVR, of the repair ship HMS *Cyclops*. In recommending Rouse to be Mentioned in Despatches, Captain Altham stated that in all probability, had there been time before the evacuation, *Sword Dance* could have been saved.

HMS *Humber* barely escaped the same fate by removing 70 tonnes of three inch armour plating into the Dvina. Royal Navy warships are not designed to be disassembled at sea and it took a full fortnight of work to remove the armour plating, a tremendous splash as each plate fell into the Dvina being greeted each time by rousing cheers from the crew. The crew then set to work constructing dummy guns from stove pipes and blocks of wood painted black in an attempt to deceive the enemy that the ship had not lost any of its bite.

Archangel: Dvina River Front September 1919: Final Operations

The Bolsheviks had no intention of allowing the British to evacuate North Russia without a fight, and resumed their attacks on the British advanced positions on both banks of the river on 6 September 1919 supported by the guns of the Bolshevik flotilla. Rumours had reached Sadleir-Jackson that the Bolsheviks had been reinforced by Red Finns (considered much hardier than the average Bolshevik conscript) and plans were underway for a counter-attack to interfere with the British plans for withdrawal by the end of the month. The attack against the British garrison at Puchega on the western bank of the river was particularly strong and the village was easily outflanked by the enemy, forcing the Fusilier garrison to fall back across the River Kodema. Two 45th Royal Fusiliers were wounded in the withdrawal and a further two Fusiliers cut off and taken prisoner.

Lieutenant Ralph Martin's naval gun battery of 20 seamen had swapped the 60 pdrs used in support of the 10 August attack for naval 12 pdrs and were rushed forward from Yakovlevskoe to Chudinova. Without adequate roads and using pack mules which had not pulled guns before, the three mile journey from Seltso to Lipovets took six hours alone, the guns having to be manhandled by the sailors most of that distance.

On the morning of 7 September, the enemy advanced on Kodema but suffered heavily from fire from the naval 12 pdrs which shelled the village and destroyed the bridge over the river, eventually forcing the Bolshevik troops to withdraw back into the village itself.

On the eastern bank the Bolsheviks had made a similar attack at 0600 on the morning of 6 September when a party of about 40 enemy were spotted moving into the village of Ivanovskaya. The Red troops made a half-hearted attempt to attack the British line but were driven off with little effort. A platoon of 46th Royal Fusiliers and 20 Royal Fusiliers Mounted Infantry counter-attacked at 0230 on the morning of 7 September and drove the Bolsheviks back into the forest, Sergeants John Whammond, MC, MM, and William Gale were both awarded the DCM for their gallantry during the counter-attack. On interrogation some of the prisoners revealed that the Bolsheviks were holding two battalions in reserve at nearby Nijni Toima.

On the western bank, the Bolsheviks holding Kodema received a nasty surprise on the morning of 7 September when a party of two platoons of 'B' Company, 45th Royal Fusiliers under Captain Charles Foulkes, MC (attached form South Wales Borderers), which had crossed the river during the night, launched a bayonet assault on the village at 0300. A number of enemy were killed outright, the remainder of the Bolshevik force fled headlong into the forest for which Foulkes was awarded an MC Bar.

The following day a patrol from the Royal Fusiliers Mounted Infantry spotted a large force of about 300 Red troops advancing north-west towards Chudinova and plans were made for an immediate attack. Just after midday Captain Alistair Pearse, MC (attached from Middlesex Regiment) and Lieutenant Vashon James Wheeler, MC (attached from Rifle Brigade) led their platoons forward in a wild bayonet assault, completely routing the enemy. The Red troops were pursued into the forest where a number more were killed and captured. When the bodies were counted, the enemy had lost three machine guns, 81 men killed and 99 taken prisoner for the loss of only one Fusilier wounded. Both Pearse and Wheeler were awarded MC Bars for the action and Sergeant Percy Petter a DCM.

On the eastern bank, 46th Royal Fusiliers were having a particularly hot time repelling an attack by 500 Red Finns on the village of Ivanovskaya. The Fusiliers managed to hold on to the village

110. Royal Navy gun battery firing naval 12 pdr in support of
final operations on the Dvina. (IWM 35017)

inflicting a number of casualties, including 30 enemy killed. The Finns withdrew out of range of the Fusiliers' Lewis guns and attempted to dig in but were driven off by fire from the naval 12 pdrs on the opposite bank at Chudinova.

The Bolshevik attacks of 6–8 September demonstrated that despite the heavy losses of 10 August, the enemy were determined to disrupt the British evacuation. Time and time again the Red commanders demonstrated an apparently inexhaustible quotient of offensive spirit, regardless of losses or setbacks. Unfortunately for the Bolsheviks, the Fusiliers were just as determined to stand their ground. For the loss of one 45th Royal Fusilier (Private James Sliney) and sixteen others wounded, the Bolsheviks had suffered 163 killed, 200 wounded and 148 taken prisoner.

On the morning of 9 September, the Bolshevik gunboats began a heavy bombardment of the 46th Royal Fusiliers at Ivanovskaya followed by an assault on three sides at 0800 by two battalions of Red Finns which had been held in reserve at Nijni Toima, cutting the village off from reinforcements from Borok. Besieged in the village, a small detachment of Royal Fusiliers Mounted Infantry under Lieutenant Luke Green, MC (attached from Rifle Brigade) fought doggedly, fighting their way through to Borok. Green himself killed three Bolsheviks at close range in desperate hand-to-hand fighting for which he was awarded the DSO, an award rarely given to junior officers.

Having driven the Fusiliers from Ivanovskaya, the Finns pushed on towards Borok where they encountered 'D' Company, 45th Royal Fusiliers under Captain De Miremont (attached from Royal Welsh Fusiliers). After a brisk fight the Finns were driven off and returned to Ivanovskaya.

On the western bank of the Dvina an RAF seaplane observed a column of approximately 300 enemy arriving by barge at Puchega at 1000. At 1130 the enemy gunboats and land based artillery began a heavy bombardment of Sludka, Chudinova and Kodema as if in preparation for an attack. The expected attack did not materialise and gradually the enemy bombardment petered out and stopped. During the barrage the enemy artillery paid particular attention to Lieutenant Ralph Martin's naval 12 pdrs, three 6 inch shells fell within 10 yards of one of the naval guns. Regardless of the fire, Martin kept his two guns in action against the enemy infantry and monitors over open sights until ordered to withdraw. For services with the Royal Navy gun battery during the Bolshevik attacks of 6–9 September, Lieutenant Martin, Sub Lieutenant Basil Brewster and Mate Arthur Ingram were awarded the DSC whilst Petty Officer Dennis Smith and Able Seaman Albert Greenway received the DSM.

During the night of 10 September, the first stage of the evacuation commenced with the embarkation of troops on barges at Yakovlevskoe and Troitsa for the secondary defence line at Shushunga-Pless. The Bolsheviks, apparently aware that the evacuation was taking place that night, shelled the British forward areas but no casualties were sustained.

As the troops were embarking, Chief Gunner Daniel Enright, RN, was busily in charge of the naval demolition party which laid charges on the bridges at Selmenga, Topsa and Kurgomen as the last troops crossed over. For his services as Chief Gunner of the River Flotilla, particularly during the 10 August offensive and in command of naval demolition parties ashore during the evacuation, Enright was awarded a DSC Bar. Enright's first DSC had been awarded for attacks on enemy U-boats in the Mediterranean whilst in command of a Motor Torpedo Boat. In 1922 as a Commissioned Gunner, he was awarded an MVO on board HMS *Renown* for services to the Prince of Wales during his visit to India and Japan. Enright was still serving during the Second World War as an instructor of naval cadets at HMS *St. George* on the Isle of Man at the age of 67.

Large amounts of stores which could not be transported downriver to Archangel were stockpiled and set alight lest they fall into the hands of the enemy. Nothing was to be left behind, not even the pontoons at Troitsa and Yakovlevskoe – 'Luby's Landing', built by the pioneers of 385th Field Company, RE – which were soaked in oil and set alight.

An officer recalled the mixed feelings amongst the troops as they left: 'It seemed a great tragedy to leave the ground we had fought for to the enemy, but it was imperative. All we left behind of material value was the white cross on Troitsa heights that marked the resting place of our dead comrades.'[1]

111. Able Seaman Albert Greenway, RN, awarded the DSM for services ashore with the naval gun battery during the final operations near Chudinova, 7–9 September 1919. (Author's collection)

At 0830 on the morning of 11 September, the Bolsheviks launched attacks on Yakovlevskoe and Troitsa. Indeed, the Bolsheviks pushed so far so quickly that there were clashes near Pless and Shushunga between the Royal Fusiliers and Bolshevik advanced patrols. The attackers were subsequently identified as a combined force of civilian partisans and deserters from 4th North Russian Rifles who had mutinied and gone over to the Bolsheviks during the Slavo-British Legion mutiny on 7 July.

The Royal Fusiliers Mounted Infantry under Lieutenant Luke Green was in action during the withdrawal, patrolling the forests and acting as forward scouts. On the night of 11–12 September, two parties of mounted infantry numbering 60 horsemen each set out to patrol the forest west of Kurgomen where they encountered parties of Red troops. The enemy followed through with a strong attack on the outpost line west of Kurgomen which was driven off after a stiff fight by 0300. Patrols sent out to inspect the enemy dead found quantities of British uniforms and equipment, suggesting the attackers were also deserters from the British-equipped White Russian forces.

Desertions were not all on the White side however and on 13 September the entire 9th Company of the Red Army 161st Regiment defected to the British near Tulgas. Their commander, a former Imperial officer, had been pressganged into service and took the first opportunity to desert, the entire company following his example. For many Red troops deserting to the British, the prospect of

---

1   Singleton-Gates, *Bolos and Barishynas*, p.161.

112. Dedication ceremony of the tri-service North Russia Expeditionary Force Memorial next to the churchyard at Troitsa, August 1919, South African Lieutenant Colonel H. Jenkins, CO, 46th Royal Fusiliers in foreground. The memorial was destroyed by the Bolsheviks only a matter of months later. (Public domain)

proper clothing and better rations was likely a powerful enticement, at least until the time was right to desert back to the Bolsheviks.

That same night a party of 200 Bolsheviks made a strong attack on the village of Nevonovskaya under the cover of an enemy searchlight from Tulgas church. The attack was eventually driven off after a very hard fight in which Privates Peter McKenna, John McLaggan, Leslie Robertson and William Wright of 45th Royal Fusiliers were killed.

CMB 36 (Lieutenant Andrew Welchman, RNR) was sent up river with Captain Francis Milton, MC, RFA, on board to investigate the searchlight and put it out of action if possible. Conditions were difficult, there being virtually no moon with a hard wind blowing. Due to the combined factors of low water level and poor visibility, the CMB ran aground on a sand bank and could not be moved. There was little point waiting for daybreak when the stricken boat would be a sitting target for the Bolshevik gunners so Welchman, Milton and a rating assembled a small collapsible boat and set off for assistance. The wind was so strong that the boat nearly capsized on a number of occasions but the three men managed to retain control and paddle furiously towards a friendly artillery barge.

On board the barge, the picket noticed a black shape slowly approaching through the night. He called a challenge but could not hear any reply in the pelting wind and rain. Suspecting an enemy mine or boarding party he again hailed the black shape when it was just 150 yards distant but once again heard no response. With the unidentifiable shape less than 100 yards distant, the sentry opened fire with a Lewis gun. The black vessel quickly sank as other objects became visible struggling in the water and screaming was heard. A small boat set out from the barge in the pitch dark and discovered with horror that they had opened fire on their own men. All three men were rescued, Welchman was badly wounded with a broken arm and the rating received a bullet to the foot. Welchman was particularly lucky: having refused to be rescued before Captain Milton and the Able Seaman, he was pulled aboard the launch just as he was going under.

On 14 September, the enemy continued to shell the river from Tulgas in the hope of hitting one of the evacuation barges whilst Bolshevik patrols pushed forward and skirmished with the Royal

113. Volunteers from 46th Royal Fusiliers in the forest on the Dvina, September 1919.
Shorts and shirts were commonly worn in the heat of summer in North Russia where
the sun rarely sets and temperatures rise to as high as 35°C/95°F. (Public domain)

Fusiliers Mounted Infantry acting as mobile rearguard. Interference by Red troops from Tulgas was proving a great annoyance to the evacuation and Sadleir-Jackson ordered the mounted infantry to secure the village.

The following day a party of 78 mounted infantry supported by trench mortars and Lewis guns under the command of Lieutenant Frederick Whalley, Rifle Brigade attached 45th Royal Fusiliers, raided the village of Nevonovskaya near Tulgas, pushing the enemy back into the forest to Bulanovskaya which was also captured, enemy casualties being counted at 127 killed and four prisoners, for which Whalley was awarded the MC.

Australian volunteer Private Norman Brooke, awarded the DCM for scouting work during the 10 August 1919 attack, now serving with the Royal Fusiliers Mounted Infantry, recalled:

> We went up the river bank and came to a ravine, the ravine was on the edge of the village, the village was high up above on the banks. The ravine ran out after three or four hundred yards. Some of us got up the end of the ravine where things got a bit easier but we were pinned down by a lot of fire and a bit of barbed wire. We were sitting in a shell hole under the barbed wire for about half an hour or more not able to shift … The Reds liked to occupy houses and get up the upstairs windows with machine guns and rifles … There was a terrible lot of rifle and machine gun fire. What settled the affair was the bringing up of a trench mortar which landed two or three shells near the enemy positions. After that the firing died down and we were able to withdraw. We lost six men killed that morning [out of a strength of 78 men in the Royal Fusiliers Mounted Infantry], I don't know how many wounded. It was rather a disastrous thing for us.[2]

The raiding party withdrew at 0430 just prior to a strong enemy counter-attack supported by artillery commenced 30 minutes later. As the enemy flooded back through Tulgas a barrage was

---

2   AWM: S00180, Interview (1984) with Private N.M. Brooke, DCM.

opened on them by Lieutenant Ralph Martin's naval gun battery which had been landed west of Kurgomen under the cover of a CMB smokescreen. Along with a captured 3 inch trench mortar, Martin's guns bombarded Kurgomen and Tulgas intermittently for the following six hours.

During the initial attack on Tulgas, Private Olaf Christian Andersen, a tough little Dane who had served in the AIF and volunteered for the Royal Fusiliers Mounted Infantry from the Australian Platoon of 'D' Company, 45th Royal Fusiliers, attacked a Bolshevik machine gun post which was holding up the attack and killed the crew. They plucky Dane pushed forward alone and only ceased to fight when seriously wounded for which he was awarded the DCM, although it appears that Andersen was actually recommended for the Victoria Cross. In the letter home to his mother in which Corporal Arthur Sullivan broke the news of his own award, Sullivan makes mention that he was not the only member of the AIF detachment so recommended: 'Another of our chaps, a little Dane who was in the A.I.F. and joined this force has been recommended. We haven't heard the result of the recommendation yet, but I hope he gets it.'[3]

At five feet three inches, the diminutive Danish-born Andersen had been naturalised an Australian-British subject by the time he enlisted into the AIF in 1917 although due to illness or injury he did not embark for the reinforcement depots in England until July the following year. The war ended before he had the chance to see active service, likely the primary motivation for his volunteering for the NRRF the following year. Andersen survived his wounds and lived to receive his DCM (it was one of his few possessions when he died a recluse many years later) but the belief that he was actually awarded the VC seems to have persisted. In 1924 the Danish Consulate in Melbourne wrote to AIF Record Office seeking further information on the award of the VC to Andersen, his mother in Denmark having reportedly received an official document notifying her of the award. No such confirmation was forthcoming from AIF Records as Andersen had not been gazetted for award of the VC.

Whilst recovering in hospital Andersen likely wrote to his mother (who in all probably could not read English) that he had been recommended for award of the VC. At some point Andersen's VC recommendation was downgraded to that for the DCM (perhaps the fact that 45th Royal Fusiliers had already received two VCs, the only such awards for North Russia may have been a factor) and when his mother, as Andersen's next of kin, received notification of award of the DCM in English which almost certainly she could not read, she likely made an assumption that the official notification which was that of the award of the Victoria Cross.

'B' Company, 45th Royal Fusiliers was the last unit to embark for Archangel on board the river boat *Perekat* on 16 September. The company had been left behind at Shushunga to act as rearguard on the western bank during the final stages of the withdrawal and did not embark until 0930, just as the last bridges were being blown by Chief Gunner Enright's naval demolition party.

Just as *Perekat* was passing the Dvina–Vaga junction a machine gun opened fire from the western bank of the river. The task of securing the confluence of the rivers had been given to a company of 1st Oxs and Bucks which had fought on the Vaga River, but due to a mix up of timings and the late arrival of the relieving White Russian unit, the Oxs and Bucks had evacuated their positions before the last Dvina Force barge had passed.

A barge carrying two 18 pdrs under Captain Francis Milton, MC, RFA (who had a narrow escape from being machine-gunned by the Army barge during the storm two days earlier) was brought into action against the machine gun and Lieutenant Clive Sergeant's Royal Marine landing party put ashore to disperse the enemy, killing the three machine gunners but not before Sadleir-Jackson had a close call himself when a bullet struck *CMB 36* (on this occasion commanded by Sub Lieutenant Isaac Newton, RNR) just two inches above his head. Even the RAF seaplane supply barge *S.S.B.1* following behind with half the seaplane flight on board got in on the action, opening fire on the tree line with Lewis

3   Quinlivian, *Forgotten Valour*, p.171.

guns, rifles and a 3 inch gun mounted on the bow for anti-aircraft defence, surely one of the few occasions, if not unique in the history of the RAF, that riggers and fitters have engaged the enemy ashore whilst afloat.

Tragically, Captain Alister Pearse, MC and Bar, Middlesex Regiment attached, Corporal Edward Nash, Sergeant Percy Petter, DCM, and Private George Scott were killed by the initial burst of machine gun fire and another 13 Fusiliers wounded. They were to be the last casualties sustained by Dvina Force in North Russia. One of those wounded, losing two fingers from his right hand, was a young Fusilier Lieutenant who would go on to a notable career with the RAF during the Second World War.

114. Lieutenant/Wing Commander Vashon Wheeler, MC and Bar, DFC and Bar, Rifle Brigade attached 45th Royal Fusiliers and RAF. (Public domain)

Vashon James Wheeler served as a subaltern with the Rifle Brigade 1916–18 and volunteered for service with the NRRF in 1919, being posted on attachment to the 45th Royal Fusiliers with whom he was awarded two MCs within a week of each other during actions 2–9 September. The loss of two fingers did not stop Wheeler from qualifying as a pilot during the 1920s and embarking on a career as an early airline pilot. By the outbreak of the Second World War, Wheeler was serving as an RAFVR transport pilot flying Avro Ansons before transferring to No. 85 Squadron with whom he flew 71 missions in Hurricane, Havoc and Beaufighter aircraft, claiming two enemy aircraft destroyed and several others 'damaged' and 'probable' for which he was awarded the DFC. After posting in the rank of Squadron Leader to No. 157 Squadron, the first RAF unit to convert to De Havilland Mosquito aircraft, Wheeler flew 29 night fighter missions in defence of England before flying his first intruder mission over Germany on 23 March 1943, being awarded a second DFC that same year. Promoted Wing Commander and given command of No. 207 Squadron flying Lancaster heavy bombers, 'Pop' Wheeler flew in every operation in which the squadron took part from the time he took command until he did not return from his 158th operational mission on the night of 22–23 March 1944, a raid over Frankfurt. Aged 46 at the time of his death, Wing Commander Vashon James Wheeler, MC and Bar, DFC and Bar, was buried in Durnbach Military Cemetery.

True to form and despite ample notice in advance, the White Russian forces were still not prepared for handover of the forward positions by the time the final British withdrawals were taking place. On 17 September, the same day the Royal Navy were reluctantly blowing up four stricken vessels of the Dvina River Flotilla rather than leave them for the Bolsheviks, appeals were being made by the White Russian leadership for General Ironside to delay the evacuation for a few extra days to allow the Russian troops time to take up their positions. Having already delayed the evacuation due to the enemy attacks in September, Ironside had no such intention and was perhaps understandably rather unsympathetic. Having been given every opportunity, training, equipment and support to act for themselves for more than a year, the White Russian forces remained as ineffective, incompetent and corrupt as ever.

Although Sadleir-Jackson had achieved considerable success with his 10 August offensive, his final report of operations to General Ironside expressed his belief in the ultimate futility of the expedition.

The military authorities at home, despatched two brigades complete in every detail less artillery and transport, in addition to these two Brigades, an Advanced River Base, and other reinforcements were sent

115. Royal Navy and Army officers of the NRRF/Dvina Force rearguard. (Public domain)

out. These do not appear to have been adequate to meet relief requirements of the Archangel Force. One relief Brigade was completely disintegrated, and never acted as a Brigade, the ambulance of the other Brigade and a considerable portion of its Signal Company were detached, and were never with the Brigade. Not a single man who was evacuated sick, or wounded, from his unit, ever rejoined: the balance of the Infantry, Engineers, and Machine Gunners, who came out after the arrival of the Volunteer Brigade, never joined their units. This disintegration and dispersion naturally reduced the striking value of the two Brigades, which were destined for the advance ... With a low river sown with several minefields, with the enemy's Flotilla practically intact and possessing an open line of retreat, without a light railway on the left bank, it is extremely improbable that no matter how successful a military operation was fought, that transport facilities would have precluded the possibility of reaching Kotlas before the ice made it imperative to withdraw.[4]

On 24 September, whilst still at Archangel, announcement was made of the award of the Victoria Cross to Corporal Arthur Percy Sullivan from Crystal Brook, South Australia. Amongst much backslapping and congratulations from his mates, Sullivan expressed his shock in a letter to his mother two weeks later:

You will be pleased to hear that for pulling a few of our chaps out of a marshy river under fire on 11 Aug. I have been awarded the V.C. I cant say I earned it but there were none in the Batt. up to then & I suppose they wanted someone to get one ... They tell me I will have to go up and see the King to get my cross. Cant say that I fancy that much ... None of us were sorry to get out of Russia. The whole country is rotten with Bolshevism and there was as much danger from the supposed loyal troops as from the Bolo.[5]

Interestingly, the date of action described in the *London Gazette* entry, 10 August, and actually inscribed on the medal itself, is incorrect: the event for which Sullivan was decorated actually took place during the withdrawal the following morning. On 1 October, *The Times* carried a story

4   The National Archives: WO 95/5430, Sadleir-Jackson Brigade, War Diary.
5   Quinlivian, *Forgotten Valour*, p.171.

of the memorial service held for Lieutenant Lord Settrington. The next column over carried an announcement of the award of the Victoria Cross to Arthur Sullivan, there being no connection made between the late Lieutenant and the award of Sullivan's Victoria Cross.

The final evacuation of Archangel took place on the 27 September 1919, 'C' Company and the Lewis Gun Company of 46th Royal Fusiliers covering the embarkation of the last troops ashore whilst seaplanes patrolled the skies overhead and CMBs stood alert at the river mouth. With the dramatic background of huge clouds of thick black smoke from the tonnes of stores being burnt on the wharf, the North Russia Expeditionary Force embarked on troop ships for home, monitors HM Ships *M.26*, *M.31*, *M.33* and battleship HMS *Fox* standing ready with guns covering the shore watching for any sign of trouble. What couldn't be burnt was taken out to sea and dumped, some 90 million rounds of small arms ammunition were thrown overboard and sent to the bottom of the White Sea.

General Ironside had offered up to 18,000 berths on the departing troopships for any local inhabitant who wished to leave. Only 6,000 took up the offer. Archangel resembled a ghost town, curfew was in effect and not a soul stirred. 'C' Company, 46th Royal Fusiliers was the last was to leave, taken on board a tug and out to sea to join the remainder of the battalion on board *Kildonan Castle* bound for Plymouth. The decks of the transports and ships were so crammed with men and equipment that one of the CMBs had to be sunk by machine gun fire as there was no room for it on board any of the departing ships. The convoy of 45 ships of all sizes slowly steamed out the harbour into the White Sea bound for England via Murmansk. The only ship not bound for 'Old Blighty' was the monitor HMS *Erebus*, its massive 15 inch guns seeing further service with Admiral Cowan's Royal Navy Eastern Baltic Fleet until the withdrawal of the fleet in December.

In a curious event, the last British soldier to leave North Russia was lucky not to have been left behind altogether:

> The third tug stopped close to us and announced that they had one soldier on board. The skipper was smiling broadly as he told us that he had been found sitting forlornly on a pile of baggage all by himself. When asked what he was doing there he shouted out, 'I am Captain Snodgrass's servant and he told me to wait here till he came.' This last man to leave North Russia was quite unperturbed. I found out later that we really did have a Captain Snodgrass in the Archangel Force [He had in fact commanded the 'Australian Section' of 201st Battalion, MGC on the Railway Front].
>
> I have often wondered where his faithful servant eventually caught up with him, and what they said to each other when he did.[6]

Kildonan Castle docked at Plymouth on 9 October, but delays meant it was several hours before the men were allowed to disembark, by which time they had become increasingly restless. When the tanned soldiers of the North Russia Relief Force finally disembarked, about 150 of their number broke through the police picket and made their way into town and the nearest public house. When local authorities attempted to round the men up, a fight between the soldiers and police broke out. Faced with the prospect of a riot on their hands, local military authorities ordered troops from a nearby barracks to restore order with bayonets fixed.

The NRRF volunteers arrived in London two days later, conspicuous by their identifying insignia:

> London streets are full of troops back from North Russia. Nearly every other officer or man to be seen yesterday wore the white star on the blue background, the Force's sign, on their sleeves. They are a tough looking crowd, too, the majority of them displaying some decoration granted for personal bravery … They

---

6   Ironside, *Archangel 1918–19*, p.186.

116. Royal Fusiliers of the NRRF march to the Dvina to embark on barges
to return to Archangel, September 1919. (Public domain)

seemed very glad to be in town once more, and were crowding round the shop windows, a thing they have not been able to do for many a long day.[7]

No sooner had General Ironside stepped ashore at Liverpool quay on 6 October, he was asked by a reporter if he wished to say anything about the expedition to North Russia. Ironside replied that he thought that too much had been said already and that he believed that the NREF had accomplished its mission, and that the White Russian would be able to stand alone against the Bolsheviks.

Ironside would not have been so foolish to believe that the White Russians would be able to hold the Red Army at bay for any length of time, his words likely being dictated by political expediency rather than any hand on heart belief. The Bolsheviks did not even wait for the winter snow to thaw before marching into Archangel on 21 February 1920.

White Russian General Eugene Miller held out until the end, fleeing across the White Sea with a number of other White Russian officers in icebreaker *Kozma Minin*, captained by Grigory Chaplin, the former Russian Imperial Navy officer who had fermented the coup in Archangel timed to coincide with the Allied attack and occupation of the city in August 1918. The Bolsheviks took command of the icebreaker *Kanada* and gave chase and a running gun battle ensued between the two ships, neither scoring any effective hit. The *Minin* eventually reached the open waters of the Barents Sea and was able to escape, three other refugee ships stuck fast in the ice and were captured with all on board.

From Murmansk the White Russians fled to Norway and then France where a large Russian exile community was established which spent the following two decades futilely dreaming of one day returning to their homeland. On 22 September 1937, Soviet agents lured Miller to a Paris apartment and drugged and smuggled him by ship to Russia where on 11 May 1939, after 19 months of interrogation and solitary confinement, the 71–year-old was executed.

One of the White Russian officers who escaped across the White Sea with Miller was Captain Vassily Prootkovsky who had been awarded the MM with the Slavo-British Legion for service with Colonel Thornhill's party in the capture of Onega in July 1918. Prootkovsky eventually settled in Australia where he served with the merchant fleet early in the war, until he was arrested by military intelligence and interned in 1942 for his advocacy of the overthrow of the Soviet government, the

---

7   *Sheffield Evening Telegraph*, 11 October 1919.

very objective for which the British had fought towards in Russia 1918–20. In a pleading letter to the British High Commission in February 1944 written from Loveday internment camp at Barmera, South Australia, Prootkovsky wrote:

> In 1918 I accepted the invitation of the British Military Authorities to join the British Forces to fight for the Allies' cause and I signed an agreement with those authorities. By that agreement I was obliged to serve under the British Flag where-ever and whenever ordered and I fulfilled my obligations honestly. On the other hand that agreement promised to one the full protection of Great Britain against her enemies whom I might be ordered to fight ... Early in 1919, while visiting Archangel I was invited to the British Garrison Mess where General Ironside explained to me that I was decorated in the name of His Majesty-King George V and that in future I would receive Great Britain's protection in any part of the British Empire against the enemies whom I fought under the British flag ... During my internment my teeth have been destroyed. I am on diet with duodenal ulcer. My eyesight has been destroyed and lately I developed heart trouble ... I wish to protest before you, Sir, as the representative of Great Britain against such a treatment, which is in full contrast to the obligations made to me by Great Britain 25 years ago ... as an ex-servicemen of the British Army I apply to you, Sir, for your assistance in my release and in the re-establishment of my good name.
> Yours faithfully,
> V. Prootkovsky, M.M.[8]

Prootkovsky was released just in time to hear of the Allied landings in Normandy but never fully recovered from his injuries sustained during the war and the conditions of his internment. He died in 1975, estranged from his wife and step-children, and lies buried in an unmarked grave in Sydney's Rookwood Cemetery.

Overall the White Russian troops had proven themselves largely ineffective on the battlefield, however there were many brave men amongst their number. Major John Bryan, Tank Corps, who commanded the NREF Tank Corps detachment sent to Archangel, wrote in the Tank Corps Journal in 1920 that he had received a cable from Colonel Kentovich, 'North Russia Tank Corps' stating that he had taken his tanks into action on the Railway Front soon after the British withdrawal, 'Proud keep traditions, English Tank Corps. Took in glorious fight five fortified points and Plesetskaya Station.' A volunteer detachment of nine officers and 60 other ranks under Major Bryan had arrived at Archangel on 29 August shortly before the evacuation with four Mark V and two Medium Mark A 'Whippet' tanks, tasked with training White Russian crews in their rudimentary use before handing the tanks over to the Russians. Colonel Kentovich's Mark V Tank, No. 9303, remains on display in Archangel as a reminder to its residents of the strange little war that took place near their small city all those years ago.

As the first Red troops of 154th Regiment entered Archangel, the population turned out to greet them with cheering crowds lining each side of Troitsky Prospekt, just as they had upon the arrival of the North Russia Relief Force seven months earlier. The Soviets knocked down the Cathedral of the Archangel Michael after whom the town was named, destroying the historic building and its large fresco of 'The Last Judgement', constructing a bleak government building where the Cathedral once stood.

General Ironside went on to serve in Northern Persia 1920–21 and was appointed Chief of the General Staff on 3 September 1939, the day Britain declared war on Nazi Germany, and for a short time as Commander-in-Chief Home Forces before his retirement in September 1940. Promoted Field Marshal in August, he was conferred a Peerage by the King in the New Years

---

8   National Archives of Australia: Series D1901, Barcode 919705, Loveday Internment Camp Files.

117. British Mark V tank 9303 supplied to the North Russian Tank Detachment and subsequently captured by the Bolsheviks. (Public domain)

Honours, choosing the title 'Baron Ironside of Archangel'. Field Marshal William Edmund Ironside, 1st Baron Ironside of Archangel, GCB, CMG, CBE, DSO, died in Queen Alexandra Military Hospital London on 22 September 1959 aged 79, and was buried with full military honours near his home in Norfolk.

Sadleir-Jackson's active service did not end with command of a brigade in North Russia. He went on to be appointed to command the Iraq Levies in 1921 and died in a car crash in France on 22 May 1932, near Peronne, whilst visiting some of his old battlefields on the Western Front.

Lieutenant Edward Sutro, MC, who had commanded the 'Australian Platoon' of 45th Royal Fusiliers on the Dvina River, took with him back to England a small dog which he named 'Dvina'. Sutro spent 15 years as a sheep farmer in New Zealand before returning to England and was noted in his later years as being rather eccentric, wearing a long cape and driving a white Rolls Royce, but also a great lover of theatre. He held the Guinness World Record for attending 6,000 theatrical opening nights within his lifetime and would in his later years fly to Australia or Canada to attend opening nights of his favourite performers. He never allowed hunting on his estate as he said he knew what it was like to be hunted in the forests of North Russia.

Ironside wanted a medal struck with a white ribbon as an award for service in North Russia but instead the criteria for award of the 1914–18 British War and Victory Medals was extended to cover operations in Russia up to July 1920. Given that more British and Commonwealth servicemen died in Russia 1918–20 than in other campaigns during the same period (all of which had individual clasps to service medals awarded in respect of service there), it is perhaps unfortunate that those who fought in the campaigns in North Russia, South Russia, Eastern Baltic, Siberia and Caspian, were not recognised with at least a 'Russia 1918–20' clasp to the General Service Medal (Army and RAF) and Naval General Service Medal.

Interestingly, consideration was given to issuing clasps to the British War Medal to commemorate specific campaigns and battles. Seventy-nine clasps were proposed by the Army and 68 by the Navy before the scheme was abandoned as impractical. The 79 clasps proposed by the Army are not known but of the 68 proposed by the Navy, clasps included 'North Russia 1918–19'; 'Eastern Baltic 1918–19'; 'Siberia 1918–19'; 'Black Sea 1918–20' and 'Caspian'.

Following its policy of repatriating bodies of its servicemen who had died overseas, the United States exhumed the graves of its soldiers in Archangel Allied Cemetery before embarking in July 1919. Some bodies buried in outlying areas or in territory since occupied by the Bolsheviks had to be left behind until a small 1929 mission operating outside of official diplomatic channels was granted permission by the Soviet Government to very quietly exhume and repatriate any remains they could locate 10 years after the last US troops had left North Russia. The remains of 89 soldiers were recovered and repatriated home to the US. Arriving at New Jersey, the convoy of coffins were carried ashore and reinterred with full military honours.

The French and Poles also repatriated the bodies of their soldiers who had died in North Russia. Only the British dead remained where they were buried, Archangel Allied Cemetery falling under the remit of the newly formed 'Commonwealth War Graves Commission', tasked with maintaining British and Commonwealth War Cemeteries of the First World War around the globe.

Archangel Allied Cemetery remains in a lonely corner of Archangel today, forlorn and overgrown, the brickwork walls surrounding the cemetery crumbling through age and lack of maintenance. Compared to the well kept, well visited CWGC cemeteries in France and Belgium, it is a sad and shabby place. The headstones made from local granite are much less distinctive than those made of white stone used in other CWGC cemeteries. During 1918–19, burials were made in the cemetery regardless of nationality, British, US, French and Polish soldiers all buried next to each other. After the other nations exhumed their dead for repatriation, gaps were left between the British headstones, giving the cemetery a disorganised, haphazard appearance. The cemetery itself contains 224 burials and 140 'Special Memorial' plaques dedicated to those who were buried in outlying cemeteries whose graves are known. The Archangel Memorial to the Missing consists of panels

118. Archangel Allied Cemetery today with Special Memorial plaques along the wall in the background commemorating those who are missing in action, buried in outlying areas or whose graves have been lost to time. (Public domain)

along the eastern wall of the cemetery with the names of a further 219 officers and men whose graves are not known, including that of Sergeant Samuel Pearse, VC, MM, whose grave at Obozerskaya has been lost to time and the elements.

The British government attempted to cover up its military involvement in Russia, 1918–20 by classifying official documents relating to the campaign under the '50 year rule'. By the time the documents were quietly released to the public in 1969–70 there was little interest in the obscure and unpopular campaign and very few books were ever published by its participants. It is little wonder therefore that the campaign remains one of the least known ever fought by the British Army in modern times. Few people in Britain today know that their country ever fought a war against the Soviet Union and the sacrifice of those British and Commonwealth servicemen and women who fought, suffered and died in North Russia 1918–19, is today largely ignored and forgotten.

In the West, Allied intervention in the Russian Civil War was quickly forgotten as trade agreements were signed and the Soviets recognised as the legitimate government in power. The Russians had a much longer memory, however, and during a 1957 visit to the United States, Soviet Premier Nikita Krushchev likely caused some confusion amongst US diplomats when he stated, 'Never have any of our soldiers been on American soil, but your soldiers were on Russian soil. Those are the facts.'[9] Few of the politicians and diplomats present would have known what he was referring to.

During a state television appearance during his 1972 visit to the Soviet Union, US President Richard Nixon mistakenly stated, 'We have never fought one another in war.'[10] An erroneous claim which was repeated by President Reagan during his presidency the following decade.

Large China gunboat HMS *Cicala*, which had seen such sterling service on the Dvina, met a sad fate on 21 December 1941 when it was sunk in the defence of Hong Kong by Japanese aircraft. Ship's captain at the time of the sinking was Lieutenant Commander John Boldero, RN, who had

9   Halliday, E.M., *The Ignorant Armies, The Anglo-American Archangel Expedition 1918–1919* (London: Weidenfeld & Nicolson, 1961), p.218.
10 Richard Nixon, Radio and Television Address to the People of the Soviet Union, 28 May 1972.

119. Monitor HMS *M..33* in drydock at the Royal Navy Museum Portsmouth, the only ship which served on the Dvina River 1918–19 surviving today. (Public domain)

been awarded the DSC as a young Sub Lieutenant in *CMB 31* during the Kronstadt Raid in the Baltic Sea on the night of 18–19 August 1919, for which captain of *CMB 31*, Commander Claude Congreve Dobson, was awarded the VC. Boldero (who had lost an arm in an accident before the war) survived his imprisonment at the hands of the Japanese and was gazetted with the award of a DSC Bar after his release.

Monitor HMS *M.33*, the only surviving Royal Navy ship which saw service on the Dvina, remains on display at Portsmouth Historic Dockyard. After returning to the UK from Russia, *M.33* was laid up before recommissioning as HMS *Minerva* in 1924, serving as a tender at the RN torpedo and anti-submarine warfare school HMS *Vernon* until 1939 when she was converted to a boom defence workshop vessel on the River Clyde. Post war she continued to serve as a floating office and workshop at the Royal Clearance Yard, Gosport, before being acquired by Hampshire County Council in the late 1980s as one of only two surviving vessels which had seen service during the First World War. After considerable restoration from 1997, and under her original name, *M.33* has been on display in a dry dock having under gone a further restoration as recently as 2010.

Australian NRRF volunteer Private Norman Brooke (awarded the DCM for the 10 August 1919 attack on the Dvina River) recalled in an interview 65 years after his service in North Russia: 'I was glad I volunteered but I don't think any of us were very proud of having been there. I have never spoken to a soul about it. Not even my family know.'

'ELOPE' Force original AIF volunteer Sergeant John Kelly likely surmised the feelings of many North Russia veterans when he spoke to a *Sydney Morning Herald* reporter nearly 60 years after last setting foot in Russia: 'Had I known beforehand what the aim and nature of the mission was, I for one, would never have volunteered for the job.'

Part III

Russia 1918–20: Campaigns on Other Fronts

The Navy

Situated on Russia's Pacific coast close to the border with Chinese Manchuria, the city of Vladivostok was not annexed by the Imperial Russian Empire until the mid 19th Century. Originally founded as a naval outpost, the township gradually expanded as the Tsar's subjects began arriving from the east, attracted to the burgeoning prosperity of Russia's eastern ice-free port. After Russia's humiliating defeat in the Russo–Japanese war of 1905, the Tsar lost to the Japanese his only other ice-free port in the region at Port Arthur on the Korean Peninsula. After 15 years of construction, the completion of the Trans-Siberian Railway in 1916 directly connected west and east Russia and Vladivostok become the receiving point for thousands of tonnes of war supplies shipped across the Pacific from Canada and the United States.

On 3rd April 1918, in response to the murder of Japanese civilians by Bolshevik agents in the city, Allied ships in Vladivostok harbour (among them British, American and Japanese warships) put ashore landing parties to maintain order and protect their respective interests in the city. The cruiser HMS *Suffolk*, (which had arrived in Siberia in January) put ashore a small party of Royal Marines to guard the British Consulate. The 'bootnecks' became the first British troops to see service in Siberia as part of military intervention in Russian Civil War.

Further seamen and marines from *Suffolk* were landed on 22 May and by 29 June unrest in the city led to the Allies enacting martial law and taking charge of essential services and utilities. Around 250 Bolsheviks, determined not to be disarmed, barricaded themselves in a government building and refused to budge until they were forcibly ejected at bayonet point by soldiers of the Czech Legion.

On 2 August, a combined Allied naval and military force steamed into Archangel harbour in North Russia and attacked the city, removing the local *soviet* from power. Although tensions had already become strained between the British and Bolshevik governments, the Allied attack and capture of Archangel marked the commencement of open hostilities. Britain and the Bolshevik government were thus in a state of undeclared war.

As a result of the attack on Archangel and in order to support White Russian Admiral Kolchak's drive west along the Trans-Siberian Railway to Moscow, in early August orders were issued by the Admiralty in London to make preparations to mount two 12 pdr guns from HMS *Suffolk* onto railway trucks for use at the front against the Red Army in the Ussuri River district, 70 miles north of Vladivostok.

The first two guns, crewed by Plymouth Division Royal Marines (Sergeant J. Cridland, Corporals C. Hoit, E. Wallis, J. Purdie, C. Kingdom and 12 Privates) from *Suffolk* under the command of Captain John Bath, RMLI, and Warrant Gunner John Moffatt, RN, left for Ussuri on 16 August followed five days later by a further two rail mounted 12 pdrs with Royal Navy 'bluejacket' crews under Commander James Wolfe-Murray, RN. Additional preparations were made after Wolfe-Murray's departure to mount two further 12 pdrs and a single 6 inch gun for service.

After two weeks in action, Captain Bath's Royal Marine gun detachment returned to Vladivostok to resupply with ammunition followed soon after by Wolfe-Murray's Royal Navy detachment. There would be no rest for the RM/RN gunners. The day after their arrival in Vladivostok orders were

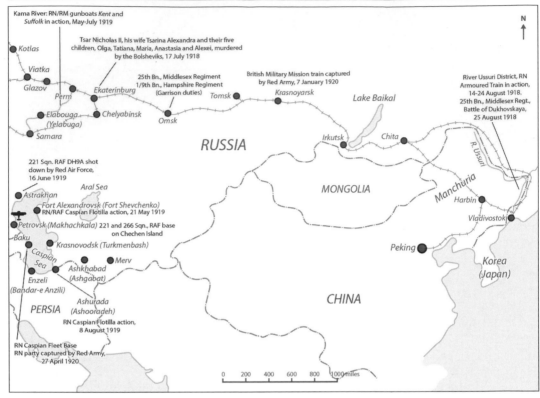

Map 4. Siberia, Caspian and Turkestan operations 1918–20

received to set out with the newly mounted 6 inch gun on a 3,500 mile long train long journey to Perm in western Siberia.

A number of awards were granted for service with the naval guns on the Ussuri during August 1918:

Distinguished Service Order (DSO):
     Commander James Wolfe Murray, RN
Distinguished Service Cross (DSC):
     Surgeon Lieutenant Neville Smith, RN
     Captain John Bath, RMLI
     Gunner John Moffatt, RN
Distinguished Service Medal (DSM):
     212126, Petty Officer George Rowe, RN
     PLY/14786, Sergeant John Potter Cridland, RMLI

After an epic train journey via Harbin, China, the Royal Marine 12 pdrs under Captain Bath and 6 inch gun under Commander Wolfe-Murray arrived at Ufa in western Siberia on 12 November 1918, the day after the Armistice on the Western Front, although word did not reach the men of the cessation of hostilities until the following day.

The 6 inch gun was first brought into action against Red troops on 16th November, followed by the 12 pdrs four days later. The temperature averaged minus 10 degrees and working the guns in such extreme conditions required exceptional stamina. Although the Bolshevik counterfire proved

120. The sheltered harbour at Vladivostok with warships in foreground. (Public domain)

inaccurate, one enemy shell did burst next to the British train sending shell splinters into its side although there were no casualties and little damage.

An enemy offensive towards the end of December drove the White troops back from their positions and the RM/RN trains were forced to flee along the congested line to Ufa which was reached two days after Christmas. There were some hairy moments during the escape when the boiler ran dry, the marines and sailors resorting to hand-carrying buckets of snow and water until steam could be raised again. The British trains escaped in time but most of those following behind were overwhelmed by the advancing Red Army.

Another close call followed on New Year's Day 1919 when a coupling broke, sending 20 carriages downhill into the engine of another train. Sabotage was suspected but could not be proven, fortunately there were no casualties. By the time the trains reached Omsk in late January the temperature was close to minus 15 degrees; the crews sitting out the savage winter in the barracks of the garrison from 25th Battalion, Middlesex Regiment.

After an uneventful couple of months in barracks the sailors and marine gunners reboarded their respective trains on 7 March 1919, and on 11 April had their firepower further increased with the arrival of a new 6 inch gun from HMS *Kent*, brought to Omsk by Canadian Army Service Corps soldiers of the Canadian Siberian Expeditionary Force (CSEF).

On 13 April both RN and RM gunners entrained for the long return trip to Vladivostok. By the time the eastern port city was reached on 6th May the original gun detachment from HMS *Suffolk* had travelled overland in excess of 12,000 miles, surely a record in the history of the Royal Navy and Royal Marines.

The officers of the gun detachment were subsequently assigned to the British 3n to Admiral Kolchack, commander of White Russian forces in Siberia, to assist with the formation of a small naval flotilla to operate on the Kama River, 5,000 miles inland from Vladivostok after the thaw. Commander Wolfe-Murray was appointed to lead the Naval Mission (considered a component of Major General Alfred Knox's larger 'British Military Mission' to Admiral Kolchak) and given acting rank of Army Captain. He proposed that the naval guns which had been mounted on train carriages for service at Ussuri could be transferred to converted gunboats and gun barges on the Kama River and be used as river-based artillery support with the White Russian flotilla at Perm.

Wolfe-Murray put the proposal to the Royal Marines of HM Ships *Kent* and *Suffolk* that a crew of volunteers would be needed to man the vessels. Of the 64 Marines on both cruisers all but one volunteered, the odd man being confined to the cells and having no vote. The volunteers were assigned according to need based upon the manning requirements of the single 6 inch gun and the four 12 pdrs which would be taken with the detachment to Perm, and not all volunteers could be chosen. The final detachment selected consisted of four officers, seven NCOs and 24 other ranks under the command of Captain Thomas Jameson, RMLI. His command was to become unique in the annals of the Royal Marines.

The British High Commission suggested that the detachment take along with it a young Russian officer to act as interpreter. The officer chosen for the job, Lieutenant Ewing, was an Anglo–Russian serving with Kolchak's forces. Born of an English father and Italian mother, Ewing had been educated in Paris where he qualified as a barrister and had been working in Russia when war had broken out. He at first attempted to join the British forces but was rejected due to poor eyesight before deciding to try the Russian Navy, with whom he was accepted. The Admiralty gave permission for Ewing to be granted the pay and allowances of a Lieutenant in the RNVR serving in the appointment of interpreter. After the detachment returned to Vladivostok later in the year Captain Jameson found a place for Ewing on General Knox's staff at the Military Mission. He was subsequently captured by the Red Army at Nijnuidrusk in February 1920, never to be seen or heard from again.

On 16th April 1919, the Marines' train finally pulled into the station at Omsk, the seat of Kolchak's White Russian Siberian Provisional Government. There, Captain Jameson met Commander Wolfe-Murray and two other officers comprising the entirety of the British Military Mission's Royal Navy representation at Omsk. After a 10 day wait the Marines boarded a train to take them across the Ural mountains on the last 1,000 miles of their journey from Vladivostok to Perm, which was reached on 28 April.

During the first night at Perm the men were woken by a tremendous roar. The Marines were understandably alarmed until they were told by humoured local Russians that it was only the sound of ice thawing on the Kama River with the onset of spring. Within 48 hours the three foot thick ice had broken up and been carried downriver by the current.

When Captain Jameson made contact with White Russian Admiral Smirnoff and his staff of the White Russian Kama River Flotilla, he was informed that two vessels had been earmarked for conversion into British-crewed gunboats, one a tug which used to work the Perm to Astrakhan (Caspian Sea) route and the other a river barge of a size suitable to mount the 6 inch gun.

The combat arm of the River Flotilla was organised into three divisions: 1st and 3rd Divisions operating from Perm on the Kama River and 2nd Division operating on the Ufa River, a tributary of the Kama. Each division consisted of six combat vessels, each armed with either 3 inch or 4.7 inch guns and several machine guns. Additionally, an anti-aircraft vessel and a 6 inch gun barge and various minelayers, repair and stores ships were assigned to each division. Equipment and supplies were scarce, and improvisation and imagination, particularly in converting field artillery to naval guns, was required.

Both of the vessels assigned to the British for conversion had to be fitted out from scratch and the naval guns fitted and mounted. The gunboat was christened *Kent* and the barge *Suffolk* after the Marines' two parent ships docked at Vladivostok, some 4,500 miles away.

The smaller *Kent* was 170 foot long and 40 foot wide with two eight foot paddles on each side. The *Suffolk* had its own tug for towing and was large enough that the 6 inch gun could be fired without fear of capsize. The two vessels were berthed within close proximity to the Motovilska railway engine factory where the mountings for the British guns were manufactured.

Complicating the installation of the 12 pdrs, the British Naval Mission had ordered that the pedestals for the guns be removed so that overhead cover could be installed for the long train journey, the plan being that pedestals could be manufactured locally once the train arrived at Perm. Without these pedestals the guns would have sat much lower on deck than regulation height, forcing the gunners to kneel down in order to load, aim and fire the guns. A wooden substitute was manufactured at the local Russian works and bolted to the newly reinforced deck of *Kent*. After a series of test firings at different elevations the pedestals proved to be up to the task.

Whilst work continued on the pedestals for the 12 pdrs, the much larger task of installing the 6 inch gun onto the deck of *Suffolk* was ongoing, chiefly owing to the fact that a crane capable of lifting the seven tonne barrel and equally heavy mounting was hard to find in Perm in 1919. Needless to say, converting a tug into a gunboat entails a lot of work. The decks had to be reinforced, sleeping quarters built as well as storerooms, magazines for ammunition and armour plating around the gun platforms and wheelhouse.

The skilled labour force at Perm were so overstretched due to so many vessels struggling to be converted at the same time that the Marines had to do much of the work themselves. It may have been the long period of boredom and inactivity during the journey to Omsk and then Perm, but the men fell to the task with enthusiasm and within a surprisingly short time *Kent* was ready on 7th May to proceed downstream to take her place with 1st Division.

Two days later, *Kent* passed Sarapaul, some 300 miles from Perm, where Captain Jameson met with Kama Flotilla commander Admiral Smirnoff and his staff. In the meantime *Suffolk* had left Perm and was heading downriver to conduct final testing before joining the division. During a test firing of the 6 inch gun it was discovered that the springs were faulty. This had been caused when the gun was first test fired from a railway carriage when the recoil cylinder fluid had been frozen, although the problem had not been discovered until the firing trials on the Kama. Installing washers to strengthen the springs meant the gun could be fired but its performance was greatly reduced. Spare springs would have to make the long train journey from Vladivostok to Perm but in the meantime *Suffolk* would continue on without them.

HMS *Suffolk* arrived at Elabouga on 14 May 1919 where it was promptly attacked by two Bolshevik seaplanes. Three small bombs dropped by the attacking aircraft straddled either side of *Suffolk* but no damage was done. Anti-aircraft fire from the flotilla forced the first seaplane down and soon after the second seaplane also landed and surrendered. It was discovered that engine trouble had forced down the first aircraft, whilst its wingman, seeing the first plane landing, had assumed that the flotilla they had just attacked was in fact their own. It was a costly mistake for the second pilot to make, as both men were executed by the White Russians shortly after their capture.

Later in the day the Red Flotilla made its first appearance, opening fire on the guard ship *Gregiasshi* of 3rd Division. The Bolshevik armament far outranged the White Russians' 3 inch guns and in a brisk action a shell penetrated *Gregiasshi*'s boiler, putting her out of action. Six ships of the White Flotilla steamed through to take on the Bolsheviks but their fire did not register any hits due to the limited range of their own guns, whilst a Red Army field battery in command of the high ground ashore kept the White flotilla at a distance.

Suffolk opened fire on one of the Red Army batteries concealed next to a church in the village of Salkoka and managed to drive the gunners from their positions. *Kent* was also in action but not able to engage the enemy as accurately as her sister ship due to the fact that no range finders were available, and the Marines were relying exclusively on observation and estimation to make corrections to their fire. The British Kama River detachment's first action against the enemy had been fought with mixed results.

On 23rd May the flotilla was ordered to make its way down the Kama to Elabouga after dusk. The Bolsheviks were in possession of the low ground and the British were advised to expect contact with the enemy. Taking all precautions to avoid detection, the flotilla arrived at Elabouga at 0340 the following day. The intelligence department reported that Bolshevik vessels were expected to make their way upstream at about midday to provide artillery support to Red Army units advancing on the northern bank the river in a drive to capture Elabouga.

At 1300 a forward guard ship reported that Bolshevik vessels were approaching. Thirty minutes later the White flotilla with the two British gunboats weighed anchor and advanced to contact with the enemy. Jameson wrote of the engagement:

> The enemy had chosen a good position with a dark background (their ships were painted dark green) at a range of 8 versts from Elabouga (approx. 5 miles), and immediately opened fire on our base. Though under heavy fire our Flotilla lost no time in getting within range. Fire was opened by Kent at 8,100 yards at the leading enemy ship. We used lyddite as the Russian ships only possessed common shell, and we could identify our fall of shot by the conspicuous yellow colour of explosion. At first we were short but soon our approach brought us within maximum range, and, laying on the flashes of the enemy guns, effective fire caused the leading ship Terek to beach herself in a burning condition. The Enemy had 11 ships in action and after their leading ship was lost the remainder sought to turn and proceed downstream. Kent's fire was directed at their second ship first by the one of her after guns which could bear by firing over the intervening land on the inside of the river bend, and then by the two foremost guns. Repeated hits by lyddite were scored on her at a range of 4,700 yards. This ship, named Roosal, was their Flagship and she also was compelled to make for the bank, reaching it in a sinking condition and burning fiercely. Her crew jumped on shore wearing white life-belts and provided an ideal target for our machine guns.[1]

The volume of fire took the Bolsheviks by surprise and quickly demoralised their crews. One of the White vessels proceeded alongside the Bolshevik flagship in an attempt to salvage her while the 3rd Division Flagship followed by *Kent* continued the chase. As the ships rounded the next curve in the river the Red flotilla was almost out of view, however one straggler presented an excellent target to the crew of *Kent* and was sunk next to the river bank, the survivors scurrying ashore.

As *Kent* and Captain Fiersdosiff in the flagship *Gordi* rounded the next bend they were met with a hail of fire. *Gordi* was badly mauled, both her foremost guns knocked out and the bridge taking a hit. Fiersdosiff requested that *Kent* move into a position to cover *Gordi's* withdrawal. By burning fuel oil *Kent* was able to make an effective smokescreen and cover *Gordi's* retreat by bursting shrapnel above the enemy's heads as both ships withdrew. The Red Flotilla did not push their luck and decided not to follow. The superior range of *Suffolk's* 6 inch gun gave covering fire to the flotilla as it withdrew to safer waters.

During the action *Kent* had fired 288 shells and *Suffolk* 42. Neither of the two British vessels had been damaged but both had received a few minor shell splinters. The battle had been won by the White Flotilla, and the attacking Bolsheviks were repulsed from Elabouga without loss but it had not been an overwhelming victory and before long the Red Flotilla was bound to make another appearance.

Reports were received that Red Army troops had succeeded in taking the junction of the Bielaya and Kama Rivers and were making attempts to destroy some White Russian barges that had been cut off from their tugs when the Red troops arrived. These barges contained many tonnes of stores critical to the operation of the flotilla and Smirnoff decided to make an attempt to recapture them rather than risk their loss to the enemy.

Grosni, the only available White ship that could attempt a rescue, was promptly despatched. Arriving at the mouth of the Bielaya, Red troops were waiting in ambush and opened fire with rifles and machine guns causing several casualties on board *Grosni*, including the gunnery officer. But the valiant little ship managed to come alongside one of the barges and hook a wire around the anchor cable. As *Grosni* slowly made steam the anchor was raised and the tug towed away under fire.

---

1   Thomas Jameson, *Expedition to Siberia, 1919: The Great War, Eastern Front* (Portsmouth, England: Royal Marines Historical Society, Special Publication No. 10, 1987), p.29.

The advance of Red troops to the junction of the Bielaya and Kama Rivers forced Smirnoff to order the White Flotilla to make a strategic withdrawal to a more secure position under fire. Four of the flotilla's abandoned barges were set alight by the Bolsheviks and used as illumination to shoot at the passing White vessels. Some Bolsheviks actually boarded one of the captured barges and opened up an intense fire from it although their shots were high and only the passing ships funnels and masts were hit. *Kent* covered the other vessels running the gauntlet of Bolshevik fire with 12 pdrs and machine guns but the effectiveness of the fire in keeping the Bolsheviks' heads down in the dark was uncertain.

During this engagement *Suffolk* was targeting Red Army units at the mouth of the river and later reports from Army HQ confirmed that at least one enemy battery had been disabled by their fire. *Suffolk*'s bombardment of the village of Dirabigski also drove Red troops from a strong position in the town which threatened to rain down fire down on the passing White Flotilla.

Although it had already given good service, *Suffolk*'s 6 inch gun was still giving its crew trouble and it was decided to send the barge to the repair ship at Sarapaul. Each time the gun was fired it had to be run out manually as there was not enough compression in the damaged springs. Sarapaul was a small city on the Kama about 50 miles from the junction of the Bielaya which the River Flotilla had been using as a base.

Facing not only the Red flotilla on the Kama, the Marines also had to contend with local Russian rations of a consistently poor quality. Jameson's description of the rations was distinctly unappetising:

> Black bread, a loaf usually some eighteen inches across, meat in casks, often bear's meat, which had been packed into the cask with ice and salt before the end of the winter, and potatoes. There was little variation and not infrequently the bread was sour, even moist and green at the centre of the loaf whereas the meat had not always kept edible owing to faulty casks.[2]

Whilst *Suffolk* was undergoing repair at Sarapaul, *Kent*'s engines began to give trouble and the gunboat was ordered out of the line for an overhaul. On 2 June, orders were received for *Kent* to proceed 25 miles downstream to Nikola Berezooka. Only a few minutes after passing beneath the span of Sarapaul bridge, Captain Jameson observed a battery of Red artillery digging in only two miles from the city. Returning to Sarapaul, Jameson notified Admiral Smirnoff of what he had observed. The Admiral replied that a message had just been transmitted on the wireless (the Admiral's flagship was the only one so equipped) that Sarapaul was under attack. The flotilla commanders held a conference where it was decided to send *Grosni* and *Kent* (the two fastest ships) forward to hold and harass the enemy until the remainder of the flotilla could arrive. Jameson recalled:

> The sun was coming up, an uneasy silence prevailed and though we observed some troops moving, it was deemed prudent to maintain observation only until such time as the rest of the Flotilla arrived. At 5.35am the Flotilla, carrying barges and tugs appeared coming around the bend below the bridge, the 1st Division engaging enemy artillery on the right bank. At 5.50am Grosni and Kent were told to lead the Flotilla and all ships to proceed at full speed. Targets were difficult to locate and enemy guns put down barrage fire on point after point upstream into which we ran unavoidably at maximum speed. We opened fire independently at any moving troops or occupied buildings. I pointed out a field gun firing at us through the back door of a house close to the edge of the water, and a lyddite shell blew house and all sky high. Captain. Fierdosiff, referring to the Kent, made the remark: 'they used their guns like revolvers and it was a heartening sight'.[3]

2   *Ibid.*, p.31.
3   *Ibid.*, p.33.

Despite the number of Bolshevik guns firing over open sights, only one ship of the flotilla immediately astern of *Kent* was sunk. *Kent* itself was near-missed on several occasions, one shell bursting on the port side slightly damaging the paddle wheel. Jameson continues:

> Another shell burst abreast the foremost gun platform just as a box of 6 shells, with points upward, was being brought up by a gun number from the magazine below, and I noticed that this man's face was covered with blood. I thought the bursting shell might have been the cause, but actually the blast of the near miss had blown the box upwards and the shell points had hit his face, making a superficial but nonetheless bloody mess. Our one casualty![4]

That the Red Army could set up field artillery virtually within sight of Sarapaul, a White Army HQ and garrison town, and launch an attack with complete surprise was a damning indictment on the White command. It also pointed to the complete lack of military intelligence and situational awareness so crucial to a battlefield commander.

After the battle at Sarapaul, Sergeant Alfred Taylor (Senior Royal Marine NCO) went ashore from *Suffolk* to stretch his legs and take his dog (also the detachment mascot) for a walk. Once ashore Taylor witnessed the filthy condition of the White soldiers and their equipment and the columns of refugees fleeing the fighting. Taylor was so absorbed by the human tragedy unfolding before him that he almost missed his launch back to *Suffolk*.

No sooner had the small launch sent to collect Taylor touched land, a rush was made by panic-stricken White soldiers and refugees towards it, almost swamping the vessel. To save the launch from being overturned, Taylor had to threaten the crowd with his revolver:

> To make matters worse, after I had got into the boat, I found that our dog was still on shore so I ordered the boat to put back to get him, and then there was a real row. To finish up with I threatened to shoot the whole damn lot of them if I had any more trouble, and what was more, I meant it! By this time the Reds were already in the town and coming down the main street. I got my way and went back for the dog, and then there was some more fun. Everything seemed against me; the dog was in for a skylark and as I went for him he would run away. The people in the boat were still swearing, but they knew now that I would not come without him and so they helped me catch him. We were away and just in time for, as we shoved off, the Reds were fairly close, their cavalry leading four deep.[5]

On 7 June, *Kent* and *Suffolk* were kept busy engaging Red Army artillery and infantry near the town of Galiana which changed hands several times during the fighting but was finally lost to the Bolsheviks. The following day fire from *Suffolk*'s 6 inch gun forced an enemy infantry unit to withdraw into the cover of a wooded area. As the Bolsheviks came out the other side of the forest, gunboats of the Flotilla opened fire with lyddite and shrapnel causing many casualties.

The water level of the Kama falls significantly in late summer which led to an unexpected lull in the fighting. Both sides took advantage of the relative quiet to reposition and resupply their units in the field. *Kent* and *Suffolk* spent much of their time ferrying troops and supplies from one side of the river to the other.

Despite the chaos and disorganisation, plagues of mosquitoes and the poor quality of rations, the health and morale of the British detachment remained very high. In recognition of their sterling service, Admiral Kolchak awarded the Marines a number of decorations, including St. Vladimir, St. Anne and St. George awards. When the British High Commissioner at Vladivostok was notified of

---

4   *Ibid.*
5   *Ibid.*, p.34.

the awards he informed Jameson that the British government would no longer recognise the Omsk government and all British forces in Siberia were to be withdrawn. As a consequence of the non-recognition of Kolchak's government, the decorations could not be accepted and would have to be returned. Jameson recorded, 'This was a disappointment as they would have been a treasured souvenir to the recipients of this expedition, and especially so when we learnt that Russian awards to British servicemen on the north and southern fronts had been accepted.'[6]

In early June, Jameson had a surprise visit by intelligence officers of Admiral Smirnoff's staff wishing to interrogate *Kent*'s Russian engineering officer and one of his local mechanics. During the investigations, incriminating documents were discovered (or planted) in the mechanic's kit. The papers were claimed to be irrefutable proof of a plan being hatched by the two men to sabotage and scuttle *Kent*. The mechanic was summarily executed without trial and the engineering officer taken away for further interrogation, likely eventually meeting the same fate as the mechanic.

The plot to sink *Kent* and the instability of the White Russian forces led to a series of rumours amongst the Marines of impending defeats and Bolshevik plots to sink their vessels whilst they were on board asleep. The rumours began to take a toll on crew morale so Jameson took steps to isolate the Russian and British crews from any further contact with each other, White troops or civilians where possible.

On 12th June, *Suffolk* was again in action together with two White Russian gun barges which engaged and forced out of action three enemy artillery batteries and also destroyed a large ammunition dump. The Royal Marine gunners had become so skilled in the use of the 12 pdr and 6 inch guns that they could sight, range and fire on the enemy in a very short time.

By late summer 1919 the Kama was becoming too shallow for the larger ships to operate and the flotilla was forced to gradually make its way back to deeper water at Perm as the water level fell. As the gunboats moved upstream they stopped occasionally to pick up refugees fleeing eastwards whenever it was safe to do so. In discussions with Captain Jameson, Admiral Smirnoff agreed that once the river level dropped to a point where the bulk of the flotilla had withdrawn to Perm, the guns on *Suffolk* and *Kent* would be of little use. Jameson suggested removing the guns from the two vessels and transferring them onto field mountings for service ashore where artillery was in desperately short supply.

When Jameson finally arrived at Perm, due to the chaotic White command situation he was unable to ascertain any real reports of enemy movements and was concerned that *Suffolk* (*Kent* had already returned to Perm because of her deeper draught) would be left behind by the retreating White Army and the crew completely cut off. As a result of the worsening situation and collapse of Kolchak's forces, Wolfe-Murray's British Naval Mission had already withdrawn its staff to Omsk.

Before the Naval Mission had left Perm, Wolfe-Murray had delegated to Jameson the responsibility of withdrawing *Kent* and *Suffolk* in the event of Perm being threatened with capture. Although reports of enemy movements were intermittent, inaccurate or non-existent, there was little doubt that the front was collapsing.

The Russians pleaded with Jameson not to withdraw but the Red advance and fragility of the White line meant that there was only one prudent decision that could be made. *Kent* was withdrawn from the line and its guns and ammunition removed and transferred onto the detachment train which had brought them to the Siberian interior. Soon after the decommissioning of *Kent* had commenced, Jameson received news that the Bolsheviks were within 70 miles of Perm on the main railway line. This left the only viable escape route as the single line running east to Ekaterinburg, a distance of 300 miles.

---

6   *Ibid.*, p.36.

The following day, in the wake of further reports of White retreats, the order was given for *Suffolk* to return to Perm immediately. Upon her arrival, Gunner Cedric Clarke, RN, reported to Jameson that *Suffolk* had exhausted its ammunition the previous day but had no way to communicate this fact and without any orders to withdraw to Perm had remained on station. In the two days that *Kent* had left *Suffolk* and returned to Perm, *Suffolk* had expended all of its 256 rounds of 6 inch ammunition against the enemy.

Chaos and panic had set in at Perm as thousands of refugees, clutching as many of their most valuable possessions as they could carry, fled eastwards through the city. The northern railway was packed to capacity with refugees and clogged up to military traffic.

As *Suffolk* arrived, work was immediately begun on dismounting her 6 inch gun. This task was completed solely by *Suffolk*'s crew, there being no local Russian labour in the chaos available for the task. The crew had not slept for two days but set to the task without complaint. Work was temporarily interrupted when all the spare ammunition, some hundreds of rounds of both 6 inch and 12 pdr arrived in a sinking barge and all hands were diverted to unloading the ammunition before the barge sank.

After a few difficulties with inadequate tools, the 6 inch gun from *Suffolk* was successfully remounted onto a train carriage, the difficult task of moving the guns, ammunition, stores and equipment being carried out almost entirely by the Marines themselves. With the permission of Flotilla Commander Admiral Smirnoff, both *Kent* and *Suffolk* met the inglorious end of being towed out to deeper water and scuttled.

Although the guns had been mounted on railway carriages with ammunition and stores there was still no engine, so an armed party of Marines was despatched to the engine repair sheds nearby where they found the remaining engines getting up steam for an imminent departure. Gentle persuasion (or perhaps not so gentle) convinced the Russian stationmaster to relinquish one of the engines and crew to the British. With an armed escort of Marines on the footplate all the way, the engine made its way back to the siding where the remainder of the detachment had been waiting without incident.

With every carriage near overflowing with Marines, equipment, ammunition and stores, the train steamed out of Perm on 29 June, only hours before the city came under enemy shellfire. With no defence to speak of, Perm fell to the Bolsheviks later the same day.

The engine pulling the British train broke down early the following morning and with no possibility of repair a difficult decision had to be made by Jameson. It was still a further 300 miles to Ekaterinburg where he might hope to find another train to take the Marines further eastwards. Jameson decided to source horses and *droskies* to carry rations and equipment for the trek whilst the men would march the 300 miles on foot with as few rest stops as possible lest Red cavalry catch them before they reached safety.

The Royal Marine detachment began unloading stores in preparation for the trek (the guns would be disabled and abandoned) when unexpectedly an engine came steaming up from the east. The train had been sent from Ekaterinburg by Admiral Smirnoff on learning that the detachment had been forced to use an engine taken from the repair workshop of dubious serviceability. The Marines were understandably relieved to not have to make the 300 mile forced march on foot and the remainder of the journey to Omsk was without incident.

On arrival in the relative, albeit temporary, security of Omsk, the detachment volunteered to crew an armoured train and head back up the line to continue the fight but their offer was refused. The White forces already had several armoured trains which could not operate because the lines were so congested with refugees. In any case the Admiralty had decided to withdraw the Marines and orders had been received to return to Vladivostok as soon as suitable train accommodation became available.

Although the Marines could prepare to defend against the danger of a derailment from saboteurs – an extra engine with a truck carrying spare rails preceded the main train a mile or so ahead, and

121. General Alfred Knox, CB, CMG (seated left), and officers of the British
Military Mission to Admiral Kolchak, summer 1919. (IWM Q81130)

additionally, armed lookouts were posted on top of some of the carriages – an unseen danger that remained ever present was the scourge of typhus sweeping across the country, taking the lives of thousands of Russian refugees. With few facilities to treat the sick or adequately bury the dead, bodies were routinely disposed of by throwing outside an open carriage door onto the railway siding below.

Vladivostok was finally reached on 18 August, 52 days after the detachment had set out from Perm. Jameson marched at the head of the British Kama River Flotilla detachment to Vladivostok docks to board HMS *Carlisle*, accompanied by the band of the 25th Battalion, Middlesex Regiment (who would leave Siberia for the UK via Canada on 7 September followed by 1/9th Battalion, Hampshire Regiment on 1 November). The lower decks of *Carlisle* were cleared and a roaring cheer given by the ships company.

And so ended a minor but fascinating (although largely forgotten) episode in the history of the Royal Marines. The officers and men of the detachment had performed sterling service and the Admiralty was not sparse in awarding decorations for their efforts:

Gunboat *Kent* (4 x 12 pdr)

Distinguished Service Order (DSO):
    Captain Thomas Jameson, RMLI
Distinguished Service Cross (DSC):
    Mate Horace Noel Barnes, RN
Meritorious Service Medal (MSM):
    PO/16219, Corporal George Henry Odey, RMLI
    PO/17719, Lance Corporal Dudley Gerald Stepney, RMLI
    PO/11169, Private Edward Nixon Stevenson, RMLI
    PLY/15043, Private Frank James Williamson, RMLI

Gunbarge *Suffolk* (1 x 6 inch)

Distinguished Service Cross (DSC):
>   Gunner Cedric William Clarke, RN

Distinguished Service Medal (DSM):
>   PO/14899, Sergeant Arthur Taylor, RMLI

Meritorious Service Medal (MSM):
>   M/8666, Armourer Crew 1st Class J. Whyte, RN
>   PO/19113 Private James Brown, RMLI
>   PLY/15061 Private Albert Haile, RMLI
>   PLY/16418 Private Melbourne James Netherway, RMLI

Mentioned in Despatches (MiD):
>   PLY/15154, Corporal Edwin Frank, RMLI
>   Surgeon Lieutenant H.C Joyce, RN (borne in HQ ship *Mariana*)

The Army

Despite the large number of British and Commonwealth soldiers who served in Siberia, 1918–19, encounters with the Red Army were very few. Although Siberia was geographically the largest theatre of military intervention in Russia it was also the relative quietest in terms of action with the enemy. The British and Canadian role in Siberia was almost exclusively to train and equip White Russian Admiral Kolchak's forces and not to take part in offensive operations.

To this end the 4,200 strong Canadian Siberian Expeditionary Force (CSEF) despatched to Siberia in late 1918 was entirely a garrison and non-combatant force. Indeed the CSEF did not suffer a single battle casualty during seven months of operations in Siberia. The force was commanded by Major General James H. Elmsley, a cavalry officer who had served with the Royal Canadian Dragoons in South Africa during the Boer War, where he had been wounded. From June 1916 he had commanded 8th Canadian Infantry Brigade on the Western Front but was invalided home in May 1918 just in time to be appointed to command of the CSEF in August of the same year.

An unusual component of the CSEF were the approximately 135 Russo–Canadians selected to join the force and formed into a 'Russo–Canadian Company'. All had served with the Canadian Expeditionary Force (CEF) on the Western Front but had conflicted loyalties in the campaign against the Bolsheviks. A number expressed that whilst they were willing to fight Germans, they would not fight fellow Russians, be they Bolshevik or not. As a result the company was broken up, 35 of their number being discharged and the remainder sent back to their units.

Despite the failure of the ill-conceived Russo–Canadian company a number of Russian names still appear on the CSEF nominal roll. Corporal Filip Konowal was a Ukrainian-born volunteer who had been awarded the Victoria Cross with 47th Battalion, CEF, for leading his section in mopping up German bunkers and machine gun emplacements at Hill 70 in August 1917, his citation noting that during two days' fighting he had alone killed 'at least sixteen of the enemy.'[7]

Ably assisted by CSEF supply units, the British landed enough supplies at Vladivostok to fully equip 200,000 men with everything from artillery, rifles, machine guns, munitions, equipment, boots and medical stores. To facilitate the moving of supplies westward, an American Railway Service Corps contingent was tasked to repair the Trans-Siberian railway and keep the stock cars rolling. Commander of the 8,000 strong American Expeditionary Force Siberia (AEF Siberia), General William S. Graves' mandate from US President Woodrow Wilson was specifically non-combatant, to ensure the safe arrival of the Czech Legion at Vladivostok and to protect supply dumps near the

---

7   *The London Gazette*, 23 November 1917.

docks. Unlike their British and Canadian allies, US troops saw a number of brisk fights with Red troops in Siberia during summer 1919 and sustained a number of casualties.

The CSEF was originally intended to be an all volunteer force and whilst there was a surplus of officer volunteers, more than could be accepted, there was a shortfall of enlisted volunteers, leading to some 1,600 men conscripted under the Military Service Act being drafted into the contingent. The Canadian government remained uneasy about sending conscripted men to Siberia but did so out of necessity. The issue of the despatch of conscripted men to Siberia was raised by William Heart, Member for Sault Ste. Marie, in a 10 March 1919 session of the Canadian parliament:

> Canada committed a national crime in sending to Russia, to participate in a domestic quarrel, men who had no business to interfere with this country's striving after freedom, no matter how blind its efforts may be. The crime is doubly heinous when you think that men who refused to go were nevertheless forced to embark for Siberia. It is a flagrant violation of the law of the country which allows men to be sent beyond the borders of Canada 'for the defence of Canada' only. No matter what distortion is made of the phraseology of this clause it can never be claimed that men sent to Siberia to interfere in the quarrels of factions at war with one another are fighting 'for the defence of Canada'.[8]

In fact the only all-volunteer unit in the CSEF was not military at all but rather 'B' Squadron of the RNWMP. The squadron had been formed to act in a paramilitary role as the force cavalry component of the CSEF. The only incident in which the mounted policemen came close to encountering the enemy was a train derailment on 4th June 1919 in which Private Philip Bossard was awarded the Military Medal for saddling up uninjured horses and rounding up those which had broken away and bringing them back to the train. Farrier Sergeant J.E. 'Ted' Margetts was awarded the Meritorious Service Medal for the same incident for organising White Russian soldiers to rescue injured from the derailed carriages. Bossard's decoration would be the only 'in action with the enemy' gallantry award made to the CSEF.

Authorised in August 1918, the advance party of 680 CSEF men (including one officer and 20 other ranks, RNWMP) sailed for Vladivostok from Victoria, British Colombia, on board the Canadian Pacific liner *Empress of Japan* on 11 October. Arriving two weeks later, the first Canadian troops to set foot in Siberia were played ashore by the brass section of a Czech Legion band. A further 898 men of the 259th Overseas Battalion sailed from Victoria on 22 December, disembarking at Vladivostok on 13–14 January 1919.

The main body of 1,808 troops, mostly from the 260th Battalion and associated brigade units embarked at Victoria on *Teesta* and *Protesliaus* on 21 and 26 December respectively, the latter after an elaborate Christmas dinner provided by local councillors. Conditions on board *Protesliaus* were horrendous and the men had a terrible time during the three week journey. A court of enquiry held the following year determined that the ship was overcrowded and food and accommodations inadequate.

Problems had however begun even before embarkation. During the march to the quay, a platoon of soldiers of the 259th Battalion, mostly men conscripted under the Military Service Act, refused to embark. Officers fired their pistols into the air and ordered loyal soldiers within the battalion to remove their canvas belts and whip the mutineers into submission. The march towards the quay continued escorted by an armed guard to quell any further dissent and after a short delay the battalion was embarked as ordered. Approximately 12 men charged with 'mutiny and wilful disobedience' did not embark and were court-martialled but their sentences commuted with the withdrawal of the CSEF from Vladivostok in mid 1919.

Of the incident, Lieutenant Stuart Tompkins in a letter to his wife recalled:

---

8   MacLaren, *Canadians in Russia 1918–19*, p.187.

122. A section of Canadian Machine Gun Corps serving with
CSEF. (City of Vancouver Archives, Mil P41)

You may not know that we have had quite a lot of trouble here. This is strictly 'sub rosa' and is not to be repeated. There has been a lot of socialistic agitation here and two weeks ago there was a meeting here largely attended by 259th men – French Canadians. At this meeting the Siberian Expedition was discussed and a strong resolution taken against it. Last Sunday night our fellows went down and broke up the meeting but the harm was done. When two companies of the 259th were marching down town yesterday to embark some of the men were egged on by agitators refused to go on. They were (forcibly) escorted.[9]

After a nightmare journey across the Pacific during which Private Harold Butler was killed by a sliding locker which had broken loose from its mountings in heavy weather, and the ship lost its port propeller, *Protesliaus* finally limped into Vladivostok harbour on 15 January 1919.

Vladivostok in early 1919 was a diverse but miserable city. One officer described his impressions of the 'dirty, evil-smelling seaport':

Trade was almost at a standstill. Penniless refugees thronged the town, crime and licence grew unchecked, and there was universal and feverish speculation in foreign exchanges. On the streets an extraordinary motley of races, creeds and tongues passed and repassed. Allied soldiers, carefree and with money to spend – Americans, British, Canadians, French, Italians, Japanese, Chinese, and Serbs – British, French and American sailors, tanned by the open sea and now ashore in search of a girl or a scrap; ex-Tsarist officers in grey greatcoats lined with scarlet silk; Russian soldiers in the homely drab supplied by the British Government; a sprinkling of soberly dressed foreign consuls and businessmen; soldiers of the new nations, Poles, Letts and Czechoslovaks, many of them ex-prisoners of war, now clad in fresh uniforms; fat Chinese merchants and lean coolies; Koreans in flowing white with strange stove-pipe hats; bearded

9   Doris Pieroth, *A Canadian's Road to Russia: The Letters of Stuart Ramsay Tompkins: Letters from the Great War Decade* (Edmonton: University of Alberta Press, 1989), p.358.

Russian priests trailed by numerous offspring; fierce looking Cossacks in mighty fur caps; tight-lipped American nurses in hard blue hats and billowing cloaks; pretty ladies with scarlet lips, high French heels, and expensive furs; Jews in gabardines and Jews in soiled frock-coats; hook-nosed Armenians; ragged refugees; indescribable beggars; lean-faced Turks, Germans and Austrians – prisoners of war awaiting repatriation; fat speculators; decent bourgeois; hooligans; grey-clad militiamen; a never ending stream of polyglot humanity.[10]

After spending most of its time in Siberia performing garrison duties around Vladivostok, in early 1919 the CSEF received orders to prepare to embark for home. General Elmsley and the last of the CSEF embarked at Vladivostok for Canada on board the transport *Montenegro* on 5 June 1919. Although no such concession was made to Canadian soldiers serving in North Russia sent home the same month, permission was given for a number of volunteers from the CSEF to remain behind in Russia on attachment to the British Military and Railway Missions; some even volunteered to work in a civilian capacity with the Canadian Red Cross.

Particularly unpopular amongst 'B' Squadron, RNWMP (one of the last CSEF units to embark for home) was the decision to leave behind all CSEF mounts to the White Russians. Some of the horses had been ridden by RNWMP on police duties in Canada. Reluctantly the horses were handed over and the last of 'B' Squadron embarked for home in August.

Despite seeing no action against the Bolsheviks, the CSEF left behind one officer and 17 other ranks buried in Siberia not including Private Butler, killed on the *Protesliaus* en route, who was buried at sea. Most of those who died succumbed to pneumonia, meningitis and influenza but Lieutenant Henry Thring of the 260th Battalion, the sole CSEF officer fatality, was to die under particularly tragic circumstances.

Having served in South Africa during the Boer War, Thring enlisted in Princess Patricia's Canadian Light Infantry in December 1914 and served on the Western Front where he was thrice wounded. By 1917, shattered in mind and body, Thring was invalided back to Canada in a state of complete physical and mental exhaustion. After eight months in a convalescent hospital he was classed as fit for active service just in time to volunteer for the CSEF, sailing for Vladivostok on the *Protesliaus* during that ship's calamitous voyage. On 18 March his body was found in a ditch with a self-inflicted gunshot wound to the head, his right hand still clutching his service revolver with torn letters and photographs of his wife lying beside his body.

A court of inquiry held into the death established from witness statements that Thring had been suffering pain from his wounds, was in a state of 'constant morose depression' and was terrified of sleep due to reoccurring nightmares. Witnesses testified that Thring had made the comment, 'I hope that we have a clash with the Bolsheviki so I can go out clean.'[11] The finding of the court was that Thring took his life in a fit of temporary insanity caused by a head wound sustained in action in France. In order that his wife's pension might not be jeopardised, members of the court officially listed his cause of death as 'accidentally killed'. Like other CSEF fatalities, Henry Thring was buried with full military honours in Churkin Russian Naval Cemetery (CWGC) where his grave remains today.

The leadership of the Japanese force in Siberia (70,000 strong, more than all the other Allied contingents combined) were quite willing, overly eager in fact, to fight the Bolsheviks but only if the engagements intersected with Japan's colonial expansion interests into maritime Russian and Manchuria. Before the war had ended in November 1918 the Allies had hoped that the Japanese in Siberia would be sent westwards to form a new Eastern Front against the Central Powers however the Japanese, although technically allies of Britain, had absolutely no intention of advancing any

---

10   Phelps Hodges, *BRITMIS: A Great Adventure of the War. Being an account of Allied intervention in Siberia and of an escape across the Gobi to Peking* (London: Jonathan Cape, 1931), p.54.

11   J.E. Skuce, *CSEF, Canada's Soldiers in Siberia, 1918–19* (Access to History Publications, undated), p.17.

123. Farriers and veterinary soldiers of CSEF at work in
Siberia. (City of Vancouver Archives, 99-662)

further than Irkutsk, it was not in their interests to do so. The ambitions of the Japanese were
exclusively to expand their influence and control of Siberia, Manchuria and the Pacific, ambitions
which would come to a head with the invasion of China in 1937 and attacks on Pearl Harbour and
Malaya four years later.

Although theoretically allies, the Japanese showed only slightly less disdain for White Russians
than Bolsheviks and behaved very much like an occupying army. Lieutenant Colonel John Ward,
CO, 25th Middlesex recorded:

> I was standing on Nikolsk platform waiting for a train, there was a crowd of Russian people, a Japanese
> sentry was standing near. He quite suddenly darted forward and jammed the butt of his rifle in the centre
> of a Russian officer's back which knocked him flat on the floor in such pain that he rolled about for a
> few minutes, while the Jap, grinning, held his bayonet at the 'On Guard'. No Russian, though there were
> many standing near, had the pluck to shoot him, and not wishing to mix myself up in the affair, I took no
> action but watched further developments.
>
> Ten minutes later another Jap sentry repeated the performance, this time the victim was a well-dressed
> Russian lady. So cowed were the Russian people that this time even her friends were afraid to help her. I
> stepped forward to assist, the Jap standing over me, but continued to laugh as though it was a huge joke. A
> few Tommies were attracted to the spot, and the Jap saw that things were beginning to take a serious turn.
>
> I proceeded to the Japanese Headquarters situated in a carriage near by and reported the occurrence.
> This officer seemed astonished that I should interfere on behalf of mere Russians, who, he said, may have
> been Bolsheviks for all he knew, and enquired whether the sentry had ever treated me so. I answered
> that the first Japanese that touches an English officer or soldier in my presence will be a dead man. This

seemed to surprise the Japanese officer, who pointed out that the Japanese were in occupation of Siberia, and were entitled to do what they liked.[12]

The 25th Battalion, Middlesex Regiment was in 1918 a garrison battalion, made of up 'B1' class men not fit enough to fight on the Western Front. The battalion had spent the war years on garrison duties in India and from 1917 in Hong Kong with two companies detached to Singapore. Commanded by Lieutenant Colonel John Ward, CB, CMG, MP, the battalion embarked for Vladivostok on board SS *Ping Suey* on 27 July 1918 under orders from the War Office although virtually no information had been relayed to Ward on the exact nature of his duties when they arrived, nor what special equipment might be required.

The journey would not to be a pleasant one. No less than two typhoons were encountered during the voyage, one passing only 10 miles from *Ping Suey*. It was a very rough passage and the men were well pleased to reach calmer waters off the coast of Japan.

On arrival at Vladivostok, 25th Middlesex were escorted into harbour by two Japanese destroyers to much fanfare. At 1000 on the morning of 3 August 1918 the battalion disembarked to the marching band of the Czech Legion and a guard of honour from HMS *Suffolk*, to be greeted by various Allied representatives. The battalion marched to the city centre past crowds of cheering Russians who had come to see the 'Angliski' soldiers.

The very day that the battalion landed, a large battle had been fought on the Ussuri River front between some 3,000 poorly armed Czechs and White Russian Cossacks and a vastly superior force of Red Army troops reportedly led by German and Austrian officers, former prisoners of war on the Eastern Front, 1914–17 who had been released and joined the Bolsheviks. When the Red troops made an inevitable further attack, a White withdrawal would be necessary and the railway junction at Nikolsk in danger of capture, threatening communications between White forces.

The situation was so dire that the Russian council at Vladivostok made a request to the War Office for the Middlesexes to be despatched to the Ussuri front without delay. Ward pointed out that his men were all 'B1' category and not combat troops but gave an assurance that should he be required to render assistance he would do all in his power to do so.

After a long train journey, the battalion took up position in front of a wooded area and began constructing defences. The Bolsheviks had recently advanced on Rumovka on the opposite side of the Ussuri River and it was the Middlesexes' job to prevent any further advance. At daybreak the Bolsheviks began to shell the wood behind the British positions but some of the shells fell short near the British trenches, however no casualties were sustained.

The Bolshevik artillery appeared to be randomly accurate and managed to knock out the two Cossack field pieces that were protecting the approach along the railway and a further two guns that were supporting the infantry which were moved to take their place, leaving the infantry without critical artillery support. Ward cabled Captain Christopher Payne, RN of HMS *Suffolk* (acting as Senior Naval Officer, Vladivostok) informing him of the lack of artillery and requesting that he send naval artillery and gunners with all possible haste.

Payne did not drag his heels and shortly despatched to the Ussuri two armoured trains fitted with two 12 pdr naval guns each and several machine guns crewed by Royal Marines and Royal Navy sailors from HMS *Suffolk*, the detachment commanded by Captain John Bath, RMLI with Commander James Wolfe-Murray, RN second in command. The arrival of the naval gunners put great heart into the Middlesexes and gave the British and Czechs fire power superiority over the Bolsheviks, at least for the time being.

---

12 John Ward, *With the 'Die-Hards' in Siberia* (London: Cassell, 1920), p.74.

124. Lieutenant Colonel John Ward, CB, CMG, MP, commanding 25th Battalion, Middlesex Regiment, Siberia 1918–19. (Public domain)

The following day the Bolsheviks sent up an armoured train of their own and began to shell near the British position but their fire was wildly inaccurate, their shells landing some 400 yards short of the British positions, 'affording much amusement and causing many caustic Cockney comments.'[13] Their shelling having no effect, the Bolsheviks sent up a troop train but accurate fire from *Suffolk*'s gunners, including a direct hit on the engine, made the Reds think better of the idea and begin to withdraw, steam escaping violently from the damaged engine.

Gains by the Bolsheviks on the Ussuri front forced a withdrawal by the Allies from their positions to a new front line near the village of Dukhovskaya. The withdrawal was covered by the naval gunners from *Suffolk* who blew up the railway bridge to the Middlesexes' front and did considerable damage to the line before withdrawing. The Bolsheviks wasted no time and within three days the bridge and line was repaired and Red Army patrols were probing the Allies' new front.

Throughout the night of 22 August, the Middlesexes fought a series of indecisive brief skirmishes with Bolshevik patrols until it was realised that the Japanese on the right flank had retired without notice leaving the British line dangerously exposed. Undiscovered, Red troops advanced onto a ridge just 100 yards from a British observation post manned by some of the *Suffolk*'s bluejackets under Gunner John Moffatt, RN (later awarded the DSC). From their position on the ridge and still undiscovered, the Bolsheviks attacked.

In command of the Middlesex machine guns, Lieutenant King moved his guns forward to cover the RN observation post but was forced to withdraw in a leapfrog manner as the enemy attacked, keeping one gun firing whilst another withdrew before resuming firing, repeating the process as they went. The Russian Maxim machine guns that the Middlesex had been issued with locally were plagued with defective ammunition and despite Lieutenant King's best efforts to get one of the guns going again he was forced to abandon it to the Bolsheviks. Of King's actions, Lieutenant Colonel Ward wrote:

He gallantly tried to restart the gun, but the enemy were now upon him, and he had no alternative but to retire without the gun. The small naval party in the advanced lookout were practically surrounded, but under

13   Ward, *With the 'Die-Hards' in Siberia*, p.13.

petty officer Moffatt, who was in charge, they managed to get out, with the enemy on their heels. This party was saved by a young marine named Mitchel, who, seeing Moffatt in difficulties, dropped on his knee and faced his pursuers. Their fire was erratic, but his was cool and accurate, and after three or four rounds the Magyars kept their heads well down in the long marsh grass, which allowed the party to escape.[14]

The confusion among the British had allowed a Bolshevik armoured train to advance up the line to a point where it could have easily enfiladed the Middlesex trenches, but once again smart shooting from the naval gunners saw the Bolshevik train off.

On the morning of 24 August 1918, a force of Japanese troops under Colonel Oie launched an attack to clear Red forces opposing the Allied hold on Dukhovskaya village. Ward believed that the orders given to the Allied contingents were deliberately issued so late as to permit only the Japanese to take part in the battle. It appeared to Ward that Colonel Oie was under orders from his superiors to limit any Allied participation in offensive operations which might later compromise Japanese plans for annexation of the maritime provinces of Siberia.

Despite the late orders, Ward was determined not to sit out the engagement. He gave immediate orders for the battalion to assemble in marching order for an advance. The Japanese had given the Middlesexes only 15 minutes to cover four miles at night but Ward was determined to play some part in the action, even if he arrived late. When the British reached the rendezvous point the Japanese were long gone but a Bolshevik armoured train could be seen some 400 yards distant. The advance had thus far been silent, rifles carried unloaded to prevent any accidental discharge which might give away the British positions, until one soldier in the process of loading his rifle accidentally fired: fortunately the errant projectile did not cause injury. Ward sent an officer to investigate followed only seconds later by the loud 'crack' of yet another rifle being accidentally fired. It was a very undistinguished and unmemorable start to the Middlesexes' participation in the battle of Dukhovskaya.

As Bolshevik shrapnel began to fall, the Middlesexes scattered into a cornfield. With his batman's rifle in his hand, Ward lead his men forward, filling a gap between two Japanese regiments. A Maxim machine gun opened fire near the British axis of advance at about 100 yards range but was quickly put out of action by some Czech Legion soldiers on the flank, who made it so hot for the Red gunner that after firing only about 150 rounds the enemy fled, abandoning a well positioned gun and 5,000 rounds of ammunition.

As the Middlesexes advanced a Bolshevik soldier suddenly rose from the ground and taking standing aim from about 400 yards range fired a shot straight at Lieutenant Colonel Ward. The shot missed but hit a Czech soldier standing nearby. Sixty shots answered the Bolshevik and the enemy rifleman fell to the ground dead. Captain Clark picked up the dead Russian's rifle and used it with great effect on the retreating Red soldiers.

The Middlesex pushed onto the railway and there disabled an armoured train mounted with a 6 inch gun. A second enemy train further up the track fired on the British troops but in their panic the fire was wild and inaccurate. By skilful manoeuvre a battery of Japanese field guns had taken up position in a tree line in advance of the infantry. A lucky shot from the Japanese gunners destroyed the railway behind the Bolshevik trains, cutting off their line of retreat. Another shell fell on the armoured train closest to the Allied advance which caught alight and within minutes was engulfed in flames, all in full view of the enemy troops. The enemy fire began to waver and become erratic as the Red troops lost the will to continue the fight. A white flag appeared over the Bolshevik positions which the Japanese cavalry ignored, attacking the Red troops from their flank, killing all in their path regardless. There were reportedly no prisoners taken.

---

14   *Ibid.*, p.54.

The pace of the advance was beginning to show on the Middlesex men, almost to a man classified unfit for combat. Ward decided to leave behind the men who were struggling and with a party of 60 of the fitter men, including Captain Clark, the battalion Padre Captain Roberts, Lieutenant Buckley, RSM Gordon and Sergeant Webb, set off to locate more of the enemy. The party advanced to within 50 yards of the burning train amid a shower of debris of exploding ammunition, then continued on through the railway siding without meeting any opposition.

Two hundred yards past the train the Middlesex heard a fusillade of shots from behind. Ward turned around to see one of the trains which had appeared to have been abandoned, firing point blank into some advancing Japanese troops. The Japanese Colonel ordered a charge and his men swarmed over the carriages, bayoneting and clubbing every Bolshevik they could find inside, hurling the bodies of their dead enemies onto the tracks below.

Ward could not believe his luck that his party had walked straight past the train without the Bolshevik troops inside firing a shot:

> My great regret was that no Bolshevik was left alive to tell us the reason why they allowed about sixty English officers and other ranks to pass unmolested at point-blank range of forty yards, and only began to fire when the Japanese soldiers came under their rifles. Many explanations were given at the time, none of which seemed to me quite satisfactory, so the mystery remains.[15]

Ward had been hoping to take at least one prisoner for interrogation and the opportunity presented itself when a Bolshevik who had evaded the Japanese scampered towards the British. Ward fired a shot in front of the enemy soldier, and the terrified man dropped to the grass so suddenly that Ward was sure that he had accidentally shot him. The British ran to near where the man had fallen and their Russian liaison called out for his surrender. The Bolshevik replied that the Japanese killed all their prisoners, to which the Russian officer replied that they were British troops, not Japanese, and that his life would be guaranteed. The bedraggled man ran almost headlong into Ward for protection. The prisoner's papers showed the prisoner to be a demobilised Imperial soldier who had served on the Eastern Front before the revolution:

> I placed him under a guard of two men with orders to see him safely to the rear. Time after time demands were made to his guards [by White Russians] to allow the murder of the prisoner. But those two British bayonets made his life as safe as though he had been in Trafalgar square. I could tell by the atmosphere which the incident created that our Allies thought this regular conduct wholly out of place on a battle field, but it fulfilled its purpose, and surrenders were accepted during the further operations.[16]

With the new prisoner under guard the Middlesexes' advance continued on to the railway station at Kraevesk. As Ward turned a curve in the line he could see a Bolshevik armoured train in the distance. A Red Army officer stepped out from the platform onto the line and walked calmly to the front of the engine. As the enemy officer strode forward he stopped and stared directly at Ward, mouth ajar, as if he was not quite sure of what he was looking at. Ward took a bead on the Bolshevik with his rifle and squeezed the trigger. The bullet missed but flew close enough to make the Red officer flee back into the station house. The shot also alerted the crew of the armoured train and within seconds they had responded with shell and machine gun fire. One 2 inch shell flew so close to Ward's head that he instinctively ducked and felt the top of his skull to reassure himself that it was still there.

15   *Ibid.*, p.67.
16   *Ibid.*, p.69.

124. Lieutenant Colonel John Ward, CB, CMG, MP (left), commanding 25th Battalion, Middlesex Regiment poses with officers of the Czech Legion. (Public domain)

The machine gun and shrapnel fire from the armoured train probed up and down the Japanese advance, causing them to scatter in all directions. The British and Japanese reorganised and began to return fire on the train but the long advance had far outranged the supporting Japanese artillery.

Using the railway buildings as cover the British and Japanese advanced on the train to a point where they could fire at the gunners' heads as they appeared above the edges of the gun carriages. A Japanese attempt to outflank the train and cut off its retreat was detected by the Bolshevik commander and in a hail of shell and machine gun fire the train withdrew towards Shamakovka. After an advance of six hours in which the battalion covered 12 miles on foot, 25th Middlesex's involvement in the battle of Dukhovskaya came to an end. In one of the station buildings RSM Gordon discovered a breakfast of fried potatoes abandoned by the retreating Bolsheviks which he ensured did not go to waste.

Although the part played by the Middlesexes had been relatively minor, the battle of Dukhovskaya had been a great success and destroyed virtually all the Red Army units east of the Ural mountains. The Japanese had sustained over 600 fatal casualties but thankfully not a man of the Middlesexes had been hit. The Battle Honour 'Dukhovskaya' was later granted to the Middlesex Regiment for their participation in the battle.

Following the Red Army defeat at Dukhovskaya, the Czech Legion began their push west of Lake Baikal, the largest freshwater lake in the world. As more territory was captured from the Bolsheviks it was decided by the War Office in London that the Middlesexes should be relocated further west to Omsk, a train journey of some 2,500 miles, where they would be joined by another British infantry battalion being sent from India via Vladivostok.

Converse to the lower category garrison soldiers of 25th Middlesex, 1/9th Battalion, Hampshire Regiment, commanded by pre-war civil servant, Lieutenant Colonel Robert Johnson, comprised 32 officers and 945 other ranks classed as 'A1', the highest physical category possible. A Territorial Army unit, the Hampshires had originally been a 'Cyclist' battalion sent to India in 1915 as garrison troops to replace regular army battalions that were being sent to fill the gaps caused by horrendous casualties at Mons. By 1918 the battalion had spent three years in India and participated only in a minor campaign in Waziristan. After spending virtually the entire war without firing a shot in anger, the Hampshires were certainly not expecting to receive orders to embark at Bombay for Vladivostok on 29 October 1918. There was some talk amongst the more gullible men that they would be marching over the Himalayas and through Tibet and China to get there. When the Hampshires received word en route to Siberia of the signing of the Armistice, the men assumed the transport ship would turn around and return to India as the war was now over. They were not so fortunate.

125. White Russian soldiers under instruction by British officers of the Military Mission to Admiral Kolchak on the Maxim machine gun at Irkutsk, summer 1919. (AWM A01070)

After disembarkation and fitting out by the CSEF with cold weather clothing, the Hampshires, like the 25th Middlesex before them, entrained for the 2,500 mile, month long train journey to Omsk. The trip was to prove less than luxurious. The train travelled at a speed of 15 miles an hour, the men in modified cattle trucks that had been supplemented with a roof, boards to sleep on and most importantly, a stove which was in almost constant use. The Hampshires spent Christmas day en route about 100 miles from Omsk, celebrating with a tot of rum whilst they travelled. The temperature was recorded as minus 20°C.

When the Hampshires arrived at Omsk the White Russian authorities billeted the battalion in a girls' school. Much to his horror Johnson learned that the students had been kicked out and had nowhere else to go, so the Hampshires' commander insisted that the girls be given a wing of the school in which to live. There were no baths and only one kitchen but the men counted themselves lucky: there were thousands of refugees outside with no shelter in a Siberian winter. Many thousands of the refugees either froze or starved to death or succumbed to typhus. Bodies piled up at the train station and on sledges became a common sight to the British soldiers.

Like most members of the battalion, Johnson had a rather stagnant and uneventful war. He had taken over the battalion as a Territorial Army Lieutenant Colonel in 1911 but by 1919 had not advanced in rank or appointment whilst some of his colleagues had brilliant careers at the front winning promotion and distinction. A religious man, Johnson expected the highest standard of moral behaviour from his men of whom he was extremely proud.

On one occasion the Hampshires' Canadian Anglican padre was returned to Vladivostok and replaced at Omsk by a Baptist. Johnson by his own admission was not a 'narrow sectarian' but returned the Baptist padre to Vladivostok and insisted on a 'C. of E.' replacement. The poor Baptist minister was sent to the other side of the world, enduring a tedious month long 2,500 mile, typhus-ridden train journey to minister for the souls of the Hampshires only upon his arrival to immediately be told to return to Vladivostok as the battalion commander would prefer an Anglican.

Numbed by the arctic cold and boredom of garrison operations, the Hampshires became increasingly frustrated with their inactivity whilst at home servicemen already demobilised with a lot less service were taking all the good civilian jobs. The average soldier could see little reason why they should be separated from their homes and families just to sit around killing time in a godforsaken corner of the earth.

The task of keeping the men of the Middlesex and Hampshire regiments occupied was not an easy one. The weather was too severe to conduct any form of training outdoors so the men spent most of their time cooped up indoors, a sure recipe for 'cabin fever'. The men amused themselves with games of ice hockey, boxing, dances and even an amateur theatrical group which put on a show for representatives of Admiral Kolchak's White Russian government.

The role of the Hampshires at Omsk was essentially to protect Kolchak from threats both external and internal, a role Johnson did not relish at all:

I am getting to regard the situation here as pretty hopeless … their [White Russian] army is useless … I never saw such an incapable lot … the army has no discipline. The regimental officers are useless. Kolchak is, I think, a determined man but he stands quite alone and may be murdered or upset at any moment and that would be the end. Indeed but for our own presence here he would already have gone, but what a hopeless situation if the head of the government here rests solely on 1,000 British bayonets.

The men of the 9th Hants escort found a full general dead drunk in their railway carriage one afternoon and as he wouldn't or couldn't go away when they asked him, they had to lift him up and throw him into the snow. The next day he turned out on parade with his division to be inspected by Kolchak. He was still drunk.

In all sorts of ways the Russians are hopeless, unbusinesslike, unpunctual, corrupt, intriguing and without internal discipline of any sort, the latter the result of the Revolution. Then they are fearfully lazy and expect the Allies to do all the work for them while they sit tight and enjoy themselves – or try to make money.

I fancy that [the Bolsheviks] are better organised and have more enthusiasm … and I should be surprised if they didn't give these people here a good hiding … I am afraid the Russians are completely hopeless and we are wasting time and energy and money in trying to help them.[17]

The assessment of another officer serving with the British Military Mission was equally as harsh:

They [the Whites] are a class which has forgotten nothing and learnt nothing, and is in every way unfit to rule. As soon as the White officers in Siberia began to recover from the effects of the Red Terror to which they had been subjected, they reverted at once to the courses which had brought about their downfall. They intrigued in the most shameless manner for posts in the rear, so that Kolchak had more officers in his G.H.Q. than Foch had in his at the time of the Armistice. Thousands of those who should have been at the Front spent practically all their time revelling in Omsk. Regimental commanders neglected their soldiers for months and then treated them with brutal severity … The intelligentsia spent half their time criticizing the British troops for not going into the firing-line, and the other half in 'wangling' safe jobs for their own officer-sons in the rear.[18]

The long winter and boredom began to take its toll on the Hampshires, many of whom were young conscripts who had joined the battalion just before it had left India. Some of the men were receiving letters from their civil employers informing that they had kept positions vacant for the duration of the war but, with the return of the male workforce, could not afford to do so any longer. In a letter to his mother, Johnson wrote:

17   Dobson and Miller, *The Day We Almost Bombed Moscow*, p.236.
18   Francis McCullagh, *A Prisoner of the Reds: the story of a British officer captured in Siberia* (London: J. Murray, 1921), pp.323-324.

126. Soldiers from 259th Battalion, CSEF pose with a Lewis gun, April 1919. Steel helmets were rarely worn in Siberia. (Public domain)

The regiment has got used to me and I am not the power I was. Last week I had a very anxious time. Pilfering of government stores and I had to take strong action. As a result there was very nearly a mutiny incited by the draft men. It was touch and go for a short while but we succeeded in averting anything really serious-about a dozen poor fools who have been severely punished … We have had a rather nasty time-an attempt on the part of ten draft men to incite the rest to a kind of mutiny. It was an anxious moment but the discipline held and only a dozen men broke out of barracks and even they returned quietly in a very short time.[19]

In an attempt to keep the Hampshires occupied with a worthwhile project, British Military Mission commander Major General Alfred Knox planned to utilise the battalion to raise and train a Russian unit with British officers and NCOs along the lines of the Slavo-British Legion in North Russia. The unit was dubbed the 'Anglo–Russian Regiment' but despite no shortage of volunteer officers and NCOs from the Hampshires (who preferred their own title given to the unit, the 'Hampshire Russian Brigade') the regiment barely got off the ground.

The Russian conscripts allocated to the unit were found to be malnourished and mostly underage boys of 14–15 years, many of whom were Mongolian and spoke little Russian. One in three had to be rejected by the British as unfit and it was immediately obvious that the Russians were sending only their lowest class of conscript. It was not long before Anglo–Russian Regiment soldiers were being beaten in the street by White Russian officers for saluting in the British style as they had been trained. One British officer recorded that the only way to obtain water supplies for the unit was for a party of British troops to provide armed escort. The regiment was abandoned as a failure in June 1919 (incidentally just before the Slavo-British Legion mutiny at Archangel in July), its conscripts returned to Kolchak's army without having fired a shot in anger, its British officers and NCOs returned to their units even more despondent at the apparent pointlessness of their presence in Siberia than they had already been.

The Hampshires had by May 1919 spent six months in Siberia, and Johnson was beginning to feel that they had been forgotten by the War Office; via his wife he lobbied to have the battalion either

---

19   Dobson and Miller, *The Day We Almost Bombed Moscow*, p.237.

relieved or sent home. The ploy worked and in early June, Johnson received a telegram from the Ministry of Labour informing that they had applied for his release from service to take a post in the Ministry. At first Johnson thought of declining the offer, he could hardly leave if his men were not going with him, but then considered that he could much more effectively lobby to have the battalion relieved and sent home from England than from Omsk.

From western Siberia it was be quicker to travel north-west to Archangel than returning to Vladivostok and on 4 June, Johnson and 12 married men who had been granted compassionate discharges left Omsk for Ekaterinburg and in an amazing journey travelled an arduous 1,800 miles to the Barents Sea, where they were picked up by the Royal Navy. Soon after Johnson's arrival in England the Red Army advance cut off the route.

It was during Johnson's journey that Czech Legion General Gajda made his big push north-west in an attempt to link up with British forces at Kotlas, south-east of Archangel on the Dvina River, but was routed by Red Army troops fewer in number than his own force, for which Admiral Kolchak dismissed Gajda from his command shortly thereafter. The attack had been part of Kolchak's grand strategy to link up with the British forces in the north and White Russian General Denikin in the south before combining forces to advance on Moscow. Over 130,000 of Kolchak's troops were involved in the offensive supported by 210 artillery pieces and 1,300 machine guns. Initially the offensive was successful, Kolchak's men reaching as far as 450 miles east of Moscow. Secretary of State for War, Winston Churchill, himself an ardent anti-Bolshevist, was quite pleased with the success and campaigned for Prime Minister Lloyd-George to recognise Kolchak's regime, the 'Provisional Government of Siberia'.

Kolchak's larger offensive eventually ran out of momentum and petered out, stopped in its tracks as the Red Army threatened to outflank the White Russian advance. By early June 1919, Kolchak had retreated 100 miles, then on 17 June, Gajda's column in the north-west was repelled, Red troops streamed through the Ural Mountains taking by surprise and destroying the White Army's 12th Division. The Siberian front was collapsing horribly and on 25 July the War Cabinet deemed imperative that the Hampshire and Middlesex battalions be withdrawn to Vladivostok immediately. The Admiralty applied the same rule to the Royal Marine-crewed gunboats operating on the Kama River which were scuttled and the crews entrained for Vladivostok.

Kolchak lost Ekaterinburg followed by Chelyabinsk but it was not a complete rout. In September the Whites halted the Bolshevik Army advance, counter-attacked and pushed the Red Army back 100 miles. Kolchak left Omsk in November and travelled 1,500 miles east to the city of Irkutsk where he set up a second line of defence.

Major Phelps Hodges, an officer serving with the British Military Mission to Admiral Kolchak, expressed the frustration many in the Mission felt with the ineffectual and incompetent White leadership during the retreat. Recalling a meeting with a particular White Russian general, Hodges wrote:

> He complained in a pained voice that the Bolsheviks were conscripting and arming peasants, and sending them straight into action without any training at all. It seemed to him most unsportsmanlike, but it apparently did not occur to him that to retire hastily, without firing a shot, before an undisciplined mob of unwilling conscripts was the most damning proof of his own side's cowardice and incompetence. I felt like advising him and his companions for the sake of their own honour, to draw their oft-rattled sabres and commit hara-kiri on the spot.
>
> It was too discouraging to think of England pouring out arms and money to these men, who did nothing but boast loudly until an enemy was heard of fifty versts away, and then retire hurriedly in the opposite direction. Here was this Army Staff, large enough for a force ten times in size, issuing lying communiqués, talking grandly in terms of brigades, divisions, counter-attacks, and retirements according

to plan, and doing nothing to make the Army a fighting force.[20]

Captain Ernest Latchford, MC, an Australian Imperial Force officer serving on secondment with the British Military Mission, had travelled to Siberia directly from North Persia where he had been serving with Dunsterforce. Latchford experienced his own frustration with the incompetence and greed of the White Russian military leadership:

We had issued a unit with a complete set of British gear, and were surprised to hear rumours of a few days later that Chinese storekeepers were selling some of the stuff. The C.O. was approached and admitted having disposed of certain articles. His native reason being that the men had only been accustomed to having one shirt, singlet etc. so it was a waste giving them two.[21]

Another Mission officer, Captain Francis McCullagh (taken prisoner by the Reds on 7 January 1920 and held in Moscow) wrote similarly of the waste, incompetence and corruption within Kolchak's forces:

127. Ukrainian-born Corporal Filip Konowal, VC, CSEF. Konowal received his award for bravery on the Western Front in 1917 and is the only Victoria Cross recipient known to have served in Siberia 1918–20. (Public domain)

We sent in all 200,000 sets of equipment to Kolchak, but they all seemed to pass through Kolchak's hands as water goes through a sieve, and the Reds got most of them. They told me that in Perm they had captured enough uniforms to clothe a whole division. They had found them unpacked in a storehouse, where they had probably been forgotten by the Whites, though at the time Kolchak's soldiers were very badly clad and his Generals were pressing us to send more uniforms. More frequently the uniforms walked over to the Reds, thousands at a time, with the Whites inside them. A Red General was nearly scared out of his wits once, during the fighting in the Urals, by seeing what he took to be the whole British Army bearing down on him; but the alarming manifestation turned out to be only a detachment of Whites in British uniforms anxious to surrender. Such phenomena became so frequent, later on, that the Reds got quite used to it; and, by the time Krasnoyarsk had been lost, about one-fourth of the Red soldiers wore the khaki of King George.[22]

By late 1919 the Hampshire and Middlesex garrison battalions and CSEF had left Siberia. General Alfred Knox's British Military Mission which remained continued to train and equip the remnants of Kolchak's White Russian Army and were caught up in the headlong retreat eastwards from Omsk when that city fell to the Bolsheviks on 14 November. Amongst the men and material captured were 50,000 soldiers (including 10 of Kolchak's generals) and huge amounts of arms and

20   Hodges, *BRITMIS*, p.122.
21   Ernest Latchford, 'With the White Russians', *Reveille*, August 1933.
22   McCullagh, *A Prisoner of the Reds*, pp.67–68.

ammunition, much of it donated by the British government. The stores were rapidly appropriated and distributed to the Red Army and remained in use for the remainder of the Russian Civil War.

By the time Latchford arrived in Siberia in mid 1919 the British Military Mission was already well established:

> The Mission consisted of about 250 officers and about the same number of N.C.O.s, and with a few exceptions, was made up entirely from the Regular Army. Many of the officers were 'Mons' people, who had been 'picked up' in 1914, and who were now, after four years as prisoners of war, being given the opportunity of seeing more service. They were, almost without exception, a fine crowd of fellows ... A number of these officers had the bad luck to be caught by the 'Bolos' when 'our show' collapsed later in the year, and they had to undergo another term of imprisonment.[23]

Knox, a fluent Russian speaker, had served as British military attaché to the Imperial Russian Army before the Revolution and witnessed first hand the Bolshevik capture of the Tsars winter palace. During the period of Kerensky Provisional Government rule, March–November 1917, Knox lobbied the new government to preserve the alliance with Britain and maintain the Eastern Front against the German and Austro-Hungarians which lasted until Lenin's Bolsheviks took power in November.

On 4 January 1920, Kolchak relinquished his position as 'Supreme Ruler' to General Denikin in South Russia, handing over what remained of the White Russian Siberian Army to Cossack Ataman Semenov. Kolchak fled to Irkutsk, arriving on 14 January only to find that the allied military missions had already left and the city was under the control of a leftist alliance which surrounded his train and the Czech Legion soldiers guarding it. The Admiral was arrested and imprisoned and on the morning of 7 February led out to the River Ushakova and executed, his body pushed through a hole in the ice into the river never to be recovered.

With Kolchak's forces decimated and the collapse of the White Russian Provisional Government in North Russia – the last British forces had been evacuated from North Russia in October 1919, and Archangel was captured by the Red Army the following February – the Bolsheviks consolidated, halting their advance eastwards and diverting resources and troops against White Russian General Denikin in South Russia.

With the transition of leadership of White Russian forces in Siberia from Kolchak to Semenov, US President Wilson ordered the withdrawal of AEF Siberia in the new year, the last US soldier left Vladivostok on 1 April 1920. The Japanese had no such intention of leaving and desperately held on to their political and military foothold in Siberia, withdrawing neither troops nor support for Semenov who became for all intents and purposes a Japanese puppet and Vladivostok a Japanese protectorate. For a time the city became a haven for White Russian soldiers and civilians fleeing from the west, a small peninsula of Russia which remained free from Bolshevik control until the Japanese finally abandoned Vladivostok to the Red Army in late 1922, and did not return to the region until their annexation of the maritime provinces of north-west China in the early 1930s in the lead up to the Sino–Japanese War.

For 12 members of the British Military Mission and two members of the CSEF attempting to elude the Bolshevik advance and make their way back to Vladivostok during the winter of 1919–20, the masses of rolling stock slowly creeping eastwards along the severely congested line caused significant anxiety. Stops were frequent followed by a wait of hours or even days until the track could be cleared enough to continue. The rate of the Bolshevik advance exceeded the rate with which the fleeing trains could steam eastward and inevitably on 7 January 1920, the Mission train was overrun

---

23   Ernest Latchford, 'With the White Russians', part II, *Reveille*, September 1933.

128. CSEF Memorial in Churkin Naval Cemetery, Vladivostok. The
cemetery contains the burials of 37 British and Canadian soldiers and
memorials to a further 13 buried in other parts of Siberia. (CWGC)

a few miles west of Krasnoyarsk. The officer in command of the detachment, Major Leonard Vining,
RE, wrote of the surprise of their capture:

> We were having supper about this time when a soldier with a large red cockade in his fur cap came into
> our carriage and asked us who we were. We replied that we were members of the British Mission … in a
> flash we saw that we were captured by the 'pukka' reds.[24]

The Bolsheviks were not quite what the British officers had expected at all. After asking if they
might join the British for breakfast, the Red Army soldiers chatted in a friendly manner and even
allowed the captured Britons to retain their arms. The Bolsheviks permitted the British to live
independently of other prisoners (held under guard in the nearby town) and walk the streets as they
pleased although they were eventually ordered to surrender their weapons.

Remarkably for one of the officers taken prisoner, Captain Francis McCullagh, Royal Irish
Fusiliers, it would be his third period of captivity. Having been taken prisoner during the Boer War,
on the Western Front in 1914 and now in Siberia, McCullagh posed and maintained an identity
as a journalist and was permitted to make his way to Moscow independently of the other British
prisoners; where, as a British civilian, he was evacuated to Finland many months before the release
of the remainder of the party, a remarkable escape made on bluff alone.

---

24   L.E. Vining, *Held by the Bolsheviks: the diary of a British officer in Russia, 1919–1920* (London: The Saint Catherine Press, 1924),
     p.141.

After killing time at Krasnoyarsk for over a month awaiting word of their fate, Major Vining was called into the local Commissars office where he was informed that the British were 'guests' of the Bolshevik government but at the Commissars discretion they could also be put to work in the nearby prisoner of war camp. Vining acquiesced to being placed in the typhus-riddled compound (not that he had much choice) but flatly refused that the officers should be put to work. The refusal visibly aggravated the Commissar and Vining was surprised to hear a few days later that the detachment would be allowed to remain in their railway carriages after all and would not be required to work. In fact the Bolsheviks delivered a most generous consignment of food to the prisoners in preparation for the journey west to Moscow:

> Jove, the Reds are not going to let us starve. We have got 2 ½ carcases of meat, heaps of flour, some rice, etc., and also, wonder of wonders, some tobacco and matches. We cannot understand this generosity on the part of the Reds. They have certainly treated us very well as regards our provisions for the journey.[25]

Second in command of the British Military Mission prisoners was an officer who had already spent nearly four years as a prisoner of war in Germany and would during the Second World War famously command 30 Corps during the 'Market Garden' operations of 1944, portrayed by actor Edward Fox in the 1977 movie *A Bridge Too Far.* Then Captain Brian Horrocks, MC, a pre-war graduate of RMC Sandhurst, had been serving with 1st Battalion, Middlesex Regiment at Armentieres in October 1914 where he was wounded and taken prisoner. A persistent escaper, on one of his attempts Horrocks made it to within sight of the Dutch border before recapture. Incarcerated in a POW camp which also held Russian officer prisoners and with not much else to do to kill time, Horrocks became proficient in the Russian language. Three weeks after his capture by the Bolsheviks, announcement was made in the *London Gazette* of the award of the Military Cross to Horrocks for services in attempting to escape captivity.[26]

Horrocks and fellow prisoner Captain George Hayes were unfortunate enough to contract typhus and were left behind when orders were received for the British and Canadian prisoners to entrain for Moscow to join prisoners captured on other fronts. Vining obtained permission from the Bolshevik authorities to take two prisoners, an Austrian and a Hungarian, to act as cooks and batmen during the long journey. Both men had been captured on the Eastern Front at the beginning of the war and were quite keen to leave Krasnoyarsk. For them every mile westwards towards Moscow was a mile closer to home.

Vining was informed by the Bolsheviks that a number of British prisoners taken in North Russia were held in Moscow and that negotiations between Whitehall and Kremlin for a prisoner exchange were well underway. It was even possible that by the time the Mission prisoners reached Moscow they would be immediately repatriated to England. The captives were understandably buoyed by the news.

On 28 March, nearly two and a half months after their capture, the Mission prisoners finally commenced the journey west to Moscow. The train only got as far as Irkutsk before orders were received by the local commissar for an indefinite halt whilst negotiations took place between London and Moscow. The days passed slowly into weeks waiting for the order to continue westwards. It was not all boredom for the British and Canadian officers, they were free to roam the streets and attended several operas and ballets using a stipend provided by the local Bolshevik authorities. The prisoners even formed a team in the local soccer league. It was certainly a strange kind of imprisonment. Considering the hardships some other British and Commonwealth prisoners of the Bolsheviks had to endure, the Mission officers captured in Siberia had perhaps the most comfortable term of imprisonment.

25   *Ibid.*, p.312.
26   *The London Gazette*, 30 January 1920.

The Red guards posted to the Mission train car even worked for the prisoners collecting firewood and carrying water, services for which the British paid the guards with tobacco and cigarettes supplied to them for free by the Soviet government. At both Krasnoyarsk and Irkutsk the British were fortunate that the treatment from the Bolshevik authorities was exceedingly good:

> It was extraordinary how much we received from the Authorities at Krasnoyarsk towards the end of our stay there. We made many requests, more in the way of a demand, and we got all that we put in for in the way of foodstuffs which could possibly be obtained in the town. At Irkutsk also we have received extraordinarily good treatment and have been given quite good food considering the scarcity of stuff and the hard times.[27]

On 12 June, the order finally came for the train to resume its journey westward through Omsk and the Ural Mountains, arriving in Moscow 11 days later. The party was marched into Ivanoffsky Monastery which had been converted into a temporary prison where the Britons and Canadians in their strange uniforms were quite a curiosity amongst the other prisoners. It appeared that the good treatment which had been extended to the detachment since their capture at Krasnoyarsk would not be extended during their stay in Moscow, although they were permitted to retain their Austro-Hungarian servants. Vining wrote, 'We roared with laughter sometimes to think that we, prisoners, should successfully have demanded of the Reds to supply other prisoners to wait upon us.'[28]

The prisoners' hopes that they would soon be released began to fade as the weeks dragged on, and the men began to suffer from the sparse diet of black bread and boiled grain each morning followed by watery soup in the evening. Despite their privations the British prisoners fared better than many of the civilian population who were dying in the streets of starvation and typhus.

After a transfer and further imprisonment and hardship at Andronoffsky Monastery with prisoners of the French Military Mission the prisoners were finally released on 20 October 1920 to entrain for Petrograd, where they arrived 36 hours later. After being escorted to the Finnish frontier the men boarded a train to Terrioki and freedom. During the entire nine months of his imprisonment Vining had been able to conceal his diary from the Bolsheviks and in 1924 published it under the title *Held by the Bolsheviks*, one of very few accounts of the experiences of an officer of the British Military Mission Siberia.

On 25 October 1922, the Japanese occupation forces in Siberia finally withdrew from Vladivostok as the Red Army entered the city. The crew of HMS *Carlisle* watched from Vladivostok harbour as the Bolsheviks took control of the city, before slowly steaming out to sea and bringing British and Commonwealth Military intervention in Russia and the Russian Civil War to a close.

---

27   Vining, *Held by the Bolsheviks*, p.196.
28   *Ibid.*, p.217.

15

Eastern Baltic: December 1918–December 1919

The Navy and RAF

Other than a small Tank Corps detachment which operated in Estonia during the summer and autumn of 1919 and a small British training mission, British operations in Finland and the Eastern Baltic as part of military intervention in the Russian Civil War were exclusively a naval affair. Unlike North Russia (specifically the Dvina River) where the Royal Navy operated a small flotilla of monitors and gunboats on the Northern (Severnaya) Dvina River, the Royal Navy in the Baltic Sea operated as a fleet at war opposed by enemy surface ships and submarines.

During 1914–18, the Baltic Sea had been blockaded by the German Imperial Navy and had been inaccessible to Royal Navy surface ships, although a small flotilla of British submarines had forced the Baltic and wrought havoc on German shipping during 1915. The German Navy had heavily mined the western Baltic as a defensive measure to prevent British interference from their northern coast, whilst the Russians had mined the eastern Baltic to prevent any moves by the Germans against their strategically important naval base on Kronstadt Island in the Gulf of Finland, only miles from the Imperial capital of St. Petersburg, renamed 'Petrograd' in 1914.

Home to the Imperial Russian Navy's Baltic Sea Fleet, Kronstadt Island had been the scene of large scale mutinies by sailors during the revolution which followed Russia's humiliation by Japan in the war of 1905. To pacify the people, the Tsar relinquished some of his autocratic control and allowed the creation of an elected representative council, the *Duma*, although the new assembly was limited in powers. The reforms also brought limited autonomy to the ethnically and culturally diverse Baltic territories of Lithuania, Latvia and Estonia.

On the outbreak of war in August 1914, the Tsar sided with Britain and France against his cousin Kaiser Wilhelm (King George V, Kaiser Wilhelm and Tsar Nicholas II were all cousins). The first offensive by the Imperial Russian Army on the Eastern Front only weeks after war was declared ended in disaster. Between 23–30 August 1914 an entire Russian army corps was surrounded and annihilated near the east Prussian city of Tannenberg. By Christmas 1914 the Western Front had stagnated in stalemate and Germany once again turned its attentions eastwards. German and Austro-Hungarian forces pushed far into Russian territory bringing all of Lithuania and the Baltic coast of Latvia under German occupation.

The Allies did their best to supply the Tsar's army with arms, ammunition and supplies through the northern ports of Murmansk and Archangel in preparation for the Tsar's 1916 Carpathian offensive, timed to coincide with the British attack on the Somme, but their efforts were hampered by the overstretched domestic railway transport system and the stores and equipment began to pile up at the docks.

The Imperial Army made great advances into Austro-Hungarian territory but the Central Powers responded strongly and were able to slow and eventually halt the offensive. Although the 1916 offensive had been a minor victory for the Russians, it was the final straw for the people at home. Years of oppression and hardship and the loss of millions of men killed wounded and missing, more than any other combatant nation in the First World War, with no end to the war in sight, was more than the Russian people could bear.

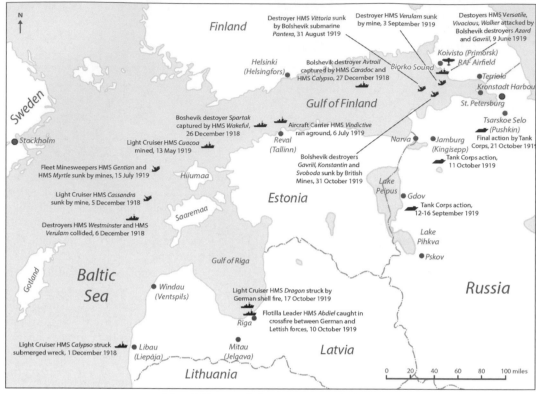

Map 5. Eastern Baltic operations 1918–19

The Petrograd workers struck in March 1917 and the local garrison mutinied, joining together to establish a soviet workers' council and soldiers' deputies. The unrest spread outwards from Petrograd as towns, villages and cities rose up against the Tsar's government.

With the Tsar's abdication and dissolution of the Imperial regime, Finland and the Baltic territories seized their opportunity for independence. Of all the Baltic territories, Lithuania had suffered the worst during the war. In 1915 the retreating Russian Army had razed the country of anything useful to the advancing Germans, a forerunner to Hitler's 'scorched earth' policy enacted 25 years later, albeit the roles reversed.

During their occupation of Lithuania, Germany squeezed the tiny country nearly dry for any resources that could be shipped to Berlin to aid the war effort. The German government also had an ulterior motive of attempting to incorporate Lithuania into Eastern Prussia. The Lithuanian independence movement had perhaps naively hoped the 1917 Bolshevik revolution would lead to their recognition by the new Russian leadership as an independent republic.

In Latvia, Letts had rallied to the Tsar's call in 1914 and rapidly mobilised troops of the famed 'Lettish Rifle Regiments' into the Imperial Army. When German troops first set foot on Latvian territory in 1915, Lettish riflemen (renowned in the Imperial Army as solid fighters) successfully defended the capital city Riga for more than two years. The Letts too had desire for independence and in the aftermath of the revolution made moves towards autonomy.

Estonia, the northernmost of the Baltic territories had been fortunate to have escaped the war mostly unscathed. Occupying German troops did not arrive until as late as December 1917 after the Petrograd revolution. Within a fortnight of the Bolshevik 'November' revolution (October in the Julian calendar, in use in Russia at the time) the Estonian independence movement had declared secession from the Russian empire with the intent to establish a unified autonomous government.

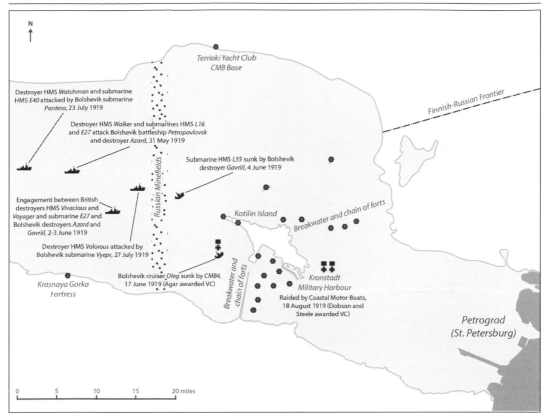

Map 6. Gulf of Finland operations 1919

As a means to encourage Finnish support for the war against Germany (the Finnish independence movement was quite strong), the Tsar had authorised the *Duma* to take a more ambiguous stance towards Finnish independence. Few Finns believed that Russia, which had ruled Finland since the early nineteenth century, had Scandinavian interests at heart and although large numbers of Finns joined the Russian forces, large numbers also fought with the German Army. When the Bolsheviks seized power in November 1917, the Finnish parliament (Finland was a Grand Duchy of the Russian Empire with its own parliament, with the Tsar as Head of State) declared independence from Russia which lead to a power struggle within the country between pro-Bolshevik 'Red' and pro-German 'White' factions.

One of Germany's first demands of the Bolsheviks during negotiations leading to the signing of the Treaty of Brest-Litovsk in March 1918 was the secession of Finland, the Baltic states, Poland and western Ukraine to German control. The German government threatened to send troops into Russia unless the Bolsheviks accepted the terms but People's Commissar for Foreign Affairs, Leon Trotsky (later People's Commissar for the Red Army and Navy during the Civil War), stood strong:

> We do not agree to shed any longer the blood of our soldiers in defence of one side against the other. We are giving the order for a general demobilization of all our armies in the strong hope that other peoples will follow our example. We are going out of the war. But we will not sign the [German] peace treaty.[1]

---

1   Geoffrey Bennett, *Cowan's War: the story of British naval operations in the Baltic, 1918–1920* (London: Collins, 1964), p.24.

129. Bolshevik battleship *Andrei Pervozvanny*, one of the main
threats to the British Baltic Fleet, 1918–19. (Public domain)

The German government responded by mobilising troops to march on Petrograd. Recognising their precarious position, Lenin acquiesced to sign the treaty as a temporary expediency until the war-weary people of Germany had their own revolution and joined the Bolsheviks. In mid 1918 a revolution seemed inevitable given the rumblings of dissent from within the blockaded German population and open sympathy was displayed by many Germans towards the Bolsheviks.

Thereafter known as the 'Treaty of Brest-Litovsk', other senior Bolsheviks were not convinced and it was not until Lenin threatened resignation that a new delegation was sent to sign the treaty on 3 March 1918, a condition of which compelled Russian troops to be withdrawn from Finland and the Baltic states whilst allowing German forces to remain.

The Allies refused to recognise the right of the Bolsheviks to sign the treaty and landed troops at Murmansk, Archangel and Vladivostok to prevent the large amount of Allied-donated war stores from falling into German or Bolshevik hands, and also to protect the ice-free port at Murmansk from use by German submarines which could menace North Atlantic convoys bringing the United States Army to France.

In Finland, bands of workers with Bolshevik sympathies (so called 'Red Finns') were making their own attempt to introduce a Bolshevik-aligned government in the country. In response, Baron Carl Gustav Mannerheim steadfastly raised a force of pro-German 'White Finns', which culminated in the Finnish Civil War. Mannerheim had been born in Sweden and had served in the Imperial Russian army as a cavalry commander until the revolution. Despite pleas to neighbouring Sweden for support, Mannerheim's country of birth maintained its neutrality and declared it would not provide aid or support to either Finnish faction.

Without Swedish support, Mannerheim made a request to Germany to send troops to aid in putting down the Red Finn insurgency. Germany despatched 12,000 troops under German General Count Rüdiger von der Goltz who together with Mannerheim's White Finns, drove the Red Finns over the frontier into Russian Karelia.

130. Bolshevik armoured cruiser *Pamiat Azova*. (Public domain)

With the Red Finns exiled to Russia, the German government asked the Finnish government to aid German troops in a drive east to cut off British held Murmansk, however before the plan could be hatched the Germans were forced to withdraw their troops from Finland to France in an attempt to stall the offensive launched there by the Allies on the Somme in early August.

The German Army proved incapable of holding back the great Allied offensive launched on 8 August 1918 on the Western Front and by November there seemed little chance that Germany could win the war. German civilians at home, like their Russian counterparts the year before, were fed up with the war and its human cost and privations, and were on the verge of revolution themselves. The Imperial German Navy was in a mutinous state and the German Army was not far behind, indeed some German troops occupying Estonia had revolted, thrown down their arms, formed *soviets* and demanded to be returned home.

The Armistice between the Allied nations and Germany signed on 11 November 1918 was not a peace treaty but rather a ceasefire agreement with stipulations to ensure Germany could not renew hostilities until a peace treaty had been negotiated and signed but it also contained clauses in which the Allies could make use of German troops occupying the Baltic territories to protect the area from Bolshevik annexation.

The Armistice also gave the Allies access to the Baltic Sea which (apart from a small British submarine flotilla that had broken the blockade early in the war) had been denied to the Royal Navy since 1914. The opening of the Baltic Sea also allowed the Royal Navy to protect Finnish and Baltic independence from either German or Bolshevik influence. On 13 November, Whitehall agreed to supply the Baltic territories with arms and supplies for which a small military mission under Major August Keenan, MC, Royal Highlanders, was formed to supervise training and distribution. Warships were seen as the more expedient option and much easier to withdraw should the need arise than ground troops.

Although the Baltic territories had been granted limited autonomy by the Bolsheviks via the Treaty of Brest-Litovsk in early 1918, the arrival of the Royal Navy Baltic Fleet in December 1918 caused Moscow considerable concern. The Bolshevik and British governments had by default been at war since the Allied attack and occupation of Archangel in August, and with the end of the war between Britain and the Central Powers the British had considerable reserves at their disposal to further prosecute a war against the Bolsheviks.

338   CHURCHILL'S SECRET WAR WITH LENIN

131. Bolshevik Bogatyr Class protected cruiser *Oleg*. (Public domain)

On 21 November 1918, the light cruiser HMS *Cardiff* had just led the German High Seas Fleet into internment at Scapa Flow when she and the other ships of the 6th Light Cruiser Squadron (HM Ships *Cassandra*, *Caradoc*, *Ceres* and *Calypso*) were ordered to steam to join the Baltic Fleet. Accompanying the cruisers were nine 'V' and 'W' Class destroyers from the 13th Destroyer Flotilla and seven minesweepers from the 3rd Fleet Sweeping Flotilla. Command of the force was given to Rear Admiral Edwyn Alexander-Sinclair, KCB, MVO, RN.

Sinclair was tasked with protecting the Baltic territories from Bolshevik influence and 'to show the British flag and support British policy as circumstances dictate.'[2] Arms to be supplied to the Estonian and Latvian provisional governments (at the time Lithuania was still under German occupation) were also transported on minelayers *Princess Margaret* and *Angora*. The British government wished Sinclair to stress to the Estonian and Latvian representatives that the arms were for use in their own self defence against either Germans or Bolsheviks. The British would not guarantee military support in the event of a Red Army invasion although the Admiralty informed Sinclair that a further squadron of warships could be called upon should the need arise.

Confusingly for Sinclair, Britain and Bolshevik Russia had not declared war, so should he consider an act by the Royal Navy in response to a Bolshevik invasion tantamount to a British declaration of war? Sinclair expressed his frustration:

> It was extremely difficult to get the Foreign Office to understand that, to frame orders for a naval force, the officer in command must be told whether he is at war or not. It may be possible under some circumstances to tell a land force, 'We do not want war if we can help it, and therefore you must let the other man fire first before you fire on him.' But with a naval force you cannot do that. The first time the other man fires it may be a torpedo, and then you may not have very much more to say, if the torpedo hits. So you must be told whether when you see a suspect you are entitled to open fire on him at once.[3]

Whilst in Copenhagen refuelling, Sinclair received word from the British Ambassador to Estonia that the presence of the fleet was urgently required to prevent 'anarchy'. Only 48 hours after their

2   Kinvig, *Churchill's Crusade*, p.137.
3   Bennett, *Cowan's War*, p.34.

arrival at Copenhagen the fleet less minesweepers sailed for the Eastern Baltic relying on paravanes (a minesweeping device) and charted 'safe routes' through the minefields.

The fleet arrived off Libau on 4 December and a day later proceeded north to Reval in line ahead formation, the cruisers in the lead with the nine destroyers following behind. Around midnight HMS *Cassandra* (Captain E.G. Kennedy, RN) second ship in line, was 'lifted bodily' into the air by a massive explosion just below the engine room compartment. The British cruiser had struck a German mine left over from the war. *Cassandra* was crippled by the explosion, her back broken in two places, and immediately began to sink. It was only the alertness of the officer of the watch on HMS *Caradoc* (Captain William Kerr, RN) following closely behind that avoided a collision with the stricken ship. *Caradoc* sent across her engineer officer to assist where he could whilst other ships in the convoy illuminated *Cassandra* with searchlights. Within 20 minutes of striking the mine, *Cassandra*'s upper deck was underwater and the ship abandoned.

Lieutenant Commander F.G. Glossop, RN, brought the destroyer HMS *Westminster* alongside the crippled cruiser but only managed to take off 14 ratings before the crashing of his ship against *Cassandra*'s hull in the heavy swell threatened to cause the smaller destroyer significant damage and Glossop was forced to abandon his rescue attempt.

Commander L.G. Ramsey, RN, (later Admiral Sir Gordon Ramsey) next brought the destroyer HMS *Vendetta* alongside and all remaining men (except one who fell overboard but was rescued) managed to board *Vendetta* without getting their feet wet.

The Royal Navy Baltic Fleet had suffered its first casualties to sea mines: sadly they would not be the last. Perhaps miraculously only 11 men had been killed by the massive explosion, and another 440 rescued from the sinking ship. A subsequent court of enquiry concluded that the starboard paravane had swept a mine but failed to cut the wire, dragging the mine into *Cassandra*'s side.[4]

The loss of *Cassandra* was a serious blow, particularly as the fleet was yet to reach station in the Gulf of Finland. The fleet was further reduced when *Cassandra*'s sister ship HMS *Calypso* (which had struck a submerged wreck at the entrance of Libau harbour on 1 December) was recalled to the UK for repairs escorted by destroyers HMS *Westminster* and HMS *Verulam* which were also in need of repair after colliding in thick fog the day after the evacuation of *Cassandra*.

When Alexander-Sinclair finally arrived at Reval his ships were warmly greeted by the Estonian people. The withdrawal of German troops from Estonia had left the country in political chaos, there had been no time to organise for the winter and there was a serious shortage of food and coal.

On 28 November, before Sinclair's arrival at Reval (renamed Tallinn after Estonian independence), the Soviet 7th Army, commanded by Latvian-born Colonel Vacietis, assisted by the guns of the Soviet Baltic Fleet, launched an amphibious attack against the town of Narva on the northern Estonian coast close to the Russian frontier. Red troops were now just 120 miles from the Estonian capital. The Estonian Provisional Government leader Konstantin Päts asked that his country be granted a guarantee of British protection and that a military mission be sent to train and equip his troops. The White Russian 'North West Army' under General Nikolai Yudenich, exiled from Russia to Estonia, requested the same protection.

Alexander-Sinclair reassured Päts that the British fleet would assist Estonia against the Bolsheviks where they could, but without full 'warlike backing' from the Admiralty, assistance would be limited. Sinclair's orders were that unless his ships were engaged by an enemy force he was to limit his fleet to coastal reconnaissance. Whitehall was not the Baltic, however, and Sinclair knew that with a Bolshevik force threatening Reval he would have to act in contravention of his orders or stand by and watch Estonia fall to the Red Army.

---

4   The National Archives: ADM1/8545/315, HMS Cassandra. Sunk by mine in Baltic. Casualties.

132. Bolshevik Gangut Class dreadnought *Petropavlovsk*. (Public domain)

On 13 December, Sinclair exceeded his orders and took cruisers HMS *Cardiff*, HMS *Caradoc* and five accompanying destroyers along the northern Estonian coast to Narva where they proceeded to shell elements of the Soviet 7th Army from the rear. The shelling was accurate and destroyed the only bridge across the Estonian frontier, cutting off the Red troops from their line of supply to Petrograd, and effectively ending the Bolshevik offensive on Reval. On Christmas Eve a small force of Estonian troops landed behind enemy lines at Kunda to harass the Red force from the rear. Sinclair returned to Libau in HMS *Cardiff* accompanied by *Ceres* and half the destroyers leaving *Calypso*, *Caradoc* and the remainder of the destroyers to stand guard off Reval.

On Boxing Day HMS *Calypso*, HMS *Caradoc*, and escorts were anchored at port in Reval, *Princess Margaret* and *Angora* having just delivered 5,000 rifles and other equipment for the Estonian Army, when the sound of gunfire echoed from the horizon and shells began falling into the harbour. An unidentified vessel was seen on the horizon, and orders were given to raise steam and proceed to contact at once.

The destroyer HMS *Wakeful* was first out and fired a couple of shots towards the unidentified ship which, taken by surprise at the arrival of the Royal Navy, immediately raised a white flag and surrendered. The British force had captured the Bolshevik destroyer *Spartak*, without loss of life on either side. *Spartak*'s crew seemed only too happy to be captured and immediately began to sell their hoard of furs and other items, looted from Estonian homes, to the British sailors for exorbitant prices.

The capture of *Spartak* had been more a comedy of errors than a stirring naval engagement. Upon commencement of the chase by British ships, *Spartak*'s forward gun returned fire but the gun was trained too far aft and the concussion knocked down the charthouse, damaged the bridge and concussed the helmsman. The engine room was unable to make full speed due to inexperience of the ship's stokers. Ten minutes after the engagement had begun, *Spartak* ran aground on a shoal and lost her screws. Such was their incompetency, ill training and inefficiency, the crew of *Spartak* had contributed more to their own defeat than had the prowess of the Royal Navy. The crippled destroyer had to be towed into Reval harbour by HMS *Vendetta*.

Papers from *Spartak* indicated that the Bolshevik cruiser *Oleg* was at anchor off Hogland Island, probably unaware of the British half fleet's presence. The cruisers HMS *Calypso* and HMS *Caradoc* and a destroyer were despatched to *Oleg*'s last indicated position, under Sinclair's instruction to sink the cruiser in direct contravention of his orders from London to only fire if fired upon.

As the half fleet set out for Hogland in the hope of catching *Oleg* just before dawn, the British ships passed a vessel in the distance sailing under blackout conditions. Both officers of the watch on board *Calypso* and *Caradoc* wanted to open fire but were overridden by their captains; the British cruisers were so close to the mystery vessel that if it was indeed a Bolshevik ship, the British would have been unable to put her out of action before she could fire torpedo tubes, at least one of which would probably have claimed *Caradoc*. When the half fleet arrived at Hogland they were disappointed to discover *Oleg* was long gone, if she had even been there in the first place.

On the way back to Reval the British again encountered the mystery ship that had been passed on the way out to Hogland. A couple of salvos were enough to convince the unidentified ship's captain that escape was impossible and the Bolshevik destroyer *Avtroil* was taken intact, the second Bolshevik destroyer captured without casualties in 24 hours. Captain (later Admiral) B.S. Thesiger, RN, of *Calypso* later wrote: 'I am not pretending this was war, but these were the first two ships (apart from the Great Surrender [of German ships after the Armistice]) that had been captured since the beginning of the war; all others had been sunk.'[5]

It later transpired through agents that *Oleg* had indeed been at anchor at Hogland but having received no radio messages from *Spartak* and warnings of enemy sightings from *Avtroil*, she had weighed anchor and steamed home to Kronstadt.

The Royal Navy half fleet had taken prisoner seven officers and 95 men on board *Spartak* and another seven officers and 138 men on board *Avtroil*. Both captured destroyers were relatively new, albeit poorly maintained, and were subsequently donated to the fledgling Estonian Navy where *Spartak* was renamed *Wambola* and *Avtroil* as *Lennuk*. Prior to the acceptance of the two destroyers, the largest vessel in the Estonian fleet had been a gunboat.

To add insult to injury, Political Commissar of the Russian Navy, Admiral Raskolnikov, was discovered hiding on *Spartak*. The Bolsheviks so highly valued Raskolnikov that in 1920 they negotiated his exchange for British prisoners held in Moscow. The crews of *Spartak* and *Avtroil* did not fare as well as Admiral Raskolnikov: in February 1919 the Estonian provisional government ordered the arbitrary execution of 40 of their number.

On 29 December 1918, with the Red Army just 25 miles from Riga (and an evacuation of 350 British and Allied subjects underway) one of the Lettish rifle regiments mutinied. Kārlis Ulmanis, Prime Minister of the Estonian provisional government, sought Germany's assistance to put down the mutiny but seeing their position of advantage, the Germans refused.

That same night HMS *Ceres* opened fire on the mutineers' barracks and after only a few shells the Letts gave up and surrendered. A Royal Navy landing party from *Ceres* was put ashore to supervise the mutineers' surrender and the evacuation of foreign nationals. With capture of the city by the Red Army inevitable, on 2 January 1919 the British fleet withdrew to Copenhagen, and the Bolsheviks occupied Riga the following day.

In the wake of the evacuation of Riga, destroyer HMS *Valkyrie* led the British force towards the mouth of the Western Dvina River (not to be confused with the 'Northern' or 'Severnaya' Dvina which runs south-east of Archangel, scene of much bitter fighting by British troops in the summer of 1919), Riga burning on the horizon behind them. HM Ships *Ceres*, *Princess Margaret*, *Cardiff* and destroyers, packed to the brim with refugees, landed their precious cargo at Copenhagen where they rendezvoused with *Caradoc*, *Calypso* and the remainder of the Royal Navy Baltic Fleet from Reval.

On 4 January 1919 cruisers HMS *Caradoc* and HMS *Calypso* and escorting destroyer *Wakeful* left Reval and proceeded to the northern Estonian coastal city of Narva where they pounded Red Army positions ashore in support of Estonian troops. The fire was accurate and Bolshevik soldiers could be observed fleeing across the snow-covered hills before the Estonians attacked.

In the meantime Admiral Alexander-Sinclair in HMS *Cardiff*, accompanied by *Ceres* and the remainder of the destroyers, had been stationed off the coast of Riga. The Latvian people were in a much more dire predicament than their Estonian neighbours. Whilst a majority of the Lettish population supported the provisional government of Kārlis Ulmanis whose aim was to establish a democratic, independent state, a not insignificant number of Letts also vehemently supported Bolshevism. To complicate matters further there were also the 'Baltic Barons' of Teutonic descent who wished to regain their positions of power and privilege with a view to incorporation in the German Empire as part of East Prussia. When the occupying German army left Estonia and withdrew from northern Latvia, the Lettish forces were unable to stem the advance of some 20,000 Red Army troops intent on filling the vacuum left by the German withdrawal.

133. General Rüdiger von der Goltz, commander of the German Army 'Iron Division' in the Baltic 1918–19. (Public domain)

Sinclair despatched HMS *Ceres* and two destroyers to the mouth of the Dvina, which on arrival at Riga on 19th December reported the military situation was much worse than Sinclair had anticipated. The 40,000 German troops still in Latvia were intending to withdraw as soon as possible, leaving most of their stores and heavy equipment behind to fall into Bolshevik hands. There was only a small formation of several hundred Balts (authorised by the Germans after the Armistice to form a Baltic militia) standing between the retreating Lettish riflemen and 12,000 Red Army troops.

HMS *Ceres* landed a party of Royal Marines to train the Lettish volunteers as best they could whilst Whitehall put political pressure on the Germans to observe the terms of the Armistice. In a letter to the German High Commissioner and High Command, Captain Harry H. Smyth, RN, outlined the British expectation of German forces occupying the Baltic:

> The Germans are to retain sufficient force in the district to hold the Bolshevik forces in check, and are not to permit them to advance beyond their present positions; the forces not required for the above are to retire with all dispatch in accordance with the Armistice conditions now in force.[6]

Article 12 of the Armistice agreement required that German forces maintain order, by use of force if necessary, in previously occupied territories at the request of the Allied governments until they were returned to Germany. Just weeks after the end of the war, the British government were demanding that armed German military forces act as a deterrent and possibly engage in actual fighting with British enemies – all in British interests.

The Germans had their own interests and had no intention of leaving the Baltic quietly, and so long as being seen to be acting in British interests would help them achieve their aim they would

---

6   *Ibid.*, p.48.

continue to do so. In reply to Smyth's letter, German General Rüdiger von der Goltz disingenuously wrote, 'the defence of the Baltic countries lies close to our hearts. We are not only here to defend a German race, but consider ourselves morally bound to protect a country which we have freed from the former governmental organisation.'[7] The British request played directly into Goltz's hands. He could use it as pretence to keep his troops in Lithuania as long as possible whilst claiming that troop demoralisation and lack of support from the Estonian and Lithuanian governments meant he could not actually carry out the British demands.

The Germans were well aware of their position of advantage in the negotiations as there was no British force that could be sent to the Baltic in time to prevent a Bolshevik takeover. To this end the German commander stipulated that he should be given command of all ground forces, German and Lettish, and that his German 'volunteers' should be guaranteed Latvian citizenship when the war was over, thus increasing the percentage of ethnic German citizens in the Baltic States and giving Germany greater claim to territorial sovereignty. The Germans had little interest in fighting the Bolsheviks unless it would benefit their own expansionist aims.

Having failed to protect Latvia from its first period of Soviet occupation, the Royal Navy Baltic Fleet sailed from Copenhagen for Rosyth on 10 January 1919. To have held the Red Army back would have required the landing of significant numbers of British troops at the height of a Baltic winter, something that the British government was unwilling to commit to.

On 23 December 1918, Admiral of the Fleet Lord Wemyss wrote a memorandum detailing what he believed to be the way ahead for British policy in the Baltic:

> The time has come for a decision as to our future policy. We have lost one new and efficient light cruiser and 11 lives. The existence of the Bolshevik Navy, though it is believed to have little efficiency, cannot be ignored. Ice conditions may at any time necessitate the withdrawal of our squadron. If we are to support and assure the independence of the Baltic Provinces, we should put in hand the immediate preparation of a land expedition of considerable strength.[8]

The Admiralty began to look into the matter but all attentions were at the time being put into preparations for the Treaty of Versailles. The only thing which could assure the independence of the Baltic states was the one thing that neither the British nor their Allies were willing to commit to in Russia: the landing of a corps-sized expeditionary force.

On New Year's Eve, the Foreign Office concluded that a land force should be sent to the Baltic but the War Office was opposed, preferring the 'safer' option of the return to the Baltic of a reinforced fleet. Command of the bolstered naval presence was given to an old sailor, a man whose name would become synonymous with the Royal Navy Baltic Fleet, Rear Admiral Walter Cowan.

A charismatic leader who loved horses and hunting, Cowan had been born in 1871, the son of a soldier in the Royal Welch Fusiliers garrisoned at Plymouth. Cowan joined the Royal Navy as a 13-year-old midshipman on HMS *Britannia* in 1884, and two years later was drilling with steam engine ships in the Mediterranean when he was struck down with sunstroke and sent home to England to recover.

After his recovery Cowan was posted to a training ship in the UK but soon fell sick once again and was invalided from the service. His naval career might have been short and undistinguished but after six months the Admiralty reviewed the young midshipman's condition and he was reinstated and returned to the Mediterranean Station.

---

7   *Ibid.*
8   *Ibid.*

Cowan next sailed for the West Indies where he was promoted to sub lieutenant and from there to the East Indies flagship, however he disliked being a junior sub lieutenant on a large warship. Unlucky enough to be struck down with dysentery, Cowan was again invalided home to England.

After being reviewed as fit by yet another medical board, Cowan requested posting to the Cape Station where he took part in campaigns in West Africa including the Bass River and Mwele expeditions and the campaign to capture Benin. In 1898, after avoiding a posting to the Royal Yacht, he was given command of the gunboat HMS *Sultan* operating on the upper Nile during the reconquest of the Sudan. He was present at the Battle of Omdurman where Winston Churchill charged with the 21st Lancers, for which Cowan was Mentioned in Despatches and awarded the DSO.

On the outbreak of war in South Africa in late 1899, Cowan managed to convince Lord Kitchener, General Roberts' Chief of Staff, that he would be of great use as his naval aide-de-Camp. Before the Admiralty had made a decision about the appointment, Cowan was already in South Africa with the Army where he spent many months on the veldt and was again Mentioned in

134. Rear Admiral Walter Cowan, KCB, DSO and Bar, MVO, Senior Naval Officer, Royal Navy Baltic Fleet, 1919. (Public domain)

Despatches for his service. Whilst in South Africa rumour reached Cowan that due to his extended absence from the service he had been struck off the Navy List for unauthorised absence. He hurriedly made his way home in an attempt to rescue his up to that point promising career in the navy.

Cowan had been on active service for more than five years, but half of that time had been with the Army in the field without formal Admiralty approval, and thus it was decided by the Admiralty that the 'Army' service could not count towards promotion. Already 30 years of age, Cowan married before posting to battleship HMS *Prince George*, shortly thereafter being promoted commander.

The following decade was relatively quiet for Cowan after a hectic turn of the century until the outbreak of war in August 1914. He received promotion to captain at age 35 and commanded a variety of destroyers and cruisers, and the battleship HMS *Zealandia*. It was in command of this ship on 10 September 1914 that Cowan rammed and sank German submarine *U-13*.

In early 1915, Cowan was given command of battlecruiser HMS *Princess Royal* and fought with her at Dogger Bank in January 1915 and at Jutland on 31 May–1 June 1916 where *Princess* suffered more than 100 casualties, subsequently requiring six weeks of repairs. Cowan was appointed Commander of the Order of the Bath for his command during the battle.

Command of HMS *Caledon* and the 10th Light Cruiser Squadron and further service in the North Sea 1917–18 followed. Cowan was held in such esteem by his superiors that in a letter from Admiral Keyes in May 1918, the commander of the amphibious raid on the Belgian port of Zeebrugge on St. George's Day the previous month (an iconic Royal Navy action of the First World War) wrote, 'I want you to know that, if you had only been free, no one but you should have commanded *Vindictive* [at Zeebrugge]'.[9] In September 1918, Cowan was promoted rear admiral and in December of the same year informed that he would be taking his squadron into the Baltic in the New Year, just in time to be made Knight Commander of the Order of the Bath for his services during the war.

Before sailing for the Baltic, Cowan was issued a directive on British policy in the region which makes interesting reading:

> The primary object of yours is to show the British Flag and support British policy. The Estonian and Latvian Governments have been supplied with 10,000 rifles, together with machine-guns and ammunition, by Rear-Admiral Sinclair. Any further supply should only be granted should you be reasonably convinced that the Estonian or other Government is of a stable nature and can control the Army, and that it will not be used in a manner opposed to British interests which may be summed up as follows: to prevent the destruction of Estonia and Latvia by external aggression, which is only threatened at present by Bolshevik invaders. The Germans are bound under the terms of the Armistice to withdraw from the ex-Russian Baltic Provinces, and in no case should you have any dealings with them. Whenever we are in a position to resist Bolshevik attacks by force of arms from the sea we should unhesitatingly do so. A Bolshevik man-of-war or armed auxiliary operating off the coast of the Baltic Provinces must be assumed to be doing so with hostile intent and treated accordingly. It is essential that you should not interfere with local politics, nor give colour for the assumption that Great Britain is favouring one part or another. You should be careful to raise no hope of any military assistance other than the supply of arms. No men are to be landed from your squadron unless under some exceptional circumstances.
>
> On arrival at Copenhagen, you should, if Rear-Admiral Sinclair has left a light cruiser and destroyers at Libau, relieve these ships from the force under your command. Riga and Reval are not to be visited without Admiralty authority, except that a destroyer may be sent for purposes of communication, and to acquire intelligence.[10]

The orders were vague at best, little more than a rough guide to furthering British interests without any instruction on how to handle the occupying German troops which could be considered to be as great a threat to Baltic states sovereignty as the Bolsheviks. Cowan would have to carry out his mission as best as he could and hope that the outcome would be equally agreeable to both the Admiralty and the Foreign Office.

With so many differing cultural and political groups all with their own interests at heart it was a delicate political situation that Cowan found himself faced with. The same White Finns that British General Maynard had fought at Murmansk the previous year were now seeking British recognition and support in return for working with the White Russians to capture Petrograd. Latvia was virtually occupied by the Bolsheviks whilst Estonia was fighting off Red Army incursions. German General von der Goltz (who had commanded the German invasion of Finland) held a large garrison in the Latvian port city of Libau and was awaiting the arrival of reinforcements from Russia.

The man who believed himself capable of leading the coalition of White Russian forces in defeating the Bolsheviks in the Baltic was General Nikolai Yudenich. Not short on self-belief, Yudenich had proclaimed himself commander of all White Russian forces on behalf of Supreme Commander of White Russian forces Admiral Kolchak. Yudenich was a hero of the war with the Japanese in 1905 and during the First World War had commanded Imperial Russian forces in the Caucasus fighting the Turks. Yudenich was so confident his forces would capture Petrograd that he established a 'Political Council' of Tsarist refugees to govern the city when it was captured. Like many White

9   *Ibid.*, p.59.
10 *Ibid.*, p.70.

135. German 'Iron Division' troops in Latvia, 1919. (Public domain)

Russian commanders, Yudenich was plagued by the indecision, corruption and quarrelling of his subordinates and was never able to bring a united front against the Bolsheviks.

Immediately after the Armistice the British government viewed German forces in the Baltic as a useful tool to defend the area from Red Army advances, but it soon became apparent that although the Germans had been defeated in the west, Goltz still believed that Germany was yet to be defeated in the east, and that the Baltic states, with their high population of ethnic Germans, would be some consolation for the loss of German colonies in the Pacific and Africa.

In early January, soon after Cowan's arrival in the Baltic, the Admiral requested permission from London to proceed to Estonia to carry out occasional bombardments of Bolshevik positions. The request was immediately turned down, the Admiralty citing that neither Riga nor Reval were to be visited. In the meantime Cowan despatched HMS *Royalist* and two destroyers to Libau to investigate the current situation in the city.

HMS *Royalist* returned with information that there were 2,000 German troops garrisoned in Libau. It was also learnt that German troops had been responsible for throwing into the sea some of the 5,000 rifles and ammunition landed by HM Ships *Princess Margaret* and *Angora* for the Lettish volunteers. Cowan's orders were not to interfere with the occupying German force, conversely Goltz was most definitely intent on interfering with British plans. The Germans did not wish for British influence on the Latvian government to exceed their own and were willing to take direct action to ensure this did not occur. Already having an established garrison in the city, the Germans clearly had the advantage.

By early 1919 the Red Army were camped just 78 miles from Libau. If the Bolsheviks attacked, the city could not be expected to hold out without significant reinforcements. The Red troops, however, were quite content to wait until the German garrison was withdrawn towards the end of the month before making a final advance on the city.

The only force available to bolster the Latvian defenders was a contingent of anti-Bolshevik Swedish volunteers. Consideration was given by the War Office to providing the Swedes one million *kronor* per month to further recruit volunteers; by the end of January the arrival of two French destroyers and a change in the attitude of the German command led the British to abandon the plan although many Swedish volunteers continued to serve with Yudenich's White Russian Army.

On the same day, 31 January 1919, Cowan learned that 500 Bolshevik troops had captured Windau on the northern Courland Peninsula, bringing Red troops to within just 40 miles of Libau. After an attempt by the plucky Lettish troops to recapture the town had failed, Cowan was relieved to receive a request from Latvian Prime Minster Ulmanis for British ships to shell the Bolshevik positions.

Cowan had likely already despatched his flagship HMS *Caledon* to Courland when he cabled the Admiralty to request permission to carry out the bombardment which was in turn duly granted. The fire from *Caledon*'s 6 inch guns was deadly accurate, destroying Bolshevik artillery batteries along the harbour entrance and driving out the Red troops in great haste.

Meanwhile at Kronstadt, a meeting of Bolshevik commanders of the Soviet Baltic Fleet had been held on 17 January where a declaration was passed that the Red Fleet in its entirety was unfit for active service. Trotsky advocated that in order to create an effective fighting fleet the ships' *soviets* should be dissolved, replaced by trusted commissars to ensure the crews loyalty and all authority be granted to the ships captain, former Tsarist Navy officers willing to serve the new Bolshevik government. Despite his best efforts, by the spring of 1919 the only Soviet ships at Kronstadt ready for the open sea were battleships *Petropavlovsk* and *Andrei Pervozvanny*, cruiser *Oleg*, destroyers *Azard* and *Gavriil*, and two submarines. More critical to the Soviet Baltic Fleet than lack of warships was lack of fuel.

On 2 March, British agents reported that the Latvian Balts were planning a coup to overthrow Ulmanis and his government. Although there was no direct evidence to link the plot to Goltz and his troops, the 'German hand was most evident'. The news prompted Deputy Chief of Naval Staff Admiral Fremantle in London to write a memorandum:

> I fear it is only too probable that the Balts may be planning a coup d'état in which they count on the support of the Germans now 8,000 good troops, well commanded, and being reinforced. The obligation is on the Germans to ensure the security of the Baltic Provinces against the Bolsheviks, but they are sending many more troops than seem to be necessary for that. We have asked four times for a decision from the Supreme War Council as to whether we should stop further reinforcements from being landed, the last time being yesterday. The only reply received has been that the question was in the hands of Marshal Foch.[11]

In response, the Secretary of the Admiralty wrote a formal letter to the Foreign Office:

> The work of the British naval officers in the Baltic would be much facilitated if they could be informed of the policy which they are required to support, and my Lords desire urgently to impress on the Secretary of State for Foreign Affairs the necessity for formulating such a policy.[12]

The British government was unable to formalise a policy on military intervention in Russia simply because they were unable to decide which course to take. In an attempt to stop the flow of German soldiers into Latvia, the British issued Goltz an explicit instruction that there were to be no further movements of German troops or supplies between German and Baltic ports and that the blockade of German Baltic coastal ports would be strictly maintained.

General von der Goltz knew that the British were stuck in a corner without him. In the absence of the landing of an Allied expeditionary force the British government needed his German troops to keep the Red Army at bay. In a thinly veiled rebuke Goltz's reply read:

11   *Ibid.*, p.83.
12   *Ibid.*

In face of the shortage of provision, munitions, equipment and reinforcements, no course remains open but to evacuate the occupied territory of Latvia, as the supply of German and Lettish troops cannot be maintained without sea transport. I am thus compelled to relinquish the repulse of the Bolshevik troops which had already been successfully commenced, to expose Latvia to Bolshevikism, and to withdraw my troops towards the German frontier.[13]

The British bluff had well and truly failed. The only way German troops could be withdrawn from Russia would be if they were replaced by an equal number of British or Allied troops which would not be approved by London any time soon. The British had to allow German troops and supplies to continue to flow into the Baltic or risk a Bolshevik takeover.

The German occupation in Latvia boiled over on 16 April when German troops attacked the Latvian Headquarters, arresting senior officers and setting the building ablaze. In response, Cowan immediately ordered 'S' Class destroyers HMS *Seafire* (Captain Andrew Cunningham, RN) and HMS *Scotsman* (Lieutenant Commander J.D. Noble, RN) to berth in Libau harbour awaiting further developments. The situation culminated in a standoff when a group of ethnic German Balts, armed and supported by Goltz, surrounded the Lettish government offices whilst German machine gunners took up position at the end of the wharf.

Cowan despatched HMS *Seafire* to steam into Libau harbour to recover a Lettish transport packed with rifles and ammunition supplied by the British government to the Letts. After recovering the vessel, Cunningham lay off the coast bombarding German troops along the approaches to the city for which he was awarded a second Bar to his DSO. Cunningham went on to greater fame during the Second World War as First Sea Lord and Chief of Naval Staff, services for which he was knighted by King George VI.

On 22 April, Cowan met with delegations from the French military mission to the Baltic (the French also had a number of warships operating with the British Fleet) in which consensus was reached that the Allies should demand of Goltz the immediate removal of the officer in charge of the party that arrested the Latvian government, and that the Lettish troops that had been disarmed should immediately have their weapons returned without interference. Initially Goltz was predictably reluctant but eventually capitulated and agreed to the terms put before him, ending the crisis and restoring British hopes for an Estonia free from German or Bolshevik interference.

With the arrival of spring 1919, the Gulf of Finland began its annual thaw and on 25 April the Red Fleet sailed from Kronstadt into the Gulf of Finland and Eastern Baltic Sea. In response to the activity of the Soviet fleet Cowan replaced HMS *Caledon* with HMS *Curacoa* and moved his flag to the newly arrived cruiser. In the second week of May (after a quick congratulatory visit to applaud Baron Carl Gustaf Mannerheim on Finland's declaration of independence from Russia) Cowan ordered his flagship to steam west along the Estonian coast towards Libau. It was to prove a fateful decision as early the following morning, 13 May 1919, HMS *Curacoa* struck a mine 70 miles east of Reval.

The British admiral was in his cabin at the time of the explosion and rushed to the bridge in his bathrobe to discover that the damage was fortunately not as bad as could have been expected. Several compartments along the starboard side had flooded but miraculously there had been only a single fatality, Ordinary Seaman George Plunkett, aged just 18 years.

After rudimentary repairs led by Warrant Shipwright George Byrne, RN (services for which Byrne was awarded the DSC), HMS *Curacoa* returned to the UK to undergo further repairs, leaving Cowan to transfer his flag to *Cleopatra* (Captain C.J.C. Little, CB, RN).

On 17 May, the Bolshevik destroyer *Gavriil* and four minesweepers were observed from HMS *Cleopatra* steaming west from Kronstadt. Shortly after 0900 the following day the British cruiser

---

and its escorting destroyers HMS *Shakespeare* (Commander F.E.K. Strong, DSO, RN), HMS *Scout* (Lieutenant Commander E.F. Fitzgerald, RN) and HMS *Walker* (Lieutenant Commander A.T.N. Abbay, RN) weighed anchor, hoping to catch the Bolshevik ships before they could withdraw behind the safety of the minefields.

HMS *Cleopatra* opened fire with her 6 inch armament at maximum range of 16,000 yards which was enough to convince the minesweepers to pull all stops and flee to safety although the plucky *Gavriil* answered *Cleopatra*'s fire with her much smaller guns. The range was so great that *Gavriil*'s shots fell well short of the British ships but in return *Cleopatra*'s fire was accurate enough to score 'splinter' hits before the proximity of the Russian minefields, and fire from one of the Bolshevik island forts, precluded the British ships from continuing the pursuit.

The day after the action, the cruiser HMS *Dragon* (Captain Francis Arthur Marten, RN) joined the Baltic Fleet from Danzig to replace the mined *Curacoa*.

On 23 May, Cowan sailed to Reval to welcome the arrival of the 7th Submarine Flotilla (submarines *E27*, *E39*, *E40*, *L11*, *L12*, *L16* and *L55*) under Captain Martin Nasmith, VC, RN, in depot ship HMS *Lucia*. Nasmith had been awarded his decoration for gallant deeds in submarine *E11* in the Dardanelles in 1915. Incidentally, Nasmith's younger brother Reginald was serving in North Russia as an officer with 8th Battalion, MGC at the same time Martin was serving in the Baltic.

The submarines were useful to Cowan as guard ships which could be stationed at entrances to the swept minefield channel into Petrograd Bay, freeing up other surface ships for duty elsewhere. Soon after their arrival, several other ships arrived to reinforce the Baltic Fleet, including the remainder of 1st Destroyer Flotilla under Captain G.W.M. Campbell, RN, flagship HMS *Wallace*. Particularly welcome were the Racecourse Class minesweepers HMS *Banbury*, HMS *Hexham*, and HMS *Lanark*, of 11th Minesweeping Flotilla, which were immediately put to work clearing passage between Reval, Libau and Copenhagen.

Also in May, HMS *Galatea* (Lieutenant C.M. Forbes, DSO, RN) arrived at Helsinki with the head of the new British Military Mission on board. The Mission's role was to support and arm General Yudenich's White Russian forces with the ultimate goal of capturing Petrograd and forcing German General von der Goltz to withdraw and comply with the conditions of the Armistice. The Mission would be based in Helsinki where both Yudenich and Goltz had their respective headquarters, one in each of Helsinki's two finest hotels, each flying the national flag of their occupant.

The Mission comprised 44 officers and 45 other ranks commanded by Lieutenant General Sir Hubert Gough, GCB, GCMG, KCVO, no stranger to political controversy. In July 1914, whilst a brigadier in command of 3rd Cavalry Brigade, Gough had been an instigator of the 'Curragh Incident' in which 57 British Army officers based at Curragh in County Kildare, Ireland, threatened to resign their commissions rather than enforce the Home Rule Act of 1914 which granted Ireland limited autonomy, the first steps towards the creation of the Irish Republic in 1922.

The incident did not appear to harm Gough's career and by age 46 he was in command of the 5th Army in France, however his distinguished services in the earlier years of the war were overshadowed by the horrendous failure at Passchendaele in 1917. The controversy and public outrage became so great that in March 1918, after he had been unable to stem the tide of the German Spring Offensive, Prime Minister Lloyd-George ordered his recall to London.

Gough had the unique honour of having a father, brother and uncle, all of whom had been awarded their nation's highest honour, the Victoria Cross: his father and uncle during the Indian Mutiny 1857 and his brother (who was later killed in action in France in 1915) in Somaliland, 1903.

The British Military Mission to the Baltic States differed from those sent to North Russia, Siberia and South Russia in that it was purely administrative with a mandate to identify ways the Allies could most effectively assist the Baltic states resist Bolshevik and German influence, rather than directly recruiting, training, arming and equipping local troops as in other theatres of British military intervention in the Russian Civil War. With the Mission came a consignment of British supplies, eight 6 inch howitzers, sixteen 18 pdr field guns, 10 trucks, and medical supplies for 10,000 troops. The supplies were mainly war surplus but were vital to the critically underequipped White Russian forces.

Throughout 1919 much of the British Fleet was primarily tasked with bottling up Bolshevik warships in Kronstadt, the island fortress and Red naval base guarding the entrance to Petrograd Bay. Protected by a ring of forts and man-made submerged breakwaters, Kronstadt was almost impregnable. The Red Fleet blockaded in Kronstadt was not a token force. The Bolshevik battleships *Andrei Pervozvanny* and *Petropavlovsk* armed with 12 inch guns were far stronger than anything in the British Baltic Sea Fleet, the largest of which were the 'C' Class cruisers with guns only half the size. Also blockaded in Kronstadt were the cruiser *Oleg* armed with 6 inch guns, the submarine depot ship *Pamiat Azova*, a destroyer squadron, the minelayer *Narova*, seven submarines and several fleet auxiliaries.

During spring 1919 the cat and mouse game continued as *Oleg* would steam out of Kronstadt harbour with an escort of destroyers to raid along the Estonian coast but upon sighting of the British fleet would flee to the safety of the Kronstadt minefields and blaze away at the pursuing British ships. The British cruisers were forced to turn away before they came in the range of the forts which ringed Kronstadt harbour.

On 29 May 1919, Cowan received an intelligence report that the Bolsheviks would imminently attempt an amphibious attack on the northern Estonian coast close to the Russian border, supported by the Red Fleet out of Kronstadt. Cowan set out from Reval in HMS *Cleopatra* accompanied by *Dragon*, *Galatea*, *Wallace*, *Walker*, and four other destroyers of the 4th Flotilla at 0500 on 30 May, and anchored off the Estonian coast in preparation to make an attack should the opportunity present itself. All ships remained at anchor except HMS *Walker* which accompanied submarines *E27* and *L16* on patrol just off the minefield to try and lure the Red ships out.

A day later destroyer *Azard* was sighted coming west with battleship *Petropavlovsk* and two other small warships behind the minefield. HMS *Walker* engaged *Azard* at 8,000 yards range and chased the destroyer eastwards under fire from *Petropavlovsk*. A Bolshevik aircraft also made an appearance, dropping a few bombs near Cowan's force until it was sent packing by anti-aircraft fire. A Red observation balloon was also launched to direct fire from the Bolshevik forts. *Azard* withdrew towards the safety of *Petropavlovsk* which kept up a well-disciplined fire on *Walker* with her huge 12 inch guns, hitting *Walker* twice with shell splinters but causing no significant damage and wounding one rating only, Able Seaman Edward Quinn.

Cowan patrolled his force up and down the minefield but the Bolsheviks showed no intention of coming out to fight and retired back towards Kronstadt after firing a few more salvos in anger. Two of Nasmith's submarines were in action during the engagement: *L16* (Lieutenant Commander Alfred Hine, RN) fired two torpedoes at *Azard* at a range of 4,000 yards and *E27* (Lieutenant Alec Carrie, RN) a single torpedo at a range of 5,000 yards, neither submarine had success.

Had *Petropavlovsk* stayed to fight it out the British casualties may have been much more severe but Soviet Admiral Zelenoy, commanding the Soviet Baltic Sea Fleet, saw the greatest use for his ships in the defence of Petrograd rather than offensive action.

The lesson learnt from the 31 May engagement was that opportunities to take the Bolshevik ships head-on would not present themselves often and if Cowan wished to have a decisive engagement he would need to position his ships further east than Reval, from where he could attack the Soviet ships as soon as they appeared. Cowan chose Biorko Sound in Finland, just 20 miles from the Bolshevik minefield and the perfect position from which the enemy could be observed coming out of Kronstadt.

On 2 June, Cowan sent destroyers HMS *Vivacious* (Commander C.L. Bate, RN) and HMS *Voyager* (Lieutenant Commander C.G. Stuart, DSC, RN) to patrol north of the minefield as a precaution, should the Bolsheviks attempt to mine Biorko harbour before the bulk of the fleet

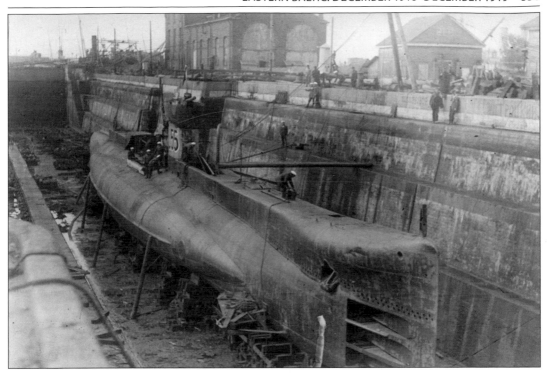

136. Above: Submarine HMS *L55* in dry dock at Kronstadt after recovery by the Soviets from the bottom of the Eastern Baltic Sea, 1928. (Public domain)

137. Below: Coffins containing the remains of the crew of HMS *L55* taken on board HMS *Champion* at Reval. (Public domain)

arrived. In transit to the Finnish coast the two British destroyers encountered *Azard* and *Gavriil* still safely behind the minefield. The destroyers exchanged a few shots at long range without effect. The following day *E27* made another failed attack on a Bolshevik ship, both torpedoes malfunctioned and exploded short of their intended target.

Two days later, destroyers HMS *Versatile* (Commander G.C. Wynter, RN), HMS *Vivacious* and HMS *Walker* had another brief engagement with the two Soviet destroyers, supported in the far distance by the guns of *Petropavlovsk*. The engagement was inconclusive but ended in disaster for the British.

Royal Navy submarine *L55* (Lieutenant Charles Chapman, DSC and Bar, RN) had been secretly lurking beneath the surface with the British destroyers as they steamed eastwards. As the British destroyers engaged *Azard* and *Gavriil*, Chapman made an unsuccessful torpedo attack. What occurred next is subject to much conjecture. Soviet sources state *L55* was struck by fire from *Gavriil* while surfaced, whilst others state the submarine struck a sea mine when submerged. What is known is that *L55* was sunk with the loss of all hands.

Although Lieutenant Blacklock's (submarine *L12*) report indicted there was little chance of survivors, Cowan and Nasmith refused to lose hope and continued to search until finally accepting the inevitable a few days later. The deaths of 43 officers and ratings on board *L55* would remain the largest single day loss of life for the Royal Navy during British military intervention in the Russian Civil War, 1918–20.

When the Soviet Navy salvaged *L55* from the bottom of the Baltic on 11 August 1928, the Admiralty made a request via the Swedish government for the crew remains to be repatriated to the United Kingdom. The Soviets insisted that no British warship would be allowed into Russian territorial waters but a compromise was made and the British merchant ship *Truro* was delivered the coffins at Kronstadt. The remains were then transferred to HMS *Champion* at Reval on 30 August with full ceremony from an Estonian honour guard. The remains of the crew of *L55* were interred in a mass grave at Haslar Royal Navy Cemetery (CWGC) on 7 September 1928 with a single headstone to mark their final resting place.

L55 was repaired and commissioned into the Soviet Fleet but lost three weeks later with all hands during trials. Recovered from the ocean floor for a second time, *L55* was recommissioned and served with the Soviet Navy until scrapped in 1953. The Soviets went on to use *L55* as the basis of design for the Leninets Class submarines which saw service with the Soviet Navy during the Second World War.

On 7 June, Cowan established an observation station east of Biorko to guard against any surprise moves from the Bolshevik Fleet. The station required a rotation of three destroyers at anchor facing seaward at all times at five minutes notice to move. Cowan's preparations were all for naught when on the night of 9 June, *Azard* and *Gavriil* left Kronstadt without being observed and attacked HM Ships *Versatile*, *Vivacious* and *Walrus* at anchor. The British destroyers returned fire whilst Cowan despatched ships from Biorko in support. After firing 80 rounds the Soviet ships returned to cover behind the minefield without either side having scored a hit. It was the most aggressive move made by the Bolsheviks to date and could have ended much worse for the British.

Amongst the most potent weapons Cowan had available were not the cruisers or destroyers of his fleet but two 40 foot coastal motor boats. The CMB had been developed by Thornycroft during the war for hit-and-run operations along the French and Belgian coasts, the combination of speed and manoeuvrability proving to be extremely effective. Equipped with up to 950 horsepower engines and a wooden hydroplane hull, the CMB could exceed speeds of 40 knots. Equipped with Lewis guns and either mines or torpedoes (one 18 inch torpedo for the 40 foot boats and two for the 55 foot model) they were heavily armed for their size. CMBs also served in the Caspian and on the Dvina River south-east of Archangel but it was in the Baltic that they truly made their name in Royal Navy history.

CMB service was voluntary and almost entirely made up of young officers of the RNR, many of whom had spent the war patrolling the North Sea in minesweepers and armed trawlers. CMBs had

138. Lieutenant Augustus Willington
Shelton Agar, RN, prior to service
in the Baltic. (IWM Q114301)

been successfully used during the Zeebrugge Raid on St. George's Day, 23–24 April 1918 and during the Ostend Raid the following month, primarily to create smokescreens and guide larger warships to the attack. After the Armistice, in December 1918 several CMBs were despatched to the Caspian Sea where a ramshackle flotilla of converted Russian trawlers with Royal Navy/Royal Marine and White Russian crews were operating against a Bolshevik flotilla.

The next task for the CMBs was in North Russia where several were used for communication duties on the Dvina River south of Archangel. CMBs were also used on the Rhine River in conjunction with the British army of occupation in Germany. In mid 1919 an urgent call came from the Admiralty for two of the smaller 40 foot CMBs to be immediately despatched for special service in the Eastern Baltic Sea. The two CMBs were intended to use their speed and agility to navigate through the chain of forts and breakwaters to transport couriers between the Finnish coast and Petrograd and bring back reports right under the noses of the Bolsheviks.

Having joined the Royal Navy as a 14-year-old midshipman in 1905, Lieutenant Augustus Agar had already qualified as a pilot in 1913 but was not accepted into the Royal Naval Air Service (RNAS) due to a lack of aircraft. He served with the Grand Fleet on battleship HMS *Hibernia* and at Murmansk with Admiral Kemp's White Sea Squadron on HMS *Iphigenia* before she was sunk as a blockship at Zeebrugge in April 1918. Before the end of the war Agar was serving with CMBs on Osea Island on the River Blackwater in Essex.

Early in February 1919 Agar was called to the London offices of the British Secret Intelligence Service (SIS) where he met head of SIS Captain Sir Mansfield George Smith-Cumming, RN, codenamed 'C'. Smith-Cumming outlined to Agar the situation in Russia and the evacuation of British SIS agents there but stated there was one British agent who had remained behind in Russia to gather intelligence of vital importance. It was imperative that this agent be got out alive as he had first hand knowledge of matters of the utmost importance. It was also critical that his carefully assembled network of couriers between Finland and Estonia be safely transported across the Gulf of Finland, as of late several had been caught attempting to cross the Russian frontier.

After the killing of Naval Attaché Captain Francis Cromie, RN, by Red troops storming the British Embassy in Petrograd on 31 August 1918, the escape from Russia of SIS agents Sidney Reilly and George Hill, and the expulsion of Robert Bruce Lockhart, William Hicks and Ernest Boyce, the SIS network in Russia had effectively ceased to exist. The Soviet secret police, the dreaded *Cheka*, were hot on the heels of the only British agent remaining in Petrograd and it was imperative that he be 'lifted' and replaced by a new spy whose cover was intact. The new agent was Paul Dukes, codename ST25 (Stockholm Station, Agent 25). Dukes had first visited Russia in 1909 as a student of classical music. As a member of the Anglo–Russian committee and a King's Messenger, he had travelled throughout Russia studying conditions in the country for the Foreign Office until June 1918 when he was summoned to return to London. Dukes believed that the Foreign Office must have been dissatisfied with his work and was understandably surprised when he was offered a job by 'C' to work in Russia as a spy for British SIS.

Dukes agreed to return to Russia to secretly report on the Bolsheviks, their weaknesses and vulnerabilities and in particular the level of German influence (the war with Germany was still ongoing) and the possibility for regime change to a return to monarchy or other pro-British government. Dukes stepped ashore at Archangel in September 1918 (under occupation by the British since the previous month) and made his way overland to Petrograd under an assumed identity.

The task for Agar was to establish a CMB base in Finland from where he could run couriers and money to Dukes as well as relaying any information and reports for analysis by the Foreign Office, and also to maintain a sea link to Petrograd. Agar was codenamed ST34; he and the crew of the two CMBs would cease to work under Admiralty authority but would come under direct command of British SIS operating independently of the Royal Navy Baltic Fleet. The CMBs were painted light grey to resemble civilian motor launches and the crew issued an allowance to purchase civilian clothes to wear in place of uniforms.

Agar was given free rein to select two volunteer crews from those at the CMB base on Osea Island. He chose three young RNR officers all under 21 years of age: Sub Lieutenants Edgar Sindall and John Hampsheir and Midshipman Richard Marshall. Each of the two crews would have their own Chief Motor Mechanic (CMM) from the Royal Naval Volunteer Reserve (RNVR) to manage the engines, CMMs Hugh Beeley for *CMB 4* and Albert Piper for *CMB 7*. Additionally, CMM Richard Pegler would be based in Helsinki to source engine spares and supplies.

In early May, Agar, Marshall and Hampsheir boarded a small Swedish steamer for passage to the Baltic with Sindall, Beeley and Piper following on another vessel soon after. The men felt somewhat uncomfortable in their new civilian clothes, Agar commented, 'It was the first time I had worn any for five years.'[14]

Immediately upon Agar's arrival in Finland planning began in earnest. He chose the small sheltered cove at Terrioki (just over 10 miles from the chain of forts flanking Kronstadt) as his base and billeted the CMB crews in the local yacht club. Agar's next move was to work out how to get his CMBs from Abo in Sweden, where they had been deposited, to Terrioki some 150 miles away. To do so he required assistance from Admiral Cowan's Baltic Fleet destroyers to tow the CMBs to their destination at night under the cover of darkness. A meeting was arranged between Cowan and Agar on board one of the destroyers to discuss the matter. To maintain his cover, Agar presented himself in civilian clothes as a 'consular official' from Reval. Cowan was most receptive to assisting to transport the CMBs to Terrioki and was particularly excited to hear of the young Lieutenant's plans to run the gauntlet of forts surrounding Kronstadt to reach Petrograd.

Before departing, Agar made a request which would greatly influence later events. Although under strict instructions that his CMBs were to be used only for the secret service operations for which they had been sent, Agar requested that the Admiral provide him with two torpedoes, one for each of the two CMBs. Cowan was not keen on the idea of two unmarked CMBs with RN crews in civilian clothes zipping across the Eastern Baltic with torpedoes, but relented when he was told of the concession given by 'C' that allowed the crews to carry a set of uniform and the Royal Navy Ensign stowed away in case of emergency.

The two CMBs were towed by HMS *Voyager* to Biorko sound where the cables were thrown off and the CMBs made their own way to Terrioki. Agar did not wait to establish himself at the new base before setting out on a series of trials to test the serviceability of the engines. An engine failure whilst attempting to cross the chain of forts would have disastrous consequences.

---

14 Augustus Agar, Baltic Episode: *A Classic of Secret Service in Russian Waters* (London: Hodder & Stoughton, 1963), p.32.

139. *CMB 4* and *CMB 7* berthed at Terrioki yacht club, Finland, 1919. (IWM Q114311)

It was fortunate that Agar took the precaution to conduct trials, as during one run *CMB 7* developed serious engine trouble. Under normal circumstances an entirely new engine would have been installed but at a remote base on the Finnish coast no such luxury existed, and with the assistance of the crew of a small oiler despatched by Cowan to set up a fuel dump for the boats Agar set to work making rudimentary repairs.

On 10 June, a dramatic event occurred just across the sea from Biorko at the fort of Krasnaya Gorka, 40 miles west of Petrograd. The Bolshevik soldiers stationed at the fort had mutinied, imprisoned their commissars and hoisted a white flag as a plea to the White Russian and Allied forces to come to their aid.

The following day Hampsheir barely escaped with his life when he fell overboard from *CMB 4*. The fully clothed midshipman sank below the surface and was only saved by the gallant actions of Hugh Beeley, who dived overboard and dragged the semi-conscious junior officer to the surface. Hampsheir was revived but very badly shaken by the experience.

On 13 June, Agar left the yacht club on his first covert mission, to land a courier at Petrograd unseen. He took an extra crew member in Hampsheir to familiarise himself with the route in the darkness. In the event of being 'rumbled', Agar intended to make a fight of it and Hampsheir would also be needed to man the CMB's twin Lewis guns. With the guidance of a local smuggler, Agar navigated the treacherous maze of forts and breakwaters for the first time without being observed and landed his precious cargo in the marshes near Petrograd before turning for home, running the gauntlet of Bolshevik patrols, searchlights, minefields, breakwaters and forts for a second time.

Agar successfully picked up the courier and his critical despatches from ST25 the following night as had been previously arranged. The pickup went off flawlessly. The exhausted agent hadn't slept for days and spent most of the trip back to Terrioki collapsed below deck, despite the tremendous noise and vibration of the engines.

As Agar had predicted, Bolshevik warships *Andrei Pervozvanny* and *Petropavlovsk* left Kronstadt early on the morning of 14 June and were soon in action bombarding the mutinying Red troops in Krasnaya Gorka fortress. Agar had already started to formulate in his mind a plan to attack the Bolshevik ships but to carry out an attack was not only contrary to his orders to use his boats for intelligence purposes only: the loss or damage of one or both of the CMBs would jeopardise his ability to bring ST25 out of Petrograd.

Returning from a run to pick up a courier, Agar encountered the Bolshevik battleships with destroyer escorts west of Kronstadt and despite the risks decided to attack one of the dreadnaughts. Four miles out from the enemy ships the engine failed and torpedo launching speed could not be maintained. Agar was forced to return to the yacht club with the torpedo still on board.

On return to Terrioki, Agar sent a cipher to London requesting permission to attack the Bolshevik ships, citing that he had already fulfilled his mission in establishing contact with ST25 in Petrograd. It would take at least several hours for a reply to be received and Agar and his crews spent the time loading both CMBs and preparing for action, followed by a few hours' restless sleep in preparation for the operation.

From the church steeple at Terrioki, Agar could observe the Bolshevik battleships bombarding Krasnaya Gorka fortress but could do nothing but wait for the reply from London. When the response did finally come he was to be disappointed. The cable read, 'BOATS TO BE USED FOR INTELLIGENCE PURPOSES ONLY – STOP – TAKE NO ACTION UNLESS SPECIALLY DIRECTED BY S.N.O. BALTIC'.[15]

Not to be discouraged, Agar took the cable from the Admiralty as permission to go ahead with his plan as long as he had Admiral Cowan's agreement. Whilst the Admiralty had no desire for Agar to use his CMBs for anything other than courier missions, they had left a loophole whereby Senior Naval Officer Baltic could overrule London's orders.

If the Red ships were to be attacked before they could return to the safety of Kronstadt there would be no time for Agar to travel to Biorko and get orders directly from Cowan himself. In a bold and risky decision for a junior officer he decided to carry out an attack without the Admiral's approval in the hope that Cowan would sanction his actions retrospectively. It was a risky gamble.

Having already had several hours to prepare, both CMBs were armed and ready to leave Terrioki on the night of 16 June, the crews eager but anxious at the prospect of action. Agar took Hampsheir and Beeley with him in *CMB 4* whilst *CMB 7* was crewed by Sindall in command with Marshall at the helm and Piper at the engines. Agar's plan was for the two boats to make their attack run together and launch both torpedoes at a single target, doubling the chances of a hit. The young lieutenant planned to attack before dawn when there was just enough sufficient light from the west to silhouette their target whilst the darkness to the east would cover the CMBs' approach through the enemy destroyer screen.

At midnight on 16 June, both CMBs set out from Terrioki. On this mission the crews wore Royal Navy uniform with both boats flying the Royal Navy Ensign. The CMBs had only just entered the open sea when Sindall in *CMB 7* struck a floating mine which fortunately did not detonate: sea mines had enough explosive to sink a cruiser, let alone a 40 foot motor boat. The propeller shaft had been badly broken in the collision and Sindall was unable to continue the attack. Agar had no choice but to abandon the mission and throw a cable to tow the stricken boat back to Terrioki.

On arrival at the yacht club both crews were understandably shocked at the near loss of Sindall, Marshall and Piper but perhaps relieved that the attack had been scrapped. Piper's examination of the underside of *CMB 7* confirmed what Agar already feared, the propeller shaft had been broken clean through and the boat would require extensive repairs before returning to service.

Agar now had only *CMB 4* remaining with which to maintain communication with ST25 and if necessary evacuate British SIS agent Paul Dukes from Petrograd. Agar made the decision to risk his only serviceable boat to make an attack on the Bolshevik warships off Krasnaya Gorka himself and on the following night, 17 June 1919, set off with Hampsheir and Beeley in *CMB 4* armed with a single torpedo.

---

15 *Ibid.*, p.82.

140. Crew of *CMB 4* who attacked and sank Bolshevik cruiser *Oleg* in the Gulf of Finland on the night of 17–18 June 1919. From left to right, Sub Lieutenant John Hampsheir, RNR, Lieutenant Augustus Agar, RN, Chief Motor Mechanic Hugh Beeley, RNVR. In recognition of their bravery Agar was awarded the VC, Hampsheir the DSC and Beeley the CGM. (IWM Q114337)

Agar brought *CMB 4* out of Terrioki harbour, past Tolbuhin Lighthouse and into the Eastern Baltic, the engine running smoothly. Within a matter of only minutes the CMB was nearing the protective Bolshevik destroyer screen. Agar reduced the engine to low revolutions to keep the visible wake in the moonlight to a minimum and began the nerve-wracking task of creeping under the guns of the destroyer screen. Without warning the silence was shattered by a deafening crash and severe vibration across the entire length of the boat. The hydraulic charge used to launch the stern-mounted torpedo had been accidentally fired, but due to a fault the discharge had not been at full power. Thanks to the safety clamps the torpedo had not been launched, although the hydraulic ram had caused a massive shudder through the boat. Hampsheir emerged from below ashen-faced. Whilst he had been installing the charge it had accidentally fired leaving him badly shaken.

It would be impossible to replace the charge at speed in the choppy seas and Agar was forced to bring the CMB to a complete stop within view of two Bolshevik destroyers whilst the charge was replaced. The CMB sat bobbing in the water as Beeley and Hampsheir fumbled in the swell to install a new cartridge. Reloading the charge took 10 minutes but to the crew in their precarious position it must have seemed like hours. The sun was already rising from the east and the dark silhouette of the cruiser *Oleg* could be made out in the near distance. With every passing minute the chances of the boat being spotted by one of the escort destroyers increased dramatically. Agar recalled:

Beeley remained wonderfully calm. There was nothing to be said. It was a time for deeds and not words. At last Hampsheir popped up from the hatch. 'Its all right, sir, we have reloaded.' With a sigh of relief, I slipped in the clutch. Throwing all caution to the winds, I put on full speed and headed straight for the

Oleg, which was now clearly visible. In a few moments we were nearly on top of her. I fired my torpedo less than five hundred yards away, just as the first shot from her guns was fired at us in return. Then I quickly put the helm over, turning almost a complete circle, and, with the sea now following us, headed back westwards towards the same direction from which I had approached.

We looked back to see if our torpedo had hit, and saw a large flash abreast the cruiser's foremost funnel, followed almost immediately by a huge column of black smoke reaching up to the top of her mast. The torpedo had found its mark. We tried to give three cheers but could scarcely hear ourselves for the din of the engines. Yet we could hear the whistle of shells overhead, telling us that both forts and destroyers were firing at us. But in the uncertain light just before early dawn, speed made us a very difficult target to hit.[16]

Oleg listed badly and sank within minutes, resulting in the deaths of 40 Red sailors. The water level was so low in the Gulf of Finland during summer that part of *Oleg*'s superstructure remained visible above the surface, an eerie reminder to the Red sailors of the presence of the CMBs, thereto likely unknown to the enemy. Agar and crew returned to Terrioki to a warm welcome from Sindall, Marshall and Piper who had heard the explosion and gunfire from the yacht club. Agar, Hampsheir and Beeley were freezing but waiting cups of sweet tea quickly revitalised all but Hampsheir. The stress and fear of the accidental discharge of the firing mechanism, the attack on *Oleg* and the previous courier missions to Petrograd under the noses of the Bolsheviks had all taken their toll on the young midshipman. In August he was struck down with 'battle shock' and sent to a Finnish hospital for rest, and took no further part in the Baltic operations.

Agar need not have worried about exceeding his orders and his attack on *Oleg* not meeting with Cowan's approval. When the two next met the Admiral was delighted with the success of Agar's bold attack and promised to back the young lieutenant's actions to the Admiralty.

For the sinking of the cruiser *Oleg* by a 40 foot CMB with a single torpedo, Agar was awarded the Victoria Cross, Hampsheir the DSC and Beeley the CGM, all three awards published in the *London Gazette* with the secretive citation, 'in recognition of his conspicuous gallantry, coolness and skill under extremely difficult conditions in action.'[17] Agar's was the only Victoria Cross never to be gazetted with a full citation and was thereafter known as the 'Mystery VC'.

In the days following the sinking of *Oleg*, *CMB 7* was repaired and Agar continued his courier runs to and from Petrograd. The Bolshevik secret police, the *Cheka*, had begun to close in on British agent Paul Dukes and SIS chief 'C' Smith-Cumming gave the order to pull the British agent out.

Agar and Sindall rotated command and crews of *CMB 4* during the subsequent courier missions to give all crews an equal rest from operations. It was during one of these courier missions that Sindall was spotted by the Bolshevik garrison passing through the chain of forts. Agar, watching from ashore at Terrioki, could see flashes in the distance followed by an anxious wait until Sindall was sighted bringing *CMB 4* into the yacht club as if nothing at all had happened.

Sindall, the CMB and all crew were unscathed thanks to inaccurate fire from the Russian gunners in the chain of forts. Inexplicably, the Bolsheviks did not turn on their searchlights and the CMB was able to escape back to Terrioki at high speed without a scratch.

Agar and Sindall both made several attempts to extract Dukes from Petrograd but were foiled on all occasions. On 8 August, Dukes came heartbreakingly close to rescue until the boat he and a courier had stolen to row out to *CMB 4* had sunk and both men were forced to swim back to shore. As the two men lay panting in the safety of the reeds they could hear the CMB patrolling up and down the coast looking for them but dare not signal for risk of compromise.

---

16   *Ibid.*, p.86.
17   *The London Gazette*, 19 August 1919.

In early July 1919 the offensive capability of the Royal Navy Baltic Fleet was significantly increased with the arrival of the converted aircraft carrier HMS *Vindictive* under Captain H. E. Grace, RN, son of the famous cricketer 'W. G.'. Originally christened HMS *Cavendish*, the Hawkins heavy cruiser had been converted into an aircraft carrier during construction and renamed *Vindictive* in honour of the cruiser of the same name which saw service during the Zeebrugge Raid in April 1918 and was sunk as a block ship during the Ostend Raid the following month. The new HMS *Vindictive* carried a complement of 12 aircraft, variously Griffins, Sopwith Camels, Short Seaplanes and two-seater Sopwith Strutters commanded by Major (RAF ranks were not introduced until September) David Donald, RAF.

Any hopes for HMS *Vindictive*'s aircraft to begin offensive patrols immediately on arrival were dashed when to Captain Grace's great embarrassment the carrier inadvertently struck a shoal and ran aground. *Vindictive* was stuck fast and it took eight days of offloading guns and stores combined with the efforts of two cruisers with towing cables and a favourable westerly wind before she came unstuck on 14 July. With *Vindictive* aground the aircraft were flown off her deck to a rudimentary airfield cut out of the forest at Koivisto in Finland.

The original aircrew of 'RAF *Vindictive*' were:

Commanding Officer:	Major David Graham Donald
Aeroplane pilots:	Captain Thomas Melling Williams, MC, DFC
	Lieutenant Eric Brewerton
	Lieutenant James MacGregor Fairweather
	Captain Arthur Clunie Randall
	Lieutenant Walmsley
Seaplane Pilots:	Captain Wilfred Reginald Dyke Acland
	Captain Colin Boumphrey
	Captain Albert William Fletcher, AFC
	Lieutenant Geoffrey Peploe Wiseman Earle
Seaplane Observers:	Lieutenant Alexander Lees
	Lieutenant Lionel James Booth
	Lieutenant Louis James Chandler
	Lieutenant William Sidney James Walne
	Lieutenant Frank Clifford Jenner

On 12 July, Cowan sent six ships of the 20th Destroyer Flotilla back to England to collect eight new CMBs and their crews and tow the craft back to the Baltic. The CMBs were the larger 55 foot version which could carry two torpedoes instead of the one carried in the 40 foot boats such as *CMB 4* and *CMB 7*.

Despite bad weather which caused one boat to capsize and sink and the tow lines for the others breaking no less than 16 times, the seven remaining CMBs reached Biorko on 30 July 1919. After dropping off their charges, the destroyers immediately resumed station escorting HMS *Princess Margaret* (Captain Harry H. Smyth, CMG, DSO, RN) on mine laying duties.

On 15 July, Flower Class minesweepers HMS *Myrtle* and HMS *Gentian* were on duty sweeping an enemy minefield west of Kronstadt. *Myrtle* had just swept up four mines and was making preparations to disarm when one of the mines detonated. With *Myrtle* crippled and sinking from underneath him, ship's captain Lieutenant Commander Richard Scott, RN, and Lieutenant Henry MacDonald, RN, immediately took action to evacuate the crew to another vessel which had come alongside. Moments after the last man had transferred across to the rescue vessel, part of *Myrtle*'s bow broke away and sank. On hearing that a member of the crew was unaccounted for, Scott gallantly returned to the hulk of the sinking ship which was on fire, rolling heavily and in danger of drifting into another mine. At extreme personal risk Scott searched below decks but despite his best efforts was unable to locate the missing rating.

Later in the day HMS *Gentian* (Lieutenant Cecil Hallett, RN) met the same fate as her sister ship *Myrtle* when she also struck a mine and sank. Within hours two minesweepers had been lost, 12 men killed (six each from *Myrtle* and *Gentian*) and a number more wounded.

Scott was awarded the Albert Medal for his gallantry in going back on board *Myrtle* in an attempt to rescue the missing man and Lieutenant MacDonald the DSC for his conduct in supervising the evacuation of the ship. Petty Officer John Canty was awarded a Bar to his DSM awarded for minesweeping in 1917 for his conduct during the incident, whilst Able Seaman Albert Reeve of *Gentian* was awarded the MSM.

During the night of 23 July, the Bolshevik submarine *Pantera* left Kronstadt and the following morning sighted the British submarine *E40* and destroyer HMS *Watchman* in the Gulf of Finland. Keeping his boat up sun to conceal his presence, Soviet Navy Captain A.N. Bakhtin brought *Pantera* to within half a mile of the British vessels and fired a single torpedo at *Watchman*, turned and immediately made another attack on *E40*.

Watching through his periscope Bakhtin saw *Watchman* steam away south-east but *E40* remained stationary as if unaware of the danger. Bakhtin closed to within four cables before firing both forward tubes. The torpedoes shot out towards their target and ran true until the British submarine turned, both torpedoes passing on either side of *E40*'s hull.

Soon after making the final attack on *E40*, *Pantera* was rocked by depth charges fired from HMS *Watchman*. Bakhtin managed to escape *Watchman*'s best efforts and returned to Kronstadt undamaged. The attack by *Pantera* came as a shock to Cowan. To date it had been the most aggressive move made by the Soviet Navy and led to a request for anti-submarine nets to be sent to Biorko and destroyers to be fitted with submarine detection equipment.

Before the submarine nets could arrive, on 27 July the Soviet submarine *Vyepr* entered the Gulf from Kronstadt to pick up where her sister submarine had left off. *Vyepr* wasted no time attacking a minesweeper and the destroyer HMS *Valorous* before being herself attacked with depth charges from *Valorous* and her sister ship HMS *Vancouver*. *Vyepr* was damaged so badly that depth could not be maintained and the crew were barely able to limp back to Kronstadt, arriving some two hours later just as seawater was beginning to enter the forward hatch and flood the batteries. *Valorous* was officially credited with the probable destruction of *Vyepr* for which Fire Control Officer of *Valorous*, Lieutenant Hugh Hollond, RN, was awarded the DSC.

Construction of a military base on Kotilin (Kronstadt) Island had begun in 1703 under Tsar Peter the Great. By 1919, Kronstadt was one of the most heavily fortified and well protected naval bases in the world, virtually impregnable from the sea. Over time, as the fortifications were extended and expanded, huge underwater breakwaters and a chain of forts were constructed north-west and southwards from the island controlling the channel to and from Petrograd.

On 30 July, several assorted aircraft from Major Donald's RAF squadron took off from *Vindictive* (the airstrip cut out of the forest near Koivisto had not yet been completed) and made a sneak attack on the military harbour. Immediately after take-off the aircrew spotted coloured flares fired from the Finnish coast, evidently enemy spies warning the Kronstadt defences that an air raid was on the way.

The mission, codenamed 'DB' in honour of Cowan's great hero Admiral David Beatty, comprised two waves of 11 aircraft dropping a total of 16 bombs over the harbour. Heavy anti-aircraft fire kept the aircraft above 4,000 feet and the bombing was largely ineffectual, but it did serve to familiarise the pilots and observers with Kronstadt from the air. Several hits were registered on the docks and the oil tanker *Tatiana*, however the 112 lb bombs were too small to cause serious damage.

Beyond the range of the chain of forts, Agar with Hampsheir and Beeley in *CMB 4* and Sindall with Marshall and Piper in *CMB 7*, lay in wait to rescue the crews of any of the aircraft that might be forced down into the Gulf. When it became clear that all the aircraft had returned to Finland,

141. RAF Sopwith Camel at Koivisto, Finland, autumn 1919. (Public domain)

Sindall requested permission from Agar to make an attack on a Soviet patrol boat which had been patrolling near the breakwater, likely as a result of the spotting of the CMBs by the chain of forts.

Agar gave permission for one hit and run attack only but not to follow the enemy gunboat if it withdrew to the east. As Sindall brought *CMB 7* up to full speed to launch his torpedo, two of the forts opened fire on the tiny motor boat forcing the young sub lieutenant to commence a zigzag course towards his target to avoid the enemy fire.

Sindall's aim was off and the torpedo missed. Rather than turning for home as he had been ordered, he continued at full speed on a collision course with the enemy vessel. The Red gunners on the motor boat fired at the CMB which was returned by Midshipman Marshall with *CMB 7's* twin Lewis guns, sending a spray of tracer bullets into the patrol vessel, silencing the deck gun crew.

The Red captain thought better than to continue the engagement and sped for the safety of the chain of forts pursued all the way by Sindall with Marshall letting fly on the Lewis guns. The enemy forts (which had ceased fire for fear of hitting their own patrol boat) began blazing away at the pursuing CMB until Sindall broke off the pursuit. Rendezvousing with Agar in *CMB 4*, both CMBs turned north-west for Terrioki.

The Bolsheviks operated their own squadron of assorted aircraft over Kronstadt from the old Imperial airfield at Gatchina near Petrograd, the beginnings of what would become the mighty Soviet Air Force. The RAF and Soviet aircraft never met each other in the skies over the Baltic apart from a single observation balloon shot down by the RAF over Kaporia Bight. The balloon was in fact shot down by the RAF twice but was patched up and sent aloft again.

On 5 August, Lieutenant Eric Brewerton with Observer Lieutenant William Walne took off from Koivisto in a Griffin to bomb Kronstadt. Approaching from 8,000 feet Brewerton shut off the engine and glided in to target with the sun behind him, opening the engine at 1,500 feet to release the bomb load, which set a large building alight. The Bolsheviks replied with anti-aircraft fire but Brewerton was able to make his getaway without being hit.

The RAF suffered their first aircrew fatality on 13 August, when Lieutenant Norman Taylor crashed Sopwith Camel *N6825* on take-off from Koivisto. He was buried with full military honours by his comrades in the small village cemetery and is one of few British servicemen ever to have been killed on active service in Finland.

On the same day, Brewerton and Walne were returning from a reconnaissance over Kronstadt when only 10 miles out from Koivisto the engine oil pressure dropped. Brewerton attempted to make the airstrip but was forced to ditch heavily in the sea. Rescued by Finns in a motor boat, the aircraft was salvaged but subsequently declared unserviceable.

On 2 August, seven of the larger 55 foot CMBs arrived at Terrioki, the eighth vessel having been lost to a North Atlantic swell on the way out from England. The CMBs had been specifically requested from England by Admiral Cowan to fulfil an ambitious plan he had been formulating since Agar's successful sinking of *Oleg* in June. The boats were accompanied by the commander of the CMB Flotilla, Commander Claude Congreve Dobson, RN, with a further 17 officers and 19 CMMs to act as crews.

Cowan believed that the CMBs could use their speed, small size and shallow draught to pass through the chain of forts, cross the breakwater, mount a surprise attack on Kronstadt Harbour and speed home before the Reds had time to recover from the shock. The ambitious plan would result in one of the most highly decorated operations in the history of the Royal Navy.

The objective of operation 'RK' (so named after Cowan's good friend Admiral Roger Keyes who had planned the great raid on Zeebrugge the previous year) was the destruction of the Soviet capital ships at berth in Kronstadt Harbour. Cowan's plan was for a timed and combined naval and air operation. The assorted RAF aircraft flying from Koivisto would attack Kronstadt from the air, distracting the anti-aircraft gunners and shooting out searchlights along the breakwater, whilst under cover of the bombing and strafing, Agar in *CMB 7* would lead the flotilla through the chain of forts to the entrance of the harbour where Lieutenant Laurence Napier, RN, in *CMB 24* would attack the guard ship destroyer. The remaining six CMBs would use gun cotton to breach the boom at the harbour entrance, speed into the harbour in two waves, fire their torpedoes in order and leave the harbour at full speed before the enemy could react. Cowan would position his destroyers and cruisers just behind the minefield to ward off any pursuers in the eventuality that the sneak attack provoked a response form the Soviet Navy.

In preparation for the raid, each CMB's engines were thoroughly serviced and torpedoes loaded into firing troughs, two for the larger 55 foot boats (except Lieutenant William Bremner's *CMB 79* and Napier's *CMB 24* which carried only one torpedo) and one for the smaller 40 foot *CMB 7*. Agar's *CMB 4*, the boat in which he had sunk *Oleg*, would not be taking part in the raid and would remain at Terrioki.

Eight CMBs would take part in the raid:[18]

CMB 7	Lieutenant Augustus Agar, VC, RN
CMB 24A	Lieutenant Laurence Napier, RN
CMB 31BD	Commander Claude Dobson, DSO, RN
CMB 62BD	Lieutenant Commander Frank Brade, DSC, RNR
CMB 72A	Sub Lieutenant Edward Bodley, RNR
CMB 79A	Lieutenant William Bremner, DSC, RN
CMB 86BD	Sub Lieutenant Francis Howard, RNR
CMB 88BD	Lieutenant Archibald Dayrell-Reed, DSO and Bar, RN

A further eight RAF aircraft from HMS *Vindictive* would attack the breakwater, forts and harbour from the air:

Sopwith Strutter	Lieutenant Thomas Williams, MC, DFC
Sopwith Strutter	Lieutenant Eric Brewerton

---

18   The letter designations after the CMB number indicate engine type and armament. 'A' indicates two Thornycroft V12 engines and one torpedo, 'BD' indicates two Green 12-cylinder engines and two torpedoes. They are recorded here for reference but will not be used hereafter.

142. The 55 foot Thornycroft Coastal Motor Boat (CMB) of the type used by the Royal Navy in the Baltic Sea, 1919. (Public domain)

Griffin Seaplane	Lieutenant James Fairweather/Observer Lieutenant William Walne
Sopwith Camel	Captain Arthur Randall, DFC
Short Seaplane	Captain Wilfred Acland/Observer Lieutenant Alexander Lees
Short Seaplane	Captain Colin Boumphrey/Observer Lieutenant Lionel Booth
Short Seaplane	Captain Albert Fletcher, AFC/Observer Lieutenant Frank Jenner
Short Seaplane	Captain David Donald/Observer Lieutenant Louis Chandler

Dobson's targets listed in order of priority were:

Andrei Pervozvanny – battleship
Petropavlovsk – battleship
Pamiat Azova – submarine depot ship
Rurik – cruiser
Dry dock

The crews practiced manoeuvring at high speed in the days leading up to the raid using buoys to represent target ships and the exact dimensions of the harbour. Entering the harbour and launching the torpedoes at speed without colliding with the target ships or harbour wall would prove to be extremely difficult within the confines of the harbour.

The plan was finalised after an aerial reconnaissance by Lieutenant Walmsley with Observer Lieutenant Frederick Whippey in a Sopwith Strutter provided photographs showing the current positions of the guard ship destroyer at the mouth of the harbour and the position of the ships at anchor. Dobson was not satisfied with photographs only and both he and Bill Bremner took off from Koivisto in the observers' cockpits of two RAF aircraft to make their own observations over Kronstadt. It was the first time either naval officer had been in an aircraft.

A planned interval of 15 minutes between the first and second waves entering the basin would allow the first wave to make its attack and depart the harbour just as the second wave would be entering. Dobson was particularly concerned about the possibility of collision between the CMBs and in the planning limited the number of boats in the small harbour at any one time. Dobson favoured a delay of 20–30 minutes between attacks but the crews vetoed the idea as they felt that the second and subsequent waves would have little chance of survival.

On 15 August, a storm broke over the eastern Baltic which for three days and nights blew a strong westerly accompanied by heavy rain and a two to three foot rise in water levels in the Gulf of Finland. The deeper water level made the task of navigating through the channel to Kronstadt much simpler and the firing of torpedoes in the harbour slightly easier. CMBs could only launch torpedoes from the trough at the rear of the boat at high speed, any slower and the torpedo simply nosedived to the bottom. The few extra feet of depth gave the CMB captains a slightly greater margin of error.

The weather cleared on 17 August and Admiral Cowan immediately ordered Operation 'RK' to commence that same night. Dobson and Bremner flew a final reconnaissance over the target courtesy of the RAF before returning to find crews and boats prepared and awaiting an address from Admiral Cowan. The eight CMBs left Biorko at 2200 and rendezvoused off a small island in the Gulf of Finland where they were met by Agar in *CMB 7*. Once all the boats were assembled, Dobson signalled with a torch and the eight CMBs set course for Kronstadt at full speed.

By 2230 the flotilla was speeding through the northern channel at a rate of knots, the spray from their bows leaving a wake behind each boat. Sub Lieutenant Howard in *CMB 86* was having engine trouble and found it difficult to keep up with the other boats. Inevitably the forts opened fire but the aim was wild. The Russian gunners did not switch on their searchlights likely because they could hear the RAF aircraft overhead and were fearful of making themselves targets. The flotilla made a wide turn to starboard as they passed the northern edge of Kronstadt Island before a final turn east to enter Kronstadt harbour from the direction of Petrograd.

On the way through the forts the engines of *CMB 86* finally gave out and the boat and its crew had to be left behind whilst the remainder of the flotilla sped on to Kronstadt. The element of surprise, fading with every passing moment, could not be jeopardised for the sake of one CMB and its crew. Howard and the crew of *CMB 86* were left to drift in the darkness alone and helpless.

Due to the slightly shorter route taken through the chain of forts thanks to an error by the Finnish pilot, Dobson (*CMB 31*), Bremner (*CMB 79*) and Dayrell-Reed (*CMB 88*) arrived at the basin a few moments ahead of the second wave, much earlier than planned, which would have disastrous consequences during the attack.

As Bremner led the first wave into the harbour, the RAF aircraft (which had taken off from Koivisto airstrip with a full bomb load in the dark) were busily bombing and strafing the guns and searchlights on the breakwater sending the Russian gunners scurrying for cover. Bremner made straight for *Pamiat Azova* anchored in the dry dock and fired a single torpedo, striking the ship dead astern on the starboard side. Bremner turned hard to port to speed out of the harbour.

Dobson in command of *CMB 31* entered the harbour at full speed and manoeuvred his boat into a firing position to attack *Andrei Pervozvanny*. To make the turn at full speed, a delicate and difficult manoeuvre, one engine had to be put in neutral gear to turn the boat to port, and then maximum revolutions applied to bring the boat up to the speed required to fire both torpedoes.

Lieutenant Russell McBean was steady at the helm as Dobson launched the two torpedoes at exactly the right moment. Columns of spray burst high into the air as the side of the battleship was shattered by two direct hits. Dobson had barely a moment to track the torpedoes before turning and accelerating to the standby position near the harbour entrance to allow Dayrell-Reed in *CMB 88* to make his attack.

The Kronstadt garrison had scrambled from their barracks, the gun crews dashing headlong to their positions around the harbour and on the breakwater. Searchlights swept back and forth across the basin as rifles and machine guns sprayed frantically at anything moving inside the harbour. The RAF made repeated attacks along the harbour, diving and strafing until their bombs and ammunition were expended. The gunners on the CMBs were also in action, firing their twin Lewis guns loaded with ammunition supplied by the RAF, sending streams of tracer across the night sky.

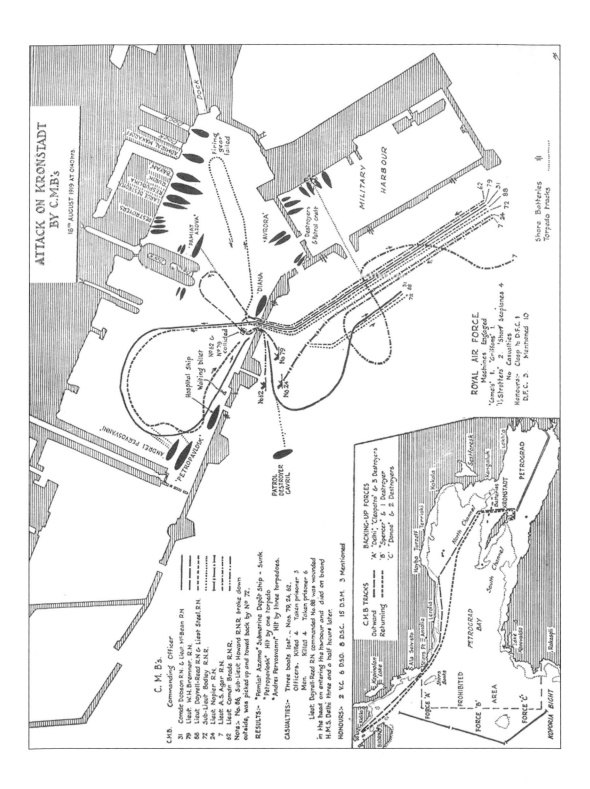

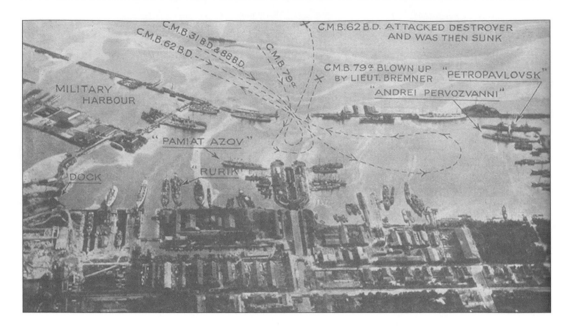

143. An RAF reconnaissance photograph of Kronstadt taken before the attack showing the route of the attacking CMBs and their targets. (IWM Q107944)

144. Overleaf: Map of the attack on Kronstadt Harbour, 18 August 1919. (Public domain)

145. Kotilin Island with Kronstadt Harbour in foreground looking towards Finland. (Public domain)

146. Some of the participants in the Raid on Kronstadt Harbour, 18 August 1919. Left–right, top: Lieutenant William Bremner, DSC, RN (awarded DSO, POW); Sub Lieutenant Osman Giddy, RN (awarded DSC, POW); Sub Lieutenant Hector MacLean, RN (killed); Left–right, middle: Midshipman Richard Marshall, RNR (awarded DSC); South African Lieutenant Laurence Napier, RN (awarded DSO, POW); Sub Lieutenant Edgar Sindall, RNR (awarded DSC); Left–right, bottom: Able Seaman William Smith, RN (killed, posthumous MiD); Sub Lieutenant Thomas Usborne, RN (killed, posthumous MiD); Lieutenant Thomas Williams, MC, DFC (awarded DFC Bar). Image 1 David Bremner; images 4, 6, 7, 9 public domain; 2, 3, 5, 8 *Illustrated London News*.

147. Photograph taken on the morning of 19 August 1919 showing Bolshevik
cruiser *Pamiat Azova* sunk in Kronstadt Harbour. (Public domain)

As Dayrell-Reed made the sharp turn to port to bring *CMB 88* into position for an attack run on *Andrei Pervozvanny*, the Lieutenant was hit and slumped at the helm, blood gushing from a terrible gaping wound to the head. *CMB 88*'s second officer Lieutenant Gordon Steele had been firing twin Lewis guns at emplacements along the breakwater but reacted instantly. Steele took over the controls, fired a torpedo at less than 100 yards range and turned the wheel hard to port, avoiding a collision with *Pervozvanny* by only seconds. Steele was so close to the battleship when the torpedo struck that spray from the explosion fell on the stern of *CMB 88*.

Most junior officers, if faced with a badly wounded commander and narrowly avoiding a fatal collision with an enemy battleship, would have quickly exited the harbour and made for Terrioki at full speed but not Steele. Only moments after escaping the blast from the torpedo which had struck *Andrei Pervozvanny*, Steele manoeuvred *CMB 88* into position to make an attack on *Petropavlovsk*. He fired the second torpedo which also ran true, striking *Petropavlovsk* beneath the forward turret. His torpedoes exhausted, Steele sped out of the harbour to join Dobson's *CMB 31* at the standby position before heading in the direction of Finland under fire from the chain of forts.

The crew of *Gavriil* (the guard ship destroyer at the harbour entrance) was slow to come into action and were only bringing their guns to bear as Bremner in *CMB 79* led the second wave into the harbour. Lieutenant Napier in *CMB 24* manoeuvred to attack the destroyer but the torpedo missed, either deflected or ran underneath the target. Seconds later a large calibre shell fired from either *Gavriil* or one of the shore batteries on the breakwater split *CMB 24* in two only yards from the destroyer. Miraculously all five officers and ratings on board survived the sinking and were left clinging to the wreckage of the CMB.

Sub Lieutenant Bodley in *CMB 72* entered the harbour at full speed and commenced to attack the ships berthed on the eastern side near the dry dock, but on the run in a single machine gun bullet disabled the torpedo firing gear and Bodley was forced to exit the harbour with his torpedoes still on board. He sped out of the basin and through the chain of forts where he encountered Sub Lieutenant Howard in *CMB 86* broken down and listing. A cable was thrown and with considerable difficulty Bodley towed Howard's stricken boat through the forts and out of danger.

Just as Lieutenant Commander Brade in *CMB 62* entered the basin and Lieutenant Bremner in *CMB 79* was leaving, Brade was blinded by a searchlight and lost direction. Brade collided with Bremner's boat at full speed in a sickening collision amidships, almost cutting Bremner's boat in half. The two boats remained stuck together as Brade kept his engines at full speed to force both boats from blocking the harbour entrance. As Bremner cleared the harbour mouth and decelerated, the wreckage of *CMB 79* broke free, the crew rapidly scrambling aboard *CMB 62*. Bremner placed the gun cotton charges originally intended to destroy the harbour's boom (which was found to have not been raised) in the crippled *CMB 79* but whilst doing so the overcrowded *CMB 62* came under fire from the guard ship *Gavriil* which had only moments earlier sunk Napier's *CMB 24*. Brade turned to meet the destroyer and launched his two torpedoes, both of which missed.

Gavriil responded with a hail of fire putting *CMB 62*'s engines out of action, and the stricken boat remained stranded until she was destroyed in a large ball of flame by *Gavriil*'s gunners. Of the 10 crewmen on board both *CMB 79* and *CMB 62* only three survived to be captured. Bremner was plucked from the water badly wounded but the gallant Brade was killed.

Agar in *CMB 7* saw the resulting fireball as *CMB 62*'s fuel tanks were hit but knew that it would be suicide to approach the scene to look for survivors. He fired his single torpedo into the outer military harbour destroying or damaging several smaller craft before speeding away to the east.

To cover the withdrawal of the CMBs through the chain of forts, the RAF fearlessly dived at the island fortresses, machine guns blazing. Agar was the last to make the run through the forts by which time the gunners were well alert having given Dobson, Steele and Bodley with Howard in tow a hot time. Being some distance behind the main waves, as Agar reached the forts daylight was already emerging over the horizon. Seeing Agar about to make his dash, a Short Seaplane overhead piloted by Captain Albert Fletcher attacked the forts in an attempt to keep the gunners' heads down. Fletcher's observer, Observer Lieutenant Frank Jenner, sprayed the forts with tracer using all his remaining ammunition. Agar successfully passed through the forts and sped to the safety of Terrioki, where the CMBs refuelled before continuing on to HMS *Delhi* at Biorko to make their reports to Admiral Cowan.

There being no medical facilities at Terrioki, Dobson and Steele continued directly to rendezvous with HMS *Delhi* where the semi-conscious and badly wounded Dayrell-Reed was transferred to ship's sick bay; Cowan attended the dying officer in his final moments. The gallant officer was later buried with full military honours in the lonely cemetery near the small airfield at Koivisto.

CMM Baden Marples Masters, RNVR, from Derby, had been demobilised in February 1919 and resumed his apprenticeship at the Rolls Royce works until he received an Admiralty telegram in July requesting he volunteer for special service. He was assigned to Dayrell-Reed's *CMB 88* and recounted in a letter to his parents:

You will be glad to hear that I am safe … We gave the Bolshies h___ on Sunday night, or rather 2 am Monday. Seven CMBs set out, but 88 B.D. had the honour of leading the attack, and was told off to put under a big battle cruiser which they have been after for a long while, and they knew that 'Blood' Reed was the only man to do it … We went straight through the forts without being seen, then into the harbour. We shot past guns of every description. The 79 CMB got a shell and it blew her to bits. Then 62 CMB got put down, and then No. 24. We made straight for our cruiser and blew it up with a torpedo, then we went for another one without our remaining torpedo which split her in two and she sank. Bullets were all the time flying through our boat until it was like a pepper box. 'Blood' Reed got shot through the head and fell dead in the sub-lieutenant's arms, and I got hit in the thigh form machine gun fire … I then got the order 'full speed ahead,' and I knew we were scooting off. Well, the bullets were flying all round and the shells too. One big shell dropped just astern of us and blew us clean out of the water. We got out of the harbour, and then we had all the forts to get through. The shelling started again, but we were doing about 55 miles per hour, and they could not touch us. All the time coming back I had to keep filling my tin hat with oil and pouring it into the oil tank as it was shot through. With one leg useless, as it had got numbed, the engines burst just as we got into safe waters, as I could not keep it up any longer. I was properly jiggered up and exhausted. I have been told that I have been recommended for the Conspicuous Gallantry Medal.[19]

Marples was indeed recommended for the CGM (as were a number of other participants in the raid) although in the end Distinguished Service Medals were awarded in place of the higher award.

Flight Lieutenant Arthur Randall's Sopwith Camel, one of eight RAF aircraft to take part in the raid, barely made the distance to Kronstadt. On the way over from Finland his engine had failed completely and stopped mid-air. Randall made preparations to ditch, the likelihood of survival from which was quite low. Just as the Camel's wheels were about to touch the waves below, the engine belched and coughed and stuttered back into life. Most pilots would have taken the prudent course of action to return to Finland but Randall continued on to Kronstadt, arriving after the raid had begun. Machine-gunning the breakwater from 500 feet, Randall made repeated passes until his ammunition was exhausted. The engine began to give trouble once again and the plucky airman decided to turn back for Finland before his luck ran out. With the engine on its last legs Randall made a crash landing on a beach on the Finnish coast.

Lieutenant Walmsley and Observer Lieutenant Frederick Whippey flew an aerial reconnaissance of Kronstadt in a Sopwith Strutter just hours later and brought back the photographs on which the success or failure of the raid rested. The submarine depot ship *Pamiat Azova* had been sunk by the torpedo fired by Bremner in *CMB 79* and *Petropavlovsk* had been sunk (although eventually salvaged and repaired) by the single torpedo fired by Steele in *CMB 88*. *Andrei Pervozvanny* had been hit and critically damaged by three torpedoes, one fired by Steele in *CMB 88* and two fired by Dobson in *CMB 31*. Several small craft had been either sunk or damaged by the torpedo fired into the military harbour by Agar in *CMB 7*. Additionally a destroyer depot ship disappeared after the raid, believed to have been sunk or damaged by the RAF.

The small flotilla had paid a heavy price for their success. Seven officers and sailors had been killed and Lieutenant Dayrell-Reed had died of wounds. An additional nine officers and sailors had been plucked from the water and taken prisoner, many of them wounded, and now faced an uncertain fate. Three CMBs had been lost and a Sopwith Camel crashed after a forced landing in Finland.

Although the primary targets of the raid had been attacked successfully none of the secondary targets had been hit. The cruiser *Rurik* and the dry dock remained undamaged and the destroyer *Gavriil* had survived no less than three torpedo attacks.

Admiral Cowan addressed all those who had participated in the raid, both RAF and RN, the following morning. Agar recorded:

> He said that the result of the action meant the end of any Russian threat by sea to Finland and freedom for the Baltic States which was what we had been sent out to accomplish. But above all things he said the action would rank as an example of British courage of which the Navy would always be proud. They were simple words, but came from the heart of this flag officer; small in stature but great in leadership, and the sailors understood him even if they did not understand the complicated policies of governments.[20]

The major threat to Cowan's fleet and the Baltic States had been effectively eliminated by the bravery of a handful of Royal Navy men and two Finnish guides in seven CMBs, an amazing achievement for which many awards would follow. Cowan ensured that the gallant services were

---

19   *Derby Daily Telegraph*, 30 August 1919.
20   Agar, *Baltic Episode*, p.178.

148. British SIS agent Paul Dukes,
codename ST25. (NPG x120742)

suitably recognised, personally recommending nearly every participant for an award.

As a result the Kronstadt Raid became one of the most highly decorated operations in British naval history. Of the 55 participants in the air and sea, no less than 48 received an award, either being decorated or Mentioned in Despatches (MiD) including the award of Victoria Crosses to Commander Dobson and Lieutenant Steele. Of the eight officers and ratings taken prisoner, seven were subsequently gazetted awards after their release in a prisoner exchange the following year.

The pilots and observers of RAF *Vindictive* were also recognised for their bravery and skill with awards of the DFC (including one DFC Bar) to pilots and MiDs to observers. Had the assortment of RAF aircraft not suppressed the fire of the enemy batteries and generally distracted the Red gunners, it is likely that casualties amongst the CMB crews would have been much higher and the raid may well have ended in disaster. The two Finnish guides, one each on board Dobson's *CMB 31* and Agar's *CMB 7*, were rewarded for their services with double pay of £25 and a congratulatory double ration of naval rum.

On 20 August, two days after the Kronstadt Raid, two Bolshevik aircraft flew over Terrioki and dropped several bombs on the village. There were no casualties but it was clear that the Bolsheviks were well aware of the presence of the CMB base at the yacht club and their activities. The ability of Agar to fulfil his original mission as a courier for agents in and out of Petrograd had decreased exponentially. The forts were on high alert and every night searchlights could be observed criss-crossing the channels between the forts, looking for any approaching CMBs. The Bolsheviks were determined not to be caught out twice and had implemented a regime of constant observation of the approaches to Kronstadt.

By late August British SIS agent Paul Dukes, codename ST25, was desperate to get out of Petrograd. The *Cheka* were hot on his heels and it could only be a matter of time before he was captured and interrogated. Dukes was desperate to leave the city by any means. He would have to make one last attempt at a prearranged pick up by Agar in a CMB before resorting to the risky overland route to Finland or Estonia.

For Agar it was his most dangerous mission to date. Both Cowan and Dobson attempted to convince Agar not to take the risk for at least a few weeks until the Bolsheviks might relax their guard, but Agar was determined to make an attempt as soon as possible. Midshipman Marshall and trusty Chief Motor Mechanic Beeley were quick to volunteer. The three men set off in *CMB 7* from Terrioki at 2200 on the night of 23 August, with a Finnish agent and local smuggler acting as pilot on what was to be Agar's thirteenth and final passage through the forts.

As the CMB arrived at the approaches to the forts, Beeley gradually eased the throttle forward until the boat was skimming the surface at top speed. Without a torpedo loaded the CMB was able to travel at maximum speed, as yet unobserved by the enemy.

Just as Agar's confidence built that the CMB would breach the forts unseen, a searchlight lit up, then another and yet another, until Agar was completely blinded by the beams. The forts opened fire, machine gun bullets and shells splashed into the ocean on either side, and a bullet damaged the CMB's steering controls. To throttle down would invite disaster, so there was nothing for Agar to do but continue on at full speed and hope for the best. Within a few minutes he was so disoriented by the blinding searchlights that he lost all sense of direction. Unknowingly, he had brought the CMB in a large semicircle back towards Kronstadt. Suddenly there was a terrific collision and the boat stopped in its tracks. Agar described the impact 'as if one was travelling by car at fifty miles an hour and suddenly ran into a brick wall.'[21] The crew were flung violently forward, and Agar himself temporarily knocked senseless.

The CMB had struck the breakwater just off the northern shore of Kronstadt directly under Fort No. 5. So close were the British sailors to the fort that the searchlight could not depress low enough to detect the CMB, and its beam swept harmlessly back and forth above the British sailors' heads.

CMB 7 lay stranded on the breakwater, taking on water, the propeller shaft sheared off in the impact. The twinkling lights of the Finnish coast were visible just 15 miles away. Kronstadt island itself lay just a few hundred yards from the crippled boat. The fact that the CMB was still relatively intact after such a severe impact was testament to the strength of Thornycroft's all-wood hull construction.

Marshall and Beeley set to work bailing water and plugging the breach as best as they could. Given that the alternative was to remain in the CMB until dawn and await capture, through a Herculean effort the four men managed to push, shove and drag the boat back into the water where it amazingly remained afloat although low in the water due to the amount of seawater which had been taken on board.

All hands set to bailing and within an hour the CMB was relatively seaworthy, although without any means of propulsion. During the ordeal the searchlight from the nearby fort continually swept back and forth over the heads of the crew, the soldiers in the forts apparently oblivious that the CMB they had been tracking had not disappeared but lay stranded directly below them only a stone's throw away. By midnight the searchlight crew gave up and switched off.

A gentle westerly breeze and the action of the ocean current pushed *CMB 7* slowly but steadily north-west, away from the fort and towards the safety of the Finnish coast. Agar and Marshall rigged a rudimentary sail from a canvas tarpaulin and at the suggestion of Gefter, the Finnish pilot, evidently an experienced sailor, used a daisy-chain of empty petrol tins roped together to act as a sea anchor which kept the CMB stern on and heading in the direction of Finland. Agar calculated that by dawn, at their present rate of drift, the CMB would still be only three miles from the forts, not far enough to be comfortably out of range.

As the sun began to rise over the horizon the cards again fell in favour of Agar and his crew. A mist began to form which provided enough cover to drift the extra distance beyond the range of the enemy guns. As the mist began to clear in the early morning sunshine, the crew found themselves just two miles from Terrioki and safety.

Since pushing off from the breakwater the crew had been taking turns furiously bailing to keep the CMB afloat, and by dawn were completely exhausted. Marshall was using his sea boots to bail when Agar spotted two fishing boats through the mist. The small boats were crewed by Bolshevik sailors from Kronstadt on a fishing expedition to supplement their rations. Not anticipating encountering a British CMB, the sailors had left their rifles behind and were completely unarmed. Gefter was able to shout in Russian that if the Red sailors did not come closer Marshall would open fire with *CMB 7*'s Lewis guns. Fortune yet again favoured Agar and his crew as they commandeered the small

21 *Ibid.*, p.185.

149. Newly decorated Royal Navy Lieutenants Gordon Steele and Augustus Agar attend a reception at Wellington Barracks for naval recipients of the Victoria Cross. (IWM Q 66160)

boats to tow the CMB closer to the Finnish coast, where they arrived 12 hours after setting out. Agar, Marshall and Beeley were completely and utterly exhausted. Remarkably, they had sailed sixteen miles through enemy territory without a working engine.

There was little to be gained by taking the Bolsheviks prisoner, so Agar chivalrously supplied them with some additional food and a little rum and allowed the Red sailors to return to Kronstadt, where they undoubtedly had a very fanciful tale to tell of capture by the enemy and being forced to tow a stricken CMB to Finland before release with a gift of rum.

With the aid of local Finnish fisherman, *CMB 7* was salvaged and towed to the yacht club, but it was soon apparent that the boat was beyond repair. The gallant little CMB was towed out into the Gulf of Finland where it was destroyed with gun cotton.

With the Bolsheviks aware of the CMBs' presence and in the light of the failed attempt by Agar to extract ST25 there seemed little possibility that Paul Dukes would be able to escape across the Gulf of Finland in one of the CMBs as originally planned. The least risky option was now for Dukes to cross the heavily guarded frontier into Finland or Estonia.

A couple of days after Agar's lucky escape in *CMB 7*, two Bolshevik aircraft raided Terrioki before the British CMB crews were able to man the Lewis guns mounted on the balcony of the *dacha*. The Bolshevik crews were suspected of being White sympathisers as their bombs were harmlessly dropped in a nearby forest.

On 31 August 1919, the Bolshevik submarine *Pantera* (which had fired two torpedoes each at British submarine HMS *E40* and destroyer HMS *Watchman* without success on 24 July) made the first Soviet submarine kill in history when she encountered HMS *Abdiel* and HMS *Vittoria* at anchor off Seskar Point and attacked *Vittoria* (Lieutenant Commander Vernon Hammersly-Heenan, RN) with two torpedoes. Both ran true and struck their target, sinking *Vittoria* within five minutes with the loss of eight of her crew.

HMS *Abdiel* fired several shells at *Pantera* but it was already too late, the Soviet submarine snuck away beneath the waves leaving a scene of carnage behind. Captain Bakhtin of *Pantera* was so concerned that he had been spotted and pursued that he did not surface until the following day. In the 28 hours she had been underwater *Pantera* had travelled 75 miles; by the time she surfaced there was so little oxygen in the submarine that a match would not ignite and the crew could barely breathe.

The sinking of HMS *Vittoria* was a great success for the Soviet Navy and a disaster for the British that should never have occurred. Anchoring ships so close to the enemy without adequate protection from submarines in a time of war bordered on gross negligence. Cowan had issued orders that in the event of reduced visibility at night, ships could anchor until the weather cleared. Captain Berwick Curtis, RN, commanding 20th Destroyer Flotilla, took advantage of this order to give the crews of HMS *Abdiel* and HMS *Vittoria* a much needed rest from the effort required to maintain a wartime watch. Cowan was furious that Curtis had allowed two of his destroyers to anchor on a clear night but worded his report of the events leading to the sinking of HMS *Vittoria* in such a way that Curtis received no more than an expression of 'Their Lordships' [of the Admiralty] severe displeasure'.

On 1 September, a grenade was flung into the garden of the British *dacha* at the Terrioki yacht club, blowing out the ground floor windows and leaving a hole in the garden. Whether it was a Finnish Bolshevik sympathiser or a Soviet agent was never discovered and the attacker was never apprehended. The local Finnish commandant was quite embarrassed by the attack and thereafter placed a 24 hour guard on the dacha, however it was evident that Terrioki was well known to the Bolsheviks as the berth of the CMB flotilla and there was no further possibility of Secret Service operations from the yacht club.

Agar decided to close down operations from Terrioki and relocate to the fleet anchorage at Biorko. Sindall was left behind to act as liaison between the Finnish commandant at Terrioki and Admiral Cowan at Biorko, primarily to pass on any information that might come to hand about the fate of crews missing and taken prisoner at Kronstadt, of particular concern to the Admiral.

The final venture by CMBs into the Eastern Baltic occurred in early September when Agar in *CMB 4* led two of the larger 55 foot CMBs into the swept channel on the southern side of Kronstadt to lay four small anti-submarine mines carried in the torpedo troughs.

On 4 September, the destroyer HMS *Verulam* (Lieutenant Commander Guy Warren, RN) struck a mine off Stirs Point in Petrograd Bay and sank with the loss of six officers and 10 ratings, the second British destroyer sunk within four days. Regardless of the danger of further mines, Lieutenant Commander Harry Keate, RN, brought destroyer HMS *Vidette* alongside the stricken *Verulam* to evacuate casualties and take on board the survivors, saving a number of lives in the process for which he was awarded the DSO.

Lieutenant Miles Filleul, RN, had been serving ashore at nearby Stirs Point with a naval observation party when *Verulam* struck the mine and immediately proceeded with Sub Lieutenants Geoffrey Williams and Frederick Vallings in shore boats to render aid, for which Filleul was awarded the DSC.

Among the dead was Engineer Lieutenant Joseph House, DSC, RN, who had served under Cowan at Jutland on HMS *Princess Royal* which took numerous hits during the battle (and suffered 22 killed and more than 80 wounded), for which House was awarded the DSC.[22] House's body was one of eight which washed ashore on the Finnish coast over the following days, only three of which could be identified.

Three days later news was received at Biorko that British SIS agent Paul Dukes had escaped over the Estonian frontier where he was nearly shot as a Bolshevik spy by over-zealous Estonian border guards. With Dukes' arrival came news that the Bolsheviks had placed a handsome reward for the capture of any of the CMB crews, Agar himself had a bounty of £5,000 on his head.

Paul Dukes was knighted by King George for his secret work in Petrograd and for 'valuable services to His Majesty's Government'. When presenting Agar with his VC at a private investiture at Buckingham Palace, the King commented that Dukes deserved to receive a VC himself, but the conditions of the award precluded him from receiving it.[23]

With their operations in the Eastern Baltic over the CMB crews were shortly thereafter sent home, but Agar was anxious to remain behind until he heard more about the fate of the missing Kronstadt CMB crews. Bolshevik radio had broadcast the official Soviet version of the raid which omitted any mention of their ships sunk and damaged and only reported that three British torpedo boats had been sunk and four officers and six ratings taken prisoner. Eventually an unconfirmed report filtered through to Finland of the names of the survivors, and in a broadcast a few days later

---

22 *The London Gazette*, 15 September 1916.
23 Agar, *Baltic Episode*, p.215.

Soviet radio confirmed them. The joy of learning that so many had survived was tempered by the loss of so many comrades.

Agar left Biorko for London via Helsinki and Stockholm on 16 September 1919. On arrival at Kings Cross station in his worn civilian suit (like many who had enlisted as young men and grown into adulthood in uniform, it was the only one he had ever owned) he reported directly to the Foreign Office without even the time to bathe, shave or have breakfast. As he waited in the passage outside the office of British SIS chief Smith-Cumming (codename 'C'), a man carrying a briefcase exited:

> He was tall, dark-haired, and lean. Something about him and his manner arrested my attention and seemed to me to be familiar, but whether it was the eager look in his eyes, or a certain tense expression in his face, I cannot say. I looked at him again and then in a flash of intuition a thought came to my mind. 'Yes,' I said to myself, 'it must be him.' I was the first to speak. 'Are you Dukes?' 'Yes,' he replied…[24]

Despite their intertwined destinies over the past months it was the first time both men had met.

The joint meeting with 'C' went well, both men were able to recount their stories and compare notes. Agar made particular mention of the sinking of *Oleg* and Hampsheir and Beeley's bravery on the occasion. When the question was raised by Agar on the matter of accounting for the thousands of pounds of cash which he had signed for before leaving London in late May, Smith-Cumming brushed his enquiry aside and told Agar that he should not bother himself with accounts and simply hand back the balance he had remaining.

Agar also raised the issue of the Kronstadt Raid prisoners, in response to which Smith-Cumming assured him that negotiations were underway towards a prisoner exchange. In the meantime the Danish Red Cross had been charged with enquiring as to the welfare of the prisoners and had been in contact with Soviet Foreign Commissar Litvinov, who had spent part of the war in England and even had an English wife.

Smith-Cumming did not like the idea of Agar returning to the Baltic (given the large reward for his capture) but as Dukes was safely in London and the British SIS mission over, Agar was returned to Admiralty duty and could return to the Baltic as a uniformed Royal Navy officer should the Admiralty decide to allow him to do so.

After the meeting concluded, Agar and Dukes were finally able to meet alone and relate to each other their stories. Dukes' tales of avoiding arrest and escaping Petrograd would have sent chills down the spine of the most hardened spy. He told of the night of 8 August, and the failed rendezvous. Whilst rowing out to meet Agar the small rowing boat capsized and he and Gefter (the Finnish agent working for the British) had to swim to shore. There they lay exhausted on the beach and watched in frustration as Agar's CMB waited offshore before slowly moving off towards the forts and Terrioki.

Agar relayed to Dukes his own tale of miraculous salvation on the night of 23 August, after the collision with the submerged breakwater during a subsequent attempt to extract him. Dukes explained that even if Agar had been able to make the rendezvous it would have been pointless as he had been unable to steal a boat with which to paddle out to meet the CMB.

On the morning of the private investiture of the Victoria Cross at Buckingham Palace, Agar presented himself in an ordinary reefer coat (there had not been time to be appropriately kitted out) with a sword borrowed from Grieves of Bond Street. The King met Agar alone in a small private study where the monarch implored the young lieutenant to sit down and tell his story. The King asked questions about CMBs, the Kronstadt Raid and particularly insisted on a detailed account of the attack on *Oleg*. The King enquired about Agar's future in the peacetime navy and said he must

---

24 *Ibid.*

at some time serve him on the Royal Yacht. In January 1924 Agar was appointed to the Royal Yacht *Victoria and Albert*. Before presenting the VC, the King was careful to examine the reverse to ensure that the date and recipient details engraved were correct. To Agar's surprise the monarch went on to also present him with the DSO he had been awarded for his part in the Kronstadt Raid.

That night Dukes and Agar were entertained by Smith-Cumming and his colleagues at the Savoy Hotel. Included in the welcome party was Sir John Thornycroft, designer of the Coastal Motor Boat. The next morning Agar once again sailed for the Baltic.

On arrival in Helsinki on 10 October, Agar hurried to HMS *Delhi*, eager to meet with Admiral Cowan and pass on the King's congratulations for the success of the Kronstadt Raid. Cowan warmly greeted the newly decorated lieutenant and immediately appointed him as an intelligence officer under the Admiral's direct command. This appointment allowed Agar free rein to travel through Biorko, Helsinki and Riga and on any ship of the British fleet in order to fulfil his duties.

The Soviet Baltic Fleet had not been very active since the raid on 18 August and had rarely ventured out of Kronstadt since. The only occasion a Kronstadt-based vessel had steamed beyond the minefield was when the small patrol vessel *Kitteboi* snuck out to defect and was promptly put into British service as a fleet tender.

Incorporated into the British fleet at this time were several wooden-hulled Finnish vessels converted into minesweepers in anticipation of sweeping the inshore channels between Kronstadt and Petrograd, should the city be taken by General Yudenich's White Russian 'North West Army' from Estonia.

During September there was little to keep the crew of the Royal Navy Baltic Fleet occupied apart from the occasional bombardment of Bolshevik positions in northern Estonia. The RAF remained active flying missions from Koivisto and on one such sortie on 17 September, a Sopwith Strutter flown by Lieutenant Samuel Dawson, DFC, and Observer Lieutenant Francis Unwin, crashed into the Baltic, killing both men. Dawson's body was recovered and buried at Koivisto but Unwin's body was never found.

On 25 October 1919 the RAF suffered their last casualty of the campaign in the Eastern Baltic when, whilst making an attack on an enemy observation balloon over the forts near Kronstadt, Pilot Officer Fred Cardwell's Sopwith Camel was shot down by flak and he was killed. A Short Seaplane was also shot down but fortunately for its crew they were rescued by an Estonian gunboat. Dawson, Unwin and Cardwell remain commemorated on the Archangel Memorial to the Missing (CWGC).

In September, the 3rd Submarine Flotilla of 'H' Class boats under Commander Max Horton, RN, in HMS *Maidstone* arrived to relieve Nasmith's 7th Submarine Flotilla. Horton was no stranger to the Baltic and was a legend in the submarine service. Having been awarded the DSO for sinking a German cruiser and destroyer within three weeks of each other in the first year of the war, Horton had gone on to command the British submarine flotilla operating in the Baltic before the Revolution for which he was awarded a second DSO. For his service in command of 3rd Flotilla and as Senior Naval Officer at Reval, he would be recommended by Admiral Cowan for yet another DSO, making Horton one of very few naval officers in the First World War to receive the DSO three times.

Before 7th Submarine Flotilla departed for the UK in December 1919, the Admiralty gifted submarines *E27* and *E40* to the Estonian government, after mounting two 12 pdr guns taken from two of the later 'L' Class boats. The 3rd Submarine Flotilla continued to patrol the western approaches to the chain of forts protecting Kronstadt until the Baltic began to ice over. The Flotilla's arrival back in the UK on 2 January 1920 brought to a close the operation of Royal Navy submarines in the Baltic Sea, 1915–19.

On 10 October, the Foreign Office issued instructions to the Admiralty to formally authorise Cowan to blockade Petrograd from the Gulf of Finland. The legality of this order was at best extremely questionable: Britain had not declared hostilities against Soviet Russia and the formal authorisation of a blockade was a belligerent act and tantamount to a declaration of war.

By October 1919 time was running out for German General von der Goltz's 'Iron Division' in Latvia, and his dream of conquest of the Baltic states as small compensation for colonies lost to Germany during the war. The German troops would soon be required to leave the Baltic under the terms that the Allied governments had set for their withdrawal.

General von der Goltz recruited a force of some 50,000 men, both German, Russian (who were opposed to the independence of the Baltic states and their 'loss' from the former Imperial Russian Empire) and the Baltic German *Landwehr* militia, all under the command of General Pavel Bermondt-Avalof, a former Imperial Russian Cossack officer, and the troops of Goltz's 'Freikorps Iron Division' of German volunteers.

Camped on the outskirts of the capital, Riga, by early October the German force postured threateningly to attack the city. The Latvians, having already been equipped with British weapons and equipment, requested support from the Royal Navy to bombard the German encampment and send the enemy packing. Yet again Cowan faced a quandary. The Latvians were requesting a British Admiral to dislodge by bombardment White Russian troops who were ardent anti-Bolsheviks and technically under the command of General Yudenich and therefore, by default, British Allies.

Nonetheless, Cowan was obliged, under his orders from the Admiralty, to protect Latvian sovereignty: the Admiral gave Bermondt-Avalof and his German–Russian force 48 hours to abandon their positions on Riga's outskirts. General von der Goltz would not go quietly and on the morning of 8 October, just as Yudenich was about to launch his own offensive to take Narva on the far eastern Estonian coast, three German aeroplanes flew over Riga and bombed the city.

Captain Berwick Curtis, RN, with three of his destroyers of the 20th Flotilla, had previously steamed five miles up the Western Dvina River (not to be confused with the Northern Dvina south of Archangel, North Russia) to join the French sloop *Aisne* in the centre of Riga to act as observers in the event of a German–Lettish conflict. When Goltz attacked the city the British and French ships were caught in the line of fire. To escape the shooting, Curtis moved his ships to the mouth of the river and sent a motorboat (crewed by volunteers covered with mattresses to absorb shrapnel) into Riga in an attempt to run the gauntlet of fire and link up with the Allied Military Missions.

By 10 October, the Germans had advanced as far as the western bank of the Dvina whilst the Letts held the opposite western bank with the British and French ships on the river dividing the two sides. At first the Germans were cautious not to catch the Allied ships in their crossfire but later as the battle wore on they were not as careful. As they brought up field guns, shrapnel began to burst above the British destroyers forcing Curtis to weigh anchor and move HMS *Abdiel* further downriver. It was out of the frying pan and into the fire. No sooner had *Abdiel* raised steam and sailed downriver, she was again caught in the crossfire and forced to speedily relocate. There was little doubt that the aim of the German gunners was deliberate.

During the night of 11–12 October, Curtis sent destroyer HMS *Vanoc* (Commander E.O. Tudor, RN), light cruisers HMS *Dragon* and HMS *Cleopatra* and the converted minelayer HMS *Princess Margaret* to Riga, the smaller destroyers used to bring off refugees and members of the British Military Mission lined along the docks. As the launches made their way to and from the British destroyers the Germans made no attempt to hide the pot-shots they were taking at the boats from Fort Danamunde as each boat was leaving.

Cowan gave permission for the fort to be captured and under the cover of British guns, Lettish troops in small boats advanced on the fort from the sea. As the British fire lifted, the Letts stormed from their launches and sent the German soldiers into headlong retreat, being fired upon all the way by the British warships upriver, cutting off their line of withdrawal. The surviving troops were forced to surrender and the Letts eventually took some 300 German prisoners.

On 17 October, the Germans got their own back when a field battery fired on light cruiser HMS *Dragon* from ashore scoring three hits, one shell landing directly on No. 5 Gun, killing nine men and severely wounding a further five sailors. Gunner Charles Coles, RN, was at his action station in After

Control when the shell struck, and seeing that the charge that was being loaded into the gun had caught alight, rushed to smother the burning clothes of the wounded and move them out of danger, for which he was awarded the DSC. Chief Petty Officer Alfred Davis, who had survived the mining of HMS *Conquest* in the North Sea in July the previous year, was the gunlayer of No. 5 Gun and miraculously escaped injury when all those around him had been killed or wounded. Davis immediately set about extinguishing flames and evacuating wounded for which he was awarded the DSM. Two of those killed, Boys 1st Class William Frett and Alfred Payne, were just 17 years old. To this day few people know that the last British servicemen killed by German forces during the First World War died in the Baltic nearly a year after the Armistice had been signed.

On 23 October, German guns again fired on the flotilla but this time the battery could not be located and the flotilla was forced to move off without firing a shot in response. Destroyer HMS *Venturous* was straddled by the German artillery with two men wounded before steaming out of range. The following day the British ships returned and bombarded the suspected German firing position. The enemy artillery fired a few shells in reply but soon thereafter remained silent, possibly put out of action by the British shelling directed by an observation party of sailors with a wireless in the Lettish frontline trenches under the command of Lieutenant A.F. Brown, RFA of the British Military Mission. For their services in maintaining communication and spotting for the ships guns whilst under fire, Signalman John Taylor and Leading Telegraphist George Lamb were both awarded the DSM.

Spurred on by the British naval bombardment, Latvian forces eventually succeeded in pushing Bermondt-Avalof's German force back along the railway all the way to Lithuania and beyond into East Prussia. Two days later the ships were relieved and Captain Curtis' 20th Destroyer Flotilla (less HMS *Vittoria* and HMS *Verulam*) made preparations to return home.

During the period 10–25 October, a volunteer motor boat crew from HMS *Abdiel* under Lieutenant Harold Morse, RN, with Able Seamen Robert Flight, Donald Thomas, Ernest Wright and Signalman Thomas Rumble, kept communications between the British fleet and Riga open despite coming under fire from German troops ashore each time they set out. For his command of the motor boat Morse was awarded the DSO and the ratings the DSM.

A 3 inch anti-aircraft gun detachment under Sub Lieutenants Neville Pisani, RN, and John Campbell, RN, had also been landed during this period from HMS *Vortigern* and was active in defending Riga from attack by German aircraft. When the Letts counter-attacked in November, the gun was mounted on a railway truck and used to support the advance on Mitau, driving off German aircraft which were attacking the Letts with machine guns. For their services both Pisani and Campbell were awarded the DSC whilst the 10 ratings who acted as gun crew were Mentioned in Despatches.

During the second week of October, Yudenich and his 40,000 strong White Russian 'North West Army' began their offensive to take Petrograd, however the General's leadership was hampered by ethnic divisions within his command. For reasons of jealousy and ambition, Yudenich (an ethnic Russian and former Imperial Army officer) had abandoned to the Bolsheviks ground which had cost the Estonians many lives to capture earlier in the year. Although General Gough (commanding the British Military Mission) had managed to convince the Estonians to unite under Yudenich's overall command, such actions alienated the Estonians from a high command of which they were already extremely suspicious. The Estonians distrusted Yudenich and the White Russian leadership who openly opposed the establishment of an independent Estonian state. Consequently, when Yudenich made what would be his final advance into Russia, the Estonian troops refused to move beyond their own frontier and their own nationalist interests.

Among the forces operating under Yudenich's command were a hardy detachment of Swedish volunteers. They were accompanied into battle by their own nursing staff, one of whom, Sister

150. Danae Class cruiser HMS *Dragon*, stuck by German fire from
ashore, 17 October 1919, killing nine sailors. (Public domain)

Matart Kurkinen was awarded the Military Medal by General Gough for her bravery and resource
in ensuring the medical welfare of the Swedish troops:

> Where the Swedish troops went she went. If they were front line infantry, as on this occasion, she walked
> with the front line. She carried a heavy load of hospital stores and must have been the saviour of many
> a man.[25]

West of Kronstadt, Soviet Admiral Zelnoy decided to set a trap for the British by laying a
minefield directly in the path that the British ships would need to follow to continue supporting
the advancing Estonian forces. Destroyers *Azard*, *Gavriil*, *Konstantin* and *Svoboda* set out from
Kronstadt on 21 October, but soon after ran into a minefield previously laid on Cowan's orders to
prevent exactly the move Zelnoy was making. *Gavriil* (which had caused such trouble to the British
CMBs during the Kronstadt Raid), *Konstantin* and *Svoboda* all struck submerged mines and were
sunk. Only *Azard* escaped, picking up just 25 survivors from the other destroyers before fleeing the
minefield and returning to Kronstadt. Some of the survivors were able to cling to wreckage and drift
ashore before they were taken prisoner by Estonian troops.

By late October 1919, the military situation had turned against Yudenich largely due to the arrival
at the front of 11,000 Soviet Navy volunteers from Petrograd. By 28 October, the 'North West Army'
had been pushed well back from Petrograd and on their left flank the Estonians had failed to take
the fortress at Krasnaya Gorka.

Cowan had previously made an urgent request that a large-calibre armed monitor be sent to the Baltic
for the express purpose of bombarding the Bolshevik forts. On 24 October, HMS *Erebus* (Captain J. A.
Moreton, RN) and its huge 15 inch guns arrived from North Russia where the monitor had covered the
evacuation of the last British troops from Archangel and Murmansk earlier in the month.

Three days later HMS *Delhi* and HMS *Erebus* were in action bombarding Krasnaya Gorka as
the destroyers HM Ships *Spenser*, *Walpole*, *Vectis*, *Mackay* and *Winchelsea* provided a submarine
screen, the latter two ships joining in the shelling at 0800. An observation balloon was used by the
Bolsheviks to direct the artillery fire from the fort; it was evidently filled with non-flammable gas as

---

25   Dobson and Miller, *The Day We Almost Bombed Moscow*, p.264.

it was 'frequently riddled' by aircraft of the RAF but never caught fire. For a full 90 minutes HMS *Delhi* and HMS *Erebus* rained fire down on the Bolshevik forts.

The RAF too were kept extremely busy dropping over 300 bombs on Krasnaya Gorka and on positions holding up the Estonian advance. Squadron Leader Donald was relieved to hear that the world's first true aircraft carrier HMS *Furious* would arrive in the Baltic shortly, taking the strain off the original hard-worked detachment from HMS *Vindictive* which had been operational almost continuously since their arrival in July. When HMS *Furious* and its cargo of 20 aircraft finally arrived at Biorko it was discovered that the planes had all seen extensive service during the war and were not suitable for further difficult service in the climatic extremes of the Baltic.

The RAF continued to fly patrols despite deterioration in weather conditions as the Baltic winter arrived in full force: on one occasion two seaplanes attacked a Bolshevik destroyer during a snowstorm. The seaplanes were too vulnerable to be used during daylight bombing raids so Sopwith Camels were despatched from England, but even at their operational ceiling they were still vulnerable to being hit by Bolshevik anti-aircraft fire. By the end of November the airstrip at Koivisto was covered with snow, making further sorties impossible. Before they were completely snowed in, the aircraft were reloaded on board HMS *Vindictive* in preparation for the trip to Libau where three Sopwith Camels were landed and despatched to Riga with two RAF pilots to train the newly formed Lettish 'Air Corps' in their use.

The RAF remained in action throughout the freezing over of the Eastern Baltic right up until their withdrawal from Finland on 11 December 1919. During their service over the Baltic the squadron had lost four aircrew and one ground crewman killed and two aircrew wounded; they had flown a total of 837 operational hours and lost 33 aircraft, three shot down by enemy anti-aircraft fire, nine force landed in the sea, seven crashed on take-off or landing and 14 damaged beyond repair by climatic conditions.

The arrival of HMS *Erebus* alone could never have been the deciding factor in the capture of Petrograd, and by the end of October Yudenich's troops had been pushed so far back that any hopes of capturing the city had to be abandoned. With every passing day the Red Army grew stronger whilst his own White Russian forces became weaker through desertion.

Since the raid on Kronstadt in August, Admiral Cowan had been particularly concerned for the welfare of the CMB prisoners held by the Bolsheviks, and requested that the Estonians hand over the survivors of *Gavriil*'s crew to the British in case they could be used as leverage in a prisoner exchange should the opportunity arise. Cowan's foresight was warranted as just a few months later in Copenhagen agreement was reached with Bolshevik Foreign Secretary Maxim Litvinov for an exchange of Bolshevik and British and Commonwealth prisoners held in Moscow.

Whilst the Estonians and White Russians had failed to defeat the Bolsheviks in the north, the Latvians were making great gains against the Germans in the south. On 3 November, light cruiser HMS *Dragon* and four 'V' and 'W' Class destroyers anchored at the mouth of the Dvina and fired in support of Lettish troops as they advanced along the banks of the river, pushing the Germans back from Riga's western suburbs as they went. For eight days and nights the German and Lettish troops fought it out on the city's outskirts whilst the British and French ships crept along the Gulf of Riga to stay within shelling range of the fighting. By 11 November 1919, the anniversary of the Armistice, reports were received that the Germans were fleeing in confusion and the Letts had recaptured Riga, in no small part assisted by the guns of the Royal Navy.

Whilst HMS *Dragon* and its escorts had been busily shelling German troops along the Gulf of Riga, cruisers HMS *Phaeton* and HMS *Dauntless*, and destroyers HM Ships *Winchester*, *Whitley*, *Valorous* and *Wryneck* had been waiting at Libau for the German attack expected there. On 4 November the attack came and the British ships were quickly in action in support of the Lettish garrison. HMS *Winchester* was hurried to Windau to ascertain the situation there only to find the garrison of 300 Lettish riflemen under attack from a German force more than double their size.

Captain L. Dundas, RN, on board HMS *Phaeton*, ordered *Wryneck* to embark 500 Lettish troops and proceed to relieve Windau at haste.

The Germans resumed their attack on Windau on 6 November but did not advance far under heavy fire from the British ships' guns. They scrambled a plane to bomb the British cruisers and destroyers in the harbour but it was driven down under a hail of fire from the Letts. Two days later snow began to fall and the German advance stalled in the freezing temperatures. On the same date HMS *Erebus* arrived and joined the other ships in counterfire missions against German batteries firing on Windau port.

The Germans reorganised and resumed the attack on 14 November, succeeding in overrunning the Lettish frontline and entering the outskirts of the city. The Lettish counter-attack under heavy covering fire from the British and French fleet pushed the Germans from the front line they had held over the previous week. Yudenich's North West Army would not advance as far again.

On 15 November the Bolsheviks retook Jamburg and continued to advance on the Estonian frontier until a halt was ordered by Moscow. The North West Army was disbanded in Estonia in late November when the once proud Army could call to arms less than 5,000 men. The remainder were incorporated into the new Estonian national army.

By late 1919 the Royal Navy Baltic Fleet was suffering a crisis of low morale amongst its sailors. A combination of poor pay (sailors serving under warlike conditions whilst not in a state of war in the Baltic were not entitled to extra pay, whilst Merchant Navy operating in the Baltic and the Army in North Russia were), slow demobilisation and the use of 'Hostilities Only' enlistees for continued active service in Russia and the Baltic had resulted in an increase of ill feeling amongst the sailors, most of whom had seen extensive wartime service and wished to return home to their families. Life as a sailor in the Great War was still very tough: pay and conditions had changed little since Victorian times and sailors' families were finding it hard to exist on a paltry wage as the cost of living in post-war Britain continued to rise. These grievances culminated in a series of incidents within the Baltic Fleet that were covered up by authorities at the time and to this day are little known.

The 1st Destroyer Flotilla had only recently returned to England from a period of active service in the Baltic in August 1919 when they received orders in October to return to station. On learning of the order, around 150 men deserted their ships and went ashore. One of the ratings who jumped ship was Leading Seaman Herbert Frank Greatwood, who served six months imprisonment for the refusal to serve: 'We had enough of it out there, getting shelled and Christ knows what ... When Churchill wanted to send us out again the war had finished ... it had been finished before we went out the first time![26] When the flotilla sailed on 14 October, the crew shortages from the desertions were made up by sailors seconded from the Atlantic Fleet.

Most of the deserters were apprehended soon after, but a group of 44 men were able to make their way to London intending to present a petition to Parliament. The deserters were promptly arrested on arrival at King's Cross Station and escorted under armed guard to the Royal Naval Barracks at Chatham, where they were held whilst the Navy considered how to respond. Court-martials were conducted and most of the mutineers sentenced to periods of imprisonment.

A court of inquiry into the desertions was conducted on board HMS *Valiant* on 20–21 October in which the assembled officers considered the sailors grievances:

> The Ships' Companies are of opinion that service in the Baltic is war service, but they do not consider that it is or has ever been recognised as such. Considerable fighting and fairly heavy casualties have occurred without the Country even being aware of the fact that the Flotillas were on Active Service. Mention was made in the Press that the First Destroyer Flotilla was at Southend when they were, in fact, actually on

---

26   IWM sound, 9024, Greatwood, Herbert Frank.

Active Service in the Baltic. This may, in itself, appear a trivial matter but it is not considered as such by the men.[27]

Although the ratings had committed one of the worst crimes under harsh Admiralty regulations, that of refusing to serve, tantamount to mutiny at sea, the findings of the court were overwhelmingly sympathetic, one senior naval officer recording a finding that bordered on editorial comment:

As to the men's desire to know why they are fighting, they are not the only people who are asking that question. The whole public is asking it and so far as I know no satisfactory answer has been given. Everyone is asking what good or use is there in this Baltic Force, they are not stopping Bolshevism nor are they advancing peace. If the force is not withdrawn or sound reasons given for the service, it seems to me that further trouble of this sort is inevitable. An Englishman is a good fighter but he must know what he is fighting about.[28]

In November 1919, the aircraft carrier HMS *Vindictive* was at anchor in Copenhagen harbour replenishing stores when grievances amongst some of her crew boiled over. Due to bad weather all leave had been revoked and there was also a shortage of canteen stores and comforts for the men. Some of the crew, particularly the stokers, felt they were being treated harshly. Around 40 sailors paraded on the quarterdeck demanding to see the ship's captain. The men were informed that Captain Grace would see representatives individually but the crowd refused to disperse. Two men were placed under arrest and sent below, and after a few minutes the remainder were persuaded to leave the quarterdeck. Soon thereafter the men returned, shouting their demands for leave. In response Captain Grace ordered the Royal Marine detachment to fall in. The sailors realised they could do no more to have their opinions heard and returned to the mess deck where they continued to chant and sing. The incident seemed to have ended there, until HMS *Vindictive* was underway: the engineering officer reported that two stokers had been caught trying to sabotage the engines and Petty Officer guards had to be posted prevent any further attempts of sabotage.

After HMS *Vindictive* reached station in the Baltic, Captain Grace ordered the entire crew aft where he made an address. The two stokers who had been caught attempting to sabotage the engines were brought forward, immediately arrested and taken below deck. Grace went on to state that if possible, leave would be granted the following day, but none of the 40 men who had assembled on the quarter deck would be allowed ashore and would be punished as he saw necessary. Grace recorded:

On the following morning, many of these men did not turn to, so I arrested five of the worst, charged them, and sent them off to England for 90 days hard labour, after which I trust that they will be discharged from H.M. Service. I arrested six more, and followed the same procedure. Next morning, 14 men still refused duty; these were at once arrested. Finally, late of Thursday evening, two seamen refused duty. I dealt with them at once. There has been no further trouble.[29]

An equally serious incident occurred when virtually all the 'Hostilities Only' ratings serving on the fleet minesweepers went on strike. Most of the minesweepers were crewed by the RNR Trawler service, professional seamen who had volunteered for naval service for the duration of the war. Minesweeping was one of the most dangerous naval jobs of the war and as far as the RNR ratings on the Baltic Fleet minesweepers were concerned, hostilities had long since ended on 11 November

27   The National Archives: ADM 1/8570/291: Request of payment of 2s/6d a day to crews of Destroyers ordered to the Baltic.
28   *Ibid.*
29   Bennett, *Cowan's War*, p.201.

151. British aircraft donated to the fledgling Estonian Air Service. (IWM Q69732)

1918 and they should not have been sent to serve in further warlike operations, particularly as the British Government was proclaiming in the press that only volunteers were being sent to Russia.

Even Admiral Cowan's own flagship HMS *Delhi* was not immune from the discontent, and experienced its own mutiny when a number of ship's company refused to turn out to duty. The refusal came as a result of the ship's visit to Reval in early December when the men, already weary of active service, feared that they would not be home to spend Christmas with their families before the Gulf of Finland froze them in. There was also a shortage of cold weather clothing and the ship was not fitted with arctic heating equipment. When *Delhi* stopped off at Reval the crew were anticipating some much overdue shore leave, however only Admiral Cowan and a few senior officers went ashore. An unidentified officer on board *Delhi* wrote:

> As usual Walter Cowan was ashore within a few minutes of anchoring … About 1100 the barge was seen returning, whilst the Commander was discussing with some of us what leave should be given. Up the gangway tripped the trim little figure of Walter Cowan … As he came over the side he barked out in his little nasal voice, 'Prepare for sea at once, please, Captain Mackworth; we are returning to Biorko.' Even the most loyal among the ship's company felt that this was 'a bit 'ard.' No Christmas shopping, no run ashore, nothing but an immediate return to bloody Biorko. So when the Commander ordered, 'Both watches prepare ship for sea,' the response was very poor; only about 25% of the ship's company obeyed the bugle.[30]

There followed anxious moments as officers consulted with Petty officers and Petty Officers with senior ratings. After a couple of hours to cool off the men fell in for duty and HMS *Delhi* proceeded back to Biorko.

Some critics have blamed Cowan for the mutinies amongst the Baltic Fleet in 1919 and used the refusal on board HMS *Delhi* as an example to illustrate the point, but it is unfair to place blame for the disaffection in the fleet solely at the feet of its commander. For the most part the men did not want to be there. The war for which many of them had volunteered had been over for a year and they had not volunteered for further active service, nor did they wish to die seemingly needlessly in an undeclared war for which those back home cared little. Even Cowan himself was retrospect, recalling

---

30 *Ibid.*, p.201.

in his 70s, 'When I commanded a squadron [in the Baltic] I made the mistake of expecting too high a standard of discipline.'[31]

During the first week of December 1919, an Armistice was signed between the Estonian and Bolshevik governments. The peace talks were a success granting full concession by the Soviets for Estonian independence. Agar took advantage of the Bolshevik–Estonian peace conference to tag along with the Estonian delegation to test the waters with the Bolsheviks for a prisoner exchange, the fate of the Kronstadt Raid prisoners still foremost on his mind.

At Helsinki, Agar changed into civilian clothes and travelled by train to the location of the conference at Dorpat. The Bolshevik delegation had been told that a junior officer from the British Fleet had come to meet with them unofficially. At the conclusion of the conference the Soviet representatives called for the British officer to discuss the departure of the British Fleet from the Eastern Baltic. Agar met with the Bolshevik delegation and the British Fleet's withdrawal from the Baltic was discussed in detail, after which Agar moved on to the subject of the Kronstadt Raid prisoners. The Bolshevik representative informed that the prisoners had been sent to the Andronikov Monastery outside Moscow where they were imprisoned with other 'counter-revolutionaries' and Allied POWs from other fronts. All officers and men had been kept together except for Lieutenant Bill Bremner, RN (*CMB 79*), who was in hospital receiving treatment for his wounds. The ratings were considered by the Bolsheviks to be 'conscripts' and were permitted to roam free in Moscow (accompanied by an escort) where they could barter at local markets for provisions although no such privilege was granted to officer ranks. The meeting ended well with the Bolshevik delegation promising to inform the British POWs that a prisoner exchange would be forthcoming.

On New Year's Eve the drifter HMS *Catspaw*, which had been serving as a fleet minesweeper, was making its way back to England when it foundered in bad weather off the Swedish coast, likely due to engine failure, and sank with the loss of all hands. The bodies of the crew (three officers and 11 ratings) were recovered by the Swedes and buried in Kviberg Cemetery (CWGC). Lieutenant Geoffrey Williams, RN, and Sub Lieutenant Frederick Vallings, RN, were both posthumously Mentioned in Despatches for their work rescuing crew members of HMS *Verulam* on 3 September.

The Letts continued to push the occupying German troops from their homeland and on 18 November the German commander asked for an armistice. The Letts, having fallen for German false promises before, rejected the request and continued to push further. On 21 November the Letts liberated Mitau, and the German commander again requested a cessation of hostilities to allow his troops to leave Latvia. The Letts ignored the request and by the end of November had pushed the Germans from Latvia completely before quickly relocating to the east of the country to keep the Red Army at bay. By 24 November 1919 the last German troops left the Baltic as General von der Goltz's 'Iron Division' was recalled to Germany.

The British Fleet spent a freezing Christmas Day at Biorko without Christmas dinner, as the Finnish ship bringing festive supplies had been struck by a mine and sunk. The Finns kindly gave what they could and Cowan ordered a double issue of rum and promise of a proper Christmas dinner on return to England. The men spent the day ashore playing soccer in the snow or ice skating.

On 28 December, after witnessing the final signatures to the Bolshevik–Estonian peace treaty, Cowan left Reval on HMS *Delhi* for England via Copenhagen and Libau, with HMS *Dragon* and the 1st Destroyer Flotilla in tow, leaving only HMS *Dunedin* and a few destroyers of the 4th Flotilla behind to sit out the winter in the Gulf of Finland. On New Year's Day 1920, Cowan and the remainder of the Royal Navy Baltic Fleet returned to Britain, arriving at Plymouth without fanfare.

---

31   Harry Ferguson, *Operation Kronstadt: the true story of honor, espionage, and the rescue of Britain's greatest spy, the Man with a Hundred Faces* (Arrow Books, 2008), p.78.

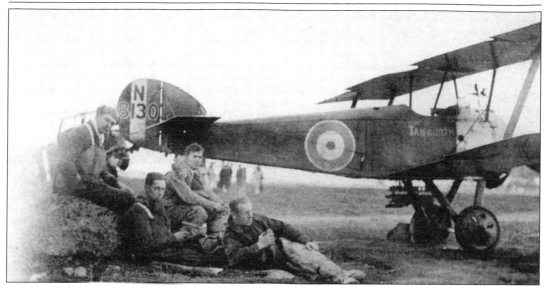

152. Sopwith Camel and aircrew from HMS *Vindictive* on the
airstrip at Koivisto, Finland. (IWM Q69732)

By 1921 the last British cruiser and two destroyers had left the Baltic, bringing to an end the Royal Navy presence there.

Agar went on to captain cruiser HMS *Dorsetshire* during the Second World War until she was sunk by Japanese aircraft along with her sister ship HMS *Cornwall* off Ceylon on 5 April 1942, with the loss of nearly 250 of her crew. After nearly a day and a half in the water, a spotter plane sighted the survivors and an hour later rescue ships arrived. Agar had suffered shrapnel wounds to the leg which became infected, and he became ill from swallowing engine oil. Deemed unfit for further active service, Commodore Augustus Agar, VC, DSO, RN, spent the remainder of the war in administrative appointments.

In retirement Agar ran a strawberry farm in Hampshire until his death on 30 December 1968. The year before his death, *CMB 4* (which had spent a short time post-war on display in the Imperial War Museum before being placed on long-term display at the Thornycroft yard at Platt's Eyot) was moved to Southampton after the closure of the Vosper works, where it was returned to the Royal Navy. The route was planned so the low loader would pass directly in front of Agar's house in Hampshire. As the CMB passed by, the elderly Agar stood by his front gate and saluted his former command. After restoration *CMB 4* was moved to Imperial War Museum Duxford where it remains on display, one of only two CMBs surviving today.

On return to England, Sub Lieutenant Edgar Sindall, RNR, joined British SIS and was based in Stockholm until 1924, his career thereafter remains unknown. Another Baltic CMB officer also joined SIS: Lieutenant William Bremner, RN, joined the service after his release from Bolshevik prison in 1920, although the extent of his service thereafter is unknown. Midshipman Richard Marshall, RNR, possibly also joined SIS but after demobilisation from the Royal Navy his service is unknown. Sub Lieutenant John Hampsheir, RNR, evacuated from the Baltic and hospitalised with combat stress, never fully recovered from his war service. He was demobilised a broken man in 1920 and married, but died in 1936 aged just 38. Both Chief Motor Mechanics Hugh Beeley, CGM, and Albert Piper, DSM, were demobilised on return to England in late 1919 and their lives thereafter remain unknown.

Having added to his illustrious career with a distinguished period of service in the Baltic for which he was made Baronet in 1921, Walter Cowan went on to further extraordinary deeds as one of the

153. Captain Augustus Agar, VC, DSO, RN, salutes his old command *CMB 4*
as it passes his home in Hampshire, 1967. (IWM HU 46103)

oldest British servicemen of the Second World War. When Germany invaded Poland in September 1939, Cowan was already 68 years old but immediately volunteered his services directly to Second Sea Lord, Admiral Sir Charles Little. Despite his age Cowan was appointed in the rank of Commander and posted to the staff of his younger brother, the Naval Control Service Officer at Lowestoft.

Staff work did not satisfy Cowan and when his old friend Admiral Roger Keyes became Director of Combined Operations, he appealed to be appointed Naval Liaison Officer to Army Commandos. Despite his age Cowan participated in Commando combined operations training and in February 1941 a very happy Naval Liaison Officer embarked for the Middle East with No. 11 (Scottish) Commando. Once the Commandos reached Alexandria, Cowan called on the Senior Naval Officer, Mediterranean Fleet, Admiral Andrew Cunningham (later Admiral of the Fleet Lord Cunningham of Hyndhope) who had been awarded a DSO second Bar as ship's captain of destroyer HMS *Seafire* in the Baltic and had been Cowan's Flag Captain on the West Indies station during the early interwar years. Before long Cowan was again at sea in the Mediterranean on board the battleship HMS *Warspite*, the first time he had heard the sound of ship's guns in action since his command in the Baltic more than 20 years earlier.

Stepping ashore in Libya, Cowan attached himself to 18th King Edward's Own Cavalry of the Indian Armoured Corps as a naval liaison. On 26 March 1941 the regiment was in action at Bir Hakim where the nearly 70-year-old Cowan saw action against the Afrika Korps. In a letter to Roger Keyes from an Italian Prisoner of War Camp (Campo P.G.N. 29, P.M. 3200) Cowan wrote:

We were holding with 500 men an unprepared position … They attacked us with many tanks and a whole Division, and the first wave went clean through, and everyone near me was either knocked over or captured. I got behind an empty Bren gun carrier and they missed me.

After a lull the second wave came on. I'd got into the carrier. An armoured car stopped about 40 yards off, and four men got out and came at me. I let drive at them with my revolver and one dropped in front. The others ran back behind their A.C. Then the captain of it shouted and gesticulated that I should put my hands up, but this I could not do, so he fired a burst at me and missed. He again hailed me and got no response, so fired another burst and again missed … I felt after missing me twice that was enough, and

I got out of the carrier and pointed to my empty pistol, and walked up and asked what he wanted. He motioned me to get up on to my car, and that was the end, and I grieve that it's all over.[32]

After nine months of captivity Cowan was released and repatriated to England on account of his age but was soon back in action as Naval Liaison Officer with No. 9 Commando in the Mediterranean. He participated in several operations against enemy-held islands in the Adriatic and in the assault on Mount Ornito in Italy in February 1944. That same year the 73-year-old was awarded a DSO Bar for service with the Commandos, some 46 years after receiving his first DSO for command of a gunboat in the Sudan, 1898. Cowan remains the oldest recipient of the DSO and the only officer to have been awarded two DSOs 46 years apart. By mid 1944, Cowan was forced to return home to England and leave his beloved Commandos behind. Operations had become too hard for him to continue although he did visit 4th Special Service Brigade (Royal Marine and Army Commandos) in Holland after the capture of Walcheren in 1944. After VE day Cowan received one of his most cherished honours when he was gazetted as Honorary Colonel of the 18th Indian Cavalry, the unit with which he had been captured at Bir Hakim in 1941. Rear Admiral Sir Walter Henry Cowan, Baronet, KCB, DSO and Bar, MVO, RN, died at Kineton, Warwickshire in 1956 aged 85.

During its service in the Baltic and Gulf of Finland, 1918–19, the Royal Navy Baltic Sea Fleet employed a total of 238 vessels of all shapes and sizes. Additionally, Admiral Cowan had under his command at one time or another, 26 French, two Italian and 14 US ships of varying classes and sizes.

A total of 133 officers, petty officers and ratings of the Royal Navy were killed during operations in the eastern Baltic, the majority due to enemy action, whilst one officer and two soldiers of the British Military Mission died of illness and four officers and one aircraftman from the RAF were killed. The cruiser HMS *Cassandra*, destroyers HMS *Vittoria* and HMS *Verulam*, submarine HMS *L55*, fleet minesweepers HMS *Myrtle* and HMS *Gentian*, drifter HMS *Catspaw* and seven coastal motor boats had all been sunk either as a result of either direct enemy action or sea mines.

The Royal Navy had performed exceptionally well under difficult circumstances and upheld the highest traditions and honour of the service. Overall, in contrast to other theatres of British military intervention in the Russian Civil War, the Baltic operations can justifiably be considered a success, as they did achieve the goal of protecting the Baltic States from both German and Bolshevik occupation and had largely kept the Soviet fleet blockaded in Kronstadt.

The three Baltic States, Lithuania, Latvia and Estonia, enjoyed their hard-won independence until 1940 when the Red Army achieved what they had failed to accomplish during the winter of 1918–19. The Soviets had long memories and it was undoubtedly with smug satisfaction that they forcibly annexed the Baltic States into the Soviet Union whilst the British Expeditionary Force was being evacuated from Dunkirk. The Soviets also never forgot from where Agar and his CMBs had attacked Kronstadt Harbour, and after the 1939–40 Russo–Finnish War Finland was forced to hand over territory north of Leningrad (formerly Petrograd) to the Soviets including Terrioki and its yacht club.

In 2006 the British government sold the former Royal Navy minehunter HMS *Sandown* (built at the Vosper–Thornycroft shipyards which built the CMBs that attacked Kronstadt) to the Estonian Navy, who rechristened the vessel *Walter Cowan* in honour of the British Admiral who had commanded the Royal Navy Baltic Fleet nearly 90 years earlier.

In July 2010 the wrecks of HMS *Cassandra*, HMS *Myrtle* and the bow section of HMS *Gentian* were discovered by the Estonian Navy where they had sunk off the Estonian coast. Parts of HMS *Myrtle* had been located as long ago as 1937 but the ship itself remained undiscovered until 70 years later. All three ships have since been declared war graves.

32   Roger Keyes, 'Admiral Sir Walter H. Cowan, BT., KCB, DSO', *The Naval Review*, Vol. XXX, No. 4 (November 1942), pp.267–268.

The Army

The only British ground force to see action in the Baltic was a Tank Corps detachment equipped with six Mark V tanks, commanded by Rhodesian Major Ernest Hope Carson, MC. Carson had served during the Mashonaland Rebellion, Boer War and in German South West Africa in 1915 where he had been awarded the Military Cross. Formed in England on 19 July 1919, the detachment of 22 officers and 26 men, all of whom had specially volunteered for service in Russia, arrived at Tallinn on the night of 5 August with the first four tanks of the detachment on board transport ship SS *Dania* and spent the following two weeks unloading and servicing the tanks for operations.

Whilst the tanks were being unloaded, Lieutenant Frank Waine went ahead of the detachment to Narva to organise billets and arrange construction of a ramp from which the tanks could be unloaded at the railway siding. By the end of August two tanks were sent by train 100 miles south from Narva to the town of Pskov, 20 miles inside the Russian frontier. The Estonian troops there were under heavy pressure from the Red Army, and it was hoped that the arrival of the tanks would bolster the defenders.

Soon after arriving at the railway station at Pskov and before the tanks had been unloaded, the town was attacked and overrun by Bolshevik troops. Swift action brought the two tanks out of the town before capture, the train transporting the tanks crossing the railway bridge only minutes before it was blown by the retreating Estonian forces.

After the abortive attempt to attack the Bolshevik positions around Pskov, General Yudenich ordered the creation of a special White Russian unit, the 'Tank Push Battalion', formed specifically to work in close conjunction with the tanks. During the first weeks of September the tanks trained with the battalion, which honed its skills in moving forward behind the tanks to attack enemy positions in their wake. Two further tanks under Captain Stephen Craven arrived in September bringing the detachment total strength to six Mark Vs. The newly arrived tanks were in rather poor condition, their service and repair supervised by Lieutenant George Wilson who was awarded the MC for his services as detachment engineering officer.

On 11 September, the Tank Push Battalion and three Mark Vs were despatched 35 miles south from their base at Narva to Gdov, a small town on Lake Pepsi. Major Carson had been asked by Yudenich to provide two tanks only but had sent one extra as a reserve in case another broke down. During the following four days fighting the Tank Push Battalion and Tank Corps detachment saw their first action and were of great assistance in pushing the Red Army back from their fortified positions. The tanks were all named, and it was estimated that during this period *Captain Cromie* (Lieutenant Stanley Welch), named after Captain Cromie, RN, killed whilst resisting Red Guards storming the British Embassy in Petrograd in August 1918, travelled 99.5 miles, *Brown Bear* (Captain Frederick Manning) traversed 96 miles and *First Aid* (Captain Lancelot Battersby) covered 81 miles. The two other tanks not deployed to Gdov were named *White Soldier* and *Deliverance*, unfortunately the name of the sixth tank of the detachment is not known. *First Aid* had been the tank inspected by General Yudenich immediately upon the detachment's arrival at Tallinn and had been named for this event.

The Tank Corps detachment saw much action during the latter half of September but were hampered by unreliability of the tanks, one of which had broken down and had to be guarded whilst it underwent repairs. On 2 October, the three tanks finally returned to Narva under the command of Captain Hugh McCrostie, who would be awarded the DSO for his work as second in command of the detachment. Upon arrival at Narva, Hope Carson found preparations underway for a final attempt to capture Petrograd and was a little frustrated that the operations around Gdov had prevented him from using his full force of six tanks to support the offensive.

On 11 October *Captain Cromie*, *Brown Bear* and *First Aid* participated in an attack on the town of Jamburg, 20 miles east of Narva. Attacking at dawn, they led the assault on the town but were too heavy to cross the bridges over the River Luga and reach the centre of the town, and thus played only a supporting role for the remainder of the battle. The attack was a complete success and White Russian General Glazenap made special mention in his report of the three British tanks:

> To the lot of the troops in our sector, feeble numerically but strong in spirit, has fallen a splendid success. We have captured Jamburg. Four Bolshevik regiments have been decimated and 300 prisoners taken; also machine-guns, an armoured car and a great deal of military booty. This success is due not only to the smart work of the troops but also to the excellent work of the tanks and their gallant British Officers. In the name of the Service and of the people who we have rescued from the Bolsheviks I congratulate all units under my command with this victory and thank all ranks, particularly Lt-Colonel Hope-Carson, for their excellent work.[33]

On 15 October, work was completed on the bridges and the tanks were finally able to cross the river and reach Jamburg railway station. *The Daily Express* special correspondent wrote of the detachment:

> The Tank Corps continues to win a golden reputation, indeed it appears to be considered impossible to take a step without their aid. Reliance is played to such an extent on the Tanks that the crews find it difficult to obtain the necessary rest. A remarkable feat reflecting credit upon Colonel Carson and his men was performed in crossing the River Luga which was considered impracticable.[34]

On 17 October the tanks were despatched by train to Gatchina, just 25 miles south-west of Petrograd and location of the old Imperial Air Service aerodrome, which had been captured by Yudenich's forces two days earlier. On 19 October *First Aid*, *Captain Cromie* and *Brown Bear* were sent to Ontolovo, eight miles north of Gatchina where a Bolshevik force had held up the White Russian advance. Two of the tanks (it is unknown which) did not make the distance due to engine trouble but one did reach the front line before nightfall. The two broken down tanks were repaired and Hope Carson ordered all three to spend the night in Ontolovo because of reports of a Bolshevik armoured train about a mile further up the railway from the town.

At dawn the following morning the attack was resumed with the tanks operating on the eastern side of the main road to avoid fire from the armoured train, if it made an appearance. *First Aid* supported by infantry advanced six miles to within a few hundred metres of Tsarskoe Selo, location of the Tsar's 'Winter Palace', just 12 miles from Petrograd. *Captain Cromie* attacked along the right flank encountering Red Army infantry in two small villages near Tsarskoe Selo. *Brown Bear* had been slowed by mechanical problems but caught up on the right flank and dealt with the enemy in a third small village. By midday the tanks were short of fuel and suffering from mechanical problems. Carson had no choice but to inform Yudenich that his tanks would be unable to continue the attack that day.

By 21 October only *First Aid* was serviceable enough to continue the attack and saw much action south of Tsarskoe Selo over the next three days, commanded by a White Russian officer with a Russian crew trained by the British. *Captain Cromie* and *Brown Bear* were forced to return to Gatchina for repairs and were met there by the three remaining tanks of the detachment.

By 24 October, the Bolsheviks were gaining the upper hand and Carson was asked to provide three tanks to counter-attack between Gatchina and Tsarskoe Selo. Two of the tanks newly arrived from Narva, *Deliverance* and *White Soldier*, were tasked to attack along with *Brown Bear*. During the counter-attack the tanks were commanded and crewed entirely by White Russian officers and

---

33   Dobson and Miller, *The Day We Almost Bombed Moscow*, p.263.
34   *The Times*, 30 October 1919.

154. British Mark Vs of the Tank Corps on the docks at Tallinn,
Estonia, 6 August 1919. (IWM Q69731)

soldiers The counter-attack was unsuccessful, and on the night of 25 October Hope Carson gave orders to entrain the tanks and return to Jamburg. The town was reached the following day and repairs and maintenance on the tanks continued. A few days later they returned to their base at Narva, crossing the river via a temporary bridge.

The success of the detachment during operations in September and October had created amongst the White Russian leadership a dependency on the use of tanks for any and all offensive operations. When Yudenich learned that the tanks were to be withdrawn he was aghast, and stated that his troops would not advance without them. Hope Carson later wrote:

> It was now obvious that the staff were relying on three lame tanks to get the column through … Many of the senior officers were incapable of understanding that the tank was a machine and had its limitations. It was seriously suggested … that by placing a tank on either side of the line it would be an easy matter to catch the [enemy] armoured train.[35]

By 4 November the Bolsheviks had taken Gatchina, two days later the North West Army evacuated Gdov, and on 12 November Jamburg was recaptured by Red troops. Shortly thereafter Yudenich's forces collapsed. The remnants of the army fled to Estonia where they made preparations to resist the Bolshevik advance. An outbreak of typhus swept through the remnants of Yudenich's army taking many of its soldiers who had neither medical supplies nor shelter. Yudenich was arrested in January 1920 whilst trying to flee to Europe with embezzled North West Army funds, which were confiscated and distributed to North West Army veterans as a final payment. Diplomatic pressure by the British Government led to his release by the Estonians; Yudenich promptly fled to France although kept himself isolated from the White Russian émigré community there. General Nikolai Yudenich died as a refugee in Nice, France, in 1935.

The Bolsheviks attempted to take Narva on 18 November by breaking the Estonian positions surrounding the town. The Estonians held fast, however, and the Red troops were unable to advance. On 3 January 1920, both sides signed the Treaty of Tartu ending the war between the Bolsheviks and Estonians and ensuring independence of the Baltic states from Russia.

---

35   Dobson and Miller, *The Day We Almost Bombed Moscow*, p.263.

The Tank Corps detachment was withdrawn from Narva on the day the Bolsheviks began their attack. Major Carson wrote a series of articles published in the Royal Tank Corps Journal in 1927 but omits to mention on what date the detachment actually left Estonia. Four tanks were left behind to the new Estonian Government.

As part of the Molotov–Ribbentrop Pact of 1939 which divided the Baltic into Nazi and Soviet 'spheres of influence', Red troops annexed the Baltic states to Soviet control in 1940. In August 1941 the four British Mark V tanks left behind by the Tank Corps detachment were thrown into action against the *Wehrmacht* steamroller. No match for the modern German tanks, all four were either destroyed or captured, the last time Mark V tanks were used in action.

For service in Estonia the Tank Corps detachment received the following awards:

Distinguished Service Order (DSO):
      Major Ernest Hope Carson, MC
      Captain Hugh McCrostie
Member Order of British Empire (MBE):
      Lieutenant Harold Cole
Bar to Military Cross (MC Bar):
      Lieutenant Frank Waine, MC
Military Cross (MC):
      Captain Lancelot Battersby
      Captain Frederick Manning
      Lieutenant Sidney Vaughton
      Lieutenant Stanley Welch
      2nd Lieutenant Robert Edgell
      2nd Lieutenant Gilbert Scott-Eames
      2nd Lieutenant George Wilson
Distinguished Conduct Medal (DCM):
      308353 CQMS Herbert Attwood
Military Medal (MM):
      309251 Private Harold Huntington
      112335 Private Evan Jones
      200596 Private Alexander Lawson
      310773 Private Thomas Lechmere
Meritorious Service Medal (MSM):
      77543 Sergeant Fred Godley
      200213 Private Percy Prigmore

16

South Russia and Crimea: November 1918–June 1920

The Army

The British presence in South Russia during the period of military intervention in the Russian Civil War stemmed from the post-Bolshevik revolution Anglo–French agreement of 23 December 1917. Much as they had done in dividing the Middle East, the British and French governments agreed on separate 'areas of influence' in South Russia, the French taking control of territory west of the Crimean peninsula and River Don at Odessa and the British to the east at Novorossiysk, including Transcaucasia.

After the Armistice of 11 November 1918 (the Ottoman Empire had withdrawn from the war two weeks earlier) there was relative stability in the British-controlled areas of Transcaucasia and east of the Don River. Divided along ethnic and religious grounds, the Transcaucasian nations of Azerbaijan, Armenia and Georgia were already operating governments of sorts and in the southern Don country General Anton Denikin was forming an anti-Bolshevik White Russian 'Volunteer Army' to fight against the Bolsheviks.

Ten thousand French troops were landed at Odessa on the northern coast of the Black Sea on 18 December to assist in restoring order in the city, in the vacuum left after the Bolshevik revolution and deposal of the Imperial Russian government by the Bolsheviks in Petrograd the previous month. Other countries also contributed to the security force: the Greeks sent 30,000 men in two divisions whilst the Poles sent a Brigade of 3,000 and the Romanians 32,000 to add to the 15,000 White Russian troops Denikin had raised.

The force was formidable in number, some 90,000 men, however the Allied governments were divided on strategy to tackle the Bolshevik issue and lacked the leadership and resolve to respond aggressively to the various Russian factions competing for control. After French troops came under attack within Odessa itself and with the French Black Sea Fleet on the verge of mutiny, the French government gave up on the whole situation and evacuated Odessa on 15 April 1919. The French had their own problems to deal with, rebuilding their shattered nation, let alone handle those of Russia. They took with them some 30,000 Russian civilians and 10,000 White Russian troops but destroyed many thousands of tonnes of supplies and equipment on the docks that would have been invaluable to the White Russian forces. The French also failed to destroy six Renault light tanks which were captured by the Bolsheviks and later used with varying success against Denikin's troops.

Despite being allies, the British were concerned that the French might gain too much influence on Denikin and were keen to start delivery of supplies through Novorossiysk as soon as possible. To this end General Frederick Cuthbert Poole (most recently Commander-in-Chief, North Russia Expeditionary Force until the arrival of General Ironside at Archangel in October 1918) was appointed to temporarily head the fact-finding mission. Poole immediately set about informing the White Russian leadership of Britain's aim to restore 'United Russia' (exceeding his orders not to 'extend any promises of assistance of any kind'[1]) on the same day that the War Office was advising of its support for strong, independent states in the Caucasus and Baltic, territory which had before the war formed part of the Russian Empire.

---

1   Kinvig, *Churchill's Crusade*, p.99.

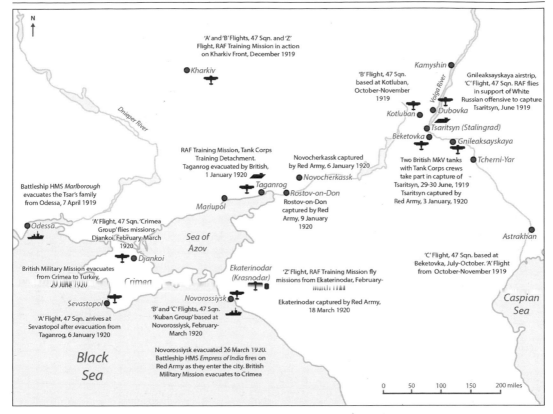

'A' and 'B' Flights, 47 Sqn. and 'Z'
Flight, RAF Training Mission in action
on Kharkiv Front, December 1919

Kharkiv

Kamyshin

'B' Flight, 47 Sqn.
based at Kotluban,
October-November
1919

Gnileaksayskaya airstrip,
'C' Flight, 47 Sqn. RAF flies
in support of White
Russian offensive to capture
Tsaritsyn, June 1919

Kotluban

Dubovka

Tsaritsyn (Stalingrad)

Beketovka

Gnileaksayskaya

RAF Training Mission, Tank Corps
Training Detachment.
Taganrog evacuated by British,
1 January 1920

Novocherkassk captured
by Red Army, 6 January 1920

Novocherkassk

Two British MkV tanks
with Tank Corps crews
take part in capture of
Tsaritsyn, 29-30 June, 1919
Tsaritsyn captured by
Red Army, 3 January, 1920

Tcherni-Yar

Taganrog

Battleship HMS *Marlborough*
evacuates the Tsar's family
from Odessa, 7 April 1919

Rostov-on-Don
Rostov-on-Don
captured by Red
Army, 9 January
1920

Mariupol

Odessa

'A' Flight, 47 Sqn. 'Crimea
Group' flies missions
Djankoi, February-March
1920

Sea of
Azov

Astrakhan

Djankoi

'C' Flight, 47 Sqn. based at
Beketovka, July-October. 'A' Flight
from October-November 1919

British Military Mission evacuates
from Crimea to Turkey,
29 June 1920

Crimea

Ekaterinodar
(Krasnodar)

'Z' Flight, RAF Training Mission fly
missions from Ekaterinodar, February-
March 1920

Caspian
Sea

Sevastopol

Novorossiysk

Ekaterinodar captured by Red Army,
18 March 1920

'A' Flight, 47 Sqn. arrives at
Sevastopol after evacuation from
Taganrog, 6 January 1920

'B' and 'C' Flights, 47 Sqn.
'Kuban Group' based at
Novorossiysk, February-
March 1920

Black
Sea

Novorossiysk evacuated 26 March 1920.
Battleship HMS *Empress of India* fires on
Red Army as they enter the city. British
Military Mission evacuates to Crimea

0   50   100   150   200 miles

Map 7. South Russia and Crimea operations 1919–20

After an extended stay of several weeks beyond his planned return date, Poole finally submitted a 50 page report on 14 February 1919 with recommendations that, 'material assistance in guns, tanks, and cars and aeroplanes alone is not sufficient.'[2] Poole advocated the landing of an expeditionary force in South Russia along the lines of that already operating in North Russia.

Poole's mission achieved little but did bring about agreement between Ataman Krasnov and General Denikin that Krasnov's Don Cossacks would serve under Denikin's command in the Volunteer Army. By the time Poole's long overdue report was published, a permanent British Military Mission had already been announced on 31 January, its first commander, General Sir Charles Briggs arriving at Ekaterinodar (now known as 'Krasnodar') the same day Poole's report was published.

The first shipment of war supplies was unloaded at Novorossiysk docks from SS *Twickenham* on 10 March 1919, but on inspection many of the guns – leftovers from the campaign against the Bulgarians at Salonika – were found to be nearing the end of their useful life if not in some cases completely unserviceable or missing critical spare parts. By the time Briggs was recalled to London on 14 June, the quality of war stores had not improved despite the establishment of a committee in London on Briggs' recommendation to ensure only serviceable equipment was shipped.

There were further problems associated with the unloading and warehousing of the stores. Captain Malcolm Goldsmith, DSO, RN (who would receive a DSO Bar for command of destroyer leader HMS *Montrose* in the Black Sea) wrote that supplies were 'pouring' into Novorossiysk but the Russians were so 'apathetic and lazy' that the ships were unloaded by Turkish prisoners who 'dumped

2   *Ibid.*, p.101.

155. White Russian General Sidorin, Commander of the White Russian
Don Army, addressing troops at Balashov, July 1919. The officer in the topee
is Major Noel Williamson, DSO, MC, RA. (IWM Q75924)

unceremoniously' the supplies onto the docks were they lay unguarded, becoming the 'target of every pilferer in town.'[3] Novorossiysk became awash with black market goods from soap to uniforms to tinned rations, all openly available for sale in the city's markets.

Having been delivered thousands of tonnes of military stores, the White Russian leadership seemed largely incapable of transporting the supplies to the front where they were badly needed. Officers in Novorossiysk strolled through town in their best new British-supplied uniforms whilst troops at the front went without shoes. To protect against pilfering each trainload of supplies had to be guarded by a detachment from the British Military Mission to ensure it reached its destination.

The British government had a huge surplus of supplies left over in the Middle East from the war, tonnes upon tonnes of which were sent to equip Denikin's Army, enough arms and equipment were sent for 250,000 men. Among the arms were 1,200 howitzers and field guns and tens of thousands of rounds of ammunition and even poison gas shells. Millions of tonnes of supplies of every imaginable type, uniforms, food, stores, equipment and even divisional stationary were eventually sent.

The British Military Mission South Russia consisted at its peak in March 1920 of 356 officers and 1,102 other ranks of all three services commanded from November 1918–February 1919 by General Poole, from February–June 1919 by General Briggs and from June 1919–March 1920 by Major General Herbert Holman, with its headquarters located at Taganrog on the north-eastern edge of the Sea of Azov. To encourage officers and men to volunteer for the Mission, enticements of greatly increased pay were offered. One of the pilot instructors who served with the RAF Mission recalled that as a young lieutenant (Army ranks were still in use until the introduction of RAF ranks in October 1919) he was paid the same rate as a lieutenant colonel. The generous rates of pay also attracted officers who had little interest in Russia other than the opportunity to avoid the widespread 'chopping' of junior officers as part of the dramatic reduction in strength of the post-war army. One

---

3   *Ibid.*, p.109.

156. White Russian gunners of III Don Corps training in the use of a British
18 pdr gun, near Novocherkassk, June 1919. (IWM Q75898)

officer described the prevailing air amongst the officers of the Mission as 'a pronounced indifference
… nobody knew anything, nobody seemed to want to find out anything, and nobody cared.'[4]

Recruiting for volunteer officers for the British Military Mission began immediately, but despite
the drastic reduction of the wartime establishment those coming forward were few and far between
and were in many cases (particularly those selected only because they could speak Russian) entirely
unsuitable for the challenging independent work required of a Mission officer. A number had also
spent years in prisoner of war camps, some since the first months of the war and lacked the experience,
confidence and resilience required to work alone many miles from headquarters. Some too were
apparently interested only in profiteering from the illegal sale of British stores or the pilfering of funds.

Major Herbert Sayer, a Tank Corps veteran of the Western Front, arrived in South Russia in
mid 1919 when the Mission was still critically short of personnel and recorded in his diary:

> I hear that he [Holman] is hopelessly understaffed and was badly staffed at the commencement, when
> the B.M.M. was being mis-run by a lot of square pegs in round holes. He has sent home some people
> and considers his staff now to be fair but manageable. I can believe the latter, since I actually found him
> typing his own papers![5]

There were undoubtedly many talented and capable officers who served with the Mission but
there were also many, particularly in its early incarnation, for whom the type of service required was
beyond their capability.

One officer who volunteered for service with the Mission was Captain Hugh Boustead, attached
from the South African Infantry Brigade which had served on the Western Front. Bored with the
post-war army, he had jumped at the chance to volunteer for further active service with the Mission:

---

4   H.N.H. Williamson, *Farewell to the Don; the Russian Revolution in the journals of Brigadier H.N.H. Williamson.* (London:
     Collins, 1970), p.24.
5   Major Herbert Sayer, *A Somewhat Unusual Journey: Victoria Stations to Taganrog. A War Office Mission to Russia, 1919* (Chertsey:
     Sayer Press, 2014), p.22.

157. General Herbert Holman, Chief of the British Military Mission (wearing topee) and Major Wynter (left) with White Russian officers at Poltava, August 1919. (IWM Q75865)

Out of the blue an officer called Pougnet, a regular staff officer in the South African Defence Force who was serving with the Brigade, told me that the Brigade had requests for officers to go out to a mission in Russia to assist the White Armies in their campaign against the Bolsheviks. He had the forms with him and said that it appeared that the applicants might go to either North or South Russia according to their need. I told Pougnet that he could send in my application straight away.[6]

The British had much less complicated issues to deal with in the Kuban region than the French in the Crimea. The area over which the British had responsibility had not been occupied by the Central Powers and was well under control of Denikin, with few disturbances. Unlike the French, there was never the need for a force of occupying British troops to be sent to fill the void of a withdrawing enemy power, this being one of the main reasons no British infantry battalions were despatched to South Russia or the Crimea.

Tanks Corps officer Major Herbert Sayer wrote of the challenges in training uneducated and 'simple hearted' Russian working class soldiers:

There exists no middle class Russian, owing to the policy of former governments which set out with the definite object of destroying all forms of education and advancement to the poorer masses under the mistaken impression that riches would then flow into the pockets of the better classes. It was thought too, that, if the workers were kept in outer darkness, they would have neither the courage nor the intelligence to revolt – in their words a dog has no hair therefore it will not bite.[7]

6   Colonel Sir Hugh Boustead, *The Wind of Morning: An Autobiography* (London: Chatto & Windus, 1974), p.47.
7   Sayer, *A Somewhat Unusual Journey*, p.21.

158. White Russian tank crewman servicing a British donated Mark V tank. The writing on the tank reads 'GENERAL DROZDOVSKY' after a White Russian general. (Public domain)

In addition to aircraft a number of tanks were despatched to Russia, the first six Mark V and six medium Mark A 'Whippet' tanks arriving with a contingent of 10 officers and 55 other ranks under the command of Major McMickering at Ekaterinodar in mid April 1919. The tank had shown its effectiveness on the battlefields of the Western Front and there were high hopes that its capability would be further increased operating on the open Russian steppe rather than in the mud and trenches of France and Flanders.

The training of White Russian troops under Colonel Khaletski (who had served with Russian Armoured Cars on the Eastern Front) to crew the tanks was rushed through, the Russian-crewed tanks seeing their first action without their British instructors present (the British Military Mission was officially non-combatant) on 8 May near Poltava. The Russians were unable to use the tanks effectively due to lack of training and experience but in the end this counted for little as the arrival of the tanks on the battlefield put the Red troops into an instant panic. The enemy fled their trenches after barely firing a shot.

In late May the tanks were moved from Ekaterinodar to their new home at the 'Baltic Works' at Taganrog, where a 'Tank Corps Training Depot' was established under the command of Major Ewen Cameron Bruce, MC. Located on the Sea of Azov, Taganrog was a pleasant setting for the Tank Corps men, most of whom had been fighting on the battlefields of France only months prior. The men made good use of available leisure activities such as sailing, going to the cinema or attending performances of General Denikin's personal string orchestra.

As members of the British Military Mission, the Tank Corps men were not permitted to participate in offensive operations against the enemy, only to train and equip Russian crews to take the tanks into action themselves. However at least two British tank crews took part in the offensive to capture Tsaritsyn (12 June–1 July 1919): one Mark V commanded by Bruce and another by Captain Rupert Walsh, who had been awarded the MM as a sergeant with the Gordon Highlanders on the Western Front before commissioning into the Tank Corps with whom he was awarded the DSO, a rare award to a junior officer.

159. British Medium Mark B tank supplied to Denikin's White Russian forces, captured
by Red troops and put back into service with the Soviet Army. (Public domain)

On 29 June, Bruce achieved the rather remarkable, if not unique feat by a Tank Corps officer, of shooting down an observation balloon whilst flying in the observer's cockpit of a DH9 on a reconnaissance mission over the Bolshevik lines. That same day Walsh earned an MC for gallantry in action near Tsaritsyn when a tarpaulin on top of his Mark V caught fire and fell back onto the petrol tank. At great risk and under fire from enemy machine guns only a short distance away, Walsh exited the tank and extinguished the fire. Two of the Russian-crewed tanks had broken down on the way to battle leaving only four Mark V's to make the final assault. Immediately upon the tanks making an appearance, crushing wire entanglements in front of the enemy positions, the Bolsheviks lost their nerve and fled, chased all the way by White Russian General Wrangel's cavalry which pushed forward to consolidate the captured ground.

Bruce successfully led three tanks into action the following day against an enemy counter-attack near Tsaritsyn under heavy fire. For his gallantry and devotion to duty in shooting down the enemy observation balloon and leadership on 30 June, Bruce was awarded the DSO.

The Russians were greatly impressed by the tanks in the battle, although one of the British tank crews took it all in his stride: 'this is a trifle. We are accustomed to work in tanks in France, where the Boche fired at us an enormous mass of shells. Out in the West there was a regular war, here is only a manoeuvre.'[8]

Additional tanks arrived at Novorossiysk in July and at its peak strength the Tank Corps Training School could call on some 57 Mark Vs and 17 Whippets. The Russian crews were never efficient enough to utilise the tanks to their full potential in offensive operations, although they were successfully used during Denikin's great withdrawal of winter 1919 and again during the final operations before the White Russian collapse the following year.

---

8   *Ibid.*, p.60.

On his return to England after service in South Russia, Bruce faced criminal charges for running a lottery fraud scheme. The case was dismissed but Bruce was ordered to pay 24 guineas in costs. This large debt was likely the cause for his volunteering to join the Auxiliary Division of Royal Irish Constabulary, the feared 'Auxies'. The Auxiliary Division, recruited mostly from former officers who had seen service during the war had a reputation for brutality and heavy-handedness and were particularly despised by Irish republicans. Like Bruce, a number of 'Auxies' had been decorated for gallantry during the war, including three recipients of the Victoria Cross. Bruce's sterling military record did not extend to service in Ireland. He was dismissed from the service for striking a civilian without cause and immediately court-martialled for robbing £75 from the Kells Country Creamery for which he was imprisoned for 12 months.

Bruce's decorations, so hard earned on the Western Front and in Russia, were officially withdrawn in 1921, 'in consequence of his having convicted by General Court-Martial'[9] but perhaps the most incredible aspect of his service in South Russia and Ireland was that he had lost an arm on the Western Front.

Some years later whilst writing the history of the Tank Corps, historian B.H. Liddell-Hart speculated that an organised force of British tanks operating in South Russia could have significantly altered the eventual outcome of the campaign:

> The evidence of what could be achieved at that time by a solitary tank handled in the 'Fear Naught' spirit, in a primitive land where such a machine was a terror-spreading novelty, suggests that the course of history might have been changed by quite a small British armoured force, properly organised, even on the basis possible in 1919.[10]

One of the very few published accounts of service with the British Military Mission was written by Major Noel Williamson, RA. Having seen extensive service as an artillery officer on the Western Front, Williamson had been wounded and awarded the MC before volunteering for South Russia. During a trip to the front with Russian gunners he had trained, Williamson had his first encounter with the Red Army.

The war on the southern steppes of Russia was fought largely for control of the vital railway, and in many cases fighting only extended as far as 15 miles either side of the line. Armoured trains were extensively used by both sides as mobile blockhouses and artillery support. Just beyond the village of Korlova the railway line took a wide bend which could allow a single 18 pdr field gun (if it could be brought forward far enough undetected) to have a good chance of knocking out any Soviet armoured train which approached the village. The bridge at Korlova had been destroyed, which meant the White Russians could not bring their own armoured train any further forward until it had been repaired. Williamson's plan relied on his belief that the Bolshevik armoured trains would likely act boldly in the knowledge that the bridge was still down. Some 50 years later he recalled:

> I saw the Bolshevik train appear over the brow of the hill and slowly begin moving down the slope in front of us at a distance of about 5,000 yards. On it came, stopping only once to fire a few rounds into the village, until as far as I could judge, it must have been in the very spot where we had expected it to be. I waited in a tense silence, watching it carefully as it halted again, the snouts of its guns moving slowly in search of a target. Over the still air, I even heard the clang of a gun port as another gun was prepared for action. There was a Russian word, probably the name of the train, they all had sonorous and war-like

9   *The London Gazette*, 29 July 1921.
10   B.H. Liddell-Hart, *The Tanks: The History of the Royal Tank Regiment and its Predecessors, Heavy Branch, Machine-Gun Corps, Tanks Corps, and Royal Tank Corps, 1914–45* (New York: Prager, 1959).

titles painted on the side in Cyrillic letters, and I could almost smell the metal and see the eyes peering nervously through the gun slits.[11]

The seconds passed agonisingly slowly but nothing happened. Williamson rushed to the White Russian gunners' position to find them asleep in the shade next to the British-supplied gun. After rousing the snoozing men with swift kicks and choice expletives, the Russian subaltern (who had also been napping) gave the order to fire. After another long wait for the Russian gunners to roll out, load and aim the 18 pdr, fire was commenced and after a few minutes of firing the enemy train had been fairly bracketed and struck twice. The Red armoured train quickly responded and within moments, shrapnel and high explosive shells were landing uncomfortably close to Williamson's position:

> Despite the firing, I was just beginning to enjoy myself when, for some unknown reason, having obtained two direct hits on the train and stopped it dead, my friend alongside me [the White Russian officer] … changed from high explosive, which would have blown it off the rails, to shrapnel which was quite useless even against the thin armour of the carriages.
>
> 'For God's sake, not shrapnel!' I shouted.
>
> … I wondered what certain well-known instructors at the Gunnery School at Larkhill in England would have said at the sight of a British Gunner standing on the box seat of an ancient two-horse victoria under a broiling sun in the middle of the Russian steppes endeavouring to knock out an armoured train – momentarily stationary and quite helpless – with the assistance of a range table and shrapnel![12]

Although Williamson was a British Army Major it was the Russian officers' gun, all Williamson could do was watch in frustration as ineffective shrapnel shells exploded above the train until a Russian Sergeant rode up to inform the White Russian subaltern that the small stock of ammunition had been expended. Williamson continues:

> I felt like exploding, but the gunners appeared to be again thinking of going to sleep in disgust and a few of them were already making themselves comfortable on the ground. There seemed little I could do with them, so I borrowed a horse and went off at full speed to look for Sachs [White Russian officer] to ask for more ammunition or for another battery to come into action and mop up the train.
>
> 'We must bring the 4.5 howitzer into action and smash it up,' I said.
>
> He laughed gaily. 'Oh, no' he said cheerfully. 'It's not necessary. The train's already finished. Our infantry will capture it now.'
>
> I didn't agree and, sure enough, in a quarter of an hour's time smoke appeared from the distant train and, slowly and silently, it steamed away with not a single short fired after it to hinder it. I was livid.[13]

An opportunity to completely destroy the Red armoured train had clearly been missed, but for a single 18 pdr with inadequately trained crew to successfully range the target with relatively few shots and score two direct hits remained quite an achievement for which Williamson was awarded the DSO.

Despite the best efforts of the Military Mission to train and equip the White Russian forces, they were at all turns thwarted by the gross incompetence and lack of administration and coordination of Denikin's forces. Despite millions of pounds worth of military supplies arriving daily at Novorossiysk, Williamson experienced first hand just how little was being distributed to the front line where it was needed most. During one visit to the front, he joined British Military Mission commander General

---

11   Williamson, *Farewell to the Don*, p.124.
12   *Ibid.*, p.126.
13   *Ibid.*, pp. 127–8.

160. General Anton Denikin inspecting the White Russian tank detachment equipped with a British Mark V tank, summer 1919. (Public domain)

Holman in inspecting a platoon of the 12th Regiment which had just returned from the front. Normally when a General asks to inspect a group of soldiers the regimental commander parades his best men however the twelve who appeared before Holman and Williamson were amongst the most 'miserable' the British officers had ever witnessed:

They had only five boots among the lot, one man had no rifle, and that of another was clogged up with dirt. Their clothes were hanging in rags, one man had no trousers and wore woollen underpants, and they looked half-starved.[14]

The gross negligence, incompetence and corruption of Denikin's forces meant that despite the tonnes of stores being unloaded at Novorossiysk every day, few supplies were actually distributed to pitifully equipped front line units whilst officers in rear areas made a fortune selling on the black market stores meant for troops at the front. Williamson described his frustration:

The sheer inability of the White Russians to organise themselves, and of the generals to act in concert with each other to coordinate their attacks, by the inevitable corruption, laziness and indifference of many officers and officials and by the curious Russian inability to react swiftly to events or to take even the simplest precautions against disaster.[15]

Serving as a Lewis gun instructor with the Don Plastuni Division, South African Captain Hugh Boustead experienced his own frustrations with the White Russian leadership. Writing of his first encounter with a Russian General:

When I had reported to him, he sent for coffee and launched into a lengthy conversation in French. After several unsuccessful attempts to get away, I finally excused myself and said I would report to the senior instructor. 'Work is not a bear,' he replied, and when I looked puzzled, explained, 'it won't run away into the woods. It will still be here tomorrow.'[16]

Boustead also recounted the difficulty in training White Russian recruits in the use of the Lewis gun:

Training the soldiers was delightful since they were so gentle and straightforward, and at the same time maddening because they were forgetful and lazy. Their interest was intense for a short time, and then

---

14   *Ibid.*, p.141.
15   *Ibid.*, p.194.
16   Boustead, *Wind of Morning*, p.51.

quite suddenly they would say to themselves, 'I know it all now,' and nothing but firm driving or bitter experience at the front would make them learn more.[17]

Boustead was awarded an MC Bar for gallantry in action with the Plastunis on 25 August 1919 when the Lewis gunners under his command repulsed a Red cavalry attack on the Division's flank. Boustead went on to win further distinction in what could only be described as a remarkable life. Born in Ceylon to English parents, by the time war broke out the young Boustead was serving as a midshipman on HMS *Hyacinth* on the Cape Station when faced with the likelihood of an uneventful war patrolling the high seas, in 1915 he jumped ship and enlisted with the South African Scottish. Wounded in the South African Brigade's epic defence of Delville Wood on the Somme in 1916, he was commissioned and later awarded the MC at Arras where he was wounded on a second occasion. Posted for service in India with the Gurkhas, he returned to the Western Front in October 1918 during the final weeks of war. Volunteering for service with the British Military Mission, Boustead was notified of the King's pardon for his desertion from the Royal Navy whilst serving in South Russia, reputedly being the first man in history to be so pardoned.

Immediately after his return to the UK from South Russia in 1920, Boustead enrolled at Oxford University where he read Russian, before interrupting his studies to captain the British Modern Pentathlon team at the Antwerp Olympics of the same year. Commissioned into the Gordon Highlanders, Boustead transferred in 1924 to the Sudan Camel Corps with whom he would serve for 25 years, becoming its commander in 1931.

A member of the 1933 Everest Expedition, for which he was awarded the OBE, Boustead became District Commissioner in Darfur and was present at the time of the Italian invasion of Ethiopia in 1935. In 1940 he was tasked with raising a battalion of Abyssinian levies which saw extensive service fighting against Italian forces in the Horn of Africa, for which he was awarded the DSO in 1941. Appointed in various post-war political and development roles on the Arabian Peninsula he was present when oil was discovered in Abu Dhabi. A recipient of the Lawrence of Arabia Memorial Medal in 1966, Colonel Sir Hugh Boustead, KBE, CMG, DSO, MC and Bar, died in April 1980.

By mid 1919, Denikin had at his disposal the equipment and supplies necessary for an attack towards Moscow, but neither the manpower nor leadership within his army to carry out the offensive. Denikin did not have enough men to garrison captured territory but gambled that he would be able to consolidate his gains when he reached Moscow. Both White Russian General Baron Wrangel and General Holman of the British Military Mission advised Denikin to wait until he could be sure of securing captured territory but regardless Denikin gambled everything on the success of the offensive.

The Royal Navy

On the eve of the French evacuation of Odessa in April 1919, the remnants of the Russian Royal Family were whisked away from Yalta on board battleship HMS *Marlborough* (Captain C.D. Johnson, RN). Johnson was serving with the post-war Royal Navy Mediterranean Fleet when *Marlborough* was called to the Black Sea Crimean port city on 7 April 1919. Among those taken on board were Dowager Empress Marie Feodorovna, sister of Queen Alexandra, Grand Duchess Xenia Alexandrovna, sister of Tsar Nicholas II, and Grand Dukes Nicholas and Peter, the Tsar's cousins. A total of 20 members of the Royal Family including a number of princes, princesses, countesses and barons were rescued, representing four generations of the Romanov dynasty. Additionally a further 63 servants and 200 tonnes of luggage were taken on board and evacuated to Constantinople. HMS *Marlborough* departed Yalta on 11 April 1919 with the Royals on board, thus ending the dynasty which had ruled Russia

---

161. Crew of HMAS *Swan* with Don Cossack representatives, December 1918. (AWM H15280)

since 1613. On return to the Crimea from Constantinople, HMS *Marlborough* saw further service bombarding the Red Army ashore for which (in addition to the evacuation of the Royal Family) a number of Imperial Russian decorations were awarded to the crew.

In order to adequately support Denikin's forces the British government first needed to ascertain the extent to which his army required equipment and training, and the status of his forces. For this purpose a small Allied naval squadron comprising light cruiser HMS *Liverpool*, a French cruiser and Royal Australian Navy destroyer HMAS *Swan* passed through the Dardanelles into the Black Sea and steamed on to the port city of Novorossiysk. On board HMS *Liverpool* was a small military mission from the French and British governments tasked with inspecting Denikin's forces and reporting back to their respective governments.

Arriving on 23 November, the following day the commander of the British Mission, Lieutenant Colonel A.P. Blackwood, DSO, Border Regiment, was immediately ashore busily meeting with representatives of the various White Russian factions. A lavish civic reception was held for the ships' crews after which Blackwood met with Denikin privately. Three days later a number of Royal Marines were landed from the Black Sea Fleet at Novorossiysk, the landings of the Military Mission and Marines marking the beginning of British military intervention in South Russia in support of White Russian forces.

Soon after disembarking, Blackwood set out on a two week tour of Denikin's 'Volunteer Army', taking with him a handful of officers from the Mission as escort. The party met with a number of Kuban Cossack Atamans who all took pains to vastly inflate their own strength in the hope of receiving as much military aid from the British as possible. Blackwood made a number of recommendations aimed at bringing White Russian forces together under a single unified command, particularly in the case of the Cossacks and Muslim tribesmen from the Caucasus; however although ostensibly under the command of General Denikin, the White Russian forces in South Russia remained under fractured tribal leadership.

At the same time Blackwood was making his tour, a naval mission under Commander Arthur Bond, RAN (HMAS *Swan*) set out to investigate the harbours in the port cities of Mariupol and Taganrog on the Sea of Azov to assess their suitability to accept the large amount of war stores intended to be sent by the British government. The party also travelled further inland to investigate territory controlled by the Don Cossacks, where Blackwood's Mission was yet to visit. They were feted at every turn by independence-minded Cossack Atamans, keen that they should not be overlooked when the British were distributing military aid. On conclusion of the tour Bond and all those who accompanied him were awarded on the spot a number of Imperial Russian decorations in acknowledgement of their visit.

On 14 October 1919, an ammunition dump at Novorossiysk harbour caught fire and exploded, setting fire to SS *War Pike* docked nearby. *War Pike* was carrying a cargo of ammunition which was being unloaded at the time of the explosion and which also caught fire. Serving at Novorossiysk with the British Military Mission, Lieutenant Colonel Arthur Cotton, RA, cleared bystanders from the dock and assisted to cast off the hawsers for *War Pike* to be towed out of the harbour by cruiser HMS *Grafton*.

Most of the crew of HMS *War Pike* had fled the ship, leaving Master Thomas Knill, in spite of the flames and explosions, to cast off hawsers from the quay and make fast other cables to *Grafton*. As *War Pike* was being towed out of the harbour, Colonel Cotton followed closely behind in a commandeered tug with a volunteer crew of sailors and marines. Immediately on reaching a safe distance from the harbour and despite the flames, Cotton led a volunteer firefighting party aboard *War Pike* and with the assistance of Knill, managed to get the fire under control before *War Pike* was towed towards shallow water where she ran aground.

A number of bravery decorations were awarded for the incident. Both Cotton and Knill received the Albert Medal whilst Lieutenant Robert Watson, RNR, was awarded the OBE. Seven MSMs were also awarded to members of the volunteer firefighting party which boarded *War Pike* and got the fire under control.

In late January 1920 the Military Mission received word of the fate of one of their missing officers, Captain William Frecheville, RE. The unfortunate officer had been cut off in a village near Rostov during the retreat and subsequently captured by the Bolsheviks on 9 January. It is known that Frecheville was killed whilst a prisoner although the circumstances of his death are unclear. A Bolshevik soldier was subsequently captured wearing Frecheville's tunic during a raid by Cossacks across the frozen Don River, the Red prisoner reportedly being beaten to death by the White cavalrymen with 'steel ramrods'. Frecheville is the only British Military Mission officer known to have died at the hands of the Bolsheviks in South Russia 1919–20.

The RAF

A number of modern aircraft were despatched to South Russia as military aid to General Denikin, primarily DH9 and DH9A models but also a large number of brand new RE8s still in their packing crates. It was estimated that the total value of supplies given to Denikin eventually amounted to £35.9 million, an extraordinary amount of money for the time. Most of the supplies sent were war surplus that could not be sold elsewhere but it was still a hugely expensive task to equip Denikin for war.

Amongst other types of aircraft, 130 RE8 two-seaters were supplied to the White Russian forces in South Russia by the British government. The task of training Russian aircrew in their use fell to the RAF Training Mission under Lieutenant Colonel Arthur Maund, which operated independently of the British Military Mission. Training was rudimentary and rushed, there being little time to adequately train pilots before they were expected to fly solo: a pitiful four hours dual flying time was the average. In fact the Russians crashed so many RE8s that they began to spread a rumour that the aircraft had been condemned for service with the RAF. To prove to their Russian students that the RE8s were entirely airworthy, the British instructors took to the air and flew low over Rostov in formation at full throttle. Not everyone was impressed by the display, however, and complaints were later filed that the aircraft flew too low for safety.

The laziness and gross incompetence of the White Russian pilots and ground crews was a continual vexation to members of the RAF Mission sent to train them. The experiences of Flying Officer W.R. Harrison and Flight Sergeant Frederick Nunn, sent to a Russian squadron equipped with DH9 aircraft, are characteristic of the trials and tribulations of an RAF instructor:

> On Saturday morning Machine No. 8088 was crashed at LEZEVAIA by apparently being flown into the ground with the engine half on. The pilot complained that the reason for this was that his throttle would not work but continued to run at 1000 revs whether the throttle was open or closed. On enquiry I found that the pilot never thought of switching off or turning off petrol to avoid crashing his machine … During the first bombing raids on the Thursday the pilots on return claimed that their bombs failed to burst and promptly blamed the British bombs. I enquired if they had been properly fused and they replied, 'Yes.' However on the next bombing raid I gave them further instructions as to how the bombs were to be fused and all the bombs thereupon burst … On Thursday afternoon on return of the pilot flying the machine 2841, he complained that his machine was running harshly. On examining the machine on Friday morning I found that the water tank had become adrift and with very little more flying it would have fallen into the pilots face. All the magneto terminals were loose and nearly off on the port magneto and the forward air intake was almost falling off. On enquiry I found that as long as the machine ran it is not the custom in this squadron to inspect the machine, either by pilots or mechanics … possessing few spare parts, the whole desire of the Captain of the Squadron whenever the least trouble or need presented itself, to have the part replaced, rather than carry on and adjust same.

Harrison's final assessment was the most damning:

> I wish to bring to your notice that giving a high class of machine as the DH9, with such tremendous powers of offence and destruction, to a squadron as incapable as No. 1 Squadron is almost a crime … I strongly request not to be sent again to instruct or assist this squadron.[18]

Despite their significant difficulties, Harrison was Mentioned in Despatches and Nunn awarded the MSM for their services with the RAF Training Mission.

No. 47 Squadron, RAF, had ended the war flying against the Bulgarians in Macedonia and was still cooling its heels and avoiding the malarial mosquitoes in the Balkans well into 1919. The Bulgarians had capitulated on 30 September 1918 (some six weeks before hostilities ended on the Western Front) and the squadron immediately set about overhauling its aircraft in readiness for despatch to other theatres of war, most likely against the Ottomans, however Constantinople surrendered a month later before the squadron saw any further action. In April 1919 an advance party of 21 officers and senior NCOs (including some aircrew who had flown with No. 17 Squadron in Macedonia) under Captain H.G. Davis sailed from Salonika for Novorossiysk. Some of the squadron members were not pleased that having just survived one war they were being ordered to embark for another without having any home leave, but generally the men were in good spirits.

Prior to the arrival in South Russia of Commanding Officer, Canadian ace Raymond Collishaw, DSO Bar, DSC, DFC, 47 Squadron was temporarily commanded by Captain Sydney Frogley (formerly 17 Squadron) who would go on to distinguish himself in South Russia as commander of 'C' (DH9) Flight. Although the Royal Air Force had been established as an amalgamation of the

---

18   The National Archives: AIR/1/1960/204/260/37: Reports on Russian Units, RAF South Russia.

162. 'C' Flight, No. 47 Squadron, RAF at Beketovka, summer 1919. Identified are front row from left: Lieutenant Mercer; Lieutenant Simmons; unknown former RNAS pilot; unknown. Middle row from left: two unknown White Russian officers; Captain Frogley ('C' Flight commander); Major Collishaw (Commanding 47 Squadron); Captain Anderson; unknown; Lieutenant Elliot. Back row from left: unknown; Lieutenant Hatchett; unknown; Lieutenant Mitchell. (Public domain)

Royal Flying Corps (RFC) and Royal Naval Air Service (RNAS) on 1 April 1918, the new RAF ranks had not yet been brought into effect and officers were still addressed by their equivalent RFC or sometimes RNAS ranks.

Collishaw was the British Commonwealth's third highest-scoring ace of the war with 60 confirmed kills over the Western Front, where he had commanded No. 3 Squadron, RNAS and latterly No. 203 Squadron, RAF. Collishaw recruited many of his best pilots to join him in Russia, among them Captain Samuel Kinkead, DSC Bar, DFC Bar, a South African RNAS ace with 33 victories who would command 'B' (Sopwith Camel) Flight. Command of 'A' (DH9) Flight was given to another South African RNAS ace, Captain Leonard Slatter, DSC Bar, DFC, who had scored seven kills over the Western Front. A third 'C' (DH9) Flight would be commanded by Captain H.G. Davis and would arrive in South Russia before the other two flights.

One officer who volunteered for service in South Russia was Lieutenant Marion Aten, an American serving as a Sopwith Camel pilot in the RAF. His father was a retired Texas Ranger of some reputation who owned a large ranch in California where Aten had worked before joining the RFC in Canada. Aten co-authored a book under the pretence of a factual memoir recounting his service in South Russia dramatically titled, *Last Train Over Rostov Bridge*, which combines large passages of fiction mixed in with fact to the point that the fiction and fact are blurred and hard to distinguish. In the book Aten claims to have shot down several Bolshevik aircraft during his service in South Russia including a black Fokker Triplane flown by a Red Air Force ace. There is no evidence to support these claims. By comparing Aten's narrative with other accounts and official documents it is possible to sift much of the fiction from the fact but because of the unreliability of *Last Train* as a factual memoir of 47 Squadron's service in South Russia, much of its content must be taken with a large pinch of salt.

Upon arrival in Russia, to enable the squadron to travel the vast distances over the Russian steppe, four specially equipped trains were provided, one for each flight and Headquarters. The trains also provided capability for each individual flight to operate independently as self-contained units with their own workshop and supplies. During its entire period of service in South Russia, The three flights of No. 47 Squadron were rarely in the same place at the same time.

'C' Flight was first into action ahead of the arrival of the remainder of the squadron, leaving for the Volga Front on 10 June 1919. 'C' Flight's five DH9s took off at 0745 for an improvised aerodrome at Velikoknyajeskaya on the Tsaritsyn railway, a distance of some 180 miles. Only four of the aircraft arrived, the fifth flown by Lieutenant E.C. White with Observer Lieutenant J.N. Webb was forced down with engine trouble at Dinskaya in a cornfield. Both crew were unhurt.

On hearing of the downed aircraft, equipment officer Lieutenant Dumas promptly left Ekaterinodar with a small party to repair or if necessary salvage the machine. At Dinskaya, Dumas commandeered an express train and held up the entire train service in that region of South Russia for the few hours it took to load the aircraft onto a flatbed carriage. The men were treated exceedingly well by the locals, Dumas wrote in a letter home:

> They gave us an excellent meal, heaps of eggs, butter, and milk but no tea or sugar. According to what I can hear, it is the same all over the country, masses to eat in the country places, but they refuse to sell it in the towns because they do not trust the paper money used everywhere … Next morning for breakfast again an enormous dish of fried eggs – about eighteen for the three of us, beautiful white bread and butter, and fresh milk.[19]

After encountering all kinds of difficulties with unreliable train services, destroyed bridges and even the weather, 'C' Flight with Lieutenants White and Webb arrived at Gnileaksayskaya, sixty miles from Tsaritsyn on the Volga on 20 June. Lieutenant Gordon Clavey crashed his machine on landing but was unhurt.

The Bolsheviks had indicated their intent to defend Tsaritsyn against the Whites at all costs, declaring the city would be the 'Red Verdun'. Despite the atrocious weather and almost constant rain, the clouds cleared enough on 22 June for a four aircraft raid against Tsaritsyn. After flying twenty-five miles the weather closed in and visibility was reduced to almost zero right up to 10,000 feet. The flight was forced to return to Gnileaksayskaya where Lieutenant Reynolds crashed on landing due to a strong gust of wind. 'C' Flight had not had a distinguished introduction to operations in South Russia, crashing three aircraft before a shot had been fired.

The following day the three remaining undamaged machines carried out the first successful raid on Tsaritsyn at 1030. The raid was led by Captain Davis (OC 'C' Flight) with pilots Lieutenants White and Verity and observers Lieutenants Douglas Blaxland Thompson (not to be confused with William Burns Thomson of Kinkead's 'B' Flight), McEwan and 2nd Lieutenant Mann. The target was the railway station on the south-eastern side of the city which was successfully bombed from a height of 5,000 feet with 20 lb and 112 lb bombs. Damage was done to the station buildings and rolling stock before the flight continued on to the Volga River where an additional 1,000 rounds of machine gun ammunition was fired at Bolshevik barges and Red cavalry near Elshanka. The following day Captain Davis led 'C' Flight in a second attack on Tsaritsyn with good results bombing barges, houses and the south-east station and firing 450 rounds into the barges, wharves and streets.

19   H.A. Jones, *Over The Balkans and South Russia 1917–1919: being the history of No. 47 Squadron Royal Air Force* (Elstree: Greenhill Books, 1987), p.141.

On one mission a 112 lb bomb landed squarely on the building where a meeting of commissars was underway, reportedly killing all but two of the forty attendees.

The pattern of raids by 'C' Flight continued until the end of the month with missions flown nearly daily. By 29 June the Red Army was observed retreating north of Tsaritsyn and by the end of the month the city had been captured by Denikin's Volunteer Army thanks in no small part to the efforts of Davis and 'C' Flight. White Russian General Pyotr Nikolayevich Wrangel's Caucasian Cavalry pushed forward and 'C' Flight went with them on 6 July to a new airfield at Beketovka. During a daring low-level reconnaissance from Beketovka on 17 July, Lieutenant Edward Cronin, a Canadian from New Brunswick, earned the squadron's first DFC in South Russia.

Captain Davis was one of the original observers from 47 Squadron's early days in Salonika where he had done excellent work over the Vardar front and was often chosen for the most difficult jobs. Davis went to a training establishment in Egypt and qualified as a pilot before rejoining the squadron in 1918. After his service in South Russia he left the RAF and went to Africa, where sadly he died of tropical fever shortly after his arrival. He was awarded the DFC in the New Year's Honours 1919 for his services over Salonika and later awarded the Imperial Russian Cross of St. George for his bravery in South Russia.

In late June 1919, Collishaw arrived at Novorossiysk with a party of 10 officers and 255 NCOs and airmen to bring the squadron up to strength and set about preparing 'A' and 'B' Flights for operations. The party was comprised entirely of volunteers who had served with No. 17 and 47 Squadrons on the Salonika front.

In the meantime at Novorossiysk, Headquarters was making efforts to secure a train to take Samuel Kinkead's 'B' Flight up the line, a task that was proving difficult as equipment and spare parts were slow to arrive via Constantinople, and Collishaw could not secure the services of a train appropriate for purpose. The party finally arrived at Ekaterinodar on 11 July to discover the local aerodrome, a large muddy field next to a racecourse, was barely suitable for flying. The airfield was shared with a White Russian squadron being equipped and trained by the RAF Training Mission commanded by Squadron Leader Arthur Maund.

On 15 July, Captain Frogley led 'C' Flight on a successful raid against the Bolshevik flotilla operating on the Volga in support of a Russian attack on the town on Kamyshin. After the Russians had captured the town, Frogley led 'C' Flight on a low-level strafing run against the retreating enemy who were mercilessly machine-gunned as they fled, for which Frogley was awarded the DFC.

'C' Flight spent most of July and August bombing and strafing enemy river barges, troop concentrations and railway stock near Kamyshin and Tcherni-Yar, as well as carrying out reconnaissance for Wrangel's forces. On 25 July, two 'C' Flight DH9s were returning from an early morning raid on enemy barges and a railway station when they were attacked by a Bolshevik Nieuport scout. The forward-firing Vickers of the DH9 flown by Lieutenant John Hatchett was inoperable but he was able to manoeuvre his aircraft into a position where his observer, Lieutenant Horace Simmons, engaged the Nieuport with a 50 round burst. The enemy aircraft turned away sharply, went into a dive and was seen to crash, the squadron's first 'kill' in South Russia.

On 30 July, two DH9s took off on a bombing and photographic reconnaissance mission against Red cavalry formations near Tcherni-Yar on the Volga north of Tsaritsyn. The lead aircraft was flown by Captain Walter Anderson with Lieutenant John Mitchell as observer. The aircraft descended to 1,000 feet to photograph enemy positions when the aircraft following as escort (piloted by Lieutenant William Elliot with Observer Lieutenant H. Laidlaw) was badly damaged by ground fire and forced to land five miles behind the enemy line. Collishaw continues the story:

> Anderson was just setting course for Beketovka when he saw Elliot's DH9 going down, apparently in trouble. The engine of the escort machine had been hit and put out of action and Elliot had no choice but to bring it down for a landing. Several squadrons of Red cavalry were in the area and as they saw the DH9

163. Left–right: Captain Walter Anderson and Lieutenant John Mitchell, both recommended for the Victoria Cross for actions near Tcherni-Yar on 30 July 1919; Lieutenant William Elliot, awarded a DFC Bar for the same action. (All public domain)

come down they wheeled about and galloped towards it. As they approached, however, they were brought up sharply by accurate bursts of fire from Laidlaw's Lewis gun. Although he had troubles enough of his own, Anderson did not hesitate for a moment after seeing what had happened. Pushing his stick down he took his machine in for a landing and taxied up close to Elliot's aircraft. It was a rough landing for the ground was bumpy but fortunately nothing gave way. The two observers kept the Bolshevik cavalry at bay while Elliot set fire to his disabled DH9. He and his observer then dashed across to Anderson's aircraft, scrambled aboard and both jammed themselves into the rear cockpit, Mitchell having resumed his place on the lower wing. Anderson, who had kept his prop ticking over, gunned his engine and the DH9 gathered speed, bumped across the ground and finally became airborne just as the irate Red cavalry closed in. The flight back to base took 50 minutes and for the whole of this time Mitchell stayed perched precariously on the wing, keeping the bullet holes plugged. The weather was hot and because they were operating at such low altitudes the flyers were dressed in shorts. The hot exhaust gases played on Mitchell and by the time the DH9 landed at base he was painfully burned, in addition to being exhausted by clinging to his exposed position. The incident brought both Anderson and Mitchell the DSO and they later each received also the DFC, in further recognition of their services in South Russia. Their DSOs must surely rank amongst the best-earned ever awarded and had the incident occurred on the Western Front instead of in such an obscure backwater as South Russia I am sure it would have resulted in a pair of VCs.[20]

As well as recommendations for the Victoria Cross to Anderson and Mitchell, Elliot received a DFC Bar for the incident, his first DFC having been awarded for service during Allenby's final advance in Palestine the previous year. Collishaw's comment that the Victoria Cross was warranted for Anderson and Mitchell is interesting as the action is almost identical to the one in which Lieutenant Frank MacNamara of the Australian Flying Corps received a Victoria Cross for his bravery in Palestine on 20 March 1917. Although wounded, MacNamara landed behind Ottoman lines near a force of Turkish cavalry and rescued another member of his squadron who had been forced down before taking off with Turkish cavalry snapping at his heels. Laidlaw unfortunately was not awarded any British decoration for his part in the rescue, although he later received the Imperial Russian Order of St. Vladimir and Cross of St. George.

---

20   Raymond Collishaw, *Air Command: A Fighter Pilot's Story* (London: Kimber, 1973), pp.186–7.

164. White Russian General Wrangel, commander White Russian forces South Russia from March 1920. (Public domain)

The 5 August 1919 was one of 'C' Flight's hardest days in South Russia. The Flight took off in the early morning light to bomb and strafe Red troop concentrations around Tcherni-Yar, returned to Beketovka, refuelled, rearmed and repeated the process a number of times. In total 'C' Flight flew for nearly 16 hours on 5 August alone. The three DH9s involved dropped 67 bombs of varying sizes and fired 2,300 rounds of ammunition causing significant casualties to the enemy.

Tragedy struck on the night of 15 August when Captain Robert Eversden was accidentally shot dead by a sentry. The RAF guards had been fired on several times during the night and on challenging Eversden, who reportedly failed to reply, the sentry shot and killed him instantly. Eversden had previously served with the Suffolk Yeomanry at Gallipoli, Palestine and East Africa. His remains were not recovered after the British withdrew from South Russia and he is commemorated, like many others whose graves are unknown in southern Russia, on the Haidar Pasha Memorial (CWGC) in Istanbul.

On 20 August, Lieutenant Edward Cronin (who had earned the squadron's first DFC the previous month) and Observer Lieutenant Howard Mercer were attacked by a Red Nieuport northeast of Tcherni-Yar. Mercer, a veteran of air combats over the Western Front, managed to get off several good bursts, hitting his target: the Nieuport was seen to go down in a marshy area and credited as a 'kill'.

Five days later a DH9 flown by Lieutenant John Hatchett with Observer Lieutenant Horace Simmons (who had scored the squadron's first aerial victory in South Russia on 25 July) were attacked by a Nieuport with distinctive colour markings of a red nose, red disc on the rudder and black crosses on the fuselage. Hits were observed from Simmons' Lewis Gun which then jammed and the engagement broken off without result.

On 27 August, Frogley led 'C' Flight in an attack against Bolshevik shipping on the Volga near Tcherni-Yar. Despite heavy enemy anti-aircraft fire the British airmen caused significant damage with bombs and machine guns. DFCs were awarded for the raid to Flying Officers Norman Greenslade and Horace Simmons (both of whom had previously been awarded the MC) and John Hatchett.

The squadron suffered its first combat fatality on 28 August when a DH9 flown by Captain Anderson was struck by enemy ground fire after making a low-level attack on a Bolshevik observation balloon near Bilklei. The balloon was destroyed but Anderson's observer, fellow Canadian Captain John McLennan was hit during the intense barrage of ground fire and was found to be dead by the time the aircraft reached Beketovka. McLennan's body was transported to Krasnodar where he was buried with full military honours. White Russian General Baron Wrangel decorated both men with the Cross of St. George for the incident, McLennan posthumously.

Whilst 'C' Flight had been in action on the Volga, Collishaw had been busy supervising the unloading of new aircraft, spares and stores at Novorossiysk and arranging their transport by rail to Ekaterinodar. The work gave Collishaw ample opportunity to familiarise himself with Denikin's White Russian forces. He found Denikin's air mechanics to be capable of great ingenuity and innovation but he was less enamoured with the Russian officers, whom he described as a 'mixed bunch'. Some were charming, energetic and dedicated but many others only charming, suitable for 'gracing the sidewalk cafes of Ekaterinodar with their immaculately turned out persons.'[21]

During August and September the squadron received further shipments of aircraft to bring the three Flights up to operational strength. On 3 August seaplane carrier HMS *Ark Royal* arrived at Novorossiysk with a shipment of DH9s which had seen service with No. 221 Squadron on the Caspian. A number of former No. 221 Squadron aircrew were also taken on strength at the time. The following month several Sopwith Camels arrived from the RNAS station on Mudros Island, destined for 'B' Flight.

In the closing days of August the Bolsheviks launched an offensive to recapture Tsaritsyn and by 2 September had advanced far enough that 'C' Flight had to abandon Beketovka for the safety of Gnileaksayskaya further south. The interruption was only temporary as three weeks later the Red advance had been halted and pushed back far enough for the Flight to return to Beketovka. The reversal was due in no small part to the work of 'C' Flight in support of Wrangel's forces, particularly against the Volga flotilla. White Russian General Kravtsevitch was so pleased with 'C' Flight's performance that he despatched a congratulatory message to Colonel Maund on 18 September which read:

> These last few days I have had the pleasure of reading in the daily report of flying of 47 Sqdn. R.A.F., about the extraordinary work of the British pilots, and especially about Major Collishaw. I beg you to accept and transmit to Major Collishaw from the whole Russian Aviation, our sincere admiration of his brilliant activity.[22]

By mid September enough administrative arrangements were in place that Collishaw was himself able to travel to the Volga Front where he arrived on 15 September. Keen to see further operational flying himself, Collishaw immediately began flying operations in one of 'C' Flight's DH9s. A week later Kinkead's 'B' Flight and their newly arrived Sopwith Camels flew out for the front. Shortly after take-off Captain Burns Thomson was forced down with engine trouble, perhaps legacy of the fact that the Camels were veterans of the Salonika front and most had their best days behind them.

Just an hour after Thomson was forced down, Lieutenant Bill Daly was seen to waggle his wings and descend rapidly for the steppe below. Within minutes, flight commander Sam Kinkead was also having engine trouble. What should have been a relatively simple flight had descended into farce. Just in time for Kinkead the Volga River came into view, and on its western bank Beketovka aerodrome. The South African ace was able to make the grass strip and taxi to a row of camouflaged hangers where several DH9 bombers were parked, four with the red, white and black insignia of the White Russian air force and the remainder with the red, white and blue cockade of the RAF. On the railway siding next to the aerodrome 'B' Flight's equipment amd supply trains were being busily unloaded.

The arrival of Canadian pilot Eddie Fulford at Beketovka via Ekaterinodar soon after the move brought 'B' Flight up to full strength. It was a very cosmopolitan sub-unit with pilots representing all corners of the globe, South Africa (Kinkead), United States (Aten), Scotland (Burns Thomson), England (Daly) and Canada (Fulford).

21 *Ibid.*, p.189.
22 *Ibid.*, p.196.

165. 'B' Flight Commander, South African ace Captain Sam Kinkead, DSO,
DSC Bar, DFC Bar, standing next to his Sopwith Camel bearing White
Russian Air Service black, blue and white roundel. (Public domain)

No. 47 Squadron spent much of September and October bombing and strafing Bolshevik gun barges as they steamed down the Volga to Tsaritsyn. Collishaw himself flew on some of these missions, and on one flight just two days after his arrival at the front scored two direct hits with 230 lb bombs on a Red gunboat, causing a violent explosion and clouds of black smoke.

In response to No. 47 Squadron's dominance of the skies over Tsaritsyn the Bolsheviks had established an airfield at Dubovka with the aim of disrupting RAF operations. On 16 September, DH9s flown by Lieutenants Cronin and Day were attacked by a Red Nieuport. The incident was related in their 'Combats in the Air Report':

> The enemy scout dived in between the tails of our machines and was met with heavy and effective cross fire from Lewis Guns, his propeller was seen to stop and he went down in a long steep dive followed by our machines, which were unable to overtake him. Enemy scout was last seen ten feet above ground over Dubovka flying south.[23]

The Squadron flew a number of raids against the Red airfield, the most successful of which took place on 17 September when two DH9s flown by Captain Anderson and Lieutenant Day with observers Lieutenants Buckley and Addison sank a large barge carrying seaplanes and destroyed and damaged several Bolshevik Nieuports parked on the airfield.

During three missions flown on 20 September, 'C' Flight dropped a total of fourteen 112 lb and seventy 20 lb bombs on Dubovka airfield. One DH9 was hit by anti-aircraft fire but managed to return to friendly territory before force landing, the aircraft was set alight as irretrievable and the crew rescued. Two days later, 'C' Flight moved back to their base at Beketovka, flying a further 11 raids against enemy troop concentrations on that day alone.

On 23 September, 'C' Flight flew yet another attack against the enemy flotilla on the Volga, bombing and strafing enemy vessels despite heavy anti-aircraft fire. Lieutenant Howard Mercer was awarded the DFC for the raid (to add to a previously earned MC) for making four attacks from just above the water, machine-gunning the enemy ships as he flew by.

On the last day of September, Kinkead scored his first aerial victory over South Russia during a combined 'B' and 'C' Flight raid on the enemy Volga flotilla. Two Red Nieuports attacked 'C' Flight's DH9s and were in turn attacked by 'B' Flight Camels; Kinkead shot one Nieuport down whilst the other fled. The Russian pilot crashed into the Volga and escaped the wreck but was unable to swim ashore and drowned. The pilot was reportedly D.N. Shchekin who on 6 June had shot down over Astrakhan a No. 221 Squadron DH9 flown by Lieutenants Mantle and Ingram, who were both taken prisoner and held in Moscow. In another encounter with a Red Nieuport over Dubovka on 7 October, Kinkead claimed his second aerial victory over South Russia bringing his total victories on the Western Front and South Russia to 35.

The White Russian squadron sharing Beketovka aerodrome with No. 47 Squadron were nicknamed by the British pilots the 'Wanderers', because of their tendency to fly such loose formation that 'B' Flight Camels were continually snipping around the heels of the stragglers to try and push them back into formation, making escort duties far more dangerous than they otherwise should have been. American Marion Aten described them less than favourably:

> Incapable of keeping formation, their planes would wander off in all directions, and we would have to shepherd them in like a flock of stupid sheep. In a fight the guns of their observers were likely to jam, and even if they didn't jam, they missed. Sometimes their planes disappeared altogether, and on several occasions we had landed to find them neatly hangared, with the Russians on their third glass of vodka.[24]

On a previous mission one of the Russian observers had reportedly mistaken Kinkead for a Bolshevik and put a burst of machine gun fire in front of his Camel's nose.

Although the aircrew of No. 47 Squadron were almost daily risking their lives flying and fighting in the skies over South Russia, few would have been able to give an answer if posed the question, 'What are you fighting for?' Of the pilots in 'B' Flight only Canadian Eddie Fulford actually closely followed political and military events both in Russia and at home. If any of the other men had a question about the Revolution or civil war, it was Eddie that they always asked, and a detailed and well thought out explanation would always be forthcoming.

On the other hand information about the political and military situations in Russia did not exactly flow freely down the chain of command. In fact Aten felt that the British Military Mission was deliberately withholding information in its own interests:

> The British Military Mission was somewhat ambivalent about telling the troops in Russia what was going on. It was an attitude that reflected that of Lloyd George and the government itself. Officer personnel might attend these lectures if they wished; if not, no pressure was brought to bear upon them. It was as if the government hadn't quite decided whether keeping the men informed was really necessary or if – and this was more to the point – whether such a course of action was actually desirable at all. The same old story: muddle in the interests of an amiable vacillation. How expertly led and superbly performing military units could result from such a policy I could never understand.[25]

In late September 1919 as British forces were preparing to evacuate North Russia, discussions were well underway in Whitehall on the fate of No. 47 Squadron in South Russia. Four years of horrendous casualties and the enormous cost both physical and fiscal had left the United Kingdom

---

24   Marion Aten, *Last Train Over Rostov Bridge* (New York: Julian Messner, 1961), p.69.
25   *Ibid.*, p.138.

tired and broke. The public was war weary and wanted nothing more than to put the traumatic war years behind them. They were suspicious of the new military enterprise being asked of them in Russia, especially of the vague political objectives. Even those who were opposed to the Bolsheviks saw little merit in expanding British involvement in Russia without an end in sight.

Proposals were made that as Britain would no longer take a front line role in Russia that the squadron should be recalled from the Volga and attached to the RAF Training Mission in a non-combat role. Colonel Arthur Maund, DSO, commander RAF in South Russia, would have none of it. Maund was a staunch supporter of the combat flying done by the squadron and wrote:

166. Canadian ace Squadron Leader Raymond Collishaw, Commanding Officer, No. 47 Squadron, RAF in South Russia and Crimea 1919–20. (Public domain)

> The value of this squadron, the damage it has done to the Bolsheviks, and the moral effect it has had on the volunteer army are so great that to withdraw it will have a most deplorable effect. They are worth as much as the whole Russian Air Force put together.[26]

The squadron had been so effective (and Wrangel was so loath to lose them) that a compromise was reached. The squadron would not be withdrawn or disbanded but would cease to be an operational unit of the Royal Air Force, instead becoming 'A' Detachment of the RAF Training Mission. All members of the squadron were invited to volunteer for further service, virtually all officers and men of the squadron duly did so. Although some men of 'A' and 'C' Flights elected to return home, not a single officer or enlisted man of 'B' Flight chose to leave. The squadron went on operating as before with little change other than the unit title. Squadron members continued to wear RAF uniforms and their aircraft retained RAF insignia and numbering. Collishaw recorded:

> None of this, of course, made the slightest difference to any of us nor to the squadron's operations but I suppose that it permitted someone to stand up on the floor of the House of Commons in Westminster and solemnly state that No. 47 Squadron of the Royal Air Force was no longer employed as a combatant unit.[27]

In early October 1919 the Bolsheviks launched their final offensive against Tsaritsyn by which time 'A' Flight had arrived from Ekaterinodar to join 'B' and 'C' Flights at Beketovka. The squadron for the first time operated as a complete unit and was immediately put into action to help stem the enemy advance. On 2 October, Burns Thomson carried out a daring raid on a heavily defended enemy battery position, machine-gunning the crews from his Camel until the battery was nearly destroyed, for which Thomson was awarded the DFC.

---

26   Jones, *Over The Balkans and South Russia 1917–1919*, p.156.
27   Collishaw, *Air Command*, p.198.

During October Collishaw participated in several 'B' Flight missions. The Camels would go in first bombing and strafing the enemy whilst the colourful White Russian cavalry charged with sabres glinting in the sun. Some of Wrangel's horsemen came from Muslim areas of the Caucasus and rode into battle flying green banners inscribed with passages from the Koran. Collishaw described the scene from his cockpit as if one had been transported back in time and was 'watching a battle that had taken place a hundred years or more before.'[28]

During a mission flown on 9 October, Collishaw encountered a Bolshevik Albatross DV, 20 miles north of Tsaritsyn. In a short dogfight Collishaw shot the Red aircraft down into the banks of the Volga, Collishaw's 61st and final kill. There has been suggestion that Collishaw exaggerated his service with No. 47 Squadron in South Russia, flying fewer missions than he claimed in his memoir, *Air Command*, and that Collishaw did not shoot down the enemy aircraft on 9 October which he claimed in his logbook.[29] In his book *Gone to Russia to Fight*, John Smith cites an absence of squadron records and 'Combats in the Air' report for the engagement with the Albatross, but it is also true that 47 Squadron's records for the period are in many cases incomplete. For most of its service in Russia, the squadron's individual Flights served many hundreds of miles apart from each other, sometimes on entirely different fronts, and in some cases there was a blurred line between personnel and aircraft of the RAF Training Mission and No. 47 Squadron.

There is also potentially confusion between the Gregorian calendar dates used by the RAF in Russia and the Julian calendar in use by the White Russian forces. When No. 47 Squadron transferred administratively to 'A' Detachment for service with Denikin's Volunteer Army in early October 1919, this confusion was likely further compounded.

It seems incredulous that a squadron commander could shoot down an enemy aircraft and it not be recorded in squadron records, particularly such an obscure aircraft as an Albatross DV. No other German aircraft other than Aten's fictitious 'Black Fokker Triplane' are recorded as having been encountered by the squadron in Russia. Collishaw did record the 'kill' in his logbook albeit with an apparently incorrect Sopwith Camel aircraft number for an aircraft crashed in 1917.[30] It also seems unlikely that with such a small number of Camels operating in South Russia that Collishaw could have got the number wrong, but it would also seem incredulous that the highest-scoring RNAS fighter ace and sixth highest-scoring ace of any nation of the First World War who had shot down 60 enemy aircraft over the Western Front would embellish his logbook with a fraudulent entry for a single enemy aircraft. Without any of the original participants left to ask it will likely remain a mystery.

The following day, 10 October, 40 armed vessels of the Bolshevik Volga flotilla broke through the White Russian blockade north of Tsaritsyn. A DH9 flown by Flying Officer Arthur Day (RAF ranks were introduced in Russia in October 1919) with Flying Officer Observer Roger Addison, made repeated attacks on the enemy ships with bombs and machine guns from very low altitudes, causing heavy casualties and forcing the flotilla to retreat back up the Volga. Day continued to make attacks until wounded by enemy machine gun fire, for which both Day and Addison were awarded the DFC.

During attacks on the same day, Flight Lieutenant Anderson was wounded by ground fire and on 24 October, Flight Lieutenant Keymer and Flying Officer Douglas Blaxland Thompson (not to be confused with W 'Tommy' Burns Thomson of 'B' Flight) were killed in a tragic landing accident:

It wasn't the Bolshies, but two poor chaps of A Flight who had broken out of formation with engine trouble and returned to the field. As they came in to land at fifty feet, the observer stood up to look ahead over the pilot's shoulder. The bomb toggle at his seat caught in the pocket of his flying suit and released

28   *Ibid.*, p. 200.
29   John T. Smith, *Gone to Russia to Fight: The RAF in South Russia 1918–20* (Stroud: Amberley, 2010), Appendix 1.
30   *Ibid.*

the bomb pull. The first bomb blew the wings off the DH-9; the wingless fuselage fell straight to the ground; and the rest of the full load of one-hundred-twelve-bombs exploded.[31]

On 12 October, Red cavalry under General Dumenko broke through the line and were threatening to cut off 'B' and 'C' Flight at Beketovka by advancing on Tsaritsyn from the west. The countryside south west of the city was flat and bare with occasional ravines leaving the Red cavalry exposed and in the open. Kinkead and Burns Thomson took off in two of 'B' Flight's Camels and after dropping their four 20 lb bombs each, Kinkead led Thomson in a series of devastating low passes, mercilessly strafing the enemy cavalry from as low as ten feet. Both pilots fired more than 1,400 rounds during the attacks, completely unsettling the assembled enemy horsemen who turned and fled on the arrival of White Russian cavalry on the scene.

After three days of fierce fighting the Bolshevik advance was halted and by 19 October the Red troops were in headlong retreat. It was a massive victory for the Whites. Over 40,000 prisoners were taken and mountains of arms, equipment and supplies. For his gallantry and leadership during the attack Kinkead was awarded the DSO to add to his DFC and Bar and DSC and Bar awarded in air combats over the Western Front.

After a move to Kotluban, north west of Tsaritsyn, 'C' Flight resumed its attacks on Bolshevik ships on the Volga. On 15 October, Flying Officer Sydney Frogley, DFC, led a formation of aircraft that bombed the flotilla from 1,000 feet, dispersing the enemy with several well-aimed bombs and sinking several vessels for which, in conjunction with his command of 'C' Flight over the previous difficult months, he was awarded the DSO.

The Red flotilla on the Volga had suffered heavy losses from No. 47 Squadron's attacks since August but had been reinforced with a number of new vessels, some equipped with 9.2 inch guns. The flotilla assembled some 40 vessels at Dubovka and positioned themselves along the river adjacent to Tsaritsyn in preparation to bombard the city whilst Red troops attacked from the landward approaches. All three Flights of No. 47 Squadron were just minutes flying time away and over the next two days flew missions non-stop, bombing and strafing the Bolshevik vessels until their ammunition and bombs were exhausted, returning to Beketovka only for as long as it took to rearm and refuel. After two days of attacks in which 11 enemy vessels were sunk, the severely mauled flotilla withdrew in disorder. Fortuitously, despite heavy anti-aircraft fire, none of the attacking British aircraft had been lost.

The following week, despite all members of the squadron taking precautions against contracting the disease, Collishaw came down with typhus (which was in epidemic in South Russia at the time) and immediately evacuated by train. As no British officer could be spared to accompany him, Collishaw was escorted by a trusted White Russian officer named Feodor. It would be no easy journey for Collishaw, and his life was quite literally in the hands of the trusted Russian. Trains were constantly under the threat of attack from 'Green Guards', peasant militias fighting to protect control of their land and resources from outsiders who were quite happy to attack anybody, be they Tsarists or Bolsheviks. When Collishaw's train rolled into Tsaritsyn a gun battle erupted between Red saboteurs and Cossacks. The engine driver had no choice but to push on through at full steam and did not stop until some miles from the city and well out of danger, but also some distance from Tsaritsyn hospital.

It was here that Feodor made a decision that probably saved Collishaw's life. The loyal Russian decided not to leave his charge at Tsaritsyn but to push on to Novocherkassk. It was to prove a fortuitous decision. The typhus ward at Tsaritsyn was packed full of cases and had run out of medicines days before, and in these conditions it would have been unlikely that Collishaw could have

31   Aten, *Last Train Over Rostov Bridge*, pp.87–88.

167. Sopwith Strutter of the RAF Training Mission in White Russian
Air Service colours, Kuban 1919–1920. (Public domain)

survived the disease. Before reaching Ekaterinodar the Canadian ace took a turn for the worse and Feodor instructed that he be taken from the train at a small village, where an elderly Russian refugee who had heard of the stricken British officer gave instructions for the stretcher to be carried to the small cottage where she lived. In a state of unconsciousness Collishaw was nursed back to health by the woman, who spoke no English. Once he had recovered enough to be moved, Feodor arranged for Collishaw to spend his final weeks of recovery in a Russian hospital at Novocherkassk; however by the time he was able to return to the village the kindly old lady had already fled. He was never able to thank her for her kindness and charity, without which he most certainly would have died. After surviving numerous air combats over France and Flanders, Collishaw had almost been bested by the bite of a Russian louse.

Denikin arrived at Tsaritsyn after its recapture in late October and announced plans for an immediate advance before Wrangel even had time to consolidate the line. With the Bolshevik forces in retreat, Denikin was keen to push on towards Moscow without delay. His plan was for columns under each of his three Generals to push forward in a large encirclement which would culminate in an attack on Moscow itself. Wrangel's Caucasian forces were to take Saratov and then move on Moscow via Nizhni-Novgorod, Sidorin's Army of the Don was to push through Norronezh-Ryazan, and Mai-Maievsky's Volunteer Army was to proceed directly into Moscow taking Kursk, Orel, and Tula along the way. Wrangel vainly protested to Denikin that such an advance so early would over-extend the 'Volunteer Army' but Denikin was in no mood to listen: it was the beginning of a large rift between the two generals.

Shortly after Tsaritsyn's capture, the pilots of 'B' Flight entered it to have a closer look at the city that they had only previously seen from the air. What they witnessed horrified them:

> In every street bodies, animal and human, lay rotting. We could smell the unburied Red victims who lay in the ravines on the outskirts. In every breath we took was the heavy, sweetish odour of decay. The looted shops were empty, the churches, with the exception of the cathedral, desecrated. In the rubbled streets with their shattered houses our whispers came back to us in hollow echoes. People staggered through doorways into the sun, and sat witlessly picking at their rags of clothes. Starving children looked at us blankly. In such a place it seemed sacrilege to be alive.[32]

---

32 *Ibid.*, p.88.

Whilst Collishaw and his pilots had been fighting their own little war around Tsaritsyn, Denikin had swept the Bolsheviks aside from Kharkov and Kursk and was advancing on Orel, just 200 miles from Moscow, which he took on 15 October. Denikin was confident he would be in Red Square for Christmas and there were few that doubted he could do it. Lieutenant Charles Roberts, an artillery instructor with the British Military Mission attached to Denikin's staff, noted after Orel's capture: 'We were deciding which horse we should ride during the triumphal entry into Moscow'.[33]

Denikin over-extended his flanks, leaving his rear and lines of communication open to attack by guerrillas and Bolshevik raiding parties. The collapse of his front line was rapid. Just a week after White forces took Orel they were ejected from the city by a reorganised Red Army. Only a week later the Don Cossacks turned against Denikin. By the time sub-zero temperatures set in during late October the trickle of desertions from Denikin's forces had became a flood, and by Christmas the White Russians were in full retreat. The capture of Orel would mark the closest to Moscow the Whites would advance during the Russian Civil War.

By the time Collishaw arrived back at Beketovka on 27 November the Russian winter had well and truly set in with thick snowfalls and sub-zero temperatures. 'C' Flight had exchanged its aircraft for RE8s, handing over the DH9s to the White Russian Air Service. Soon after the exchange, 'A' and 'B' Flights relocated to the Kharkov Front where they spent the final months of the year operating over the frozen Ukrainian steppe attempting to stem the Red advance from Orel. 'C' Flight had been due to join the squadron but was unable to do so due to a lack of rail transport, and spent November and December on the Volga Front supporting Wrangel's attempts to hold his line at Tsaritsyn.

In an effort to provide as much support as possible to Denikin's forces during the critical last months of 1919, Colonel Maund gave orders to hastily equip a flight of RE8s and assemble volunteer air and ground crews from members of the RAF Training Mission. The new unit would be designated 'Z' Flight and would operate independently of the Training Mission and No. 47 Squadron. Command of the Flight was given to Squadron Leader John Archer, OBE. The Flight was equipped with its own train to transport its aircraft, personnel, and supplies; it first saw action near Kharkov at No. 47 Squadron's temporary airstrip at Peschanoe, north east of Kharkov.

'Z' Flight's operations in December 1919 would form the basis for the title of one of the few books published about British involvement in the Russian Civil War, *The Day We Almost Bombed Moscow*. Based largely on an interview with 'Z' Flight pilot Vic Clow, Dobson and Miller recount how Squadron Leader Archer reportedly cabled Colonel Maund requesting permission for 'Z' Flight to bomb Moscow. The distance was far beyond the operational range of an RE8, however, and in the absence of a significant White Russian advance permission was denied.

In light of Denikin's dramatic advance Whitehall had anticipated that such a request might have been made and on 19 September Secretary of State for War Winston Churchill cabled General Holman (commanding the British Military Mission to Denikin) stating it was 'inadvisable that British airmen should be used in present circumstances to bomb Moscow.'[34] With Denikin on the verge of advancing on Moscow and the British government under pressure to distance itself from further entanglement in the Russian Civil War, Churchill saw 'no military value' in the mission. In light of his cable, whether the events described by Clow (which seem improbable) actually transpired will probably never be known so many years after the fact, and with so few original sources available.

'B' Flight arrived at Peschanoe on 5 December with 'A' Flight following a few days later. Both Flights flew a number of missions against the Bolsheviks over the next few days until the continued enemy advance forced the squadron to withdraw further down the line. Its Camels in particular had seen extensive service and were virtually worn out.

---

33   Dobson and Miller, *The Day We Almost Bombed Moscow*, p.21.
34   *Ibid.*, p. 24.

168. Observer Lieutenant Horace Simmons, MC, DFC, 'C' Flight, No. 47 Squadron, RAF. Simmons shot down an attacking Bolshevik Nieuport fighter on 25 July 1919 and damaged another a month later. (Public domain)

On 19 December during a visit by General Holman to 47 Squadron, Collishaw took him as observer in a DH9 on a reconnaissance mission. Sighting an enemy armoured train the Canadian ace took the aircraft down to make an attack run, dropping several bombs around the train. It was only on their return to the airfield that Collishaw learned that the train had been one of Wrangel's, an unfortunate incident of 'friendly fire'. Collishaw took Holman on several other flights over enemy held territory although they appear to have been uneventful.

'A' Flight flew a number of missions against the advancing Red Army during the final days of 1919, one of which nearly ended in capture for two of its aircrew. On 23 December, two DH9s flown by 'A' Flight commander Flight Lieutenant Leonard Slatter and Flying Officer John Breakey with Pilot Officer observers Spalton and Gordon, flew a reconnaissance mission near Litchansk where they discovered the railway bridge had been captured and two enemy armoured trains were proceeding south to Popasnaya at full steam. Slatter led the attack and was credited by a White Russian report kept in the squadron war diary as 'undoubtedly saving many troops and much rolling stock from falling into enemy hands.'[35] Returning from the mission, the aircraft flown by Breakey was hit by ground fire and forced to hastily land in enemy-held territory. After setting fire to their machine, Breakey and Gordon set off on foot through the frozen steppe, arriving back at the Flight the following day. Breakey was subsequently awarded a DFC Bar for service in South Russia although not specifically for this incident alone.

Slatter had a narrow escape himself near Krinichnaya on 29 December when the DH9 he was flying with Pilot Officer observer Allan Hesketh lost its propeller mid-air. With no prior warning the propeller disintegrated but Slatter was skilfully able to land the aircraft after a terrifying few minutes. Both men were shaken but unhurt.

Further east the mass influx of refugee trains fleeing the advancing Red Army was causing innumerable delays along the line, and 'B' Flight's train did not reach Taganrog until 11 December after a most eventful journey. During an overnight stay in a railway siding one of the sentries, an aircraftman named Carstairs, caught and killed a Bolshevik saboteur in the act of setting explosive charges on one of the carriages. On another night the engine was very sneakily stolen, leaving the Flight stranded, and it took some time to arrange a replacement. The danger of sabotage was so great that orders were issued for all officers and men to be in possession of a rifle and 150 rounds of ammunition at all times.

It was during the tedious withdrawal to Taganrog that No. 47 Squadron suffered one of its few fatalities in South Russia. Aircraft Mechanic James Garvey had contracted pneumonia and succumbed to the illness on Christmas Eve. Garvey was buried in the frozen ground alongside the

35   The National Archives: AIR 1/408/15/232/1: War Diary of RAF Mission South Russia Dec. 1919–Jan. 1920.

village of Gorlovo; in lieu of a chaplin, 'B' Flight commander Samuel Kinkead conducted the burial. With his grave lost to time Garvey's name remains commemorated on the Haidar Pasha Memorial (CWGC) in Istanbul.

Upon 'B' Flight's arrival at Taganrog (location of the RAF Training Mission since its move from Ekaterinodar) Kinkead set his mechanics to work, taking advantage of the workshops and spares which had not been available in the field. Collishaw's intention to have 'B' Flight quickly refitted and returned to the front was quashed, however: by the time the squadron was ready to resume service at the front the Bolsheviks had advanced so far that it had to be evacuated back to Ekaterinodar, in such haste that 'B' Flight's newly refurbished Camels and equipment had to be abandoned to the Bolsheviks.

About twelve miles from Rostov, 'B' Flight encountered a stranded train with a number of British Military Mission officers on board. The boiler had blown, leaving some one hundred men of the Mission stuck at Taganrog until another engine could be found. It transpired that the White Russian command at Taganrog had fled at the first sign of the Bolsheviks, without warning the Military Mission. Upon

169. Lieutenant Howard Mercer, MC, DFC, RAF. An observer with 'C' Flight, No. 47 Squadron, shot down a Soviet Nieuport fighter on 20 August 1919. (Author's collection)

learning of the stranded train and the British officers' predicament, General Wrangel despatched another engine from Rostov with General Holman on board, however not far out from Rostov the rescue train's own boiler blew. Concerned for the welfare of his stranded men, Holman exercised his rank and position to relieve 'B' Flight of their engine and steam off to Taganrog at full speed to rescue the Mission officers.

'B' Flight were stranded until they could hitch a ride on another engine, and after a long and nervous wait a White Russian Major arrived and offered to tow 'B' Flight's engineless train on to Rostov. By nightfall the British airmen were half a mile from the city and early the following day the Flight finally steamed into Rostov. In the near distance Rostov Bridge could be seen teeming with an endless procession of refugees and fleeing White soldiers. The entry into the city by 'B' Flight was hardly triumphant. The streets were deserted and the stores had been closed and boarded up, the owners having either fled or barricaded themselves inside. The hospital was jammed with thousands of patients both military and civilian, a few with wounds from battle, most stricken with typhus.

By New Year's Day 1920 no engine had yet been found for 'B' Flight and within a few days Red troops were approaching the railyards from the nearby hills. Rostov had been nearly encircled by the Bolsheviks and if the British airmen could not find another engine they would have to abandon their supplies and equipment to the Bolsheviks and make their way across the bridge on foot to escape the tightening noose. Rescue seemed a forlorn hope and Kinkead began to make preparations to march the Flight across the bridge along with the rest of the fleeing refugees.

Brigadier Alan Brough, CMG, CBE, DSO, a Royal Engineers officer with the Military Mission, visited the 'B' Flight train and informed Kinkead that Red troops had already entered the city and a Russian icebreaker, the *Donskoi Gerla*, under the command of Lieutenant Norman Peploe, DSC,

RN (accompanied by Corporal William Smith, RASC and Private Arthur Funnel, Royal Sussex Regiment from the Mission) was on its way up the River Don to rescue any British personnel still stranded at Taganrog (Peploe was subsequently awarded a DSC Bar for the mission whilst Smith and Funnel received MSMs, an unusual occurrence of Army MSMs awarded for service afloat). Kinkead received word that White Russian engineers were planning to blow up Rostov Bridge in one hour, and it being too risky to wait for *Donskoi Gerla* to arrive, 'Kink' gave orders for 'B' Flight to cross the bridge on foot. Forming up the Flight in ranks, he marched them across the bridge in step as a military formation. It was not possible to set fire to the 'B' Flight train because the sidings were so crowded with refugees. Instead all the equipment and supplies were left to the Bolsheviks. The men marched the 11 miles in silence, stepping through the human carnage as they went. As they marched, weeping refugees clutched at their sleeves pushing babies and young children on them, begging that they be taken with the British to safety. It was a very different reality to that of seeing the war from the air and an experience that none of those who participated would likely forget.

A British Military Mission train was waiting for 'B' Flight on the opposite side of the Don River, which took them straight to Ekaterinodar where all British forces in South Russia were gathering in preparation for the final evacuation. Marion Aten recalled the final parade of the British Military Mission South Russia:

> Here, in a hollow square, stood most of what was left of the British contingent in South Russia; staff, infantry Tommies, tankmen, gunners, airmen. Among them were officers and enlisted men from the Irish, Welsh, Grenadier and Coldstream Guards, the Seaforth Highlanders and the Black Watch – proud and famous regiments that had fought to glory at Aisne, Mons and Le Chateau, on the Somme, at St. Quentin, and Ypres. Altogether we numbered about nine hundred men.[36]

General Holman moved to the head of the hollow square to address the assembled officers and men and pulled no punches as to their predicament. Ekaterinodar was being abandoned by the White Army, only a few companies were fighting a delaying action on the outskirts of the city. Within the city itself and surrounding area there were 15,000 civilians fleeing the advancing Red Army. The fate of the families of the White Russian soldiers was of particular concern to Holman. When the White retreat had begun he had been ordered by the War Office to evacuate all British personnel to Novorossiysk but had given his word to his White Russian friends and allies that he would not leave their families until they were safely on board a British ship.

All that stood between the families of the White soldiers and the Bolsheviks were the 900 officers and men of the RAF and British Missions. Holman could not order the soldiers and airmen to stay to accompany the White refugees to Novorossiysk, indeed if the Red Army captured the railway siding they would have to cover the 90 miles to Novorossiysk on foot in a Russian winter with the enemy snapping at their heels. Holman instead offered that any man who wished to depart on a train leaving for Novorossiysk immediately could do so and no one would think less of them for it. Three soldiers stepped forward and took up the offer, undoubtedly a difficult decision to make in front of their comrades who had decided to stay.

The following morning the evacuation of the families of the White soldiers and civilians to Novorossiysk began. Those who could not fit in the already crowded refugee trains were packed into carts and sleighs and sent on the southbound roads with an armed Mission escort. Major Noel Williamson, RA, who had been awarded the DSO with the British Military Mission for a dual with a Bolshevik armoured train the previous year described the scene:

---

36   Aten, *Last Train Over Rostov Bridge*, p.306.

170. Officers of the British Military Mission with a wrecked French Renault
FT tank, captured by the Bolsheviks after the French evacuation of Odessa
and put into service with the Red Army. (IWM Q75933)

Desolation and anguish ... dead horses, abandoned wagons, guns and equipment blocked the roads. Thousands of wounded died untended when hospitals had to be evacuated and they were hurried to the railway on improvised stretchers, only to succumb to cold or lack of care ... Desertions from the army were now in the thousands, and officers lost all sense of responsibility in the need to escape, and the troops straggled to the seas without any adequate rearguard, pressed all the time by the Reds ... Amazingly enough, during this time, there were many Russian officers who were still busily engaged in exchanging and selling loot, and those employed on equipment work had enormous sums of money ... The army was utterly exhausted. Skeleton regiments trudged southwards, their feet wrapped in cloth and sacks, artillerymen dragging their rusted guns, the exhausted men falling from their horses to freeze to death before they woke.[37]

Williamson was fortunate that he himself did not succumb to illness. He fell ill with typhus the day of the evacuation and was presented with his DSO by General Holman whilst lying semi-delirious on a stretcher on one of the evacuating ships.

Those Mission men not escorting refugees were crammed aboard one of the last trains to leave Ekaterinodar and along with 'B' Flight set out for Novorossiysk. When the train finally arrived at Novorossiysk harbour the city was in a state of panic. The docks were packed with refugees standing shoulder to shoulder pleading for a place on one of the outbound merchant ships. William described the chaos:

Troops were throwing away their shoulder straps and officers were tearing off their epaulettes ... others shot themselves in despair, whilst fat merchants offered suitcases full of paper roubles for the chance of a passage. Young girls were trying desperately to get themselves married to Englishmen – not for love but to get out of the country as British subjects – and several actually did, making arrangements to part as

---

37   Williamson, *Farewell to the Don*, p.256.

soon as they were in safety. Distraught fathers offered money to British soldiers to marry their daughters, and young girls – some of high birth – prostituted themselves to earn enough money to pay the passage for themselves and their families to ruthless and money-grabbing barge captains … Invariably, even as they earned the money, the prices went up as others also clamoured for places, and some of the girls committed suicide. It was a sick, desperate, terrified city.[38]

The wharves were scattered with every conceivable form of military equipment no longer of any use. Army Service Corps men of the Military Mission were working in shifts to push container after container of supplies into the Black Sea to prevent their capture by the Bolsheviks. Brand new tanks, unassembled aircraft still in their packing crates, field guns, tonnes of ammunition, uniforms, weapons and equipment all went over the side. Some of the supplies being destroyed had only recently been unloaded. Despite efforts to destroy the stores, a huge amount of British supplies and equipment still fell into the hands of the Bolsheviks and by the time the Russian Civil War ended in 1922 a considerable portion of the Red Army had been equipped and supplied by the British taxpayer.

To guard the dock and assist in the evacuation of the RAF and British Military Mission and destruction of stores, 2nd Battalion Royal Scots Fusiliers, under Lieutenant Colonel R.K. Walsh, CB, CMG, DSO, were despatched from the British Army of the Black Sea based at Constantinople. The battalion remained at Novorossiysk for a difficult two weeks leading up to the final evacuation on 26 March 1920. The Bolsheviks began shelling the harbour as the final evacuation was underway, the British battleship HMS *Empress of India* and French *Waldeck-Rousseau* replying in kind, lobbing their huge shells into the city's outskirts. Red troops had entered the city and snipers were firing at groups of refugees and White soldiers from the rooftops. A massive cloud of black smoke from burning stores filled the sky, blocking out the sun. The docks were crammed with refugees and soldiers all clamouring for the few places left on the ships, barges and boats of every size and description. A swarm of refugees attempted to rush the Royal Scots Fusiliers guarding entry to the evacuating ships, who were forced to disperse the crowd at bayonet point. Orders had been given that only White troops, their dependents and those who had worked for the British would be allowed to embark.

A number of Sopwith Camels, RE8s, DH9s and other aircraft met a rather inglorious end, crushed beneath the tracks of a British tank. Some forty DH9s still in their packing cases were destroyed in the same manner before the tank itself was driven off the end of the wharf. On 24 March, most of what remained of 'A' Detachment, RAF, 'Kuban Group' (No. 47 Squadron) was evacuated from South Russia for Constantinople on board *Baron Beck*.

The Bolsheviks entered Ekaterinodar on 17 March; on the following day Lieutenant Colonel William Bingham, OBE, 69th Punjabis (Indian Army), attached British Military Mission, suicided by shooting himself with his service revolver. Bingham had served in China during the Boxer Rebellion and at Gallipoli, the Western Front and during the campaign against the Bolsheviks in Turkestan, 1918, before volunteering for attachment to the British Military Mission. Bingham had attended a dinner with Kinkead and other RAF officers the day before his suicide, his dining companions noting he appeared strained and was drinking heavily. During conversation Bingham related that the Mission had been besieged by refugees whom he feared would be captured by the Bolsheviks if they could not be evacuated, and his anguish at orders that transport was to be used for military families only and no further civilians were to be evacuated. Despite the order Bingham evacuated a number of civilian families before returning to his billet and taking his own life. His body was hastily buried in Novorossiysk New Cemetery and his name later commemorated on the Haidar Pasha Memorial (CWGC) in Constantinople.

---

38   *Ibid.*, p.277.

On 26 March the inevitable orders were given for all British personnel to immediately evacuate from Novorossiysk via any means necessary. The remnants of 'B' Flight were amongst 4,000 British servicemen and refugees assigned to board the captured German merchantman SS *Bremerhaven* (which had berths for only 1,500) whilst the Military Mission were crammed aboard SS *Hannover*. Before boarding for Constantinople, General Holman handed over command of the much reduced Mission to Brigadier John Samuel Jocelyn Percy, CB, CMG, DSO, who would take it to the Crimea to continue operations in support of Denikin. Percy had been born under the name 'Baumgartner' and served during the Boer War and North West Frontier before changing his name to 'Percy' during the first years of the war.

The chaos and panic can hardly be imagined as thousands of soldiers and civilians jostled for positions on board the ships. The great Russian writer Konstantin Paustovsky (who would be nominated for the Nobel Prize for Literature in 1965) was a witness to the disaster and recalled the horrible scene on the docks at Novorossiysk that day:

> For a very long time afterwards, I was haunted and burdened by the feeling that at some time, in some picture by a pitiless artist, I had already witnessed this epic flight-gaping mouths, torn open by cries for help, eyes bulging from their sockets, faces livid and deeply etched by fear of death, of people who could see nothing but the one, blinding, terrible sight: rickety ships' gangplanks with handrails snapping under the weight of human bodies, soldiers' rifle butts crashing down overhead, mothers stretching up their arms to lift their children above the demented human herd, the children desperately crying, and the trampled body of a dying woman still squirming and screaming on the quay.
>
> People were senselessly destroying each other, preventing even those who reached the gangway from saving themselves. The moment anyone gained a hold on the plank or the rail, hands grabbed and clutched at him, clusters of bodies hung on him. He inched his way forward, pulling them along, but lost his hold, fell together with his terrible human load into the sea and drowned, powerless to shake it off…
>
> Crushed suitcases, bundles, and baskets slithered downhill under foot, like monstrous living creatures. Clothes spilled out and wound themselves round shoes and ankles. Women's petticoats and lace, children's frocks and ribbons trailed after the fugitives, and the sight of these homely things made their flight even more tragic…
>
> Ships slowly listed under the weight of people clinging to the deck rails and scrambling aboard. Sailors and soldiers tried to keep them out, but were pushed back and borne down…
>
> We saw the mooring lines being hacked through, and ships sailing away without stowing the gangplanks. The gangplanks slid into the sea, with people still clinging on them…
>
> Suddenly the docks emptied. People hurled themselves back into the alleys, disappeared into the chinks of the port.
>
> Riding slowly down the slope littered with broken luggage, torn clothes and here and there a body trampled to death, came a Soviet mounted patrol.
>
> The men rode with heads bowed, as though lost in thought. They pulled up beside the bodies, dismounted and bent over them, trying to see if any were still alive – but none were.
>
> The horsemen rode to the end of the breakwater, halted and for a long time watched the ships.[39]

The last British ships left Novorossiysk that night as shells dropped into the harbour from Bolshevik artillery in the surrounding hills. The big guns of British and French warships of the Black Sea Fleet kept the Red Army at bay as the overcrowded transports left the harbour. The British battleship HMS *Empress of India*, cruiser HMS *Calypso*, flotilla leader HMS *Stuart*, destroyer leader

---

39   Konstantin Paustovsky, *The Story of a Life: Vol. 3, In that dawn* (London: Harvill Press, 1964, repr. New York: Pantheon Books, 1982), p.220.

171. Captain Sydney Frogley, Commanding 'C' Flight, No. 47 Squadron, RAF. Frogley was twice decorated for service in Russia with both the DSO and DFC for work bombing ships and barges of the Bolshevik flotilla operating on the Volga River. (Public domain)

HMS *Montrose* and destroyers HM Ships *Steadfast*, *Seraph*, and *Sikh*, and seaplane carrier HMS *Pegasus* eventually evacuated more than 5,000 of Denikin's troops to Constantinople. The Imperial General Chief of Staff, General Sir Henry Wilson, made the entry in his diary after the evacuation, 'So ends in practical disaster another of Winston's military attempts. Antwerp, Dardanelles, Denikin.'[40]

On 4 April, Denikin fled to political asylum in England leaving Baron Wrangel the poisoned chalice of Commander-in-Chief Armed Forces South Russia. Wrangel knew the war was all but lost but believed one last successful White offensive would leave him in a much better position to negotiate with the Bolsheviks. In spite of some brilliant victories, Wrangel's heavily outnumbered forces in the Crimea could never have made any real progress, especially as the British government, in an effort to normalise relations with the Bolsheviks and commence talks, had withdrawn their support. Wrangel considered it a great betrayal. The small British Military Mission attached to Wrangel was also withdrawn and the Royal Navy withdrew its support in the Black Sea. The British government was so concerned that any success by Wrangel's forces (using previously donated British arms, equipment and supplies) would damage its standing with the Bolsheviks in the upcoming Anglo–Soviet Trade Agreement talks, that they actually offered to mediate with the Soviet leadership on his behalf. With the writing on the wall and a Bolshevik victory in Russia inevitable, Whitehall had made a complete turnaround.

In the meantime whilst 'B' and 'C' Flights had been in action on the Volga Front, 'A' and 'Z' Flights had remained in action further west on the Kharkov Front, leapfrogging southwards down the railway line as the Bolshevik advance threatened to overrun the White line completely. Collishaw recalled that the procedure was for the senior pilot to lead the flight down the line until he picked out a flat area adjacent to a railway siding suitable for a landing strip. The aircraft would then land and await arrival of the train carrying the rest of the Flight, which could take anywhere from hours to days depending on how congested the railway line was. Once the train had pulled into the siding the Flight resumed operations until a few days later when the advancing Red Army would force a repeat of the process.

'A' Flight spent Christmas Day in the midst of a blizzard in the eastern Ukraine. Disaster nearly followed on Boxing Day when a fire broke out in the HQ train which threatened to spread to the other carriages and neighbouring 'Z' Flight train, the consequences of which would be catastrophic. The men could not hope to survive for long in the midst of the Ukrainian winter without the warmth and shelter of their passenger carriages. Swift action to unhook the burning coach saved

40   Sir Charles Edward Callwell, *Field Marshall Sir Henry Wilson: His Life and Diaries*, vol. 2 (London: Cassell, 1927), p.231.

other carriages from catching fire but the HQ carriage was destroyed, including, much to Collishaw's dismay, a large diamond which he had purchased from a once-wealthy refugee for a fraction of its value. A search was made in what was left of the train the following day but the diamond was not found. The ace later lamented, 'Whether I lost that Boxing Day night a small fortune or merely a glittering chunk of glass for which I had paid – by my standards – a lot of money I shall never know, and perhaps it is just as well.'[41]

An increasingly heavy snowfall and rapid Bolshevik advance conspired to make further flying operations impossible, and Collishaw ordered that all aircraft and supplies be loaded and trains to make their best time eastwards to Kuban territory post haste. One of 'A' Flight's DH9s could not be loaded and was set on fire to prevent its falling into enemy hands. A reserve train set up to carry additional squadron supplies and equipment had to be abandoned and was captured complete by forward units of the Red Army.

172. Captain Leonard Slatter. OBE, DSC and Bar, DFC, Commanding Officer 'A' Flight, No. 47 Squadron, RAF. South African Slatter was later a member of the 1926 RAF High Speed Flight with fellow 47 Squadron veteran Captain Sam Kinkead. (Keith Chiazzari)

'Z' Flight's train with General Holman on board safely crossed the railway bridge at Rostov-on-Don; however by the time 'A' Flight's train arrived Bolshevik cavalry had cut the line, forcing Collishaw to abandon plans to evacuate from Novorossiysk, redirecting the Flight through Taganrog and then south-west into the Crimea. Collishaw did what he could for the thousands of refugees by adding as many carriages as he dared to the RAF train and mounting Vickers and Lewis machine guns on the roofs of several coaches as defence against Red cavalry. Most of the Russian engine crew had fled on hearing that Rostov had been cut off, and it fell to the squadron's adaptable mechanics to act as firemen and engineers.

It was slow and hard going, wood was scarce and the boilers had to be filled with snow. Word had also reached Collishaw that a Bolshevik armoured train had been despatched down the line to pursue the British airmen. The Squadron Leader's anxiety was not eased by the slow speed of 'A' Flight's withdrawal. Bolshevik saboteurs were constantly damaging the line and work parties were organised from amongst the airmen to repair damaged sections of track, which sometimes meant ripping up the line over which the train had just passed and relaying in front of the engine to allow the train to continue its escape. On one occasion the pursuing Red armoured train was spotted in the distance coming around a bend but could not bring its guns to bear before 'A' Flight steamed out of range.

Typhus took a heavy toll on the crowded refugee carriages and Collishaw was forced to make the difficult decision to order the bodies of the dead to be thrown from the moving train. Some distraught mothers concealed the bodies of their dead children, which accelerated the spread of the disease, but Collishaw found it difficult to condemn the mothers for their actions.

---

41   Dobson and Miller, *The Day We Almost Bombed Moscow*, p.207.

173. Senior officers of the British Military Mission on its departure from the Crimea, 29 June 1920. Standing left to right: Captain Oldfield (ADC); Lieutenant Colonel Barnes; Lieutenant Colonel Ling, RA; Lieutenant Colonel Symonds (ADQS); Captain Treloar. Sitting left to right: Lieutenant Colonel Reid; Brigadier General Brough; Brigadier-General Percy (GOC Commanding); Captain Phillimore, RN (Commanding, RN Mission); Colonel Roche. (Public domain)

A stop to refuel shortly before reaching the Crimea nearly ended in disaster after a runaway locomotive sent down the line by the Bolsheviks careered into the rear of most of 'A' Flight's carriages, which fortunately carried only supplies, not passengers. After a Herculean effort to clear the damaged wagons and leave nothing of use to the Bolsheviks the train was able to continue on to the Crimea, where it arrived on 4 January 1920.

After dropping off the refugee carriages the train continued on to 'A' Flight's new home at the Russian aerodrome at Simferopol, where the DH9s were unloaded, reassembled and after a brief refit and service, back in the air flying missions from 17 February. At this time Collishaw's HQ and 'A' Flight were redesignated the 'Crimean Group' whilst 'B' and 'C' Flights were redesignated 'Kuban Group'.

On 30 January 1920, Colonel Maund resigned as head of the RAF Training Mission to be replaced by Squadron Leader John Archer who had previously commanded 'Z' Flight, disbanded on arrival in the Crimea. Archer had started the war as a subaltern in the Seaforth Highlanders before completing pilot training in early 1916 and posting to an RFC squadron in Egypt. Awarded the OBE for his services during Allenby's final push on Damascus, Archer's award was upgraded to the CBE in recognition of his services in South Russia.

'A' Flight remained in action throughout February, flying a number of missions despite the severe weather. On one mission flown on 18 February to bomb the railway station at Novo-Alexeyevka, a DH9 flown by Flight Lieutenant John Grigson with observer Flying Officer Cedric Gordon encountered a Red Sopwith Strutter fitted with skis for operations during winter. After completing their bombing run, Grigson dived on the Red aircraft to put Gordon in a position to open fire at it from the rear cockpit. After being on the receiving end of several bursts from Gordon's Lewis gun, the enemy pilot decided that discretion was the better part of valour and attempted to flee. Grigson pursued him but was unable to keep pace and the enemy Sopwith was seen to land in a snow-covered field adjacent to Novo-Alexeyevka station. Although not for this specific encounter alone, both

Grigson and Gordon were subsequently awarded DFCs for their service with 47 Squadron in South Russia.

Despite the inevitable outcome, 'A' Flight continued to fly daily missions other than when weather conditions made flying impossible. On one of these missions in late February, Collishaw had a very lucky escape after his DH9 was forced down after his engine cut out mid-air. After a forced landing on fortuitously hard-packed snow the DH9's engine continued to turn over, and the Canadian ace was able to taxi the aircraft over the snow the entire 20 miles back to base.

On one rather unusual mission during March in the waning days of the British presence in the Crimea, 'A' Flight dropped bundles of supplies and ammunition to the White Russian vessel *Kornilov*, which had become stuck fast in the frozen Sea of Azov. On this mission and a number of other occasions Collishaw flew a Nieuport scout, supplied to the RAF by the White Russians who had in turn received the aircraft as war supplies donated by the French before the revolution.

On 17 March, whilst flying an 'A' Flight DH9 on a bombing mission over Novo-Alexeyevka station, pilot Flight Lieutenant Matthew Langley with observer Flying Officer T.W. Brockley were attacked by two Red Nieuport fighters. During the engagement Brockley shot down one enemy fighter 'completely out of control'. Langley's 'Combats in the Air' report stated:

> Nieuport Pilot was evidently an experienced pilot and made several determined attacks from all positions. As he was doing a heavy banked turn a burst of 20 rounds was fired into him from the rear gun, the tracers going right into him. He dropped into a vertical side slip for about 1,000 feet and then was seen to turn over into a vertical nose dive.[42]

By mid March, Denikin's retreating forces could barely outpace the advancing Red Army and orders were issued for all British forces in the Kuban to withdraw to Novorossiysk for evacuation. 'A' Flight in the Crimea flew its last mission on 28 March, bombing and strafing Red cavalry and artillery, also scoring direct hits on an armoured train. The following day Collishaw flew a long reconnaissance over enemy held territory, his last mission flown over Russia; on his return orders were received to withdraw to the port of Theodosia. On 31 March 1920, 'A' Detachment (No. 47 Squadron, RAF) 'Crimean Group' embarked at Theodosia on board HMT *Katoria* for Constantinople via Sevastopol.

On 4 April, the same day that Baron Wrangel replaced Denikin as Supreme Commander of White Russian Forces South Russia, the new British Military Mission commander General Percy (who had taken command of the Mission from General Holman on its withdrawal from Novorossiysk to the Crimea on 26 March) addressed the last of the Mission personnel on Theodosia pier immediately prior to evacuation. The dissolution of the Mission brought to an end organised British military intervention in South Russia and Crimea, although a handful of advisers remained in the Crimea until June when the British government finally ordered all British military personnel withdrawn from Russia.

Wrangel's forces managed to hold out in the Crimea until November when he and 146,000 military and civilian personnel, the remnants of Denikin's 'Armed Forces South Russia', fled to Turkey and then Belgrade, where a large Russian exile community had been established. In the 1930s it was estimated that there were two million Russian refugees of the Russian Civil War spread across the globe, the largest refugee diaspora in modern history up to that time. Many settled in the Balkans and France, some as far afield as China, Australia and the Americas. Where officers had once led regiments into battle they now built roads and railways, dug coal and worked plantations. Wrangel died in mysterious circumstances in Brussels in 1928, Denikin in Michigan in 1947. Both their wives lived in New York and became lifelong friends.

---

42   The National Archives: AIR 1/408/15/232/3: War Diary of 47 Squadron, RAF, South Russia, 1–31 March 1920.

Kinkead and Aten resumed active service with the RAF in Baghdad in 1921, whilst Collishaw saw further service in North Persia. From 1922–24 the Canadian and South African aces were reunited and flew together in the Kurdistan campaign. Collishaw went on to command the RAF at El Alamein in 1942 and retired from the service after the Second World War in the rank of Air Vice Marshall to his native British Columbia.

William Burns Thomson was killed in a flying accident at Kantara, Egypt, in 1924 whilst performing aerobatics in his Camel at low altitude. Even the great Samuel Kinkead's life ended early in a flying accident: 'Kink' died as a member of the RAF High Speed Flight (commanded by fellow South African Leonard Slatter) in 1928 when his Supermarine S5 seaplane crashed into the sea off the Isle of Wight during an attempt to break the world speed record. Bill Daly of 'B' Flight died in an air collision over Northampton in 1923. Eddie Fulford, the brilliant pilot who struggled to reconcile the British cause in Russia, served during the Second World War and in 1942 survived the sinking of his troopship en route for North Africa.

'A' Flight commander Leonard Slatter went on to a distinguished career in the RAF, and was commanding the Schneider Cup team at the time of Kinkead's death. Slatter rose through the ranks to Air Marshall and served through to the Second World War in several senior appointments including command of RAF Coastal Command, for which he was knighted. He died in England in 1961, aged 66.

Marion Aten retired from the RAF and returned home to California to take over his father's '8 N-Bar' ranch. In 1961 his book *Last Train Over Rostov Bridge*, co-authored by Arthur Ormont, was published in the US shortly after his death to only moderate interest.

Of his time in South Russia Collishaw reminisced: 'We all took home with us many memories, and I am sure that I am not the only member of the squadron who has since tried – with little success – to banish some of these from my mind.'[43]

On 18 November 1920, the British government began trade agreement negotiations with the Bolsheviks and officially recognised the Soviet leadership as the legitimate government in power in Russia. With the signing of the Anglo–Soviet Trade Agreement on 16 March 1921, British intervention in the Russia Civil War officially came to an end.

---

43   Collishaw, *Air Command*, p.213.

17

Turkestan and Caspian: August 1918–May 1920

Turkestan

In mid 1918 Major General Wilfred Malleson, CB, CIE, was commanding a small joint British-Indian force at Meshed in northern Persia, near the eastern bank of the Caspian Sea on the border of modern day Turkmenistan; Malleson's task was to prevent any Turkish/German force from landing at Krasnovodsk on the east coast of the Caspian, and using the railway to travel southwards towards the Afghan border and threaten the British jewel in the east: India.

Malleson was an Indian Army intelligence officer who had originally been sent to North Persia in June 1918 to keep an eye on events across the border in Transcaspia, where the Bolsheviks were in almost complete control. In the event of a Turkish breakthrough, Malleson had orders to sabotage the Trans-Caspian Railway and destroy the large stockpiles of cotton warehoused in storage facilities down the line.

The political situation across the border did not remain stable for very long. There was a feeling of dissatisfaction with Bolshevik rule amongst the local population, most of whom were ethnic Russian, and taking advantage of the political situation a group of opposition Mensheviks and Socialist Revolutionaries (socialist factions not aligned with the Bolsheviks) established a government, calling themselves the 'Ashkhabad Committee'. The Bolsheviks could not allow a rival party to function within what would become the Soviet Union and were determined to unseat the flimsy government.

With so few Red troops in the region the local Bolsheviks armed some of the 35,000 German and Austro-Hungarian prisoners of war in Turkestan as auxiliaries and sent them down the line towards Ashkhabad. In fact nine out of ten 'Red' troops in Turkestan were German-Austro-Hungarian with the remainder 'low-class Russians with a sprinkling of Sarts and bad characters of the countryside. Their numbers included some ex-officers of the old Imperial Army and also men of the working classes. An ex-convict commanded a battalion composed entirely of felons from the Tashkent jail.'[1] Total enemy forces were estimated to be 4,000 strong with up to 30 field guns and 60 machine guns. The initial German-Austro-Hungarian assaults were repulsed but the Ashkhabad Committee knew they could not hold out indefinitely and appealed to the British for assistance.

Malleson had been issued instructions on what his actions should be in such an event by Commander-in-Chief of the Indian Army, General Sir C.C. Munro: he gave Malleson authorisation to afford limited military and financial aid to the Trans-Caspian government to prevent an Ottoman-German advance down the railway, and by extension the same moves by the Bolsheviks. Malleson signed a formal agreement with the Ashkhabad Committee on behalf of the British government affirming Whitehall's support to 'guarantee the continuance of military and financial help so long as the Trans-Caspian government remains in power and continues to place at the head of its political program the restoration of order and the suppression of Bolshevik and Turk–German intrigue and plans for invasion.'[2]

---

1   J.A.C. Kreyer and G. Uloth, *28th Light Cavalry in Persian and Russian Turkistan, 1915–20* (Oxford: private publication, 1926), p.135.
2   Dobson and Miller, *The Day We Almost Bombed Moscow*, p.93.

Through a series of events Malleson's men were soon in action against the Bolshevik-sponsored German-Austro-Hungarian troops near the ruins of the ancient city of Merv, 350 kilometres down the line from Ashkhabad. On 15 August at Bairam Ali, a section of machine guns under Lieutenant Walter Gipps, 19th Punjabis with Havildars Ilam Din and Nand Singh, were left to face an overwhelming enemy attack and defend an Anglo-Indian armoured train without support after the local defenders abandoned their trenches. During a difficult withdrawal in which Singh was wounded, and with no rest and little food and water, the gallant Punjabis finally reached safety at Dushak three days later.

The 19th Punjabi infantry had spent the war garrisoning the North-West Frontier and were latterly in Persia, protecting approach routes to Afghanistan from Ottoman interference. At the time they were ordered into southern Turkestan in mid-1918 the battalion officers were as follows:

Commanding Officer:	Lieutenant Colonel Dennis Erskine Knollys
Second in Command:	Captain G.E.F. Shute
Adjutant:	Captain R.F.G. Adams
Quartermaster:	Lieutenant F.W. Stewart
Subadar Major:	Isar Singh
No. 1 Company:	Lieutenant J.F. Stephen
	Major J. Drummond (from Dec. 1918)
	Lieutenant E.A. Cuevilier (from Dec. 1918)
No. 2 Company:	Lieutenant W.F. Gipps
No. 3 Company:	Captain Geoffrey Pigot
	Lieutenant L.S. Ingle (from Dec. 1918)
Attached:	Major William Bingham, 69th Punjabis
Attached:	Captain R.J.D. Teague-Jones, 12th Pioneers
Attached:	Captain K.H.W. Ward, KRRC
Attached:	Captain George Dmitry Lamkirk, DSO, MC, General List

The Punjabis were again in action stopping the Bolshevik advance from Tashkent in its tracks at Kaakha on the morning of 28 August. Lieutenant Colonel Knollys commanded the battalion during the defence, the first occasion that the Punjabis used the Lewis gun in action, employed to great effect from a rooftop by Sepoy Natha Singh until wounded.

As the enemy advance threatened the British flank, Quartermaster Lieutenant F.W. Stewart took command of the battalion followers and led them into action in a last ditch attempt to protect the regimental bivouac. Just as the Red troops were enveloping the Indian troops, Lieutenant J.E. Stephen led No. 1 Company in a bayonet charge against the enemy, driving them back in disorder, although four Punjabis died in the assault and a further 14 were wounded.

British officer casualties included Tasmanian-born Captain Kenneth Ward, KRRC, Captain Reginald Teague-Jones, 12th Pioneers and Lieutenant Stewart wounded. Stewart was also subsequently awarded the Military Cross for his bravery and leadership.[3] Ward succumbed to his wounds two days after the battle, aged 33. Prior to the outbreak of war he had travelled from Australia to accept a commission in the British Army and had spent five years campaigning on the North-West Frontier of India before resigning his commission in 1913. In August 1914 he enlisted as a private in the KRRC and saw action on the Western Front where he was twice wounded before resuming a commission. Ward is today commemorated with other Anglo-Indian soldiers who died in Turkestan on the Tehran Memorial, Iran.

---

3   *The London Gazette*, 15 October 1918.

The day after the battle at Kaakha, reinforcements arrived in the form of a company of 1/4th Battalion, Hampshire Regiment under Captain John Fardell from Enzeli via Krasnovodsk, and on 5 September a battery of 18 pdr guns of 44th Battery, Royal Field Artillery under Captain Harrison. Further skirmishes followed on 11 and 18 September, on the latter date an attempt was made by Red cavalry supported by an armoured train to turn the left flank of the Anglo-Indian defensive line near Kaakha but they were driven off by the Punjabis (who had lost three men in a skirmish with Red troops on 15 September) and Hampshires. Malleson's force was significantly bolstered on 21 September with the arrival of 'C' (Captain J. Lothian) and 'D' (Lieutenant R.G. Vines) Squadrons, Indian 28th Light Cavalry (accompanied by a party of Sistan Levy Corps) under Major J.A.C. Kreyer which had spent the war in Persia protecting the Afghan–Indian frontier from German–Ottoman interference.

The local British-allied Mensheviks operated an unarmed Henri-Farman biplane reconnaissance aircraft in the area, and the Bolsheviks a Morane-Saulnier monoplane which occasionally ineffectually bombed and machine-gunned Kaakha railway station. The aircraft never met in the air and the Henri-Farman eventually crashed and was written off. A scare occurred in September when intelligence reported that the enemy would soon use gas shells against Kaakha, and Russian respirators were issued to all Anglo-Indian troops although the reports did not transpire.

Malleson's force now numbered under 1,000 Anglo-Indian troops which combined with locally enlisted Turkmen and anti-Bolshevik Russians, were enough for offensive rather than defensive actions. Malleson wasted no time before moving on the enemy line near Dushak. Leaving the Hampshires company in reserve, the 19th Punjabis, 28th Light Cavalry and 44th Battery RFA set out on the night of 13 October and reached the starting line for the attack without mishap. As the troops formed up to await dawn, two patrols of Punjabis encountered each other in the dark and fired on each other, alerting the enemy. The decision was made to continue the attack in spite of the loss of the element of surprise. There was little cover and the Punjabis suffered terribly during the advance from machine gun and artillery fire. However under cover of the guns of 44th Battery, RFA the Punjabis again demonstrated keen use of the bayonet and soon drove the defenders from their positions straight into the lances of 28th Light Cavalry, who killed 60 of the enemy with lances alone. A shell fired by 44th Battery detonated three wagons carrying explosives in a railway siding, causing a huge explosion.

Soon after entering Dushak the enemy launched a determined counter-attack which threatened the Punjabis' line of retreat. With all the company officers killed or wounded, command of the forward companies fell to Subadar Major Isar Singh who was himself wounded. Running short of ammunition and water and with Lewis guns choked with sand, the order was given to withdraw, the Punjabis taking with them some of the six field guns and 16 machine guns captured at Dushak. The wounded were treated by an Indian field ambulance commanded by Captain John Sinton, VC: he had received his award during the campaign in Mesopotamia, when although wounded in both arms and torso he refused to go to hospital and remained treating Indian soldiers under heavy fire.

The Punjabis suffered heavily in the attack, losing Lieutenant James Eliot Stephen aged 25 killed, Captains G.E.F. Shute and Geoffrey Pigot wounded in the shoulder and throat respectively, and Lieutenant Gipps in the leg. A further 47 Punjabis and two soldiers from 28th Light Cavalry were killed, 30 led-horses killed, and more than 140 men of both units wounded. Bolshevik casualties at Dushak were estimated to be over 500. Captains Shute and Pigot were both awarded the Military Cross for bravery and leadership during the battle,[4] whilst Subadar Bal Singh was awarded the Indian Order of Merit[5] and several other ranks the Indian Distinguished Service Medal (IDSM).

---

4   *The London Gazette*, 12 September 1919.
5   *The Gazette of India*, 4 April 1919.

On 17 October Malleson received orders from the government of India prohibiting the use of Indian troops for further offensive operations. Thereafter there remained a period of relative calm until January 1919, when command of the Malleson mission was handed over from the Indian government to the War Office and transferred to the British Army of the Black Sea under General Sir G. F. Milne, GCMG, KCB, DSO. Reinforcements arrived in late October in the form of half of 'A' Squadron, 28th Light Cavalry under Lieutenant William Straker followed by 'B' and the remainder of 'A' Squadron under Lieutenant K. S. Thomson in November.

In December Captain Geoffrey Pigot, MC, rejoined the battalion from hospital and resumed command of No. 3 Company which had also been reinforced by the arrival of Lieutenant Louis Sabaux Ingle a few days earlier. At the same time Major James Drummond arrived to take command of No. 1 Company which had been without an Officer Commanding since the death in action of Lieutenant Stephen. Lieutenant Edward Augustus Cuvelier also arrived as a reinforcement company officer for No. 1 Company. During the absence of British officers the companies had been very ably led by Indian subadars.

In January 1919 command of the small Anglo-Indian force was taken over by Brigader L. N. Beatty, CMG, DSO, Indian Army. Reinforcement also arrived in the form of two platoons of 9th Battalion, Royal Warwickshire Regiment detached from North Persia Force, known as 'NORPERFORCE', commanded by Major General W. M. Thomson.

On the morning of 16 January 1919, Red troops launched a surprise attack through the early morning fog near Annenkovo Station using the fire from several armoured trains to cover the advance. The attacking force numbered some 3,000 men and included several armoured trains, 400 cavalry, nine field guns, horse and camel trains and a large number of infantry.

No. 1 Company under recently arrived Major Drummond and Lieutenant Cuvelier was heavily attacked and at risk of envelopment by the overwhelming enemy force, it was only the skilful deployment by Major Drummond of his platoons that kept the attackers at bay. Lewis guns became clogged with sand, and as ammunition in the front line began to run low, pairs of sepoys made repeated trips carrying boxes of ammunition from company headquarters to the firing line.

At a critical point Captain Pigot and Lieutenant Ingle led No. 3 Company in a bayonet charge which drove off the attackers as 28th Light Cavalry began an encircling movement, causing a rout in the fog and confusion. Both No. 1 and No. 3 Companies were so stretched out that in the confusion neither saw each other until the battle was over. Ten Punjabis died in the attack and a further 36 were wounded; 28th Light Cavalry were fortunate to escape the action without sustaining any fatal casualties. The Red force suffered more than 500 men killed and wounded and a number more taken prisoner. A reconnaissance the following morning of the left flank of the attack counted 176 enemy dead alone, the bodies already stripped by the Turkmen.

For bravery and leadership during the defence of Annenkovo, Major Drummond and Lieutenant Ingle were both awarded the Military Cross,[6] and Captain Pigot a Bar to his MC awarded for the battle of Dushak the previous October.[7] Subadar Nihal Singh and several other ranks also received the IDSM for individual acts of bravery in the defence. Lieutenant Colonel Knollys would also subsequently be awarded the DSO for his command of 19th Punjabis during the campaign.[8]

Several encounters with Red cavalry occurred during the remainder of the month. On one occasion Lance Daffadar Bola Ram of 'D' Squadron, 28th Light Cavalry was leading a patrol of eight men when they were cut off by Red cavalry three times their number. Ram ordered a charge against the enemy with lances, speared two enemy and burst through the enemy formation without loss to the

6   *The London Gazette*, 26 May 1919.
7   *The London Gazette*, 29 November 1919.
8   *The London Gazette*, 3 June 1919.

Indian cavalrymen. Ram was subsequently awarded the IDSM for his bravery and leadership and further decorated with the Cross of St. George 2nd Class by the local White Russian commander.

Another incident occurred during a patrol of 'A' Squadron on 2 March 1919 led by Lance Duffadar Manovr Khan, who found his 13-strong patrol surrounded by 150 Red cavalry. Realising there was little chance of survival without decisive action, Khan ordered a charge against the enemy and broke through the encircling Red troops. Trumpeter Murad Ali accounted for two enemy with his sword and another with his revolver. The Red force gave chase and as the patrol split up three Indian cavalrymen were separated and subsequently reported missing, two of whom – Lance Duffadar Lal Khan and Shoeing-Smith Ahmed Yar Khan – subsequently escaped captivity and many months later rejoined their regiment in Lucknow via circuitous routes. In the case of Shoeing-Smith Khan, he made his route to freedom in a remarkable journey via the British Consul in Kashgar, China, rejoining his regiment in India in 1921, and was awarded the IDSM for his resourcefulness in escaping captivity. Khan was also able to report on the fate of the third missing trooper, Sowar Gulfaraz Khan who had been killed during the frantic escape. Lance Duffadar Manovr Khan who had led the patrol was awarded the Indian Order of Merit whilst two of his troopers were awarded IDSMs.

In late March orders were received from General Milne for the withdrawal of British forces from Turkestan. By the end of the first week of April all Anglo-Indian troops had been withdrawn to Meshed bringing to an end British military intervention against the Bolsheviks in Russian Turkestan. Both 19th Punjabis and 28 Light Cavalry were subsequently awarded Battle Honours 'Persia 1915–19' and 'Merv' in recognition of their services during the campaign. Captain Geoffrey Pigot, MC and Bar later wrote a history of 19th Punjabis 1857–1946 and subtitled his work *Sherdil-ki-Paltan*, which translates from Punjabi as 'Regiment of the Lionhearted'.

Caspian

Although Germany surrendered on 11 November 1918, the end of the war came a little sooner for the Kaiser's allies: the Austro-Hungarian Empire surrendered on 4 November, the Ottoman Empire on 30 October and Kingdom of Bulgaria on 29 September.

Three days after the Armistice, the British Cabinet formally laid down its policy with regards to post-revolution Russia. British troops of the NREF were to remain at Murmansk and Archangel; an Allied presence was to be maintained in Siberia with the intent to convince the Czech Legion to remain in Russia (before the Armistice there had been plans by the Allies to ship the Legion to France); contact would be established with White Russian General Denikin in South Russia; the Baltic States of Lithuania, Latvia and Estonia would be supplied with military arms and equipment and the railway running through Transcaucasia in southernmost Russia would be occupied by British and Indian troops of the 'British Army of the Balkans and Black Sea'.

Since the commencement of commercial oil production in the nineteenth century, Transcaucasia had become one of the richest territories in all of the Russian Empire. Located on the southern edge of the Caucasus mountain range, it has both the highest and lowest points in Europe, nine of its mountains exceed the height of Mont Blanc whilst the city of Baku is 60 feet below sea level. Positioned on one of the great crossroads of history, to the west lie the shores of the Black Sea, to the east the Caspian Sea, to the south Turkey and Persia. The climate and terrain ranges from semi-tropical forest to desert. It is a land of ancient history, where wars have been fought, civilisations made and empires lost.

Baku, the capital of modern day Azerbaijan, is an ancient city built when the Turks ruled the area in medieval times, Ottoman influences which are still evident today. The city's streetscape is filled with mosques, flat-topped houses, narrow streets and crowded markets. In the early 1900s a new area of town was built using the influx of oil money into the local economy. European-style houses were constructed near the shorefront, plush new hotels were built with every imaginable luxury, many of the rooms occupied year round by Baku's oil millionaires. Like neighbouring Georgia and Armenia, the Azerbaijani capital city was made up of a diverse mix of nationalities. There were Georgians, Azerbaijanis, Armenians, Cossacks, Tartars, Jews, Persians, Turks, Bulgars and Russians amongst others. Generally, all lived together relatively harmoniously but tensions increased between Azerbaijani Muslims and Armenian Christians in mid 1918 as the Turkish Army, supported by a large number of Azerbaijani auxiliaries, advanced on Baku. Despite the apparent strategic value of Baku, it was by September 1918 no longer crucial to the Allied war effort. The German offensive on the Western front had been repulsed and with the arrival of reinforcements from the United States, Germany and the Central Powers could not hold out indefinitely. In Baku itself however there were no illusions of victory. The Turks remained outside the city whilst their Azerbaijani auxiliaries terrorised the civilian population.

After a long stalemate and stand-off, on 1 November, Malleson's force finally pushed the German–Austro-Hungarian force out of Merv. The ejection of the Bolsheviks from southern Turkmenistan combined with the Allied successes on the Western Front and capitulation of the Ottoman Empire the day before, effectively eliminated any real danger of an invasion of Afghanistan and India from the western Caspian.

The short lived and minor Anglo–Indian campaign in Central Asia is largely forgotten today, however it was during the British occupation of Baku that an event occurred which would shape Anglo–Russian relations for decades to come, namely the execution of the so called '26 Commissars'.

On 15 September, a party of Bolshevik Commissars arrived at Krasnovodsk having fled across the Caspian from Baku before its capture by a combined Ottoman–Azerbaijani force. Immediately upon arrival the Commissars were arrested by White Russian Cossacks who, aware of the importance of their prisoners, sent a message to the Ashkhabad Committee some 350 kilometres away, asking what should be done with the captives. Three days later a meeting was held to decide their fate. The only British representative present at the meeting was Captain Reginald Teague-Jones, an Indian Army intelligence officer and Malleson's liaison with the Committee. Fyodor Funtikov, the Socialist Revolutionary leader of the Committee, wanted the Commissars shot outright and stated as much. On the night of 20 September, the 26 Commissars were put onto a train, taken into the desert and shot, nine others also taken prisoner at Krasnovodsk were not executed although it is not known why.

The Bolshevik version of events is predictably quite different to Malleson's in that it places the blame for the executions solely on the British. According to the Soviet version, the Commissars were to be put on trial in Baku, but the city fell before any of these proceedings could take place and on British orders the doomed men were shipped across the Caspian to the White Russian-held city of Krasnovodsk, where they were executed at the order of British General Malleson. Malleson's own account was that he did not become aware of the capture of the Red Commissars until three days after their arrest at Krasnovodsk, but immediately saw the potential for their use in a prisoner exchange. Malleson states he made a request to the Committee that he take responsibility for the Commissars and have them shipped to India where a camp was being built to house Bolshevik prisoners captured in Central Asia.

The day after the meeting Teague-Jones, a fluent Russian speaker, stated that he went to see Funtikov where he learned that the Committee had decided to shoot the prisoners (Jones claimed that he had left the meeting before any such decision had been made). He immediately cabled Malleson, who in turn cabled the Committee representative only to discover that the Commissars had already been shot. The executions did not become public knowledge until March 1919 when a story was run in a Baku newspaper containing an interview with Funtikov, then imprisoned by the Bolsheviks at Ashkhabad. Funtikov disavowed all responsibility and laid blame squarely on the British, stating that Teague-Jones had pressured him into ordering the executions and that the 'British officer' had been pleased when news was received that the orders had been carried out. Funtikov also claimed that Teague-Jones had agreed to conspire to cover up the crime. Imprisoned

174. Captain Francis Lord, MC, MM, AIF attached Dunsterforce, on the lookout for Ottoman troops from an Armenian defensive position near Baku, September 1918. (AWM G00803)

and himself facing execution, Funtikov's claims have more than a whiff of desperation about them and were likely an attempt to indemnify his own prominent role in the executions.

Soon after the news of the executions became public, Teague-Jones changed his name to 'Miller' and went on to work with the British Military Mission to White Russian General Denikin in South Russia. A year after the executions the Commissars' bodies where exhumed and cremated at a memorial service at Baku. A famous Russian artwork of the execution depicts a British officer standing as witness to the shootings even though there were none within many miles of the scene.

The Commissars became martyrs for the Bolshevik cause and prime fodder for the propaganda machine. Factories and streets were named after the victims, statues erected in their honour and in Baku the anniversary of their executions was commemorated every year. Since the fall of the Soviet Union in the early 1990s the Azerbaijanis have been less jubilant in commemoration of Soviet rule and in early 2009 the '26 Commissars' memorial in central Baku and its eternal flame (which had been extinguished) was demolished.

After the second 'Bolshevik' revolution of November 1917, the Imperial Russian Army which had faced Ottoman forces in the south Caucasus was gradually recalled from the Russian frontier, leaving the Turks to occupy the oil-rich wells along the south-eastern coast of the Caspian Sea. The British government believed that the Georgians and Armenians, if properly equipped, trained, and bolstered by British troops, could hold the Turks at bay and deny to the enemy the oilfields of Baku on the Caspian's western shore.

To achieve this objective a small force of officers recruited from across the British Commonwealth was detached for service under Major General Lionel Charles Dunsterville, CB, CSI, Indian Army. Dubbed 'Dunsterforce', the detachment was strongly Commonwealth in composition. Dunsterville wrote of them:

> These officers and N.C.O.s were chosen from all the units in the various theatres of the war, from France, Salonika, Egypt and Mesopotamia. They were chiefly from the Canadian, Australian, New Zealand and South African contingents. All were chosen for special ability, and all were men who had already

distinguished themselves in the field. It is cretain that a finer body of men have never been brought together, and the command was one of which any man might be proud.[9]

Dunsterforce set out from Baghdad on 27 January 1918 in a caravan of Ford motor cars across northern Persia to the town of Enzeli, intending to continue on to the southern Caspian coast and thence to Baku and Tiflis in modern day Azerbaijan and Georgia. Dunsterville was tasked to assess the suitability of the overland route and the martial qualities of the local troops. In the end Dunsterville only got as far as Enzeli before being turned around by the local Bolshevik administration. Dunsterville returned to Hamadan in North Persia to await arrival of reinforcements of experienced officers from across the British Empire who had volunteered for 'a hazardous enterprise in a foreign theatre of war.' The officers were required to have 'the spirit of adventure, undoubted courage, and ability to quickly estimate difficult situations. They must be of strong character, adventurous spirit, especially good stamina, capable of organising, training and eventually leading, irregular troops.'[10]

With the assistance of 1,200 White Russian Cossacks, remnants of the Imperial Army scattered across Russia's southern frontier, the Bolshevik council was forced from Enzeli and the town occupied by Dunsterforce in late June 1918. Dunsterville quickly seized the opportunity to cross the Caspian and establish the force at Baku.

The following month, Dunsterforce was further strengthened by the arrival of support (9th Royal Warwickshire Regiment, 7th Gloucestershire Regiment, 9th Worcestershire Regiment, 7th North Staffordshire Regiment, 39th Company, MGC) which had seen service during the Gallipoli and Mesopotamian campaigns. By late August 1918 the strength of Dunsterforce at Baku had risen to 1,200, including a number of volunteer officers and NCOs from Australia, Canada, New Zealand and South Africa.

British and Commonwealth troops could not defend Baku alone, however, the situation becoming more precarious when the Armenian garrison were discovered to be incapable of contributing to the defence of the city. On 14 September, a Turkish–Azerbaijani force of 14,000 troops attacked simultaneously from several points along the line, sending the Armenian troops fleeing from their trenches in the hills above Baku. It was left to soldiers of the 39th Brigade to do all they could to keep the Turks from the docks for as long as possible to allow an evacuation. After holding out for 14 long hours and sustaining a number of casualties the British troops withdrew from the frontline and hurriedly embarked on an assortment of ships to escape across the Caspian to Enzeli on the night of 14/15 September. The Austin and Ford cars of the original Dunsterforce convoy were disabled and pushed off the pier into the Caspian whilst two damaged Martinsyde Scout aircraft that had accompanied Dunsterville were also rendered inoperable. Total casualties suffered by Dunsterforce up to the evacuation of Baku were 71 killed, 21 died of wounds, 64 wounded and 24 missing.

The Turkish advance halted after the capture of Baku as the Ottoman commander consolidated his forces. He may as well not have bothered, as by 2 October 1918 General Allenby had pushed from northern Palestine into Damascus and by the end of the month Turkey had surrendered.

A lesser-known participant in the Dunsterforce operations was a small Royal Navy detachment under the command of Commodore David Norris, RN, who would be made Companion of the Order of the Bath (CB) for his services in the Caspian, which arrived at Enzeli on 6 August and was present at Baku from 26 August until the final evacuation.

Although no other naval parties made it as far north as Baku, a further detachment of seamen and marines under Major P.W. Malcolm, RMLI, and Lieutenant Commander F.G. Charsley, RN, were kept busy at Enzeli during the final months of 1918 fitting out requisitioned Russian freighters

9   Dunsterville, L.C., *The Adventures of Dunsterforce* (London: Edward Arnold, 1920), p.9.
10   MacLaren, *Canadians in Russia 1918–19*, p.9.

SS *Kruger* and SS *Kursk* with naval guns which had been brought overland from Baghdad. SS *Kursk* was crewed by Royal Navy seamen and designated an unarmed depot ship, whilst *Kruger* was fitted out with five 4 inch guns as an armed flagship for Commodore Norris with Captain Basil George Washington, RN (who would would be awarded the CB for services in the Caspian), a lateral descendent of the first president of the United States, as ship's captain.

On 8 October 1918, the flotilla was further strengthened with the commissioning of the Royal Marine-crewed SS *Venture* (also known as *Ventuir*, 3 x 4 inch guns). The following day a number of seamen and marines under Commander Kenneth Guy, RN, sailed for Krasnovodsk on the eastern shore of the Caspian to commission oil tanker SS *Emile Nobel* (3 x 6 inch, 1 x 4.7 inch guns), followed in November by HM Ships *Bibi Abat* (3 x 4 inch guns), *Zoroaster* (2 x 4 inch guns) and *Asia* (4 x 4 inch guns).

The following day, Commodore Norris was badly injured in an accident and had to be hospitalised, command of the flotilla being

175. Commodore David Norris, CB, RN, Commanding RN Caspian Flotilla and Major General Lionel Dunsterville, CB, CSI, commanding 'Dunsterforce'. (AWM H12236)

assumed by Captain Washington until Norris was well enough to return to duty on 5 February 1919.

A much larger 'Centro-Caspian Naval Flotilla' of converted merchant ships was also operating in the Caspian out of Baku but was strictly a White Russian force, although some Royal Navy officers and crews served on these ships. The crews were mainly Russian with a sprinkling of Royal Navy officers, ratings and Royal Marines to crew the wireless sets and operate deck guns. It was not until 2 March 1919 that Commodore Norris, fed up with the inefficiency and indecision of the White Russian leadership, commandeered the flotilla in its entirety from the Centro-Caspian government and absorbed the ships into the Royal Navy Caspian Flotilla, christening the ships 'HMS' – 'His Majesty's Ships' and began flying the white ensign of the Royal Navy.

After the Armistice in November 1918 and withdrawal of Turkish troops from the western Caspian, Captain Washington led a convoy of 12 ships from Enzeli to the flotilla's new base at Baku. Arriving at the same time at Batum on the Black Sea were soldiers of the 'British Army of the Balkans and the Black Sea', an army of occupation tasked with occupying and maintaining order in areas which had been occupied by the Bulgars and Turks. The 27th (Indian) Division was assigned to the Caucasus region, some Gurkhas and Indian troops being despatched over the railway from Batum to Baku.

The Royal Navy Caspian Flotilla saw its first engagement with the Bolsheviks on 8 December 1918 when HMS *Zoroaster* (Lieutenant Commander Frederick Charsley, RN) and HMS *Alla Verdi* were fired on by three Bolshevik gunboats. Despite the falling snow obscuring visibility, the enemy gunners managed to find their target: *Zoroaster* was struck three times by enemy shells causing several shrapnel casualties amongst the naval and marine crew. Return fire from *Zoroaster* and *Alla Verdi* set one of the enemy gunboats on fire, but it escaped apparently only slightly damaged. Over 300 shells were fired by the enemy during the engagement, for which ship's captain of *Zoroaster*, Lieutenant Commander Frederick Charsley, RN, was awarded the DSO.

176. Royal Navy 40 foot Thornycroft Coastal Motor Boat operating on the Caspian Sea, 1919. (IWM Q51671)

On 29 December HM Ships *Venture* (Lieutenant Commander Richard Harrison, RN), *Slava* (Lieutenant George Robertson, RNR), *Bibi Abat* and *Asia* (Lieutenant Alexander Wilson, RN) took part in the bombardment of the Bolshevik base at Star-Tchernaya, leaving the town burning in their wake for which Robertson was awarded the DSC.

In January 1919, the Royal Navy barracks at Baku were formally commissioned by Commander Gerald Parnell, RN, and the following month the base at Enzeli was closed down in favour of establishing an advanced base further north at Petrovsk, where Commodore Norris and garrison commander Major Malcolm, RMLI, arrived on 21 January. It was imperative to blockade the Red fleet in the northern Caspian as it was known that the enemy flotilla included at least four submarines which could not effectively operate in the shallow waters south of Astrakhan. By keeping the submarines penned in the northern Caspian and at Fort Alexandrovsk to the east, they could not be deployed effectively.

Located 200 miles north of Baku, Petrovsk (modern day Makhachkala, Dagestan) was vulnerable to attack: preparations were made to strengthen the Royal Marine garrison with two 6 inch quick-firing guns which had been dismounted from a monitor in Mudros harbour and sent across the Black Sea to Batum, thence by rail to Baku and finally by ship to Petrovsk where they were dragged 100 feet up a snow-covered hill by means of an RAF truck and mule train. Mounted into concrete emplacements, the guns were test-fired as soon as the concrete was dry. Although the defence of Petrovsk itself fell to a detachment of Gurkhas, the naval 6 inch guns were crewed by Royal Marines from HMS *Alla Verdi*.

In addition to an advanced base from which Russian merchant ships could be fitted out for service with the Royal Navy flotilla, Chechen Island near Petrovsk was also established in January 1919 as the base of No. 221 Squadron, RAF who were joined in March by one flight of No. 266 Squadron (Wing Commander W. Bowhill, RAF) and later by a White Russian squadron equipped with Spad and Nieuport fighters. Several aircraft from No. 266 Squadron also flew from the seaplane carrier (converted merchantman) HMS *Orlionoch*, and latterly HMS *A. Yousanoff*, (each equipped to carry two seaplanes) captained by Lieutenant William Chilton, DSC Bar, RN, which had been equipped with two 4 inch guns as defence against prowling enemy torpedo boats.

In the spring further reinforcements arrived in the form of Thornycroft Coastal Motor Boats (CMBs) dispatched to the Caspian under Commander Eric Robinson, VC, RN, who had been awarded the VC for gallantry destroying a Turkish battery ashore during the Dardanelles campaign

An advance party of No. 266 Squadron had sailed from Lemnos in early February on board the ferry *Princess Ena* through the Dardanelles to Batum and then by train to Baku via Tiflis accompanying four CMBs on the journey. The advance party continued on to Petrovsk where they supervised construction of a seaplane jetty and crane and the conversion of existing buildings into seaplane hangars. The main body of 266 Squadron with 10 Short 184s sailed on HMS *Engadine* from Mudros on 18 February, arriving at Petrovsk on 12 March.

During test flights of the Short 184s, problems were encountered with the buoyancy of the seaplane floats due to the lack of salinity in the freshwater Caspian Sea. Special fine-pitch propellers had to be urgently sent from Malta to give the Maori III engines the extra torque required for take-off. Test flights continued without incident until 25 April when Short 184 (N9081) crashed on take-off due to a sudden gust of wind. The damaged aircraft was towed back to the jetty and hoisted ashore where repairs were commenced.

On 19 April, HMS *Asia* fought a long range engagement with two enemy torpedo boat destroyers (TBDs) which ended without result. Six days later HMS *Zoroaster* and HMS *Venture* exchanged fire with the same TBDs but the duel once again ended inconclusively.

In response to increasingly aggressive moves towards Petrovsk by the enemy, No. 221 Squadron launched their first mission against the Bolshevik flotilla base at Astrakhan on 21 April, although despite all the DH9s dropping all their bombs and expending most of their machine gun ammunition, little actual damage was done.

Strikes by workers at the Baku shipyards delayed work and it was not until 10 May that HMS *A. Yousanoff* was fitted out and ready for operations. Lieutenant (later Air Vice Marshall) Christopher Bilney, RAF, described the rather rudimentary vessel:

> By clearing the fore deck and rigging a derrick to the foremast we were able to stow two seaplanes side by side with their wings folded. On the poop deck we had a 4 inch gun, but as it was No.1 Mk.1 of its particular series and built in 1898 I am very glad we never had to fire it.[11]

On 12 May, HMS *A. Yousanoff* finally embarked Short 184s *N9080* and *N9082* and sailed for Petrovsk. The same day Captain J.A. Sadler with Observer 2nd Lieutenant F. Kingham flew 266 Squadron's first operational mission, a 3.5 hour bombing and reconnaissance flight, although no suitable targets were encountered.

On 15 May, tragedy struck 221 Squadron when a DH9 flown by Lieutenant Bertram Turner, with Observer 2nd Lieutenant George Jemmeson, one of a formation of four aircraft making a routine flight from the aerodrome at Petrovsk to Chechen Island, crashed on landing and burst into flames, killing both pilot and observer.

On 18 May, a flight of DH9As from 221 Squadron flew a raid over Alexandrovsk to bomb enemy shipping in the harbour. All the bombs fell wide and no hits were observed although one aircraft was struck by enemy machine gun fire but was able to return to Petrovsk.

In early May, word was received that the Bolsheviks intended to occupy and establish a forward base at Fort Alexandrovsk much in the manner that the British had done at Petrovsk. The Bolsheviks were in desperate need of oil and the establishment of a base at Fort Alexandrovsk, directly across the Caspian from Petrovsk and Baku, posed a significant threat to the British-held oilfields on the Baku Peninsula. In response, Commodore Norris decided to carry out a reconnaissance in force against Fort Alexandrovsk taking with him HM Ships *Kruger, Asia, Emile Nobel* (Commander Kenneth Guy, RN), *Sergie* (converted as a CMB carrier with 1 x 12 pdr and 1 x AA pom-pom) and seaplane carrier HMS *A. Yousanoff*. Leaving Baku and Petrovsk on 14 May, the force rendezvoused at Kulaly Island the following day just as a gale began blowing from the south-east making the launch of CMBs and seaplanes impossible. Norris decided instead to steam directly for Alexandrovsk with the CMBs and seaplanes still on board.

Soon after daylight on 16 May, a number of fishing boats were sighted and later a convoy of three steamers towing two large barges with TBDs acting as escort. HMS *Emile Nobel* opened long range fire on the enemy convoy with its three 6 inch guns, forcing the enemy steamers to abandon the barges and flee towards Alexandrovsk, pursued by the British flotilla. The enemy steamers disappeared on entering a thick fog, and rather than risk his ships further, Norris ordered the flotilla to make its way back to the abandoned barges, both of which were sunk and their crews taken prisoner.

---

11   IWM: 10790 DS/MISC/87, Private Papers, Air Vice Marshall C.N.H. Bilney.

The prisoners revealed that Alexandrovsk had been occupied by a large Bolshevik force and the bulk of the enemy fleet was berthed there making preparations to attack Petrovsk. The wind continued to limit operations on 17 May and the seaplanes could not launch. An attempt to launch *N9080* from HMS *A. Yousanoff* was abandoned when the aircraft was damaged against the side of the ship in the rolling sea. *N9082* was launched successfully but was unable to take off in the swell and was damaged whilst being hoisted back on board. Rendered ineffective through damage to its aircraft, Norris ordered *A. Yousanoff* to return to Petrovsk under escort of HMS *Emile Nobel*, which was in need of refuelling. On arrival at Petrovsk, *N9082* was put ashore and *N9079* taken on board. The slight damage to *N9080* was repaired on the spot and both seaplanes were on board HMS *A. Yousanoff* when it sailed to the rendezvous with HMS *Sergie*, 20 miles south of Chechen Island, in preparation for the raid on Fort Alexandrovsk. Commodore Norris had issued orders to *Sergie* to break away from the flotilla to rendezvous with *A. Yousanoff* the following day and make preparations to launch CMBs and seaplanes.

On 20 May, 2nd Lieutenant Howard Thompson with Observer Lieutenant Frank Bicknell flew the first of several bombing missions over Alexandrovsk in *N9080*, experiencing heavy anti-aircraft fire over the harbour. Second Lieutenant Robert Morrison with 2nd Lieutenant Henry Pratt took off in *N9079* to fly a second bombing mission but the engine failed whilst in a climbing turn at only 200 feet. The aircraft crashed into the sea but both men escaped unhurt and were able to scramble free, clinging to the wreckage until rescued.

Captain John Sadler with Observer 2nd Lieutenant Frank Kingham were the next to attempt a takeoff in *N9080* but had to return to *A. Yousanoff* due to condensation in the petrol tank which caused the engine to sputter intermittently. At 0415 the following day, Sadler and Kingham made another attempt to fly a bombing mission over Alexandrovsk but encountered further mechanical problems, and had to return to the seaplane carrier where the mechanics began work stripping, cleaning and reassembling the carburettors, a job that took eleven hours. With one aircraft damaged and another unserviceable, ship's captain Lieutenant William Chilton, RNR, was forced to sit out the attack in frustration. By the time *N9080's* engine had been reassembled, Commodore Norris would have already led the flotilla in the raid on Alexandrovsk harbour and returned to the open sea.

On the morning of 21 May 1919, the flotilla (less HMS *A. Yousanoff* and HMS *Sergie*) was bolstered by the arrival of HMS *Venture* and HMS *Windsor Castle* and the return of HMS *Emile Nobel*. At 1100, an enemy TBD and three smaller craft were sighted, the TBD opening fire on the flotilla before fleeing for the protection of the harbour as Norris raised full steam in an attempt to cut the enemy vessels off. An hour later both sides were exchanging ranging shots with *Venture* straddled, although not struck, by falling enemy shells. At 1213, Norris issued the order to all ships to open fire.

The third salvo fired by *Emile Nobel* struck a large armed barge which caught fire and sank, its crew taken off by small launches. During the next 30 minutes, *Emile Nobel* and *Venture* both scored hits on the enemy vessel *Kaspy* which ran aground amongst the fishing fleet.

The engagement was not all one sided, however, and by 1300 enemy fire was becoming increasingly accurate and heavy. HMS *Asia* was repeatedly straddled without being hit, but at 1257 a shell struck *Emile Nobel* in the engine room killing four sailors and a Royal Marine Bugler, and wounding seven others. *Emile Nobel's* engines were damaged but she was able to maintain speed and follow the flotilla into the harbour and continue to engage the enemy.

At 1303, the flotilla changed formation to single line with HMS *Kruger* in the lead followed by HM Ships *Venture, Asia, Windsor Castle* and *Emile Nobel*. *Kruger* could only bring two 4 inch guns to bear from which over 100 rounds were fired, both guns controlled by Commodore Norris' secretary, Paymaster Lieutenant Herbert Pertwee, RN, for which Pertwee was awarded the DSO.

The enemy 75 mm battery on the cliffs above the harbour resumed fire as the flotilla passed beneath, hitting HMS *Kruger* on the port side amidships before being silenced by fire from *Kruger's* 4 inch and a broadside of all four 4 inch guns on board HMS *Asia*. Trapped by the British ships entering the

177. HMS *Emile Nobel*, RN Caspian Flotilla, 1918–19. (IWM Q55583)

harbour the enemy vessels took refuge amongst the burning barges and fishing fleet but were one by one located and fire opened on them. The badly damaged Soviet vessel *Kaspy* was aground and on fire but gallantly continued to engage the British flotilla with a single gun still in action.

With visibility in the harbour obscured by smoke and the damaged HMS *Emile Nobel* in tow, Norris decided to end the raid and ordered the flotilla to leave Alexandrovsk harbour and make preparations to treat the wounded. The final shots of the raid were fired by the damaged *Emile Nobel*, the last ship to leave the harbour, firing her aft 4.7 inch as she went. At 1500, whilst still in sight of Alexandrovsk harbour, a large explosion was heard, followed some minutes later by two smaller explosions. At 1700 the flotilla halted to allow Surgeon Lieutenant Alan Cockayne, RN, to transfer from HMS *Zoroaster* to *Emile Nobel* to treat the wounded.

Whilst the raid had been underway, repairs had been ongoing on HMS *A. Yousanoff*'s single remaining seaplane, and at 1515 Sadler and Kingham once again took off in *N9080* to bomb and strafe the harbour from 3,000 feet, returning to *A. Yousanoff* at 1755. At 0530 the following morning, 22 May, Lieutenant Robert Morrison and Observer 2nd Lieutenant Henry Pratt flew the first of five raids on Alexandrovsk harbour flown that day in the same aircraft with alternating crews. Morrison and Pratt bombed and strafed the harbour without result and on return to *Yousanoff* to refuel and rearm, handed the seaplane over to Lieutenant Howard Thompson and Observer Lieutenant Frank Bicknell who flew the second mission of the day, scoring a direct hit on Finn Class destroyer *Muskvityanise*.

On the return of Thompson and Bicknell at 1045, Sadler and Kingham took off for the third raid, dropping a 230 lb bomb between a destroyer and Red vessel *Kaspy*. Coming down to 2,500 feet, Sadler dropped his four 16 lb bombs on the fishing fleet whilst Kingham blazed away with the observer's machine gun.

On their return to HMS *A. Yousanoff* it was the turn of Morrison and Pratt to fly their second mission of the day, taking off at 1445, followed by Thompson and Bicknell on the fifth and final raid of the day at 1630. Both Morrison and Thompson missed with their bombs and returned to *A. Yousanoff* where at 1800 Sadler and Kingham made an attempt to fly a sixth mission for the day, until fog forced their return to the seaplane carrier shortly after taking off.

The following officers' decorations were awarded for the action at Fort Alexandrovsk:

Distinguished Service Order (DSO):
      Commander K. A. F. Guy, RN (HMS *Emile Nobel*)
      Commander R. Harrison, RNR (HMS *Venture*)
      Captain B. G. Washington, RN (HMS *Windsor Castle*)

Lieutenant A.G.B. Wilson, RN (HMS *Asia*)
Distinguished Service Cross 2nd Bar (DSC):
    Lieutenant W.B. Chilton, DSC Bar, RNR (HMS *A. Yousanoff*)
Distinguished Service Cross Bar:
    Lieutenant R.M. Taylor, DSC, RN (HMS *Emile Nobel*)
Distinguished Service Cross:
    Surgeon Lieutenant A.A. Cockayne, RN (Medical Officer)
    Engineer Lieutenant T. Gardner, RN (HMS *Emile Nobel*)
    Lieutenant A.B. Lee, RNR (HMS *Venture*)
    Mate A. Maguire, RN (HMS *Asia*)
Distinguished Flying Cross (DFC):
    Lieutenant F.R. Bicknell, RAF (HMS *A. Yousanoff*)
    2nd Lieutenant H.G. Thompson, RAF (HMS *A. Yousanoff*)

After a night of heavy fog, HMS *Kruger* and HMS *Venture* were forced to withdraw further east after coming under accurate fire from two enemy destroyers. Sadler and Kingham were sent up to harass the enemy ships but were unable to locate the destroyers due to an increasingly heavy mist. Raiding Alexandrovsk harbour instead, they bombed a large 'Volga' barge armed with a 6 inch gun.

Unable to locate HMS *A. Yousanoff* in the mist, Sadler landed on the edge of the fog and taxied eastwards for an hour and a half hoping to sight land. A heavy swell developed during the night and at 2330 the tailplane was wrenched off and the aircraft began to sink. Both Sadler and Kingham were forced to cling to the wreckage until they were spotted and picked up by HMS *Asia* at 1830 the following day, after 20 hours in the water.

On 28 May, Captain Washington led HM Ships *Windsor Castle*, *Venture*, *Slava*, *Bibi Abat*, *Sergie*, *Edinburgh Castle* (formerly *Soyous*, CMB carrier, 1 x 12 pdr) and *A. Yousanoff* on a close reconnaissance of Fort Alexandrovsk to assess damage done during the raid a week earlier, and to ascertain enemy strength in the harbour. The CMB squadron was launched from *Edinburgh Castle* and *Sergie* and proceeded up the harbour, torpedoing a large barge and submarine depot ship on their way. On arrival in the harbour a white flag was raised and a delegation put out in a motor launch to meet with Commander Robinson in the lead CMB. The delegation of civilian merchant sailors, informed Robinson that the Bolsheviks had left Alexandrovsk, abandoning their plans to establish a naval base, taking with them several damaged ships and two submarines. Further investigation of the harbour revealed that during the raid and subsequent air attacks the British flotilla had sunk one gun barge armed with two 6 inch guns, a destroyer (the *Muskvityanise*) an armed minelayer, a submarine depot ship, an ammunition carrier and four motor boats as well as a number of other ships damaged.

HMS *A. Yousanoff*'s seaplanes flew four sorties during 29 May, bombing and strafing the mouth of the Volga where the barges and tugs which had escaped Alexandrovsk harbour on 21 May had congregated.

On 16 June, a flight of four No. 221 Squadron DH9As took off from Petrovsk to bomb Astrakhan docks. Two barges carrying flying boats were sighted, bombed and set on fire. Over Astrakhan city the flight was attacked by two Red Air Force Nieuport 17s flown by Soviet naval pilots D.N. Shchekin and A.P. Korotov. Both pilots had only recently completed training at Moscow Flight School before posting to 47th Reconnaissance Detachment at Astrakhan equipped with three Nieuport 17s, two Nieuport 25s and a handful of Sopwith Strutters. Attacking from head-on, machine gun fire from Shchekin's Nieuport struck the engine of a DH9A flown by 2nd Lieutenant Anthony Mantle with Observer 2nd Lieutenant H. Ingram, puncturing the radiator and forcing Mantle to make an emergency landing in a field 20 miles inland from Astrakhan. The two men set fire to the aircraft before fleeing the scene but were soon after captured by Red cavalry and held as prisoners of war in Moscow until their release in a prisoner exchange a year later.

178. View of the three 6 inch guns mounted on the deck of HMS *Emile Nobel*. (IWM Q51666)

In retaliation for the shooting down of Mantle and Ingram, 221 Squadron attacked the Red airfield at Astrakhan on 19 June. Three aircraft were destroyed on the ground and another forced to crash land. A further squadron-strength attack on Astrakhan was launched on 27 June, eight DH9As dropping 2.5 tonnes of bombs on enemy shipping and the aerodrome: a number of vessels and aircraft were damaged.

On 28 June, Short 184 seaplane *N9082* with crew Thompson and Bicknell launched from HMS *A. Yousanoff* which had returned to station off Chechen Island. Thompson was unable to get the aircraft airborne and released a 112 lb bomb to lighten the load. The bomb detonated, blowing the seaplane in half but miraculously neither crew member was injured, although both were badly shaken.

No. 221 Squadron continued bombing operations over the Caspian, Astrakhan and Alexandrovsk throughout July. During one mission to bomb enemy shipping a DH9A flying from Chechen Island was hit by anti-aircraft fire and force landed in friendly territory. The aircraft was too badly damaged to be repaired and was destroyed on the spot.

In mid July HMS *A. Youssanoff*'s engines had deteriorated to the point where she could no longer be used for seaplane operations, and its two Short 184s and guns were moved to HMS *Orlionoch*. On the morning of 24 July, Sadler with Observer Lieutenant Tarton-Jones in Short 182 *N9078* accompanied by Lieutenants McCughey and Wake in *N9081*, made an attack on a Bolshevik armed tugboat near the mouth of the Volga from an altitude of 800 feet. The tug returned fire with a machine gun, one shot cutting the main oil line on Sadler's aircraft causing the engine to belch thick black smoke before completely seizing 20 minutes later. Sadler managed to put the aircraft down safely as McCughey flew back to *Orlionoch* to organise a rescue by CMBs *51* and *60*, which towed the stricken aircraft back to *Orlionoch* for repair. After their heavy losses on 21 May, the Bolshevik Caspian Fleet would never again pose a serious threat against Baku or Petrovsk and by the time the enemy flotilla had undertaken reorganisation and repair, the British flotilla was already being decommissioned, the first vessels being handed over to White Russian command on 28 July 1919.

On 8 August, the Royal Navy Caspian Flotilla fought its last engagement when HMS *Bibi Abat* and *Orlionoch* attacked the town of Ashurada in the south-east corner of the Caspian on the north Persia coast. In a highly successful operation four ships, six barges and 200 prisoners were captured. Able Seaman Albert Wade of *Orlionoch* and Leading Seaman Alfred Harris of *Bibi Abat* were both awarded the Meritorious Service Medal for salvaging enemy barges and vessels which had been partially scuttled by the fleeing enemy.

179. Airco DH9 of 221 Squadron, RAF at Petrovsk, winter 1919. (IWM Q60270)

On 2 September 1919, the last members of the Royal Navy Caspian Flotilla left Petrovsk for Novorossiysk on the Black Sea, ending the operations of the Royal Navy on the Caspian Sea, although small numbers of naval personnel remained in the region on various duties.

On 27 April 1920, the Baku provisional government received an ultimatum from Soviet agents that if power was not handed over to local Bolsheviks the city would be invaded and occupied by Red troops. The provisional parliament refused and the same night Red Army troops entered Baku. This made for an embarrassing situation when five officers and 26 ratings of the Royal Navy from HMS *Emperor of India* under Commander Brian Austin Fraser, RN, tasked with taking charge and repair of the remnants of the White Russian Caspian Fleet at Enzeli, stepped off the train at Baku and straight into the hands of the Bolsheviks. One of the party, Able Seaman Stan Smith wrote of his capture:

Our job was to build up fortification in case the Bolsheviks beat Denikin's men and advanced on Persia. We had to transfer guns from ships left by the Royal Navy and set up seashore fortifications. We were also supposed to repair ships for Denikin's men but a boat arrived with a message that these ships were still in Baku and in such a state they couldn't be moved to Enzeli. So we loaded up our stores and went to Baku where the ships were in a really sorry state of repair. I don't think the guns had been moved since the Navy left. They hadn't been elevated and trained and were thick with rust.

I was part of the team which tackled guns while other men worked on the engines and other machinery. I was partnered off with a chap called Dart to repair a recoil cylinder on one of the guns when – crunch – the Bolsheviks entered the town … I was quietly working away when 'bang', I knew no more. I had been fairly effectively bashed over the head and when I woke up I was trussed up like a chicken with both hands behind my back and my feet lashed tightly together … We were roped together and marched off to the prison of Byrloft Chyrma. It was a humiliating experience because there were jeering crowds on either side of us, giving every impression that they had won a great victory.

On arrival at the prison we were split into two groups and placed in two adjoining cells with bare walls, no furniture and an earth floor, each cell measured about sixteen foot square at the most and into our cell sixteen men were crammed. We endured our first night as prisoners of war huddled together for warmth as there were no blankets or bedding of any kind … When the food came we were ready to eat anything.

It was a bowl of soup which was more like dish water-thin and absolutely tasteless – and half a round of black bread. This was to be our ration for the first twenty-four hours.[12]

The conditions of imprisonment were harsh. There was little food and the men put to work unloading trains at the railyard. Three months into the gruelling routine, on 17th July 1920, Able Seaman Eugene Marsh committed suicide. His body was later interned in Corfu British Cemetery (CWGC) although the year of burial and journey of his remains from Baku to Greece is not clear. After weeks of negotiation, on 7 November the party were released and evacuated to England, arriving at Portsmouth on 1st December 1920. The other prisoners all contributed to the purchase of a ceremonial sword for Commander Fraser which he used for his entire career, including service as an Admiral during the Second World War. It is no small irony that 23 years after his imprisonment by the Bolsheviks, Fraser was awarded the Soviet Order of Suvarov by Stalin for service in the sinking of German battleship *Scharnhorst* in December 1943.

By mid 1920 the Bolsheviks controlled the entire northern Caspian leaving the British garrison at Enzeli in northern Persia in a precarious position. On 18 May the Bolshevik Caspian Fleet encircled the 500 strong British–Indian force at Enzeli and landed troops. The British were forced to surrender, the Bolshevik commander allowing them to pass through to the lines of the British North Persia Force on condition that all ships and heavy equipment were abandoned. The Bolshevik commander was none other than Commissar F.F. Raskolnikov, the same man who had been captured by the British in the Baltic in 1919, held hostage, released in a prisoner exchange and later given command of the Bolshevik Caspian Fleet. The occupation of Enzeli was the first occasion that the Bolsheviks annexed territory that had not previously been part of the Imperial Russian Empire, and was the first town to be absorbed into the new Soviet Union.

---

12   Max Arthur, *The True Glory: The Royal Navy 1914–39: A Narrative History* (Coronet Books, 1996), pp.164–166.

18

Spies and Secret Agents: November 1917–August 1918

Britain had sent forces to support the Imperial Russian government as early as February 1915 when the Admiralty despatched battleship HMS *Jupiter* to serve as an icebreaker at Russia's northern sea port of Archangel ('Arkhangelsk') in the White Sea as the Tsar's own vessels had broken down. If the northern sea lane through the White Sea was not freed of ice, vital war supplies could not be landed at Archangel for despatch to the Eastern Front, leaving the Imperial Russian Army critically short of arms and equipment.

During the first years of the war both Britain and France established Military Missions in Russia to aid and train the Tsar's Forces to better wage war against Germany, using modern tactics and equipment and lessons learned on the Western Front. Along with the British Military Mission came several intelligence officers tasked with appraising German strength and troop movements on the Eastern Front. After the Bolshevik Revolution of November 1917, most of these officers become members of the British Secret Intelligence Service (SIS) network operating in Russia.

By mid 1918 the key British agents operating in Moscow and Petrograd were Robert Bruce Lockhart, Francis Cromie, Sidney Reilly, George Hill, Stephen Alley, Ernest Boyce, Denys Garstin and William Hicks. Alley had been head of SIS in Russia until 1918 when he was succeeded by Commander Ernest Boyce, RNVR. After the November revolution, British SIS continued to engage in intelligence operations against the interests of Germany and the Central Powers although not specifically targeting the new Bolshevik government. British SIS would learn many lessons in the black arts of espionage, deception and subterfuge in Russia that would later prove extremely valuable during the dark days of the Second World War.

Lockhart joined the Consular Service in 1911 and had been posted to Russia the following year. His early years in Russia were mostly filled with nights at the opera and ballet, caviar, vodka and parties at the mansions of wealthy Russian aristocrat friends. Lockhart could count Prince Lvov and Alexander Kerensky (both future leaders of the Provisional Government prior to the Bolshevik coup) amongst his close friends.

Lockhart showed considerable aptitude for consular work and quickly rose through the ranks of the political service, and by 1915 he was Consul General at the British Embassy in Petrograd (St. Petersburg was renamed 'Petrograd' in 1914 due to the Germanic origin of the original name). Lockhart also maintained close associations with prominent personalities in Moscow which led to his receiving much vital information on the political situation in that city. After the November 1917 revolution his despatches to Whitehall were eagerly anticipated by the Foreign Office, as the British government was anxious for news of the attitude of the Bolsheviks towards the continuance of hostilities with the Central Powers on the Eastern Front.

Lockhart may have been an astute politician but he had a major weakness in his interactions with the fairer sex which had got him in no small amount of trouble. During his rubber plantation days in Malaya he had caused quite a stir by initiating a relationship with a ward of the Sultan. Whilst in Russia he had an affair with a French aristocrat for which he was reported to the Ambassador for 'immoral behaviour'. Despite his rapid rise through the consular ranks and promise as a possible future ambassador, Lockhart's career in the consular service looked somewhat bleak. Fortunately for the young diplomat, Ambassador Sir George Buchanan had taken a liking to his protégé and to save Lockhart from embarrassment sent him home to recuperate from 'poor health'. In the months leading up to the Bolshevik coup Lockhart found himself passing the time in London whilst events that would change the course of modern history were unfolding in Russia.

On 21 December 1917 Lockhart was invited to Number 10, Downing Street by Viscount Milner (soon to be Secretary of State for War before Winston Churchill) and introduced to Prime Minister Lloyd George, already familiar with Lockhart's reports on the internal situation in Russia before his recall. The two men conversed briefly before Lloyd George declared to other cabinet members present that Lockhart was being wasted in London and should be immediately returned to Russia.

Lockhart was accompanied at the meeting by Captain William L. Hicks (formerly of the British Military Mission and a fluent Russian speaker), Edward Burse (a businessman who had lived and worked in Moscow for several years) and Edward Phelan from the Ministry of Labour working under the cover of a 'Commercial Mission'. There is little doubt that when Lockhart returned to Russia, he too was working either directly or indirectly for British SIS.

180. Robert Bruce Lockhart, British Consul General in Petrograd and Moscow. (Public domain)

Lockhart arrived in Petrograd in February 1918 by which time Sir George Buchanan had already returned to Britain. Sir George had been opposed to the absolute rule of the Russian monarchy but had developed a close relationship with the Tsar. Sir George handed over the ambassadorship of the British Embassy to Consul General Francis Lindley before returning to England. With the Tsar deposed and Lenin suspicious of British motives and under pressure from the Kaiser not to negotiate with the Allies, there would be no further constructive dialogue between the two governments.

On 18 February the German Army resumed its advance eastwards into Russia through the Ukraine, in an attempt to force the Bolsheviks into a corner when negotiating the strict terms which the Germans intended to propose at the Brest-Litovsk talks the following month. There was a genuine fear that the Germans would advance on Petrograd, and the staff at the Allied embassies fled to the Finnish frontier to escape capture although the Germans seemed content to occupy most of western Ukraine only and the embassy staff eventually returned.

Captain Francis Cromie, DSO, RN, the handsome and decorated sailor who had commanded a flotilla of British submarines operating in the Baltic at the time of the Revolution, had no desire to be appointed Naval Attaché in Petrograd, however the absence of any other naval officers of suitable rank or experience made him the only suitable candidate. Cromie was in every sense a classic naval hero but he was no spy. In September 1915 he had successfully broken the German naval blockade of the Baltic by bringing submarine HMS *E.19* through the German minefields and patrols into the Gulf of Finland. Only a week later he sank a German destroyer and in November sank the light cruiser SMS *Undine*. The following month he almost single-handedly blockaded the German sea lanes to Sweden by sinking or capturing 10 steamers flying the Imperial German flag. Cromie was awarded the DSO in 1916 along with a swag of Russian and French decorations, the same year he was given command of the joint British and Russian submarine fleet in the Baltic. The small flotilla was tendered by the depot ship *Dvina* which had previously played a significant role in the 1905 Russian Revolution under the name *Pamiat Azova*.

Despite the upheaval in Russia following the March 1917 Revolution, the resulting abdication of the Tsar and the establishment of a Provisional Government under Alexander Kerensky, Cromie tried vainly to keep the submarine flotilla operational against German shipping in the Baltic. This was to prove an impossible task, however, as the Russian sailors were mutinous, spare parts were few and far between (the British sailors had to do all minor and major maintenance themselves) and food was becoming so scarce that bread was being used as currency in Petrograd.

Cromie was not one to be put off by such difficulties and in the spring of 1917 launched several successful patrols against German shipping. However these successes were an almost solely British enterprise as the Imperial Russian Navy had ceased to function. In the confusing times which followed the Revolution the Russian sailors were only too happy to sit it out and wait to see what eventuated.

Cromie eventually moved his fleet to Helsinki in an attempt to escape the unstable atmosphere of Kronstadt; in December he received orders to return to Britain but was instead appointed Naval Attaché, a post he did not relish. Cromie pleaded with Director of Naval Intelligence, Admiral Sir Reginald 'Blinker' Hall for a reprieve:

> This is the very billet I asked you to protect me from … a position I cannot afford when I have to support a family and my mother out of my pay. Therefore I earnestly ask you not to abandon me for ever to the backwaters of diplomacy … Please don't forget I am still a submarine officer.[1]

In his role as Naval Attaché Cromie was supplied by British SIS with hundreds of thousands of pounds for bribes and expenses. At one time Cromie had £1.5 million sterling hidden within the walls of the British Embassy but only £720 in his own personal bank account. The huge sum of cash was to be used to fund the scuttling of the Russian fleet at Kronstadt and the remaining submarines of the British flotilla, should they fall into the hands of the Germans. By 1918 the mothballed Russian fleet consisted of two battleships, several cruisers, a mine-laying cruiser, a submarine depot ship and several destroyers.

In March 1918, German cruisers attacked Tallinn, just 90 miles across the Gulf of Finland from Cromie's new base in Helsinki. The following month German troops began landing in southern Finland. The time had come for Cromie to scuttle the British submarine flotilla, which proved to be a much more difficult task than initially thought. The submarines were completely iced in and had to be inched out into deeper water before they could be scuttled. This meant the British sailors had to carry out the tedious task of manually breaking the surface ice for several hundred metres in order to reach water deep enough to make recovery of the submarines difficult.

Cromie ordered the Russian contingent of his small flotilla to follow suit and they too sank their submarines. The strange goings on in the Gulf of Finland had not escaped the attentions of the local population who flocked to the docks to see what they could loot. Cromie wrote, 'I told them I would kill the first armed man that set foot aboard, backing up my words with an absurd twenty-two pistol.' His task completed, Cromie wrote to Hall, 'I am afraid the Huns will obtain much valuable material, but devil a stitch of ours.'[2]

The next prominent figure to appear in the increasingly complex political landscape was legendary 'Ace of Spies' Sidney Reilly. Born Salomon Rosenblum in Odessa to Ukrainian Jewish parents, Reilly had previously worked for British SIS in Russia during the Tsar's disastrous 1905 war

1   Dobson and Miller, *The Day We Almost Bombed Moscow*, p.104.
2   Michael Wilson, *Baltic Assignment: British Submariners in Russia 1914–19* (London: Leo Cooper in association with Secker & Warburg, 1985), p.217.

with Japan. An experienced spy by 1918, Reilly was sent by Director of British SIS, Captain Mansfield Smith-Cumming, RN (codenamed 'C') to Murmansk where he was to make contact with Robert Bruce Lockhart in Moscow. The journey by sea was uneventful but his arrival at Murmansk was to be much less congenial. The Royal Navy were suspicious of the seemingly out-of-place character who arrived unannounced at Murmansk docks, and despite his protests Reilly found himself confined in the brig of battleship HMS *Glory*. In a strange twist of fate Major Stephen Alley, MC was passing through Murmansk on his way home after the conclusion of his time as British SIS Chief in Moscow. No one in Murmansk would be more suitable to interrogate a suspected Bolshevik spy than the former head of the British SIS in Russia. At Admiral Kemp's request, Alley was sent to question Reilly and although the two men had never met, Reilly quickly deduced Alley's credentials and presented a carefully concealed message in SIS code. It was to be the beginning of a close friendship between the two spies.

181. Submarine hero Captain Francis Cromie, CB, DSO, RN, British Naval Attaché at Petrograd, 1918. (Public domain)

With his identity and credentials established, Reilly promptly continued to Petrograd where he reported to Commander Boyce before heading on to Moscow and his original rendezvous with Lockhart. Reilly's first act was to put on his Royal Flying Corps uniform (he was officially a serving 2nd Lieutenant in the British Army) and proceed to the Kremlin where, as a representative of the British Aviation Mission, he requested a meeting with Lenin. He was rejected at the gate.

After the unsuccessful attempt to hold council with Lenin, Reilly returned to Petrograd with orders to assist Cromie in planning the destruction of the Russian Fleet. Reilly also took the opportunity to spend time socialising in the city's best restaurants, all the time forming friendships and networks with various White Russian sympathisers which could be called upon at a later date.

One of Reilly's contacts was the former Minister for War in Kerensky's Provisional Government and head of the 'Union for the Defence of Fatherland and Freedom', Boris Savinkov. Members of the UDFF, many former Tsarist army officers and disgruntled Socialist Revolutionaries, were in close contact with other like-minded groups who had formed a loose anti-Bolshevik alliance. Reilly saw that there might be the opportunity to use Savinkov's anti-Bolshevik contacts to usurp the Bolsheviks from power in a coup.

Savinkov had good reason to despise the Bolsheviks. Immediately after Lenin seized power a Constituent Assembly was formed with an overwhelming majority of Socialist Revolutionaries. The Assembly's inaugural meeting was also its last as Lenin, displeased with the threat to his power the elected Socialist Revolutionary majority posed, sent in his Lettish riflemen to end the Assembly on 18 January 1918.

Britain was not the only country to operate networks of spies in Russia. The French had given Savinkov a considerable amount of money to assist organising and rallying the anti-Bolshevik movement. French spies had considerable involvement in the Czech Legion uprising in Western Siberia in 1918. Count Wilhelm von Mirbach, the Kaiser's Ambassador to Moscow, led the German intelligence operation. Mirbach was an aggressive operator and cultivated his own network of pro-German spies amongst the population. These agents were in turn commanded by Colonel Rudolf Bauer and conducted counter-intelligence operations against their British and French counterparts. It was a strange war by proxy, the three remaining largest belligerent nations fighting each other for control and influence of newly non-belligerent Russia.

Not all agents operating in Russia would become as famous as Reilly, dubbed posthumously with the moniker 'Ace of Spies'. One British agent who worked hand in hand with Reilly was codenamed IK8, real name George Hill. After a privileged childhood in Russia were his father had worked as an expatriate businessman, Hill knew the country, its customs and its people well and spoke the language fluently. Hill had himself tried his hand as a businessman in Moscow but by August 1914, seeking excitement, travel and adventure, found himself working on fishing vessels off the coast of British Columbia.

After the outbreak of war Hill promptly enlisted in the CEF and served as an intelligence officer in France. His luck did not hold out and he was wounded by a grenade and sent to London to recuperate. After being classified fit for further active duty, he was sent to Salonika where he served from 1916 with the Manchester Regiment. Bored with the lack of excitement at his new posting, Hill made application to join the RFC and was subsequently accepted.

After qualifying as a Pilot, Hill reportedly flew 'hush-hush' missions landing agents behind enemy lines. On one such mission after dropping off his precious cargo, Hill was taxing for a quick take-off when he spotted an enemy cavalry patrol charging towards his aircraft. Using skill and a little luck, Hill was able to pull his BE2 airborne before the enemy could get close enough to capture him but upon landing discovered several bullet holes throughout his aircraft.

Whilst in London on leave in July 1917, Hill received orders to join the Royal Flying Corps mission to the Imperial Russian Air Service and arrived in Petrograd shortly before the November 1917 Bolshevik revolution and subsequent cessation of hostilities between Russian and the Central Powers. The German secret service remained very active in Russia and Hill barely escaped an ambush in the street by two of their agents:

> Just as they were about to close with me I swung round and flourished my walking stick. As I expected, one of my assailants seized hold of it. It was a sword-stick, which had been specially designed by Messrs Wilkinson, the sword makers of Pall Mall and the moment my attacker had the scabbard in his fist I drew back the rapier-like blade with a jerk and with a forward lunge ran it through the gentleman's side. He gave a scream and collapsed to the pavement. His comrade, seeing that I had put up a fight and was not unarmed, took to his heels while I withdrew and fumbled for my revolver. Meanwhile the man I had run through staggered off, leaving my scabbard on the pavement, and I went back and recovered it. That swordstick had thereafter a value in my eyes.[3]

With the RFC Mission largely redundant after the cessation of hostilities, Whitehall ordered Hill to assist the Bolsheviks (in the early months of Bolshevik rule the relationship between the Allies and Lenin was cautious but amicable) by working on improving the standard of the Russian railway system with the assistance of a Canadian Colonel Joe 'Klondike Bill' Boyle. The Bolshevik authorities allowed the two officers to commandeer a railway carriage for the purpose which had belonged to the Tsar's mother, Empress Maria Feodorovna (who would be evacuated with other members of the Russian Royal Family from Yalta on board HMS *Marlborough* in April 1919) and was the height of opulence and luxury. It had an observation deck, a stateroom, a pantry and kitchen, was fully self-contained and could even produce its own electricity.

---

3   Hill, *Go Spy the Land*, p.88.

For the next seven months Hill and Boyle lived in luxury as they steamed across Russia, slowly making their way towards Petrograd. On arrival they became the first Allied officers to enter the Bolshevik Headquarters in the city at the Smolny Institute, where permission was obtained from Lenin himself to continue to assist in the upgrade of the Russian railways with the understanding that the British would withdraw their support for the ousted Provisional Government and support the Bolsheviks in their place.

Hill and Boyle set off with Lenin's mandate and proceeded to clear the congested railways and free up rolling stock for traffic. Often there was no alternative to clear the line but to push entire trains off the tracks and down an embankment. The 'restructuring' of the railway system meant that food and supplies were able to be distributed much more freely from the wheat fields in the east to the major cities in the west.

As they arrived at each town and railway siding, Hill and Boyle solved problems as they encountered them. They were also tasked with the return to Romania of its gold bullion reserves, crown jewels, foreign office archives and millions of pounds of Romanian currency which had been moved to Russia for safekeeping following the collapse of the Romanian Army. It took nine days to reach Jassy in eastern Romania during which time neither men had the opportunity to wash or shave. Considering the value of the items they were transporting and the lawlessness in Russia at the time, Hill and Boyle agreed it would be unwise to stop any longer than necessary to refuel. Both officers successfully returned the national treasures to Romanian authorities and were awarded the Order of the Star of Romania in recognition of their services.

In early 1918 (prior to the landing of Royal Marines at Murmansk in March) the Allies and Bolsheviks remained on relatively good although strained terms. The Bolsheviks were in desperate need of military assistance and Bolshevik Minister for War Leon Trotsky was willing to accept any help and advice from the Allies. Trotsky had been so impressed by Hill and Boyle's work on improving the efficiency of Russian railways that he appointed Hill, still a serving RFC officer, 'Inspector of Aviation', a position which gave Hill unprecedented access to all aerodromes and aviation personnel of the fledgling Soviet Air Force. Hill wrote:

> Two or three times a week I would spend half an hour with him [Trotsky] discussing aviation. He had marvellous powers of concentration and the knack of putting his finger on the weak spot of anything and of scenting when information was not being freely given.[4]

Hill's close association with Trotsky enabled him to build up a network within the Bolshevik leadership that would report on German troop movements in the east. It was through Hill's inside information that London learned which German divisions had been pulled out of the Eastern Front and sent to France for Ludendorff's spring 1918 offensive. The information-gathering network that Hill cultivated proved to be so effective that Trotsky later incorporated it into the 'Third Section' of the new Red Army. In 1920 the Section was renamed 'Registration Directorate' which later evolved to become the 'Chief Directorate of Intelligence' or 'GRU'. The GRU would in later years become one of the worlds leading military intelligence organizations; founded in part by a British RFC officer from a nation towards which much of its intelligence gathering arsenal would be directed.

Whilst Hill, Reilly and Cromie were hard at work in Russia, Bruce Lockhart was in London trying to convey to Whitehall the seriousness of the situation in Russia. Apart from Churchill, a vehement anti-Bolshevist, the British government were less concerned about who in particular was running Russia than their position on killing Germans. After a meeting with the Bolshevik Minister for War in February 1918, Lockhart cabled the Foreign Office: 'Trotsky will cooperate with us

---

4   *Ibid.*,p.190.

as long as it suits him. Our attitude should be the same'.[5] The Foreign Office response penned by Foreign Secretary Arthur Balfour is reflective of Britain's attitude towards the Bolsheviks at the time, 'Internal affairs in Russia are no concern of ours. We only consider them in so far as they affect the war'. Britain had no intention of interfering with the Bolsheviks where they were in power but would not abandon 'our friends and Allies in those parts of Russia where Bolshevism cannot be regarded as the de facto Government.'[6]

The Foreign Office reply left Lockhart in an unenviable position. To Balfour in London it may have been a reasonable foreign policy statement but to Lockhart in Moscow it showed how little the Foreign Office understood the situation in Russia. If Britain continued to support and aid anti-Bolshevik factions in Russia then in time the Bolsheviks would also regard the British as enemies, not to mention that throughout most of Russia it was nearly impossible to determine which government was solely in power in any region at any one time and if they were, would they still be in power the following month.

Whilst the German and Bolshevik governments were intently discussing the terms of the Brest-Litovsk Treaty, Lockhart was appealing to the Foreign Office to join with Red Army forces to continue fighting the Germans in the east. Although Lockhart's plan was in the best interests of Britain and her Allies, Lenin would never have agreed to it. Lenin's sole concern was the survival of Bolshevism in Russia at any cost which can be seen in the Bolshevik leader's attitude towards the extremely harsh conditions of the Brest-Litovsk Treaty. Whilst other Bolsheviks dismissed the terms out of hand, a decision that would resume war with Germany and possibly ultimately result in the destruction of Bolshevism, Lenin was determined against all opposition to accept the harsh terms of the Treaty.

The lack of confidence between Whitehall and its agents on the ground in Russia was becoming an increasing problem. Unconfirmed reports reached London that thousands of German and Austro-Hungarian prisoners of war in Siberia were being released and armed by the Bolsheviks. Lockhart immediately cabled London that the reports were fanciful and false and immediately received a reply to the effect that London did not believe him. Lockhart went directly to Trotsky and asked if the reports were true. Trotsky denied that prisoners of war were being released and suggested that some Allied representatives should go to Siberia to see for themselves. Lockhart took up the offer and despatched William Hicks, Raymond Robbins and Captain W.B. Webster of the American Red Cross Mission, who returned with a report that some 1,000 former POWs had been armed as protection against Semenov's White Russian Cossacks and another 1,000 formed into a local Red Guard battalion at Omsk, hardly the thousands which had been reported to London.

In fact, the Bolsheviks were so critically short of men that they were looking to the POW camps for recruits to bolster the ranks of the Red Army. In 1918 a Prisoner of War Congress held by prisoners in a camp at Samara requested they be allowed to form units which would later become known as 'International Battalions' of the Red Army. A Chinese battalion was recruited from the thousands of their countrymen serving in labour units of the Red Army; there were Czechoslovak, Hungarian, Romanian and Yugoslav battalions, eventually numbering some 50,000 men. Ironically, 20 years later most of these nationalities were represented in units of the *Waffen-SS* which fought against the Red Army on the Eastern Front.

On 6 July 1918, Savinkov's 'Union for the Defence of Fatherland and Freedom' launched a full scale uprising in Yaroslavl, roughly 250 kilometres north-east of Moscow. The UDFF managed to hold out for two weeks until Red Army field guns were brought up to pound the dissidents into submission. It is unlikely to have been a coincidence that on the same day that Savinkov launched his

5   Richard Henry Ullman, *Anglo-Soviet Relations, 1917–1921: Intervention and the War* (Princeton, N.J.: Princeton University, 1961), p.73.
6   Dobson and Miller, *The Day We Almost Bombed Moscow*, p.111.

coup the German Ambassador to the Bolsheviks, Count Mirbach was assassinated by Socialist Revolutionaries in an attempt to provoke an aggressive German response.

The assassination was the first act of the Left-Socialist Revolutionaries attempt to launch their own coup to take over Moscow. They did achieve some initial success, including the capture of the *Cheka* headquarters at Lubyanka Street along with its much-feared leader Felix Dzerzhinsky. The Revolutionaries also captured and took control of the central telephone office and issued a telegram announcing that the Socialist-Revolutionaries were now in power and that all orders previously issued by the Bolsheviks were null and void. They were a little hasty in their declaration, however, as the Bolsheviks quickly regrouped and using their praetorian Lettish Rifleman as a spearhead drove the Socialist-Revolutionaries out of Lubyanka Street and the mansion in which Dzerzhinsky and most of the *Cheka* leadership were being held.

182. 'Ace of Spies' Sidney Reilly, ostensibly an officer with the RFC Training Mission to the Imperial Russian Air Service. (Public domain)

The Bolsheviks immediately laid blame for the uprisings on French and British subterfuge. The French had to some extent financed Savinkov, and Yacov Blumkin (Count Mirbach's assassin) had stayed in a hotel room next to Lockhart, but Balfour had specifically instructed Lockhart not to become further involved with Savinkov or his plans. Blumkin was later discovered to be a double agent for the *Cheka*, which had itself been infiltrated by Socialist Revolutionary spies.

There is some ambiguity as to the extent of British involvement with Savinkov and his group at this time. Reilly and Hill never hid the fact that they maintained contact with the group and knew of Savinkov's plans for a coup. The fact that Reilly and Hill were unashamedly involved with Savinkov and the fact that Balfour had specifically ordered Lockhart to have no contact with the Russian dissident indicates that Lockhart and Reilly possibly coordinated the plot on their own. Lockhart later blamed the failure of Savinkov's uprising on the French Ambassador Joseph Noulens, who had encouraged Savinkov to launch the coup in July by telling him that the Allies were to land an expeditionary force at Archangel any day. When the Allies did land at Archangel on 2 August it was with a paltry 500 sailors and soldiers, most of whom were from the 'ELOPE' Training Mission and technically non-combatant. When Reilly learned how few troops had been landed at Archangel he was livid.

The events leading up to and after the Savinkov/Socialist Revolutionary uprisings would prove to be a turning point in relations between Whitehall and the Bolsheviks. Although there was no evidence to directly link the British government there was little doubt that the Allies had been involved. After July 1918 all contact between the Bolsheviks and Allied agents such as Hill and Reilly immediately ceased and it became no longer safe for members of the British Embassy staff or Military Mission to wear their uniforms on the street. Reilly was forced to go underground and assume a false identity.

Armed intervention by the Allies was now inevitable and the Bolsheviks would be forced to resist militarily. In later years Stalin would claim that Allied military intervention in Russia was a blatant attempt to crush the Bolshevik regime in its infancy. It is true that by August 1918 the removal of the Bolsheviks in favour of a government which would resume hostilities on the Eastern Front was an Allied objective but it had not always been so. In April and May, Royal Marines and Royal Navy sailors had actually fought anti-Bolshevik White Finns on the Finnish frontier with Russia at the request of the local Murmansk *soviet*. In southern Russia in September, British soldiers had died defending the Russian frontier from the Ottoman advance in Transcaucasia although it had also been in British interests to deny the Turks the Caspian oilfields. It is true that by mid-1918 Britain was actively attempting to overthrow the Bolsheviks or directly assist those White Russian factions with concurrent objectives although without the degree of premeditation that the Soviets would later claim.

The day after Allied forces landed at Archangel, 25th Battalion, Middlesex Regiment disembarked at Vladivostok harbour and was sent into the line against Red Army troops. Soon Moscow would be effectively encircled by British forces in the Baltic, North Russia, Siberia, South Russia and Black Sea. British troops were on the ground in Russia and they were not going to leave without a fight.

August 1918 was not a good month for the Bolsheviks. After the landing of Allied troops at Archangel the Germans broke the Brest-Litovsk treaty and ordered their troops to resume an advance into the Ukraine in an attempt to force Lenin to eject the British from Russian territory. The anti-Bolshevik Czech Legion had established itself along the Trans-Siberian Railway and White Russian General Denikin had captured Ekaterinodar in South Russia.

During the crackdown which followed the landing of British troops at Archangel, a number of British citizens in Moscow and Petrograd were detained, interrogated and put under house arrest. Cabling facilities were confiscated and offices raided for incriminating evidence. On 5 August, all Allied officers, military attaches and members of the various military missions were rounded up and incarcerated. George Hill, forewarned of the impending raid, managed to escape the sweep to his colleague Sidney Reilly's flat. They packed their bags with whatever they could carry, destroyed reports and papers, warned the US consulate (The US Navy had also participated in the capture of Archangel) and then fled themselves.

The Lettish Riflemen were the most reliable troops the Bolsheviks had: wherever there was a disturbance in the city, the Letts were the first to be sent. They guarded the Kremlin and all the banks, prisons, munitions dumps, railroads and gold reserves in Petrograd. If the Letts could be convinced to join the Allies' cause the Bolsheviks would find themselves exposed and vulnerable. To this end a secret meeting was arranged between Lockhart, Reilly, the French Consul General and a Lettish colonel. Reilly later reported to Hill that there was a real possibility of the Letts being won over, as quite a few officers were expressing disappointment with the Bolsheviks. The enterprise was later dubbed 'The Lockhart Plot'.

With so much cash circulating and so many people involved, it was only a matter of time before the *Cheka* became aware of the plot to turn the Lettish troops. The Bolsheviks later claimed they had known of the plot from its inception as the Lettish colonel whom Lockhart and Reilly had met with had remained loyal and notified his Red Army superiors. Whether this is true or not is questionable but it is probable that the Lettish officer was playing both sides for the best offer.

The Bolsheviks also claimed they had intercepted messages between Cromie in Petrograd and Lockhart in Moscow that revealed how Lockhart had spent six million roubles bribing the Letts and other Russians to join the Allies at Archangel. Lockhart was able to finance the coup by obtaining huge amounts of Russian currency from wealthy citizens who wished to flee from Russia to England. In return for many millions of roubles, Lockhart issued promissory notes for British currency to be redeemed in England.

All the scheming came to a head on 30 August when Moisei Uritsky, head of the *Cheka* in Petrograd, was assassinated by a military cadet and Kerensky Provisional Government loyalist Leonid Kanegisser. Uritsky's assassin was later caught and personally interrogated by head of the *Cheka*, Felix Dzerzhinsky. Even under torture Kanegisser was adamant he had acted alone, however Dzerzhinsky was sure that the British were in some way involved.

That same night Fanya Kaplan, a young Socialist Revolutionary, shot Lenin in the neck and chest as he was leaving a Moscow factory after making a speech to assembled workers. Lenin's wounds were so serious that he was not expected to live. One bullet had penetrated just above the heart and the other entered the neck near the artery. Kaplan was quickly arrested by the *Cheka* and summarily executed four days later. Dzerzhinsky believed that the timing of the assassination of Uritsky in Petrograd and attempted assassination of Lenin in Moscow were not a coincidence and that both had both been coordinated and instigated by the British. The Bolshevik version of events was that Uritsky had been murdered 'because he brought together the threads of the English conspiracy in Petrograd.'[7] To Dzerzhinsky Petrograd was on the verge of counter-revolution and it was imperative that he strike back immediately to maintain control.

On the following day, 31 August, the *Cheka* chief ordered Red gunboats to take station on the River Neva opposite the British Embassy in Petrograd. Whilst *Cheka* agents and Red Guards were beating down the door, Commander Ernest Boyce began burning documents and codebooks whilst Naval Attaché Captain Francis Cromie stood at the top of the stairway armed with a revolver in an attempt to block the *Cheka* from entering the Embassy. The Red Guards broke in and opened fire, and Cromie

183. Felix Dzerzhinsky, feared head of the *Cheka*, the Bolshevik secret police, forerunner of the KGB. (Public domain)

was shot and killed. The Embassy was searched and stripped of its files and documents and its military and civilian staff were arrested.

The justification given for storming the British Embassy was that the *Cheka* had tracked a group of conspirators to within its walls. Upon entering the building the *Cheka* supposedly stumbled upon a 'secret meeting' where they arrested five Russian conspirators and two dozen English agents. According to an article published in the Bolshevik newspaper *Izvestia* grandiosely titled 'An Appeal to the Civilised World', the conspirators had opened fire on the *Cheka* agents who had returned fire in self-defence, killing a Russian and wounding two others. Cromie was reportedly killed whilst resisting arrest.

Mrs Natalie Bucknall, one of the British Embassy staff who had witnessed events, wrote in a sworn statement that the *Cheka* had broken down the front door and charged up the staircase where Cromie had shouted at them to leave British territory at once, to which the Red Guards took no notice, shouting for Cromie to raise his hands. Cromie then opened fire with his revolver hitting three Red Guards, there was a flurry of shots and Cromie fell mortally wounded. Mrs Bucknall and a colleague rushed downstairs to Cromie's body: the gallant naval officer opened his eyes and spoke, but his final words were indecipherable. The Red Guards threatened to shoot the two women if they did not return upstairs and were told that the Embassy had been seized in the name of the Soviet government. The Embassy was searched at gunpoint by Bolshevik soldiers and sailors and the staff taken to the Gorokhovaya prison to be interrogated. The *Cheka* thoroughly searched the Embassy looking for incriminating evidence of British complicity in counter-revolutionary activities. On 2 September the Danish ambassador in Petrograd sent a telegram to his country's government:

---

7   Silverlight, *The Victors' Dilemma*, p. 66.

The [British] archives were sacked and everything was destroyed. Captain Cromie's corpse was treated in a horrible manner. Cross of St George was taken from the body and subsequently worn by one of the murderers. English clergymen were refused permission to repeat prayers over the body.[8]

Dutch minister W.J. Oudendijk (who had been using his country's neutrality to attempt to negotiate the release of the British diplomats) returned to Petrograd on 4 September, four days after the *Cheka* had stormed the Embassy. He was disgusted and outraged to find Cromie's body still lying in the small chapel. No funeral had been arranged and Oudendijk immediately began organising for Cromie to be buried with the respect he deserved. Strangely, the Bolsheviks gave Cromie a state funeral, probably in an attempt to maintain an ostensibly neutral position after the storming of the Embassy. In another strange incident in an already surreal event, German and Austrian diplomats attended the funeral procession. As the hearse crossed a bridge over the River Neva, crewmen of Soviet ships on the river stood to attention and saluted as the casket passed. The body of a senior decorated officer of the Royal Navy, killed by Red Guards within the walls of the British Embassy was given a state funeral by the Bolsheviks attended by representatives of nations at war with Britain. In post-Revolution Russia nothing was unusual.

The British government was outraged at the infringement of its sovereign territory and internment of its diplomatic representatives. Winston Churchill was particularly outraged and demanded that the perpetrators be brought to justice 'however long it takes'. In reprisal for Cromie's death, Bolshevik Ambassador Maxim Litvinov (Lockhart's equivalent based in London) was arrested and imprisoned in Brixton jail. The British Foreign Secretary Arthur Balfour sent a telegram to his Soviet contemporary stating:

> Should the Russian Government fail to give complete satisfaction or should any further acts of violence be committed against a British subject His Majesty's Government will hold the members of the Soviet Government individually responsible and will make every effort to secure that they shall be treated as outlaws by the Governments of all civilised countries and that no place of refuge shall be left to them.[9]

The severe tone of this message may have just saved Bruce Lockhart's life. He had been arrested the day after the failed assassination attempt on Lenin and bustled into *Cheka* headquarters, the infamous 'Lubyanka', where he claimed diplomatic immunity and refused interrogation. *Cheka* agents had searched the Briton's apartment for compromising documents but did not search Lockhart's person. In the breast pocket of his greatcoat he had concealed a notebook which recorded payments to anti-Bolshevists in code. Lockhart managed to dispose of this potentially damning evidence in the lavatory.

During his imprisonment Lockhart was interrogated by Dzerzhinsky's deputy, Jacob Peters, who had been tried in London under the moniker 'Peter the Painter' and acquitted for his role in the murder of three London policemen in the robbery leading to the 'Sidney Street Siege' of 1911. Peters, the son of a Latvian farm worker, was 18 when he became a member of the Latvian Social Democratic Labourers Party, a banned organisation under the Tsarist government. During the 1905 war with Japan he was arrested for spreading discontent amongst sailors of the Baltic Fleet and suffered imprisonment and torture at the hands of the Tsar's secret police, the *Okhrana*.

Upon his release in 1909, Peters fled to England and became a member of an anarchist revolutionary group which robbed businesses in London to finance their anti-government activities in Russia. It was during one of these robberies on a jeweller's shop in December 1910 that the gang were surprised by a

---

8   *A Collection of Reports on Bolshevism*, Foreign Office, 1920, Report No. 3.
9   *The New York Times*, 4 September 1918.

184. Head of British SIS (later MI6), Captain Sir George Mansfield Smith-Cumming, codenamed 'C'. (Public domain)

patrol of unarmed policemen. The gangsters opened fire, killing three policemen and wounding two more whilst one of the gang members was accidentally shot by a comrade. The revolutionaries were eventually tracked down, and on 3 January 1911 cordoned off in an apartment at 100 Sydney Street, Stepney, in London's East End by 200 Metropolitan Police. A gun battle broke out. The siege is significant in British history for the calling out of an armed detachment of Scots Guards from the Tower of London to assist police and the appearance on the scene of then Home Secretary Winston Churchill who authorised despatch of a 13 pdr field artillery onto the streets of London.

A fire broke out in the apartment (possibly lit by the police), however Churchill refused to allow the fire brigade access to the building. As smoke billowed from the windows of the apartment, shooting from within the building stopped and the fire brigade were allowed in; one firefighter was killed by falling debris. The bodies of two anarchists were found inside the apartment, dead from smoke inhalation, but 'Peter the Painter' had escaped the net. Peters was eventually captured and arrested but when brought to trial was acquitted on a lack of evidence, and after marrying an English girl he left London in 1917 to return to his homeland. After the November 1917 Revolution he was appointed deputy head of the *Cheka* where he gained a reputation for brutality and torture.

Both Lockhart and fellow agent William Hicks (who had also been arrested) were put in a cell and left until morning, when a woman was brought into the cell. Lockhart figured her to be Fanya Kaplan, Lenin's attempted assassin. The *Cheka* were obviously hoping she would recognise the two agents, thus implicating the British in the assassination attempt. When Kaplan showed no sign of recognising her cellmates she was taken outside and shot and her body burned.

After spending several days at Lubyanka Street, Lockhart and Hicks were moved to cells within the walls of the Kremlin itself. Despite repeated attempts to incriminate them, the *Cheka* could find no real evidence of their participation in any counter-revolutionary activities and were forced under pressure from Soviet Foreign Secretary Georgy Chicherin (who was in turn under great pressure from Whitehall) to grant their release.

Lockhart was returned to Petrograd in October for exchange with Bolshevik Ambassador Maxim Litvinov, held by the British government. Lockhart finally arrived in London on 19 October 1918, one of very few spies and secret agents to survive arrest and imprisonment by the Soviets. He was knighted and went on to have a distinguished diplomatic career, recounting his experiences in Russia in a 1932 autobiography, *Memoirs of a British Agent*.

Reilly was himself fortunate to have avoided being embroiled in the British Embassy affair. He was supposed to meet Cromie the day of the Naval Attaché's death but only later found out the reason why Cromie had been unable to keep the appointment. The following day Reilly booked train

185. Stephen Alley, head of British SIS in Russia during the November 1917 Russian Revolution. (Public domain)

passage to Moscow, travelling on false identity papers. When he arrived, he found Moscow in chaos. The British Mission had been closed down and George Hill had gone into hiding. The newspapers were full of stories of British conspiracies and the 'Lockhart Plot', and posters bearing Reilly's likeness and a reward of 100,000 roubles for his capture had been distributed throughout the city. Reilly escaped the dragnet by fleeing to Petrograd in a coach filled with German diplomats. At the Baltic coast he bribed his way onto a Dutch ship and by early November was lunching at the Savoy Hotel in London.

Reilly's colleague George Hill also managed to escape to England, arriving there on 11 November, the day the Armistice was signed. Both Reilly and Hill were subsequently despatched to South Russia to asses White Russian General Denikin's political situation before returning to England three weeks later. For their services in Russia, Reilly was awarded the MC whilst Hill was thrice decorated with the MBE, DSO and MC. Ernest Boyce was recognised with the award of an OBE whilst another British agent, Denys Garstin, went on to serve with the NREF at Archangel where he was awarded the DSO and MC but sadly killed in action on 15 August 1918.

Cromie was awarded a posthumous CB for his services as Naval Attaché:

In recognition of his distinguished services in the Allied cause in Russia, and of the devotion to duty which he displayed in remaining at his post as British Naval Attaché in Russia when the British Embassy was withdrawn. This devotion to duty cost him his life.[10]

No doubt enjoying the irony, Hill returned to Russia in 1941 as a brigadier with the British Military Mission to the Soviet government. Given the task of liaising with the NKVD (successor to the *Cheka* and forerunner of the KGB) Hill opened the first British SIS (by then MI6) station in Moscow since 1918. What a difference 20 years and a common enemy can make.

10 *The London Gazette*, 24 September 1918.

19

Moscow Prisoners of War: August 1918–October 1920

After his forced landing over enemy territory and capture south of Archangel in April 1919, South African Colonel Kenneth van der Spuy, RAF, was transported south by rail to Moscow. On arrival in the Red capital he was held at the Kremlin for about a month, before being moved to the old French Legation building and imprisoned with other British soldiers captured at Murmansk and Archangel. Information on British and Commonwealth prisoners is very scarce but it appears that those held at the Legation building were all officers; most other ranks were held at Andronikov Monastery, although it appears that some officers were held there as well.

During their time in the French Legation building the prisoners were frequently visited by the Anglican Chaplain in Moscow, Reverend Frank William North and his wife Margaret Caird North, who would bring with them small parcels of precious food extracted from their own meagre supplies. The men cherished these monthly visits as the food parcels invariably broke the monotony of the scraps of black bread and watery cabbage soup provided by the Bolsheviks.

Over five days from 26 July 1919, British prisoners captured at Onega during the mutiny of White Russian troops who defected to the Bolsheviks were forced marched more than 100 *versts* to the railhead at Plesetskaya and then crammed into a cattle truck for the journey to Moscow. Their destination was the infamous Butyrka prison where they arrived on 10 August. Lieutenant Lewis Euron Roberts, attached to 'ELOPE' Force from the Royal Welsh Fusiliers, noted the less than comfortable conditions in the prison: 'all officers were put in one big cell with canvas and iron beds along the walls, crawling with bugs and lice … Diet, only soup twice daily, and bread, and half an hour's exercise per day.'[1]

During the early stages of their incarceration, Bolshevik Foreign Secretary Maxim Litvinov (who had himself been imprisoned in Brixton prison in England the previous year until released in a prisoner exchange) stipulated that unless the British prisoners gave their word not to attempt escape they would be put in a common jail with petty criminals. Realising that their chances of escaping from the prison let alone reaching the Finnish frontier 500 miles away were virtually nil and that conditions at the Legation building were far better than anything they could expect in a local prison, the prisoners gave their parole not to escape. The parole was rescinded, however, when the prisoners in the Legation building leaed that the party of officers and men under Lieutenant Colonel R.J. Andrews, DSO, MC, Devonshire Regiment, who had been taken prisoner during the mutiny at Onega, were being held in the Butyrka prison with common criminals.

Colonel van der Spuy at once demanded that the Onega prisoners be immediately released from Butyrka and brought to the Legation building. Litvinov would not budge, however, and without the assurance of the prisoners' parole, within hours had the Legation prisoners moved from the Legation building under guard to one of several prisons run by the *Cheka*, the Bolshevik secret police. The South African airman recalled:

> The conditions at the Vetcheka are almost indescribable: We were packed into a small room only just large enough to accommodate us lying down on a wooden pallet side by side, like so many sardines. The prison

---

1   IWM, 823 99/17/2, Private papers of Lieutenant L.E. Roberts.

186. British Prisoners of War at the entrance to St. Andrews Anglican
Church, Moscow. Some British prisoners wear Russian civilian clothing. This
photograph most likely taken Christmas 1919. (IWM Q71271)

was filthy and the food really foul. Once a day for twenty minutes we were made to 'exercise' in a courtyard crowded with hundreds of the prison inmates; it was during these twenty minutes, and at no other time, that one was expected to obey the calls of nature. For years afterwards, I used to have nightmares about the so-called latrines we had to use – they were indescribably filthy, filled to overflowing, and it was difficult to find space even for one's feet when squatting. There were other happenings too, which I do not wish to recall, the horror of which haunted me for years.[2]

Colonel van der Spuy managed to scrounge pencil and paper and wrote to Litvinov in strong terms demanding that he and his men – as senior British officer held by the Bolsheviks the South African had became the de facto commanding officer of all British and Commonwealth prisoners – were prisoners of war and should be immediately transferred to the prison housing those captured at Onega. Whether the letter reached Litvinov is unknown but three days later van der Spuy and his party were marched through the streets of Moscow to Butyrka prison. The South African noted, 'I had only once in my lifetime been inside a jail proper – but only as a visitor, not an inmate!'[3]

After 10 days in Butyrka prison van der Spuy was able to make contact with Lieutenant Colonel Andrews, and a few days later both groups of prisoners were moved into the same crowded cell. The long days of imprisonment dragged on into weeks and months, the boredom and monotony being broken only by the occasional visits by Reverend North and his wife. Surviving on very little food, the prisoners began to shed much of their body weight. Sanitation was primitive and clothing became infested with lice. Although conditions were harsh the British prisoners fared much better than many Russians outside the prison gates, who were succumbing in their thousands to starvation and typhus.

2   van der Spuy, *Chasing the Wind*, p.147.
3   *Ibid.*, p.149.

187. Detail of photograph of British prisoners of war in Moscow (see image 199). The officer seated at right is Lieutenant Colonel Richard John Andrews, DSO, MC, Devon Regiment. (IWM Q71271)

Not all British prisoners were incarcerated in Butyrka, and seem to have been distributed apparently randomly across Skolniky (Lieutenant Lewis Roberts, RWF, and several officers), Butyrka (Colonel van der Spuy and four officers) criminal prisons and Andronikov Monastery (Lieutenant Colonel Andrews, eight officers and 36 men) where political prisoners were held. By far the best place to be imprisoned was the monastery where conditions were not as dire as in the criminal prisons. Apart from a newspaper reporter or two, British civilian prisoners were in most cases required to remain under supervision in Moscow but were not imprisoned.

On 1 September, Private Edward Blunden, RASC (who had been Orderly Room Sergeant at Chekevo at the time of the White Russian mutiny at Onega on 20 July) died of heart failure as a result of severe dysentery, the only British serviceman to die whilst a prisoner of war of the Bolsheviks. He was buried in Moscow, although the location of his burial is unknown and he remains commemorated on the Archangel Memorial. The day after Blunden's death the first prisoners of the North Russia Relief Force arrived at Butyrka, captured in operations along the Vaga and Dvina Rivers the previous month.

The lack of activity and stimulation left the prisoners to create their own entertainment, primarily in the form of gossip. The rumours floating up and down the corridors were almost always the highlight of the day. Colonel van der Spuy wrote of the emotional rollercoaster of being a prisoner in Moscow:

It is extraordinary but perhaps only natural how in prison life one's hopes soared or fell on the slightest grape-vine rumour. After all, we had no one to discuss things with but ourselves – no newspapers, no news from the outside world, no means of knowing whether things were going well or badly, whether our troops were continuing to fight the Bolsheviks or withdrawing ... Every rumour was, therefore, avidly seized upon and chewed threadbare; out of them each one of us probably drew his own mental picture, and for a day or two remained elevated or depressed.[4]

Even the relatively harmless pastime of playing cards, associated with gambling and considered a vice by the Bolsheviks, was denied the British prisoners. Regardless of the ban, some of the British prisoners managed to cunningly construct an improvised deck from scrap cardboard and coloured chalk. Playing cards was one of the prisoners favourite time-passers until one day a guard made an unexpected roll call and caught the huddle of conspirators in the act. As punishment, early the next morning the cell door crashed open and a startled van der Spuy was frogmarched towards the solitary confinement cells. Having resigned himself to a spell away from his comrades which he believed would be at most a few days, van der Spuy went without complaint. Little could he have known that he would spent two months in solitary confinement during which time he was allowed only limited sleep and no mental stimulation. After two excruciating months van der Spuy was overjoyed to be returned to the cramped cell with his comrades and quickly fell back into the old routine.

On 1 October two new RAF prisoners arrived: Captain Ronald Sykes, DFC, (a former RNAS ace with six kills over the Western Front) whose Sopwith Camel had been forced down on the Murmansk Front after engine failure, and Observer Lieutenant Bugg, who had been captured at Archangel on 10 August in an incident in which his pilot Captain John D'Arcy-Levy had been killed. Both airmen were kept in isolation for two weeks and had their meagre rations supplemented by small food parcels lowered from an upper story window by some of the other British prisoners.

Sykes recounted his capture after crash landing in the forest:

I set off to walk back … I got onto a forest track and there I met a group of Russians wearing British khaki. I thought they were some of our White Russian friends but they turned out to be White Russians who had discovered that the British were going to evacuate and they had decided to change sides and go south to join the Red Army, so they took me along with them.

I went to Moscow by train. As I reached Moscow the snow had began. It was snowing hard when I walked through Red Square past St. Basil's Cathedral. I was taken to a group of British officers, some of them were RAF, they had force landed all round the fringes of Russia, the others had been on liaison duties with the White Russian army … At first they had been on parole but the senior officer Colonel Andrews objected to the armed guards which had been put on them and said that if they did not take the armed guards away he would withdraw parole. They would not take them away, he withdrew parole and we were all locked up in the Butyrka prison not very far from the Lubyianka [*Cheka* Headquarters].

Then one day the Russian guards came and took Colonel van der Spuy who had force landed somewhere near Archangel and been captured, and me and three others. The five of us were taken away to another building, put in single cells and told we were hostages…

To begin with we wrote letters and sent messages to everyone we could think of, Lenin, Trotsky and the prison commandant the result of which was they allowed to have our cell doors open for 12 hours a day so we could visit one another, we made up a pack of cards [to pass the time].

The British padre in Moscow, Mr. North, was left free and he was a sort of unofficial contact with the Foreign Office … he also collected potatoes out in the country and his wife would boil them up and he sent in bags of cold boiled potatoes to us to supplement our ration of rye bread. He wasn't allowed to write us letters or send us any messages but he could write a list of the contents of his parcel so instead of a list of the contents he used to send us a message in a form that looked like a list.

We got a parcel in from Mr. North and the message on the piece of paper said the British government was '…holding Lenin and Trotsky responsible for your safety'. A few days later they came to us and said,

---

4   *Ibid.*, p.151.

'you are no longer hostages, you are prisoners of war on parole, you can leave the prison now and go across Moscow and live in the [Andronikov] monastery on the other side where all the others are living.'[5]

Six weeks after their capture on 18 August 1919, the Kronstadt Raid prisoners were transferred from Petrograd to Andronikov Monastery. Sub Lieutenant Osman Giddy, RN, taken prisoner when *CMB 24* was sunk, later wrote an account of his incarceration:

During the three days journey from Petrograd to Moscow we were given no food, except at one station where soldiers brought us bread and weak tea. We were desperate with hunger and at one stop where a farm cart drove up with potatoes and carrots, we grabbed handfuls and ate them raw much to our subsequent discomfort.

Eventually we arrived at Moscow … we refused to march, as Bremner [Lieutenant William 'Bill' Bremner, DSC, RN] was incapable of walking, and after much heated discussion a cart was found for him…

Our party consisted mostly of Russians with as many women and children … Next to us, an old lady in a faded black satin dress hobbled along on high-heeled shoes, bent under the weight of a sack, bulging with old belongings. When we relieved her of this she thanked us in fluent English. She was born a princess…

The monastery lies on top of a small hill overlooking the city and is most impressive. We passed through the great gateway and halted inside the walls which enclosed a cemetery and were kept there for some time, until Napier [Lieutenant Laurence Napier, RN], myself and the six ratings were taken to a separate building containing two large rooms. In the darkness it was some seconds before I realised the rooms were full of people. They were British soldiers.

We had heard there were British prisoners of war in Moscow, but to stumble on them like this was wonderful. Our depression vanished and our hunger as well, for, crowding round to hear our story, they pressed on us precious food they had carefully hoarded for emergencies…

They were a mixed collection. Several officers captured in a White Russian mutiny at Onega, R.F.C. officers force landed in Odessa and Murmansk. Soldiers serving in regiments in North Russia and so on … We spent five months at this monastery … Conditions were appalling … our personal cleanliness sadly deteriorated and lice never left us until we left Russia.

With the coming of the New Year the temperature fell to below zero and it was excruciatingly cold. We slept on trestle beds made of straw and had one small stove only, which burned wood. The soldiers' ears were frostbitten as they had no woollen headgear … Once the temperature dropped to 30 degrees below zero…

It was little better outside where the soldiers could walk freely in the city if they wished while officers were restricted to the monastery walls on the principle that privileges were for men only and not for officers. At last relief arrived with our exchange in April [1920].[6]

In November 1919 a rumour reached the prisoners that British Labour Member of Parliament James O'Grady was scheduled to meet with Soviet Foreign Secretary Litvinov at Copenhagen to discuss the exchange of Russian and British prisoners. After a week of anxious waiting the prisoners learnt that the talks had come to nothing. The British government had offered 100 Red prisoners and a number of concessions for the release of all British and Commonwealth prisoners but the Bolsheviks were adamant they must have all Russian prisoners held by Allied countries repatriated,

5   IWM sound, 301, Sykes, Ronald.
6   Agar, *Baltic Episode*, pp.218–220.

188. Detail of photograph of British Prisoners of War in Moscow (see image 199). Seated left is Reverend Frank North, CBE, to his left South African Lieutenant Laurence Napier, DSO, RN, and to his left Mrs Margaret Caird North, CBE. (IWM Q71271)

including the many thousands still interred in prisoner of war camps in Germany who had not been returned to Russia after the Bolshevik revolution.

With the failure of the talks and no end to their imprisonment in sight the men began to fall into despair. Lieutenant Roberts described 19 December (the day the prisoners learned of the failure of the Copenhagen talks) as 'a BLACK DAY'. Colonel van der Spuy was also despondent:

> What could I hope for? It seemed to us that the British Government was taking no live interest in us and rumours merely served to wear down our resistance. Hope grows thin when one has to live in a cold, dreary, cement-floor cell, seeing the same faces daily, discussing the same things daily, eating the same food daily, de-lousing ourselves daily or whiling away the long hours by playing a game with our vermin tormentors … Hope grows even thinner when good news on one day turns to bad news the next, with nothing to cling to in the way of fact.[7]

As negotiations moved into 1920 without any sign of conclusion, van der Spuy and the other prisoners were moved from Butyrka to the Andronikov Monastery where they were united with a number of other British prisoners, mostly other ranks who had been imprisoned under less harsh conditions than their officers. For the other ranks it was a strange kind of incarceration. They were granted permission to visit the local markets to barter for supplies (although at all times under armed guard) as the Bolsheviks considered the other ranks to be 'conscripts' who had unwillingly been sent

---

7   van der Spuy, *Chasing the Wind*, p.159.

189. Lieutenant William Bremner, DSO, DSC, RN (centre), recently released from imprisonment in Moscow, is greeted by his father and brother at Harwich, 8 February 1920. (David Bremner)

by the military hierarchy to Russia. The market currency was purely that of commodity trading, the rouble by this time being completely worthless.

Even without the armed escort there was little chance of escape from Moscow. Freedom meant a 1,000 mile trek to the Finnish frontier through extremely difficult terrain in a country where there was little food and the people only spoke Russian, of which few of the prisoners could muster more than a handful of words and phrases.

Officers were also allowed out of the monastery (although not granted the freedom of the other ranks) to be taken on trips around Moscow where they were forced to sit through lengthy sessions of Bolshevik indoctrination. Towards the end of their imprisonment the Bolshevik treatment of the officers softened and likely in an attempt to influence the 'bourgeois' officers before they returned home the Bolsheviks organised a number of excursions around Moscow. Sub Lieutenant Giddy recalled:

> Before long our 'education' started-that is, we were propagandised as thoroughly as possible. Every day a smart lady commissar would be assigned to us and we would be taken on foot to see museums, art galleries, the open market, the Kremlin and the Crown Jewels, on which visit I passed the room where I had first been detained ... This and that would be pointed out to us as exemplifying Soviet 'progress'. The prisoners 'education' extended to nights at the opera where one of the Russian prisoners was even allowed to play the principal part of 'The Barber of Seville'. One never-to-be-forgotten night we visited the Royal Opera House, where some of us occupied the royal box and I actually sat in the Czar's red velvet, gold-embossed chair.[8]

After an unforgettable Christmas Day, early in the New Year the rumours of release began to arrive more and more frequently until news was received that the first prisoner to be released on 27 January 1920 would be Lieutenant William Bremner, DSO, DSC, RN, who had been badly

---

8   *Ibid.*, p.172.

wounded and taken prisoner during the Kronstadt Raid. Also three wounded soldiers: Corporal Alfred England, 45th Royal Fusiliers; Lance Corporal Edwin Sylvester, Devon Regiment attached 1st Oxs and Bucks, taken prisoner after the failed raid on Ignatovskaya on 27 June 1919 in which he was badly wounded, losing an eye; and Private Lambert, 17th Liverpools. They were followed by Corporal Harris, RE, sent home with a bad lung on 27 February.

Bremner's party arrived at Harwich via Copenhagen on 8 February to a small fanfare. A photographer from *The Daily Mirror* was present and photographs of the four men appeared in the *Mirror*'s edition the following day. The photographs show a handsomely bearded but otherwise healthy looking Bremner whilst Sylvester's left eye is covered by bandages. All four men of the party wore civilian clothing in place of military uniform. The *Mirror* article states a figure of 120 British prisoners of war and 34 civilians as being held as 'hostages' in Russia.

After an excruciating wait the remaining prisoners learnt they would be released some time in early March via a train bound for Petrograd, thence to Finland and freedom. Then the blow came: only half the remaining prisoners would be released immediately, the others would follow at a date and time yet to be specified.

On 8 March all of the remaining other ranks were detailed to entrain for the week long train journey to Finland via Petrograd. Some of the soldiers were reluctant to leave the officers behind but knew they had little choice. The officers themselves were understandably disappointed that they would not be joining the other ranks but happy that the men were on their way home. In a curious case a German officer prisoner indicated he would shortly be repatriated home as a result of negotiations between the British and Soviet governments. Not surprisingly the remaining British officers were none too pleased. Lieutenant Lewis Roberts, 17th Liverpools, taken prisoner during the mutiny at Onega on 20 July 1919 wrote. 'fancy our government obtaining the release of German officers whilst their own subjects remain in prison! What a paradox!'[9]

On 21 March the remaining officer prisoners at Skolniky and Butyrka prison were moved to Andronikov Monastery where they awaited orders to entrain for the Finnish frontier. The Bolsheviks were keen to keep a senior officer behind just in case negotiations broke down, informing van der Spuy that he would be the last to leave. In an act of kindness and chivalry, Captain George Roupell, VC, East Surrey Regiment (who had been taken prisoner at Onega, 20 July 1919) volunteered to remain behind with the South African airman to keep him company.

After a week of anxious waiting the remaining officers were detailed on 25 March to board a dirty and smelly fourth class railway carriage for the two day journey to Petrograd. Accompanying the soldiers were the Reverend and Mrs North and other British civilians also to be repatriated to England. Both Reverend and Mrs North were awarded CBEs in recognition of their self-sacrifice in the service of British and Commonwealth prisoners of war in Moscow.

At the Finnish frontier the prisoners' elation at their release almost turned to utter despair. Reverend North and his wife had spent almost 20 years in Russia but after the Revolution they had no intention of ever coming back. They had packed all their belongings into suitcases which contained mainly clothes, books and a few pieces of silver tableware, their only possessions in the world that they were allowed to take out of Russia. Although they had written authority from Moscow to take their meagre possessions out of the country, the guards at the border, probably keen on keeping the valuables for themselves, confiscated the lot and refused to allow the suitcases across the border, leaving the Reverend and his wife with only the clothes they were standing in. The local commander then decided they were not going to let the Norths cross into Finland at all and instructed the distraught husband and wife to board the train for the return trip to Moscow.

---

9   IWM: 823 99/17/2, Private papers of Lieutenant L.E. Roberts.

In solidarity with the Norths whom had done so much for the British prisoners in Moscow, every single one of the British prisoners refused to cross the border unless they were accompanied by the Reverend and Mrs North. This left the border guards in an embarrassing situation. The prisoner exchange had been arranged at the highest levels of the British and Bolshevik governments. If the British prisoners did not cross the Finnish frontier that day there would be hell to pay for those responsible and the guards knew it. The local commander had no choice but to let the prisoners and the Reverend and Mrs North cross the frontier and walk the few hundred yards to Finland and freedom.

After a short time recuperating in a Finnish hospital the prisoners boarded a slow boat for Southampton where they were quietly disembarked without any fanfare and given rail tickets to their various depots, without so much as a new set of civilian clothes. The ship docked on a Saturday morning but the ex-prisoners were not allowed to leave until late afternoon, lest members of the public should spot them and begin to ask questions as to who the haggard looking men in shabby service uniforms were. It would appear that the British government, who had made such efforts to keep their war with the Bolsheviks outside of public view, did not want the public asking questions as to why almost 100 prisoners of the Bolsheviks, many of whom had not been volunteers despite government claims that only volunteers were being sent to Russia in 1919, had been secreted into the country after more than a year of imprisonment of which the public knew virtually nothing. Lieutenant Colonel van der Spuy himself disembarked at Southampton wearing the same clothes he had been captured in and had worn through more than a year of imprisonment in appalling conditions.

Several decorations were awarded to prisoners of the Bolsheviks after their release, most notably awards of the DSO to Lieutenants William Bremner, DSC and Laurence Napier, RN, the DSC to Sub Lieutenant Osman Giddy, RN, and DSMs to Chief Motor Mechanics Henry Dunkley, Benjamin Reynish and William Whyte, RNVR and Stoker Petty Officer Samuel McVeigh, RN, all awards for the Kronstadt Raid 18 August 1919. Recommendations for the awards had been made by Admiral Cowan immediately after the raid (when it was still unknown if the officers and ratings had survived the sinking of their coastal motor boats) but announcement of the awards withheld until after the prisoners' release.

Private Thomas Pyle, 6th Battalion, Royal Marines had been badly wounded and taken prisoner during the failed attack on Koikori on 8 September 1919. The wound to his left leg was so severe that it necessitated amputation by Soviet doctors. Pyle was gazetted for award of the DCM after his release, his award being unique to the Royal Marines for the Russian Civil War and also for its citation: which made specific reference not only to his gallantry in action bombing enemy sangars at Koikori but also for his determination under trying conditions whilst a prisoner of war, the only British gallantry decoration awarded (at least in part) for services whilst a prisoner of war of the Bolsheviks.

Appendix I

Roll of Honour: British and Commonwealth Servicemen

North Russia (Murmansk)						
Name	Age	Number	Rank	Unit	Date	Comments
ASBURY, Henry T.	36	262808	LCpl	248FldRE	01.02.19	Acc. killed in barracks fire sabotage
ATWOOD, H.			Fireman	MercMne	11.10.19	SS *Welshman*
BELLIS, William Francis	21	M/20240	Armr	RN	07.11.18	HMS *Glory*
BENTLEY, Peter	23	37011	Pte	11RSussR	21.10.18	Killed in train accident
BLACK, Neville Victor	21	36679	Pte	11RSussR	13.10.18	
BOHIN, Richard			Fireman	MercMne	09.10.19	SS *Welshman*
BOOTHROYD, Richard	20	PO/18942	Pte	6RMBn	27.08.19	Attack on Svyatnavolok
BOSWORTH, Frederick, MM Bar	23	840058	Cpl	240RFA	30.06.19	
BREMNER, Archibald		243012	Dvr	420RFA	08.07.19	Acc. drowned, *Jolly Roger* incident
BRENTNALL, Percy John	18	69801	Pte	2HLI	23.09.19	Raid on Red Finnish hideout
BURTON, Richard, DSC	29		Capt	6RMBn	08.09.19	Attack on Ussuna
CARPENTER, Alan Bazil		3818/DA	Deckhd	RNR	09.01.19	HMT *Mitres*
CHARLOTTY, John		75855	Pte	2HLI	29.08.19	
CHOLMELEY, MC			Capt	ChesR	16.08.19	Drowned in Lake Onega
COLLINS, Hugh		69914	Pte	2HLI	23.09.19	Raid on Red Finnish hideout
COOK, Charles Henry	45	522942	Spr	RE	01.03.19	Died (TB)
CREMER, Albert Edward	20	J/28070	AB	RN	29.10.18	Died of illness, HMS *Glory*
CUBBON, Fred		T4/110307	Cpl	1123RASC	22.10.18	Died (pneumonia)
DANBY, Frederick William	23	36848	Pte	11RSussR	23.10.18	
DEARLOVE, Reginald Alfred	18	PLY/17106	Pte	RMLI	12.11.18	HMS *Glory*
DEVINE, Ames		69893	Pte	2HLI	23.09.19	Raid on Red Finnish hideout
DOCHERTY, James	19	74839	Pte	2HLI	23.09.19	Raid on Red Finnish hideout

Name	Age	Number	Rank	Unit	Date	Circumstance
DRAKE-BROCKMAN, Lewis	30		Maj	RMLI	10.05.19	Defence of Karelskaya
DRAPER, Richard James		4137/ES	EngMn	RNR	15.10.18	HMS *Glory*
ELLENDER, Reginald, MM	31	495231	Pte	53HosRAMC	02.07.19	Died (pneumonia)
ELLIOTT, William Bloemfontein		20278	Pte	6RMBn	27.08.19	Attack on Svyatnavolok
ERICKSON, Cail Ivar	29	3034411	Sgt	CEF	11.04.19	Attack on Urosozero
FAWCETT, Henry			Maj	RMLI	29.12.18	Acc. killed
FAZAKERLY, W.E.		CH/19560	Pte	6RMBn	09.09.19	Attack on Koikori
FERNS, James		63739	Pte	13YorkR	24.02.19	Died (pneumonia)
FOX, Fred Marshall		5255/TS	Deckhd	RNR	07.10.18	HMS *Glory III*
FRASER, Jack D.		74730	LCpl	2HLI	23.09.19	Raid on Red Finnish hideout
GOTTS, Abraham	19	69871	Pte	2HLI	27.09.19	D. of wounds, raid on Red Finnish hideout
GRAHAM, Lancelot	20	75162	Pte	2HLI	23.09.19	Raid on Red Finnish hideout
GREEN, A.J.			Civilian	YMCA	08.08.19	
GREEN, William Sidney Allen		CH/19654	Pte	6RMBn	09.09.19	Attack on Koikori
GRIFFITHS, Thomas	59		Bosun	MercMne	21.08.19	SS *Welshman*
HALE, Wilfred	21	K/18261	Sto1	RN	25.10.18	HMS *Glory*
HARLOW, Maurice Charles	40	010333	Pte	RAOC	08.02.19	
HARTLEY, Frederick George		13833	Cpl	19MGC	13.09.19	Killed in action
HAWKES, Thomas William		CH/22061	Pte	6RMBn	08.09.19	Attack on Koikori
HITCHEN, Bertie Thomas	22	CH/18521	Pte	RN	03.05.19	Defence of Maselskaya, HMS *Glory III*
HOBBS, Arthur		8796	Gnr	420RFA	08.07.19	Acc. drowned, *Jolly Roger* incident
HOLDEN, John William	39	231628	LCpl	248FldRE	01.02.19	Acc. killed in barracks fire, believed sabotage
HOLLIDAY, Henry		273274	Gnr	420RFA	08.07.19	Acc. drowned, *Jolly Roger* incident
HUGHES, Albert		75138	Pte	2HLI	23.09.19	Raid on Red Finnish hideout
JACKSON, James		WR/220004	Spr	RE	04.09.19	Railway Operations Division

JENKINS, Arthur		CH/17498	Pte	6RMBr.	08.09.19	Attack on Koikori
JENNISON, William		14324/DA	Deckhd	RNR	09.10.18	HMT *Queen IV*
JOHNSON, Christopher M.		34477	Pte	11RSussR	21.10.18	Killed in train accident
JOHNSON, Frederick Walter		13/962	Sgt	EYorksR	19.02.19	Attack on Segeja Bridge, attd. 237th TMB
JOHNSON, Victor		SK/10423	AB	MMR	07.10.18	HMT *Ralco*
KEAVENY, Michael		PLY/1977	Pte	RMLI	04.10.18	HMS *Glory III*
KELLY, Hugh J.	27	75067	Pte	2HLI	23.09.19	
KENNY, J.L.			Master	MercMne	20.08.18	SS *Asturian*
LANGFORD, Henry		36921	Pte	11RSussR	08.05.19	Died of accidental wounds (burns)
LETT, Alfred George		L/12614	LCpl	1ESurrR	15.09.19	Attack on Siding 5
MARDELL, Charles Frederick		G/35888	Pte	11RSussR	11.05.19	Died (typhoid)
MARDLE, Herbert George Joseph	19	13039	Cpl	1ESurrR	15.09.19	Attack on Siding 5
MARSHALL, Peter		S/9421	LCpl	RAOC	04.08.19	
MARSHALL, Robert Barnaby	23		Lieut	1ESurrR	14.09.19	Died of wounds 13.09, ambush nr. Siding 6
McDONALD, James Francis		88767	Sgt	19MGC	09.09.19	Attack on Koikori
McLEAN, Frank	25	CH/17765	Pte	RMLI	18.08.18	HMS *Glory*
McLEOD, George		18588	Pte	253MGC	15.09.19	Drowned attempting to save a fellow soldier
MILLER, George Gordon Darley	19		2Lt	RFA	15.09.19	Attack on Siding 5, attd. armoured train
MILLER, James		13573	LCpl	1ESurrR	15.09.19	Attack on Siding 5
MILNER, Tom	29	16832	Deckhd	RNR	12.10.18	HMS *Glory III*
MITCHELL, James		76363	Cpl	SYRENSigRE	08.07.19	Acc. drowned, *Jolly Roger* incident
MOFFATT, Thomas		74918	Pte	2HLI	23.09.19	Raid on Red Finnish hideout
MOULL, William F.		L/11844	Pte	11RSussR	21.10.18	Killed in train accident
MUIR, Allan	35		Capt	17LpoolR	15.05.19	Killed in action, attd. 237th TMB
MURRAY, Wallace		PO/20779	Pte	6RMBn	27.08.19	Attack on Syatnavolok

Name	Age	Number	Rank	Unit	Date	Notes
MUZNER, Albert	28	17484/DA	Deckhd	RNR	14.10.18	HMT *Ariadne*
NEALE, Arthur Albert	34	CH/16383	Sgt	6RMBn	09.09.19	Attack on Koikori
NICOLSON, Alexander	21	18839/DA	Deckhd	RNR	22.10.18	Died (influenza), HMS *Glory*
NORGATE, Frederick James, MM	25	46087	Cpl	19MGC	22.09.19	
NORRIS, William Henry	26	J/7635	PO	RN	14.05.18	HMS *Cochrane*
OAKLEY, James Percival	25	PO/16997	Pte	RMLI	15.10.18	Died of illness, HMS *Glory*
OXFORD, Stanley Charles	19	254580	Dvr	1203RFA	18.06.19	
PARKINSON, Harry	19	CH/2250(s)	Pte	RMLI	10.10.18	HMS *Glory*
PATRICK, Ernest Arthur	32	467097	Sgt	RAMC	05.10.18	
PERRY, Walter	24	36872	Pte	11RSussR	21.10.18	Killed in train accident
PHILLIPS, Thomas Henry		63778	Pte	13YorksR	04.03.19	
PIGGOTT, William G. Clifford	21	CH/19459	Pte	6RMBn	09.09.19	Attack on Koikori
PLUMPTON, Robert			2Lt	6YorksR	25.12.18	Murdered by White Russian soldier
POLLINGTON, Arthur Bertie	24	SS/116444	Sto1	RN	02.07.19	HMS *Glory*
POTTER, Joseph William		64835	Pte	6YorksR	05.01.19	
PURNELL, Robert	32	69865	Pte	2HLI	23.09.19	Raid on Red Finnish hideout
RAISTRICK, Charlie	24	CH/17633	Pte	6RMBn	09.09.19	Attack on Koikori
RENDALL, William George	21	18931	Pte	6RMBn	27.08.19	Attack on Svyatnavolok
RILEY, William Parkinson	29	100520	Sgt	MidxR	02.01.19	NREF Interpreter
ROBINSON, Henry G.		16373	Pte	2HLI	23.09.19	Raid on Red Finnish hideout
ROBINSON, John	22	239097	Dvr	420RFA	08.07.19	Acc. drowned, *Jolly Roger* incident
ROWE, H.		465033	Pte	RAMC	14.12.18	
ROXBURGH, Albert Edward			Waiter	MercMne	10.09.18	HMT *Czar*
RUMSEY, Frederick Harold	23	K/20868	Sto1	RN	06.10.18	HMS *Glory*
SCOTT, Thomas C.		CH/20282	Pte	RMLI	01.10.18	HMS *Glory*

Name	Age	Service No.	Rank	Unit	Date	Remarks
SCOTTER, Harry		3305/TS	Trimmer	RNR	02.10.18	HMT *Ralco*
SHAKESBY, James	30	1634/DA	Deckhd	RNR	04.10.18	HMT *Ariadne*
SHARPLES, Thomas		S/9380	Pte	RAOC	05.08.19	
SHERWIN, Benjamin Disraeli		M/2744	VictPO	RN	14.10.18	HMS *Glory*
SHOWELL, George Albert	23	L/16796	Pte	SpCoyMidxR	23.06.19	Died of wounds
SLATER, Herbert Hopwood	19	PO/2609	Pte	RMLI	11.11.18	HMS *Glory*
SLOPER, Gerard Orby, MC	33		Capt	NorthdFus	08.02.19	
SMART, Walter Henry	29	2019/EA	ERA	RNR	18.10.18	HMS *Glory*
SMITH, Charles		14921/DA	Deckhd	RNR	05.10.18	HMT *Ariadne*
SMITH, Thomas Henry		243937	AC2	RAF	03.07.19	
SMITH, William Seth		36994	Pte	11RSussR	21.10.18	Killed in train accident
SNOWDEN, George Isaac		1275/DA	Deckhd	RNR	12.11.18	HMT *Sarpedon*
STOPFORD, Frederick Leonard		18449	Pte	6RMBn	27.08.19	Attack on Svyatnavolok
STRACHAN, James		04213	Pte	RAOC	15.03.19	
TAYLOR, James Pearson		CH/21551	Pte	RMLI	07.01.19	HMS *Glory*
TERRY, Horace John	19	L/13071	Pte	1ESurrR	13.09.19	Died of wounds
THOMPSON, Leonard Frederick	22	L/17651	Pte	SpCoyMidxR	15.05.19	Killed in action
THURSTON, Albert Arthur		S/39256	Pte	RASC	06.03.19	
WEIZA, J.			AB	MercMne	24.09.19	SS *Magpie*
WICKENS, Thomas Stanley Alfred	18	13935	Pte	1ESurrR	01.09.19	
WILLIAMS, Joseph		PLY/20082	Pte	6RMBn	01.09.19	Died of illness
WORROLL, E.H.	19	RMA/15055	Gnr	RMA	03.05.19	Defence of Maselskaya, HMS *Glory III*

North Russia (Archangel)

Name	Age	Service No.	Rank	Unit	Date	Remarks
ADAM, Gerald Wallace	20		2Lt	13YorksR	10.08.19	
ADAMS, William		T/327001	Dvr	1122RASC	17.03.19	Killed in action

Name	Age	Number	Rank	Unit	Date	Cause
AGGIO, Alfred George	19	130870	Pte	46RFus	15.08.19	Accidentally killed, GSW head
AINSWORTH, Charles Henry	34	266299	Pte	17LpoolR	07.12.18	Attack on Seletskoe
AITKEN, Thomas	30	377016	Pte	2/10RScots	16.09.18	
ALDWINKLE, Bernard			Lieut	421RFA	03.11.18	Acc. killed, GSW head during pistol practice
ALEXANDER, Walter	28	311118	Sto1	RN	03.07.19	HMS *Fandango* mined and sunk
ALLIN, Albert Edward	42	33307	Pte	2/10RScots	06.01.19	
ALMOND, George Henry	47	TR/51966	Cpl	1102RASC	01.09.19	Defence of Ust-Vaga, served Boer War
ANDERSON, Arthur	20	66246	Pte	2/10RScots	13.10.18	Defence of Borok
ANDREWS, Thomas Archibald		129315	Pte	46RFus	10.08.19	Dvina offensive
ARAM, Arthur	30	60724	Pte	6YorksR	05.05.19	Died of wounds
ASHER, Hyman	24	301392	Pte	2/10RScots	29.10.18	Died of wounds, attack on Kulika
AYRES, Joseph	22	L/6251	OStwd2	RN	25.08.19	Acc. killed, HMS *Glowworm* explosion
BAILEY, Tom E.G., MC	35		Capt	6YorksR	02.04.19	Attack on Bolshie Ozerki
BARDELL, Ernest Henry		66056	LCpl	2/10RScots	30.08.18	
BARR, David Buik, MC	25		Capt	ELancR	13.07.19	D. wounds, mutiny of Slavo-British Legion
BARRETT, Wilson		220150	Pte	138RAMC	18.07.19	
BARRY, Christopher		130804	Pte	45RFus	10.08.19	Dvina offensive
BASSETT, William Frederick, MC			Lieut	2/10RScots	27.10.18	Attack on Kulika, 10th Bn., R. Highl's attd.
BATES, John		205526	Pte	6YorksR	03.04.19	Defence of Shred Mekhrenga
BATH, Valentine		9655	Pte	2HantsR	05.06.19	Accidentally drowned, SLI attd.
BATTEN, John	33	6549	Sgt	2HantsR	20.06.19	Attack on Troitsa
BEAK, Alfred George	29	65131	Cpl	6YorksR	03.04.19	Defence of Shred Mekhrenga
BEATTIE, John Linton	22	K/33831	Sto1	RN	01.10.18	HMS *Attentive*
BEGLEY, Henry Frederick	27	11027	Pte	2HantsR	27.06.19	Direct hit on blockhouse, Conn't Rgrs. attd.
BELL, Harold	26	66054	Sgt	2/10RScots	13.10.18	Defence of Borok

Name	Age	Number	Rank	Unit	Date	Notes
BELL, John	39	129796	Pte	45RFus	10.08.19	Dvina offensive
BELL, William		155065	Pte	55HosRAMC	17.03.19	
BENTLEY, Richard Leslie	20	377020	Pte	2/10RScots	10.10.18	Defence of Borok
BEST, Norman Victor	21	377089	Cpl	2/10RScots	21.11.18	Died of wounds, defence of Tulgas
BEST, Reginald Robert	21	64594	Pte	6YorksR	25.03.19	Killed in action
BETTANY, James Albert		128952	LSgt	45RFus	10.08.19	Dvina offensive
BLAND, Cecil, F.R., MC			Lieut	RBerksR	07.07.19	Murdered, mutiny of Slavo-British Legion
BLUNDEN, Edward George		S/436619	Pte	RASC	01.09.19	Died (dysentery) whilst POW in Moscow
BOOTH, E.W.		998910	OS	MMR	25.08.19	Acc. killed HMS *Glowworm* explosion
BOOTH, Edward Arthur			Lieut	Gen List	23.09.19	
BOYLES, Charles	22	J/12947	AB	RN	14.09.18	Killed, naval landing party, HMS *M.25*
BRIDCUTT, Arthur Elijah	23	40822	Gnr	RGA	11.08.19	attd. RFA
BROADBENT, William Sidwell		129126	Pte	45RFus	10.08.19	Dvina offensive
BROWN, Allan	28		Capt	AIF	20.07.19	Murdered, mutiny at Onega
BROWN, George Henry	30	114148	Pte	17LpoolR	06.11.18	Died (pneumonia)
BROWN, John S.		52382	Pte	2/10RScots	13.10.18	Defence of Borok
BROWN, Robert	23	33092	Pte	17LpoolR	07.12.18	Attack on Seletskoe
BROWN, William	18	131804	Pte	46RFus	10.08.19	Dvina offensive
BROWN, William	22	65048	Cpl	6YorksR	19.04.19	Killed in action
BUCHAN, William John	19	66055	LCpl	2/10RScots	18.09.18	Killed in action
BUCKINGHAM, Ernest Albert		J/27084	AB	RN	14.09.18	Killed, naval landing party, HMS *Glory IV*
BUCKLEY, Arthur		T/438768	Dvr	1122RASC	17.03.19	Killed in action
BULMER, John Joseph	24	292934	Gnr	443RFA	01.08.19	Amphibious attack on Onega
BURFORD, F.W.	24	100302	AB	MMR	03.08.19	HMS *Walton Belle*
BURGESS, William Edwin		A/437681	Pte	RASC	05.11.18	

Name	Age	Number	Rank	Unit	Date	Notes
BURNS, James McN.	19	52455	Pte	2/10RScots	27.10.18	Attack on Kulika
BURROWS, Albert Arthur	23	130850	Pte	46RFus	13.09.19	Defence of Nevonovskaya/Bulandovskaya
BUSS, John William		J/2144	AB	RN	03.07.19	HMS *Fandango* mined and sunk
BUTCHER, Wilfrid James	24	129673	Pte	46RFus	15.10.19	Died of wounds
BYGRAVE, William		J/22825	AB	RN	04.12.18	HMS *M.25*
CAIRNS, John	33	133378	Pte	46RFus	29.08.19	Attack on Emtsa
CARD, John Victor, MC	32		Capt	ESurreyR	25.03.19	Killed in action, attd. RANB
CASEY, Patrick	33	227466	YeoSig	RN	25.08.19	Acc. killed, HMS *Glowworm* explosion
CASSIDY, Thomas		11768	LCpl	2/10RScots	27.10.18	Attack on Kulika
CHALLONER, George		59639	Pte	2/7DLI	26.10.18	
CHANDLER, Geoffrey		5188393	Pte	390RASC	07.04.19	
CHAPMAN, Frederick V.		02	Pte	2HantsR	19.06.19	Acc. drowned, advance on Troitsa, SLI attd.
CHEESEBROUGH, Thomas M.		J/85493	OS	RN	02.07.19	Killed attempting to defuse enemy sea mine
CHILD, Archibald Ernest		J/31371	AB	RN	02.07.19	HMS *M.24*
CHISMAN, Stanley		J/20791	AB	RN	18.08.19	HMS *Fox*
CLARKE, William John		PO/11179	Pte	RMLI	28.08.18	HMS *M.25* struck by enemy shellfire
CLAXTON, Herbert George		277109	LCpl	2/7DLI	25.03.19	
CLAYTON, Herbert		58043	Pte	6YorksR	02.04.19	Attack on Bolshie Ozerki
CLEVELAND, Robert George		J/16266	LS	RN	25.08.19	Acc. killed, HMS *Glowworm* explosion
CLUBB, John Charles	21	376978	Pte	2/10RScots	06.10.18	Defence of Borok
COASE, Edward Henry	22	J/16309	AB	RN	25.08.19	Acc. killed, HMS *Glowworm* explosion
COCKELL, John Charles	20	66075	Pte	2/10RScots	10.10.18	Defence of Borok
COLEMAN, Thomas		SS/119415	Sto1	RN	27.07.19	HMS *Haldon*
COLLEDGE, Arthur Vincent	21		Lieut	45RFus	10.08.19	Dvina offensive
COLLINS, William		52265	Pte	2/10RScots	11.11.18	Defence of Tulgas

COLLISHAW, William		64920	Pte	6YorksR	13.03.19	
CONNOLLY, Thomas Patrick		36325	Pte	253MGC	11.06.19	Died (septicaemia)
CONVILLE, Walter		313866	Gnr	67CFA	11.11.18	Defence of Tulgas
COOK, Frederick		244534	Dvr	55RFA	20.08.19	
COOPER, Charles Crook	19	53410	Pte	2/10RScots	27.10.18	Attack on Kulika
COPE, George	40	64626	LSgt	6YorksR	06.04.19	D. wounds, attack on Bolshie Ozerki 03.04
CORK, F.T.		998921	Bosun	MMR	26.08.19	D. wounds, HMS *Glowworm* explosion
CORLETT, Charles E.	30	381327	Pte	17LpoolR	09.02.19	Defence of Kodish
CREE, William		130197	Pte	45RFus	10.08.19	Dvina offensive
CROAL, Kenneth McFarlane	21		2Lt	2/10RScot	19.10.18	Shelling of VP445, 6th Bn., R. Fus. Attd.
CROSBY, Ernest Leonard		109922	Pte	2/7DLI	29.10.18	
CROUCHER, Nathaniel Frank	22	311534	Dvr	238SigRE	14.07.19	
CRUISE, Charles Thomas		131035	Pte	45RFus	10.08.19	Dvina offensive
CURALL, George		55080	Pte	201MGC	10.07.19	
CUTTS, Sydney Albert		57834	Pte	6YorksR	12.05.19	Died of wounds
DALLAS, George B.			Lieut	8MGC	15.09.19	Ambush near Bolshie Ozerki
DALZIEL, John Morrison			2Lt	2/10RScots	14.11.18	
DAMMS, Joseph		294631	AC2	RAF	23.07.19	
DANCY, G., MC, DCM			Lieut	1OBLI	02.06.19	Self-inflicted gun shot wound (suicide)
D'ARCY-LEVY, John Martin			Capt	RAF	10.08.19	Landed enemy territory, bayonetted to death
DARLING, H.H.			Laundn	MercMne	29.05.19	HMHS *Garth Castle*
DAVEY, Herbert		CH/17711	Pte	6RMBn	08.09.19	Attack on Koikori
DAVIDSON, Norman	18	L/7256	Dvr	421RFA	04.11.18	Died (pneumonia)
DAWES, George	25	J/12434	AB	RN	25.08.19	Acc. killed, HMS *Glowworm* explosion
DAY, George Albert		66009	LCpl	2/10RScots	11.11.18	Defence of Tulgas

Name	Age	Number	Rank	Unit	Date	Notes
DE MATTOS, Gerald Chamber	27		Maj	45RFus	11.08.19	Died of wounds, Dvina offensive
DEARDEN, James William	20	376877	Pte	2/10RScots	14.10.18	Died of wounds, defence of Borok
DENNISON, William Webster		271982	AB	RN	03.07.19	HMS *Fandango* mined and sunk
DIXON, Frederick A.J.		66274	Pte	2/10RScots	27.10.18	Attack on Kulika
DIXON, George Bell	19	376825	Cpl	2/10RScots	12.11.18	Died of wounds, defence of Tulgas
DOGETT, Alfred	31	O/24085	Sgt	RAOC	29.07.19	
DOWNING, Willfred Weston	30	66277	Pte	2/10RScots	27.10.18	Attack on Kulika
DOYLE, Alfred Richard	28	129393	Pte	46RFus	01.08.19	Raid on blockhouses near Selmenga
DRIVER, H., DSO, MC			Capt	46RFus	10.08.19	Dvina offensive, Befordshire Regt. attd.
DRURY, George Henry, DCM	21	265418	Cpl	BedfR	26.03.19	Killed in action
DUNLOP, Thomas McLean	19	66279	Pte	2/10RScots	11.11.18	Died of wounds, defence of Tulgas
DYER, Royce C., DCM, MM Bar			Capt	CEF	30.12.18	Died of illness
EELS, Alfred Henry	30	K/4447	Sto1	RN	03.07.19	HMS *Fandango* mined and sunk
EVANS, Daniel Goronwy	25	PLY/1843	Pte	RMLI	18.10.18	HMS *Glory*
FARMER, Thomas William	20	J/33401	AB	RN	25.08.19	Acc. killed, HMS *Glowworm* explosion
FAWDEN, William Herbert	19	L/0619	Stwd3	RN	01.08.19	HMS *Pegasus*
FENSOME, George Alfred	21	65103	Pte	6YorkR	31.08.19	Acc. killed, fell from moving train
FERRIES, J.R. (survived)		24699	LCpl	1OBLI	27.06.19	Attack on Ivanovskaya, R. Scots attd.
FINCH, Aubrey Malcolm Cecil	22		Capt	SeaHighrs	07.07.19	Murdered, mutiny of Slavo–British Legion
FIRTH, Clarence		244009	Pte	13YorksR	17.04.19	
FISHER, William Henry	22	5176	Pte	8MGC	01.09.19	Defence of Ust-Vaga
FITCH, Matthew Craig, MC	29		Capt	2/10RScots	09.12.18	
FITZGIBBONS, Frederick Thomas	24	998936	AB	MMR	22.07.19	Acc. drowned, HMS *Lobster*
FITZHERBERT-BROCKHOLES, Roger Hubert			Lieut	RN	02.07.19	Killed attempting to defuse enemy sea mine
FORSTER, Ernest Wilson	21	142131	AC1	RAF	28.05.19	Acci. drowned in Dvina River near Bereznik

FOSTER, Fred		66285	Pte	2/10RScots	27.10.18	Attack on Kulika
FOSTER, Thomas William	31	129109	Sgt	45RFus	06.07.20	Died of wounds
FRASER, D.		41064	A.Bdr	67CFA	13.11.18	Ambushed, mounted patrol nr Ust-Padenga
FRENCH, Thomas	20	376883	Pte	2/10RScots	11.11.18	Defence of Tulgas
FULBROOK, John	20	129176	Pte	45RFus	10.08.19	Dvina offensive
GALLAGHER, Edward		129220	Pte	45RFus	10.08.19	Dvina offensive
GALLON, William		133332	Pte	46RFus	03.08.19	
GARNHAM, G.T., MM		128930	CSM	45RFus	10.08.19	Dvina offensive, fmly. CSM, 17LondR
GARSTIN, Denis N., DSO, MC	28		Capt	10Hussars	15.08.18	Posthumous DSO/MC
GILLETT, John William		66291	Pte	2/10RScots	27.10.18	Attack on Kulika
GILLIES, John	18	66108	Pte	2/10RScots	07.10.18	Defence of Borok
GIRDLER, William	41	037473	Pte	RAOC	28.01.19	
GLANVILLE, Leonard	19	90427	AB	RN	25.08.19	Acc. killed, HMS *Glowworm* explosion
GLEDHILL, Philip Coulson	19	130269	Pte	45RFus	10.08.19	Dvina offensive
GONDRE, Jean	19		2Lt	RAF	20.07.19	Killed in aircraft accident on Dvina River
GORDON-LENNOX, Charles	20		Lieut	45RFus	24.08.19	Died of wounds, Irish Guards attd.
GORMAN, Donald Thomas, MC			Capt	2HantsR	22.06.19	Died of wounds, attack on Troitsa 20.06
GOSLING, Gerald Noel, MC	20		Lieut	GloucR	07.07.19	Murdered, mutiny of Slavo-British Legion
GOUGH, Ernest J.	19	49181	Pte	1OBLI	27.06.19	Attack on Ignatovskaya, Devon. Regt. attd.
GOULD, Cyril	19	CH/2100	Pte	RN	18.10.18	HMS *Glory*
GRACIE, Hamilton Cameron	25	84381	Gnr	55RFA	30.06.19	Died of wounds
GRAHAM, George	32	31500	Pte	2/10RScots	27.10.18	Attack on Kulika
GRAHAM, William	19	108580	Pte	17LpoolR	07.09.19	Attack near Kodish
GRAY, Ernest Henry		CH/2547	Pte	RMLI	23.11.18	Died of sickness
GREANY, Percy Marks, MM		24938	Sgt	17LpoolR	07.12.18	Died of wounds, attack on Seletskoe

GREEN, Albert Leonard		249477	AC2	RAF	04.09.19	
GREEN, Sebald W.B., DSO			Cdr	RN	25.08.19	Died of wounds, HMS *Glowworm* explosion
GREEN, William MacDonald		50505	Pte	2/10RScots	27.10.18	Attack on Kulika
GRIFFITH, Thomas Comber	24		Lieut	LNLR	08.07.19	Murdered, mutiny of Slavo-British Legion
GRIFFITHS, Harry	22	57701	Pte	13YorksR	28.08.19	
GROHEIT, Arthur Leslie	23	30807	Sgt	RSussR	07.07.19	Died of wounds, 17th Bn.
GRUNDY, Ernest		66102	LCpl	2/10RScots	10.10.18	Defence of Borok
GWATKIN, Henry Albert		66545	Pte	2/10RScots	11.11.18	Defence of Tulgas
HALE, Francis	23	66111	Cpl	2/10RScots	10.10.18	Defence of Borok
HALE, Harry	24	57801	Pte	13YorksR	04.04.19	Died of wounds
HAMILTON, Gordon	19		Midsh	RNR	28.08.18	HMS *M.25* struck by enemy shellfire
HAMMOND, George Robert	19	SS/119282	Sto1	RN	09.07.19	Acc. killed, HMS *Glowworm* explosion
HAMMOND, Henry Pat	39	377109	LCpl	2/10RScots	08.10.18	Defence of Borok
HANSFORD, Archibald Revening	30	J/18293	LS	RN	24.06.19	HMS *Sword Dance* mined and sunk
HARE, Andrew Alfred John	19	131559	Pte	45RFus	10.08.19	Dvina offensive
HARKINS, Philip		130339	Pte	45RFus	22.09.19	Died of wounds
HARRIGAN, George		66293	Pte	2/10RScots	07.10.18	Defence of Borok
HART, Howard Victor	29		Lieut	6LondR	23.03.19	Attack on Bolshie Ozerki, 6LondR attd.
HAWKER, Robert Harcourt	19	155424	Pte	201MGC	19.06.19	Acc. drowned in Dvina River
HEALY, William		53290	Pte	2/10RScots	22.03.19	
HEGARTY, Patrick		S/9485	Pte	RAOC	21.07.19	
HENRY, Frederick William	17	133181	Pte	1OBLI	26.06.19	Attack on Ignatovskaya, 45RFus attd.
HERBERT, Peter John, DCM	20	17669	Sgt	1OBLI	27.06.19	Attack on Ignatovskaya, Devon Regt. attd.
HEYWORTH, John Richard	32	63899	Pte	13YorksR	04.04.19	
HULL, Sidney (CWGC 'Hill')		SS/8798	AB	RN	25.08.19	Killed, HMS *Glowworm* explosion

Name	Age	Number	Rank	Unit	Date	Notes
HILL, Samuel	22	128947	Cpl	45RFus	10.08.19	Dvina offensive
HILLS, William Henry		S/20833	Sgt	404RASC	01.03.19	
HINSON, William	19	130934	Pte	45RFus	10.08.19	Dvina offensive
HOGARTH, Robert Stevenson	19	66113	LCpl	2/10RScots	10.10.18	Defence of Borok
HORLE, James		314290	Pnr	385FldRE	12.07.19	
HORN, Arthur		7503/DA	2Hand	RNR	10.10.18	HMT *William Spencer*
HORNE, Frederick Augustus		130062	Pte	45RFus	10.07.19	
HOUGHTON, James	24	58354	Pte	17LpoolR	07.12.18	Attack on Seletskoe
HUGHES, Norman Labrey	19		2Lt	1OBLI	27.06.19	Attack on Ignatovskaya, Devon Regt. attd.
HUMM, David		18530	Pte	252MGC	01.02.19	
HUNT, Percival Victor		73843	Pte	2HantsR	20.06.19	Attack on Troitsa, R. Fus. attd.
JACKSON, Arthur		57755	Pte	13YorksR	05.05.19	
JACKSON, Harry		129780	Sgt	46RFus	10.08.19	Dvina offensive
JACOB, Gwynne, DCM, MM Bar			Lieut	46RFus	01.08.19	Raid near Selmenga, E. Yorks Regt. attd.
JARDINE, John		SS/115744	Sto1	RN	28.08.18	HMS *M.25* struck by enemy shellfire
JAY, William Robert	17	53460	Pte	2/10RScots	27.10.18	Attack on Kulika
JOHNSON, John Joseph	25	292934	Gnr	443RFA	01.08.19	Amphib. attack on Onega (alias BULMER)
JOHNSON, James Edward		243197	AC1	RAF	31.03.19	Ambush near Bolshie Ozerki
JOHNSTON, William	37		EngOff	MMR	05.03.19	HMS *Lobster*
JONES, Elias	29	WZ/250	LdgSea	RNVR	19.11.18	SS *Corfe Castle*
JONES, Francis Ernest	19	130253	Pte	45RFus	10.08.19	Dvina offensive
JONES, Joseph		8656	LCpl	252MGC	15.09.18	
KALTERSON, Harold William		128992	Pte	45RFus	13.07.19	
KEITH, Alexander		195605	LSea	RN	25.08.19	Acc. killed, HMS *Glowworm* explosion
KELLY, Edward	32	131583	Pte	45RFus	10.08.19	Dvina offensive

Name	Age	Number	Rank	Unit	Date	Remarks
KEMP, James	19	66306	Pte	2/10RScots	27.10.18	Attack on Kulika
KEMP, John Miller	19	192239	Pte	8MGC	27.08.19	
KENWORTH, John		114116	Pte	17LpoolR	09.02.19	Defence of Kodish
KIDD, David	27	66131	LCpl	2/10RScots	13.10.18	Defence of Borok
KNIGHT, Clarence R.W.	21		Lieut	RAF	21.06.19	Died of wounds (shrapnel)
LAMBERT, Marie L.B.H.	39		Maj	RASC	24.08.19	Served Boer War
LARAD, R.			2Off	MercMne	20.10.18	HMT *Clan Macrae*
LARLHAM, George	28	365385	LdgCk	RN	28.08.18	HMS *M.25* struck by enemy shellfire
LAUDER, T.			EngOff	MercMne	10.10.18	HMT *Clan Macrae*
LAVIN, James	21	52489	Pte	2/10RScots	11.11.18	Defence of Tulgas
LAWTON, Henry	31	130807	Pte	45RFus	15.09.19	R. Fusiliers Mounted Inf. attack on Tulgas
LeMOINE, Claude Melvin		J/20444	2Lt	RAF	20.08.19	Acc. killed, aircraft accident on Dvina River
LEADBETTER, William George			AB	RN	25.08.19	Acc. killed, HMS *Glowworm* explosion
LEES, Charles	32	377104	Pte	2/10RScots	20.02.19	Died of wounds
LEES, Peter	22	376806	LCpl	2/10RScots	27.10.18	Attack on Kulika
LEGATE, George			EngOff	MercMne	29.10.18	HMT *Seattle*
LEWIS, Ernest William		287608	Mech	RN	06.10.18	HMS *Glory IV*
LIVESY, James Trevor	35		Gnr	RN	03.07.19	HMS *Fandango* mined and sunk
LIVINGSTONE, John	22	43156	Cpl	2/10RScots	11.11.18	Defence of Tulgas
LODGE, Henry William		K/37239	Sto1	RN	06.10.18	HMS *Attentive*
LOGAN, Robert Gibson	25	129594	Pte	45RFus	10.08.19	Dvina offensive
LOVE, Joseph Tracey Taylor		133180	Pte	45RFus	29.06.19	
LYNE, William John	21	161296	Pte	252MGC	25.01.19	
MacDOUGALL, Dugald, DFC	23		Capt	RAF	25.08.19	Acc. killed, HMS *Glowworm* explosion
MacFARLANE, Thomas L.			Lieut	RNVR	25.08.19	Acc. killed, HMS *Glowworm* explosion

Name	Age	Number	Rank	Unit	Date	Description
MacMILLAN, Douglas	19	66317	Pte	2/10RScots	27.10.18	Attack on Kulika
MAHER, Cyril	24	18619	Pte	17LpoolR	09.02.19	Defence of Kodish
MAHONEY, John	29	129213	Pte	46RFus	11.09.19	Bolshevik ambush
MAHONEY, Michael	40	220057	Pte	RAMC	26.08.19	
MAIN, Donal Alexander, MC	25		Capt	2/10RScots	05.09.18	6th Bn, HLI, attd.
MALONE, James		66313	Pte	2/10RScots	27.03.19	
MANN, Stephen William, MM			Lieut	2LondR	27.03.19	Killed in action, attd. RANB
MANSFIELD, Maurice Charles			Lieut	GenList	11.02.19	
MARTIN, Charles		129617	Pte	45RFus	10.08.19	Dvina offensive
MARTIN, John Anthony	32		Lieut	RN	06.10.19	Drowned, HMS *Lobster*, New Zealander
MARTINDALE, William	37	T/1096	Sgt	RAOC	24.05.19	
MAYER, Constantine Anton	30	342085	Sgt	331WksRE	01.06.19	Latvian national
McALPINE, Charles Brown			Lieut	RNR	04.11.18	HMS *Glory*
McCARDLE, John McE.	19	140811	AC1	RAF	01.04.19	Ambush near Bolshie Ozerki
McCOY, John Robert		SS/7701	AB	RN	25.08.19	Acc. killed, HMS *Glowworm* explosion
McCRAE, John	24	K/22922	Sto1	RN	25.08.19	Acc. killed, HMS *Glowworm* explosion
McDONALD, John J.	31	41842	Gnr	68CFA	07.05.19	Died of illness
McDONOUGH, William		29664	Pte	17LpoolR	09.02.19	Defence of Kodish
McKENNA, Peter Joseph		131257	Pte	45RFus	14.09.19	Defence of Nevonovskaya/Bulandovskaya
McKENZIE, James Simon		141175	Pte	8MGC	01.09.19	Defence of Ust-Vaga
McLACHLAN, Thomas		130143	Pte	45RFus	10.08.19	Dvina offensive
McLAGGAN, John	24	130011	Pte	45RFus	14.09.19	Defence of Nevonovskaya/Bulandovskaya
McLAUGHLIN, Cyril Edward			Lieut	RN	11.03.19	Killed attempting to defuse enemy sea mine
McLAUGHLIN, Edward D.		62419	Pte	2/10RScots	21.12.18	Killed in action
McLAUGHLIN, William	18	52288	Pte	2/10RScots	27.10.18	Attack on Kulika

Name	Age	Number	Rank	Unit	Date	Notes
McMILLAN, Michael	26	48141	Pte	8MGC	26.06.19	Killed in action
McWATTIE, John James Hartley			Lieut	RNR	02.01.19	HMT *Aspasia*
McWHIRTER, Samuel	22	52403	Pte	2/10RScots	22.02.19	
MEACHEM, Albert James	25	PO/15568	Pte	RMLI	30.10.18	
MEAD, Edward Maurice Leslie		CH/2569	Pte	RMLI	13.02.19	HMS *Glory*
MELTON, Albert J.		161231	Pte	252MGC	05.05.19	
MERCY, Francis Joseph	49	66436	Sgt	2/10RScots	15.03.19	
MERRITT, Henry George	26	66144	Pte	2/10RScots	10.10.18	Defence of Borok
MESTON-REID, J.			Capt	RE	06.11.18	
METTHAM, James Arthur			Capt	RE	12.11.18	
MICHIE, David	26	377057	L./Cpl	2/10RScots	07.10.18	Defence of Borok
MICHIE, James B.			Lieut	RAMC	31.12.18	
MIDDLEMAS, Robert	26	92102	Gnr	421RFA	09.03.19	Defence of Vistafka
MIDDLETON, George Hilton			Lieut	RAMC	10.08.19	Dvina offensive
MIDGLEY, Percy Beaumont		114275	Pte	17LpoolR	15.12.18	Died (pneumonia)
MILLER, Hugh	21	52277	Pte	2/10RScots	11.11.18	Defence of Tulgas
MILNER, Dermod Ross			Chpln	RN	17.09.19	Killed in fall, HMHS *Garth Castle*
MILSON, William Ewart Emmatt		377059	Pte	2/10RScots	10.10.18	Defence of Borok
MILTON, Charles Lewis	20	50785	LCpl	17LpoolR	09.02.19	Defence of Kodish
MOODY, Henry Hardy		8637	LCpl	1OBLI	15.09.19	Died of wounds, Devon Regt. attd.
MOORE, Alfred		144186	PO	RN	16.10.19	HMS *Chelmsford*
MORRELL, Arthur		62918	Pte	6YorksR	03.04.19	Defence of Shred Mekhrenga
MOWAT, Oliver Alexander, MC	25		Capt	68CFA	27.01.19	Died of wounds, defence of Shenkursk
MULHALL, Peter		133306	Cpl	45RFus	23.07.19	Raid on enemy position near VP450
MURPHY, Joseph		108666	Pte	17LpoolR	05.05.19	Defence of Mala Bereznik

Name		Age	Number	Rank	Unit	Date	Remarks
MURRAY, Bernard			114100	Pte	17LpoolR	28.06.19	
MURRAY, Frederick	20		J/44493	AB	RN	25.08.19	Acc. killed, HMS *Glowworm* explosion
NASH, Edward Robert			128960	Cpl	45RFus	16.09.19	Withdrawal of Dvina Force
NELSON, Charles William	25		L/4055	Stwd2	RN	03.07.19	HMS *Fandango* mined and sunk
NELSON, John	27		22738	Pte	1OBLI	01.09.19	D. wounds, defence of Ust-Vaga, KOSB attd.
NEWTON, Arthur			65046	Sgt	6YorksR	27.03.19	Attack on Bolshie Ozerki
NIMMO, Robert			52791	Pte	2/10RScots	11.11.18	Defence of Tulgas
NUNAN, Noel Daniel	27			2Lt	RAF	24.02.19	D. wounds after forced landing near Onega
NUTTER, Richard			T/440204	Pte	39€RASC	27.08.19	Died of illness
O'DRISCOLL, William			133199	Pte	45RFus	30.06.19	
O'NEILL, John	23		376686	Pte	2/10RScots	27.10.18	Attack on Kulika
O'NEILL, John			129217	Pte	45RFus	10.08.19	Dvina offensive
OLIVER, Robert Stewart	19		53494	Pte	2/10RScots	11.11.18	
OWENS, Alfred	24		330381	Pte	17LpoolR	07.12.18	Attack on Seletskoe
PARKER, Frank Bryan	22			Capt	6YorksR	23.03.19	Attack on Bolshie Ozerki, 7YorksR attd.
PARKER, William, MM			36479	LCpl	280MGC	04.05.19	
PATON, David Smith	20		52241	Pte	2/10RScots	27.10.18	Attack on Kulika
PEARMAN, Ernest			130866	Pte	46RFus	10.08.19	Dvina offensive
PEARSE, Alister Cullen, MC Bar	21			Lieut	45RFus	17.09.19	Died of wounds, Middlesex Regt. attd.
PEARSE, Samuel G. VC, MM	22		133002	Sgt	45RFus.	29.08.19	Attack on Emtsa
PERCY, William John	26		377068	LSgt	2/10RScots	28.10.18	Died of wounds, attack on Kulika
PERETZKER, Abraham			66036	Pte	2/10RScots	13.11.18	Died of wounds, defence of Tulgas
PETTER, Percy Edwin, DCM			128970	LSgt	45RFus	16.09.19	Withdrawal of Dvina Force
PHILLIPS, Henry	19		60197	Pte	1OBLI	01.09.19	Defence of Ust-Vaga, R. War. Regt. attd.
PHILLIPSON, Alfred John			10087	LCpl	1OBLI	11.06.19	Drowned Dvina River, Cheshire Regt. attd.

Name	Age	Number	Rank	Unit	Date	Notes
PICKLES, Arthur	21	377006	LCpl	2/10RScots	09.04.19	Died of wounds
PIMM, Nathan		18536	Pte	1OBLI	01.09.19	Defence of Ust-Vaga, attd. 239th TMB
PINE-COFFIN, Tristram James		33	Lieut	DevonR	23.09.19	
POLLARD, Alexander		109571	Pte	2/7DLI	26.10.18	
PONTING, Denis Lawrence	19	60227	Pte	1OBLI	01.09.19	Defence of Ust-Vaga, R. War. Regt. attd.
PORTER, John J.		280719	Dvr	RFA	16.09.19	Died of wounds (accidental)
POWELL, Richard		66326	Pte	2/10RScots	27.10.18	Attack on Kulika
POWER, Richard		131122	Pte	45RFus	10.08.19	Dvina offensive
POWNALL, John Alfred		66171	Pte	2/10RScots	10.10.18	Defence of Borok
PRICE, Alexander Thomas	28	192237	Cpl	8MGC	09.06.19	
QUAKLEY, William	21	66178	Pte	2/10RScots	10.10.18	Defence of Borok
RALPHS, Arthur	24	66541	Cpl	2/10RScots	11.11.18	Defence of Tulgas
RAMSDEN, A., MM		131176	Pte	46RFus	23.11.20	Died of wounds
READ, Frederick		19546	Pte	2HantsR	01.09.19	Ambush near Bolshie Ozerki, Wilts Rgt attd
RHODES, Isaac Atkinson		62866	LCpl	6YorksR	23.03.19	Attack on Bolshie Ozerki
RHODES, Jack Richard	19	104385	Pte	2/7DLI	15.02.19	
RICHARDSON, Peter Welsh	19	129843	Pte	46RFus	10.08.19	Dvina offensive
ROBERTS, Benjamin	21	129057	Sgt	45RFus	05.01.20	Died of wounds sustained in North Russia
ROBERTS, John Williams		114144	Pte	17LpoolR	09.02.19	Defence of Kodish
ROBERTS, Walter Stanley		97669	Pte	RAMC	12.03.19	
ROBERTSON, Leslie G.D.	19	128979	Pte	45RFus	14.09.19	Defence of Nevonovskaya/Bulandovskaya
ROBINS, George Edward		376940	Pte	2/10RScots	11.11.18	Died of wounds, defence of Tulgas
ROBINSON, Arthur Henry		L/9906	Pte	1OBLI	27.06.19	Died of wounds, attack on Ignatovskaya, RWKR attd.
ROBINSON, George		130256	Pte	45RFus	10.08.19	Dvina offensive

Name	Age	Number	Rank	Unit	Date	Notes
ROSS, Thomas	19	53400	Pte	2/10RScots	14.10.18	Defence of Borok
RUDDELL, Richard	31	40845	Dvr	443RFA	26.07.19	
RUSSELL, Frank H.		87238	Gnr	67CFA	13.11.18	Ambushed, mounted patrol nr. Ust–Padenga
SALISBURY, Frederick Thomas		131015	Cpl	45RFus	10.08.19	Dvina offensive
SALMONS, Christopher DCM		66539	Sgt	2/1CRScots	11.11.18	Defence of Tulgas
SCOTT, George		375288	Sgt	2/1CRScots	27.10.18	Attack on Kulika
SCOTT, George Frederick	26	131222	Pte	45RFus	16.09.19	Died of wounds, withdrawal of Dvina Force
SCOTT, Robert	21	53443	Pte	2/10RScots	07.06.19	
SCUDDER, Henry William		227344	AC1	RAF	02.07.19	Killed attempting to defuse enemy sea mine
SELBY, Thomas	34	302718	Pte	2/7DLI	31.10.18	
SEMENKO, J.	25		Motor1	MMR	12.10.18	HMY *Josephine*. Belgian national
SEVIOUR, William	21	9176	Pte	2HantsR	20.06.19	Attack on Troitsa, Wilts Regt. attd.
SEXTON, Frederick William	29	129587	Pte	46RFus	09.09.19	Defence of Ivanovskaya
SEXTON, John	23	J/24832	LS	RN	02.07.19	Killed attempting to defuse enemy sea mine
SHAW, Frederick Charles	18	194903	AC2	RAF	04.09.19	
SHEPHERD, S.LeFl., MC Bar			Maj	45RFus	10.08.19	Dvina offensive
SIME, Thomas Burness		66350	Pte	2/10RScots	27.10.18	Attack on Kulika
SIMM, Edwin	24	291166	Dvr	RFA	30.03.20	Died of wounds
SIMPSON, Arthur C.	21	159317	Pte	8MGC	13.07.19	
SIMPSON, Eric	20	237635	Spr	103SigRE	24.07.19	
SIMPSON, Harold, DCM	24	66186	CSM	2/10RScots	13.10.18	Defence of Borok, fmly. 6th Bn., SLI
SIMPSON, William Ernest		J/56335	OS	RN	18.09.18	HMS *Glory IV*
SLADE, Robert Henry	19	131555	Pte	45RFus	10.08.19	Dvina offensive
SLINEY, James		129303	Pte	45RFus	08.09.19	Attack on Kodema
SMART, William		301636	Pte	RAMC	03.10.18	

Name	Age	Number	Rank	Unit	Date	Notes
SMITH, Lancelot William Henry	23	J/14515	AB	RN	25.08.19	Acc. killed, HMS *Glowworm* explosion
SNELLGROVE, Ernest		J/43244	AB	RN	25.08.19	Acc. killed, HMS *Glowworm* explosion
SNYDERS, Emanuel Leon	47		2Lt	RASC	17.03.19	
SOUTHERN, James Henry	42	S/9319	Pte	RAOC	07.07.19	
SPACKMAN, Arthur Patrick	27	376822	Sgt	2/10RScots	11.11.18	Defence of Tulgas
SPEIGHT, Albert Thomas	24	S/359064	Sgt	RASC	05.05.19	
SPEIRS, William George	20	66354	Pte	2/10RScots	27.10.18	Attack on Kulika
SPINK, David Martin		66196	Pte	2/10RScots	16.09.18	
STARK, James Chalmers	18	66358	Pte	2/10RScots	27.10.18	Attack on Kulika
STEVENSON, Eric Arthur			2Lt	17LpoolR	07.02.19	Attack near Kodish, Yorkshire Regt. attd.
STODDART, John		133354	Pte	46RFus	29.08.19	Attack on Emtsa
STONELEY, Arthur	40	114307	Pte	17LpoolR	30.05.19	
STRASMAN, Albert	29	376946	Pte	2/10RScots	11.11.18	Died of wounds, defence of Tulgas
STRICKLAND, Alfred Edward		109711	Cpl	2/7DLI	01.06.19	
STUART, Walter Scott		11261/DA	Deckhd	RNR	14.10.18	HMT *William Spencer*
SUGDEN, Ben Roy	21	114187	Pte	17LpoolR	30.12.18	Attack on Tarasova–Kochmas road
SUMMERFIELD, John	33	277263	Pte	2/7DLI	23.01.19	
SWAIN, Frank		910188	FarrSgt	421RFA	01.12.18	
SWAN, James	19	53267	Pte	2/10RScots	27.10.18	Attack on Kulika
SYKES, Harold	19	J/55280	Armr	RN	25.08.19	Acc. killed, HMS *Glowworm* explosion
SYKES, Jesse		57700	Pte	13YorksR	16.07.19	
SYKES, John Bertram		109835	Cpl	2/7DLI	25.10.18	
TASKER, Albert George		109712	Pte	2/7DLI	23.10.18	
TAYLER, William Ulric Chevallier			Lieut	46RFus	10.08.19	Dvina offensive, 1st Bn, RWKR attd.
TAYLOR, Francis Mortimer, MC	30		Maj	RAMC	17.03.19	

TAYLOR, George Leonard		97783	Pte	2HantsR	20.06.19	Attack on Troitsa, R. Fus. attd.
TENSON, W.	40	37360	Cook	MMR	04.05.19	RFA *Belgol*
TEVENDALE, William	20	6116	LCpl	2/10RScots	16.01.19	Wife A. Tevendale, N. Fitzroy, Melbourne
THOMAS, Leonard A., DSM		1937/ST	Trimmer	RNR	18.10.18	HMS *Glory*
THOMSON, George		376116	Pte	2/10RScots	27.10.18	Attack on Kulika
THURSFIELD, R.M.R.	33		SurgLt	RN	25.08.19	Acc. killed, HMS *Glowworm* explosion
TILLEY, William		131286	Pte	RAMC	17.07.19	
TOMBLER, William		403292	Sgt	RAMC	07.02.19	Enemy shell hit aid post, attack on Kodish
TROTTER, John S.		131476	Pte	45RFus	10.08.19	Dvina offensive
TUCKER, Hubert Frederick	19	J/50198	AB	RN	04.08.19	Acc. drowned, HMS *Nairana*
TURNER, Henry James		114356	Pte	17LpoolR	07.12.18	Attack on Seletskoe
TYAS, Samuel	33	220213	Pte	139RAMC	28.08.19	
VESCARDI, Vittore		T/440168	Pte	390RASC	11.06.19	
WAGANOFF, W.G.			Lieut	RN	25.08.19	Acc. killed, HMS *Glowworm* explosion
WALKER, Gerald Francis	36	377084	Sgt	2/10RScots	10.10.18	Defence of Borok
WALKER, Harry		47302	Pte	1OBLI	26.06.19	Attack on Ignatovskaya, 2/10RScots attd.
WALKER, John Sydney		66434	Pte	2/10RScots	27.10.18	Attack on Kulika
WALLACE, John		129840	Pte	46RFus	09.09.19	Defence of Ivanovskaya
WAREHAM, Stanley Belben, MM		42763	Cpl	67CFA	11.11.18	Defence of Tulgas
WARREN, Christopher Frederick	35	308634	Mech	RN	03.07.19	HMS *Fandango* mined and sunk
WARWICK, Walter	25	66381	Pte	2/10RScots	10.10.18	Defence of Borok
WATSON, John Allan	31	129840	2Lt	RGA	31.01.19	Murdered by US soldier
WEBB, James	22	K/19636	AB	RN	03.07.19	HMS *Fandango* mined and sunk
WEDDELL, William John	19	S/389685	Pte	390RASC	29.03.19	
WEIR, Thomas Steel		376535	Cpl	2/10RScots	27.10.18	Attack on Kulika

Name		Service No.	Rank	Unit	Date	Notes
WELSH, W.W.			Pte	1OBLI	27.06.19	Attack on Ignatovskaya, Devon Regt. attd. Not recorded CWGC
WHITE, John Henry, MM		036	Sgt	1OBLI	26.06.19	Attack on Ignatovskaya
WILKES, Charles	22	9615	Sgt	1OBLI	01.09.19	Defence of Ust-Vaga, R. War. Regt. attd.
WINTON, A.		11716	EngOff	MercMne	31.10.18	HMT *Kyleakin*
WOOD, Charles		07058	Sgt	RAOC	31.10.18	
WOODRIFFE, Harry Herbert		M/520	ERA3	RN	15.09.18	HMS *Glory IV*
WORTHINGTON, Cecil John		312887	Cpl	68CFA	24.01.19	Enemy shell, defence of Shenkursk
WREN, Christopher George	19	130961	Pte	45RFus	10.08.19	Dvina offensive
WRIGHT, Albert Henry		114191	Cpl	17LpoolR	10.02.19	Defence of Shred Mekhrenga
WRIGHT, H.		J/35323	AB	RN	25.08.19	Acc. killed, HMS *Glowworm* explosion
WRIGHT, Stanley	20	J/22771	OS	RN	14.09.18	HMS *Glory IV*
WRIGHT, William Edward		131207	Pte	45RFus	14.09.19	Defence of Nevonovskaya/Bulandovskaya
YACAMINI, Clarence William	19	66045	Pte	2/10RScots	13.11.18	Defence of Tulgas
ZIGOMALA, John C., MBE	21		Lieut	Irish Guards	25.08.19	Killed, HMS *Glowworm* explosion, attd. RE

Siberia

Name		Service No.	Rank	Unit	Date	Notes
ANNELLS, Thomas, MSM	31	PW/2618	CSM	25MidxR	31.07.19	
BIDDLE, Edward		77103	Pte	CSEF	22.10.18	Died (influenza), buried at sea
BONIFACE, Benjamin		G/39718	Pte	25MidxR	15.08.19	
BOSTON, Walter	26	3212961	Pte	CSEF	16.04.19	16th Fld. Amb., CAMC
BREWER, Albert Edward James		J/51017	AB	RN	05.11.18	HMS *Suffolk*
BRITTON, Gilbert		K/40777	Sto1	RN	14.07.18	HMS *Suffolk*
BUNGAY, James		TF/208204	Pte	25MidxR	09.02.19	
BURT, Leonard Robert		355728	Pte	1/9HantsR	29.05.19	
BUTLER, Harold Leo		2768761	Rfmn	CSEF	31.12.18	Acc. killed, buried at sea, 259th Bn.
CARTER, H.F.H., MC			LtCol	KOYLI	28.02.19	

CROSSLEY, George William		G/99184	Pte	25MidxR	17.12.18	
CRUSE, Edward John		G/39145	Pte	25MidxR	29.01.19	
DAVIES, C.		0844	Pte	1/9HantsR	16.03.20	
DIGBY-JONES, Charles Kenelm			Capt	RE	25.09.18	
DODD, William Edwards	35	2770021	Pte	CSEF	05.04.19	Died (toxaemia), 260th Bn.
ELLIS, Richard	35	39732	Pte	1/9HantsR	17.03.19	
FELLEGER, Ralph		L/15784	Pte	25MidxR	02.07.19	
FORD, William Lew			Chpln	RN	09.05.18	HMS *Suffolk*
FULLER, John		TF/208200	Pte	25MidxR	16.01.19	
GILLESPIE, Earl		2770501	Pte	CSEF	19.03.19	260th Bn.
HARDING, Charles		G/49205	Pte	25MidxR	20.11.18	
HENDERSON, William John	19	2772673	Pte	CSEF	29.12.18	Died (meningitis), RNWMP
HIGGINS, David		3209524	Bugler	CSEF	06.03.19	Died (pericarditis), 260th Bn.
HOWARTH, Thomas	21	J/20280	AB	RN	28.04.18	HMS *Suffolk*
KAY, Frank Joseph		3139773	Pte	CSEF	28.12.18	Acc. killed, buried at sea, 259th Bn.
LARVIERE, Romeo		3091184	Pte	CSEF	11.03.19	Died (pneumonia), 259th Bn.
LAWES, Charles Albert		355186	Sgt	1/9HantsR	28.04.19	
LEONARD, Frederick Samuel		0953	Pte	1/9HantsR	05.02.19	Formerly 37689, SLI
MANION, James Floran	17	3214452	Pte	CSEF	22.02.19	Died (pneumonia), 260th Bn.
MANSON, Samuel	28	3567	Sto	RNR	18.02.19	Died of illness, HMS *Kent*
MARSH, Henry		K/14716	StoPO	RN	22.10.19	HMS *Carlisle*
MARTIN, Alfred John		G/39414	Pte	25MidxR	22.01.19	
MASSEY, Richard		3356470	Pte	CSEF	30.05.19	Died of illness, CAOC
MAY, Alfred		39771	Pte	1/9HantsR	19.06.19	
McDONALD, Joseph Emmett		2769528	LCpl	CSEF	28.02.19	Died (pneumonia)

Name	Age	Number	Rank	Unit	Date	Notes
McMILLAN, Peter		3040731	Pte	CSEF	06.06.19	Died of illness, 259th Bn.
OSOLL, Ernest Karl Waldemer			Civilian	BMM		Date unknown, CSEF
REED, William Henry		PO/20028	Pte	RMLI	09.09.19	HMS *Carlisle*
SMITH, David John	30	297225	LSto	RN	24.09.19	HMS *Carlisle*
SOTHERN, Roy		3348086	Pte	CSEF	04.03.19	Died (pneumonia), 260th Bn.
STEEL, Edward Anthony, DSO	38		LtCol	RFA	14.10.19	Formerly West African Frontier Force
STEPHENSON, Edwin Howard	33	261974	Pte	CSEF	24.05.19	Died (smallpox), 11th Stat. Hosp., CAMC
TAYLOR, William Humphrey	35	39829	Pte	1/9HantsR	30.07.19	
THRING, Alfred Henry			Lieut	CSEF	18.03.19	Gun shot wound (suicide), 260th Bn.
TONG, Alfred		G/39726	Pte	25MidxR	17.05.19	
WADE, Edward Charles		G/39623	Pte	25MidxR	16.09.18	
WARD, Frederick Eaton		3181048	Pte	CSEF	02.03.19	Died (pneumonia), 20th Coy, CMGC
WEBB, Samuel James	42	G/39394	Sgt	25MidxR	13.09.18	
WELLS, Henry		G/39750	Pte	25MidxR	08.02.19	
WORTHINGTON, Ernest	39	479930	QMS	CSEF	06.03.19	
WRIGLEY, William		G/102791	Pte	25MidxR	31.08.19	
WYNN, John Shirley Murray	35	2006180	Sgt	CSEF	14.01.19	16th Fld. Coy, CE

Baltic Sea

Name	Age	Number	Rank	Unit	Date	Notes
ACKLAND, John, MSM	36	S/717	SQMS	RAMC	18.08.20	BMM Baltic
ADAMS, Herbert James	22	K/24581	Sto1	RN	04.06.19	HMS *L.55* sunk
ALMOND, Percy James	23	J/22758	AB	RN	17.10.19	HMS *Dragon* struck by German artillery
AMEY, John Edward Herr	33	MC/360	Sto1	RN	15.07.19	HMS *Myrtle* sunk by mine
ANGUS, Donald Meikeljohn	27	272470	ERA3	RN	04.06.19	HMS *L.55* sunk
ASHLEY, Alexis William	18		Midsh	RN	03.09.19	HMS *Verulam* mined, sunk
BAMBRIDGE, Herbert, DSM	27	J/3947	AB	RN	31.08.19	HMS *Vittoria* sunk

Name	Age	Number	Rank	Service	Date	Notes
BARTON, William Edward	25	J/7515	LS	RN	04.06.19	HMS *L.55* sunk
BENNETT, George Hicks		191017	PO	RN	31.12.19	HM Drifter *Catspaw*, sunk
BIRCH, Alexander	27	MC/375	Sto1	RN	15.07.19	HMS *Myrtle* sunk by mine
BOULTON, John	20	J/450369	AB	RN	03.09.19	HMS *Verulam* mined, sunk
BOWERMAN, Thomas John	19	M/14502	ERA5	RN	31.12.19	HM Drifter *Catspaw*, sunk
BOYD, William	36	297445	POSto	RN	15.07.19	HMS *Gentian* sunk by mine
BRADE, Frank Tomkinson, DSC	32		LtCdr	RNR	18.08.19	*CMB 67*, Kronstadt Raid
BREWER, Arthur Bertie	31	310926	Mech	RN	31.12.19	HM Drifter *Catspaw*, sunk
BROAD, Charles William	23	J/20915	AB	RN	17.10.19	HMS *Dragon* struck by German artillery
BULLOCK, James W.	23	J/21915	AB	RN	27.09.19	HMS *Phaeton*
BUNTING, Arthur		21090	Pte	ManchR	13.12.18	
BULLOCK, James W.	23	J/21915	AB	RN	27.09.19	HMS *Phaeton*
BUTLER, Harry	26	K/15724	Sto1	RN	04.06.19	HMS *L.55* sunk
CARDWELL, Fred	20		P/O	RAF	25.10.19	Shot down by flak over Kronstadt
CHAPMAN, Manners, DSC Bar	30		Lieut	RN	04.06.19	HMS *L.55* sunk
CLAREY, Albert Webb	25	J/7631	PO	RN	31.08.19	HMS *Vittoria* sunk
CLARK, Thomas Joseph	23	SS/117078	Sto1	RN	03.09.19	HMS *Verulam* mined, sunk
CLARKSON, Albert	25	J/28603	LS	RN	04.06.19	HMS *L.55* sunk
CLIFTON, Frederick		K/18374	Sto1	RN	04.06.19	HMS *L.55* sunk
COOKSON, Edgar Charles			S/Lt	RN	03.09.19	HMS *Verulam* mined, sunk
COWLES, Edward James	24	J/12334	LSig	RN	20.10.19	Died of illness, HMS *Abdiel*
CRAIG, Henry David Cook, MC	32		Maj	HLI	13.02.20	DAQMG, BMM Baltic
CROMIE, Francis N.A., CB, DSO	36		Capt	RN	31.08.18	Killed defending British Embassy
CROOK, Herbert	26	J/4894	PO	RN	04.06.19	HMS *L.55* sunk
CRYSELL, Albert William	23	J/15756	AB	RN	04.06.19	HMS *L.55* sunk

Name	Age	Number	Rank	Service	Date	Notes
DAGG, Charles Frederick	26	J/3758	POTel	RN	04.06.19	HMS *L.55* sunk
DAVIES, Leonard Frank	25	J/7627	LSig	RN	04.06.19	HMS *L.55* sunk
DAWSON, Samuel, DFC	24		Lieut	RAF	17.09.19	Shot down by flak over Kronstadt
DINGLE, Edward Henry	23	K/24623	Sto1	RN	31.12.19	HM Drifter *Catspaw*, sunk
DAYRELL-REED, Archibald, DSO and Bar	31		Lieut	RN	18.08.19	Died of Wounds, *CMB 88*, Kronstadt Raid
EBLING, Francis John	25	M/2182	ERA3	RN	04.06.19	HMS *L.55* sunk
EDGECOMBE, Arthur Wilfrid	18		Midsh	RN	03.09.19	HMS *Verulam* mined, sunk
EGGLESTON, Charles Henry	24	K/31712	Sto1	RN	05.12.18	HMS *Cassandra* sunk by mine
ELLIOTT, John	27	K/13388	Sto1	RN	03.09.19	HMS *Verulam* mined, sunk
ENGLAND, Charles Henry	19	249558	AC1	RAF	22.07.19	Listed as 'Died', buried Koivisto, Finland
FENN, William	23	J/18493	AB	RN	04.06.19	HMS *L.55* sunk
FINNIS, Jack Files	28	K/16255	Sto 1	RN	04.06.19	HMS *L.55* sunk
FLOCKHART, William	56	MC/400	ERA4	RN	15.07.19	HMS *Gentian* sunk by mine
FLODIN, Robert	27	K/8277	LSto	RN	04.06.19	HMS *L.55* sunk
FRENCH, Henry George Hazelden	17	J/79157	BoyTel	RN	04.06.19	HMS *L.55* sunk
GASCOYNE, Archibald Thomas	24	J/11344	AB	RN	04.06.19	HMS *L.55* sunk
GIDDY, Joseph	42	279642	POSto	RN	05.12.18	HMS *Cassandra* sunk by mine
GILHOOLY, John Joseph	34	305788	POSto	RN	05.12.18	HMS *Cassandra* sunk by mine
GILLIES, James Cunningham		MC/410	ERA4	RN	15.07.19	HMS *Myrtle* sunk by mine
GILLINGWATER, Lewis T.E.	20	J/34181	AB	RN	17.10.19	HMS *Dragon* struck by German artillery
GISSING, Joseph	25	J/8374	AB	RN	04.06.19	HMS *L.55* sunk
GRIFFITHS, Clifford		K/12149	LSto	RN	04.06.19	HMS *L.55* sunk
GUY, James	31	226859	CPO	RN	04.06.19	HMS *L.55* sunk
HAIGH, Ernest	19	J/44770	AB	RN	15.07.19	HMS *Gentian* sunk by mine
HAMMERSLEY, Rupert Lawrence	25	J/5015	LS	RN	04.06.19	HMS *L.55* sunk

Name	Age	Number	Rank	Service	Date	Ship/Remarks
HANDEL, Thomas Henry	25	M/7794	SBA	RN	04.10.19	HMHS *Berbice*
HARNESS, John David	22	J/31257	AB	RN	31.08.19	HMS *Vittoria* sunk
HAWKINS, Veines James, DSM	25	J/13592	LS	RN	02.05.19	Accidentally drowned, HMS *Vindictive*
HIRST, John	21	TZ/9031	AB	RNVR	12.07.19	HMS *Gentian*
HOLMES, Sidney Davison		J/15841	LS	RN	18.08.19	*CMB 62*, Kronstadt Raid
HOUSE, Joseph, DSC	40		EngLt	RN	03.09.19	HMS *Verulam* mined,
HOWES, James	26	K/23105	Sto1	RN	04.06.19	HMS *L.55* sunk
HUTCHINGS, Ernest	19	J/41101	AB	RN	31.08.19	HMS *Vittoria* sunk
JACKSON, Arthur Frederick	21	J/41800	AB	RN	03.09.19	HMS *Verulam* mined, sunk
JARVIS, Harold William		K/488	LSto	RN	03.09.19	HMS *Verulam* mined, sunk
JENKINS, David James		SS/120469	Sto1	RN	31.12.19	HM Drifter *Catspaw*, sunk
JENNINGS, Harry Clarence	29		Lieut	RN	04.06.19	HMS *L.55* sunk
JOHNSON, Robert	29	M/13305	Shpwr3	RN	15.07.19	HMS *Myrtle* sunk by mine
JUSTIN, Thomas Henry	23	J/20176	AB	RN	31.12.19	HM Drifter *Catspaw*, sunk
KING, William	42	286715	ChSto	RN	03.09.19	HMS *Verulam* mined, sunk
KINGSBURY, Walter Stenhouse	30	K/52659	Sto2	RN	05.12.18	HMS *Cassandra* sunk by mine
LARN, William		J/84897	OS	RN	17.10.19	HMS *Dragon* struck by German artillery
LEADON, John	22	SS/6815	AB	RN	31.12.19	HM Drifter *Catspaw*, sunk
LEES, Arthur	19	K/55385	Sto1	RN	31.12.19	HM Drifter *Catspaw*, sunk
LEES, Charles C.D.	25		Lieut	RN	03.09.19	HMS *Verulam* mined, sunk
LEVEN, Bernard	27	K/11579	LSto	RN	04.06.19	HMS *L.55* sunk
LILLEY, Roger Arthur	21	M/29898	ERA4	RN	04.06.19	HMS *L.55* sunk
LOWE, George William	20	J/38578	AB	RN	17.10.19	HMS *Dragon* struck by German artillery
MacLEAN, Hector Forbes			S/Lt	RN	18.08.19	*CMB 62*, Kronstadt Raid
MADDEN, Edward	36	MC/1688	LSto	RN	12.06.19	HMS *Hexham*

Name	Age	Number	Rank		Date	Fate
MARCEL, Hedley Augustus	19	J/91014	OS	RN	31.12.19	HM Drifter *Catspaw*, sunk
MARTIN, Richard	35		SurgLt	RN	25.12.19	Accidentally drowned Reval, HMS *Grenville*
MILES, Ernest Arthur	26	J/8763	LS	RN	31.08.19	HMS *Vittoria* sunk
McCREA, Robert Litterick, DSM	25	MC/49	POSto	RN	15.07.19	HMS *Gentian* sunk by mine
McGILLIVRAY, William		309172	Sto1	RN	05.12.18	HMS *Cassandra* sunk by mine
McVEIGH, John Marmion	22	MC/433	Sto1	RN	15.07.19	HMS *Gentian* sunk by mine
O'BRIEN, Daniel		304458	Mech	RN	05.12.18	HMS *Cassandra* sunk by mine
O'CONNELL, Denis	28	K/9557	LSto	RN	04.06.19	HMS *L.55* sunk
ORME, Louis	23	J/22122	AB	RN	04.06.19	HMS *L.55* sunk
OWERS, Leonard George		J/36904	AB	RN	31.08.19	HMS *Vittoria* sunk
PACKMAN, Thomas Robert	32	M/23475	CERA	RN	15.07.19	HMS *Myrtle* sunk by mine
PARNELL, William	27	K/5042	POSto	RN	04.06.19	HMS *L.55* sunk
PARSONS, Randall Robert	28	238893	LS	RN	03.09.19	HMS *Verulam* mined, sunk
PARTRIDGE, Richard Harold	22	K/43684	Sto2	RN	05.12.18	HMS *Cassandra* sunk by mine
PAYNE, Alfred John	17	J/90873	Boy1	RN	17.10.19	HMS *Dragon* struck by German artillery
PENDRILL, Reginald Joyce		J/38465	AB	RN	03.09.19	HMS *Verulam* mined, sunk
PERKINS, Cyril Edward		K/41030	Stoker 1	RN	05.12.18	HMS *Cassandra* sunk by mine
PETFORD, Ernest	23	M/10275	Cook	RN	02.11.19	HMS *Maidstone*
PETITT, John Edward	19	J/48470	AB	RN	31.08.19	HMS *Vittoria* sunk
PLUNKETT, George Harry	18	SS/9510	OS	RN	13.05.19	HMS *Curacoa* struck by mine
POLLEY, Frank Alfred Richmond	21	J/32369	AB	RN	03.09.19	HMS *Verulam* mined,
POTTER, Cyril Charles Nicholas	30	M/2722	ERA2	RN	04.06.19	HMS *L.55* sunk
POTTS, Bertram Edwin	28	J/1511	AB	RN	04.06.19	HMS *L.55* sunk
POWELL, Owen Philip	21		S/Lt	RN	03.09.19	HMS *Verulam* mined, sunk
PRIMMETT, Arthur	27	K/2814	LSto	RN	15.07.19	HMS *Myrtle* sunk by mine

Name	Age	No.	Rank	Service	Date	Ship/Notes
RAMPTON, Frederick George		183835	CPO	RN	30.07.19	HMS *Princess Margaret*
RAXWORTHY, Henry F.	21	J/34915	AB	RN	11.12.19	HMS *Dragon*
REID, John Stewart Gilchrist, DSC	33		Lieut	RN	04.06.19	HMS *L.55* sunk
REYNOLDS, Patrick	40	287229	POsto	RN	05.12.18	HMS *Cassandra* sunk by mine
REYNOLDS, Roland	21		Lieut	RN	31.12.19	HM Drifter *Catspaw*, sunk
RUFFELL, William Frederick	19	J/84918	OS	RN	03.09.19	HMS *Verulam* mined, sunk
RYDER, Thomas	28	K/9251	POsto	RN	05.12.18	HMS *Cassandra* sunk by mine
SEARLES, Walter	21	J/25694	AB	RN	31.08.19	HMS *Vittoria* sunk
SHAW, William Fleetwood, DSM	29	271948	ERA2	RN	04.06.19	HMS *L.55* sunk
SHRAPNELL, Arthur Frederick	22	J/26736	AB	RN	05.12.18	HMS *Cassandra* sunk by mine
SLEATH, James William	19	SS/8121	OS	RN	17.10.19	HMS *Dragon* struck by German artillery
SMITH, William George	23	J/18754	AB	RN	18.08.19	*CMB 79*, Kronstadt Raid
SOUTHWELL, Henry K.M.	24		Lieut	RN	04.06.19	HMS *L.55* sunk
STAINES, John Patrick		K/15531	Sto1	RN	04.06.19	HMS *L.55* sunk
STEPHENS, Francis Edward	21	MB/3005	CMM	RNVR	18.08.19	*CMB 72*, Kronstadt Raid
STROUD, John Stephens		204391	PO	RN	17.10.19	HMS *Dragon* struck by German artillery
TAYLOR, Norman Samuel	20		Lieut	RAF	13.08.19	Crashed on take off at Koivisto
TAYLOR, Thomas James Charles	24	J/13653	PO	RN	04.06.19	HMS *L.55* sunk
THATCHER, Francis Leslie Howe	20	MB/1974	CMM	RNVR	18.08.19	*CMB 62*, Kronstadt Raid
TRETT, William Robert Harper	17	J/86811	Boy1	RN	17.10.19	HMS *Dragon* struck by German artillery
TRICKETT, Charles	26	K/14239	Sto1	RN	04.06.19	HMS *L.55* sunk
TUNDERVARY, John Herbert		K/10680	LSto	RN	04.06.19	HMS *L.55* sunk
UNWIN, Francis John	22		Lieut	RAF	17.09.19	Shot down by flak over Kronstadt
USBORNE, Thomas Richard Guy	18		S/Lt	RN	18.08.19	*CMB 79*, Kronstadt Raid
VALLINGS, Frederick Francis Orr	20		S/Lt	RN	31.12.19	HM Drifter *Catspaw*, sunk

Name	Age	Number	Rank	Branch	Date	Notes
WAKELY, Alfred Henry	35		ERA	RN	04.06.19	HMS *L.55* sunk
WASH, Walter Herbert	24	J/12352	AB	RN	04.06.19	HMS *L.55* sunk
WEBB, Charles Stephen	20	J/40368	AB	RN	31.12.19	HM Drifter *Catspaw*, sunk
WEIR, Alexander	18	MC/913	Sto1	RN	15.07.19	HMS *Gentian* sunk by mine
WELLS, Charles Tingay	23	J/23612	AB	RN	04.06.19	HMS *L.55* sunk
WESTCOTT, Grenfield	33	K/1139	LSto	RN	04.06.19	HMS *L.55* sunk
WILDING, Thomas Edward	28	K/16770	POSto	RN	31.12.19	HM Drifter *Catspaw*, sunk
WILKS, Frank		J/7669	PO	RN	04.06.19	HMS *L.55* sunk
WILLIAMS, Geoffrey H. Collman	21		Lieut	RN	31.12.19	HM Drifter *Catspaw*, sunk
WILSON, Thomas Matthew	19	J/76227	AB	RN	08.10.19	HMS *Windsor Castle*

South Russia

Name	Age	Number	Rank	Branch	Date	Notes
ADAMS, Herbert George	18	161234	AC2		26.10.19	Worked Bristol Aeroplane Company
ANDERSON, William Oliver		J/25289	AB	RN	28.08.19	HMS *Theseus II*
BALDWIN, Sidney	20	367531	Spr	RE	22.07.19	
BARDWELL, George Frederick	31	200140	Cpl	RAMC	16.01.20	
BARRITT, Douglas Reynolds	39	S/10639	Pte	RAOC	12.02.20	
BEAVERS, John Robert		69470	Sgt	RFA	01.02.20	
BINGHAM, William Henry, OBE	43		LtCol	IndArmy	18.03.20	69th Punjabis attd., BMM, suicide
BLEWITT, Albert Pretoria	18	J/54766	OS	RN	03.01.19	HMS *Temeraire*
BROCKS, Leslie Baden	18	L/8944	OStwd3	RN	12.12.18	HMS *Superb*
BROWN, M.		92579	Pte	RWelchFus	12.01.20	2nd Battalion
BRUNDRED, William	23	329969	AC2		23.01.20	
BUSHELL, Charles Henry	19	61188	Pte	EssexR	08.02.20	2nd Battalion
BUTTIGIEG, Antonio	23	886	Labr	MaltLCorps	31.05.20	
CASSIDY, James		37082	Sgt	RGA	01.11.19	

Name	Age	Number	Rank	Unit	Date	Remarks
CAZALET, Ronald De Bode			Capt	GenList	08.01.20	Att. South Russia Detachment, Tank Corps
COUCHE, Henry John, MC	25		Lieut	MGC	09.01.20	
COX, William		33823	Sgt	GloucsR	26.02.20	7th Battalion
CUNLIFFE, John		110447	Pte	TankCps	15.12.19	
DAMARY, Frederick William	23	68341	Dvr	RFA	10.08.19	101st Brigade
DAWSON, James William	19	42127	Sgt	DWR	16.01.20	2nd Battalion
DE COUNDOUROFF, George	27		Lieut	SpList	25.07.19	
DOCHERTY, John	19	36538	Pte	AVC	09.10.19	
DUFF, Edward Algernon			Capt	TankCps	22.09.19	Died of sickness, 8th Battalion
ELLIOTT, John		308084	Cpl	TankCps	06.03.20	
EVERSDEN, Robert Ernest	24		Capt	47SqnRAF	15.08.19	Acc. shot by sentry
FARRUGIA, Guiseppe	30	365483	OClerk3	RN	30.12.19	HMS *Blenheim*
FRECHEVILLE, William Ralph	24		Capt	RE	09.01.20	Murdered whilst POW of Red Army
FREEMAN, Frank Oliver	20	331013	AC2	47SqnRAF	27.12.19	
GARVEY, James Thomas		331023	AC2		24.12.19	
HALL, Henry John	37	209947	Sgt	221SqnRAF	23.07.19	
HUNTER, David	44		Maj	SpList	18.10.19	Army Gym Staff
JAGGER, Norman Victor		M/7104	ERA4	RN	15.12.19	HMS *Theseus II*
JEMMESON, George Edwin	20		2Lt	221SqnRAF	15.05.19	
KEYMER, Basil, DFC Bar	20		Capt	47SqnRAF	24.10.19	Killed in flying accident
LACEY, William		37999	Sgt	RGA	25.07.19	
LANE, Jack Cecil		377142	Spr	RE	15.11.19	
MacKENZIE, Alexander Smith		PLY/2180	Pte	RMLI	19.12.18	3rd RM Battalion
MacMILLAN, John	27	2753	Sto	RNR	21.05.19	HMS *Grafton*
McLENNAN, John Lawrence, MC	36		Capt	47SqnRAF	28.08.19	Killed in action near Tsaritsyn

Name						
MILNE, W.K.A.			AB	MercMne	13.01.20	SS *Grodno*
MOORE, William Ellender	31	235944	LS	RN	08.02.20	HMS *Julius*
MORGAN, Cecil Edgar	28	ES/49811	Pte	RASC	27.01.20	
NICKLEN, Reginald James	19	J/45235	AB	RN	22.09.19	HMS *Caradoc*
NIXON, Herbert	27	ES/58659	Pte	RASC	25.01.20	Motor Transport
O'NEILL, Ambrose	39	M/280547	Cpl	RASC	03.08.19	
PATTERSON, William George		228491	AB	RN	09.08.19	HMS *Victory*
PRICHARD, Francis Hesketh			Capt	RGA	01.02.20	
PUPLETT, Joseph Robert	27	RMA/1973	Gnr	RMA	28.12.18	
REYNER, Maurice Percy	24	S/7148	2Cpl	RAOC	22.08.19	
RICHARDSON, John Thomas		587490	Pte	RASC	25.01.20	Labour Corps attached
RICHARDSON, William Francis	37		Capt	RE	07.02.20	
ROCK, Sydney James	19	62845	Pte	RWarR	01.02.20	3rd Battalion
SAMPSON, William James	22	36024	Pte	WorcsR	24.05.19	9th Battalion
SKINNER, Charles Edwin	35		Maj	RFA	13.01.20	
SKINNER, Leslie	19	23451	Cpl	RAPC	20.01.20	
STREVENS, Charles Edward	28		Bosun	RN	08.12.18	HMS *Superb*
SUMPTER, George, DSO, MC Bar	28		Capt	RFA	20.08.20	
TAIT, Leonard Henderson	19	261765	AC1	47SqnRAF	12.10.19	
THOMPSON, Douglas Blaxland	27		Lieut	47SqnRAF	24.10.19	Killed in flying accident, formerly RFA
TREMLETT, Francis Frederick		212980	PO	RN	05.05.20	HMS *Benbow*
TURNER, Douglas Blaxland			Lieut	221SqnRAF	15.05.19	
WEEKS, Ernest Henry	34	305276	LSto	RN	22.01.20	HMS *Concord*
WILLIAMS, Griffith		K/1591	LSto	RN	22.02.20	HMS *Caesar*
WINCH, Robert William		670039	Pte	Labour Corps	25.07.19	

Turkestan

ALAM, Nur	2152	Sepoy	19Punjabi	14.10.18	Battle of Dushak
ALI, Bahadur	744	Naik	19Punjabi	14.10.18	Battle of Dushak
BEG, Muhammad	2851	Sepoy	19Punjabi	14.10.18	Battle of Dushak
DAD, Jahan	1100	Sepoy	19Punjabi	14.10.18	Battle of Dushak
DIN, Karm	2483	Sepoy	19Punjabi	23.10.18	
DINA		Follwr	28LtCav	26.10.18	
GUL, Haji	1307	LNaik	19Punjabi	28.08.18	Defence of Kaakha
GUL, Hasan	1282	Naik	19Punjabi	14.10.18	Battle of Dushak
HAKIM, Abdul	2822	Sepoy	19Punjabi	14.10.18	Battle of Dushak
HAMID, Abdul	2862	Sepoy	19Punjabi	28.08.18	Defence of Kaakha
HASA, Gul	441	Hvldr	19Punjabi	16.01.19	Defence of Annenkovo
HAYATULLAH	3365	Sepoy	19Punjabi	14.10.18	Battle of Dushak
ISRARUDDIN	3541	Sepoy	19Punjabi	14.10.18	Battle of Dushak
JINDA		Follwr	19Punjabi	16.01.19	Defence of Annenkovo
KHAN, Abdullah	2479	Sepoy	19Punjabi	14.10.18	Battle of Dushak
KHAN, Chaudri	455	Hvldr	19Punjabi	28.08.18	Defence of Kaakha
KHAN, Farid	989	Hvldr	19Punjabi	16.01.19	Defence of Annenkovo
KHAN, Gulfaraz	2479	Sowar	28LtCav	02.03.19	Skirmish with Red cavalry
KHAN, Lal	2165	Sepoy	19Punjabi	14.10.18	Battle of Dushak
KHAN, Makhan	2770	Sepoy	19Punjabi	14.10.18	Battle of Dushak
KHAN, Mehdi		Subdr	19Punjabi	14.10.18	Battle of Dushak
KHAN, Nawab	3320	Sepoy	19Punjabi	15.09.18	Skirmish near Kaakha
MAKHATUDDI	3386	Sepoy	19Punjabi	14.10.18	Battle of Dushak
MUHAMMAD, Din	2760	Sepoy	19Punjabi	14.10.18	Battle of Dushak

MUHAMMAD, Din		Follwr	28LtCav	26.10.18	Skirmish near Kaakha
MUHAMMAD, Dost	3560	Sepoy	19Punjabi	15.09.18	Defence of Annenkovo
MUHAMMAD, Fateh	711	Naik	19Punjabi	16.01.19	Defence of Annenkovo
RAKHMAN, Gul	1605	LNaik	19Punjabi	16.01.19	Defence of Annenkovo
RAM, Basanta		Jmdr	28LtCav	17.10.18	Died of Wounds, Battle of Dushak
SAPURA	3199	Sowar	28LtCav	26.10.18	
SHAH, Walayat	1542	Sepoy	19Punjabi	14.10.18	Battle of Dushak
SHAH, Walayat	1596	Naik	19Punjabi	16.01.19	Defence of Annenkovo
SINGH, Amar	714	Sepoy	19Punjabi	14.10.18	Battle of Dushak
SINGH, Amar	714	Sepoy	19Punjabi	14.10.18	Battle of Dushak
SINGH, Barisal	2784	Sowar	28LtCav	23.10.18	
SINGH, Barisal	2784	Sowar	28LtCav	23.10.18	
SINGH, Bela	2833	Sowar	28LtCav	14.10.18	Battle of Dushak
SINGH, Budh	1801	Sepoy	19Punjabi	14.10.18	Battle of Dushak
SINGH, Channan	3004	Sepoy	19Punjabi	14.10.18	Battle of Dushak
SINGH, Channan	3004	Sepoy	19Punjabi	14.10.18	Battle of Dushak
SINGH, Dharm	1895	Sepoy	19Punjabi	14.10.18	Battle of Dushak
SINGH, Ganga	2423	Sepoy	19Punjabi	14.10.18	Battle of Dushak
SINGH, Harnam	2670	Sepoy	19Punjabi	15.09.18	Skirmish near Kaakha
SINGH, Hazara	1165	Sepoy	19Punjabi	14.10.18	Battle of Dushak
SINGH, Hukam	2617	Sepoy	19Punjabi	14.10.18	Battle of Dushak
SINGH, Hukam		Subdr	19Punjabi	16.01.19	Defence of Annenkovo
SINGH, Idan	2528	Sowar	28LtCav	23.10.18	
SINGH, Jagat	2122	Sepoy	19Punjabi	14.10.18	Battle of Dushak
SINGH, Jawahar	1280	Sepoy	19Punjabi	16.01.19	Defence of Annenkovo

Name		Number	Rank	Regiment	Date	Event
SINGH, Khushal		2610	Sepoy	19Punjabi	14.10.18	Battle of Dushak
SINGH, Kishn		1455	Naik	19Punjabi	14.10.18	Battle of Dushak
SINGH, Lachman		236	Naik	19Punjabi	14.10.18	Battle of Dushak
SINGH, Lakha		2343	Sepoy	19Punjabi	14.10.18	Battle of Dushak
SINGH, Lal		2024	Sepoy	19Punjabi	14.10.18	Battle of Dushak
SINGH, Mainga		3024	Sowar	23LtCav	23.10.18	
SINGH, Mangal		1369	Sepoy	19Punjabi	14.10.18	Battle of Dushak
SINGH, Mula		2132	Sepoy	19Punjabi	14.10.18	Battle of Dushak
SINGH, Munsha		2935	Sepoy	19Punjabi	14.10.18	Battle of Dushak
SINGH, Munsha		2481	Sepoy	19Punjabi	14.10.18	Battle of Dushak
SINGH, Munsha		2534	Sepoy	19Punjabi	14.10.18	Battle of Dushak
SINGH, Naranjan		4959	Hvldr	19Punjabi	14.10.18	Battle of Dushak
SINGH, Narayan		245	Naik	19Punjabi	14.10.18	Battle of Dushak
SINGH, Nikka		1862	Sepoy	19Punjabi	16.01.19	Defence of Annenkovo
SINGH, Pabudan		2469	L/Dfdr	28LtCav	14.10.18	Battle of Dushak
SINGH, Pheru		339	L/Naik	19Punjabi	14.10.18	Battle of Dushak
SINGH, Puran		2542	Sepoy	19Punjabi	14.10.18	Battle of Dushak
SINGH, Rur		2331	Sepoy	19Punjabi	14.10.18	Battle of Dushak
SINGH, Rur		1277	Sepoy	19Punjabi	16.01.19	Defence of Annenkovo
SINGH, Sabi		2679	Sepoy	19Punjabi	14.10.18	Battle of Dushak
SINGH, Sewa		1171	L/Naik	19Punjabi	28.08.18	Defence of Kaakha
SINGH, Sukha		2874	Sepoy	19Punjabi	14.10.18	Battle of Dushak
SINGH, Teja		1414	Sepoy	19Punjabi	14.10.18	Battle of Dushak
SINGH, Ugam		2745	Sowar	28LtCav	23.10.18	
SINGH, Wariam		2881	Sepoy	19Punjabi	14.10.18	Battle of Dushak

SINGH, Wasankha		818	Sepoy	19Punjabi	14.10.18	Battle of Dushak
STEPHEN, James Eliot	25		Lieut.	19Punjabi	14.10.18	Battle of Dushak
WARD, Kenneth Hilary	33		Capt	KRRC	30.08.18	DOW, Defence of Kaakha
WAZIR		2650	Sepoy	19Punjabi	14.10.18	Battle of Dushak
Caspian Sea						
BESSANT, Frederick Arthur	33	K/35840	Sto1	RN	21.05.19	Attack on Alexandrovsk, HMS *Emile Nobel*
BURNETT, Oliver	32	309917	POSto	RN	21.05.19	Attack on Alexandrovsk, HMS *Emile Nobel*
COLLARD, William Albert	22	J/36559	AB	RN	21.05.19	Attack on Alexandrovsk, HMS *Emile Nobel*
DARKE, Herbert Robert	32	M/1	CERA	RN	21.05.19	Attack on Alexandrovsk, HMS *Emile Nobel*
MARSH, Eugene		J/42309	AB	RN	17.07.21	Suicide whilst POW at Baku, Azerbaijan
WHEATON, Harold	19	CH/19979	Bugler	RMLI	21.05.19	Attack on Alexandrovsk, HMS *Emile Nobel*

British and Commonwealth Known Prisoners of War of the Soviets

Baltic Sea

Name	Number	Rank	Unit	Date	Comments
BOWLES, Herbert James	J/49783	AB	RN	18.08.19	Kronstadt Raid, *CMB 24* sunk
BREMNER, William Hamilton, DSO, DSC		Lieut	RN	18.08.19	Kronstadt Raid, *CMB 79* sunk
DUNKLEY, Henry John, DSM	MB/2714	CMM	RNVR	18.08.19	Kronstadt Raid, *CMB 79* sunk
GIDDY, Osman Cyril Horton, DSC		S/Lt	RN	18.08.19	Kronstadt Raid, *CMB 24* sunk
HARVEY, Charles Alfred	J/44035	AB	RN	18.08.19	Kronstadt Raid, *CMB 24* sunk
McVEIGH, Samuel, DSM	312495	StoPO	RN	18.08.19	Kronstadt Raid, *CMB 62*
NAPIER, Laurence Egerton Scott, DSO		Lieut	RN	18.08.19	Kronstadt Raid, *CMB 24* sunk
REYNISH, Benjamin, DSM	MB/574	CMM	RNVR	18.08.19	Kronstadt Raid, *CMB 24* sunk
WHYTE, William Eric, DSM	MB/3006	CMM	RNVR	18.08.19	Kronstadt Raid, *CMB 24* sunk

North Russia (Archangel)

Name	Number	Rank	Unit	Date	Comments
ANDREWS, Richard John, DSO, MC		LtCol	DevonR	20.07.19	Mutiny of White Russian troops, Onega
ASHTON, J.	22005	Pte	156RAMC	11.08.19	Attack on left bank of Dvina River
ASKEW, W.		Spr	RESigs	20.07.19	Mutiny of White Russian troops, Onega. Escaped
BENDRY, B.	377027	Pte	2/10RScots		Unknown circumstances
BERESFORD, ?		2Lt	RASC	20.07.19	Mutiny of White Russian troops, Onega. Escaped
BLACKWELL, W.		Capt	WYorksR	20.07.19	Mutiny of White Russian troops, Onega

Name	Number	Rank	Unit	Date	Circumstances
BLUNDEN, Edward George	S/436619	Pte	RASC	20.07.19	Mutiny of White Russian troops, Onega. Died Moscow, 01.09.19
BOLTON, H.A.		2Lt	RE	20.07.19	Mutiny of White Russian troops, Onega
BRAY, S.W.	128982	LCpl	45RFus		Unknown date/circumstances
BRINDLE, Frank	7878	Pte	156RAMC	11.08.19	Dvina offensive
BUGG, ?		ObsLt	RAF	10.08.19	Landed enemy territory, pilot killed
CARTER, Frank	061	Pte	1OBLI	27.06.19	Attack on Ignatovskaya, Devon Regt. attd.
CHAMPION, Oliver, DSC		Lieut	RNVR	20.07.19	Mutiny of White Russian troops, Onega. Escaped
CLEMENTS, John T.	022	Pte	1OBLI	27.06.19	Attack on Ignatovskaya, also wounded. DevonR attd.
COATES, L.A.E.		2Lt	MiltyCtrl	20.07.19	Mutiny of White Russian troops, Onega. Escaped
COCHRANE, H.T., MM	220044	Pte	156RAMC	11.08.19	Dvina offensive
CONNOR, Alfred	19909	Pte	8MGC	01.09.19	Defence of Ust-Vaga
COOK, Horatio Wilson		2Lt	GenList	20.07.19	Mutiny of White Russian troops at Onega. Escaped
CORLETT, Cyril Norman		Lieut	6YorksR	20.07.19	Mutiny of White Russian troops, Onega. HLI attd.
DAVISON, J.		Pte	6YorksR		Unknown date/circumstances, repatriated UK Nov 1919
DAWSON, Robert	66282	Pte	2/10RScots	27.10.18	Attack on Kulika
DODDS, MC, DCM, MM		2Lt	RESigs	20.07.19	Mutiny of White Russian troops, Onega
DOGGETT, Alfred	24085	Sgt	RAOC	20.07.19	Mutiny at Onega, rescued, very seriously wounded
DOYLE, B.	12756	Pte	156RAMC	11.08.19	Dvina offensive
ECCLES, L.W.G., MC		Lieut	ColdGds	20.07.19	Mutiny of White Russian troops, Onega
ENGLAND, Alfred	129956	Cpl	45RFus		Unknown date/circs. Also wounded, released Feb 1920
FAICHNEY, Ernest	53276	Pte	2/10RScots	13.10.18	Defence of Borok
FARLOWE, H.	130430	Pte	46RFus		Unknown date/circumstances
FOX, George Frederick		Lieut	RAOC	20.07.19	Mutiny of White Russian troops, Onega. Escaped
FRASER, Cyril Lloyd		Maj	RASC	10.18	Near Obozerskaya, repatriated June 1919
FUSZARD, Charles A.	S/407453	Pte	RASC	20.07.19	Mutiny of White Russian troops at Onega. Escaped

Name	Number	Rank	Unit	Date	Circumstances
GAY, George	63912	Pte	13YorksR		Unknown date/circumstances
GOODES, Arthur G.	66220	Pte	2/10RScots	13.10.18	Defence of Borok
HAMLETT, Frederick	131264	LCpl	45RFus		Unknown date/circumstances
HARRISON, Hugh L.	109661	Pte	2/7DLI	20.07.19	Mutiny of White Russian troops, Onega. Escaped
HARVEY, J.	220143	Pte	156RAMC	11.08.19	Dvina offensive
HAY, George Harold, DSO		Maj	2/10RScots		Mutiny at Onega
HOPKINS, G.	220053	Pte	156RAMC	11.08.19	Dvina offensive
HUGHES, J.H.		Pte	2/10RScots	13.10.18	Defence of Borok
HYNDMAN, ?		Pte	2/10RScots	13.10.18	Defence of Borok
KING, Reginald Henry		Capt	RASC	20.07.19	Mutiny of White Russian troops, Onega
LAING, William S.	66433	Pte	2/10RScots		Unknown date/circumstances
LAMBERT, ?		Pte	17LpoolR		Unknown theatre/date/circs., repatriated Feb 1920
LANSDOWNE, George, DFC		Lieut	RAF	14.07.19	Force landed seaplane behind enemy lines
LEISHMAN, John L.	52442	Pte	2/10RScots	13.10.18	Defence of Borok
LEVINSON, Asher M.	S/407191	Pte	RASC	20.07.19	Mutiny of White Russian troops, Onega. Escaped
LINDFORD, Francis	66225	Pte	2/10RScots		Date/circumstances unknown
MACK, J.	131048	Pte	45RFus		Unknown date/circumstances
MARKS, D.	131363	Pte	46RFus		Unknown date/circumstances
MARSHALL, Harold L.		ObsLt	RAF	14.07.19	Force landed seaplane behind enemy lines
McDONALD, J.		SSgt	RAOC	20.07.19	Mutiny of White Russian troops, Onega. Escaped
McKENZIE, Harold S.	7117	Pte	HAC	20.07.19	Mutiny of White Russian troops, Onega. Escaped
McPHEE, W.J.	131232	Sgt	46RFus		Unknown date/circumstances
MILLER, ?				20.07.19	Details unknown, mutiny of White Russian troops, Onega
MONAGHAN, M.J.		Lieut	RifBde	20.07.19	Mutiny of White Russian troops at Onega
MULVANEY, ?				20.07.19	Details unknown, Mutiny of White Russian troops, Onega

Name	Number	Rank	Unit	Date	Circumstances
ORR, Andrew	62720	Pte	2/10RScots	13.10.18	Defence of Borok
PARKER, Percy	129086	Pte	45RFus		Unknown date/circumstances
PENNYCOOK, Rodger	66176	Pte	2/10RScots	27.10.18	Attack on Kulika
PICKARD, C.		Pte	6YorksR	04.19	Unknown circs., wounded, repatriated November 1919
PRESTON, Ernest J.	128954	Pte	45R.Fus		Unknown date/circumstances
RHODES, J.W.	200119	Pte	156RAMC	11.08.19	Dvina offensive
RICHARDS, Albert W.	6404	Pte	13YorksR		Unknown date/circs., repatriated November 1919
ROBERTS, Lewis Euron		Lieut	17LpoolR	20.07.19	Mutiny of White Russian troops, Onega, 13th Bn., RWF attd.
ROCHE, ?		Chpln		03.04.19	Near Obozerskaya, returned blindfolded three days later
ROE, F.		LCpl		20.07.19	Mutiny of White Russian troops, Onega. Escaped
ROUPELL, George, VC		Capt	ESurrR	20.07.19	Mutiny of White Russian troops, Onega
SEARLE, N.E.	129662	Pte	45RFus		Unknown date/circumstances
STONE, Harry	131005	Pte	45RFus		Unknown date/circumstances
SWEETING, Albert	129626	Pte	45RFus		Unknown date/circumstances
SWINDON, F.	131253	Pte	45RFus		Unknown date/circumstances
SYLVESTER, Edwin A.	79022	LCpl	1OBLI	27.06.19	Attack on Ignatovskaya, lost left eye, Devon Regt. attd.
TATTAM, Francis		2Lt	RAF	31.03.19	Ambush near Bolshie Ozerki, also wounded
TODD, Thomas	131584	Pte	45RFus		Unknown date/circumstances
TRIGG, R.G.		SCondr	RASC	20.07.19	Mutiny of White Russian troops, Onega
TWINER, E.	131200	Pte	46RFus		Unknown date/circumstances
UNDERWOOD, Jessie F.	32709	Pte	1OBLI	27.06.19	Attack on Ignatovskaya, also wounded, KOSB attd.
UNIACKE, C.D.W. OBE		LtCol	RFA	20.07.19	Mutiny of White Russian troops, Onega. Escaped
VAN DER SPUY, Kenneth		LtCol	RAF	04.19	Force landed in enemy territory, engine failure
WALL, H.	200244	Pte	156RAMC	11.08.19	Dvina offensive
WYNNE, John	131063	Pte	45RFus	11.08.19	Dvina offensive

North Russia (Murmansk)

Name	Number	Rank	Unit	Date	Notes
COPESTAKE, William, MSM	217160	AB	RN	21.07.18	Shore duty HMS *Attentive*, released POW exchange, May 1919
PYLE, Thomas, DCM	CH/22549	Pte	6RMBn	08.08.19	Attack on Koikori, severely wounded in action, leg amputated
SYKES, Ronald, DFC		Capt	RAF	31.08.19	Force landed in enemy territory, engine failure

South Russia

Name	Number	Rank	Unit	Date	Notes
GRACEY, George		Capt	IntelCorps		Unknown date, repatriated June 1919

Siberia

Name	Number	Rank	Unit	Date	Notes
EYFORD, ?		2Lt	CSEF	07.01.20	British Military Mission train, Krasnoyarsk
HAYES, G.		Capt			Unknown unit/date/circs., attd. British Military Mission
HORROCKS, Brian, MC		Capt	MidxR	07.01.20	British Military Mission train overrun, Krasnoyarsk
ILLINGWORTH, ?		Sgt		07.01.20	British Military Mission train overrun, Krasnoyarsk
JAMES, ?		Pte		07.01.20	British Military Mission train overrun, Krasnoyarsk
LILLINGTON, ?		Sgt		07.01.20	British Military Mission train overrun, Krasnoyarsk
MacMILLAN, David	12626	RSM	GordHighrs	07.01.20	British Military Mission train overrun, Krasnoyarsk
McCULLAGH, Francis, MBE		Capt	GenList	07.01.20	British Military Mission train overrun, Krasnoyarsk
NEVILLE, ?		Capt	RFA	07.01.20	British Military Mission train overrun, Krasnoyarsk
OSBORNE-DEMPSTER		Lieut	RASC	07.01.20	British Military Mission train overrun, Krasnoyarsk, Canadian
PRICKETT, ?		Capt		07.01.20	British Military Mission train overrun Krasnoyarsk
ROONEY, ?		Sgt		07.01.20	British Military Mission train overrun Krasnoyarsk
SMITH, ?		Pte	CSEF	07.01.20	British Military Mission train overrun Krasnoyarsk
STEPHENS, ?		2Lt		07.01.20	British Military Mission train overrun Krasnoyarsk
VINING, Leonard Edward		Maj	RE		British Military Mission train overrun Krasnoyarsk
WALTERS, ?		RSM	RE		British Military Mission train overrun Krasnoyarsk

Turkestan and Caspian Sea

FRASER, Brian Austin		Cdr	RN	27.04.20	Commanded RN party captured at Baku
GRANT, ?		Pte	GloucsR		Unknown date/circumstances, captured at Baku
INGRAM, H.		Lieut	221SqnRAF	16.06.19	Shot down over Astrakhan, pilot 2nd Lieut. A.J. Mantle
KHAN, Lal		LDfdr	28LtCav	02.03.19	Escaped via Persia, rejoined regiment
KHAN, Ahmed Yar		SSmth	28LtCav	02.03.19	Escaped via China, rejoined regiment
MANTLE, Anthony, DFC		Lieut	221SqnRAF	16.06.19	Shot down over Astrakhan
SMITH, Stanley		AB	RN	27.04.20	RN party captured at Baku

Theatre Unknown

BATCH, Percy James		LtCol	Special List		Unknown unit/date/circumstances, repatriated June 1919
GOGAS, Christo	G/102426	Sgt	MidxR		Unknown theatre/date/circumstances
GOLDSMITH, George M.		Capt	IntelCorps		Unknown theatre/date/circumstances, repat. June 1919
HARRIS, ?		Cpl	RE		Unknown theatre/date/circumstances, repatriated February 1920
NASH, George Nathaniel		Capt	RGA		Unknown date/circumstances, repatriated June 1919
THORN, Arthur Charles		Maj	MGC		Unknown theatre/date/circumstances
WILSON, ?		Capt	RESigs		Unknown theatre/date/circumstances

Roll of Australians known to have served in Russia 1918–20

Name	Service with AIF			Service with British Army			
	Rank	Number	Unit	Rank	Number	Unit	Comments
ABERCROMBIE, Brian	Pte	2220	2Bn	Pte	133056	45RFus	WIA 08.08.15, Gallipoli
ALEXANDROFF, Alex	Pte	6823	4Bn	Sgt	L/21564	MidxR	Born Vladivostok, Russia
ALLISON, Robert Richard	WO1	2856	AIFHQ	Pte	192142	201MGC	
ANDERSEN, Olaf Christian	Pte	55324	6Bn	Pte	133025	45RFus	DCM (L.G. 21.01.20). Wounded 15.09.19 Tulgas
ARMSTRONG, Rowley Rutherford	Lieut		LabCps	Lieut		RwyTrspt	See Rockhampton *Morning Bulletin*, 09.03.20
ATKINS, David Thomas	Pte	3252	5Bn	Pte	133043	45RFus	WIA 10.08.18, W. Front
ATTIWELL, Keith	Pte	56029	AAVC	Pte	133040	45RFus	
BAKER, Edward	Pte	3363	55Bn	Cpl	133004	45RFus	WIA 22.03.18, W. Front
BARBER, Glen Joseph	Gnr	18833	7FAB	Gnr	293025	443RFA	Admitted hospital Archangel, 07.08.19, insane
BARTLETT, Allan Edward	Pte	54864	59Bn	Pte	193024	201MGC	
BAUER, Oscar Leonard	Pte	5348	11Bn	Pte	133015	45RFus	POW, 16.04.17, Western Front
BAVERSTOCK, William	Pte	51079	4Bn	Pte	192217	201MGC	
BENNETT, Albert Horace	Gnr	695	2SgeBty	LCpl	192228	201MGC	MM AIF; C. of St. Geo. Gassed 28.05.17, W. Front
BORELAND, Stanley John	Pte	2135	56Bn	Pte	193018	201MGC	WIA/POW 02.04.17, W. Front
BREWSTER, Arthur Claude	Pte	5310	23Bn	Pte	192207	201MGC	WIA 20.03.17, gas 03.10.1918, W. Front
BROOKE, Norman	Gnr	4376	2TMB	Pte	133029	45RFus	DCM (L.G. 21.01.20), Dvina offensive
BROWN, Allan	Capt	121	49Bn.			'ELOPE'	WIA 14.07.15 Gallipoli, 14.07.17 W. Front, killed Onega 20.07.19 (MiD x 2)

Name	Rank	No.	Unit	Rank	No.	Service	Notes
BURKE, Allan Frederick	Sgt	8/1419	2Otago	Capt		NZEF	MBE (LG 03.06.19), & MM (L.G. 13.03.19) – Archangel. Born Adelaide, South Australia
BURROW, William Henry	Cpl	2073	4PnrBn	Sgt	133078	45RFus	
CAREY, Alfred David	Dvr	7186	4AASC	Lieut		RAF	OBE (L.G. 22.12.19 – Archangel), St. A/St. S
CHEESEMAN, Joseph	Pte	2760	55Bn	Pte	133071	45RFus	WIA 28.05.18, Western Front
COLLIER, Douglas	Pte	2632A	47Bn	Pte	192219	201MGC	WIA 07.06.17, 12.10.17, Western Front
COLLINS, Joseph Michael	Pte	5803	20Bn	LCpl	133018	45RFus	MM (L.G. 03.01.20 – Archangel)
CORMACK, Cornelius	Pte	2584	10Bn	Pte	133019	45RFus	WIA 01.07.18, gas 11.08.18, Western Front
DAISH, Ernest Ethelbert				SBA	M/25525	Royal Navy	B. NSW. Served Dvina River, HMS *London Belle*
DALE, John Thomas	Pte .	2115	4PnrBn	Pte	133022	45RFus	WIA 09.06.17, W. Front
DARBY, Harry	Pte	3307	5Bn	Pte	193033	201MGC	WIA 29.09.18, W. Front. ANMEF, 1921
DAVIES, Charles Stuart	Brig		8InfBde	LtCol		45RFus	DSO, AIF, CMG (L.G. 03.02.20 – Archangel)
DAVIES, Thomas Henry	Maj		RE	Maj		RE	DSO/MC – W. Front; born Tasmania. See *IWM Review* (No. 12, 1999)
DENVILLE, Harold	Cpl	50A	3MGBn	Pte	193044	201MGC	WIA 18.09.18, Western Front
DIDSBURY, James	Pte	1298	8Bn	Pte	133079	45RFus	WIA 27.04.15, Gallipoli, 23.08.18. W. Front
DONLON, Marcus	Pte	2647A	49Bn	Pte	133030	45RFus	WIA 24.04.18, Western Front
DORRINGTON, Louise Coles	Nurse		Red Cross	Nurse		Red Cross	See *Adelaide Register*, 03.07.20. American Red Cross Hospital, Vilnius, Lithuania, 1919–20.
DOUGLAS, Edgar Francis	Pte	250	3LHR	Pte	MR47892	RASC	WIA 11.06.15, Gallipoli
DRUMMOND-HAY, Robert A.	PO	148	RANBT	Lieut	RNR	HMS *Nairana*	MiD (L.G. 12.12.18 – White Sea)
ELLIS, Charles Howard	Pte	201989	LondR	Capt		MidxR	OBE (L.G. 25.11.21 – Turkestan). B. Sydney
FAGAN, John	Pte	1920	18Bn	Pte	133042	45RFus	WIA 27.10.15 Gallipoli, 08.08.18, W. Front
FLINTON, James Patrick	Pte	3540	10FAB	Pte	193047	201MGC	
FRANCIS, Frank	Pte	61389	AAPC	LCpl	192144	201MGC	

Name	Rank	Number	Unit	Rank	Number	Unit	Notes
FRANCIS, James	Pte	1268	16Bn	Pte	133066	45RFus	Wd. 02.05.15, Gallipoli; POW 11.04.17, W. Fr.
FRENCH, Bernard Russell	Maj		RMunFus	Maj		RMunFus	DSO (L.G. 01.01.19 – Egypt); St. Stan./St. Vlad. See *Sydney Uni Book of Remembrance*
GAFFEY, Ernest	Pte	3153	53Bn	Pte	133035	45RFus	WIA 29.08.19, Emtsa, North Russia
GARDINER, Stanley	Gnr	6547	4FAB	Lieut		RAF	MBE (L.G. 22.12.19 – Archangel); St. Anne
GASCOIGNE-ROY, Heatlie Fletcher	Capt		BordR	Sgt	130525	46RFus	DCM (L.G. 21.01.20 – Dvina offensive), OBE (L.G. 13.06.59)
GIPPS, Horace Bridges	Lieut	1043	14FAB	Cpl	133028	45RFus	DCM (L.G. 21.01.20 – Emtsa), WIA 24.08.18, W. Front
GOATES, Ernest Henry	Pte	61142	6Bn	Pte	133045	45RFus	
GOODING, Frank	Pte	4713	20Bn	Pte	193045	201MGC	WIA 14.11.16, gassed 25.05.18, W. Front
GORMAN, Thomas	Pte	256	1Bn	Capt		2HantsR	MC (L.G. 11.12.16, W. Front); died of wounds 22.06.19, attack on Troitsa
GRAHAM, Robert Louis	2Lt	20	3Bn			'ELOPE'	DCM, Gallipoli; WIA 09.09.15, 13.12.15, Gallipoli; 03.07.17, Western Front
GRAY, James Gordon	Sgt	27811	3FAB			MMR	MM, AIF; see *Evening Post*, 12.04.20, RN Lake Onega Flotilla
GREATOREX, Michael	Pte	56324	AAMC	Pte	193023	201MGC	
GUHL, Avery Cyril	Pte	56334	11Bn	Pte	133012	45RFus	WW2 WX10309, 2/13th Fld. Amb.
GUINEA, John Denes	Pte	57673	9Bn	Pte	133008	45RFus	WW2 NX41955, 2/18Bn, d. POW, Sandakan
HANKE, Theodore	Pte	60072	AAMC	Pte	193032	201MGC	Enlisted RAF, 22.04.21
HART, Harry George	Pte	1538	RE	2Lt		RE	See *Sydney University Book of Remembrance*
HAYES, Stanley George	Cpl	53591	55Bn	Pte	133027	45RFus	
HEAD, Edward John	Sgt	9	68RAF	Capt		RAF	AFC (L.G. 12.07.20 – South Russia). See *The Australasian*, 19.06.20. South Russia
HENEY, John Henry Waldo	Lieut		ColdGds	Lieut		45RFus	MC (L.G. 10.12.19 – W. Front); See *Sydney Morning Herald* 23.02.20.

Name	Rank	No.	Unit	Rank	No.	'ELOPE'	Notes
HICKEY, Charles John	Sgt	1668	11Bn	Pte	133014	45RFus	WIA 24.08.15, Gallipoli; lost left eye, 02.07.16, Western Front
HICKEY, John Joseph	Pte	4809	Dental	Sgt	133031	45RFus	
HILL, Charles Godfrey	Pte	59749	55Bn	Pte	133024	45RFus	WIA Emtsa, 29.08.19. Leg amputated
HODSON, William	Pte	2668	4MGBn	Pte	133034	45RFus	WIA 05.04.18, Western Front. MM (L.G. 22.01.20 – Archangel); also Cross of St. George
HOOPER, Archie Gordon	Pte	137	10Bn	Pte		45RFus	WIA 04.11.17, Western Front
HOWARD, Claude	Pte	6928	28Bn	Pte	193043	201MGC	Enlisted 18.08.15, ANMEF
JAMES, Stanley Edward	Pte	3094	22Bn	Pte	192221	201MGC	Gassed 23.07.18, W. Front
JONES, Arthur Edward	Pte	5872	27Bn	Cpl	133080	45RFus	
JONES, Joseph	Pte	5659	18Bn	Pte	133033	45RFus	Gassed 28.05.16, France
JONES, Walter (real name William)	Pte	6332	18Bn	Pte	193013	201MGC	WIA 09.08.18, W. Front. MM, AIF; MM Bar (L.G. 22.01.20 – Archangel); also C. of St. G.
JUDGE, Cecil Guildford Kimmorley	Capt		4Bn	Capt		BMM Siberia	MC Bar, AIF. WIA 07.05.16, 15.04.17. Dunsterforce, 1918
KELLY, Edward Patrick	Pte	3411A	53Bn	Pte	133077	45RFus	WIA 20.07.16, Western Front
KELLY, John Robert	Sgt	453	30Bn			'ELOPE'	
KELLY, Patrick	Spr	157	5PnrBn	Pte	133073	45RFus	WIA 26.06.18, Western Front
KENNARD, William	Sgt	2972	31Bn	Sgt	133057	45RFus	MiD (L.G. 03.02.20 – Archangel)
KEVAN, John McLure	Pte	58591	55Bn	Pte	133026	45RFus	WIA, GSW head, lost eye, 29.08.19, Emtsa
KING, Edgar Arnold	Pte	20717	AAMC	Pte	133013	45RFus	WIA Russia, GSW knee, arm. Also C. of St. G.
KIRVALIDZE, Paul Ippolit	Pte	3088	3Bn	Pte	3088	MidxR	WIA 20.07.16, Western Front; interpreter with BMM South Russia 1919–20.
LAMB, Vernon Waghorn	Dvr	13980	AASC	Lieut		RAF	See *Argus* 29.06.19; prev. ANMEF (RAN)
LATCHFORD, Ernest William	Capt		38Bn	Capt		BMM Siberia	MC, AIF; Dunsterforce, 1918
LEE, Leslie	Pte	377	3MGBn	LCpl	193041	201MGC	Gassed 16.10.17, W. Front

Name	Rank	Unit	Number	Corps	Number	Notes
LLOYD, Ernest George	Lieut	3MGBn		MercMne		See *Daily Commercial News*, 05.04.22. Previously PO, RAN
LOHAN, Paul Francis	Capt	51Bn		'ELOPE'		WIA 13.07.17, Western Front
LUTHERBORROW, Allan John	Pte	7Bn	5701	45RFus	133005	DCM (L.G. 21.01.20 – Railway Front). Severely WIA 24.07.19, VP445
MABBOT, George	Pte	17Bn	429	45RFus	133036	Gassed 23.07.18, W. Front
MADDEN, Norman	Pte	2Bn	60483	45RFus	133060	Enlisted RAN, 09.02.21
MAHER, William	Pte	41Bn	225	45RFus	133052	
McCREADY, Robert	Sgt	NZEF	12/4228	'ELOPE'		See NZ *Evening Post*, 12.06.22. Born NSW
McDONNELL, Sydney	Pte	49Bn	2710	45RFus	133023	WIA 05.04.18, Western Front
McLEAN, James Duncan	Pte	55Bn	58612	45RFus	133037	
McLEOD, Samuel	Gnr	5MTCoy	15710	45RFus	133047	
MEERIN, Robert	Pte	3MGBn	2845	MidxR		Born Riga, Latvia. NRRF interpreter
MERCER, John Dawson	Spr	13FCE	5496	45RFus	133016	
METCALFE, Francis	Pte	4Bde	7583	45RFus	133020	Deserted RAN 03.10.17, enlisted AIF
MILLER, Stanley	Pte	53Bn	3244	MercMne		See *Charleville Times*, 23.06.39.
MINKSHLIN, Anthony	Pte	13LHR	1328	45RFus	133006	MSM (L.G. 03.01.20 – Archangel)
MORGAN, James Harold	Lieut	11Bn		WelshR		WIA 25.04.15, Gallipoli. Suicide, see *West Australian*, 27.04.39
NAVEAU, Frank Alfred	Dvr	5DAC	4065	45RFus	133061	
NEWMAN, Victor	Pte	4Bn	6769			MIC does not state NRRF unit or number
O'BRIEN, John Murdock	Capt	ICamelC	960	BMM Sib.		Dunsterforce, 1918
ODLIFF, Ivan (Jack)	Pte	MGReo	3177	201MGC	193040	B. Russia; prev. Russian Navy. WIA 24.07.16
OLIVER, Charles	WO1	6Bn	6865A	201MGC	192110	WIA 05.06.18, Western Front. C of St. George
OLSEN, Edward James	Pte	18Bn	5849	201MGC	193014	
O'REILLY, Peter Joseph	Pte	19Bn	5378	45RFus	133053	

Name	Rank	Number	Unit	Rank	Number	Unit	Notes
OSBORNE, Robert August	Pte	2664	6Bn	Pte	192227	201MGC	MM, AIF
PARSONS, James Luke	LCpl	586	AAVC	Cpl		201MGC	
PEARSE, Samuel George	Cpl	2870	1MGBn	Sgt	133002	45RFus	WIA 19.05.18, W. Front. Killed 29.08.19, Emtsa; posthumous VC (L.G. 23.10.19)
PEDEN, James	Pte	60985	9GSR	Pte	133039	45RFus	
PEITI, Jack	Pte	7514	11Bn	Pte	133050	45RFus	WIA 29.08.19, Emtsa. Born Italy
PERRY, Bertram Harold	LSgt	487	30Bn			'ELOPE'	MM, AIF
PIOCH, Edward Henry	Pte	2188	4PnrBn	Pte	133075	45RFus	WIA 05.07.18, W. Front
PORTEOUS, Ernest	Pte	2034	16Bn	Pte	133064	45RFus	WIA 17.08.15, Gallipoli
PURDUE, Joseph	Pte	60748	7Bn	Pte	133007	45RFus	DCM (L.G. 03.02.20 – Dvina Offensive). WIA 06.09.19. WW2 VX78974, RAE
QUAMBY, Leslie	Pte	7786	AIFHQ	Pte	192218	201MGC	
QUARELL, William Frederick	Gnr	10897	5FAB	Pte	133059	45RFus	DCM (L.G. 21.01.20 – Emtsa) WIA 29.08.19. WW2 as WX2794, RAE
RAWLINS, Edward Bland	Pte	2063	24Bn	Pte	133058	45RFus	WIA 05.08.16, 15.06.18, Western Front
REA, Harry	Pte	60025	AASC	Pte	133017	45RFus	
REDMOND, Edward	Pte	56128	10Bn	Pte	133046	45RFus	Enl. RAN 08.06.1916 as 5719 J.E. Boag
REVIERE, John William	Pte	1727	55Bn	Pte	133074	45RFus	
RIORDAN, Thomas De B.	Pte	433	4MGBn	Pte	193051	201MGC	WIA 27.03.18, Western Front
ROBERTS, Frederick	Pte	2705	5PnrBn	Pte	133072	45RFus	
ROBINSON, Wilfred John	Pte	61464	1MGBn.	Pte	133038	45RFus	Severely WIA 29.08.19, Emtsa
ROBINSON, William John	Sgt	1006	11Bn	Sgt	133001	45RFus	DCM (L.G. 21.01.20 – Dvina offensive). WIA 11.07.15, Gallipoli, POW 16.04.17, W. Front
ROCHE, John Francis	Gnr	30948	5TMB	Sgt	133063	45RFus	MM (L.G. 03.01.20 – Archangel)
RUSSELL, John James	Pte	5450	53Bn	Pte	132258	201MGC	Lied about age; disch. aged 53 yrs 3 mths
SAUNDERS, Arthur George	Maj		RE	Maj		RE	See IWM Review (No. 12, 1999) & Kalgoorlie Miner, 27.08.46.

Name	Rank	Number	Unit	Rank	Number	Unit	Notes
SLEEMAN, Thomas Oliver	Sgt	33920	2DAC	Sgt	20896	MMR	See *Evening Post*, 12.04.20. RN Lake Onega
SMIRNOFF, Paul	Pte	59174	17Bn			MidxR	NRRF Interpreter. Born Vologda, Russia
SMITH, Peter	Pte	4026	23Bn	Pte	192209	201MGC	MM, AIF, MM Bar (L.G. 21.01.20 – Archangel). WIA 04.08.16, 18.3.17, 04.10.17, W. Front
SPARKE, Alan Everard	Pte		RHA	Capt		RHA	See *Sydney Morning Herald*, 15.04.20
SPIES, Harold John	Pte	1770	AIF HQ	Cpl	133054	45RFus	MM, AIF; MM Bar (L.G. 03.01.20 – Archangel). Gassed 11.08.18, Western Front
STEPHENSON, Alfred	Pte	66321	20GSR	Pte	133041	45RFus	
STEWART, George E.				Col		US Army	Born NSW. MoH, Philippines, 1900
SULLIVAN, Arthur Percy	Cpl	56133	Artillery	Cpl	133003	45RFus	VC (L.G. 29.09.19 – Dvina offensive). Acc. killed, Aus. Coronation Contingent 09.04.37
SUTTON, James Norman	Pte	5403	18Bn	LCpl	133032	45RFus	MM (L.G. 22.01.20 – Archangel). WIA 03.05.17, gassed 07.04.18, Western Front
TARRANT, Richard	Capt		45Bn			'ELOPE'	WIA 27.04.15, Gallipoli; 07.08.16, W. Front
THOMPSON, James	Gnr	3265	2FAB	Pte	133081	45RFus	WIA, 07.11.16, later RAOC, British Army
TILEY, Ernest Leslie	Pte	55701	7Bn	Pte	133009	45RFus	Joined RAN, 10.02.20; WW2 QX7269
VON DUVE, Arthur F.	Sgt	3948	10Bn			'ELOPE'	MM, AIF. WIA 21.09.17, W. Front
WADE, Bert	Pte	55010	59Bn	Pte	133067	45RFus	Enlisted in AIF alias Frederick Lonnergan
WARD, Kenneth Hilary Wodehouse	Pte	11691	KRRC	Capt		KRRC	See *The Mercury*, 27.04.15, Died of wounds, 30.08.18, Turkestan
WATSON, George	Pte	408	4Bn	Pte	133010	201MGC	Previously served Royal Irish Rifles
WATTS, Bernard Joseph	Pte	5792	1AGH	Pte		45RFus	
WHATSON, Frederick	Pte	58180	9Bn	Pte	193042	201MGC	WIA 10.08.19, Dvina River
WILLIAMS, Benjamin	Pte	59835	55Bn	Pte	133069	45RFus	See *Farmer & Settler* 03.10.19
WILSON, William Alfred	Pte	54538	34Bn	Pte	193025	201MGC	
WOODS, Cecil	Pte	133051	45RFus	Pte	193025	201MGC	

Name	Rank	Number	Unit	Rank	Number	Unit	Medals
WRIGHT, Roderick John	Pte	736	18Bn	Pte	133048	45RFus	
WYATT, Claude Howard	Cpl	2244	27Bn			'ELOPE'	MM, AIF; MM
YEAMAN, Wilfred	Pte	1106	46Bn	Pte	192143	201MGC	

AIF men previously incorrectly identified as serving with the North Russia Relief Force 1919

MIC = Medal Index Card, a card index of those eligible for issue of WW1 service medals by the British Government in respect of service with Imperial (British) forces.

Name	Rank	Number	Unit	Comments
ASKEW, Arthur	Pte	3433	15Bn	Disch. UK intending to enlist in NRRF but did not do so, AIF disch. cancelled
BROWN, Robert	Pte	491	5LTMB	Disch. UK intending to enlist in NRRF but did not do so, AIF disch. cancelled
CROOK, Albert Thomas	Pte		5DivTrain	Enlisted in NRRF but deserted 18.06.19, did not embark for Russia
FLEMING, Jack Cyril	Pte	2481	26Bn	Disch. UK intending to enlist NRRF but joined RAF, did not embark for Russia
GASGOIGNE, Herbert Frederick	Pte	1547	5DAC	Disch. Australia 18.07.19. Previously misidentified as Heatlie Fletcher Gascoigne-Roy, DCM, 46th Royal Fusiliers.
HENDERSON, Claude	Pte	3679	5PnrBn	Disch. UK, enl. NRRF 201MGC, did not embark. AIF disch. cancelled
JENKYN, Richard, DCM	RSM	3635	2FAB	Disch. from AIF in the UK but did not enlist in the NRRF and does not have a MIC. Married UK 30.09.19
LARKINS, Francis Edwin	Pte	7036	6Bn	Disch. UK but did not enlist in NRRF, married UK 30.09.19
MORRIS, John	Pte	2846	50Bn	Disch. UK, enlisted RASC, 27.08.19, did not serve in Russia
RUSSELL, Sydney	Pte	6054	2TunCoy	Disch. UK, enlisted NRRF 133068, 45RFus, did not embark. Disch. 25.07.19
WOODYARD, Ernest	Pte	3812	57Bn	Disch. UK, enlisted NRRF 133065, 45RFus but did not embark for Russia

AIF men who may have served with the NRRF 1919 but whose service in Russia cannot be confirmed

BOYLE, Richard Henry	Pte	5670	2FAB	Disch. UK intending to enlist NRRF but no evidence he did so, no MIC
ELLIOTT, George	Pte	2317	46Bn	disch. in UK intending to enlist in NRRF, returned to Aust. 25JUL20, no evidence he served in Russia, no MIC
FLORAS, Francis	Dvr	602	2AASC	disch. in UK intending to enlist in NRRF but no evidence he did so, does not have MIC

HERBERT, Stanley A.	Pte	128943	45RFus late LonR	Australian Red Cross enquiry made (WIA 24 July 1919 – Railway Front) although there is no evidence he was Australian
HUGHES, Douglas	AM1	1279	AFC	Disch. UK 16.07.19 intending to enlist NRRF, no evidence he did so, no MIC
HYNDES, Roy Eric	Pte	3127	1PnrBn	Disch.UK intending to enlist in NRRF but no evidence he did so, no MIC
KEVORKIAN, Elias	Pte	804	5MGBn	Disch. UK but no evidence he intended to enlist in NRRF, no MIC
MURRAY, James Daniel	Pte	4136	4FCE	Prev. RAN & ANMEF. Disch. in UK intending to enlist in NRRF but no evidence he did so, does not have MIC

Appendix IV

Roll of South Africans & Rhodesians known to have served in Russia 1918–20

No South African units served in Russia: all South Africans who served in Russia did so attached to British units. Each entry covers two rows: first is the soldier's service with South African/British forces, then his service in Russia.

Name	Service with SA/Brit Forces			Service in Russia				
	Rank	Unit	Awards	Rank	No.	Unit	British Awds	Imp Ru. Awds
ALBU, Walter George	Capt	RAF		Capt		RAF		St. Stan. 2 Cl.
ATKINS, Arthur Samuel	2Lt	ColdGds		2Lt	ColdGds			
BEVERLEY, Robert	Capt	2SAInf	DSO/MC	Capt		BMM Sib.		
BORNMAN, William John				Pte	193002	201MGC		
BOTHA, Bennie				Pte	193003	201MGC		
BOTHA, Jacobus				Pte	193037	201MGC		
BOUSTEAD, Hugh	Capt	SAInf	MC	Capt		BMM S.Ru.	MC Bar (L.G. 24.04.20)	St. Vlad. 4 Cl.
BRIGHTON, Walter James				Pte	193007	201MGC		
BROWNE, Claude Melville	Maj	SAInf	MC	Maj		BMM S.Ru.	OBE/MiD (L.G. 16.07.20)	St. Anne 2 Cl.
BUDLER, Xavier Harry Barker		SAInf		Pte	192149	201MGC		
BURGER, Jacobus				Pte	193004	201MGC		
CHAMBERLAIN, D'E						2HantsR		
CLARKE, William James		SAInf		LtCol		201MGC	OBE/MiD (L.G. 03.02.20)	St. Stan. 2 Cl.
CRESSWELL-GEORGE, Estcourt	Pte	1SAInf		Pte	193049	201MGC		Cross of St. George
DE CLERK, John				Cpl	192141	201MGC		

Name	Rank	Unit	Award	Rank	No.	Unit	Award (L.G.)	Notes
DOGSON	Capt	RAF		Capt		RAF		
ECCLES, L.W.G.	Cpl	ColdGds	MC	Capt		ColdGds		POW Moscow, 1919–20
EPSTEIN, Maurice George	Lieut	RAF		Lieut		RAF	MC (L.G. 21.01.20)	
FEATHERSTONE, Clive	Capt	SAInf		Capt		45RFus		
FERENCZY, Peter				Pte	193048	201MGC		
FRASER, R.D		SAMtRif		Maj		2HantsR		
FRICKER, Edward Guy	Lieut	ESurrR		Lieut		ESurrR		
GREEN, Luke Lot	Lieut	SpRes	MC	Lieut		46RFus	DSO (L.G. 03.02.20)	
GWATKIN, R.D.S	Capt	RFA		Capt			MBE (L.G. 03.03.19)	Dunsterforce, 1918
HASELDEN, F.	LtCol	SAInf	DSO/MC	LtCol		'ELOPE'	WIA 30.12.18	
HERSCHELL, Allan	Capt	SAInf	MC	Maj		RE	OBE (L.G. 12.12.19)	Dunsterforce 1918
HEYDENRYCH, L.R.	LtCdr	RNVR		LtCdr		BMM S.Ru.		St. Anne/St. Stan.
HOPE CARSON, Ernest	Capt	TankCps	MC	LtCol		TankCps	DSO/MiD (03.02.20)	St. Vlad. 4 Cl.
HUGHES, Owen	Sgt	SAInf		Sgt	131306	46RFus		
JACKSON, William				Pte	193039	201MGC		
JENKINS, Herbert Harold	LtCol	SAInf	DSO	LtCol		46RFus	CMG/MiD (L.G. 03.02.20)	St. Anne 2 Cl.
JUBELIN, Lewis	Pte	SAInf		Pte	131866	46RFus		
KILPIN, D.	Capt			Capt				
KINKEAD, Samuel Marcus	F/Lt	RAF	DSC*/DFC*	F/Lt		47SqnRAF	DSO/MiD (L.G. 01.04.20)	St. Vlad./St. Anne/ Cr.St.G.
KNOWLES				LtCol				North Russia

Name	Rank	Unit	Decorations	Rank	No.	Unit	Awards	Notes
LUNN, W.S.	Capt	SAHA	MC	Capt		RE		Dunsterforce, 1918
MACFARLANE, B.N.		SAInf	MC	2Lt				
MACFIE, Thomas Girdwood	Lieut	4SAInf	MC	Capt		'ELOPE'	DSO/MiD (L.G. 03.10.19)	St. Anne 3 Cl.
MacLEOD, Donald Macleay	Pte	4SAI	DSO/MC/DCM	LtCol		2HantsR	MiD (L.G. 03.02.20)	St. Anne 2 Cl.
MASON, Frederick C.		SAInf		Pte	133646	46RFus		
McCABE, Frederick H.				Pte	193046	201MGC		
McCORKINDALE, Malcolm				Sgt	193038	201MGC	MiD (L.G. 03.02.20)	Cross of St. George
McKENZIE, D.M.R,		6DnGds		Lieut		'ELOPE'		
MURRAY, Thomas W.		SAInf		Pte	192163	201MGC		
NAPIER, Lawrence Egerton	Lieut	RN		Lieut		RN	DSO (L.G. 04.05.20)	POW Moscow, 1919-20
NORCUTT, H.J.		SAHA	MC	Capt		'ELOPE'		St. Anne 2 Cl.
OLSEN, Alfred Gunder	Capt	6LNLR		Pte	193009	201MGC		
REID, Oswald Austin	LtCol	NorfR	VC	Maj		'ELOPE'		
SHERWOOD-KELLY, John			VC/CMG/DSO	LtCol		2HantsR		
SLATTER, Leonard Horatio	FLt	RAF	DSC*/DFC	FLt		47SqnRAF	OBE (L.G. 12.07.19)	St. Stan 2 Cl.
SMITH, A.				Lieut		46RFus		
SNYMAN, Jacobus		SAInf		Pte	21498	NRRF		
SUMNER, Harold Lawrence	Cpl	4SAInf	MC/MM	Lieut		240TMB		
THOMPSON, Humphrey Q.F.				Dr		RedCross	Cross of St. G.	Anglo-Russ. Hosp. 1917
THOMPSON, John				Pte	193036	201MGC		

Name								
VAN DER BYL	RAF					RAF		
VAN DER SPUY, Kenneth Reid		MC		LtCol		RAF	Ord. St. G./St. Vlad.	POW Moscow, 1919-20
WHAMMOND, John	LovatSc	MC	Lieut	Sgt	129381	46RFus	DCM/MM (L.G 21.01.20)	
WHITELAW, William	RhodR		Pte	LCpl	129240	45RFus		WIA
WIESE, Cornelius				Pte	193010	201MGC		
WILKINS, Gordon Ralph				Pte	193001	201MGC		
WILLIAMS, Thomas Melling	RFC	MC/DFC	Lieut			RAF	DFC Bar (22.12.19)	
WOOD, Charles L.	SAHA		Gnr	LBdr	292960	443RFA	WIA 01.08.19 Onega	
WOOLVEN, Duncan C.	SAI			Pte	129686	46RFus		

Roll of New Zealanders known to have served in Russia 1917–20

| Name | Service with NZ/Brit Forces | | | Service in Russia | | | | |
	Rank	Unit	Awards	Rank	No.	Unit	Brit. Awds	Imp Ru. Awds
BANKS, D.W.		KEH				ELOPE		
BUDDLE, R.	Cdr	RN	OBE	Cdr		RN		
BURKE, Allan Frederick	Sgt	OtagoR		Capt		ELOPE	MBE/MM (L.G. 03.06/13.03.19)	C. of St. G; b. Adelaide, S. Australia
CAMPBELL, Alan Le Grande	Lieut	HLI		Lieut		RAF		Caspian 1918-19
CAREY, Frank				Gnr	L/4565	420RFA		Lake Onega Flotilla
CARR, Charles Roderick		RNAS				RAF	DFC (L.G. 18.11.19)	St. Anne/St. Stan.
CARTER, John Herbert	ChOff	MercMne	DSC	Lieut		RNR	C'dn. 02.09.19	
CASON, Arthur Thomas	Sgt	4NZRB				YMCA		
DENT, Bertie	Cpl	CantR						See *Evening Post* 11.02.22
EASTWOOD, Thomas Ralph	Maj	Samoan	DSO/MC	LtCol		RifBde	Brev. LtCol (L.G. 03.02.20)	
HANNA, Samuel Jackson	Capt	MMGC		Lieut		RNAS	DSC (L.G. 30.11.17)	RNAS Amd. Cars, 1917
HULL, Clive Benson	Cpl	NZESigs		SLt		RNAS		RNAS Armd. Cars, 1917
HUTCHISON, L.G.D.	Maj	LpoolR	MC	Maj		LpoolR		

JACK, Archibald	LtCol	RE	CMG/CBE	Brig		BMM Sib.	CB/MiD (L.G. 14.01.20)	Japan O. of Rising Sun
KIRKALDY, Grange I.	Capt	RHighrs		Lieut		45RFus		WIA 10.08.19
MACKY, John	Lieut	MMGC	MC	SLt		RNAS		RNAS Amd. Cars, 1917
MARTIN, John A.	Lieut	RNR		Lieut		RNR		Died Archangel, 06.10.19
McCREADY, Robert	Sgt	AuckR		Sgt	12/4228	ELOPE		B. NSW, Died NZ 1922
MENDOZA, Frederick George	Pte	AuckR		Pte	192197	201MGC		Prev. RN (NZ)
PARK, William Henry	Cpl	AuckR	MC/DFC	Capt		RAF	St. Anne, 2nd Cl.	Pigeon Flight, Murmansk
PERRY, Herbert	Sgt	OtagoR		Lieut		ELOPE		
PETTIGREW, Gordon Thompson				Lieut		RAF		
QUINN, Charles	Pte	Samoan		Pte	192205	201MGC		
SKINNER, Arthur H.	Pte	CantR		Lieut		RAF		
SMITH, Peter	Pte	23AIF	MM	Pte	192209	201MGC	MM Bar (L.G. 21.01.20)	
STEELE, Hector	BQMS	RFA	MC	Lieut		443RFA	MiD (L.G. 03.02.20)	From Waikato
STUBBS, Leslie	Lieut	RNVR		Lieut		RNVR		From Auckland
WHITCOMBE, Alec Noel Hawkes						RFA	MC (L.G. 03.10.19)	St. Anne 3 Cl.
WILLIAMS, Aubrey L.	L/Cpl	1NZFCE		Civn		For. Off		Brit Embassy
WILLIAMS, Harold		CivnJourn				CivnJourn		
WOODS, Basil Arthur Naden	Pte	AuckMR		Lieut		RNAS	St. Vlad./St. Stan./St. Anne	RNAS Amd. Cars, 1917
WORSLEY, Frank	LtCdr	RNR	DSO	LtCdr		RNR	DSO Bar (L.G. 17.10.19)	St. Stan.

NREF Order of Battle including Allied Contingents, 15 December 1918

Murmansk Command

Murmansk:

British General Headquarters: Major General Maynard	
French Headquarters: Colonel Begou	160
Italian Headquarters: Colonel Sifola	180
120 Railway Battery, 6 x 18 pdrs	150
1 section 155 mm howitzers	60
2 sections Royal Marines	60
492nd Field Company, Royal Engineers	200
1 Company 13th Battalion, Yorkshire Regiment	180
No. 1 Stokes Mortar Battery	130
New Armoured Train	60
Miscellaneous, ASC, RAMC, AOC	1,000
Total	2,180

Kola

Headquarters 236th Brigade: Lieutenant Colonel Rowlandson	100
Headquarters 6th Brigade RFA: Colonel Sawins	60
420th Battery, RFA, 6 x 4.5 inch howitzers	480
434th Battery, RFA, 4 x 18 pdrs	120
2 Sections 65 mm mountain guns	60
1 Section Royal Marines	60
1 Company 13th Battalion, Yorkshire Regiment	180
1 Battalion Italian Infantry (Neapolitans)	1,100
1 Italian Reserve Company (Besagliers)	160
1 Section Italian Carabinieri	30
253rd Machine Gun Company (less two sections)	60
Total	2,410

Drovianoi (on Kola Gulf)

1 Company 13th Battalion, Yorkshire Regiment	180
Total	180

Loparskaya

1 Section Royal Marines 2 x 12 pdrs	60
1 Section British Infantry	25
1 Company French Ski Battalion	140
Total	225

Imandra

1 Section British Infantry	25
1 Company Yorkshires	180
Total	<u>205</u>

Kandalaksha

Headquarters 238th Brigade: Colonel Burton	150
61st French Field Artillery, 4 x 75 mm	130
1 Section Artillery, Slavo-British 2 x 3 inch	60
1 Mountain Battery, 4 x 2.75 inch (Finnish Legion)	120
2 Sections 548th Field Company, Royal Engineers	60
2 Companies 11th Battalion, Royal Sussex Regiment	360
1 Company 29th Battalion, London Regiment	180
238th Trench Mortar Battery	120
2 sections 253rd Machine Gun Company	60
Finnish Legion	800
1 Section Royal Engineers	60
Total	<u>2,100</u>

Kem

Headquarters 237th Brigade: General Turner	150
62nd Battery, French Field Artillery 4 x 75 mm	130
Armoured Train, 2 x 18 pdrs	30
1 section Royal Engineers	30
Demolition Party	40
13th Yorkshire Regiment (less 2 companies)	720
Karelian Regiment	2,000
Detachment RAF, 6 x RE8	60
1 Company Slavo-British Legion	300
Total	<u>3,460</u>

Soroka

Headquarters Advanced Post: Colonel Leckie	
Canadian Malamute Company	50
1 Battalion Serbians (less 1 company), Colonel Markovitch	500
235rd Machine Gun Company (less 2 sections)	120
1 Section Royal Engineers	60
1 Company Slavo-British Legion (Sumski Posad)	200
1 Company Lithuanians	100
Total	<u>1,030</u>

Alexandrovsk

1 Section Italian Infantry	50
1 Section French Ski Company	30
Total	<u>80</u>

Pechenga
Lieutenant Colonel Elliott

2 Companies 11th Royal Sussex	360
1 Serbian Company	200
1 Serbian Field Artillery 4 x 75 mm	120
435th Battery, RFA, 4.5 inch howitzers	130
Total	810

Summary	British	French	Italian	Serbian	Russ'n	Finnish	Karel'n	Total
Murmansk	1,840	160	180					2,180
Kola	1,120		1,290					2,410
Drovianoi	180							180
Loparskaya	85	140						225
Imandra	205							205
Kandalaksha	1,050	130				920	60	2,160
Kem	1,020	130			300		2,000	3,460
Soroka	280			500	300			1,030
Olympia	60			250				310
Alexandrovsk		30	50					80
Pechenga	490			320				810
	6,330	**590**	**1,520**	**1,070**	**600**	**920**	**2,060**	**13,050**

Archangel Command

Archangel:
Headquarters: Major General W.E. Ironside
Headquarters US Forces: Colonel Stewart

British	2,700
US 339th Infantry Regiment	900
French	100
Russian volunteers in training	1,600
Total	5,300

Pinega:
2 Companies US 339th Infantry Regiment	500
Total	500

North Dvina River:
Headquarters at Semenovskoe: Gen. Finlayson

British and Canadians	1,200
US 339th Infantry Regiment	500
Russians	300
Total	2,000

Vaga River
Headquarters at Shenkursk: Lieutenant Colonel Colby

Seletskoe:
British	300
US 339th Infantry Regiment	200

Total **500**

Shred-Mekhrenga:
US troops	450
Russians	100

Total **550**

Shenkursk:
US 339th Infantry Regiment	750
Russians	100

Total **850**

Archangel–Vologda Railway:
Headquarters at Obozerskaya: Lieutenant Colonel Lucas

Obozerskaya and *Verst* 445:
US 339th Infantry Regiment	450
French	120

Total **570**

Onega River:
British	150
Russians	50

Total **200**

Shekuvo:
	50
US 339th Infantry Regiment	200
Russians	50

Total **300**

Summary	British	US	French	Russ'n	Total
Archangel	2,700	900	100	1,600	5,300
Pinega		500			500
North Dvina	1,200	500		300	2,000
Vaga River	300	1,400		200	1,900
Archangel Railway		450	120		570
Onega River	200	200			400
	4,400	**3,950**	**220**	**2,100**	**10,670**

Appendix VII

Allied Dispositions Archangel Command, Midnight 9 August 1919

General Officer Commanding:
Major General Sir. E. Ironside, KCB, CMG, DSO

General Headquarters, Archangel:
Staffs and Departments

VOLOGDA FORCE

GOC: Brigadier General A.J. Turner, CMG, DSO
HQ: Obozerskaya
Front: *Verst* post 455 – Bolsheozerki

British:

'HQ', 'Y' and 'Z' Companies, 2nd Battalion, Hampshire Regiment	530
'HQ' and 'D' Companies, 8th Battalion, MGC	193
Half 238th Trench Mortar Battery	24
Special Company, 6th Battalion, Yorkshire Regiment	123
Special Company, 45th Battalion, Royal Fusiliers	113
Special Company 46th Battalion, Royal Fusiliers	105
Special Section, 201st Battalion, MGC	66
Detachment, RA	91
Detachment, RE	101
No. 1 Armoured Train (1 x 8 cm, 1 x 18 pdr, 2 x 77 mm howitzers)	22
HQ and Details	132
Total	1,500

Local Allied Troops:

Slavo-British Legion Details	56
Total	56

Russian National Army:

6th Northern Rifle Regiment	1,539
1st Light Trench Mortar Battery	86
1 Troop, 1st Squadron, Northern Dragoons	28
1st Field Company, Engineers (less two sections)	125
2nd Artillery Division	547
1st Battery (8 x 75 mm guns)	
3rd Battery (6 x 75 mm guns)	
2nd Heavy Battery (1 x 60 pdr, 2 x 6 inch and 4 x 155 mm howitzers)	
No. 4 Armoured Train (2 x 75 mm, 1 x 155mm, 1 x 77 mm howitzer)	33
No. 5 Armoured Train (2 x 6 inch naval guns, 1 x 77 mm howitzer)	40

Attached No. 1 Armoured Train		28
	Total	2,426

Polish Legion:

Infantry and Machine Gun Company		233
	Total	233
	Total Vologda Force	4,215

SELETSKOE COLUMN

OC: Lieutenant Colonel H.E. Lavie, DSO, DLI
HQ: Seletskoe
Front: Kodish Bridge–Shred Mekhrenga

British:

Special Company, 13th Battalion, Yorkshire Regiment		65
Special Section, 252nd Company, MGC		40
'A' Company, 8th Battalion, Machine Gun Corps		75
1 Platoon, 'X' Company, 2nd Battalion, Hampshire Regiment		50
421st Battery, RFA (4 x 4.5 inch howitzer, 2 x 18 pdrs)		112
HQ and Details		96
	Total	438

Local Allied Troops:

'HQ', 1st, 2nd and MG Companies, French Foreign Legion		274
1st Battery, Slavo-British Legion (4 x 3.7 inch howitzer, 2 x 2.75 inch)		181
Details Slavo-British Legion		33
	Total	488

Russian National Army:

7th Northern Rifle Regiment		1,617
1 Troop, 1st Squadron, Northern Dragoons		19
1 Section, 1st Field Company, Engineers		49
HQ and Details		35
	Total	1,720
	Total Seletskoe Column	2,646

DVINA FORCE

GOC: Brigadier General L.W. de V. Sadleir-Jackson, CB, CMG, DSO
HQ: Troitsa
Front: Nyuma River–Selmenga River

British:

45th Battalion, Royal Fusiliers	1,068
46th Battalion, Royal Fusiliers	1,048
1 Platoon, 'D' Company, 1st Oxs & Bucks LI	31
201st Battalion, MGC ('HQ' and two companies)	309
240th Light Trench Mortar Battery	54

241st Light Trench Mortar Battery		53
385th Field Company, RE		175
250th Signal Company, RE		107
1153rd Heavy Transport Company, RASC		95
155th Field Ambulance, RAMC		145
55th Battery, RFA (6 x 3.7 inch howitzers)		309
HQ and Details		160
	Total	3,554

Local Allied Forces:

2nd Battery, Slavo-British Legion (4 x 12 pdrs)		145
1 Section, MG Company, Slavo-British Legion		52
VAGA Squadron, Slavo-British Legion		150
2 Companies, 1st Labour Battalion, Slavo-British Legion		542
RASC Lithuanian Platoon, Slavo-British Legion		42
	Total	931

Russian National Army:

3rd Northern Rifle Regiment		2,359
4th Northern Rifle Regiment (less 3rd Battalion)		1,789
2nd Russian Trench Mortar Battery		79
2nd Field Company, Russian Engineers (less two sections)		129
1st Squadron, Northern Dragoons (less detachment)		98
2nd Squadron, Northern Dragoons		131
Line of Communications Company		172
Labour Company		198
Details		27
HQ, Marousi's Brigade		151
1st Russian Artillery Division (less 1st and 3rd Battalions)		422
2nd Battery (4 x 18 pdrs)		
4th Battery (4 x 4.5 inch howitzers)		
1st Heavy Battery (4 x 18 pdrs)		
	Total	5,555

	Total Dvina Force	10,040

VAGA COLUMN

OC: Colonel W.M. Dodington, 1st Battalion, Oxs & Bucks LI
HQ: Seltso
Front: Nijni Kitsa–Mala Bereznik

British:

1st Battalion, Oxs & Bucks LI (less 'D' Company)		547
2 Sections, 'C' Company, 8th Battalion, MGC		51
239th Trench Mortar Battery		53
1 Section, 384th Field Company, RE		41
Details		46
	Total	738

Russian National Army:

3rd Battalion, 4th Northern Rifle Regiment	508
1st Battery, 1st Artillery Division (4 x 18 pdrs)	101
Detachment, 1st Heavy Battery	27
1st Mobile Veterinary Section	25
Total	<u>661</u>

Total Vaga Column	<u>1,399</u>

PINEGA FORCE

GOC: Brigadier General George W. St. G. Grogan, VC, CB, CMG, DSO
HQ: Pinega
Front: Shcelinskaya–Piligori–Lake Soyala

British:

'W' and 'X' Company (less one platoon), 2nd Battalion, Hampshire Regt.	323
'C' Company, 8th Battalion MGC (less two sections)	102
Half 238th Trench Mortar Battery	32
348th Field Company, RE (less one section)	136
348th Signal Company, RE	83
1152nd Heavy Transport Company, RASC	70
Motor Transport section, RASC	16
British Mission	29
HQ and Details	150
Total	<u>941</u>

Local British Troops:

MG Company, Slavo-British Legion (less one section)	96
3rd Battery, Slavo-British Legion (4 x 18 pdrs, 1 x 4.5 inch howitzer)	139
Total	<u>235</u>

Russian National Army:

8th Northern Rifle Regiment	1,894
1 section, 2nd Field Company, Engineers	53
3rd Battery, 1st Division Artillery (4 x 3 inch guns)	188
Detachment Heavy Artillery (2 x 6 inch howitzer, 1 x 47 mm)	
HQ and details	166
Partisans	158
Total	<u>2,459</u>

Total Pinega Force	<u>3,635</u>

DANILOV'S DETACHMENT

OC: Colonel Danilov, Russian Army
HQ: Unski Posad
Front: Nijmozero

Russian National Army:

1st Northern Rifle Regiment ('HQ', three companies, one MG section)	567

Special Section, Field Artillery (2 x 18 pdrs)	83
Total Danilov's Detachment	<u>650</u>

KONETSBOR DETACHMENT

OC: Major MacDonald, 1st Battalion, Oxs & Bucks LI
HQ: KONETSBOR

British:

D Company, 1st Bn., Oxs. & Bucks. L.I. (less one platoon)	123
Mounted Detachment	14
Light Trench Mortar Section	12
Details	15
Total Konetsbor Detachment	<u>164</u>

LINES OF COMMUNICATION

Commander: Colonel Russell Johnson, DSO, Essex Regiment
HQ: Ust Padenga
Rear: Bakharitza

RAILWAY SECTOR:

HQ: Isako Gorka

British:

B Company, 8th Battalion, MGC	111
Naval picquet	20
No. 2 Armoured Train (1 x 6 pdr, 1 x 75 mm naval howitzer)	13
No. 3 Armoured Train (2 x 47 mm naval guns)	10
HQ and Details	35
Total	<u>189</u>

Local Allied Troops:

Chinese Labour Company, Slavo-British Legion (less two platoons)	139
Railway Company, Slavo-British Legion	174
Slavo-British Legion details	55
Total	<u>368</u>

Russian National Army:

Attached No. 2 and 3 Armoured Trains	27
Total Railway Sector	<u>574</u>

RIVER SECTOR:

HQ: Yemetskoe

British:

HQ and Details	40

Local and Allied Troops:

Two Platoons Chinese Labour Company, Slavo-British Legion	65
Details	39
Total	104

Russian National Army:

Town Guards and Details	198
Total River Sector	198
Total Lines of Communication	916

BASE

Commandant: Brigadier General J.D. Crosbie, CMG, DSO
HQ: Archangel

British:

Cadre, 2/7th Battalion, Durham Light Infantry	125
Cadre, 17th King's Liverpool Regiment	76
Cadre, 6th Battalion, Yorkshire Regiment	92
Cadre, 13th Battalion, Yorkshire Regiment	70
Cadre, 252nd Company, MGC	13
Cadre, 280th Company, MGC	9
'Campion's' Battery, RFA (4 x 3.7 inch howitzers)	60
'Stevenson's' Battery, RFA (2 x 18 pdr Mk IV, 2 x 4.5 inch howitzers)	39
Base Details and Administrative Services	-

Local and Allied Troops:

1st Labour Battalion, Slavo-British Legion (less two companies)	550
Pioneer Platoon, Slavo-British Legion	54
Bakharitza Guard, Slavo-British Legion	101
Artillery Details, Slavo-British Legion	76
Depot, Polish Legion	-
Depot, French Foreign Legion	-
Slavo-British Legion Base Details & Administrative Services	-

Russian National Army:

Archangel Reserve Regiment	239
1st Northern Rifle Regiment (less Danilov's Detachment)	643
Artillery Training at RA School	520
4th Battery, 2nd Division (4 x 4.5 inch howitzers)	
1st Battery, 4th Division (4 x 2.75 inch)	
2nd Battery, 4th Division (4 x 3.7 inch howitzers)	
3rd Battery, 4th Division (4 x 18 pdrs)	
AA Section (2 x 13 pdrs AA)	
1 Section, 2nd Field Company, Engineers	53
3rd Works Company, Engineers	103
1st Automobile Division	259
1st Labour Battalion	486
HQ Base details and Administrative services	1,751

His Majesty's Ships, North Russia, March 1918–October 1919

Battleship:	HMS *Glory*	01 Sep 1916–Oct 1919
Cruisers:	HMS *Cochrane*	03 Mar–10 Nov 1918
	HMS *Attentiv*	08 Jun–19 Oct 1918
	HMS *Glory IV*[1]	03 Aug 1918–30 Apr 1919
	HMS *Fox*	27 Apr–07 Oct 1919
Yachts:	HMS *Salvator*	May–29 Nov 1918
	HMS *Josephine*[2]	03 Aug 1918–21 Apr 1919
	HMS *Alvina*[3]	03 Aug 1918–15 Jul 1919
	HMS *Ladas*[4]	30 Apr–6 Oct 1919
	HMS *Kathleen*	Aug 1918–Sep 1919
Q-ships:	HMS *Tay and Tyne*	24 May–Dec 1918
	HMS *Hyderabad*	10 May–06 Nov 1919
Icebreakers:	HMS *Alexander*[5]	13 Mar–04 Sep 1918 and 27 Oct 1918–12 Jun 1919
	HMS *Sviatogor*[6]	03 Aug 1918–21 Jul 1919
Aircraft Carrier:	HMS *Argus*	24 Jul–02 Aug 1919
Seaplane Carriers:	HMS *Nairana*	07 Jul–08 Oct 1918 and 26 Apr–12 Oct 1919
	HMS *Pegasus*	11 Apr–03 Oct 1919
Monitors:	HMS *M.23*	25 Jul 1918–04 Nov 1919
	HMS *M.24*	10 May–03 Oct 1919
	HMS *M.25*[7]	25 Jul 1918–17 Sep 1919
	HMS *M.26*	10 May–11 Oct 1919

1   The Russian Cruiser *Askold* was commandeered 3 August 1918, and commissioned as HMS *Glory IV.* Paid off at the Clyde 30 April 1919.
2   The Russian Yacht *Gorislava* was commandeered 3 August 1918 and commissioned as HMS *Josephine*. Returned to White Russian forces 21 April 1919.
3   The Russian Yacht *Sokolitza* was commandeered 3 August 1918 and commissioned as HMS *Alvina*. Returned to White Russian forces 15 July 1919.
4   HMS *Ladas* was an ex-paddle minesweeper converted to Admiral's yacht.
5   HMS *Alexander* was built for the Russian Government but commandeered by the Royal Navy before its delivery.
6   The icebreaker *Sviatogor* was commandeered from the Russians 3 August 1918.
7   HMS *M.25* was scuttled 17 September 1919 when the water level of the River Dvina fell to a level that made its passage to Archangel and the White Sea impossible.

	HMS *M.27*[1]	12 Apr–17 Sep 1919
	HMS *M.31*	10 May–25 Oct 1919
	HMS *M.33*	10 May–14 Oct 1919
	HMS *Erebus*[2]	01 Aug–Oct 1919
	HMS *Humber*	14 May–06 Oct 1919
Large China Gunboats:	HMS *Glowworm*[3]	17 Oct 1918–08 Nov 1919
	HMS *Cockchafer*	17 Oct 1918–23 Oct 1919
	HMS *Cicala*	17 Oct 1918–23 Oct 1919
	HMS *Cricket*	17 Oct 1918–23 Oct 1919
	HMS *Moth*	05 Jul–23 Oct 1919
	HMS *Mantis*	28 Jun–22 Oct 1919
Paddle Minesweeper:	HMS *Haldon*	13 May-17 Oct 1919
Tunnel Minesweepers:	HMS *Sword Dance*[4]	26 Apr–17 Sep 1919
	HMS *Step Dance*	26 Apr–03 Nov 1919
	HMS *Morris Dance*	15 May–03 Nov 1919
	HMS *Fandango*[5]	15 May–17 Sep 1919
Repair Ship:	HMS *Cyclops*	26 Apr–Oct 1919
Russian Paddle Steamer:	HMS *Borodino*	Aug 1918–Sep 1919
Hospital Ships:	HMHS *Braemar Castle*	
	HMHS *Kalyan*	
	HMHS *Garth Castle*	
Hospital Carriers:	HMS *London Belle*	06 May–Oct 1919
	HMS *Walton Belle*	06 May–Oct 1919

---

1   HMS *M.27* was scuttled 17 September 1919 when the water level of the River Dvina fell to a level that made its passage to Archangel and the White Sea impossible.
2   HMS *Erebus* sailed from North Russia direct to the Baltic Sea, and arrived at Copenhagen 21 October 1919.
3   HMS *Glowworm* was severely damaged in an explosion 25 August 1919 whilst attempting to extinguish a fire onboard an ammunition barge on the Dvina River near Bereznik. Twenty-five men were killed in the explosion.
4   HMS *Sword Dance* was mined and sunk 24 June 1919.
5   HMS *Fandango* was mined and sunk 3 July 1919.

British Forces in North Russia, March 1918–October 1919

ARCHANGEL ('ELOPE')

Headquarters Archangel Command ('ELOPE Force'), NREF

Royal Navy (RN):
Dvina River Flotilla
Dvina River coastal motor boats
Royal Navy battery (2 x 60 pdr, 2 x 12 pdr naval guns)
Royal Navy Shore Observation Party
Russian Allied Naval Brigade

Royal Marines (RM):
Detachment Royal Marines Field Force North Russia (Russian Allied Naval Brigade)
Royal Marines Landing Party Dvina River

Royal Air Force (RAF):
'ELOPE' Wing:
    No. 1 (Slavo-British Aviation Corps) Squadron Bereznik
    No. 2 Squadron Pinega
    No. 3 Squadron Bereznik
    No. 4 Squadron Obozerskaya
Troitsa seaplane anchorage:
    RAF seaplanes (landed from HMS *Nairana*/HMS *Pegasus*)
    Seaplane Supply Barge 1
    Seaplane Supply Barge 2

Royal Artillery (RFA/RGA/CFA):
1st Battery, Slavo-British Legion (4 x 3.7 inch howitzers, 2 x 18 pdrs)
2nd Battery, Slavo-British Legion (4 x 12 pdrs)
3rd Battery, Slavo-British Legion (4 x 18 pdrs, 1 x 4.5 inch howitzer)
16th Brigade, Canadian Field Artillery:
    67th Battery, Canadian Field Artillery (6 x 18 pdrs)
    68th Battery, Canadian Field Artillery (6 x 18 pdrs)
55th 'Stevenson's' Battery, Royal Field Artillery (two 18 pdr Mk IV, 2 x 4.5 inch howitzers)
    (1st (Grogan's) Brigade, NRRF)
421st Battery, Royal Field Artillery (6 x 4.5 inch howitzers)
443rd 'Campion's' Battery, Royal Field Artillery (4 x 3.7 inch howitzers) (2nd (Sadleir-Jackson's)
    Brigade, NRRF)
No. 1 Armoured Train (1 x 8 cm, 1 x 18 pdr, 2 x 77 mm howitzers)
No. 2 Armoured Train (1 x 6 pdr, 1 x 75 mm naval howitzer)
No. 3 Armoured Train (2 x 47 mm naval guns)

Royal Artillery School, Archangel

Royal Engineers (RE):
348th Field Company
384th Field Company (1st (Grogan's) Brigade, NRRF)
385th Field Company (2nd (Sadleir-Jackson's) Brigade, NRRF)
'ELOPE' Force Army Postal Service Detachment
'ELOPE' Force Field Engineer Detachment
'ELOPE' Force Railway Detachment
Signal Service:
     1st (Archangel) & 2nd (Archangel) Divisional Signal Companies
     250th Signal Company (NRRF)
     348th Signal Company
     'ELOPE' Force Signal Company, Wireless Detachment, Cable Detachment
     Royal Engineers School, Archangel

Infantry:
1st Battalion, Oxfordshire and Buckinghamshire Light Infantry (1st (Grogan's) Brigade, NRRF)
1st (Dyer's) Battalion, Slavo-British Legion
2nd Battalion, Hampshire Regiment (1st (Grogan's) Brigade, NRRF)
2nd Battalion, Highland Light Infantry
2nd (Burke's) Battalion, Slavo-British Legion
6th, 13th Battalions, Yorkshire Regiment
2/7th Battalion, Durham Light Infantry
2/10th Battalion, Royal Scots
17th Battalion, Liverpool Regiment
45th, 46th Battalions, Royal Fusiliers (2nd (Sadleir-Jackson's) Brigade, NRRF)
45th/46th Royal Fusiliers Mounted Infantry (2nd (Sadleir-Jackson's) Brigade, NRRF)
238th, 239th Trench Mortar Batteries (1st (Grogan's) Brigade, NRRF)
240th, 241st Trench Mortar Batteries (2nd (Sadleir-Jackson's) Brigade, NRRF)
Pioneer Platoon, Slavo-British Legion
Railway Company, Slavo-British Legion

Machine Gun Corps (MGC):
252nd Company; 253rd Company (detachment – transferred from Murmansk); 280th Company
8th Battalion (1st (Grogan's) Brigade, NRRF)
201st (Special) Battalion (2nd (Sadleir-Jackson's) Brigade, NRRF)
Machine Gun Company, Slavo-British Legion

Royal Army Service Corps (RASC):
390th, 391st, 392nd, 396th, 397th, 398th, 401st, 402nd, 403rd, 404th Depot Units of Supply
130th Bakery Section
1102nd, 1122nd Horse Transport Companies
1123rd Company
1152nd Heavy Transport Company (1st (Grogan's) Brigade, NRRF)
1153rd Heavy Transport Company (2nd (Sadleir-Jackson's) Brigade, NRRF)
Remount Depot
RASC Lithuanian Platoon, Slavo-British Legion
Motor Transport School, Horse Transport School, Archangel

Royal Army Medical Corps (RAMC):
53rd, 54th, 55th Stationary Hospitals
82nd, 83rd, 85th Casualty Clearing Stations
85th General Hospital
125th, 136th, 138th, 139th Sanitary Sections
151st, 152nd, 153rd Field Ambulance
155th Field Ambulance (1st (Grogan's) Brigade, NRRF)
156th Field Ambulance (2nd (Sadleir-Jackson's) Brigade, NRRF)
No. 2, No. 3 Detention Hospitals
Ambulance Train
Dental Detachment
Hospital Ship HMHS *Kalyan*

Royal Army Veterinary Corps (RAVC):
Detachment
Veterinary School, Archangel and Base Hospital

Royal Army Ordnance Corps (RAOC):
Detachment

Army Pay Department (APD):
Detachment

Miscellaneous:
Chinese Labour Company, Slavo-British Legion
Intelligence Corps
North Russia Expeditionary Force Canteens (including YMCA)
North Russia Expeditionary Force Base Records
Russian Disciplinary Company
'ELOPE' Force Army Chaplains
'ELOPE' Force Cable Censorship Office
'ELOPE' Force Establishment of Instructors
'ELOPE' Force Establishment of Interpreters
'ELOPE' Force Field Censorship Office
'ELOPE' Force Military Landing Establishment
'ELOPE' Force Military Police Detachment

MURMANSK ('SYREN')

Headquarters Murmansk Command ('SYREN' Force), NREF

Royal Navy (RN):
'SYREN' Lake Onega Flotilla (administratively 237th Brigade)

Royal Marines (RM):
6th Battalion, Royal Marines
Royal Marines Field Force North Russia (HMS *Glory III*)

Royal Air Force (RAF):
'Duck' Flight (seaplanes) Medvyeja-Gora
'Pigeon' Flight Lumbushi

Royal Artillery (RFA/RGA):
6th Brigade, Royal Field Artillery:
  420th Battery, Royal Field Artillery (6 x 4.5 inch howitzers)
  434th Battery, Royal Field Artillery (4 x 18 pdrs)
  435th Battery, Royal Field Artillery (4 x 4.5 inch howitzers)
  1203rd Battery, Royal Field Artillery (6 x 18 pdrs)
  6th Brigade Ammunition Column
Mountain Battery, Royal Garrison Artillery (4 x 65 mm Italian mountain guns)
Armoured Train (2 x 18 pdr)
Royal Artillery School, Murmansk

Royal Engineers (RE):
492nd, 548th Field Companies
Army Postal Service Detachment
Inland Water Transport Detachment
Meteorological Section
Railway Detachment
Signal Service:
  236th, 237th Brigade Signal Sections
  6th Royal Field Artillery Brigade Signal Subsection
  'SYREN' Force Signal Company, Wireless Detachment, Cable Detachment
Royal Engineers School, Murmansk
Royal Engineers Signals School, Murmansk

Infantry:
236th Brigade:
  Karelian Regiment
  Slavo-British Legion (detachment)
  236th Trench Mortar Battery
237th Brigade:
  1st Battalion, East Surrey Regiment
  No. 1 Special Company, King's Royal Rifle Corps
  No. 1 Special Company, Middlesex Regiment
  KRRC/Middlesex Mounted Infantry
  Canadian Malamute Company
  237th Trench Mortar Battery
238th Brigade:
  11th Battalion, Royal Sussex Regiment
  29th Battalion, London Regiment (company)
  Slavo-British Legion Artillery (2 x 3 inch)

Machine Gun Corps (MGC):
19th Battalion
253rd Company (less detachment transferred to Archangel)

Royal Army Service Corps (RASC):
129th, 131st Bakery Sections
393rd, 394th, 395th, 399th, 400th, 406th, Depot Units of Supply
1123rd Horse Transport Company
Agricultural Company
Malamute Dog Train
Motor Transport School & Horse Transport School, Murmansk
Reindeer Transport Company
Remount Depot

Royal Army Medical Corps (RAMC):

55th Stationary Hospital
84th Casualty Clearing Station
86th General Hospital
127th & 132nd Sanitary Sections
154th Field Ambulance
Ambulance Train
Dental Detachment
Detention Hospital; Murmansk Detention Hospital
Hospital Ship HMHS *Braemar Castle*

Detachments:
Royal Army Veterinary Corps (RAVC)
Royal Army Ordnance Corps (RAOC)
Army Pay Department (APD)
Labour Corps

Miscellaneous:
Intelligence Corps
North Russia Expeditionary Force Canteens (including YMCA)
North Russia Expeditionary Force Base Records
'SYREN' Force Army Chaplains
'SYREN' Force Cable Censorship Office & Field Censorship Office
'SYREN' Force Establishment of Instructors
'SYREN' Force Establishment of Interpreters
'SYREN' Force Military Landing Establishment
'SYREN' Force Military Police Detachment

Appendix X

His Majesty's Ships, RN Eastern Baltic Fleet December 1918–December 1919

Commanders:
December 1918 to January 1919: Rear Admiral Edwyn Alexander-Sinclair, KCB, MVO, RN
January 1919 to December 1919: Rear Admiral Walter Cowan, CB, DSO, RN

Light Cruisers:	HMS *Cleopatra*	HMS *Danae*
	HMS *Caledon*	HMS *Dauntless*
	HMS *Calypso*	HMS *Delhi*
	HMS *Caradoc*	HMS *Dragon*
	HMS *Cassandra*	HMS *Dunedin*
	HMS *Ceres*	HMS *Galatea*
	HMS *Cardiff*	HMS *Inconstant*
	HMS *Curacoa*	HMS *Phaeton*
	HMS *Champion*	HMS *Royalist*

Aircraft Carriers:	HMS *Furious*	*HMS Vindictive*

Monitor:	HMS *Erebus*

Destroyers:	HMS *Abdiel*	HMS *Verulam*
	HMS *Bruce*	HMS *Vidette*
	HMS *Mackay*	HMS *Vittoria*
	HMS *Scotsman*	HMS *Vivacious*
	HMS *Scout*	HMS *Vortigern*
	HMS *Seafire*	HMS *Voyager*
	HMS *Sepoy*	HMS *Wakeful*
	HMS *Shakespeare*	HMS *Walker*
	HMS *Spencer*	HMS *Wallace*
	HMS *Valentine*	HMS *Walpole*
	HMS *Valiant*	HMS *Walrus*
	HMS *Valkyrie*	HMS *Warspite*
	HMS *Valorous*	HMS *Watchman*
	HMS *Vancouver*	HMS *Waterhen*
	HMS *Vanessa*	HMS *Westminster*
	HMS *Vanity*	HMS *Whitley*
	HMS *Vanoc*	HMS *Winchelsea*
	HMS *Vanquisher*	HMS *Winchester*
	HMS *Vectis*	HMS *Windsor*
	HMS *Velox*	HMS *Wolfhound*
	HMS *Vendetta*	HMS *Wryneck*
	HMS *Venturous*	
	HMS *Versatile*	

Fleet Minelayers:	HMS *Angora*	HMS *Princess Margaret*
Fleet Minesweepers:	HMS *Banbury* HMS *Gentian* HMS *Hexham*	HMS *Lanarrk* HMS *Myrtle*
Submarine Depot Ships:	HMS *Lucia*	HMS *Maidstone*
Submarines:	HMS *L.11* HMS *L.12* HMS *L.16* HMS *L.55*	HMS *E.27* HMS *E.39* HMS *E.40*
Coastal Motor Boats:	*CMB 4* *CMB 7* *CMB 24A* *CMB 31* *CMB 62BD*	*CMB 72* *CMB 79A* *CMB 86* *CMB 88BD*
Hospital Ships:	HMHS *Berbice*	

Participants in the Raid on Kronstadt Harbour, 18 August 1919

Of the 55 participants in the Kronstadt Raid no less than 48 received either a decoration or MiD.

Statistics

Royal Navy

Victoria Cross (VC)	2
Distinguished Service Order (DSO)	6
Distinguished Service Cross (DSC)	8
Distinguished Service Medal (DSM)	16
Posthumous Mentioned in Despatches (MiD)	3
Killed in Action (KIA)	7
Died of Wounds (DOW)	1
Prisoner of War (POW)	8

Sunk by enemy fire:	*CMB 24A*
	CMB 62BD
	CMB 79A

Royal Air Force

Bar to the Distinguished Flying Cross (DFC Bar)	1
Distinguished Flying Cross (DFC)	6
Mentioned in Despatches (MiD)	6

Crash landed	Sopwith Camel

Results

- Submarine Depot Ship *Pamiat Azova* sunk by a single torpedo fired by *CMB 79A*.
- Battleship *Petropavlovsk* hit and critically damaged by a single torpedo fired by *CMB 88BD*.
- Battleship *Andrei Pervozvanny* hit and critically damaged by three torpedoes, one fired by *CMB 88BD* and two fired by *CMB 31BD*.
- Several small ships in the military harbour either sunk or damaged by torpedo from *CMB 7*.
- Destroyer depot ship damaged by RAF bombing.

Royal Navy

Coastal Motor Boat No. 7 (Thornycroft 40 foot)
Agar piloted the CMB fleet through the chain of forts and patrolled the harbour mouth to protect withdrawal of the CMBs. As the surviving CMBs left the harbour after making their attacks, Agar

fired No. 7's only torpedo into the military harbour, destroying and damaging several vessels before returning through the chain of Forts to Finland.

Lieutenant Augustine W.S. Agar, VC, RN (DSO for raid)
Sub Lieutenant Edgar Robert Sindall, RNR (DSC for raid)
Midshipman Richard Nigel Onslow Marshall, RNR (DSC for raid)
Chief Motor Mechanic Albert Victor Piper, RNVR (DSM for raid)

Coastal Motor Boat No. 24A (Thornycroft 55 foot)

CMB 24A was sunk by patrol destroyer Gavriil at the mouth of the harbour after Napier's unsuccessful attack with a torpedo on Gavriil. All the crew survived the sinking but were subsequently taken prisoner by the Bolsheviks.

Lieutenant Laurence Egerton Scott Napier, RN (DSO for raid)
Sub Lieutenant Osman Cyril Horton Giddy, RN (DSC for raid)
Able Seaman Charles Alfred Harvey, RN
Able Seaman Herbert James Bowles, RN
Chief Motor Mechanic William Whyte, RNVR (DSM for raid)
Chief Motor Mechanic Benjamin Reynish, RNVR (DSM for raid)

Coastal Motor Boat No. 31BD (Thornycroft 55 foot)

Dobson led the first wave of CMBs into the harbour and successfully attacked battleship *Andrei Pervozvanny* with two torpedoes before leaving the harbour under fire and returning through the chain of forts to Finland.

Commander Claude Congreve Dobson, DSO, RN (VC for raid)
Lieutenant Russell H. McBean, DSC, RN (DSO for raid)
Sub Lieutenant John Christian Boldero, RN (DSC for raid)
Chief Motor Mechanic Ernest Yeoman, RNVR (DSM for raid)
Chief Motor Mechanic Harry Eric Sadler, RNVR (DSM for raid)

Coastal Motor Boat No. 62BD (Thornycroft 55 foot)

As it entered the harbour, *CMB 62BD* collided with *CMB 79A* which was leaving, having successfully torpedoed submarine depot ship *Pamiat Azova*. *CMB 62BD* picked up the survivors from *CMB 79A* which had been critically damaged by shellfire from patrol destroyer *Gavriil*, which had already sunk *CMB 24A*. *CMB 62BD* immediately attacked *Gavriil* unsuccessfully with two torpedoes, only to be sunk by the destroyer and guns on the breakwater. Only McVeigh survived from *CMB 62BD* but was subsequently taken prisoner by the Bolsheviks.

Lieutenant Commander Frank Tomkinson Brade, DSC, RNR (killed)
Sub Lieutenant Hector Forbes MacLean, RN (killed)
Leading Seaman Sydney Holmes, RN (killed)
Chief Motor Mechanic Francis Leslie Howe Thatcher, RNVR (killed)
Stoker Petty Officer Samuel McVeigh, RN (DSM for raid)

Coastal Motor Boat No. 72A (Thornycroft 55 foot)

Entered the harbour and commenced an unsuccessful attack on a Bolshevik destroyer, the firing gear was shot away before torpedoes could be launched. Bodley turned and left the harbour when he came across *CMB 86BD* broken down and moving very slowly. *CMB 72A* remained in company with *CMB 86BD* and eventually took her in tow through the chain of forts back to Finland.

Sub Lieutenant Edward Roland Bodley, RNR (DSO for raid)
Sub Lieutenant Roland Hunter-Blair, RN (DSC for raid)
Leading Seaman Alexander Richard Bremner, RN (DSM for raid)
Chief Motor Mechanic Edwin Thomas Clarke, RNVR (DSM for raid)
Chief Motor Mechanic Robert George Pratten, RNVR (DSM for raid)

Coastal Motor Boat No. 79A (Thornycroft 55 foot)

CMB 79A collided with *CMB 62BD* as *CMB 79A* was leaving the harbour after torpedoing submarine depot ship *Pamiat Azova*, and *CMB 62BD* was entering the harbour. Bremner managed to bring *CMB 79A* outside of the harbour before she was critically damaged by shellfire from patrol destroyer *Gavriil*, which had already sunk *CMB 24A*. The crew of *CMB 79A* were picked up by *CMB 62BD* which immediately attacked *Gavriil* unsuccessfully with two torpedoes only to be sunk by the destroyer and guns on the breakwater. Only Bremner and Dunkley survived from *CMB 79A* but were subsequently taken prisoner by the Bolsheviks.

Lieutenant William Hamilton Bremner, DSC, RN (DSO for raid)
Sub Lieutenant Thomas Richard Guy Usborne, RN (killed, posthumous MiD for raid)
Able Seaman William George Smith, RN (killed, posthumous MiD for raid)
Chief Motor Mechanic Francis Edward Stephens, RNVR (killed, posthumous MiD for raid)
Chief Motor Mechanic Henry John Dunkley, RNVR (DSM for raid)

Coastal Motor Boat No. 86BD (Thornycroft 55 foot)

Passed through the chain of forts under a heavy fire but broke down before reaching the harbour. Could only maintain a few knots before *CMB 72A* arrived and took her in tow through the chain of forts back to Finland.

Sub Lieutenant Francis Walter Howard, RNR (DSC for raid)
Sub Lieutenant Robert Leslie Wight, RN (DSC for raid)
Engineer Lieutenant Commander Francis Bertrand Yates, RN (DSO for raid)
Chief Motor Mechanic Alfred Williams Henry Tidey, RNVR (DSM for raid)
Chief Motor Mechanic Walter Montague Scales, RNVR (DSM for raid)
Able Seaman Albert Hinchcliffe, RN (DSM for raid)
Able Seaman Robert Dalley, RN (DSM for Raid)

Coastal Motor Boat No. 88BD (Thornycroft 55 foot)

Dayrell-Reed entered the harbour and made an attack run on the Battleship *Andrei Pervozvanny* but was immediately shot in the head and the boat thrown off course. Steele took the controls, steadied the boat and moved back into firing position before torpedoing *Andrei Pervozvanny* at 100 yards range. Steele immediately turned to attack battleship Petropavlovsk which was also successfully torpedoed. Steele then left the harbour and returned through the chain of forts to Finland.

Lieutenant Archibald Dayrell-Reed, DSO and Bar, RN (died of wounds)
Lieutenant Gordon Charles Steele, RN (VC for raid)
Sub Lieutenant Norman Eyre Morley, RNR (DSC for raid)
Chief Motor Mechanic Vernon Fisher Gascoigne, RNVR (DSM for raid)

Chief Motor Mechanic Baden Marples Masters, RNVR (DSM for raid)

Royal Air Force

Sopwith Strutter:
Williams bombed the Harbour as the raid was underway, possibly hitting battleship *Petropavlovsk*, and then circled overhead to attract fire from Bolshevik gunners on the breakwater.

Flying Officer Thomas Melling Williams, DFC, MC (DFC Bar for raid)

Sopwith Strutter:
Brewerton bombed the harbour and then circled overhead to attract fire from Bolshevik gunners on the breakwater.

Flying Officer Eric Brewerton (DFC for raid)

Grain Griffin:
Fairweather's aircraft was the first to arrive off Kronstadt and bombed and strafed the harbour and patrol destroyer *Gavriil*. He then circled overhead to attract fire from Bolshevik gunners on the breakwater and chain of forts to cover the withdrawal of the CMBs back to Finland.

Flying Officer James MacGregor Fairweather (DFC for raid)
Pilot Officer Observer William Sidney James Walne (MiD for raid)

Sopwith Camel:
The Camel's engine failed completely on the way to Kronstadt forcing Randall to glide towards the sea and prepare to ditch. Within 50 feet of the water the engine picked up, and he continued on to Kronstadt and attacked searchlights along the breakwater with machine guns from 500 feet. The engine again began to give trouble and Randall returned towards Finland, but when about 10 miles from Koivisto the engine gave out again and he had to force land on a beach. Although Randall was unharmed the Camel was a write-off.

Flight Lieutenant Arthur Clunie Randall, DFC (MiD for raid)

Short Seaplane:
Acland's aircraft bombed and strafed the harbour searchlights and then circled overhead to attract fire from Bolshevik gunners on the breakwater and the chain of forts, to cover the withdrawal of the CMBs back to Finland. When his petrol was exhausted Acland returned to base, refuelled and went out again on a second sortie.

Flight Lieutenant Wilfred Reginald Dyke Acland, AFC (DFC for raid)
Pilot Officer Observer Alexander Lees (MiD for raid)

Short Seaplane:
Boumphrey's aircraft bombed and strafed the harbour searchlights and then circled overhead to attract fire from Bolshevik gunners on the breakwater and the chain of forts to cover the withdrawal of the CMBs back to Finland. When his petrol was exhausted Boumphrey returned to base, refuelled and went out again in another aircraft on a second sortie.

Flight Lieutenant Colin Boumphrey (DFC for raid)
Pilot Officer Observer Lionel James Booth (MiD for raid)

Short Seaplane:

Fletcher's aircraft bombed the patrol destroyer *Gavriil* at the entrance to the harbour and strafed the harbour searchlights, then circled overhead to attract fire from Bolshevik gunners on the breakwater and the chain of forts to cover the withdrawal of the CMBs back to Finland.

Flight Lieutenant Albert William Fletcher, AFC (DFC for raid)
Pilot Officer Observer Frank Clifford Jenner (MiD for raid)

Short Seaplane:

Donald's aircraft led the bombing attack on the harbour and breakwater and then circled overhead to attract fire from Bolshevik gunners on the breakwater and the chain of forts, to cover the withdrawal of the CMBs back to Finland.

Flight Lieutenant David Grahame Donald, AFC (DFC for raid)
Pilot Officer Observer Louis James Chandler (MiD for raid)

Sopwith Strutter (Photographic Reconnaissance):

Although this aircraft did not take part in the raid due to mechanical failure, both Walmsley and Whippey flew photographic reconnaissance missions over Kronstadt in the days leading up to the raid which was critical to the success of the operation:

Lieutenant Walmsley
Lieutenant Observer Frederick Arthur Whippey (DFC for Photo Reconnaissance flights over Kronstadt)

Bibliography

Archival Documents

A vast amount of archival material has been consulted during research for this book. Those files listed below are considered by the author to be the most relevant.

National Archives (United Kingdom)

Admiralty (ADM) Files

ADM 1/8545/315, HMS *Cassandra*. Sunk by mine in Baltic. Casualties
ADM 1/8570/291, Request of payment of 2s/6d a day to crews of Destroyers ordered to the Baltic
ADM 1/8563/208, *CMB4* attempt to land Courier behind Bolshevik lines
ADM 53/48558, HMS *Marlborough*, ship's logs 1919–1920
ADM 137/1668, Baltic proceedings, November–December 1919
ADM 137/1679, Baltic various subjects, Volume II
ADM 137/1694, Archangel River Expedition proceedings (evacuation), 1919, Vol. I
ADM 137/1695, Archangel River Expedition proceedings (evacuation), 1919, Vol. II
ADM 137/1698, North Russia telegrams, Mar. 1918–Oct. 1919
ADM 137/1704, White Sea SNO's Records, Vol. I. 1918-19
ADM 137/1707, White Sea SNO's Records, Vol. IV. 1918–19
ADM 137/1708, White Sea SNO's Records, Vol. V. 1919
ADM 137/1711, White Sea SNO's Records 1918–19, Vol.VIII. 1918–19
ADM 137/3760, Report of Court of Enquiry into the burning of the Naval Transport House at Murmansk on 13th June 1918
ADM 137/3890, Record of German Baltic naval station
ADM 137/3963, White Sea telegrams, July–Dec. 1918
ADM 156/93, 6th Royal Marines Battalion, misconduct and indiscipline
ADM 186/606, Organisation of the Archangel River Flotilla 1919

Air Ministry (AIR) Files

AIR 1/10/15/1/35, Report of RAF Dvina River Expedition, July–Aug. 1919
AIR 1/15/15/1/67, South Russian Mission War Diaries 'A' Detachment (ex 47 Sqn.), 'Z' Flight of Instructional Mission
AIR 1/408/15/232/1, War Diary of 'A' Detachment, 47 Sqn., RAF, South Russia Dec. 1919–Jan. 1920
AIR 1/408/15/232/3, War Diary of 47 Squadron, RAF, South Russia, 1–31 March 1920
AIR 1/1666/204/99/12, Nominal roll in South Russia: All ranks
AIR 1/1666/204/99/13, Nominal roll in South Russia: Officers
AIR 1/1769/204/143/5, GROs, RAF Murmansk, July–Sept. 1919
AIR 1/1957/204/260/12, RAF South Russia: Recommendations for honours and awards
AIR 1/1959/204/260/28, No. 47 Sqn. War Diary, June–Nov 1919
AIR 1/1960/204/260/37, Reports on Russian Units, RAF South Russia
AIR 1/1960/204/260/39, Miscellaneous returns on Russian personnel, RAF South Russia
AIR 1/1960/204/260/40, HQ RAF South Russia, Nominal Rolls of British and Russian personnel
AIR 1/2266/209/70/16, North Russia, report on use of 'M' gas bombs, 1919

AIR 1/2268/209/70/20, Winter flying in North Russia by Lieutenant-Colonel R. Grey, RAF, June 1919

AIR 1/2268/209/70/218, Resume of events in North Russia, Major-General E. Ironside, Aug. 1919

AIR 1/424/15/258/1, HMS *Nairana* reports, 18 July–18 Sept. 1918

AIR 1/435/15/274/2. Resume of events, RAF Seaplanes, HMS Nairana, Aug.–Oct. 1918

AIR 1/435/15/274/3, Resume of events, RAF Archangel, April–June 1919

AIR 1/438/15/301/4, Reports of operations, RAF Archangel, May–Sept. 1919

AIR 1/445/15/303/18, Balloon Expedition River Dvina, March–June 1919

AIR 1/445/15/303/19, Assorted files, RAF North Russia 1918–19

AIR 1/450/15/312/9, Summary of operations, RAF Murmansk, June–Sept. 1919

AIR 1/462/15/312/122, Murmansk, RAF operations reports, 1918–19

AIR 1/472/15/312/168, Murmansk, RAF operations reports, June–Sept. 1919

AIR 1/472/15/312/169, Archangel, RAF operations reports, Feb.–Oct. 1919

AIR 1/473/15/312/171, Summary of operations, HMS Nairana, RAF Murmansk, June–Sept. 1919

AIR 1/473/15/312/173-4, Observers' logs, RAF Murmansk, June–Sept. 1919

AIR 1/473/15/312/178, Telegrams, RAF Murmansk, Sept. 1918–Sept. 1919

AIR 1/475/15/312/191, Correspondence, Duck Flight, Murmansk, June–Sept. 1919

AIR 1/769/204/143/12, GROs, 237th Infy. Brigade, Murmansk, Aug.–Sept. 1919

AIR 1/770/204/143/20, Hostile log reports, RAF Murmansk, July–Sept. 1919

AIR 1/9/15/1/33, Report of original Kem Flight, RAF Murmansk, Aug.–Sept. 1919

AIR 1/9/15/1/34, Report of HMS *Nairana* seaplanes, RAF Murmansk, Aug. 1919

AIR 2/118, Organisation and Future Organisation and Maintenance of RAF Mission to South Russia

AIR 5/1340, 'London Gazette' supplements: work of the independent air force: operations in North and South Russia

War Office (WO) Files

WO 06/1170, Report on use of smoke generators and 'M' gas bombs in North Russia, 1919

WO 95/5422, War diaries, 1st (Grogan's) Brigade, North Russia Relief Force 1919: 55th Bty., RFA, 384th Fld. Coy., RE, Bde. Sig. Coy., RE, 1st Bn., OBLI, 2nd Bn., Hants Regt., 2nd Bn., HLI, 238th TMB, 8th Bn., MGC, 155th Fld. Amb., RAMC, 136th, 137th San. Sect., RAMC, 1152nd Coy., RASC

WO 95/5423, War diaries, Archangel Force Troops, North Russia Expeditionary Force: 421st Bty., RFA, 2/7th DLI, 280th Coy., MGC, 125th San. Sect., RAMC

WO 95/5426, War diaries, Murmansk Force Troops, North Russia Expeditionary Force: 6th Bde., RFA: 420th, 434th, 435th, 1203rd Btys, RFA, 492nd, 548th Fld. Coys, RE, SYREN Force Sig. Coy., RE, No. 1. Spec. Coy., KRRC, No. 1 Spec. Coy., Midd'x Regt., 252nd Coy., MGC, 154th Fld. Amb., 127th, 132nd San. Sect., RAMC

WO 95/5427, War diaries, 236th & 237th Infy. Bdes., Murmansk, North Russia Expeditionary Force: 6th Bn., Yorks Regt., 11th Bn., R. Suss. Regt., 17th Bn., L'pool Regt., 236th TMB, Finnish Legion, 1st Bn., E. Surr. Regt., 13th Bn., Yorks Regt., 237th TMB, 253rd Coy., MGC

WO 95/5429, War diaries, Dvina Force, Archangel, North Russia Expeditionary Force 1918–19: 16th Bde., CFA, 2/10th Bn., R. Scots

WO 95/5430, War diaries, 2nd (Sadleir-Jackson's) Brigade, North Russia Relief Force 1919: 'Campion's' Bty., RFA, 385th Fld. Coy., RE, 45th & 46th Bns, R. Fus., 201st Bn., MGC, 139th San. Sect., RAMC, 1153rd Coy., RASC

WO 95/5431, War diaries, Archangel Lines of Communications Troops: 2nd Bn., S–BL, Russian Disp. Coy., 82nd & 84th CCS, 85th & 86th Gen. Hosp., 53rd Stat. Hosp., 60th Amb. Train, RAMC

WO 95/5432, War diaries, Murmansk, Lines of Communications Troops: 393rd, 394th & 400th Depot, 1123rd HT Coy., RASC.

WO 95/5487, NREF, Military Control Establishment

WO 106/1148, Report on use of 'M' gas bombs in North Russia, 1919

WO 106/1175, Report on evacuation of Shenkursk, January 1919
WO 154/336, War Diary 'SYREN' Force, 237th Infy. Brigade Nov. 1918–July.1919
WO 158/711, Lecture on river fighting, North Russia
WO 158/715, Operations, dispositions of forces Archangel, Aug. 1918–Apr. 1919
WO 158/716, Dvina Force reports, May–June 1919
WO 158/718, Report of operations near Plesetskaya, Dec. 1918–Jan. 1919
WO 158/720, 'SYREN' Flotilla reports, Aug.–Oct. 1919
WO 158/721, Operation: Report by Senior Naval Officer, May–Oct. 1919
WO 158/728, Combined operation between the Lake Flotilla and Russian troops, Aug. 1919
WO 158/729, Lake Onega: Operation Orders, Aug. 1919
WO 158/732, 'SYREN' Lake Flotilla Operations, Aug.–Sep. 1919
WO 158/733, North Russia, General Policy, 1919
WO 158/734, Lake Flotilla: Operation Orders and narrative of operations
WO 158/735, RAF Reports on operations, Sept.–Oct. 1919
WO 158/969, Court of Inquiry proceedings, 6th Royal Marine Battalion indiscipline
WO 159/717, Questions on Naval cooperation in North Russia, Nov. 1918–June 1919
WO 160/10, Dvina Force report on the Dyer's Battalion mutiny, July 1919
WO 32/3762, Conditions of Service (officers): Non British Candidates
WO 32/5411, Decision of Provisional Governments to re-establish certain Russian decorations
WO 32/5685, Employment of tanks in Russia, 1919
WO 32/5693, Offensive operations at Archangel, Aug. 1919
WO 32/5696, Tanks: proposals concerning formation of tank expeditionary force and use of tanks in Russia
WO 32/5698, Murmansk Command, Report on operations, Sept. 1919
WO 32/5699, Proposed exchange of POWs with the Bolsheviks
WO 32/5703, CinC, NREF, Report on operations
WO 32/5704, Report of Allied operations, North Russia, 10 Aug.–12 Oct. 1919
WO 32/5715, Policy concerning negotiations with Soviet forces
WO 32/5718, Account of the evacuation of Novorossiysk
WO 32/5723, Report of events connected with handing over and execution of Admiral Kolchak
WO 32/5749, Use of gas in North Russia
WO 32/9545, Mutiny in 1st Battalion, S.B.L. Dyer's Regiment, North Russia
WO 32/9567, Withdrawal of British troops from the Caspian and Caucasia: transfer of Caspian Flotilla and RAF to Denikin
WO 106/1295, Operations; Russian Military Reports
WO 106/1279, Returned British POWs: Report by Captain F. McCullagh
WO/158/727, Naval operations reports, July–Sept. 1919
WO 279/781, Notes for personnel volunteering for service with the British Military Mission in South Russia
WO 329/2308, British Military Mission in Russia officers: medal rolls
WO 388/5, Statistical records (monthly returns) of medals awarded to and received from various countries

Library and Archives of Canada

1918/08/21–1919/05/31. War diaries – North Russia Expeditionary Force, 16th Brigade, CFA
1918/10/16–1919/05/31. War diaries – North Russia Expeditionary Force, 67th Battery, CFA
1918/10/09–1919/05/31. War diaries – North Russia Expeditionary Force, 68th Battery, CFA
1918/10/11–1918/12/31–1919/01/01-1919/01/31, War Diaries – Force Headquarters, Siberia
1919/02/01–1919/02/28–1919/03/01-1919/03/31, War Diaries – General Staff, Siberia
Vol. 3057, Reel T-11119; File 962-War Diaries – 'B' Squadron, Royal North West Mounted Police, Siberia
Service Files of the First World War, 1914–1918 – Canadian Expeditionary Force

Australian War Memorial

1DRL/0158, Letters of Captain A. Brown
1DRL/0428, Australian Red Cross Society Wounded and Missing Enquiries Bureau, 1914–18 War. 133002, Sergeant Samuel George Pearse, VC, MM, Royal Fusiliers
1DRL/0527, Diary of Sub-Lieutenant D. Munro
3DRL/7086, Letters of Private W.J. Robinson
3DRL/7709, Diary of Sergeant B. Perry, MM
PR/85/324, 419/31/50, Memoirs of Sergeant John Kelly
PR89/140, Recollection of Private Ernest Heathcote
AWM ID S00180, Interview with Private N.M. Brooke, DCM (1984)
PR91/126, Diary of Private W.C. Yeaman
3DRL/6371, Private Letters of Private W.B. Baverstock
90/147, Private Journal of Sub Lieutenant B. Brewster, DSC

Imperial War Museum

10815 PP/MCR/237, Private Papers of B. Brewer
10790 DS/MISC/87, Private Papers, Air Vice Marshall C.N.H. Bilney, CB, CBE
12008 PP/MCR/56, Private Papers of Brig. G.R.P. Roupell, VC, CB
1589 87/45/1, Recollection of H.F. Goodright
209/91/11/1, Diary of S.J. Rutland
2109 92/46/1, Private Papers, Lieutenant J.D. Snow, RNR
2650/94/11/1, Private papers of R.S. Mouat
3450 86/86/1 Private Papers of E.M. Allfrey
430 PP/MCR/182, Memoir of Major-General D.N. Wimberley, CB, DSO, MC
4615/81/21/1 Diary of R. Rudd
7267 76/67/1, Recollection of Captain R. Sykes, DFC, RAF
823 99/17/2, Private papers of Lieutenant L.E. Roberts
997/88/7/1, Private Papers of P. Brentnall
14070 (Docs.), Private Papers, Commander R. Harrison, RNR
6971 (Docs.), Private Papers, Captain H.G. Pertwee, CBE, DSO, RN
751 (Docs.), Private Papers, Payr. Commander M.C. Franks, OBE, RD, RNR
4170 (Docs.), Private Papers, A. Lupton, RMLI
7679 (Docs.), Private Papers, Lieutenant H. Mercer, CBE, MC, DFC, RAF
11020 (Docs.), Private Papers, Lieutenant-Colonel L.A. Gundry-White
242 (Docs.), Private Papers, Captain J.W.C. Lancaster
20971 (Docs.), Private Papers, Major-General G.N. Wood, CB, CBE, DSO, MC
534 (Docs.), Private Papers, Major-General D.A.L. Wade, CB, OBE, MC
1366 (Docs.), Private Papers, H.A. Hill
742 (Docs.), Private Papers, Brig. C.E. de Wolff CB, CBE
8213 (Docs.), Private Papers, Major A. McPherson, DSO, MC, DCM
15273 (Docs.), Private Papers of Colonel A.P. Hodges, MC
17490 (Docs.), Private Papers of Lieutenant Commander P.L. Puxley, RN
16636 (Docs.), Private Papers of Captain E.R. Conder, DSO, DSC, RN
8535 (Docs.), Private Papers of Squadron Leader E. Brewerton, DFC and Bar, RAF

Journals & Private Papers

Private Diary of Lieutenant Roy Smith-Hill, RMLI

Private letters of Private E. Cresswell-George, 201st Battalion, MGC

Private Diary of Ernest Ethelbert Daish, SBA, RN

Private Diary of Hugh McColl, 46th Battalion, R. Fus.

Private Diary of Lt. Colonel C.H.L. Sharman, 16th Brigade, CFA. Public Archives of Canada, EE-112

E.W. Latchford, 'With the White Russians', *Reveille*, vol. 6 to 12, August 1933 (pp. 26–27) through to vol. 7, no. 8, April 1934 (pp. 23, 57)

'Admiral Sir Walter H. Cowan, BT., KCB, DSO', *The Naval Review*, Vol. XXX, No. 4, November 1942 (pp. 267–268)

A Collection of Reports on Bolshevism, Foreign Office, 1920, Report No. 3

Jeffrey Grey, 'A "Pathetic Sideshow": Australians and the Russian Intervention, 1918–1919', Journal of the Australian War Memorial 7 (October 1985): 12–17

Jeffrey Grey, 'HMAS *Swan* in Russia', *Sabretache: Journal of the Australian Military Historical Society*, vol. XXV, no. 2, April–June 1984

Peter Burness, 'The Australians in North Russia 1919' *Sabretache: Journal of the Australian Military Historical Society*, vol. XXII, no. 4, August 1976

Charmion Chaplin-Thomas, 'The Fourth Dimension', *The Maple Leaf*, Vol. 8, No. 2, January 2005

London Gazette Despatches

9 October 1919, Royal Navy Caspian Sea (Seymour, Rear Admiral Black Sea)

6 April 1920, North Russia Expeditionary Force (Poole, Maynard, Ironside, Rawlinson).

6 April 1920, Royal Navy Baltic Sea (Admiral Cowan)

19 May 1920, Royal Navy North Russia (Admiral Green, Captain Altham)

8 July 1920, Royal Navy North Russia (Admiral Kemp)

5 August 1920, Transcaspia (General Munro)

7 January 1921, British Army of the Black Sea (General Milne)

Books

Agar, Augustus, *Baltic Episode: A Classic of Secret Service in Russian Waters* (London: Hodder & Stoughton, 1963)

Albertson, Ralph, *Fighting Without a War* (New York: Harcourt, Brace & Howe, 1920)

Altham, Captain E., CB, RN, *A History of the White Sea Station, 1914–19* (London: Training & Staff Division, Naval Staff, July 1921)

Arthur, Max, *The True Glory: The Royal Navy 1914–39. A Narrative History* (London: Coronet Books, 1996)

Ashmore, Leslie, *Forgotten Flotilla: British Submarines in Russia 1914–18* (Portsmouth: Manuscript Press in association with the Royal Navy Submarine Museum, 2001)

Aten, Marion, *Last Train Over Rostov Bridge* (New York: Julian Messner, 1961)

Bainton, Roy, *Honoured by Strangers: the Life of Captain Francis Cromie CB, DSO, RN, 1882–1918* (Shrewsbury: Airlife Publishing, 2002)

Baron, Nick, *The King of Karelia. Colonel P.J. Woods and the British Intervention in North Russia 1918–1919. A brief history and memoir* (London: Francis Boutle, 2007)

Bennett, Geoffrey, *Cowan's War: the story of British naval operations in the Baltic, 1918–1920* (London: Collins, 1964)

Bennett, Geoffrey, *Freeing the Baltic* (Edinburgh: Birlinn, 2002)

Bentinck, Major V.M., *Mutiny in Murmansk: The Hidden Shame: The Royal Marines in North Russia 1918–1919* (Royal Marines Historical Society, 1999)

Blumberg, General Sir H.E., KCB, RM, *Britain's Sea Soldiers. A Record of the Royal Marines during the War 1914–19* (Devonport: Swiss and Co., 1927)

Body, Captain O.G., DSO, RFA & Bombardier W.G. Willmott, RFA, *A Short History of 421st Battery, R. F. A., North Russia 1918-19* (Privately published, undated)

Boustead, Colonel Sir Hugh, KBE, DSO, MC, *The Wind of Morning: An Autobiography* (London: Chatto & Windus, 1971)

Bradley, John, *Allied Intervention in Russia, 1917–20* (New York: Basic Books, 1968)

Bujack, Philip, *Undefeated: the Extraordinary Life and Death of Lt. Col. Jack Sherwood Kelly, VC, CMG, DSO* (Great Britain: Forster Consulting, 2008)

Callwell, Sir Charles Edward, *Field Marshall Sir Henry Wilson: His Life and Diaries*, vol. 2 (London: Cassell, 1927)

Challinger, Michael, *ANZACS in Arkhangel: The Untold Story of Australia and the Invasion of Russia 1918–19* (Richmond, Victoria: Hardie Grant Books, 2010)

Collishaw, Raymond, *Air Command: A Fighter Pilot's Story* (London: Kimber, 1973)

Dobson, Christopher & Miller, John, *The Day We Almost Bombed Moscow* (London: Hodder & Stoughton, 1986)

Dukes, Paul, *Red Dusk and the Morrow: Adventures and Investigations in Soviet Russia* (London: Williams and Norgate, 1922)

Dunsterville, L.C., *The Adventures of Dunsterforce* (London: Edward Arnold, 1920)

Edmonds, H.J., *Norman Dewhurst, MC* (privately published, 1968)

Ellis, C.H., *The British Invervention in Transcaspia, 1918–19* (University of California Press, 1963)

Ewing, Major John, MC, *The Royal Scots, 1914–19* (Edinburgh, London: Oliver and Boyd, 1925)

Ferguson, Harry, *Operation Kronstadt: the true story of honor, espionage, and the rescue of Britain's greatest spy, the Man with a Hundred Faces* (London: Arrow Books, 2008)

Fraser, Edward, *The Royal Marine Artillery: 1804–1923* (London: Royal United Service Institution, 1930)

Gordon, Dennis, *Quartered In Hell: The Story of American North Russian Expeditionary Force 1918–1919* (Missoula, MT: Doughboy Historical Society, 1982)

Haddon, Victoria (ed.), *North Russia Expedition of Summer 1919: A Diary written by Mr R A Jowett* (CreateSpace, 2014)

Halliday, E.M., *The Ignorant Armies, The Anglo–American Archangel Expedition 1918–1919* (London: Weidenfeld & Nicolson, 1961)

Hill, George A., *Go Spy the Land: Being the Adventures of IK8 of the British Secret Service* (London: Cassell & Co., 1932)

Horrocks, Lieutenant-General Sir Brian, KCB, KBE, DSO, MC, *A Full Life* (London: Collins, 1960)

Hudson, Miles, *Intervention in Russia 1918–20: A Cautionary Tale* (Leo Cooper, 2004)

Ironside, Sir Edmund, *Archangel 1918–19* (London: Constable, 1953)

Irwin, Mike, *Victoria's Cross: the story of Sgt. Samuel George Pearse, V.C., M.M.: from ANZAC to Archangel* (Victoria: Northland Centre, 2003)

Jackson, Robert, *At War with the Bolsheviks* (London: Tom Stacey Ltd., 1972)

Jameson, Captain Thomas, DSO, *Expedition to Siberia, 1919: The Great War, Eastern Front* (Portsmouth: Royal Marines Historical Society, Special Publication No. 10, 1987)

Jones, H.A., *Over The Balkans and South Russia 1917-1919: being the history of No. 47 Squadron Royal Air Force* (Elstree: Greenhill Books, 1987)

Jones, Ira, *An Air Fighter's Scrapbook* (London: Nicholson & Watson, Ltd., 1938)

Kettle, Michael, *Churchill and the Archangel Fiasco, November 1918–July 1919* (London: Routledge, 1992)

Kinvig, Clifford, *Churchill's Crusade: The British Invasion of Russia, 1918–1920* (London: Continuum, 2007)

Kreyer, J.A.C., and Uloth, G., *28th Light Cavalry in Persian and Russian Turkistan, 1915–20* (Oxford: private publication, 1926)

Liddell-Hart, B.H., *The Tanks: The History of the Royal Tank Regiment and its Predecessors, Heavy Branch, Machine-Gun Corps, Tanks Corps, and Royal Tank Corps, 1914–45* (New York: Prager, 1959)

Livock, G.E., Imperial War Museum, *To the Ends of the Air* (London: HMSO, 1973)

Lockhart, R.H. Bruce, *Memoirs of a British Agent; being an account of the author's early life in many lands and of his official mission to Moscow in 1918* (London: Putnam, 1932)

MacLaren, Roy, *Canadians In Russia 1918–19* (Lewiston, N.Y.: Maclean-Hunter Press, 1976)

Maurice, Sir F. (ed.), *Soldier, Artist, Sportsman: The Life of Lord Rawlinson* (Boston: Houghton Mifflin Co., 1928)

Maynard, Charles, *The Murmansk Venture* (London: Hodder & Stoughton, 1928)

McCullagh, Francis, *A Prisoner of the Reds: the story of a British officer captured in Siberia* (London: Murray, 1921)

Moore, Joel R., Mead, Harry H., Jahns, Lewis E., *The History of The American Expedition Fighting the Bolsheviki* (Nashville, Tennessee: The Battery Press, 2003)

Muirden, Bruce, *The Diggers Who Signed on for More: Australia's Part in the Russian Wars of Intervention, 1918–1919* (Kent Town, S. Australia: Wakefield Press, 1990)

Neville, Sir J.E.H., *History of the 43rd and 52nd (Oxfordshire and Buckinghamshire) Light Infantry in the Great War, 1914–1919* (Aldershot: Gale & Polden, 1938)

N.R.E.F., 16th Brigade, C.F.A., 67th and 68th Batteries: in North Russia, September 1918 to June 1919 (Bryant Press Ltd., Toronto)

Pautovsky, Konstantin, *The Story of a Life: Vol. 3, In that dawn* (London: Harvill Press 1964, repr. New York: Pantheon Books, 1982)

Phelps, Hodges, *BRITMIS; A Great Adventure of the War; Being an account of Allied intervention in Siberia and of an escape across the Gobi to Peking* (London: Jonathan Cape, 1931)

Pieroth, Doris, *A Canadian's Road to Russia: The Letters of Stuart Ramsay Tompkins: Letters from the Great War Decade* (Edmonton: University of Alberta Press, 1989)

Pigot, G., *History of the 1st Battalion, 14th Punjab Regiment, Sherdil-ki-Paltan (late XIX Punjabis)* (New Delhi: Roxy Printing Press., 1946)

Quinlivian, Peter, *Forgotten Valour, The story of Arthur Sullivan VC, Shy War Hero* (Frenchs Forest, NSW, Australia: New Holland, 2006)

Sayer, Major Herbert, *A Somewhat Unusual Journey: Victoria Stations to Taganrog: A War Office Mission to Russia, 1919* (Chertsey: Sayer Press, 2014)

Shackleton, Sir Ernest, *South* (London: Heinemann, 1919)

Shrive, Frank J., *The Diary of a P.B.O. (Poor Bloody Observer)* (Erin, Ontario: Boston Mills Press, 1981)

Silverlight, John, *The Victors' Dilemma: Allied Intervention in the Russian Civil War 1917–20* (London: Barrie & Jenkins, 1970)

Singleton-Gates, G.R., *Bolos and Barishynas: Being an account of the doings of the Sadleir-Jackson Brigade, and Altham Flotilla, on the North Dvina during the summer 1919* (Aldershot: Gale & Polden, 1920)

Skuce, J.E., *CSEF, Canada's Soldiers in Siberia, 1918–19* (Access to History Publications, undated)

Smith, John T., *Gone to Russia to Fight: The RAF in South Russia 1918–20* (Stroud: Amberley, 2010)

Soutar, Andrew, *With Ironside in North Russia* (London: Hutchinson & Co., 1940)

Strakhovsky, Leonid Ivan, *Intervention at Archangel;the story of allied intervention and Russian counter-revolution in North Russia, 1918–1920* (Princeton: Princeton University Press, 1944)

Swettenham, John, *Allied Intervention in Russia 1918–19, and the Part Played by Canada* (Toronto: Ryerson Press, 1967)

Thomson, John, *Shackleton's Captain: A Biography of Frank Worsley* (Christchurch, NZ: Hazard Press, 1988)

Thornycroft, John I. (and Co.), *A short history of the revival of the small torpedo boat (C.M.B.s) during the Great War and subsequently in the Kronstadt, Archangel and Caspian Sea expeditions of 1919* (Privately published, 1920)

Tomaselli, Phil, *Air Force Lives: A Guide for Family Historians* (Barnsley: Pen and Sword, 2013)

Ullman, Richard Henry, *Anglo-Soviet Relations, 1917–1921: Intervention and the War* (Princeton, N.J.: Princeton University Press, 1961)

Uloth, Gerald, *Riding to War* (Monks, 1994)

Van der Spuy, Major General K., *Chasing the Wind* (Cape Town: Books of Africa, 1966)

Vining, L.E., *Held by the Bolsheviks; the diary of a British officer in Russia, 1919–1920* (London: The Saint Catherine Press, 1924)

War Office, *Army: The Evacuation of North Russia 1919* (London: HMSO, 1920)

Ward, John, *With the 'Die-Hards' in Siberia* (London: Cassell, 1920)

Ward, William, *A Well-kept Secret: The Allied Invasion of North Russia, 1918–19* (Privately published, 2010)

Williamson, H.N.H., *Farewell to the Don; the Russian Revolution in the journals of Brigadier H.N.H. Williamson* (London: Collins, 1970)

Wilson, Michael, *Baltic Assignment: British Submariners in Russia 1914–19* (London: Leo Cooper in association with Secker & Warburg, 1985)

Wilson, Michael, *For Them the War Is Not Over: The Royal Navy in Russia 1918–20* (Stroud: The History Press 2008)

Young, E. Hilton, *By Sea and Land: Some Naval Doings* (London: T.C. & E.C. Jack, 1920)

Index

INDEX OF PEOPLE

INDEX OF PLACES

INDEX OF MILITARY UNITS

Allied Forces

Russian Forces

Bolshevik/'Red'/Soviet

INDEX OF SHIPS

Allied/White Russian

INDEX OF GENERAL TERMS